TEACHERS OF THE
INNER CHAMBERS

*Women and Culture in
Seventeenth-Century China*

Teachers of the Inner Chambers

WOMEN AND CULTURE IN
SEVENTEENTH-CENTURY CHINA

Dorothy Ko

Stanford University Press
Stanford, California

Published with the assistance of China
Publications Subventions and a special
grant from the Stanford University
Faculty Publication Fund to help support
nonfaculty work originating at Stanford.

Stanford University Press
Stanford, California
© 1994 by the Board of Trustees of the
Leland Stanford Junior University

Printed in the United States of America

CIP data appear at the end of the book

Original printing 1994
Last figure below indicates year of this printing:

04   03   02   01

To my mother and father,
Tam Kam-fook and Ko Cheuk-luen,
who sent me to the same university
as my brother

ACKNOWLEDGMENTS

I chanced upon the worlds of Shen Yixiu, Huang Yuanjie, Liu Rushi, and other heroines in this book in 1984 when I was scanning library catalogs and bibliographies for any entries with the word *nü* (female). So little was known then about how women lived before the nineteenth century that a frequent reaction to my dissertation topic was "You don't mean that women in traditional China could read and write?!"

When I finished drafting this book in fall 1992, scores of translators were collaborating on a multivolume anthology of women poets from all dynasties, an equally monumental biographical dictionary of Ming-Qing women was under way, and an international conference on women and literature in Ming-Qing China had received generous grants from virtually all major funding agencies in Chinese studies. A new field is being written into existence.

My own intellectual transitions are just as perceptible. My dissertation was a work of social history, focusing on issues of education, kinship, social networks, and mobility. Upon returning to the U.S. academic community after a long sojourn in Japan, I became fascinated by the theoretical possibilities of cultural history. I began to question my old understanding of power, gender, and culture.

Caught between momentous transitions in the field and in my own outlook, this book is an awkward creature. To some readers it may say too little, to others too much. The message I wish to convey, however, is simple: women built intellectual and emotional communities through reading and writing. This process was as gratifying to Shen Yixiu, Shang Jinglan, and Gu Ruopu as it has been for me. It is only fitting, then, to acknowledge here my growing community of teachers, colleagues, and friends.

Harold Kahn changed my life when he told a bewildered graduate student, "Read all the theory you want, but a historian's job is to tell a good story." Lyman Van Slyke steered my search for a story with unfailing sagacity even as I was migrating three hundred years away from his period of specialization. Susan Mann joined my trio of guardian angels as a role model in the archives as in daily life. She took off my blinders by insisting that the history of women in imperial China, however invisible, was knowable. She suggested the title of this book long before I had a book. The thought of being able to acknowledge these mentors here sustained me through blocs of writer's blues.

I remember the libraries I frequented as warm and nurturing places; their staffs have become part family. The Hoover Institution at Stanford University provided a home away from home, as did the Naikaku bunko in Tokyo and the Institute of Oriental Culture of Tokyo University. Custodians of other collections have spread feasts for the visitor's eyes, and I wish I could thank them one by one: the Harvard-Yenching Library; the Library of Congress; the Oriental Library at the University of California, Berkeley; the Tōyō bunko, Japan; the Gest Library of Princeton University. The last even gave me a grant just to visit.

If the financial assistance I received were loans, I would be in debt for the rest of my life. Fellowships from Stanford kept me free from worries throughout my graduate program. During a fruitful year in one of the world's most expensive cities, the Inter-University Center in Tokyo paid my tuition, and the College Women's Association of Japan brought me a comfortable existence. A pre-doctoral fellowship from the Social Science Research Council and American Council of Learned Societies sustained me for an extra year of archival work in Tokyo. I started drafting this book in the summer when a stipend from the State University of New York at Stony Brook allowed me to survive on take-out dinners. I finished the book with a bottle of champagne paid for by a Chancellor's Summer Grant from the University of California at San Diego. The Committee on Research of the same university cleaned up the mess by providing funds for final manuscript preparation.

Since transmigration is a blessing instead of a curse in the academic community, I cannot even begin to acknowledge the wheels of obligation I have incurred, let alone repay my dues. Too many teachers, colleagues, and friends have read drafts, written letters, and suggested readings that my only hope of relief is to reciprocate their kindness in private. I thank my early teachers for setting the wheel into motion: Harry Harding, Jr., David Abernethy, Robert Keohane, Albert Dien, Peter Duus, Jeffrey Mass, Estelle Freedman. I would not have survived five years in Tokyo if not for the scintillating company of Nakao Katsumi, Ueda Makoto, Ōki Yasushi, and members of the Chūgoku joseishi kenkyūkai. Professors Linda Grove, Yanagida Setsuko, Ono Kazuko, Kishimoto Mio, and Hamashita Takeshi opened many institutional and intellectual doors in Japan.

Many forerunners have watched over my shoulders. Susan Mann, Kathryn Bernhardt, Suzanne Cahill, and an anonymous reader read the entire manuscript. They each corrected embarrassing mistakes and offered valuable suggestions. Kang-i Sun Chang read the chapter on courtesans and suggested improvements. Chün-fang Yu readily responded to my pleas for help by sharing her expert knowledge on Buddhism. Wai-Lim Yip provided indispensable help in the reading and translation of poems. Taking responsibility for the mistakes that remain, I cannot thank these readers enough. I am also indebted to Shinno Reiko for her bibliographical assistance and to Mark Eykholt for help in preparing the Index.

Through the years, Charlotte Furth, Patricia Ebrey, Ann Waltner, Ellen Widmer, Katy Carlitz, Maureen Robertson, Judith Zeitlin, Paul Ropp, and Marilyn Young have generously shared their work and insights. My gratitude to this community of scholars is more than what footnotes can convey. Bill Rowe has been my best friend for being my most demanding critic. Each of these people has taught me a great deal. Muriel Bell of Stanford University Press kept the bad news from me for years, that my dissertation would make an unreadable book. Her constant encouragement is heartwarming. Li Huai, who provided one of her paintings for the book jacket, has my cordial thanks and admiration.

To my husband, Jim Impoco, I offer words of gratitude and a warning: Thank you for providing a window to the world outside academe and for putting up with my pathological myopia. Beware, I am starting my second book.

D.Y.K.

Contents

Translations of offices and official titles follow those given in Charles O. Hucker, *A Dictionary of Official Titles in Imperial China* (Stanford University Press, 1985).

Educated Chinese men and women used a variety of given names—official name (*ming*), courtesy name (*zi*), and sobriquets (*waihao*). Those that appear in this book are the ones by which that person was commonly known or with which published works were signed. Often it was the official name, but courtesy names were also used. In some cases the decision is arbitrary. Chinese and Japanese names are given in the order of family name first.

References to age have been converted to the Western count, unless otherwise noted.

SELECTED REIGN PERIODS OF THE
MING AND QING DYNASTIES, 1522–1795

MING DYNASTY (1368–1644)

Jiajing period	1522–66
Longqing period	1567–72
Wanli period	1573–1620
Taichang period	1620 (eighth–twelfth month)
Tianqi period	1620–27
Chongzhen period	1628–44

MAJOR SOUTHERN MING REGIMES (1645–61)

Hongguang period	1645 (first–fifth month)
Longwu period	1645–46
Shaowu period	1646 (eleventh–twelfth month)
Yongli period	1647–61

QING DYNASTY (1644–1911)

Shunzhi period	1644–61
Kangxi period	1662–1722
Yongzheng period	1723–35
Qianlong period	1736–95

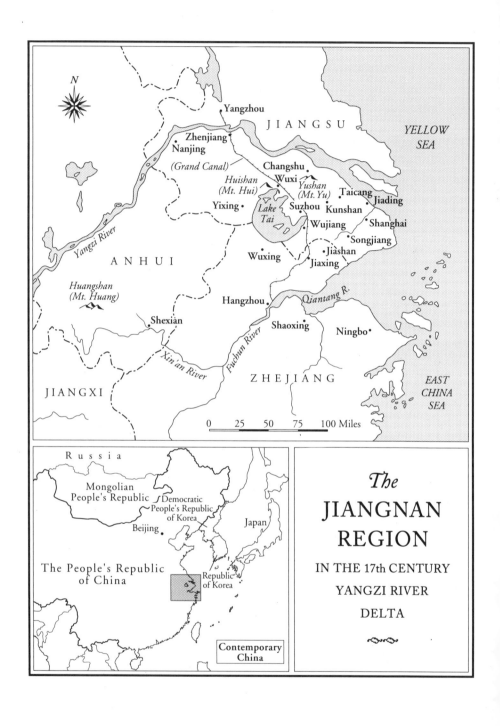

The JIANGNAN REGION

IN THE 17th CENTURY

YANGZI RIVER

DELTA

TEACHERS OF THE INNER CHAMBERS

Women and Culture in
Seventeenth-Century China

Introduction

GENDER AND THE POLITICS
OF CHINESE HISTORY

TEACHERS of the inner chambers, the heroines of this book, occupied a world larger than the inner domestic domain. The texts of their lives and their contexts can be fully illuminated only by using "gender" as a category of historical analysis. In this Introduction, I first argue that gender becomes a relevant category in Chinese history only when the historian writes against the May Fourth legacy. I then outline my method of integrating gender with Chinese history by way of summarizing the main themes of the book. I conclude that by taking gender into account, we discover how vital seventeenth-century China was and how our familiar periodization will have to be modified.

The Victimized Woman in Old China

From its inception, the study of Chinese women's history was integral to the nationalistic program of China's modernization.[1] The first general history of Chinese women, *A New History of Women of the Divine Land* (*Shenzhou nüzi xinshi*), was written by an anti-Manchu revolutionary, Xu Tianxiao, and published a year after the dynastic order collapsed in 1912. In his attempt to incite women to be worthy members of the new citizenry, Xu cited the outstanding strength of Western heroines ranging from Queen Victoria to Madame Roland. In contrast, he lamented that "women in China lack lofty goals and distinguishing thoughts; they can boast of neither an independent will nor great enterprises."[2] Chinese women, like China itself, desperately needed to catch up with the West.

The identification of women with backwardness and dependency acquired a new urgency in the May Fourth–New Culture period (1915–27). As imperialist aggressions intensified, the victimized woman became the

symbol of the Chinese nation itself, "raped" and dominated by virile foreign powers.[3] Women's enlightenment thus became a prerequisite for the
political liberation of the nation as a whole as well as for China's entrance
into the modern world. In short, women's subjugation to the patriarch
epitomized the savageries of old China, the roots of its present-day humiliation. The image of the victimized feudal woman was vested with such
powerful nationalist sentiments that it assumed the mantle of unassailable
historical truth.

So moving was the suffering of Xianglin's Wife, the protagonist in a
short story called "The New Year's Sacrifice" by Lu Xun, the foremost
May Fourth writer, that she remains the quintessential "traditional Chinese woman" in the minds of most Chinese. Xianglin's Wife, a widow, was
sold by her mother-in-law for re-marriage. After her second husband also
died and their only son was devoured by a wolf, she returned to her former
master to serve as a maid. Stigmatized as impure, Xianglin's Wife was
barred from preparing food for the New Year's sacrifice. She eventually
went insane and collapsed on the street.[4] All the traits of the victimized
woman are found in Xianglin's Wife: she is sold as a commodity, called by
her husband's name, has no identity of her own, and worst of all, is so
steeped in the ideology of her oppressor that she blames her misfortunes
on herself.

The literary portrait of victimized women was reinforced by documentary evidence presented in the most widely read history of Chinese
women, first published in 1928. In *A History of the Lives of Chinese
Women* (*Zhongguo funü shenghuo shi*), Chen Dongyuan thus described
his thesis: "From the beginning of history, our women have been the
wretched ones." Chen clearly stated his reason for undertaking the work:
"I merely want to elucidate how the concept of 'superior man–inferior
woman' [*nanzun nübei*] emerged, how the destruction of women was
intensified, and how the weight of history is still crushing their backs
today." He continued, "I now light a torch to shine upon this monstrous
burden, so that all can see in clear relief how monstrous our 3,000-year
history has been, and then we would know the shape of the new life to
come."[5] To Chen, women's history was worth writing if, and only if, it led
to their emancipation from the yoke of China's feudal past.

In contemporary China, as in the West, impressions of Chinese women
before the twentieth century are still shaped by the concerns, values, and
lexicon of such writers as Lu Xun and Chen Dongyuan. The May Fourth
image of the miserable traditional woman was reinforced by the political
agenda of the Chinese Communist Party (CCP): to claim credit for the
"liberation" of women, the CCP and its sympathizers perpetuated the
stark view of China's past as a perennial dark age for women.[6]

This a priori assumption of woman as victim has found ready support-ers among Western readers. Chandra Mohanty argues that the prevalent construction of Third World women as victims is part of an ethnocentric feminist discourse that privileges Western women as "secular, liberated and in control of their own lives." Mohanty also points out that this discourse rests on the shaky assumptions of homogeneity of women across cultures, the universality of patriarchy, and a dichotomy between tradition and modernity.[7] In the case of China, Western feminist scholarship is a mere accomplice to more persuasive Chinese nationalist concerns.

So powerful is this coalescence of Western and Chinese discourses that even Chinese scholars critical of the Orientalist lapses of Western writers are just as committed to the view of Chinese women's history as "a history of enslavement." For example, the highly articulate scholar Du Fangqin repeated the May Fourth rhetoric almost verbatim in the conclusion to her recent book: "Political authority, clan authority, husband's authority, re-ligious authority — these four thick ropes bound up the minds and bodies of Chinese women. They bound them up so tightly that the ghosts [of these patriarchal authorities] are still hovering around today." The pas-sionate phrase "four thick ropes" derives from Mao Zedong's "Report on an Investigation of the Peasant Movement in Hunan" of 1927.[8]

In short, the invention of an ahistorical "Chinese tradition" that is feudal, patriarchal, and oppressive was the result of a rare confluence of three divergent ideological and political traditions — the May Fourth–New Culture movement, the Communist revolution, and Western femi-nist scholarship. Although these traditions envision vastly different forms for modernity and the place of women in it, they concur in their indigna-tion over the cloistered, crippled, and subservient existence of women in old China.

With the demise of Maoist radicalism in 1976, scholars in China and the West began to question the success of the socialist revolution in elevat-ing women to an equal economic and psychological footing with men.[9] This revisionism regarding contemporary women, however, made the en-trenched image of women in perpetual bondage even harder to resist. Since "new China" appears to be littered with "feudal remnants," the May Fourth legacy acquires renewed relevance. Writers continue to speak of "patriarchy in traditional China" as if both "patriarchy" and "traditional China" were monolithic, unchanging entities.[10]

It is my contention that the deep-seated image of the victimized "feu-dal" women has arisen in part from an analytical confusion that mistakes normative prescriptions for experienced realities, a confusion exacerbated by a lack of historical studies that examine women's own views of their worlds. My disagreement with the May Fourth formulations is not so much that they are not "true," but that May Fourth iconoclasm is itself a political and ideological construct that tells us more about the definition of twentieth-century Chinese modernity than the nature of "traditional society." Although not without its grain of truth, the overwhelming popularity of the image of victimized women has obscured the dynamics not only of relationships between men and women but also of the functioning of Chinese society as a whole. To dispel the ahistorical bias and revise the image, historical studies of Chinese women must take greater account of specific periods and locales, as well as of the different social and class backgrounds of the women in question. Above all, women's history must be more deeply anchored in general Chinese history.

Only with this "bifocal" historical perspective can we come to understand that neither the "woman as victim" hypothesis nor its "woman as agent" antithesis can sufficiently convey the range of constraints and opportunities that women in seventeenth-century China faced.[11] Both the restrictions and the freedoms were most clearly manifested among a privileged group of educated women from the most urbanized region of the empire, the "teachers of the inner chambers." When the term first appeared in seventeenth-century China, it referred to a class of itinerant female teachers. In this book, I give it a more general and figurative usage. All the women who appear in this book, whether wives, daughters, or widows, taught each other about the vicissitudes of life through their writings. By transmitting a literate women's culture across generations, they effectively transcended the inner chambers temporally, just as the itinerant teachers defied the same boundaries spatially. Although the lives, thoughts, and circumstances of these poets, teachers, artists, writers, and readers may not have been shared by the majority of the population, they are most instructive to us for the way they highlight the possibilities for fulfillment and a meaningful existence even within the confines the Confucian system imposed upon women. Thus this book examines the lives of these women while asking them to instruct us on the historical time and space they inhabited.

As such, this book focuses narrowly on women not to highlight their isolation but to seek their reintegration into Chinese history. My twin concerns—women's history and the history of seventeenth-century China—are analytically inseparable. Born out of a curiosity about how women actually lived, this book in the end proposes a new way to conceptualize China's past. This reconception of history rests on the premise that by understanding how women lived, we better grasp the dynamics of gender relations; by comprehending gender relations, we gain a more realistic and complete knowledge of the values of Chinese culture, the functioning of its society, and the nature of historical changes.

This integration of gender and Chinese history entails the use of terminologies outside the established nomenclature of social historians of imperial China. Hence it is best to begin by outlining my idiosyncratic and eclectic approach by discussing the key concepts that structure this book: gender, class, women's culture, communities of women, Confucian tradition.

Working Definitions: Gender and Class

The most important concepts for my argument are the differences between gender and sex and the intersections between gender and class. The concept of gender is central to both pairs. According to the *Women's Studies Encyclopedia*, "gender is a cultural construct: the distinction in roles, behaviors, and mental and emotional characteristics between females and males developed by a society." As such, "gender" is conceptually distinct from "sex," although the two have often been used interchangeably: "Sex is a term that encompasses the morphological and physiological differences on the basis of which humans (and other life forms) are categorized as male and female. It should be used only in relation to characteristics and behaviors that arise directly from biological differences between men and women."[12] Although sexuality is an important subject of historical inquiry, this book is primarily concerned with gender, especially the female gender, as a cultural construct.

In the course of establishing gender as a category of historical analysis, Joan Scott has furnished a more precise definition: "The core of the definition rests on an integral connection between two propositions: gender is a constitutive element of social relationships based on perceived differences between the sexes, and gender is a primary way of signifying relationships of power." She then further delineates the first proposition into four elements: symbolic representations, normative concepts, social institutions, and subjective identity.[13] My goal is to elucidate the relationships between the last three of these. In particular, I emphasize normative concepts of gender gleaned from the Confucian classics and precepts, the key roles played by such social institutions as kinship and education in the construction of gender, and the subjective gender identities of seventeenth-century elite women as revealed in their own writings.

By highlighting in her second proposition the connections between gender and power as well as how they construct each other, Scott has called attention to the integral links between gender and other formulations of equality and hierarchy. This notion of connectedness between gender and politics is particularly relevant to China, where the husband-wife bond had served as a metaphor for ruler-subject ties and a model for all political authority since the Warring States period (fifth century to 221 B.C.).[14] In other words, we cannot conceive of the history of gender in isolation from political history, and vice versa. In this book, I speak of one aspect of this connectedness as the intersection between gender and class. My usage of "class" refers loosely to occupational groups and social stations differentiated by access to wealth, political power, cultural capital, and subjective perceptions and does not connote the Marxist meaning of economic determination.

Gender and class constituted the two primary axes against which each individual Chinese woman was to be defined in society. The Confucian dictum "Thrice Following" (*sancong*, often rendered "Three Obediences") represents an attempt to signify a woman by the occupational "class" of the paterfamilias in each stage of her life cycle: father, husband, son. Together with the admonition to demarcate the inner from the outer, which I analyze below in terms of a doctrine of separate spheres, Thrice Following is one of the twin pillars of Confucian gender ethics.

The meaning of Thrice Following is explicated in the *Book of Rites*, part of the classical canon. As translated by James Legge: "The woman follows (and obeys) the man: — in her youth, she follows her father and elder brother; when married, she follows her husband; when her husband is dead, she follows her son."[15] The same demands were reiterated in some of the most popular books of precepts, including *Instructions for the Inner Chambers* (*Neixun*), attributed to the Ming empress Renxiaowen, and Lü Kun's *Exemplars in the Female Quarters* (*Guifan*).[16] As insinuated by Legge's use of both "follows" and "obeys," however, the exact meaning of *cong*, or the nature of female submission prescribed in the idealized norms, is by no means clear-cut.

Twentieth-century scholars have often interpreted *cong* as unconditional obedience of the wife to the whims of the husband and bemoaned her "total dependence on him bodily and psychologically."[17] Whatever the philological origins of the word or the intent of Confucius, I argue that this interpretation oversimplifies the workings of gender relations and the Confucian ethical system, which I will refer to as the gender system. This distortion conveys the impression that the Chinese gender system was built upon coercion and brute oppression, which, in my view, ascribes to it at once too much and too little power. The strength and resilience of the gender system — as it unfolded in history, not on the pages of codes of conduct — should be attributed to the considerable range of flexibilities that women from various classes, regions, and age groups enjoyed in practice. These flexibilities, in turn, ensued from a number of built-in tensions and contradictions in the gender system, the most important of which is that between gender and class.

My contention is that in practice *sancong* deprived a woman of her legal and formal social identity but not her individual personality or subjectivity.[18] For this reason, I prefer the translation Thrice Following to Three Obediences. In its claims of universal applicability to women from all families and age groups, the dictum opened up the conceptual possibility of identifying women by their shared gender, or women-as-same. At the same time, by defining women according to the social station of their paterfamilias, the dictum was predicated on a divisive element, or women-as-different. This inherent contradiction accorded women a range of freedoms within their own limited spheres, but these spheres were fragmented and often demarcated by the class of their male kin. As a result, even the most mobile and articulate women in the seventeenth century had no institutional and conceptual means to forge a broadly based united front that could launch systematic and fundamental attacks on the gender system.

In her study of Northern Song (960–1126) palace women, Priscilla Ching Chung makes an astute observation on the practical meaning of Thrice Following:

Since Chinese law also confers upon a woman the same status held by her husband, it is more valuable to discuss women in terms of different social and economic classes. Albert O'Hara has suggested dividing women in China into four classes: slaves and laboring women, wives of farmers and merchants, wives of scholars and officials, and wives of nobles and rulers. Within each class responsibilities and privileges of women differed. It is, therefore, important to understand that subservience of women to men did not mean total subordination of all women to all men but the subordination of specific women to specific men within their own class, and only in terms of personal and family relationships.[19]

In other words, although it is valid to speak of an undifferentiated block of "Chinese women" on a certain normative level, any historical study of women and gender should be class-, locale-, and age-specific.

As this study of the wives and daughters of scholar-official families in seventeenth-century Jiangnan will show, this double formulation of gender and class accounts for the perpetuation of the gender system during a time of traumatic socioeconomic transition. These educated women did not support the gender system because they were whipped into submission to their fathers, husbands, and sons, as is often implied in May Fourth literature.

New Paradigms of Chinese Women's History

This book seeks to revise the May Fourth view of history, which construed the oppression of women as the most glaring failing of China's feudal patriarchal past. The pervasiveness of this formulation has distorted not only women's history but also the very nature of pre-nineteenth-century Chinese society. The widely shared assumption of universal oppression of women in traditional China logically leads one to expect these women to rebel or escape whenever they could. Hence the search for signs of "resistance" and, when that fails — when one finds instead women's seemingly voluntary compliance — allusions to the power of the Confucian tradition to "silence" women. These inquiries are faulty from the start, for they are predicated on a conception of society and gender relations that is overly mechanistic and too neatly dichotomous — man on top of woman; state over society. When scholars focused on the hoped-for imminent collapse of the system that would set women free, what I consider to be the crucial question — How did the gender system manage to function so well for so long? — was never asked, let alone answered.

In this book, I attempt to explain both the functioning and the reproduction of the gender system by focusing on women's vested interests in it. By implicating women as actors maneuvering to further their perceived interests from within the system, I see them as architects of concrete gender relations, the building blocks from which the overarching gender system was constructed. Instead of outright resistance or silencing, I describe processes of contestation and negotiation, whose meaning is ambivalent not only to us in hindsight but also to men and women at the time.

Above all, in lieu of the May Fourth dichotomous model of an oppressive patriarchy, I propose a dynamic tripartite model that construes the lives of Chinese women as the summation of three levels of shifting realities: theory or ideal norms, practice, and self-perceptions. As the chapters that follow will show, these three levels were at times in harmony and at other times at odds; in some instances they were separated by formidable gulfs, and in other cases their overlapping was seamless. Whereas the May Fourth model derived largely from static description of ideal norms, we are compelled to reconstruct the history of women and Chinese society from the gulfs and the overlappings between these three elements, transitory territories that are by nature shifting and multifarious in meaning.

The specific interplay between these three constituents of a woman's life varied not only with time but also with the social and geographical locales of the woman concerned. For the elite women from the Jiangnan urban centers that form the bulk of this study, through didactic literature and dictums transmitted orally, they were taught the ideal norms they were supposed to embrace — the Thrice Following and its corollary, the Four Virtues (*side*). In everyday life, most adhered to these dictums nominally, being bound by law and social custom to lead a domestically centered life. Although women could not rewrite the rules that structured their lives, they were extremely creative in crafting a space from within the prevailing gender system that gave them meaning, solace, and dignity. Their impressive array of tactics, as we will see, ranges from reinterpreting the dicta through writing, revamping the meaning of such dicta in practice, to boring through the cracks between the morally laudable and the permissible both in writing and in practice.

In so doing, these women opened up arenas of freedom for themselves without directly challenging the ideal norms promulgated by the official ideology. Thus in their self-representations—gleaned from poetry and other genres of writing—there is a conspicuous absence of overt attacks on the system. Indeed, the most educated members of the female population were inclined more to celebrate their role as guardians of Confucian morality than to repudiate it. In this case, the ideal norms prescribed by the official ideology and women's self-perceptions are in apparent agreement. This agreement, however, masks the complex processes of negotiation and the variegated mosaic of women's everyday life, which often defied the official norms.

This book is my attempt to reconstruct this mosaic, the context in which educated women from seventeenth-century China could speak to us about their frustrations, pleasures, and aspirations. In repudiating the simplistic May Fourth construction of the victimized women in old China, my intention is not to defend patriarchy or write an apology for the Confucian tradition. Rather, I insist that a realistic understanding of the strength and longevity of the Confucian gender system serves the agendas of the historian, the revolutionary, and women equally well.

Indeed, the distinction between "what should be" and "what is" is a key to understanding the Janus-faced nature of seventeenth-century Chinese society, which appears to be the best of times and the worst of times for women. If legal statutes and moral instruction books were accurate guides, the late Ming (1573–1644) and early Qing (1644–1722) periods would indeed be a dark age of tightening restrictions. Whereas elite women enjoyed a degree of inheritance rights and were relatively free to remarry during the Song dynasty (960–1279), by the seventeenth century they had lost their property rights and were subjected to increasingly strict sexual mores, most notably the cult of chastity.[20] Moreover, massive lists of chaste women in local gazetteers suggest that both elite and commoner women subscribed to the chastity cult.[21] Scholars have described these changes in terms of a "decline in the status of women," a decline allegedly caused by a hardening of Neo-Confucian philosophy and by the development of a market economy that commoditized women.[22]

Even a cursory look at descriptions of seventeenth-century urban life in local histories, private writings, and fiction suggests a contrasting picture of the vitality of women's domestic and social lives, as well as the degree of informal power and social freedom they apparently enjoyed. For example, Ming and Qing novels and dramas show that housewives possessed the "power of the key" to the household bursary.[23] The innumerable women's biographies and eulogies in local gazetteers and literati writings supply ample evidence of erudite scholars, able managers, avid travelers, and imposing personalities. Most relevant to our purposes, however, is a large body of writings by educated women — mostly poetry, but also letters, essays, and drama. Not only are these writings the best indicators of rising female literacy rates, but they also convey a sense of the richness of women's intellectual and social worlds.[24] They are the primary materials on which this book is based, supplemented by works of their male relatives.

The gaps between norms and actual behavior on the one hand and between formal and informal power on the other suggest that we need to pay as much attention to the everyday lives and self-perceptions of women as to overarching structures of domination.[25] What this calls for, above all, is a concept of power that focuses not on static structures or institutions but on the dynamic processes through which power is exercised. Even in imperial China — often regarded as a classic example of so-called patriarchy — there was much fluidity and possibilities for individuals to constitute themselves in everyday practice.

Power Without the King: Realities of the Patriarchal Family

The theories of power developed by French scholars Michel Foucault and Pierre Bourdieu can help us conceptualize the unofficial power that Chinese women enjoyed. Foucault cautioned that power is not "something that is acquired, seized, or shared, something that one holds on to or allows to slip away." Instead, "power is exercised from innumerable points, in the interplay of nonegalitarian and mobile relations." Rather than ask "who has power" and "who is deprived of it," he argued, the historian of sexuality should look for changing distributions of power and appropriations of knowledge, processes he called "matrices of transformations."[26]

Similarly, Pierre Bourdieu has warned that anthropologists steeped in structuralism are blind to the vast domain of "practical kinship" in which men and women operate. They are thus condemned to taking the genealogy-based "official kinship" to be the only reality. To chart the relationships of practical kinship, Bourdieu has distinguished between "official power" that men monopolize and "dominated power" that women often wield, a circumscribed power by proxy that is nonetheless real. "Even when women do wield the real power," he wrote, "as is often the case in matrimonial matters, they can exercise it fully only on condition that they leave the appearance of power, that is, its official manifestation, to the men."[27] Here, too, the appearance of kinship hierarchy and formal structures of power mask the realities of the exercise of power.

Foucault's notion of "power without the king" and Bourdieu's "dominated power" suggest that even in a society as thoroughly patriarchal as China, kinship systems and family relations may not have been the workings of men alone. The nature and degree of power that a woman could exercise depended not only on her social position and the task at hand but also on such factors as her personal skills and her position in the life cycle. This vision of kinship and power relations allows the historian to study women's lives as they themselves saw them without having to judge at the outset whether certain institutions or practices are "oppressive." Questions of judgment are important, but they can be broached only on the basis of concrete knowledge of how men and women lived, how they viewed their lives, as well as the manifold ways in which prevailing ideologies impinged upon their lives and perceptions. For seventeenth-century China, the present state of our knowledge on such matters is pitifully incomplete.

A realistic understanding of gender and power relations has to begin with the family, the basic social universe of Chinese men and women. In a historical overview, Patricia Ebrey discusses three sets of ideas and practices that characterized the early development of the Chinese family: patrilineality, filial piety, and patriarchy. These attributes, firmly established by Song times, showed remarkable resilience through time and universality across class and regional boundaries.[28] The particular expressions of patrilineality, filial piety, and patriarchy, however, were historical occurrences that varied with time, place, and the social background of the men and women concerned.

The domestic lives of gentry men and women studied in this book suggest that even if the assumptions of patriarchy were not being challenged outright in the seventeenth century, in practice they were being constantly mitigated. Although men still claimed legal rights over family property and fathers enjoyed authority over women and children, the housewife as de facto household manager, mother, and educator of children had ample opportunities to influence family affairs. In the context of everyday life, women were hardly outsiders to the family system.

More damaging to the myth of an omnipotent patriarchy was the growing availability and acceptance of women's education, which, by the seventeenth century, created a visible cohort of gentrywomen with a literary and classical education. Their very existence, and the fact that education increased their cachet as wives, called into question the foundation of patriarchal values—women as inferior moral and intellectual beings.

Whereas Joanna Handlin-Smith has examined the philosophical challenge posed by educated women to Confucian thinkers like Lü Kun (1536–1613), in this book I focus on the changes in family life and definitions of domesticity.[29] This is evident in the rising incidence of companionate marriage, changing definitions of womanhood, and the increasing vigor with which women redrew or trespassed the boundaries between the domestic and public spheres.

The Inner and Outer: Negotiated Boundaries

As mentioned above, Confucian gender ethics was founded on the twin pillars of Thrice Following and the doctrine of separate spheres (man: outer / woman: inner). Chinese society has often been said to thrive on a clear demarcation between domestic and public spheres, with women confined to the former and men controlling the latter. To the extent that the Chinese family functioned on a gender-based division of labor, with women barred from taking the civil service examination and hence from bureaucratic appointments, there is truth to this statement. Yet the formula of separation is more prescriptive of an ideal norm than descriptive of the realities of gender interactions in the seventeenth century.

This distinction has to be stressed in light of two widely held misconceptions. First is the image of the cloistered woman, crippled by bound feet and imprisoned in her inner chambers. In this book, I show that despite moral precepts admonishing women to stay at home, even gentrywomen traveled a great deal, on trips ranging from long-distance journeys accompanying their husbands on official appointments to excursions for pleasure in the company of other women. Second, and more important, the juxtaposition of a female domestic sphere with a male political sphere implies that the family is immune to politics, an erroneous assumption that anyone who has lived with a Chinese family would dismiss. The juxtaposition is misleading because it ignores the crucial interaction between family and state on the one hand, and between men and women, both inside and outside the family, on the other.

The validity of separate spheres as an analytical tool has long been questioned by scholars outside sinology. In an influential essay published in 1979, feminist historian Joan Kelly argued that women's history should be approached in relational terms and with a "doubled vision." Arguing that a "woman's place is not a separate sphere or domain of existence but a position within social existence generally," Kelly stressed that relegating "men and women" to neatly defined spheres often reflects the wishes of the patriarch more than it does social reality.[30]

Social scientists, notably Pierre Bourdieu, have proposed new theoretical constructs that break down the dichotomy of domestic versus public spheres. Bourdieu's articulation of concepts of "habitus" and "embodiment" attributes the reproduction of distinctions in society at large, especially that of male/female, to the structuring of body movements and domestic spatial arrangements. Thus linking social hierarchies with private and domestic dispositions, the concept of habitus transcends "the usual antinomies . . . of determinism and freedom . . . or the individual and society."[31] In a related attempt to construct a unitary theoretical vision, anthropologists Jane Collier and Sylvia Yanagisako have taken the entire ethnographic tradition to task for treating kinship and gender as distinct domains. No historian would disagree with their argument that binaries such as "domestic/public," "nature/culture," and "reproduction/production" are inadequate because they assume an opposition as a historical given instead of explaining its existence in the first place.[32]

Following the insights of these scholars, the organizational scheme of this book rests on a continuum of inner (*nei*) and outer (*wai*) domains as fields of action that women inhabited. Although often rendered in English as "domestic" and "public," "inner" and "outer" in their Chinese contexts are always relative and relational terms. The inner/outer construct does not demarcate mutually exclusive social and symbolic spaces; instead, the two define and constitute each other according to shifting contexts and perspectives. In the eyes of the Qing monarchy, for example, the family is the very site where public morality can be exemplified. Hence when I use the term *public* in this book, I do not mean a realm that excludes the domestic; rather, I am referring to relationships and writings in the public eye.

Building on the Chinese concept of an inner-outer continuum, I situate the lives of women studied in this book in a series of nested circles originating in the private domain of the inner chambers and extending to the social realms of kinship, neighborhood, and to the heart of the so-called public spheres of print culture, litigation, and loyalist activities. Women's social lives in these various fields of action constitute the two major themes of the book. First, I investigate the forging and emotional content of their friendship ties with other women. Second, I portray women's interactions with the men in their life — father, husband, sons, relatives, teachers, authors, and, in the case of courtesans, clients and lovers.

These two kinds of intimacies constituted the weft and warp of a woman's emotive, intellectual, and religious lives. The rich tradition that seventeenth-century literate women created and celebrated was largely separate from the world of men, although it was by no means separatist. In fact, while shared concerns, routines, rituals, and emotions distinguished the female world from the male, the very construction of such routines and rituals was a product of interactions with the prerogatives, networks, and enterprises of men. No single word such as "domination" or "subjuga-tion" can adequately describe the nature of relationships between these men and women.[33]

Since the borders between inner and outer, or between private and public, are ambivalent, shifting, and open to negotiation, cases of women crossing boundaries are particularly revealing of the nature of those boun-daries and the terms of their negotiation. Examples of such gender role reversals as girls raised as boys and professional women writers who were the breadwinners of the family, discussed in Chapter 3, will lend further support to the contention that gender boundaries were constructed, not predetermined, entities.

Women's Culture: Domestic, Social, and Public Communities

Having argued for the need to study women's history in the context of their everyday interactions with other women and men, in this section I seek to establish a seemingly contradictory argument for the distinctness of women's culture. The contradiction is more apparent than real in light of the ambivalent relationship between women's culture and so-called general culture.

My usage of *women's culture* derives from historian Gerder Lerner's explanation that the anthropological meaning of the term "encompass[es] the familial and friendship networks of women, their affective ties, their rituals." Lerner argues that "it would hardly be appropriate to define the culture of half of humanity as a subculture. Women live their social exis-tence within the general culture. . . . Women live a duality — as members of the general culture and as partakers of woman's culture."[34] For women who lived in this duality, the connectedness of the so-called female and male spheres did not detract from the exclusive meaning of the women's culture in their lives or their own awareness of it. Although gentrywomen in seventeenth-century China often depended on men to publish their verses and to expand their social networks, this dependence did not pre-clude friendship ties and emotions to which only women were privy.

The intensity and endurance of these ties are as glaring as the distinctly literary and textual expressions that the women gave them. The exclusive-ness of women's culture was built on a shared interest in literature as writers, editors, and readers. The volumes of poetry, prefaces, essays, and colophons that these women wrote with and for each other allow us to reconstruct a discourse of love, sex, and beauty in the context of everyday boudoir life. Through the exchange of verse, these women were able to express their feelings toward one another despite physical separation, in much the same way as friends exchanged letters in the age of postal communication.[35] The exchange of poetry created female networks analogous to "the female world of love and ritual" in nineteenth-century America which, as described by Carroll Smith-Rosenberg, was sustained by letters.[36] In both cases, the transmission of writings was instrumental to the maintenance of a distinct and emotive women's culture.

Furthermore, some readers were aware that being female set them apart from men, and they strove to develop their own appreciation of literature. Women who read *The Peony Pavilion* (*Mudanting*), a play by Tang Xianzu (1550–1616), were often moved to write their own commentaries because they felt that male authors did not understand the feelings of the female protagonist. The germ of a female literary criticism can be seen in the efforts of three women, married to the same man at different times, who produced the *"The Peony Pavilion": Commentary Edition by Wu Wushan's Three Wives*. The bonds developed by these women and the content of their commentary will be analyzed in Chapter 2. The self-awareness of woman readers like them is the best testimony to a distinct women's culture in the seventeenth century.

In other words, Chinese women's culture is born not only of individual women's self-perceptions, but also of their evolving relationships with other women, with the world of men, and with imaginative terrains peopled by literary characters, historical figures, and legendary heroes. The women's world may be circumscribed in the final analysis, but it surely is not cloistered, monochromatic, or repetitive.

In the seventeenth century, this women's culture also acquired informal and formal organizational existence. "Women's culture," in this sense, can be used interchangeably with "communities of women." Female associations had a long history in China; one tenth-century Dunhuang manuscript documented a society of fifteen members devoted to the promotion of friendship among women.[37] Although women in the seventeenth century were known to have gathered in groups to study Buddhist sutras or to encourage one another in the Christian faith, the most common organizational expression of gentrywomen's communities was the poetry club.[38]

I identify three kinds of women's communities based on membership and activities: domestic, social, and public communities.[39] A "domestic" community was the most informal and was constituted when mothers or mothers-in-law gathered with female relatives after dinner to discuss literature or when they composed poetry while strolling in the garden. It was "familial" in the sense that all the women were related by kinship ties and that activities were enmeshed in everyday family life. A "social" community was made up of a group of related women together with their neighbors and in some cases friends from afar. Although social communities cast their net wider than "domestic" communities, their activities were just as informal. In many ways they can be thought of as a transitional type between the other two. A "public" community is so called because it was publicly visible as a result of its publications and literary fame of its members. Similar to men's poetry societies, some of these gentry groups had formal names — Banana Garden Seven, or Ten Wuzhong [Suzhou] Poets, for example. Members came together as kin, neighbors, fellow students, or simply as like-minded writers.

Courtesans formed a different type of public network, which can be called "extra-familial." Such networks were a form of public community in that they were known to many members of the public. Although independent of the male-centered kinship system, these networks were even more enmeshed in the public networks of men than their gentry counterparts. Ironically, although courtesans led lives supposedly free of patriarchal control, their networks were the most dependent on male support and were the weakest vehicle for expressions of the members' feminine identities.

These three modes may also describe stages in the life span of a group. As a domestic community grew to incorporate outside members, it became social; a social community might eventually turn public as it gained recognition in established literati circles or embarked on editorial and publication projects. The incidence of the different types also showed a progression over time. The domestic was the most common form in the Jiangnan region in the seventeenth century; toward the end of the century and into the next, public communities dotted the landscape as local sons invoked women's poetry as evidence of the sophistication of their hometowns.

This tripartite division should not obliterate the attributes shared by all literate women's communities. First, all were extensions of an intimacy between women, created as the women's tradition was transmitted from one generation to the next in the inner chambers. As such, they were expressions of the emotional and intellectual concerns of their members *as women*. Second, this was a highly literary tradition, built on women's shared love of poetry and literature. Although the exchange of souvenir objects such as fans, portraits, paintings, and shoes was frequent, the raison d'être of the communities was the appreciation, production, and propagation of the written word.[40] Third, all three types of networks relied on the world of men for membership recruitment and expansion. The very existence of public communities, in particular, was predicated on men's recognition and promotion.

The centrality of the written word to the women's communities described in this book suggests that this particular form of women's culture was limited to elite women or women in affluent areas with opportunities for education. Although maids, concubines, and female entertainers occasionally participated in these networks, they did so only by dint of their contacts with the cultural world of gentrymen and -women.[41] The literary nature of the women's culture surveyed in this book is a function of both the cultural dominance of members of scholar-official families, male and female alike, and the powerful all-encompassing presence of the Confucian tradition.

The power of the Confucian ideological and cultural tradition is at once a constraint and an opportunity for the privileged women. The constraints of the rigid gender-based parameters were most keenly felt by the women themselves. For them to be so educated and so intimate with the male elites and yet to be formally excluded from their political world was frustrating indeed. Hence laments of "if only women could take the examination . . ." were muttered not only by talented daughters and their ambitious mothers but also by frustrated fathers of lackluster sons in the seventeenth century. Yet to speak of oppression and restrictions is to assume women to be extraneous to the Confucian tradition. Although this is true to some extent, it is more valid to recognize them as intrinsic to that tradition. They were born into it and lived by it; without overt battle calls they were manipulating and changing it from within. The power of the Confucian tradition rubbed off on the elite women in subtle but manifold ways.

Women in the Confucian Tradition

The complex and ambivalent existence of women in the Confucian tradition can be illuminated only when the propensity to treat "Confucianism" as an abstract creed or a static control mechanism is discarded. The Confucian tradition is not a monolithic and fixed system of values and practices. To be sure, the tenets of Confucian ideology as a philosophy and a way of life, laid down in the Classics, have maintained a remarkable degree of continuity through history. The very resilience of this tradition, however, was the product of constant adaptation and interpretation by individual scholars to realign it with changing social realities. In this sense, the Confucian tradition, like the boundaries between the inner and outer, was open to a certain degree of negotiation.

Instead of treating the Confucian ideological tradition as a monolith, I make an analytical distinction between (1) an "official ideology," epitomized by the Song Neo-Confucian canon, which remained the sanctioned curriculum of the civil service examination in the Ming and Qing dynasties; (2) an "applied ideology" expressed in primers and precepts that attempted to explain and propagate the official ideology; and (3) "ideology in practice," private views expressed by scholar-officials and men of letters who were fully schooled in the first two, yet as shown from their letters, diaries, and prefaces, were more accommodating to reality than were the official treatises. Although all three were responsive to social changes, the degree of responsiveness tended to be lowest for the former and highest for the latter. I am interested most in changes in the realm of "ideology in practice" despite a certain doctrinal rigidity in official ideology, for it is in this realm that new discourses on domesticity and womanhood were most evident in the seventeenth century.

In the sixteenth and seventeenth centuries, even interpretations of the official ideology were undergoing significant adjustments. In the most urbanized region of the empire, Jiangnan, male thinkers often loosely identified as followers of the Wang Yangming Neo-Confucian School were radically reinterpreting the Confucian canon. Although their philosophical concerns were as varied as their political agendas, these men shared a basic dissatisfaction with the dry rationality and scholastic orientation of the Confucian "mainstream." Instead, they championed intuition, spontaneity, and expression of emotion.[42] Focusing on its ramifications in literature and domestic life, I call one aspect of this inward turn the "cult of *qing*" (feeling, emotion, love). This introspection has far-reaching consequences not only for philosophy and religion, but also for literature, social life, and gender relations. In other words, the possibilities for change in the seventeenth century stemmed not from challenges to the Confucian system from without but from dynamic developments within the tradition itself. The women who studied men's books and published their own poetry played a visible role in these internal transformations.

As the Confucian tradition strove to regain its footing, a handful of women found enough elbow room to enter a male world of literature and civility (*wen*), albeit often as substitute or honorary men. The fact that the Chinese literary tradition consisted almost entirely of writings by men meant that the woman writer had to be initiated into a world in which she had no rightful place and no distinct voice. Yet, as the subsequent chapters will show, women artists of the seventeenth century did not seem to consider this a problem; they simply appropriated from that philosophical and literary tradition ideas and idioms that expressed their own thoughts and feelings. In choice of genre and literary voice, their writings may not have differed much from that of men's; the emotional content was nonetheless uniquely feminine.

Other women writers appeared to have wrestled with the problem of articulating their place in the Confucian literary tradition. Some sought to establish a female genealogy from within that tradition, invoking the

names of a handful of famous women of talent in history — Han scholar
and teacher Ban Zhao, Tang poet Xue Tao, Song poets Li Qingzhao and
Zhu Shuzhen, and Yuan painter-calligrapher Guan Daosheng. Others
sought to discover germs of women's culture in the Confucian canon by
arguing that many of the authors featured in the *Book of Songs* were
female.

Some women went further than seeking legitimacy; they actively embraced Confucian values and took it as a woman's duty to resuscitate the
Confucian way and to transmit it to the next generation. As examples
from this book will show, many women writers bemoaned the growing
disorder in society and saw the revival of the Confucian moral vision as
their natural duty. To them, motherhood was an exalted calling through
which women could save the world. Cults of domesticity and motherhood
may have been promoted first by male literati, but they acquired concrete
meaning only as women embraced the ideals for their own reasons. Their
affirmation of the Confucian tradition, or their interpretations of it, did
not simply serve the interests of the patriarch. In the ways that the good
mother used it to justify a sophisticated education for girls, this affirmation could even have inadvertent subversive effects.

Given the dynamic and multitudinous nature of the Confucian tradition, its relationship with educated women — although by no means equal
or reciprocal — was not as predetermined as the precepts would have us
believe. From a long-term historical perspective, the Confucian tradition
has to be understood as a constructed rather than natural order, one that is
responsive to social change. If individual men and women cannot be construed merely as the acted upon, then neither can the "dominant ideology"
itself be reduced to a preordained, static, and monolithic existence.

Women and the Social History of Jiangnan

The development of a literate women's culture in seventeenth-century
Jiangnan was possible only with the wealth generated by urbanization and
commercialization in the region. Growing opportunities for women to
receive an education, read books, publish, and travel were necessary conditions for the growth of this women's culture. The existence of a sizable
group of literate women, in turn, left an indelible mark on the urban
culture of the region. As readers, writers, painters, teachers, and travelers,
they stretched the traditional boundaries of a woman's role as good wife
and mother to encompass uncharted territories.

These women participated in regional and national lives not primarily
as economic producers but as producers and consumers of culture. Yet
their cultural activities were sustainable only with the quickened pace of

economic development in the various regions after the mid-Ming period. Scholars in China, Japan, and the United States have elucidated the enormity of the socioeconomic changes that transpired, although the historical implications of these changes are still being hotly contested.[43] The monetarization of silver in the sixteenth century, in particular, put a new face on the economic life of the empire. Commerce introduced cash crops to increasing areas of cultivation, fostered webs of trade routes and marketing networks, prompted a general retreat in government control over the economy, and cast China as a formidable exporter in the world trade system.

These economic developments went hand in hand with far-reaching social changes. Without accounting for their different effects on males and females, scholars have identified the salient aspects of such changes in terms of expanded educational opportunities, flourishing commercial publishing, fluid class and status structures, proliferation of urban centers, and the growing importance of commercial wealth in the investment portfolio of elite families. Wealthy merchants, together with absentee landlords, presided over an emergent urban culture in cities and market towns.[44] How these fundamental changes affected women from different social and geographical locations, however, has not figured as the central focus of in-depth studies. It is this gap that this book seeks to fill. Writers at the time widely considered confused gender hierarchies at once an epitome, a symbol, and a culprit of general social disarray. For this reason alone, gender is a major constituent of the social and economic histories of seventeenth-century China.

In no region were the links between gender and socioeconomic changes more pronounced than in Jiangnan, the location of this study. Jiangnan (literally, "south of the [Yangzi] River"), a millennium-old designation, evoked shared meanings and bountiful images to people in the seventeenth century. It was less a physical area with unequivocal boundaries than an economic way of life and a cultural identity.[45] In geographical terms, the heart of seventeenth-century Jiangnan coincided with the drainage area of Lake Tai in the provinces of Zhejiang and Jiangsu. In the administrative hierarchy, the prefectures of Suzhou, Songjiang, Changzhou, Jiaxing, and Huzhou covered the core of Jiangnan, with the occasional inclusion of neighboring Zhenjiang. Yet it is its mode of economic production that gave the region its perceived affluence and urbanity. The warm and well-drained area had been a rice bowl of the empire since the late Tang. In the mid-Ming, cash crops, notably mulberry leaves and cotton, began to supplant rice cultivation. With the ensuing development of trade routes, market towns, and employment opportunities for migrant population, the cotton and silk industries transformed Jiangnan into China's wealthiest, most urbanized, densely populated, and volatile region.[46]

The boundaries of Jiangnan as a cultural region are more elusive than its geographical, administrative, and economic delineations. Whereas the very name of Jiangnan, a popular poetic allusion, conjured up images of abundance, hedonism, and sensual beauty, the identities of the privileged few who could partake of these riches were always a matter of contestation. This politics of exclusion is evinced by the ambivalent location of Yangzhou, a major port on the Grand Canal and center of the Salt Administration. Although physically situated north of the Yangzi River, it was considered part of Jiangnan in the seventeenth century by dint of its riches, thriving merchant culture, and frequent traffic with the Yangzi Delta. When its fortunes plummeted in the nineteenth century, Yangzhou was relegated to Jiangbei ("north of the River"), the vulgar backwaters that was Jiangnan's Other.[47]

This politics of exclusion is intimately linked to the linguistic life of the Jiangnan localities. With the exclusion of Yangzhou came the denigration of its dialect, a variant of Jianghuai "Mandarin" (*guanhua*). The various Wu dialects from the Lake Tai area became the spoken language of choice, to the point of replacing *guanhua* in certain northern counties. Yet the Wu language is not a singular dialect; its local variants have long contested for prestige in specific Jiangnan prefectures.[48] That is to say, Jiangnan in the seventeenth century was as divided by local practices, loyalties, and dialects as it was united by its uniform depiction as the land of plenty.

The amorphous cultural identities of seventeenth-century Jiangnan have important implications for women's history. Women writers from the core areas of Suzhou and Songjiang frequently traveled to or befriended women from Hangzhou, Shaoxing, and other areas that are at best peripheral according to the stricter geographical and administrative definitions of Jiangnan. In hindsight, we see these women as inventing their own expanded geography with their literary ventures and social networks, a geography that imposes yet another layer of complexity onto the already amorphous cultural identities of the Jiangnan region. At the same time, women's loyalty to native place was a divisive force that fragmented the women's communities. These tensions between local and regional identities, or between women's culture and Jiangnan culture, can be explored fully only by unitary analyses that link private concerns to the public sphere and gender to so-called general history.

The elite women's culture portrayed in this book was also found in other regions of the empire, notably the Beijing metropolitan area and Guangdong. But only in Jiangnan did it attain such heights. The production and consumption of literature, exchange of verses, and cross-fertilization of ideas that gave birth to this literate women's culture required a critical mass of educated women and sympathetic men, as well as established publishing centers, academies, and art markets. This critical mass was first found in late sixteenth-century Jiangnan and continued to flourish, in various forms and locations, until the nineteenth century.

This book focuses on the period from the 1570's to the 1720's, during which time the socioeconomic and cultural conditions most conducive to this women's culture were in place. In subsuming this century and a half under the loose rubric "seventeenth century," I am making a deliberate statement on the periodization of Chinese history in general and the nature of historical change around the time of the Ming-Qing transition in particular. Whereas our present scheme of designating historical periods is overtly or tacitly a function of political history (the late *imperial* period; the Qing *dynasty*), the social historian sees change and continuity in a different light. From the vantage point of gender relations, the broadly conceived seventeenth century constitutes a coherent period.

This emphasis on socioeconomic and cultural continuities seeks not to discount the relevance of political changes but to suggest more encompassing frameworks of historical analysis. The political rupture in 1644 and the subsequent consolidation of an alien Manchu dynasty brought major changes in power alignments, cultural policies, ethnic politics, and military organization, many of which affected women's lives and definitions of womanhood. The fall of the Ming house, for example, effectively ended the erudite and politicized existence of Jiangnan courtesan culture, as described in Chapter 7. Not only were the verse-chanting courtesans who appeared in the company of merchants in the eighteenth century a fragment of their former artistic self, the social location and political function of the courtesan's house had also diminished.

As seminal as Manchu policies were in the areas of morality and ideology, they did not interrupt the spread of women's education and women's involvement in public print culture. As early as 1979, Jonathan Spence and John Wills called attention to the "very important secular trends that can be observed from mid-Ming [1590's] through high-[Q]ing [beginning ca. 1730], with only brief interruption by the conquest. These include commercial growth, urbanization, growing numbers of examination candidates, the wider dissemination of increasingly sophisticated classical scholarship, and discussion of 'statecraft.' "[49] These secular trends, in fact, were the power supply that fed into the continued vibrancy of women's culture and spread of women's education.

This enduring vibrancy was evident in the resilience of a host of social practices and institutions that accompanied the birth of women's culture described in this book. Ranging from the growth of a reading public to enhanced employment for women artists and teachers to the proliferation of female poetry societies, these secular developments signified a growing involvement of women in the literate culture of China as well as fundamental changes within that culture. The trajectories of some of these developments extended well beyond the seventeenth century. Hence although the narrative of this book falls almost entirely between the 1570's and 1720's, occasionally I discuss trends that were brought to fruition only in the mid- to late-eighteenth century. These include the development of teaching as a profession and the canonization of erudite women in local history.

In recognition of the many secular trends that transcended the dynastic transition, scholars in Taiwan and Japan have begun to refer to "late Ming–early Qing" (*Mingmo-Qingchu* in Chinese; *Minmatsu-Shinsho* in Japanese) as a coherent historical epoch.[50] The famous Japanese historian Miyazaki Ichisada, for example, contrasts the artistic ideal of individuality and amateurism with the reality of rampant commercialism in this period, a contrast embodied in the work of the celebrated painter and art critic Dong Qichang (1555–1635). He points out that the enormous concentration of wealth in the seventeenth century led to the maturing of an art and antique market and facilitated the proliferation of regional schools of painting. Previously prefecture-based (Suzhou, Hangzhou), these regional schools were now based in the lowest administrative unit, the county (Huating of Songjiang, Changshu of Suzhou). This fragmentation, argues Miyazaki, stemmed from the lack of public venues for exhibition that transcended parochial identities.[51] The seventeenth-century artistic world, in this sense, was a microcosm of society at large in the paradoxical co-existence of commercialism with aestheticism, of cosmopolitanism with parochialism.

Asserting that the late Ming–early Qing (or simply "the seventeenth century" in this book) constituted an integral unit in social history does not preclude recognizing the enormous changes *within* this period and the internal contradictions thus engendered. These contradictions lend an ambivalent image to the period marked by the reigns of the Wanli (1573–1620) and Kangxi (1662–1722) emperors. If we focus on the social upheavals it witnessed, it was the freest and most chaotic of times. If we focus instead on the vehement imposition of ideological control, especially those instigated by the Manchu monarchs, the same period appears to be the most restrictive and orthodox of times. The teachers of the inner chambers who populate this book knew the freedoms and restrictions equally well, although they did not portray their lives in such terms.

Comparative History: Fallacies of a Universal Modernity

Historians of China have generally considered the seventeenth century to be part of the late imperial period, which lasted from the sixteenth century through the nineteenth. The nature of the socioeconomic changes that transpired over these centuries, however, has prompted some historians to compare China to early modern Europe and to argue that "early modern" better describes the latter half of that period than "late imperial."

In his study of the development of capitalism and urban institutions in the middle Yangzi city of Hankou, for example, William Rowe argues that the national long-distance trade networks and shared sense of urban community that existed by the nineteenth century were characteristic of the early modern period.[52] Similarly, Paul Ropp, in his study of popular literature and its readership in the early to mid-Qing, has concluded that widespread educational opportunities, a flourishing publishing industry, and a higher degree of equality between the sexes were all harbingers of a new age.[53] In a more limited vein, Craig Clunas has also argued for labeling the period from the mid-sixteenth century to the fall of Ming (1644) "early modern" in his study of the discourse of luxury goods.[54]

Many of the social trends and institutions discussed in this book do bear a superficial resemblance to counterparts in early modern Europe: rising female literacy rates, the emergence of the woman writer, the growing importance of urban readers and theatergoers as consumers of culture, a general retreat into the private world of domesticity and sentimentality — to name the more salient examples. These superficial resemblances, however, mask the more substantive differences in social structure, political institutions, and historical dynamics. A case in point is the double-edged effects of the spread of printing in seventeenth-century China and early modern France. While breaking up the learned elite's monopoly by making religious tracts and novels available to an urban public, the printing industry in both countries also produced texts that promoted the orthodox creed.[55] Yet in contrast to the ultimate decline of monarchies in early modern Europe, the monarchical state in seventeenth- and eighteenth-century China retained its moral authority in the face of massive socioeconomic changes. This resilience of the state's moral authority was all the more striking in light of its de facto retreat from such public functions as water control and granary management in the eighteenth century.

If the nature of the imperial Chinese state and its political control is fundamentally at variance with that of Europe, even more salient is the difference in constructions of personhood and individuality. The use of such words as "inner emotions" and "subjectivity" in the Chinese context is not predicated on the awareness of an individuated self or clearly perceived boundaries between self and others or between inner and outer. Similarly, the study of male and female networks in this book highlights the overriding importance of family and communal ties in the construction of both the private and public spheres in seventeenth-century China, a condition that precluded the birth of the independent, privatized individual who was the Prince in early modern Europe. Hence what I describe as "privatization in Chinese life" signifies a phenomenon quite different from the one bearing a similar name in Europe.

My conviction is that while the *meaning* of Chinese history has to be sought in the unique context of China's cultural and historical dynamics, its *significance* lies in what it can teach us about the shared richness of human experience. However, without detracting from the importance of comparative history, I contend that the paucity of our present knowledge about the nature of social change in seventeenth-century China does not allow for meaningful comparisons. As is evident throughout this book, I benefit from the insights and perspectives provided by scholars of European and American experiences, yet I refrain from making what seems to me premature comparisons between China's history and those of other countries. When the very meaning of Chinese modernity is still being debated in China today, the use of "early modern" is more befuddling than enlightening. Hence rather than adopting the transplanted "early modern" rubric, I have opted for a mere chronological characterization of this period of contradictions and change: the seventeenth century.[56]

To paraphrase Joseph Levenson, this is a web book, not a line book. But the seven chapters, arranged in three parts, follow a simple logic. Part I deals with the historical contexts of seventeenth-century Jiangnan. Chapter 1 sets the stage by describing the most salient socioeconomic development from the perspective of gender: the flourishing of commercial printing and the visibility of women in the emergent reading public. Chapter 2 focuses on the primacy of *qing* as a new principle of human relations in this floating world. For all the attention it focused on women's abilities, the cult ultimately served to reinforce the notion of separate male/female spheres.

The cult of *qing* and the growing presence of educated women in real life prompted the rethinking of domesticity, a woman's place, and womanhood. In Part II, these are analyzed in terms of a struggle over the rationale and content of women's education. Chapter 3 takes up deliberations on the woman's sphere, and Chapter 4 discusses the attributes of a new womanhood: talent, virtue, and beauty.

Part III introduces four variants of women's communities that thrived on the fertile soil of print culture and new womanhood. These networks are situated in concentric circles that radiate from the inner realms of domesticity to the public realm. Chapter 5 focuses on the gentry poet's conjugal relations and her intimacies with women of her family. Chapter 6 traces the trajectories of gentry poets who traveled widely, forged networks in the social and public domains, and sought to construct a genealogy of women writers through time. These women established a distinct literate women's culture and crafted for it a respectable space in literati culture and kinship networks.

Chapter 7 portrays the most agile and boldest of all women — courtesans, professional writers, and the gentry wives who befriended them. Their transitory communities embody a paradox that kept the gender system running in the face of socioeconomic upheavals: the wider a women's community grew, the more fragmented it became; the women who were freest from domestic constraints were also the most dependent on men in the public domain.

Part One

SOCIAL AND PRIVATE HISTORIES

1

In the Floating World

WOMEN AND COMMERCIAL PUBLISHING

TWO DEVELOPMENTS IN THE late sixteenth century formed the backdrop, indeed, the *sine qua non*, of this book. For the first time in Chinese history, a considerable number of women managed to publish their writings within their lifetime; at the same time, printed books became so accessible that reading ceased to be the prerogative of the upper echelon of the traditional elite. A booming publishing industry was instrumental both in the birth of the woman reader-writer and in the emergence of a reading public.[1] The purpose of this chapter is to outline these two related developments in the context of commercial publishing in the sixteenth and seventeenth centuries.

The birth of the woman reader-writer — as a type, not an isolated individual — required the presence of a critical mass of literate women who were not necessarily legendary household names. Although almost every successive dynasty boasted a handful of women distinguished by erudition, they stood as lonesome reminders of the incongruity between their individual gifts and the yoke of their times. In the seventeenth century, in contrast, in every Jiangnan city and in every generation there were women who wrote, published, and discussed one another's works. The growth in the number of educated women, together with expanded opportunities for them to interact with one another and with society at large, created a critical mass that had not existed before. Hence the role that literate women played in the culture of seventeenth-century China was qualitatively different. This book is about these women and the culture they shaped.

The debut of women as author and audience was in itself one of the most conspicuous elements in the urban culture that had been taking shape in the Jiangnan market towns since the mid-sixteenth century. The quickening pace of commercial publishing and circulation of books created a fertile ground for cross-fertilization between the ideas of men and women, between local and cosmopolitan cultures, and between written and oral traditions. In this world in flux, men of letters envisioned new philosophical and literary possibilities in which educated women played active and constructive roles, possibilities I analyze in terms of a cult of *qing* in Chapter 2. To highlight the fluidity of boundaries that characterizes this culture of the reading public, I refer to it as the "floating world" — an allusion to the urbane world depicted in Japanese *ukiyoe* ("pictures of the floating world").

Educated women were at once consumers and producers of this new culture. As readers, writers, and editors, they emerged from their supposed cloistered anonymity to assume a visible place in literate culture, previously the prerogative of the male literati. The term *floating world* evokes a second meaning when applied to these women, who used the creative acts of reading and writing to negotiate the domestic/public boundary as well as the thin line between fiction and reality. Readers of fiction and drama, in particular, found in the fanciful plots and characters metaphors for the realities they experienced. In everyday life, in turn, they conversed with fictional characters, creating their own fantastic world by way of wordplay, games, and rituals. In other words, the reading woman inhabited a world much larger than her boudoir by exercising her intellect and imagination; she became all the more entrenched in the public world when she was moved to wield the brush herself. In this sense, reading opened up a floating world in which the familiar constraints on her life appeared less formidable and more open to negotiation.

To illustrate the import of the rise of the woman reader-writer, in this chapter I situate her in a series of larger social phenomena of which she was a part — the emergence of a reading public, commercial publishing, urban culture, and the development of a commercialized society and money economy. In the sections that follow, I first briefly examine the changes in social relations brought on by the influx of silver into China. I then turn to the pivotal roles played by book merchants as well as private and commercial publishers in heralding a new urban culture, which I refer to as the culture of the reading public. I pay special attention to one of its salient elements — the visibility of women who could read and write — by analyzing the floods of books that the commercial presses issued for and by women. Finally, I speculate on the conflicting implications of the growing presence of the woman reader-writer for greater gender equality.

Money and Disorder in Social Hierarchies

It all began with money. In the sixteenth century, silver imports from the Americas and Japan completed the transition of the Jiangnan economy into a thoroughly monetarized one. It was estimated that in the first three decades of the seventeenth century, at least 250,000–265,000 kilograms of specie reached China's coastal and Central Asian borders every year.[2] It is hardly surprising that an intrusion of such magnitude into production and exchange created havoc in social hierarchies. Traditional social distinctions — between high and low, merchant and gentry, male and female, respectable and mean — were idealized constructs best suited for a self-sufficient agrarian society. By the sixteenth century, these binary oppositions seemed at odds with the complexity of human relationships in the highly commercialized region. The ideal Confucian norms, devised to instill social harmony by perpetuating hierarchies and distinctions, became more prescriptive than descriptive, although they were no less powerful because of that.

The growing complexity of social relations in a monetary economy can be understood on three levels: definitions of personhood, principles of social organization, and the perceived boundary of so-called local society.[3] Underlying all these changes was the reduction of webs of personal economic dependency between landlord and tenant to ties of mere economic exchange. Peasants pursued new opportunities for social and physical mobility by producing for the market or by migrating to the burgeoning cities.[4] As a result, itinerant laborers and vagabonds became common sights in the Jiangnan cities and countryside. This undermining of old attributes of status and personhood, however, rarely translated into heightened personal freedom, nor did it give rise to a less stratified society. Not only did the freedom to compete breed insecurity, it also strengthened old forms of servitude and introduced new ones. A freer labor market, in fact, co-existed with heightened commendation and subjugation of bondservants to the local gentry.

The Japanese historian Kishimoto Mio astutely observes that "from the eyes of those who lived in the sixteenth century and after, their world was marked by the collapse of traditional hierarchies: high/lowly, respectable/mean, senior/junior." Yet she goes on to note that this perceived collapse by no means implies that the seventeenth-century society had disintegrated into an unstructured mass of free individuals. To the contrary, people in the Lower Yangzi formulated a complex of new social groupings structured by both vertical and horizontal ties, ranging from literati societies to friendship pacts to master-servant bondage to lineage organizations to networks of vagabonds.[5] With the decline of traditional mechanisms of social control and welfare, people became all the more ingenious in utilizing old and new organizational principles to create a modicum of collective security in a competitive and uncertain world.

The result was not only a proliferation of social groupings that arose from societal needs rather than the imperatives of the state but also a new repertoire of principles on which these groupings were organized. The most salient example of such new principles was that of the female gender, as evinced by the networks formed by literate women. Through face-to-face contacts and exchange of manuscripts, woman poets forged their own communities with like-minded readers from different families, cities, and even social stations. By way of concrete examples of these communities, we will investigate in Part III of this book how the category of female gender intersected with other existing principles of association such as kinship and neighborhood ties while maintaining a separate identity.

These women and their social networks were very much products of the commercialized society. The affluence enjoyed by many families in the Jiangnan urban areas, now sponsoring schools and publishing ventures, greatly enhanced educational opportunities for women. The gates of learning, an exclusively male vocation according to the ideal of separate spheres, increasingly became opened to women in practice. In this sense, alongside the collapse of such traditional hierarchies as high/low, the male/female division also appeared to be less strict than before. Once educated, women became all the more agile in exploiting the gap between theory and practice to expand their horizons and to construct larger and more formal women's communities. Since these issues, all major themes of this book, will be further expounded later, suffice it to note here that the growing incongruity between idealized hierarchical boundaries and the realities of mobility and fluidity in a monetarized society was conducive to the emergence of the female gender as a category of social organization.

Whereas women's communities were born of a new principle of social organization, other associations represented new applications of aggregates of existing principles. Later in this chapter, we will encounter examples of business arrangements forged on the basis of kinship and locale in the publishing trade. The Japanese social historian Ueda Makoto coined the term *circuit (kairo)* to distinguish this and other social formations in Ming-Qing society from traditional social networks. "Networks" refers to personal groupings built on individual ties, which could not last beyond its members' lifetime, but "circuits" are institutional arrangements that are fixtures in the communities in which they operate and lend them stability. Constructed on a multitude of overlapping and shifting criteria such as lineage, bureaucracy, membership in secret societies, and native place, these circuits outlived economic cycles of depression and inflation and survived the political upheavals of the Manchu conquest in the mid-seventeenth century.[6]

Both heightened mobility and the proliferation of new social organizations accelerated the demise of imperially sanctioned village chiefs and tax chiefs, which created a hiatus in local leadership.[7] This weakening of the village as a natural habitat, coupled with heightened traffic between town and country, called into question the very idea of a contiguous "local society" with clear-cut social and spatial demarcations. Instead, local society became a multivalent entity, whose boundaries and composition shifted with the task at hand and the vantage point of the viewer. For example, the field of action of the landowning gentry increasingly expanded to that of the county, the lowest administrative unit. This was in large part due to the prevalence of absentee landlordism, which meant that local disputes could no longer be resolved at the grass-roots level and had to be dealt with at the county level and above. Prominent lineages, too, often selected marriage partners from distant areas within their county.[8] Another repercussion of the hiatus in local leadership was the ascendance of lineage organizations in local society. I will elaborate on the import of growing lineage power and the marriage alliance circle to women's education in Chapter 4.

In short, the intrusion of money created a mobile and fluid society in Jiangnan, a floating world in which definitions of identity, social relations, and community were no longer predetermined but were defined by situational context and could change over an individual's lifetime. Commentators at the time were all too aware of the incongruity between realities in this floating world and the idealized Confucian order frozen in terms of such binaries as high/low, senior/junior, or male/female.

This gulf between the ideal and the real, the most important cultural legacy of the monetary economy, enabled the production of new knowledge while prompting many to seek the reinvention of old orders. The emergent world of commercial publishing and women's involvement in it were situated squarely at the crossroads of these tensions. As the women saw it, they could enjoy de facto freedoms and opportunities for personal fulfillment without overtly challenging the ideal order. These educated women were extremely skillful at exploiting the social and ideological fluidities to expand their own social and intellectual horizons. Their growing visibility as reader-writer and expanding social networks constituted the most salient examples.

The widening gap between norms and social realities affected women in a second way, by enhancing their educational opportunities. Instead of diminishing the lure of moral education, the glaring distance between ideal norms and reality prompted crusaders to redouble their didactic efforts through mass-produced texts. These crusaders, some of whom were educated women themselves, identified the cultivation of motherly virtues as the key to setting the world straight. Challenges to ideal norms wrought by social disorders, in fact, provided the strongest justification for women's education. Yet since this education was intended to strengthen the ideological underpinnings of social and gender hierarchies, its implications for women's well-being were problematic. I will return to this issue in my discussion of commercially published didactic books for women.

The inadequacy of age-old moral guidelines in providing for everyday survival created a volcano of demands for a new form of knowledge — practical, how-to guides. From the safest travel routes to terms used in real estate contracts to proper conduct in brothels and gambling dens, the vexed traveler in the floating world could draw upon an encyclopedia of know-how that the Classics did not provide.[9] The fluid commercial society now promised multiple channels to wealth and a modicum of prestige outside the civil service — manufacturing, trade, and para-bureaucratic services — but competition was stiffer than before. Books were useful in more ways than one to the social climbers: students mimicked the latest model examination essays; merchants kept abreast of market conditions; families consulted almanacs for auspicious dates before launching building projects, planning trips, or binding a daughter's feet. Those who thus rose above the fray, in turn, found book ownership a time-honored symbol of their newfound status.

In other words, heightened competition for social status increased the demand for books, both as ammunition and as token of victory. It was this new market for practical instruction that fueled the commercial publishing industry and created a distinct feature of the emerging reading public. In the gap between ideology and practice, boundless possibilities emerged. Having been engraved onto woodblocks, they would soon gain a material existence from the printed page.

The Publishing Boom and Birth of the Reading Public

The publishing industry that fed on the appetite for practical knowledge was itself part of the commercialized and monetarized society. Recent work by Japanese scholars has shown that nothing short of *revolution* describes the transition that the Chinese publishing industry went through in the Jiajing period (1522–66).[10] It was not a technological revolution — all the know-how for woodblock printing was in place by the ninth century — but a revolution in the economics of publishing and the culture of learning.[11] In the second half of the Ming dynasty, the supply of and demand for books soared, and prices plunged, triggering an unprecedented publishing boom throughout the country.

The influx of silver and the ensuing commercialization in sixteenth-century China ushered in an age of mass publishing. The proliferation of trade routes and regional markets quickened the circulation of books and ideas at the same time as it created a newly affluent class of consumers. Many of the publishing houses that thrived were centuries-old family enterprises dating back to the Song dynasty, yet they responded to changing market conditions by catering to the needs and tastes of a new group of readers who did not hail from the traditional scholar-gentry elite. Specifically, the mid-sixteenth century, which coincided with the Jiajing period, marked the transition from the age of quality printing to that of quantity printing. In the age of quality printing, which lasted from the Song to early Ming, blocks were cut and proofread with meticulous care and only high-quality paper and ink were used. Books, as objets d'art, were prerogatives of the wealthy.

The heyday of quantity printing, in turn, began in the Wanli period.[12] The advent of mass printing was propelled by a host of economic and cultural factors, namely, cheaper paper, which lowered production costs substantially; new fonts with most strokes crisscrossing at right angles, which simplified woodblock cutting; and craft specialization, which facilitated the division of labor and improved efficiency. Riding on the crest of change, private publishing ventures in the form of family or commercial presses mushroomed, outstripping official presses in both variety and volume of output.

As a result of this publishing boom, people with no previous access to the printed page or those who had previously had to expend time and effort borrowing and handcopying books could readily buy books in the open market and build a private collection.[13] These people, including aspiring students, holders of lower-degrees, petty rural landlords, owners of small businesses, and women from gentry families, joined the traditional elites to make up a new reading public. The taste of this new reading public was as eclectic as its social composition. Not only did more people come into contact with books, they also devoured a dazzling array of genres — stories, poetry, prose, plays, primers, encyclopedias, religious tracts, didactic books, travel guides, and household almanacs, besides the examination-related canon, model essays, and study aids.[14] Hence in the diversity of its constituency and taste, the reading public exemplified the plurality of the monetarized society of which it was a part.

The term *mass printing* calls attention to the soaring number and variety of books produced in the sixteenth and seventeenth centuries. Similarly, the term *reading public* highlights the end of the monopoly of the scholar-official elites as authors and consumers of literate culture. The word *public*, however, does not carry the connotations of "public sphere" or even "civil society" as it often evokes in European history. Nor do the descriptions of "mass" or "popular" press rest on the social existence of a middle class.[15] The reading public in sixteenth- and seventeenth-century

TABLE I
Sample Retail Book Prices in Seventeenth-Century China

Genre	Title and Publication Data	Price (in ounces of silver)
Travel literature[a]	*Gazetteer of Nanjing Temples* (*Jinling fansha zhi*), Nanjing, 1607; 977 pp.	0.225
Practical guidebook[b]	*Complete Guide to Letter Writing* (*Xinbian shiwen leiju hanmo daquan*), Jianyang, Fujian, 1611; 2,800 pp.	1
Novel[c]	*Romance of the Gods* (*Fengshen yanyi*), Suzhou, Wanli period; 20 *juan*	2
Song scripts[d]	*Sound of Moon Dew* (*Yuelu yin*), Hangzhou, n.d.; 4 *juan*	0.8
Household almanac[e]	*Almanac of Ten Thousand Treasures* (*Wanbao quanshu*), Jianning, Fujian, 1614; 34 *juan*	1
Household almanac[e]	*Almanac of Ten Thousand Treasures* (*Bianyong Wanbao quanshu*), Jianning, Fujian, 1628; 37 *juan*	0.1

[a]Inoue, p. 423.

[b]K. T. Wu, p. 235; Inoue, p. 423; Zhang Xiumin, *Yinshua shi*, p. 518.

[c]Zhang Xiumin, *Yinshua shi*, p. 518; Ōki, "Shuppan bunka," p. 103. (For a Tianqi period [1621–27] edition, see Han Xiduo and Wang, p. 10.)

[d]Wei, p. 124.

[e]Sakai, p. 89.

China was more an extension of the traditional elite than its enemy. A cursory survey of prices makes it amply clear that even with mass production, books remained out of reach for the majority of families.

Insufficient information makes it difficult to conduct quantitative studies of the economics of book publishing. With rare exceptions, the price of a book was not printed on the cover, and I know of no extant price list for books. But scattered references suggest that the book market was two-tiered. Song editions and other rare books were prohibitively expensive, but families of moderate means could afford to own a sampling of popular literature and practical guides. The famous late Ming bibliophile and private publisher Mao Jin (1599–1659) of Suzhou, for example, was known to have paid 200 ounces of silver per page for a prized Song book, and over 1,000 ounces for a copy of a rare Ming edition.[16] In the seventeenth century, a Song edition of *Records of the Historian* (*Shiji*) could fetch 300 ounces.[17] At the lower end of the market, prices hovered around one ounce of silver for an almanac or a novel (see Table 1). The Japanese scholar Sakai Tadao explains that mass production depreciated prices considerably: "In the Wanli period, most almanacs and practical guides were priced at about one ounce. Later, in the Chongzhen period (1628–44), a hastily printed copy could be had for one-tenth of that price."[18]

Even thornier than the question of pricing is that of purchasing power.

Leaving aside the problem of variations in degree of purity, the purchasing power of one ounce of silver varied from place to place and from year to year. Without delving into the macroeconomics of exchange rate fluctuations, it is clear that one ounce of silver was not an amount that the majority of the population could easily dispense with. To cite an arbitrary example, according to commodity prices listed in a 1585 statute book published in Nanjing, one ounce of silver could buy 3.2 *shi* of rice, or 320 catties of salt, or 80 catties of tea, or 200 sheets of bond paper, or 400 writing brushes. In terms of wages, an average agricultural laborer in Huzhou received full board and five ounces of silver in return for a year's work in the period from the 1630's to the 1650's.[19] Evidently, paying one ounce for a book was a considerable expense, but not a prohibitive one, for a family of some means. It was, however, still out of reach for a lower-class family. The newly affluent group of book buyers thus inhabited an ambivalent social position. Although they might appear rustic to holders of metropolitan degrees, to the majority of the population they still lived in a world apart.

To be sure, in a society where most were illiterate, no matter how fast the reading public was growing, it did not exceed 10 percent of the entire population. Its impact on the cultural and intellectual life of the day, however, was more profound than sheer numbers can convey. I will elaborate on the significance of this reading culture below, after surveying the two major vehicles of its production and propagation—family and commercial publishing enterprises. The phenomenal growth of these two forms of non-governmental publishing greatly enhanced the opportunities for ordinary writers, including women, to gain access to books and to have their own works published in their lifetime.

Official and Family Publishing

As books became cheaper, less sacred, and more in demand, the pace of all three forms of printing enterprises—official, private, and commercial—quickened in the sixteenth and seventeenth centuries. Official publishing (*guanke*) refers to printing financed by public funds and supervised by government bureaus, imperial princes, and bureaucrats. The most prolific bureaus were the National University system under the Ministry of Rites and the Directorate of Ceremonial of the Imperial Household Department. In the main, official publishing specialized in the Confucian canon that formed the basis of the civil service examination and printed matters necessary for governance—calendars, gazetteers, medical treatises. Extant records, however, show an occasional inclusion of such popular novels as *Romance of the Three Kingdoms* and *The Water Margin*.[20]

These books, distributed through the bureaucracy, were mostly stored away in pavilions or purchased by local academies as textbooks with government funds. The monopolistic nature of this enterprise ensured that prices were high and circulation outside official channels limited.[21]

More relevant to the needs of readers and authors in urban Jiangnan were the other two forms of publishing, family and commercial. Family publishing (*jiake*), a means of converting a family's cultural capital into prestige or even profit, could be conducted on an ad hoc or a long-term basis. In the former, gentry families would hire a team of workers for a specific project, usually the collected works of their erudite son(s) and daughter(s). These books, symbols of the financial and cultural attainments of the family, were mostly given away to cement social ties. Occasionally they were also sold in bookstores.[22] The large number of collected works of Ming and Qing individuals or families found in today's library vaults can be attributed to the popularity of this custom. Genealogies, too, were printed as ad hoc projects, with families hiring itinerant workers who traveled with a stock of movable type. The poetry collections of many gentrywomen were also published in this way. A second kind of family publishing involved full-fledged presses that prominent writers and collectors built in their villas. Staffed with permanent workers, they produced high-quality reproductions of treasures from the family library and published works penned by the master of the house himself.[23]

The flourishing of family publishing would not have been possible without the affluence generated by the commercialized economy. It is indicative of the spirit of the floating world in seventeenth-century Jiangnan in three ways, all of which had a direct bearing on the rise of the female reader-writer. First, it bespeaks the quickening pace and multiple channels through which information was generated and exchanged. The dispersion of book production from government venues into family villas meant a decentralization of venues for the production of knowledge. This is particularly crucial to the generation of a critical mass for woman readers and writers. Collected works of individual women were predominantly issued by family publishing enterprises, as were men's writings of a more private and emotional nature, which had formerly been considered unworthy of publication. The commercial presses seized upon these private musings by both men and women and manufactured a cult of emotionality from them (see below).

Second, family publishing constituted one facet of a general trend toward privatization in Chinese life in the Ming-Qing period, when the family became the locus of a host of formerly "public" activities and family life assumed increasing emotional significance. This development altered the content and texture of life for both males and females, but its impact on the supposedly housebound females was particularly drastic. Without venturing out of the family compound, the gentry daughter could devour the family's library collection, watch operas on the living-room stage, and befriend visitors from far and near. In other words, even as gentrywomen remained physically cloistered, the boundaries of the inner chambers became permeable as a brave new world came toward her from without. I will elaborate on this fundamental shift in the meaning of domesticity in Chapters 3–5.

Third, family publishing played a role in facilitating the reception of a new image of women as intellectual beings. In bringing the world of culture and scholarship to the heart of a woman's traditional domain, family publishing helped cement a new relationship between women and learning. Not only did more women learn to read and write in this conducive atmosphere, but many were even hailed as the pride of their family, who financed the publication of their works. This incorporation of women's talent into the family's repertoire of cultural capital helped promote the legitimacy of a literary education for daughters and led to the valorization of women writers in local histories. In helping to redefine domesticity, family publishing was instrumental in constructing a new womanhood.

Commercial Publishing: Books for Money

Even more so than family publishing, the organization and style of a third kind of publishing—commercial—epitomized the profound cultural changes brought about by the monetary economy. Books became firmly linked with profit, in both the economic and moral sense, in the minds of readers and publishers. In order to promote sales, merchants fused didacticism with entertainment and words with pictures. By doing so, they produced not only new kinds of books but also a new milieu for interactions between authors and readers. Directness, sincerity, and personal rapport became the order of the day.

Commercial publishing (*fangke*) grew phenomenally in the mid-sixteenth century and continued to prosper in the Qing. Like family publishing, its operation was decentralized due to the portability of the instruments needed for woodblock printing and the relatively low overhead involved.[24] The Jiangnan cities—Hangzhou, Suzhou, and Nanjing—excelled in the elite market, but publishing centers flourished in every region of the empire. Even in provinces as remote from the Yangzi heartland as Shanxi, Guangdong, Hunan, and Hebei, printers vied to issue the latest bestsellers.[25] In the Wanli period, the onslaught of mass publishing shifted the dynamics of the trade to such new areas as Wuxing in Zhejiang and Shexian in Anhui.[26] Northern Fujian, having specialized in the lower end of the market since the Song dynasty, continued to thrive until the early Qing. Its eclipse then boosted production in the establishments of Nanjing, Suzhou, and Hangzhou. In the eighteenth century, Jiangnan returned to the center stage of publishing as it increasingly catered to the mass market.[27]

Commercial publishing was part and parcel of the general commercial expansion changing the face of the empire. Publishing houses in Huizhou in Anhui and Jianyang in Fujian, in particular, heralded the new styles and genres that appealed to the eclectic taste of the reading public. Similar to the renowned Huizhou and Shanxi merchants, these printers utilized such traditional cultural resources as lineage ties to run their rationalized businesses.[28] And, just like the banking industry established by Shanxi and Ningbo bankers, there was a remarkable degree of regional and lineage specialization in commercial printing. A renowned example was the Huangs of Qiu Village, Shexian, Huizhou, who produced successive generations of woodblock illustrators from the early Ming to the twentieth century. With their earliest extant work dating from 1489, the Huangs reached their peak of productivity in the Wanli period, when they turned the works of leading painters into prints that graced the pages of novels, dramas, and books of precepts. Winning for their family the name of Dragon-Carving Hands (*diaolong shou*), these craftsmen followed the footsteps of their fellow Huizhou merchants in migrating to the major Jiangnan cities in the seventeenth century.[29]

Another example of the regional-cum-lineage specialization in the trade is provided by the Liu and Yu families in Jianyang, Fujian. The princes of mass publishing, they led the trade in volume and were renowned for speed and efficiency, if not always for accuracy and originality. Their specialty was illustrated novels and almanacs. Both northern Fujian families started business in the Song dynasty, experienced a surge in production in the early to mid-sixteenth century, and saw their fortunes peak in late Ming.[30] The Yus, the biggest printing conglomerate in Jianyang, left records of over thirty independent publishing houses that flourished in the Wanli period and produced over a thousand titles in Ming times. Emulating the names of literati studios, these houses were often called "xx *tang*," "xx *guan*" or "xx *zhai*." Each was headed by one man from the Yu lineage, entitled "master" (*zhuren*), with the combined duties of publisher, administrator, and sales manager. Very often he also wrote and edited manuscripts.

One such man-of-letters / entrepreneur was Yu Xiangdou (ca. 1560–ca. 1637), who took up his family trade in 1591 after failing the civil service examination. An expert promoter, he often included his own portrait in the books he published, as well as the names of the copyist, block-cutter, and binder. This public recognition accorded these master crafts-men, however, obliterated a new division of labor that arose in the mid-Ming. To expedite production, carvers with varied skill levels began to work in teams, with trainees concentrating on the straight lines in charac-ters and masters specializing in the more taxing strokes. Besides supervis-ing these craftsmen, Yu Xiangdou also delighted in collecting oral stories and compiling household almanacs. In modern terminology, his was a vertically integrated enterprise merging writing, editing, block-cutting, printing, retailing, and advertising. In the year 1591 alone, his publishing house issued over ten titles.[31] The fact that many portraits of Yu Xiangdou are preserved in his books but almost no biographical data survive be-speaks the preponderance of visual representations in his day.

In their efficient business operation, mass production of literature and practical guidebooks, aggressive self-promotion, and ample use of graph-ics, commercial presses such as Yus set the tone for the age. Commercial publishing made books one of the myriad commodities that money could buy. To compete for the attention of the consumer, books had to speak directly to the readers by serving their needs, be it edifying their minds, gratifying their senses, or instructing them in practicalities. When mer-chants spoke of selling books at cutthroat margins to hasten turnover and reap bigger profits, the secularization of books was complete.[32] This coup-ling of books with money was a most telling feature of the culture of the reading public.

Book Merchants: Architects of a Cosmopolitan Culture

The many meanings of the marriage of books and money were ex-emplified by the social position of the book merchant, who personified the myriad contradictions in the commercialized society. He at once inhabited previously disjointed worlds, being at the crossroads of money and cul-ture, business and scholarship, entertainment and morality, and inter-regional and local cultures. His agility in weaving these disparate worlds together helped forge a new urban culture, the culture of the reading public.

This cosmopolitan culture was neither an "elite" nor a "mass" culture, the lines of which had never been clear-cut in Chinese society.[33] Nor should it be called a "middle-class" or "merchant" culture, which presupposes an autonomous bourgeois power at loggerheads with the old scholar-official elites. In China, family members of the old elite, if not the scholar-official himself, were often entrepreneurs; merchants who struck gold, in turn, sponsored scholarship and the arts while purchasing their sons the best classical education available.[34] The new cosmopolitan culture that arose

三台山人余仰止影圖

from commercialization differs from that of an idealized agrarian society governed by Confucian gentlemen in the prominence it accorded to merchants and monetary exchange, but it was neither an entirely new creation nor a rebel against the old. For lack of a better term, we may call it the "culture of the reading public," referring to its constituency, or "the new urban culture." It is characterized by a blurring of traditional dualities and fluidity of boundaries — between gentry and merchant, male and female, morality and entertainment, public and private, philosophy and action, as well as fiction and reality. It is, in short, culture of the floating world.

The term *urban culture* has many specific connotations in the history of Western Europe. There were two salient differences in China, however. The urban culture resulting from the publishing boom was in fact trans-urban in character, in the sense that it permeated the commercialized Jiangnan cities and market towns without necessarily fostering distinct urban identities. Nor does the pivotal role played by the book merchant in shaping this culture imply a bourgeois class consciousness. In contrast to the destruction of the old aristocratic rule in Europe, commercialization in China did not pit the merchants against the imperial government in a struggle for political power. There were, in fact, no effective social or legal distinctions between scholar-officials and merchants. The culture of the reading public, in other words, cannot be contained within fixed geographical boundaries, nor can it be identified with any specific class. Born in a fluid and mobile society, its hallmark was none other than the possibilities for the mingling of disparate worlds that it engendered.

The composite possibilities opened up by commercial publishing were most evident in two sets of tensions that characterized the culture of the reading public: the uneasy co-existence of the cosmopolitan/parochial dimensions in its spatial location and the convergence of scholarship/ business in its sociocultural orientation. The ambivalent spatial location of this culture found its parallel in the patterns of commercial agriculture. Regional cash-crop specialization, which necessitated interregional trade, created the conditions for both a heightened awareness of local specialties and identity as well as the forging of a common trans-urban culture. Constant movement and fluid identities bred insecurity, prompting people to reaffirm the familiar cultures of their native place or place of residence. Book merchants catered to this revival of parochial sentiments by publishing local gazetteers and travel guides to local sights, which proliferated in

---

(*Opposite*) The publisher-author Yu Xiangdou presents himself to the readers of his household almanac as a scholar-magistrate surrounded by the refinements of literati life (Yu Xiangdou, page following contents. Courtesy of The Institute of Oriental Culture, University of Tokyo).

the seventeenth century.[35] It was also in such an environment that local sons promoted books by women writers and stories of chaste widows from their county, prefecture, village, or city, thus implicating women into contests of localism. The culture of the reading public, in this sense, was both trans-regional and local in scope, and at once coalescing and divisive in orientation. The meaning of "local" was inevitably ambiguous, since the very boundary of "local society" was no longer fixed.

Yet more significant than the forces of division were the frequent traveling and cross-fertilization among people from different areas. The most successful book merchants operated on an interregional scale. To cut costs and to ensure product quality, they routinely transported the raw materials for book production — paper, wood, and ink — as well as craftsmen from one province to another. The long-distance trade routes for a burgeoning traffic in grains and textiles were conduits for an equally profitable movement of books, people, and ideas. For example, Huizhou woodblock cutters were hired to work in Beijing, Suzhou, and Hangzhou; Suzhou copyists and cutters collaborated with those from Nanjing, Jiangxi, and Fujian; the Yus of Fujian sent relatives to Nanjing to operate subsidiaries. Through them, Nanjing books were reprinted in Fujian, and vice versa.[36]

The distribution of books was just as cosmopolitan as their production. In the late sixteenth century, bookstores thrived in such metropolitan centers as Beijing, Nanjing, Suzhou, and Hangzhou. Books produced in one region were available throughout the country, although books shipped from afar naturally cost more. Book merchants from central Zhejiang, for example, supplied the flourishing Jiangnan market with books shipped via the waterways that crisscrossed the region.[37] Even the more parochial populace had access to local book fairs, part of the periodic marketing network. The book market in Jianyang, Fujian, for example, convened every five days and attracted merchants from all parts of the empire.[38]

More conducive to cross-fertilization of ideas than the shipment of books was the mobility of the book buyers themselves. Buyers from every corner of the empire congregated in Beijing, in particular. The metropolitan examination, held every third spring, provided an ideal occasion for bookstores in the capital to peddle their wares. With candidates present from every province, Beijing book merchants set up temporary booths outside the examination hall. In addition, these merchants also tapped into the capital's monthly and annual periodic markets. Every year for three days beginning on the fifteenth day of the second month, book merchants participated in a festive early spring bazaar held at the Lantern Market in the eastern part of Beijing. On the first, fifteenth, and twenty-fifth days of every month, they joined other merchants on the grounds of the City Temple on the western edge of the city.[39] When examination candidates and other travelers to the capital returned home, they disseminated novels, model essays, and books on hobbies to readers in provinces far and near.

From among the newly affluent group of book buyers in dispersed areas reading the same books emerged a cosmopolitan culture that emulated the refined tastes of the existing literati culture but was different in social origins and raison d'etre. The civil service examination had long fostered a homogeneous culture among those who passed and became officials; in the process of preparing for the examination, they had for decades plowed through the same classical works, spoken the same language, and exchanged poetry with each other. Homogeneity was a device for cultural exclusion that perpetuated the scholar-officials' monopoly of political power. The new trans-urban culture, in contrast, was an eclectic and inclusive one, open to all who could afford it. This culture was not intended to compete with the entrenched scholar-official culture, for it had no independent philosophical or canonical base. It co-existed with literati culture, for it belonged to a different realm altogether, being concerned more with the minute and mundane pleasures of daily life than with the ultimate concerns of philosophy or governance. Most indicative of the germs of this trans-urban culture was the popularity of books on the hobbies and tastes of the refined gentleman — tasting tea, burning incense, collecting rocks and antiques, for example.[40] These guidebooks appealed to the nouveaux riches from every town, who were eager not only to buy books but also to buy into the lure of the mandarin lifestyle.

Guidebooks to genteel tastes were by no means a sixteenth-century invention. The classic on tea was written in the Tang dynasty; the Song saw an abundance of treatises on the art of calligraphy and antique collecting.[41] Yet the mass reproduction of treatise after treatise on all manners of hobbies in late Ming encyclopedias and anthologies bears witness to how widespread the problem of vulgar imitation had become in an age of commercial publishing. In a Song bibliophile treatise often reproduced in late Ming guidebooks, for example, a seasoned book collector lectured novices on correct reading habits: "Don't fold dogears; don't scratch the characters with fingernails; don't wet your fingers with saliva before turning the pages; don't use your book as a pillow."[42] There is also the frequent admonition that excess betrays vulgarity. Hence the author of a guide to flower arrangement in the course of discussing the appropriate utensils, the art of balancing the main flower with "maids," water, the need to clean the petals daily, and the like, issued repeated warnings: place the vase on a simple table bulky in feel but fine and smooth to the touch; get rid of lacquer tables inlaid with gold and mother of pearl; do not burn incense next to the

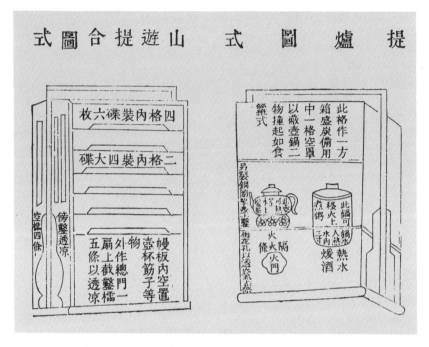

Instruments of leisure: designs for a ventilated picnic basket with ample space for food and utensils for a party of six, as well as a portable stove to boil water and warm wine (Tu Long, *Youju jian*, 8ab, in *Kaopan yushi*).

flower arrangement, lest you cannot discern the natural fragrance you so meticulously cultivated; sip tea, preferably unseasoned, in the presence of flowers and stop chattering away with friends; if you like to get drunk while watching flowers, you might as well do so in a brothel.[43] These warnings, similar to that of not using a book as a pillow, were issued as markers of distinction between the gentry connoisseurs and their imitators.

The popularity of guidebooks to polished tastes is indicative of several subtle changes that commercialization brought to the culture of sixteenth- and seventeenth-century China. Although the tastes of the old gentry still set the standards to be emulated, the growing number of people with the leisure to busy themselves with dusting flower petals now hailed from non-official as well as official families. Both old moneyed families and the nouveaux riches enjoyed a previously unmatched affluence that allowed them to pay meticulous attention to pleasures of daily life in the domestic setting, pursuing one fad after another in interior design, mundane hobbies, and decorative art objects. This constituted another aspect of the privatization of Chinese life alluded to above in the context of family publishing. In subsuming this emphasis on practicality and license given to mundane pleasures under the rubric of a new trans-urban culture, I do not mean to suggest that the old scholar-official culture was immune from these developments or that the old and the new cultures were in opposition. My interest is, rather, the key roles played by commercially produced guidebooks and the wide trading networks of book merchants in the dissemination of this new culture as well as the more diverse social base of its constituency. The new cosmopolitan culture, while maintaining continuities with the old, was more eclectic and comprehensive in its spatial and social locations.

Besides its composite spatial dimensions encompassing the local and the cosmopolitan, a second characteristic of the culture heralded by the book merchant was the convergence of commercial and scholastic pursuits, or of money and culture. The confidence with which the book merchant straddled these two worlds is graphically conveyed by a Nanjing bookseller's self-introduction in *The Peach Blossom Fan* (*Taohua shan*), a drama by Kong Shangren (1648–1718): "Nanjing ranks first among cities for the wealth of its books, and most of these are in Three Mountain Street, where I keep the largest bookshop." The successful merchant showed off his impressive stock with the familiarity of an academician: "Here are the Thirteen Classics, the twenty-one dynastic histories, all the tomes of the nine schools of philosophy, of the three religions, and the hundred thinkers, besides collections of eight-legged essays and fashionable modern novels. They cram the shelves and innumerable boxes and rooms. I have traveled north and south to gather this collection, minutely examining old editions to make fine reprints with scholarly annotations." The rewards for expertise were manifold: "As well as earning a handsome profit by these transactions, I have helped to preserve and circulate the noblest thoughts of mankind. Even the doctors and masters of literature greet me with deference. I have reason to be satisfied with my reputation."

The bookseller's business acumen brought him into the heart of bureaucratic politics. Not only did he have to keep abreast of the political fate of examiners, he even played a leading role in propagating favored literary styles and philosophies:

[He laughs:] "This year the general civil service examination will be held again, and the finest literary talents will receive due honor. The government has endorsed a proposal by the Minister of Rites, Qian Qianyi, advocating a new style of writing to express the spirit of the new reign. Consequently I have invited several leading critics to compile anthologies as models for composition. They will start work today. I'll hang up my latest advertisement. [He hangs a couplet on each side of the door, which it reads:] 'The style in vogue was created by men of renown, / Imitation of these models will please the chief examiner.' "[44]

At once bibliophile, businessman, literary trendsetter, and self-pro-
moter, the book merchant set the tone for the culture of the reading public.
Although this Nanjing book merchant was a fictional character, his agility
in both the scholar's studio and the cutthroat business world rings true
when seen against the careers of such commercial publishers as Yu Xiangdou introduced above. In addition to their ability to blend the seemingly
incompatible concerns of money and learning, book merchants like Yu
were no less skillful in imparting a personal touch to an increasingly
impersonal industry. In fact, so successful were they in doing this that the
mass-produced book became the ironic vehicle for the propagation of a
cult of personal rapport.

Facsimile of Self and Primacy of Human Communications

Product of an assembly line, a typical commercially published book has
a dull, mass-produced appearance that is a far cry from the antique book,
each volume of which is an object of art bearing the individual mark of the
artists who crafted the blocks and assembled the pages. Ironically, it was
on the uniform pages dotted with mechanical fonts of the mass-produced
book that the ideals of human sincerity and personal rapport became
widely disseminated. This primacy of matters of the heart was the most
important feature of the culture of the reading public.

Frederick Mote and Hung-lam Chu have described how mass production brought uniformity to the script style of a book printed in the sixteenth century:

In place of characters that previously could be identified as "Yen style" or "Ou-
yang style" or "Chao style," mid-Ming printers began using homogenized styles
loosely designated "Sung dynasty characters." With repeated application to
wooden blocks by ordinary craftsmen, such nondescript calligraphy came to be
called "craftsmen script." This dominance by the artisan indicates a broad trend
toward dull standardization of Chinese script, presenting an overall uniformity, as
in the mechanically produced fonts of Western alphabets; consequently, individualistic liveliness and expressiveness waned. . . . If such books gained in legibility,
they lost much of their presence and personality.

Yet as if to compensate for this dullness, commercial printers developed
the practice of printing facsimile pages of personalized calligraphy in the
front matter of a book:

Whether or not there is apparent deception in the insertion of the facsimile prefaces and postfaces in books of that age, the visual impression on the reader is one
of individuality — personalities perceived through distinctive calligraphy.[45]

This "visual impression of individuality" facilitated by the technology of facsimile reproduction epitomized the ideal of natural and truthful communications embodied in the catchwords of the day: *qing* (feeling, emotion, love), *zhen* (sincerity, truth, and, interestingly, portraiture), and *qi* (resonance). In fiction, prose, and verse, sincerity of heart was hailed as the raison d'être of human existence; so potent were torrents of emotions that they leveled even age-old hierarchies. The printed page itself emerged as a medium through which strangers developed rapport; reading and writing created new social realities by joining people from afar.

Curiously, even as valorization of matters of the heart and the popularity of visual representation of individuality created the theoretical possibility of a new construction of the individual self as an autonomous agent, this possibility was not exploited in China as it was in early modern Europe. Instead of viewing reading as a private and individual act, the Chinese reading public became fascinated by the social and communicative possibilities that reading engendered. Specifically, the printed page became the arena for the forging of three sets of personal relationships: publisher-reader, author-reader, and reader-reader. I explore the import of the latter two on the educated women who constituted the reading public in subsequent chapters; here I focus on the extent to which the publisher-reader relationship was mediated by pictorial illustrations of the publisher's face.

No reader who opened the covers of a novel or almanac would be surprised to find the publisher looking at him or her in the eye as if he were the reader's best friend. As mentioned above, the Fujian merchant Yu Xiangdou delighted in presenting portraits of himself in the almanacs and novels he published. In another example, a Nanjing publisher included a portrait of himself clasping volumes of books in a work he issued in 1615 together with this sales pitch: "First you heard my name, now you see my face. I handle all kinds of books, selecting only the finest editions." Such personal appeals first appeared in books printed in the late Yuan, but they did not become customary until the late Ming.[46] In an age of creative advertising, the publisher, in effect, rendered *himself* the commodity that was being promoted. This facade of personal rapport, expressed in the form of a supposedly truthful rendition of the advertiser's face, masked the primarily economic and impersonal nature of the exchange between the publisher and his customer.

This pictorial representation of self was just as popular outside the publishing world. In scholar-official circles, it was customary for men and women to paint and exchange self-portraits as tokens of friendship. In spite of, or because of, the prevalence of discord and rivalry that informed human relations in a competitive society, direct face-to-face communications and resonance between like-minded individuals became cherished ideals. I will return to the gendered meaning of these ideals in my discussion of the cult of *qing*.

Not only did the publisher seek to speak to the reader on a personal level, the reader also expected the same cordiality from the author. A reader who picked up a drama text, a novel, or a poetry collection did so not only to be instructed but also to engage in a dialogue with the author or even to attempt a projection of self onto the fictional world. I examine the emotional involvement of female readers with their authors in later chapters; here, I consider the import of facsimile technology for this author-reader rapport. The vogue of illustrated books in the seventeenth century helped change the very meaning of reading by inviting direct participation from the reader. The blending of textual and visual representations on the pages of an illustrated book was another characteristic of the floating world of the reading public.

The first half of the seventeenth century witnessed the golden age of Chinese woodcut prints. Color printing by woodcut, a Ming innovation, produced elegant five-color albums and maps that were collector's items. At the lower end of the market, books of every genre, be they novels, plays, encyclopedias, almanacs, books of precepts or primers, had to include at least a black-and-white picture or two.[47] So prevalent was this fad for illustration that the Hangzhou publisher of a 1625 edition of *The Peony Pavilion* sounded almost apologetic for following suit: "Books of drama simply do not sell without pictures. So I, too, ape the fashion and furnish these illustrations for your pleasure. As they say, 'Can't go against the tide.' That's all."[48]

The symbiosis of words and pictures, devised to stir the reader's heartstrings and to instill a sense of personal involvement, signified a new taste among the reading public. Less steeped in the classical education catering to those preparing for the civil service examination, the new book consumers shunned ornate literary styles and abstract speculation. Instead, practicality, instant gratification, and emotional expression were the order of the day. It was in this context that the needs of the woman reader were foregrounded, allowing her to leave an indelible mark on the general culture of sixteenth- and seventeenth-century China. According to old gender stereotypes, not only were women so likely to be uneducated that they could at most "read" picture books, they were also the temperamental sex, who inhabited a private world ruled by natural emotions. In other words, both a craze for illustrated books and the primacy of emotional rapport represented, in the minds of those who subscribed to gender stereotypes, women's tastes and concerns that had now gained currency and become universalized.

Illustrated books have long been identified with the education of women. Often mentioned in the same breath with "illiterate masses," women were supposed to be among the least educated, hence the most given to drawings and the vernacular. It is no accident that one of the earliest woodcut illustrated books was a didactic work intended for women, namely the *Biographies of Exemplary Women* (*Lienü zhuan*) produced by the Yus of Fujian, probably during the Yuan dynasty (1280–1368). Based on the classic text on exemplary women, good and bad, penned by Liu Xiang (79–8 B.C.), these illustrations are so artistically skilled that Ming and Qing carvers of illustrated novels and plays also imitated their style.[49] As we will see, illustrated editions of *Biographies of Exemplary Women* and other didactic works for women were best-sellers that inundated the market in the seventeenth century.

This equation of woman reader with pictures was a fanciful ideological construct that was undermined by social developments in seventeenth-century Jiangnan. The spread of women's education and the visibility of prolific woman writers invalidated the image of women as illiterate masses. Nor were women the only consumers of picture books: men were equally enthusiastic readers of *Biographies of Exemplary Women* and other illustrated texts. Yet both gender stereotypes — women the illiterate and emotional beings — died hard. I investigate the implications of such stereotypes for women's self-perceptions in my discussion of the cult of *qing* in Chapter 2; here a positive development — the visibility of women in the new urban culture — is more relevant. The craze for illustrated books in the seventeenth century focused attention on the different needs of the woman reader; this spilled over to more general discussions on women's abilities, their differences from men, and their rightful roles in society. In short, the very definitions of womanhood and gender differences were being articulated in a new context generated by commercial publishing. This new discourse on womanhood, which resulted in a more complex and multivalent image of the ideal woman, is the subject matter of Chapter 4.

The primacy of human communications fostered on the pages of the illustrated book was in part a creation of the woman reader-writer herself. In the next chapter, I examine how women viewed the personal author-reader relationship, one manifestation of the cult of *qing*. Here, I analyze the most important development that ensued from the cult of sincerity and emotions: the genesis of a positive image of the woman writer. In an age that valued the natural expression of emotions, some men of letters came to recognize that women's exclusion from the examination system was a blessing in disguise. Not expected to conform to conventions and spared from the rote memorization of the Classics, a woman was free to create literature purely as an expression of her true self. Hence women's writing was a corrective for the stylized and formulaic prose and verse purveyed by male scholars. The marginality of women's words, irrelevant to any claims of formal political power, was the very source of their literary salvation. Not only was a female writer different from a male, she was better.

This valorization of the woman writer was predicated on her supposed distinctions from man, distinctions perceived to have arisen from nature and reinforced by political culture. Wu Guofu, a man of letters who contributed a preface to the poetry collection of Wang Duanshu (1621–ca. 1701), a professional woman writer, focused on women's exclusion from men's public world, a result of the prevailing gender system: "Talented ladies from the inner quarters have nothing to do with the civil service examination. Since they do not aspire to fame, their words are true. Nor are they distressed by the rise and fall of empires. Since national affairs are not where their minds focus, their words are detached."[50] Another man of letters, Xu Yejun (Shijun; 1602–81), focused on the distinctiveness of women as a result of biology. In an essay defending his inclusion of women's correspondence in a volume of letters, Xu stated tersely: "Women differ from men in their appearance and constitution."

Yet Xu Yejun went on to emphasize that this biological distinction was secondary to the moral and intellectual potentials of women: "But remember that talented women composed ingenious circular poems; faithful women persevered in poverty and served their husbands with industry; virtuous women severed their arms or threw themselves off cliffs; women decorated with medals led armies out of sieges and subdued rebels. In which area are they willing to be second to men?" He went on to point out the potential superiority of women, one that was, again, rooted in their divorce from men's public world: "Although there are women who are not inclined to learn, those who do are sure to surpass men. Why? Without the distraction of external affairs, their hearts are still and their minds can concentrate better."[51] Although Xu did not question the gender inequality inherent in such female virtues as fidelity and chastity, by celebrating women's willpower and success in fulfilling the strenuous demands placed on them, he was in effect arguing that women could measure up to men. If given a chance to learn, women are men's intellectual and moral equals.

From a modern feminist perspective, both Xu and Wu can be faulted for holding up male achievements as the norm and standard for women. This male-centered bias reflected the exclusive nature of the gender system at the time. Although we should recognize both personal and systemic biases, it is also important for us to acknowledge the positive impact of their arguments on the women of their times. The conviction that women can be worthwhile intellectual beings prompted these men to promote women's education and to compile and publish women's words. Later, we will see that commercial publishing promoted an explosion of interest in anthologies of women's poetry in the seventeenth century. These volumes were often compiled and published by such men as Wu and Xu who recognized not only the market value of women's poetic voices but also their literary merits. This valorization of the female poet, which promoted a positive self-image among female readers, reverberated in the works of women who took up the writing brush. In encouraging numerous women to keep on reading and writing, this valorization was the most far-reaching legacy of the primacy of human communications engendered by commercial publishing.

Morality and Entertainment: Books That Women (Were Supposed to) Read

The novelty and significance of this valorization of female poets become more striking when seen against the educated women's highly problematic standing in the orthodox Confucian tradition. The emboldened woman readers and writers of the sixteenth and seventeenth centuries had to eke out a precarious existence in a learned tradition that allowed them no formal place. The doctrine of separate spheres relegated men, literature, and political power to the public sphere and women, procreation, and household labor to the domestic realm. Since literacy and knowledge of the Classics constituted the gateway to bureaucratic appointments and hence political power, reading and writing were deemed, at least in theory, an exclusively male privilege. A woman's contribution to this scholastic tradition was at best subsidiary and indirect, albeit indispensable. As mother, she was to give birth to sons, supervise their early education, and work incessantly at the spinning wheel and loom to support their studies. As wife, she was to provide for the family's daily needs so that her husband could concentrate on his public pursuits.

To train females to meet the demands of motherhood and household management, didactic texts were written and transmitted through the dynasties, beginning with Liu Xiang's *Biographies of Exemplary Women*. If Confucian education can be said to consist of two emphases and goals — moral cultivation and cultural education — males were supposed to excel in both, but females were to devote themselves only to the former. In other words, the orthodox Confucian tradition recognized the propriety of women's education; yet true to the ideal order of separate spheres, this education was to be distinct from men's in content and purpose. Women were to cultivate their morality by way of books of precepts written especially for them; since the Classics, histories, and literature required too much time and effort to master, they were deemed irrelevant, if not detrimental, to their socialization as self-sacrificing mother and wife.[52]

Yet the Confucian tradition was replete with internal contradictions with regard to the relationship between women and learning. Symptomatic of women's nominally marginalized existence in the learned tradition, books they were supposed to read were clearly identified as such—hence the *Four Books for Women* (*Nü sishu*), which bear no relation to the Four Books of the Confucian canon except in name, whereas the unmarked Four Books were taken for granted to be a male prerogative.[53] But to speak of books for women at all is to acknowledge an inevitable gap between the strict interpretation of ideal norms, which warned that reading was not a woman's business, and the nagging presence of wives and mothers who both read and wrote. Throughout history, highly erudite women mastered not only the didactic works but also the Classics and voluminous histories. Some of the books of precepts for women, in fact, were attributed to female writers. Their visibility and high repute suggested that in practice the relationship between women and the Confucian learned tradition was more ambiguous than the prescriptions of the ideal norms implied.

Not only were erudite women eulogized in official histories, expedient circumstances even allowed a handful of them indispensable roles in the male-to-male transmission of the scholastic tradition. The most renowned example was the historian and teacher Ban Zhao (A.D. 41–ca. 115), who authored parts of the official dynastic history of the Former Han after the death of her father and brother. In addition, Ban held a special place in the Confucian tradition as the author of the popular didactic text *Precepts for Women* (*Nüjie*).[54] Although Ban performed her literary and scholastic feats as a surrogate for her male kinsmen, to woman readers Ban's unassailable reputation bespoke the flexibility of the system despite its official strictures against women's acquiring a literary and classical education.

These age-old inconsistencies within the Confucian tradition became more glaring in the sixteenth and seventeenth centuries. Not only had economic and cultural prosperity rendered the presence of women schooled in the Classics commonplace, men and women were also deliberately exploiting the inconsistencies to champion the propriety of a literary and cultural education for girls. They evoked Ban Zhao's name constantly as proof that even by Confucian standards reading and writing constituted a respectable vocation for women.[55] Their call makes sense in an age when books earmarked for women's moral education had lost their gender-specific and purpose-specific meanings. There is no doubt that women read both the *Four Books for Women* and the Four Books they were not supposed to read, together with all the histories, plays, novels, and poetry anthologies available in the market. Conversely, men were just as enthralled by books for women. As the gulf between ideal norm and social reality became all the more apparent, the lines between books for males and books for females, as well as between didacticism, practical knowledge, and entertainment became increasingly difficult to determine.

It is in the context of the incongruity between norms and reality as well as the ambiguous meaning of feminine morality in the culture of the floating world that we should seek to understand the implications of the spread of didactic books for women in the sixteenth and seventeenth centuries. The popularity of these books is undeniable. Although many were hastily produced by profit-minded publishers, some were collector's items adorned with the finest illustrations. The number and variety of even extant copies are impressive.[56] In 1587, for example, a Nanjing printer issued a fully illustrated version of *Biographies of Exemplary Women*; the famed Huangs of Shexian followed suit in 1606. A leading Suzhou printer also produced a reprint of a supposed Song edition.[57] Other best-sellers include an illustrated *Female Exemplars (Nüfan)* produced by a Huang illustrator in 1602, and a two-colored illustrated *Exemplars in the Female Quarters (Guifan)* issued in 1600, which was so popular that it was reissued sometime between 1612 and 1615.[58] In 1618, another illustrated edition of this work was printed in Huizhou by a literati publisher. Donations for an impressive total of 1,220 copies were collected, although it is not known if that corresponds with the actual number of copies printed.[59]

The wide circulation of didactic texts, however, does not mean that their message was well received, or even that their message was unequivocal. The fluidities that characterized the culture of the floating world were amply reflected on the pages of these books. The lines between money and morality, fiction and history, didacticism and entertainment, were often blurred. Historical exemplars became fictional heroines when the *Biographies of Exemplary Women* was dramatically retold in the vernacular and issued as illustrated fiction under the name *Romance of the Biographies of Exemplary Women (Lienü zhuan yanyi)*.[60] Confucian didactic history here shaded into vulgar entertainment.

Even without this metamorphosis in genres, the very popularity of books intended for women's moral education carries a double contradiction. First, since the ideal virtuous woman was not supposed to be literate, the massive number of such books on the market calls attention to the disjuncture between ideal and reality discussed above. Moreover, since morality was supposed to be the antithesis of material profit, the commercial success of didactic books mocks the relevance of the traditional moral precepts. Yet these contradictions only seemed to have made these stories more appealing to the reading public, who thrived on ambivalence and irony.

The impulses behind the mass production and popularity of didactic books for women are manifold. In a study of late Ming illustrated moral instruction books, Katherine Carlitz points out that the motives of compilers, financiers, and publishers of these precepts were as varied as the intention of the readers. Lü Kun, compiler of the immensely popular *Exemplars in the Female Quarters*, was a scholar-official famous as a moral crusader among women and the illiterate masses. That commercial publishers shared his sincere moral conviction, however, is doubtful. Although they exploited the interest in stories of female virtues for different ends, both moral crusaders and profit-seeking publishers were aware of the appeal of the ideal of fidelity to a fluid and decadent society. In his study of the foibles of the God of Money, whom devotees believed to be desirous of young maidens, Richard von Glahn has suggested that women took on attributes of money in Ming-Qing Jiangnan: "The popular conception of wealth thus bore a striking resemblance to the conventional portrait of women as alluring but inconsistent and fickle, pregnant with destructive power."[61] To men who found the transience of economic fortunes as anxiety provoking as that of sensual pleasures, stories of women's moral steadfastness were doubly satisfying.

Most revealing of the tensions in the commercialized society is the interest displayed by local lineages in organizing and financing publication of books of precepts for women. The gap in local leadership that ensued from the demise of village chiefs prompted lineage organizations to assume more active political roles. These lineages sought to capitalize on the cultural prestige of the genre to promote regional pride while strengthening their own standing as leaders in local community. The participation of three of the most powerful Huizhou lineages in the publication of a locally printed *Exemplars in the Female Quarters* is particularly noteworthy. As Carlitz says of the intriguing links among money, morality, and local pride that this epitomized:

Women's virtue is taken very seriously . . . and a call is made for concerted efforts to revive it. These efforts are measured in money, and donations for the publication knit together different strands of the community: men and women, local degree-holders, merchants, and monks. Thus money is used to subsidize a new kind of local product . . . that cements local harmony by appealing to a kind of virtue in which Huizhou was considered preeminent.[62]

This joint project in Huizhou is revealing of the ways in which the publication of didactic books served a multitude of needs in this commercialized society. As money disrupted traditional hierarchies, the publication project provided a rallying point for a new social organization encompassing wealthy patrons from diverse social origins. The organizational strength of lineages in this fluid society was amply demonstrated by their generous contributions to the fund-raising campaign. The published book itself stood as testimony to the local pride and identity of Huizhou in a cosmopolitan age when books, people, and ideas traversed regional and social boundaries.

The uses to which readers put these didactic books were as varied as those of their publishers. One seventeenth-century man of letters who moved from Jiangnan to Beijing in search of patrons and employment wrote a friend in Hangzhou for a copy of the *Biographies of Exemplary Women*. His reasons: "I have not stocked up on tales of women in the past and today, and hence cannot very well exchange verses with the ladies here. If I had a copy of the *Biographies of Exemplary Women*, I could compose more enchanting songs in the *Lianhua luo* style. Please help me."[63] *Lianhua luo* were ballads that beggars sang. Here, this man of letters uses the term to poke fun of himself, equating writing social poems with begging for a living. The usefulness of *Biographies of Exemplary Women* to this pursuit attests both to its popularity and to its non-didactic uses. The very subject of women's morality had become a form of entertainment.

True to the spirit of the age of visual representations, this conflation of morality and entertainment was poignantly expressed on the pages of illustrated books. Katherine Carlitz has discovered that one picture block for an edition of *Biographies of Exemplary Women* was reused for a play issued by the same publishing house. Moreover, an illustrator who carved the blocks for didactic books produced more of the same for not-so-pious romantic plays, so that a chaste widow reappeared as a lovesick maiden, in the same pose and setting, in another book.[64] It is doubtful that contemporary readers knew the difference or that it mattered to them at all.

Not only did morality and entertainment become more indistinguishable, moral teaching and practical guidance were also conflated within the covers of illustrated household almanacs. An eighteenth-century handbook entitled *Golden Guide to Feminine Virtues* (*Kunde baojian*) provides a graphic example. Half its chapters preach domesticity and docility through stories of virtuous women; the other half contain tips on such chores as how to wash colored clothes, get rid of pimples, prepare garlic so that it does not cause bad breath, and turn a female fetus into a male one. The almanac concludes with a large selection of recipes, embroidery designs, and patterns for making hats and shoes.[65] Written in colloquial language and printed in large type with ample illustrations, this almanac was issued for the benefit of housewives who were not necessarily highly educated.

More ironic than the combination of didacticism with fiction and practical advice was its conflation with poetry, considered by the most doctrinal to be detrimental to the development of womanly virtues. One example of this curious juxtaposition of morality and poetry was an anthology of women's verse, *Pouch of Pearls from Famous Ladies* (*Mingyuan ji'nang*), compiled by an obscure editor known only by his pen name, Sojourner on the Pond (Chishang ke). The editor prefaced a rather pedestrian selection of women's verse from antiquity to the Ming dynasty with a short didactic text, *Analects for Women* (*Nü lunyu*). Although he did not state his intentions, judging from the hastily produced volume and its commercial success (at least two editions were printed from different blocks, one in 1592 and the other in 1595), the addition of precepts was intended to, and did, enhance sales.

Curiously, in this reprint the author of this didactic text, a Tang woman named Song Ruozhao, was mistaken for Ban Zhao. Sojourner on the Pond proceeded to write a formal biography of Ban, even lecturing his readers on the correct reading of Ban's honorary name, Cao Dagu (*gu* in other usages was pronounced *jia*). He got everything right but this line: "[Ban Zhao] wrote a twelve-volume book to instruct girls entitled *Analects for Women*."[66] The book that Ban wrote, in fact, was *Precepts for Women*. Was the Sojourner so busy pushing the beads on his abacus that his memory failed him? Or was he shrewd enough to recognize that Ban Zhao was a more marketable name than Song Ruozhao? Both explanations are plausible.[67] In any case, the appearance of moral precepts under the same cover as women's verse is suggestive of how commoditization of women's words had brought about a convergence of didacticism and poetry, both being read as, above all, entertainment.

The proliferation of didactic texts ostensibly for women — conflated with entertainment, practical advice, and poetry — is thus a complicated phenomenon that defies simple characterization in terms of intentions or results. Similarly, the casting of the woman reader in a learned culture populated by men has equally ambivalent implications. In the eyes of men steeped in Confucian orthodoxy, the many new faces of didacticism were worrisome. The wide circulation of didactic books facilitated the popularization of such virtues as domesticity and chastity but threatened to dilute their didactic meaning and relevance. Hence even a scholar-official as farsighted and pragmatic as Lü Kun, who sought to harness the power of mass publishing by promoting colloquial didactic books for women and the masses, complained that too many books on the market spelled disaster.[68] The impossibility of his position was symptomatic of the contradictions that shaped Lü Kun's moral, intellectual, and social universes. The image of a woman engrossed in a book bought from the marketplace captures many of the contradictions that commercial publishing inflicted on the Confucian tradition.

Every Fragrant Word: Books That Women Wrote

If the image of the reading woman appears awkward against the ideal moral woman, even more problematical is that of a woman wielding a writing brush — who becomes famous for it. Yet women participated in the publishing boom in Ming-Qing Jiangnan not only as readers, but also as authors and publishers. Even more so than stories of moral women, writings by women themselves were investments that promised hefty returns. Poetry anthologies appear to have been most popular, but other genres such as collections of correspondence and drama also found their way into print.[69]

Not all women's writings were issued for profit. There were two distinct venues of publication and distribution, although details on funding and number of copies printed are scant. Whereas commercial publishers printed anthologies at the behest of the market, collected works of individual women were often issued by their families for limited circulation to commemorate domestic bliss or to evidence the family's sophistication. Examples of family publishing projects will be discussed in subsequent chapters; here I concentrate on women's writing produced for the marketplace. Table 2 lists extant anthologies of women's verse and prose; although by no means exhaustive, it conveys the high profile that the woman writer assumed in seventeenth-century print culture.[70]

The valorization of woman poets discussed above, or the equation of a woman's voice with sincerity, naturalness, and truthfulness, was a major impulse behind the boom in anthologies of women's verse. The import of this valorization may be further explored from two angles: the commoditization of the female voice and the integral role it played in seventeenth-century literary reform movements.

Men of letters began to recognize the literary and market potentials of women's words around the end of the sixteenth century. From the perspective of literary history, this attention to women's writings was part of a reaction against a rigid stylistic conformity that many critics saw as prevailing in the sixteenth century. The Chinese scholar Cao Shujian has termed this movement, which flourished from the Longqing period (1567–72) to the end of the Ming (1644), "the literature of inspirational gusto" (*xingling wenxue*). Influenced by philosopher Li Zhi's (1527–

TABLE 2

Major Anthologies of Contemporary Women's Writings Published in China in the Seventeenth and Eighteenth Centuries

Year of Publication	Compiler	Title	Genre	Number of women writers represented
1557	Tian Yiheng	*Shi nüshi*	*shi* poetry	26 (Ming)
Longqing reign (1567–72)	Yu Xian	*Shuxiu zongji*[a]	poetry	17 (Ming)
Ca. 1620	Zhong Xing	*Mingyuan shigui*	*shi* poetry	110 (Ming)
1595	Chishang ke	*Mingyuan ji'nang*	*shi* and *ci* poetry	23 (Ming)
1628	Zhao Shijie	*(Jingke) Gujin nüshi*	prose and verse (31 genres — epitaphs, memorials, letters, etc.)	52 (Ming)
1636	Shen Yixiu[b]	*Yirenshi*	mostly *shi* poetry; also *ci* and a preface	46 (Ming)
1667	Wang Duanshu[b]	*Mingyuan shiwei*	*shi* poetry	about 1,000 (mostly Ming-Qing)
1673	Liu Yunfen	*Cuilou ji*	*shi* poetry	201 (Ming)
1685	Gui Shufen et al.[b]	*Gujin mingyuan baihua shiyu*[a]	*ci* poetry	26 (Ming); 45 (Qing)
1690	Xu Shumin, Qian Yue	*Zhongxiang ci*	*ci* poetry	410 (Ming-Qing)
1716	Hu Baoyi	*Benchao mingyuan shichao*	*shi* poetry	57 (Qing)
1773	Wang Qishu	*Xiefang ji*	poetry	2,000+ (Qing)

NOTE: The anthologies listed meet the following criteria: all are general anthologies, not collected works of individual writers or families; all contain the work of at least ten women; all are published works, not private manuscripts; all contain substantial portions by Ming and/or Qing women and are not reprints of Song and Yuan works; all focus exclusively on women's writings. See the Bibliography for full citations.

[a]I have not seen this volume, and the information is drawn from secondary sources.

[b]Female editor.

1602) notion of "innocence" (*tongxin*), this loosely defined movement held that the mark of good literature was the truthful expression of one's inner self.[71] Adherence to ancient or contemporary schools of literary style was denigrated, as was the regurgitation of the Classics. It is thus not surprising that many adherents of this movement were also promoters of women's writings.

Although short essays and jottings — previously dismissed as too private and trivial — gained respectability from this elevation of sincerity, it was poetry that exemplified the spirit of the age. Stephen Owen has stated that "the Chinese lyric at its best was conceived as the highest form of speaking to someone else." Poetry, in other words, is at once personal and social. "In a basic way Chinese poetry becomes a way to create community, both speaking to others in the present and creating a living community across time."[72] In later chapters, we will see that educated women fully exploited both the personally expressive and socially communicative aspects of poetry in the seventeenth century. The perceived expressive and emotional qualities of the genre coincided with literary and philosophical emphases as well as gender stereotypes that construed females as emotional beings in the private sphere. No wonder there were so many women poets, and no wonder their works carried a special appeal for the reading public.

The association of poetry, emotions, and women was particularly strong in the case of song lyrics (*ci*), a form of verse with uneven lines that was considered more expressive and hence more feminine than regular verse. Kang-i Sun Chang has observed that many Ming-Qing critics saw "a convergence of biological femaleness and stylistic femininity" of the genre, hence they thought women would make better song lyrics poets. The late Ming revival of the genre was thus integrally related to the popularity and valorization of female poets. Both were, in turn, predicated on a cult of *qing*.[73]

The most eloquent advocate of the woman poet was Zhong Xing (1574–1627), editor of the most famous of late Ming anthologies, *Poetic Retrospective of Famous Ladies* (*Mingyuan shigui*). In this comprehensive collection, one-third of the 36 *juan* are devoted to Ming women alone; the remaining two-thirds covers women poets of all the previous dynasties. In his preface, Zhong Xing, a leader of the so-called Jingling School of literature, issued a manifesto for the primacy of inspirational gusto to the poet. Central to his arguments was an antithesis between woman, nature, and the private sphere on one hand, and man, human traditions, and the public sphere on the other. Not only was true poetry, in his view, born of the former, but it was the very embodiment of female innocence and sentimentality.

"Poetry is none other than the voice of nature," Zhong proclaimed. It "cannot be mastered by following rules." He then cited the *Book of Songs*, one of the Five Confucian Classics and believed to be in large part composed by women, as the hallmark of natural expressiveness. Having criticized contemporary male poets who mistook the rules for the essence of poetry, Zhong drew an analogy between the poet's coming of age and the development of the female psychology: "A grown-up woman starts life as a girl who knows neither [the difference between] the skilled and the crude nor any hidden worries." Yet as she grows up, innocence gives way to an intuitive experience. A teenage girl slowly begins to realize that "life has its ups and downs. When she is happy, she can change ice crystals into flowers; when she is sad, dark clouds turn into snow. [Her mind can be] as serene as jade or as melancholy as flowers in dreams. All of a sudden a thread arises from nowhere, tying loose ends neatly together. This is the source of [words that are] prodigal and lush, high and lofty, slender and graceful, murmurous or vociferous." Inspirational insight, in other words, is a natural and spontaneous occurrence in the mind and cannot be forced by deliberate learning or mimicking rules. "Tomorrow's great poets are invariably those who are clumsy in poetry today."[74]

Not only are females likely to be better poets because they are less corrupted by the human learned tradition, they personify the essence of poetry. "Poetry is a creature of serenity. Her body likes leisure, not toils. She likes her place clean, not filthy. Her sphere is to be secluded, not rowdy. No one can surpass females in these aspects." Zhong then made the same argument as Wu Guofu: women's exclusion from men's public and political endeavors is a blessing in disguise. In addition, Zhong made a most interesting contrast between the materiality of a man's world and the imaginary and psychological nature of a woman's world.

A male travels to the four corners of the world, and he knows what these corners are like. [The Sui dynasty official] Yu Shiji authored the *Gazetteer of Ten Commanderies* (*Shijun zhi*) in which he conveyed a picture of mountains and waters by describing the landscape; he conveyed a picture of territorial jurisdictions by describing the commanderies and counties. . . . But females do not have to do this. They embrace villages and districts on their beds and pillows and [imagine] fortresses on the frontier in their dreams. They can do this because they are serene.[75]

Zhong Xing's conviction that serenity constituted the true nature of poetry prompted him to publish women's verse as model for men who went astray. This valorization of the female voice reversed the traditional gender hierarchy; the notion of separate spheres itself, however, became even more entrenched. The male-female distinction was construed as rooted in psychology. Women remained the intuitive and sentimental sex, whereas men continued to be identified with learning and the intellectual tradition. At the same time, however, Zhong's recognition of the female freedom in imagining and constructing a version of reality was a remarkably astute observation. This disjuncture between the physical location of a woman's body and her inner world, as we will see, was a most effective weapon for the woman reader-writer obliterating the rigidity of separate spheres and her supposed confinement in the inner chambers.

To the association of women, poetry, and spontaneity so well articulated by Zhong Xing, a fourth link should be added: money. The success of Zhong's compilation, reprinted and incorporated into other anthologies throughout the seventeenth century, inspired other publishers. The next major anthology of women's writings to appear, *Lady Scholars from Past and Present* (*Gujin nüshi*), was the work of a Hangzhou commercial publisher, Zhao Shijie, whose profit motive was much more apparent. Zhao's method of distinguishing himself in a crowded field was to include both verse and prose, unearthing an impressive array of genres of "public" writings previously considered male prerogatives. The profitability of women's words prompted comments from those who feared that women's literary integrity would be compromised. Even Zhong Xing, who published his anthology in large part as a statement of his literary convictions, was accused by another editor of "smirking of the profit-seeking merchant." The accuser, Xu Shumin, headed a team of 29 male scholar-officials and men of letters who compiled a rare and wide selection of song lyrics, *Song Lyrics from the Fragrant Crowd* (*Zhongxiang ci*). Although he also credited four male financiers, it is possible that donations were made as investment and that the team was not entirely immune from the profit motive.[76]

The competition to produce an ever bigger and newer selection of women's verse prompted an incessant search for hidden manuscripts. Hu Baoyi of Suzhou, for example, combed printer shops, the studies of relatives and friends, and warehouses of book merchants for women's verses, annotated them with the help of his wife and disciples, and published an anthology. In the introduction he included his home address and encouraged "women poets from all over" to send in their works so that he could print a sequel. The commercial purpose of the venture was betrayed by his stern warning in the end: "The blocks [of this anthology] are kept in the Lingyun ge. Issuers of pirated copies will be pursued even if they are ten thousand miles away!"[77] (Lingyun ge was Hu's studio and doubled as the name of his publishing venture.) The personal tone of such solicitations was reminiscent of the advertisements that publishers made by way of printing their own portraits.

Many of the anthologies that flooded the market were monumental works issued in sequels — if the first sold well, then the profits could finance the next, and so on. A personal invitation from publisher to reader was thus a sales pitch in disguise. One success story was that of Deng Hanyi (1617–89), a leader of Yangzhou salons and compiler of *Perspectives on Poetry* (*Shiguan*). Alongside the verses of 45 women he interposed his own comments, a practice initiated by Tian Yiheng in *Poetry of Lady Scholars* (*Shinüshi*) over a century earlier. Deng's appeal to readers at the end could not have been more personal: "As soon as this anthology is printed, I plan to compile volume two. If you have poems or comments, please send them to my home in Taizhou, or to Cheng Muqian, at Crossed-Scissors Bridge, New City, Yangzhou." Having listed the addresses of three other friends in Yangzhou, Beijing, and Nanjing, Deng cautioned overzealous readers who might show up at their doorstep that "it is most convenient to drop them in the mail." Six years later he published a sequel containing the works of 33 women.[78]

The more the demand for newer and larger selections of women's words, the stronger the incentive not only to make already popular names more visible by re-anthologizing them but also to discover previously unknown works. All this combing of dusty archives and soliciting of manuscripts smack of voyeurism on the parts of both publishers and readers. The result, however, was the heightened visibility and ready availability of a large body of women's verse that would otherwise have been lost to history. Not only did the number of poets thus brought to public view soar, but the geographical and social locations of published women also diversified. The earlier anthologies tended to feature writers from Jiangnan, often women who were personally known or indirectly related to the editors, but as the seventeenth century advanced, writers hailing from peripheral regions and even such foreign countries as Korea became common. Peasant poets, too, made their debut, although their authenticity remains an open question.[79]

More powerful than philosophical treatises, the commercial and literary interests of such men as Zhong Xing, Hu Baoyi and Deng Hanyi in women's poetry promoted women's education and popularized a positive image of woman writers. They, and like-minded men of letters who contributed prefaces to these collections, did not launch arguments for equality of the sexes, nor did they champion women's education overtly. Yet their appreciation of women's poetry for its direct and natural outflow of emotions amounted to public recognition of women's creative talent. The popularity of women's verse must have persuaded parents that it was natural for their daughters to read and write. Thus the promotion of male publishers helped create a niche for literate women, poets in particular, in the urban culture of Jiangnan.

The literate women themselves took the clue and began to compile women's poetry to serve their own ends — the creation of a women's community across time and spatial distance. In subsequent chapters I will return to the lives of two of these editors — Shen Yixiu (1590–1635) and Wang Duanshu — and their historical mission of preserving and transmitting women's writings.

Rare as they must have been, there were even women publishers. The verses of a Hangzhou woman, Liang Ying (1707–95), for example, were published separately by two printer's wives. Madame Wang, wife of the Huizhou printer Wu Dilan, issued Liang's poetry in Huizhou. Madame Li, wife of the owner of a Yangzhou press, Yuanguo tang, published Liang's poetry on plum blossoms in 1730. According to a twentieth-century scholar who saw a copy of this volume, *Every Fragrant Word* (*Zizi xiang*), both the cutting of the blocks and the printing were first-rate, making this one of the best-produced collections of women's writings.[80]

Liang Ying's husband, Huang Shugu (1701–51), was instrumental in

Liang's writing career. Huang, a fifth-generation descendant of a Hang-zhou matriarch and renowned poet, Gu Ruopu (1592–ca. 1681), initiated Liang into a family tradition of woman writers and poetry clubs. A man of letters who roamed Jiangnan for patrons, Huang was staying on the estate of Wu Yirong, a Yangzhou merchant, in the early 1730's.[81] Although it is not clear if Wu and the printers who issued Liang's verses were related, it is most likely that Huang arranged the publication of his wife's works when he was in Yangzhou. He also invited two good friends to write prefaces for her. Huang's involvement, as we will see in the later chapters, was typical of the male relatives of famous woman poets.

Reading, writing, editing, and publishing, educated women in Ming-Qing Jiangnan became visible participants in literate culture as consumers and producers. Both the print culture and their own lives would never be the same again.

Gender Relations in the Floating World

The appearance of a critical mass of women writers and readers was a striking feature of urban culture in seventeenth-century Jiangnan. This appearance, however, carries contradictory implications for gender rela-tions. The very visibility of the social and cultural changes that transpired masks their underlying contentious nature.

Visibility was the essence of the urban print culture and the monetary economy that sustained it. The new moneyed families engaged in *conspic-uous* consumption; the woman reader-writer emerged from her cloister into *public view*. The novelties of the print culture were graphically clear to all those with eyes to see at the time and in posterity: a profusion of books — books laden with mistakes, books with pictures, portraits of pub-lishers and artists speaking personally to the reader, stories of virtuous women reiterated in various genres, women's verse anthologized in series of publications. The age of visual representation demanded that hidden words be exposed and novelties be projected in exaggerated fashion.

The implications of these changes, however, were by nature controver-sial, for they depended on the values and vested interests of the viewer. What a scholar-official feared as an erosion of social and gender bound-aries could appear to his wife as an opportunity to advance her freedom and mobility. At the same time, she was likely to join him in bemoaning the degenerate and decadent age. No blanket statement can do justice to the complexity of the changing times, which often manifested itself in contradictory positions embraced by one person simultaneously.

It is therefore extremely difficult to assess the impact of the changes on women. Scholars have argued that the new urban culture sowed the seeds of more equal gender relations. Paul Ropp, for example, characterizes the eighteenth century as a battleground between the "dominant culture" of orthodox Confucianism, with its increasingly restrictive norms for women, and an "emergent culture" that arose from Jiangnan urban and commercial centers, where novelists portrayed intelligent and strong female protagonists and men of letters decried concubinage and footbinding.[82] Charlotte Furth also argues that the values and lifestyle of a "bohemian counterculture" posed a challenge to the authority of the patriarch in the family, but she cautions that the dissenting artists depended on the old elite patronage system and did not have an independent economic base.[83] Both scholars concur that commercialization created the possibilities for more equalized gender relations.

My study of women in the Jiangnan print culture is built on these pioneer works. On the location of this culture and its implications for gender relations, however, my interpretations differ. First, to call this floating world an "emerging culture" or "counterculture" is to draw too rigid a line between the Confucian tradition and the urban culture that arose in late Ming Jiangnan. As argued in this chapter, this culture was not an abnormality; instead, it grew out of developments from within "mainstream" Confucian literati culture and in turn transformed values and behavior in that world. Furthermore, the premium placed on private aesthetic expressions of emotion touched every aspect of Chinese life. Intimate matters in the bedrooms of gentry households were affected, as much as business transactions in market towns, liaisons in the pleasure quarters, the appeal of popular religious sects, and the mode of communication in literature and schools of literary criticism. The culture of the reading public has to be seen as a dominant motif in the general culture of seventeenth-century China.

My second disagreement concerns the implications of the inclusion of women in print culture for greater gender equality. From hindsight, the impact of the urban print culture can only be described as a paradox. On an individual level, some women gained parity with men in the world of learning and literature; the opposite is true on a systemic level, where the promotion of the woman writer served only to reinforce the prevalent premise of gender distinctions. This paradox is equally evident in the two primary modes of woman's inclusion in the emergent print culture: the spread of women's cultural education and the valorization of women's poetic voice.

The seventeenth-century print culture changed the theory and practice of women's education by giving legitimacy to cultural education. But cultural literacy did not diminish the strong hold of Confucian morality on the educated women's lives. In fact, never before had the vehicles for propagating Confucian ideology been more powerful and pervasive. Tales of moral exemplars, now vividly illustrated and presented as vernacular stories, reached more homes and perhaps hearts and minds than did dry treatises. Even more persuasive was the advocacy of educated women, as they composed poems and songs to teach other women the virtues of fidelity. The rise of the woman reader-writer, in other words, was a sign largely of the strength of the Confucian gender system, not its demise. The educated woman brought her new cultural resources to the service of her supposed natural duties of motherhood and moral guardianship. With the support and promotion of the new woman as erudite mother and teacher, the underpinnings of the gender system became even more solid than before.

The implications of the valorization of the female poetic voice are just as ambivalent. Because of it, more women were encouraged to pursue an education and to devote themselves to writing; they were, in this sense, becoming more like men. Yet this very valorization was predicated on an insistence of male/female distinctions in constitution, sensitivities, and outlook. The gender system as a whole, thriving on these perceived distinctions, proved to be resilient enough to survive the onslaught of socioeconomic changes.

In short, seventeenth-century Jiangnan was a transitory world full of contradictions. It allowed educated women unprecedented room for creative expression and emotional fulfillment, but these opportunities, tied to family backgrounds, were not freely available to all. Old gender stereotypes died hard, often co-existing with more sympathetic thoughts on woman in the same person. Voices of individual women were heard, but women in seventeenth-century China had yet to articulate their collective aspirations. In such a floating world, the story that matters most is that of individual and everyday struggles. As the pages that follow will show, each of these stories is woven of its own bittersweet blend of hope and frustration, freedom and bondage, friendship and loneliness.

The Enchantment of Love
in 'The Peony Pavilion'

CONTRARY TO PERSISTENT gender stereotypes that relegated females to an intuitive and sentimental existence, educated women inhabited a world rich in both intellectual and emotional meaning. In fact, it was the act of reading that joined the cerebral and sentimental into a closed circle. In the preceding chapter, I offered an objective overview of the sociocultural position of the woman reader in the print culture of seventeenth-century Jiangnan; in this chapter I examine the subjective meaning of reading — of dramas, poetry, and each other's works — to the woman herself. In particular, I focus on the craze of women for *The Peony Pavilion*, a tribute to love by the great late Ming playwright Tang Xianzu, to illuminate two significant results of reading: how reading romantic fiction helped shape women's self-perceptions, and how women projected their self-perceptions onto pages of commentaries and poems, fueling a cult of *qing* among the reading public.

The Obsessive Reader: The Three Women's Saga

Ming and Qing women did not read to master a canonical tradition in order to compete in the civil service examinations, nor did they leaf through books casually just to pass the time. They read for edification, often with an intensity that bordered on fanaticism. Drama and other fictional works were particularly engaging, for they gave shape to the reader's aspirations while offering solace for the imperfections experienced in real life. From pages of fiction woman readers built their own floating worlds in which intellectual stimulation conjoined with emotional and religious gratification.

Specifically, the meanings that the obsessive female reader found in fiction and drama can be understood in four ways, as this chapter will show. First, fictional characters provided role models for the socialization of girls. Literary critics have suggested that girls derived their expectations about the future not from observing real life but from reading fiction.[1] This is particularly true for *The Peony Pavilion*, whose heroine, Du Liniang, became the alter ego of generations of young women.

Second, reading was also an inventive act in the fundamental sense of the word. Women who read created not only their self-images but also a multiplicity of meanings with which to construct their world as they pleased. *The Peony Pavilion*, a romantic tale with a happy ending, became structurally linked in the minds of some women with the lore of Xiaoqing, a romantic tale about a reader of *The Peony Pavilion* with an unhappy ending.[2] Readers of both the romantic drama and Xiaoqing's tragedy themselves became celebrated figures and inspired new recitations of poems and tales. Readers were made into fictional characters, and the fictions, in turn, were read by more readers, who created new fictions. A simple story of the love-struck maiden Du Liniang, in the end, spun an entire tradition of tales with conflicting messages. Each reader had room to re-imagine the tales to satisfy her shifting moods and needs.

A third significance of reading stemmed from its addictive qualities. For many girls, an early love of books developed into a lifelong devotion to intellectual and literary pursuits. The fervor women brought to collating, handcopying, and circulating books and manuscripts often resembled religious fanaticism. Like all addictions, reading was gratifying but consuming; it could even be fatal. Indeed, the stories of the untimely deaths of Xiaoqing and other girls who loved literature were so prevalent that a superstition equating reading with fatality gained currency as the phenomenon of women reading became widespread.

Yet despite the power of superstition and the real dangers of consumption, women did not stop reading. Reading took on a fourth meaning as the ultimate transcendental act, offering the promise of salvation alongside the danger of fatality. To read is to partake of a world that is larger than the one defined by the four walls of the inner chambers. Reading connected women to a social world of like-minded readers and an imaginary world of fictional characters that appeared to be larger but truer than life. Books, like religious devotions, provided a way out of the drudgeries of mundane existence. It is no accident that reading itself became a religious act, as readers took flights of fancy in devising female-exclusive domestic rituals honoring heroines from such plays as *The Peony Pavilion*.

How reading engendered these four meanings is vividly demonstrated by the story of the three young women who wrote and compiled *The Peony Pavilion: Commentary Edition by Wu Wushan's Three Wives* (henceforth *Three Wives' Commentary*). Its publication in 1694 was a crowning event in the emergence of the woman reader-writer as cultural producer. The long and assiduous process of production was particularly revealing of the extent to which books made their way into the female quarters and how deeply the world of publishing in seventeenth-century Jiangnan affected the lives of women.

The three women's saga began with the innocent and private obsession of a young girl, Chen Tong (ca. 1650–65), who lived in the green hills outside Hangzhou. Like many other females of her times, Chen was absorbed in the world of love evoked by *The Peony Pavilion*, a play that was an instant success upon its first publication in 1589.[3] Chen became a devotee of the play, spending hours collating and correcting the different versions that Jiangnan book merchants purveyed. One day, from her sister-in-law, Chen obtained a copy of an authentic edition issued by the press that belonged to the playwright Tang Xianzu himself.[4] Unable to put it down, she started to scribble comments on the margins of the pages.

Chen was such an avid lover of literature that even after she fell ill she stayed up all night reading. Her mother, worried about her health, seized and burned all her books, including the second volume of her prized edition of *The Peony Pavilion*. Chen's wet nurse, however, rescued Volume 1, which was tucked away under a pillow, and used it to press dried flowers. Book burning failed to restore Chen, who died not long before her wedding. The wet nurse then took the book to the home of Chen's betrothed, Wu Ren, together with a pair of shoes that Chen had made as a memento for her future mother-in-law, and sold it to him for one ounce of silver.[5]

Wu Ren, resident of a scenic Hangzhou suburb, was a poet of some repute and moved in the circles of the famous playwright Hong Sheng (1645–1704), an old family friend, and his neighbor Mao Xianshu (1620–88), a leading early Qing poet and member of several Hangzhou poetry clubs.[6] A drama aficionado himself, Wu delighted in the tiny scribbles, full of Chan Buddhist insights, left by Chen Tong on the pages of *The Peony Pavilion* and regretted that the second half had been lost to fire.

Soon Wu Ren married another local girl, Tan Ze (ca. 1655–1675), who was as fond of the play as Chen Tong had been. Tan committed Chen's commentary to memory, completed the second half in Chen's spirit, and handcopied her comments and Chen's onto the margins of an original edition of the play that Wu had bought from the book merchants in Wuxing, a leading retail book center in Jiangnan. She lent the copy to her niece, but reluctant to appear boastful about her talent, she pretended that the commentary was her husband's work. The niece showed the copy to her tutor, and soon literary circles in Hangzhou were talking about Wu

Ren's commentary on *The Peony Pavilion.*[7] Wu himself, however, admitted freely who the true authors were. One day, in the Beijing living room of his old friend Hong Sheng, he used Chen's and Tan's expositions on dreams and emotions to debate with Hong, who was impressed.[8]

In 1675, three years after her marriage, Tan Ze also died. The ill-fated Wu Ren married a third time, a Hangzhou woman named Qian Yi, more than a decade later. She, too, stayed up all night reading *The Peony Pavilion* and the comments by her two "elder sisters." Eager to preserve the women's manuscripts, Qian told her husband, "I heard that a woman named Xiaoqing once wrote an afterword to *The Peony Pavilion* that is no longer extant. But when I read her 'cold rain lone window' poem, my heart sank. Now elder sister Chen produced her commentary, which elder sister Tan completed, but it's a pity that they have been known under your name all these years."[9] Xiaoqing, a Yangzhou concubine, wrote of the comfort she derived from reading the play in her famous "cold rain lone window" poem, as we will see later. Qian managed to convince her husband to reissue the play with commentary under the three women's names and sold her jewelry to finance the block-cutting and printing. The result was the publication of *Three Wives' Commentary* in 1694, graced by prefaces and afterwords from Hong Sheng's daughter and members of Banana Garden Seven, a women's poetry club in Hangzhou (see Chapter 6).[10]

The long and meandering process behind the production of China's first published work of female literary criticism encapsulates the major themes of this book: the connectedness between male and female networks; the spread of companionate marriage; the forging of a women's culture in the context of domestic life, through the exchange of books, manuscripts, and mementos like shoes; the central role played by the production, appreciation, and propagation of literature in this women's culture; and the significance of women writing and publishing. It is also, for the purpose of this chapter, an eloquent statement of the degree to which female readers were enchanted by *The Peony Pavilion* and its vindication of love. Chen Tong, Tan Ze, and Xiaoqing, all readers who died in their teens, testified to the potency of both the creative genius and consumptive danger unleashed by the seemingly casual act of reading a book.

Dramatization of Love in The Peony Pavilion

The social effects of reading were magnified when books were not only read quietly but were also read aloud, recounted verbally, and performed on stage. The three women's enchantment by the vindication of love in

The Peony Pavilion testifies to the persuasive power of a cult of *qing*, hallmark of the seventeenth-century Jiangnan urban culture. The popularity of this and numerous other dramas — written to be both read and performed — was particularly important to the forging of the cult. As discussed in the preceding chapter, the personal sales pitches of commercial publishers and the flood of illustrated books contributed to a cult of truthful representations and personal communications and promoted the image of women as more natural, hence better, writers. Adding to these developments in the publishing world, I attempt here a fuller view of the cult of *qing* by taking into account the performance-related aspects of drama. Above all, through the examples of *The Peony Pavilion* and the Xiaoqing plays, I explore the philosophical underpinnings of the cult, the crucial role played by women in its propagation, and the different perspectives that men and women brought to the reading of the meaning of *qing*.

The cult of *qing* was born of the sympathetic reading of fiction and appreciation of dramas on stage. Kang-i Sun Chang has aptly observed that "the blossoming of the cult of [*q*]*ing* in the late Ming took place largely through readers' imitation of the role types created in contemporary fiction and drama."[11] This is particularly true for the readers and audiences of Tang Xianzu's *Peony Pavilion*. Soon after its first appearance in 1589, the drama was hailed as the embodiment of *qing* par excellence. The thriving publishing industry and the popularity of theater in seventeenth-century Jiangnan magnified its impact, creating a cult out of the drama itself.

The appeal of *The Peony Pavilion* had much to do with both Tang Xianzu's literary innovations and the attraction of its heroine, Du Liniang, as the prototype of a new female. Many seventeenth-century critics recognized that artistically the play represented the height of Southern drama. A Japanese specialist on the play, Hirose Reiko, has shown that Tang perfected a dramatic gaze and language uniquely suited to the creation of an ethereal world of deep feelings. Emotions were elevated to the realm of aestheticism. Compared to *The Western Chamber*, a classic Yuan drama with a similar love theme, *The Peony Pavilion* appears "condensed and wet," whereas the former feels "diluted and dry." In its expert dramatization of the characters' innermost thoughts and feelings, *The Peony Pavilion* is able to enchant as no other play can.[12]

The realistic disclosure of Du's inner world accounts for her credibility, and hence the sympathy she wins for her course of action. Daughter of a magistrate, Du is well versed in both the Classics and the moral precepts for women but finds the rote memorization and moralism stifling. One day, instead of following her lessons with a tutor, Du falls asleep in the garden. In her dream she falls in love with a scholar, Liu Mengmei, and avidly pursues him. The image of Du Liniang that emerges is one of a strong-willed woman determined to live out her fantasies in defiance of social constraints.

The love-struck Du Liniang falls ill and dies at the age of fifteen, but takes care to leave a portrait of herself behind. The lover in her dream turns out to be a real person who chances upon her portrait and falls in love with her. Even in the other world, Du continues her search for Liu, and they eventually marry. In the end, Du is resurrected, Liu captures first place in the examinations, and Du's perseverance is rewarded by her attainment of true love.

Du Liniang signifies an enchanting new woman completely at home in the urban culture of her day — educated but natural, sensuous yet respectable, persistent unto death in pursuing her life's ambition. Although captivating males and females alike, she became the alter ego of her female audience.

The popularity of the drama among women reached legendary proportions. If Ming and Qing woman readers shared a common vocabulary, it was based on *The Peony Pavilion*. No other work of literature triggered such an outpouring of emotion from women. There was no lack of male devotees who rewrote the play, staged it, and wrote commentaries; almost all the better-known men of letters from Ming-Qing Jiangnan made remarks on the play in one form or another.[13] The women's response, however, was shocking in its novelty, intensity, and a certain consensus of sentiment, despite subtle differences in interpretation. True to the spirit of the cult of *qing*, women created communities transcending spatial and even temporal barriers through their shared appreciation of this play, as we have seen in the example of the *Three Wives' Commentary*.

Although existing information is insufficient to glean the actual number of copies printed, there are over ten extant Ming and Qing editions of the play, some elaborately illustrated. Issued by both private presses and the leading commercial publishers of the day, the play was no doubt a best-seller.[14] Chen Tong, the first wife of Wu Ren who initiated the *Three Wives' Commentary* project, collated twelve different versions of the play, some by the same name; Wu later bought another copy for his second wife from a book merchant in Wuxing, one of the thriving Jiangnan book markets.[15] Women also handcopied the play, and shared it among friends. Circumstantial evidence of women scribbling poems onto margins as they read suggests that many in fact owned a copy.

Written in a vernacular but refined prose, the dialogue of *The Peony Pavilion* was laced with classical allusions. Hence as a literary work, it was accessible only to the educated. However, although some dramas were intended to be read but not performed, Tang Xianzu was a practitioner

who wrote for the stage. *The Peony Pavilion*, his most popular work, was adopted for regional theaters by at least five dramatists in the Ming dynasty alone.[16] Tang supervised the production of many of these performances himself, which were at first staged by troupes in his native Jiangxi province. A measure of the popularity of these performances was provided by Tang, who estimated that there were over a thousand professional actors around his native place of Yihuang.[17] By late Ming times, selected episodes from the play were immensely popular in Beijing and Jiangnan, both in literati homes and popular theaters.[18] About one-quarter of the scenes remained a staple of the repertoire as late as the nineteenth century.[19] With stage performances, the message of the play reached well beyond a circle of literate readers.

To understand the full impact of such plays as *The Peony Pavilion*, one has to appreciate the enormous popularity of the theater in seventeenth-century China and the visibility of women in it. The Yuan dynasty (1280–1368) saw the perfection of drama as a literary genre, but the Ming was the golden age of drama, more aptly called opera, as a performing art.[20] With the proliferation of professional troupes, a vastly expanded repertoire, and increased venues for performance, the opera, in various local song styles, captivated men and women from all regions and social classes.[21]

There were three kinds of drama troupes in Ming-Qing times — court-sponsored troupes, professional groups, and private companies kept by literati and merchant families. Since performances by the first were reserved for residents of the palace and visiting dignitaries, they will not be discussed here. Similar to the publishing industry, the private sector of the world of theater experienced phenomenal growth in the sixteenth and seventeenth centuries as a result of commercialization. The social organization of both professional and family troupes was radically transformed by the spread of material and cultural affluence. Wang Anqi, a specialist on Ming Southern drama, has pointed out that private Yuan troupes were family-based, often made up of husband, wife, and their children. Groups of professional actors with no kin ties first appeared in the Ming. Many of these groups were all male, employing boys as female impersonators, but

---

(*Opposite*) Facsimile of self: The love-struck Du Liniang leaves a legacy before her death by drawing her portrait from mirror reflections. The engraver explored the ambiguities in the Chinese phrase *xiezhen* (sketching a likeness / sketching true self) by positioning the tip of the painting brush on Liniang's own face. His name, Mingqi, is visible in the upper left corner; he was a member of the famed Huang family from Huizhou (*Mudanting*. First published 1617; reprinted — Chang Bide, p. 10).

female actors became increasingly popular in the last decades of the sixteenth century. Contemporary accounts show that they performed with men, although we know nothing about their offstage living or traveling arrangements. Drama aficionados also wrote of all-female troupes.[22] One of these woman actors, Zhu Chusheng, was studious about discussing matters of diction with expert scholars. She evidently regarded herself with the dignity of a professional artist.[23]

Not only the composition of the troupes but also their repertoire and patrons diversified. Tanaka Issei distinguishes three ranks of professional troupes according to the training of the actors and the status of their patrons. The highest-ranking groups resided permanently in the local city and served wealthy lineages, local officials, and merchants. Technically most advanced, they reflected the moral preference of the local elite, staging dramas espousing loyalty and chastity. Next in rank were semi-itinerant groups based in the local city but occasionally touring the countryside. They, too, reflected the conservative taste of the village elders.[24] Lowest in rank were itinerant troupes that performed in market towns and at temple fairs. Often with ties to secret societies, their repertoire was heavy on romance and weak on virtues. Although less trained, they were more innovative than the other two. Naturally, they also met the strongest resistance from local authorities.[25] This third type was instrumental in shaping the Jiangnan urban culture in general and the cult of *qing* in particular.

Besides these professional groups for hire by the public, troupes kept by private families also existed. This practice first became popular in the late sixteenth century, especially among Jiangnan literati families. Supervised and funded by aficionados, these troupes served a variety of functions — experimentation with new tunes, private entertainment, social network building, and testimony to the family's erudition and wealth. Similar to family publishing, family troupes constituted a means of converting cultural capital into prestige and was indicative of the trend of privatization of Chinese gentry life. Besides actors, these companies often included trainers and musicians, with the size of the larger groups reaching 20 to 30 people. Some actors were recruited from professional troupes; others were maids and concubines who received special training. The popularity of family troupes attests to the degree to which the opera permeated the private and official lives of the literati class. By the eighteenth century, however, the custom had shifted from literati to merchant families.[26]

(*Opposite*) The communicative power of *qing*: the lover in Du Liniang's dream turns out to be a real person, who falls in love with her likeness / true self (*Mudanting*. First published 1617; reprinted — Chang Bide, p. 13).

Although literati wives and daughters played no formal role in the organization of family troupes, they benefited from a daily immersion in music and literature. House parties often ended with a few arias; women sometimes enjoyed them from behind a screen.[27] It is no accident that some families famous for their troupes — the Shen in Wujiang, the Qi in Shanyin, and the Yuan in Nanjing — also boasted an exceptional concentration of female literary talents. Yuan Dacheng's daughter Lizhen (d. ca. 1652) was a playwright who drafted her father's famous play, *Swallow Letters*.[28] Women from the Shen and Qi families formed poetry clubs (discussed in later chapters). One of the Shen daughters, Ye Xiaowan, also published a play.

Although commoners were usually not privy to the performances of private literati companies, their craze for opera could be satisfied through other venues. A famous drama aficionado, Zhang Dai (1597–ca. 1689), occasionally took his family troupe to perform in such public places as temples and pavilions, attracting thousands of local fans. The audience appeared to be familiar with the repertory, on one occasion chanting its disapproval of a certain character at his entrance.[29] More often than these impromptu appearances by elite companies, however, were regular performances of professional itinerant troupes. These could take two forms — religious and secular festivals in temples and temporary venues, as well as regular shows in theaters.[30] In addition, the public also enjoyed performances in inns, taverns, and brothels. Many of the better-known prostitutes in the seventeenth and eighteenth centuries relied on their operatic skills to attract clients.

Partly because of the association of prostitution with dramatics since ancient times, women played active roles in the theater in Ming and Qing China. To a certain degree, drama remained stigmatized; local authorities were incessant in outlawing plays they considered lewd, and household instructions repeatedly warned sons and daughters of the theater's vice. But the popularity of shows in the living rooms of literati households and the promotion of leading literary figures accorded the theater a degree of respectability. Gentrywomen — as playwrights, readers, critics, and audience — took drama seriously both as a literary genre and as a performing art. Commoner daughters were just as mesmerized in their roles of actors and audience. In their eagerness to dramatize emotions, women were second to none.

Male Vindication of Qing

To the extent that female readers and audience were largely responding to literary images created by men, the cult of *qing* is a collaboration of the two sexes with men taking the initiative. Although men and women shared common grounds in their recognition of the primacy of *qing*, there were subtle differences between the male and female perspectives. Generally speaking, men's discourse on *qing* was couched in philosophical jargon that reflected the prevailing fusion of Neo-Confucian morality with Buddhism and Daoism. Although women were not immune to Buddhist jargon, they tended to focus on such matters of immediate personal relevance as marriage and happiness. They also incorporated the cult into their everyday lives by devising domestic rituals.

Most representative of the male proponents of the cult of *qing* was Tang Xianzu. To Tang, the central tenet of the cult of *qing* was, in literary scholar C. T. Hsia's words, the postulation of "love as the primary and essential condition of life." The playwright's convictions were clearly stated in his preface to *The Peony Pavilion*, an often-quoted manifesto of the cult:

Love is of source unknown, yet it grows ever deeper. The living may die of it, by its power the dead live again. Love is not love at its fullest if one who lives is unwilling to die for it, or if it cannot restore to life one who has so died. And must the love that comes in dream necessarily be unreal? For there is no lack of dream lovers in this world. Only for those whose love must be fulfilled on the pillow and for whom affection deepens only after retirement from office, is it entirely a corporeal matter.[31]

Hsia has pointed out that the three key words in this passage, "life" (*sheng*), "love" (*qing*), and "dream" (*meng*), underscore the influence of the Neo-Confucian Taizhou school on Tang's philosophy in general and his affirmation of *qing* in particular.[32]

Founded by Wang Gen (ca. 1483–1540), son of a salt maker, the Taizhou school is commonly considered the popular and radical wing of the Wang Yangming Neo-Confucian school. A commoner throughout his life, Wang preached Confucian virtues to the common folk with religious fervor. His famous motto, "The streets are full of sages," encapsulates his commitment to the practical needs of the ordinary men and women. In affirming the moral and intellectual capacity of every individual to attain sagehood, Wang Gen also argued for his or her right to self-expression and self-fulfillment.[33]

With adherents drawn from the gentry, merchants, and commoners, the Taizhou school, named after Wang's native place in Yangzhou prefecture, was one of the most influential intellectual movements in mid- to late Ming Jiangnan. In membership and basic tenets, it epitomized the spirit of the emergent urban culture—a fluid status system, emphasis on the self, and celebration of the vitality of life. Many dramatists who championed the cult of *qing*, editors who appreciated women's poetry, and fathers who encouraged their daughters to be educated traced their intellectual heritage to this school.

Tang Xianzu, for example, was a student of Luo Rufang (1515–88), a third-generation disciple of Wang Gen. A charismatic speaker who often lectured to thousands of people, Luo had deep faith in the goodness of men, innate knowledge, and the "perpetual renewal of life." Some scholars even argued that Luo elevated vitality of life (*sheng*) to a position equal with *ren*, the ultimate Confucian virtue of humanity.[34] In writing *The Peony Pavilion*, according to C. T. Hsia, Tang went further than Luo in affirming *qing* as the "distinguishing feature of human existence." Yet Tang added a pessimistic note in introducing the time element: only in dreams can life and love find complete fulfillment.[35]

Tang Xianzu's championing of *qing* was echoed in the works of Hong Sheng, a leading early Qing playwright and a close friend of Wu Ren. In *The Palace of Eternal Youth* (*Changsheng dian*, finalized in 1688), a drama set against the fall of the Tang capital to a rebel general, Hong eulogized the love between Li Longji (Tang Xuanzong, r. 712–56), the toppled emperor, and his consort Yang Guifei. Following Tang Xianzu, Hong equated *qing* with basic human nature, suggesting that there are sincere (*zhen*) *qing* and insincere (*jia*) *qing* just as there are goodness and evil. In its manifold manifestations, *qing* is the key to the rise and fall of empires and other historical events.[36] Those endowed with sincere *qing* can "move stones; change heaven and earth; shine as the sun; leave their names in history," Hong wrote in Scene 1. "Ministers are loyal and sons filial only because their *qing* is sincere to the extreme."[37]

Wu Ren described the central theme of *The Palace of Eternal Youth* as follows: "The fundamental nature of *qing* is principle [*li*], something we cannot do without; but if *qing* is given a free rein it overruns principle and becomes desire [*yu*], something we should avoid. This drama clearly points to a way out, those who are indulgent should take heed and repent."[38] Disagreeing with some critics that *qing* and the Neo-Confucian moral principle are always at odds, Wu Ren stated that "*qing* stems from nature; nature is none other than principle." Defending the respectability of *qing*, he reiterated its distinction from desire: "Nature expresses itself as *qing*, but, in excess, *qing* becomes desire."[39] In distinguishing love and desire and in channeling love into the boundaries of moral principle, this notion of *qing* smacks of Confucian views of propriety.[40]

The vindication of *qing* was the central motif not only in dramas but also in short stories popular among the reading public in late Ming Jiangnan. The word *qing* itself became a cliché. Hence editor and publisher of popular literature Feng Menglong (1574–ca. 1645) issued a collection of over 800 stories on love entitled *Anatomy of Love* (*Qingshi*, literally "a history of *qing*"). In the preface, Feng wrote of love as a supreme principle that governs all human relationships:

If there were no *qing* under heaven and earth, no being could be born. . . . With *qing*, even distant ones can be together; without *qing*, even close ones are rent asunder. Having *qing* [*youqing*] and not having *qing* [*wuqing*] are worlds apart. I wish to establish a religion of *qing* [*qingjiao*] and teach all living beings: the son faces his father with *qing*; the minister faces the emperor with *qing*; the same holds true for all other relationships. Things in this world are like loose coins; *qing* is the cord. Just as loose coins are strung together by a cord, even those from far corners of the earth can become couples.[41]

Written in colloquial language in the form of a Buddhist *gatha*, Feng's manifesto for a religion of *qing* appealed to the ordinary reader in its fusion of Confucian morality and Buddhist terminology. Feng recast the father-son and emperor-minister relationships, two pillars of Confucian ethics, in a new, gentler light. What marks these relationships is not the traditional virtues of loyalty and filial piety, but resonances from the heart. Human emotions, in other words, soften the edges of hierarchical obligations and sow the seeds for more egalitarian, reciprocal relationships. The same message is conveyed in the short stories that Feng compiled. Ōki Yasushi, a Japanese specialist on Feng, argues that in selecting stories for his series of anthologies, *Sanyan*, Feng's sole yardstick for evaluating a person's worth was his or her "sincerity of heart" (*zhenqing*).[42]

Feng Menglong's reduction of Confucian virtues to sincerity and Wu Ren's apologies cited above are, as Patrick Hanan suggests, attempts to accommodate *qing* to Confucian morality.[43] Yet this accommodation was fraught with subversive implications. In some seventeenth-century dramas and prose, love-crazed prostitutes who committed suicide were equated with chaste widows who threw themselves into wells, for both exemplified the Confucian dictum of "perseverance from beginning to end; not to serve two [masters] unto death" (*congyi erzhong, zhisi buer*). These women, in turn, were as exalted as loyal ministers who died for their country. United by an ultimate act of sincerity, a dead prostitute thus shared the fame of immortal officials and generals like Qu Yuan and Wen Tianxiang. This dilution of Confucian morality led one early nineteenth-century scholar to question the real motives of chaste widows whose names were enshrined in the gazetteers. These women, he suspected, actually died for love, not moral principles.[44]

Although Tang Xianzu, Hong Sheng, Wu Ren, and Feng Menglong sought to blend their belief in the primacy of *qing* with Neo-Confucian tenets on the one hand and with Buddhism on the other, the cult of *qing* was not a philosophical abstraction. Its true meaning has to be appreciated in the lives of those galvanized by its promise of a freer and happier life. Young, educated women, above all, were frustrated by the lack of fulfillment in their lives beyond the limited repertoire of roles reserved for women. Armed with heightened sensitivities and literary skills, they sought solace from the world of love evoked in literature.

The Female World of Love and Ritual

The message of *The Peony Pavilion* — love as a natural impulse unrestrained by moral codes or even death — struck a sympathetic chord among woman readers in Ming-Qing times. Like Rousseau after publication of *La Nouvelle Heloïse*, who had to use a trapdoor to slip away from readers besieging his retreat on the Ile Saint-Pierre, Tang Xianzu became an instant celebrity upon the production of his drama.[45] The attraction of woman readers to the author was unprecedented. Some fell so madly in love with Tang that they offered themselves to him.[46] Even more powerful was the reader's identification with the protagonist. One Yangzhou woman was said to have become so obsessed with the drama that she read it day and night and asked to be buried with it.[47] An actress from Hangzhou who could not marry the man she loved became famous for her portrayal of Du Liniang. So strong was her identification with Du that she allegedly died on stage during one climactic act.[48]

The appeal of the work was by no means limited to the frustrated in love. An early Qing gentry wife from Huizhou described how popular the play was in the inner chambers of respectable households: "Ladies in the boudoir all collect the latest embroidery patterns and keep them pressed between the leaves of a book. In between cutting patterns, all our eyes are fixed onto the pages of *The Peony Pavilion*." The result could be serious: "Once we read *The Peony Pavilion*, all of us are lured into the ocean of Classics and histories and are absorbed in poems and songs."[49] A mere drama, in other words, initiated the embroidering housewife into a new world of literature and scholarship. The lure of these new horizons partly accounted for the drama's popularity in the inner quarters.

Even more alluring was Du Liniang herself. Young, talented women developed intimate bonds with Du as if she were a friend. Ye Xiaoluan (1616–32), a teenage poet from Wujiang, wrote three poems and dedicated them to the portrait of Du attached to her copy of *The Peony Pavilion*. In one of them, Ye imagined Du to be a fairy from the moon: "I fear that you will fly back to the palace of the Big Chill [the moon] before I can cast on you a long, tender gaze."[50] Ye's tenderness toward Du is indicative of the world of *qing* into which young, educated women like her were initiated.

The behavior of devotees of *The Peony Pavilion* is most revealing of their romantic sensitivity. Taking the three key motifs of the play — life, love, and dreams — to the extreme, these women turned their own lives into a dreamworld permeated by love. For example, Qian Yi, Wu Ren's third wife, set up an altar in her garden after the work was published. On the altar she consecrated a portrait of Du Liniang together with a red plum branch to symbolize Du's lover, Liu Mengmei. Under torchlight, Qian made offerings of the commentary, wine, and fruits to Du. When Wu Ren chided his wife for taking fictional characters a little too seriously, Qian retorted: "If the spirit of god is manifested even in a piece of wood. . . . how can you or I tell for sure whether Du Liniang is real or not?"[51]

This conflation of fiction with reality stemmed from Qian's belief that *qing* could bridge the gap between the phenomenal world and the fantastic. The night after she worshipped at Du's altar, Qian dreamed that she walked into a garden with her husband, the setting of which recalled the famous scene "The Interrupted Dream" in the play, in which the heroine first meets her lover in a dream.[52] Amid the dazzling colors of peony blossoms, Qian saw a beauty whom she took to be Du Liniang. When winds blinded her sight and interrupted her dream, Qian awoke her husband and told him about it. To her surprise, Wu Ren claimed that he just had the same dream. Too excited to go back to sleep, Qian and Wu called a maid to heat up some water for tea, washed up, and set down the details of the dream on paper. Wu also asked Qian to draw a picture of Du as she saw her in her dream; it turned out to resemble the woman he saw. The two commemorated their unusual resonance of "sharing a dream" with rounds of poetry. Wu then admitted that he had been wrong in chiding Qian; Du Liniang was indeed a "real" person.[53]

The fantastic world was as rich in religious meaning as in conjugal resonance. In winter 1693, one year before the publication of the commentary, Qian Yi and her husband were proofreading a handcopied manuscript against Tan Ze's original before sending it to the printers. While they were distracted by sounds of cracking bamboo from a gathering snowstorm, a draft tipped over a candle and set the original manuscript on fire. In an act that foretold the famous scene in the eighteenth-century novel *Story of the Stone*, when the maudlin protagonist Lin Daiyu buried flower petals, Qian and Wu ordered a servant to dig a hole by the garden wall, wrapped the ashes in raw silk, and buried them next to a plum tree. A burn mark was said to have appeared on the tree.[54] Tan's manuscript was more than just a memento; it embodied her spirit.

The Peony Pavilion thus inspired a host of domestic rituals — worshipping at altars, painting portraits, burying manuscripts. Emulating Du Liniang's legacy, young women also painted and exchanged portraits of themselves. In addition, Chen Lanxiu, a gentrywoman poet from Chang-shu, Jiangsu (fl. 1662–1722), selected choice verses from the play and arranged them into a wordplay. Called *paipu* ("tunes"), the arrangement was used as a game in the female quarters, although details about it are lost.[55] Such word games and the belief that manuscripts embodied the author's spirit suggest that to these lovers of literature, the world of senti-mentality, with all its fanciful aura, was intimately linked to the written word.[56]

Female Readings of the Cult of Qing

Devoted woman readers of *The Peony Pavilion* offered a range of inter-pretations of the play. It is difficult to deduce from them a single "female reading" — an interpretation shared by all women and distinct from men's. Yet these women show a consensus of sentiment in the prime of place they assigned to expositions of *qing*. Taken together, their words constitute a spectrum of women's views of the cult of *qing*.

At the heart of the *Three Wives' Commentary* is a conviction that *qing* — including romantic and sexual love — is a noble sentiment that gives meaning to human life. Chen Tong launched into what she took to be the major theme of the play at the outset. Against Tang Xianzu's line of "Daylong I polished verses for the bowels' torture / for the telling of 'love, in all life hardest to tell,'" Chen wrote: "*Qing* does not only mean love between a man and a woman, but the latter is indeed hardest to tell." Qian Yi added that romantic love and the feelings of such tragic heroes as Xiang Yu, a third century B.C. warlord, are both *qing*.[57] Similar to Feng Menglong's reduction of loyalty and filial piety to sincerity of heart, these women affirmed that *qing* is an overarching principle governing all human relationships. As such, *qing* is not the prerogative of either sex alone.

Yet they agreed that Du Liniang was the greatest embodiment of *qing* that ever lived, calling her "love-crazed" (*qingchi*) and her love "the ulti-mate" (*qingzhi*). To them the most telling episode of her devotion to love came when she, knowing that she would soon die from lovesickness, leaves a self-portrait for posterity. In the play, this scene depicts a sensuous delight that the fifteen-year-old (sixteen *sui*) Du takes in her own beauty, tinged by regret over the transiency of youth. Weeping, Du sings:

"How can it be that Du [Liniang] must sketch with her own hand the grace of her sixteen years! Ah, that time should have etched —

> These peach-blossom cheeks of youth
> so swiftly with lines of care!
> Surely a happy lot is beyond my deserving.

Or why must 'fairest face be first to age'? . . .

> Now to damp down the burning
> of desire in the soul's brief resting place of flesh,
> take brush and paper, ink and inkstones."

She then paints a self-portrait and is pleased with its sweet appeal and charm.[58]

Both the tenderness Du feels toward her beauty and her lament of its fleeting nature stirred Chen and Qian, who were about the same age as Du when they wrote their commentaries. Their comments on the above scene read: "That Liniang is the greatest love-crazed one in history is seen in this episode. Had she been without it, posterity would not have found [her love] credible." Love, embodied in Du's portrait and her ghost, is a vital life force unconstrained by the passing of time or corporeal death. In calling this *qing* the "eternal debt" (*wusheng zhai*), Chen Tong alluded to the Buddhist view that *qing* is a kind of defilement (*chi, moha*) that causes ignorance of the true nature of existence (*wuming, avidyā*).[59] The use of Buddhist terms, however, was merely a fashionable convention. These devotees seemed untroubled by the essential incompatibility between idealization of *qing* and the original teaching of the Buddha.

This transcendental quality of *qing* induced these women to equate love and dreams in their commentary and, as we have seen, to believe that dreams and fictional characters constituted part of "real" life. Chen wrote: "Liniang did not know Liu had a dream; Liu did not know that Liniang had a dream. Both were filled with love, but each was dreaming his or her own dream. Since neither thought that he or she was dreaming, they both attained truth." The word "truth" (*zhen*) also means "reality," as Qian elaborated on Chen's words: "Liu changed his name because of his dream; Liu fell sick because of her dream. Both took their dreams to be real. As long as they did, their dreams indeed turned out to be real."[60]

In the scene in which Du, having been resurrected, plans to elope with Liu, she calls her return to life "the reopening of a dream world." Tan commented: "When one lives day by day in the world of *qing*, one lives in dreams everyday."[61] This line aptly describes the world of sentimentality and fantasy in which young women like Chen, Tan, and Qian lived.

Tan Ze elaborated on the theme of the supremacy of *qing* by equating it with talent (*cai*). In the play, Du declared her love for Liu Mengmei, the man of her dreams, as they met in the underworld: "I love your unsurpassed talent." Fearing that the reader would mistake Du's admiration for a vulgar longing for examination success and high position, Tan commented: "Her love of talent is by no means snobbish." Qian added: "When one's *qing* is fair, so is one's talent. Mencius argued that the one with talent is the one with *qing*. Hence those without *qing* cannot be called talented."[62]

This pairing of love with talent denies the "man : talent / woman : love" convention in the popular genre of scholar-beauty romances. These woman critics asserted that neither love nor talent is the prerogative of one sex alone. This argument was developed on two fronts: their endorsement of Du's education and their view that Liu Mengmei is as great a devotee of love as Du. On Du's education, these women shared the playwright's delight in parodying her tutor Chen, an ossified Confucian moralist who failed to detect, let alone approve of, the budding sentiments of the pubescent Du. Yet they applauded the tutor's choice of curriculum and his decision to have Du recite poems from the *Book of Songs*, one of the Confucian Five Classics. To him, the moral of these didactic poems, chosen by Confucius himself, can be summed up in the phrase "to set aside evil thoughts." To Du, these were love songs, probably written by women, that echoed her romantic sensitivities, a view shared by the young woman critics as well: "It is indeed appropriate to speak of poetry from within the women's chambers. How else can one begin to understand the *Songs*?"[63] In other words, men do not monopolize the reading of the Classics; a woman's talent is just as important, especially with regard to poetry. This view was shared by male editors who published anthologies of women's verse discussed in the preceding chapter, and, as we will see, supporters of women's education reiterated the same argument.

Nor is love a woman's monopoly. While celebrating Du Liniang as the quintessential embodiment of *qing*, the woman critics also acknowledged the devotion of her lover, Liu. Concerning the pains that Liu took to bring Du back to life and to seek the consent of her unbelieving father to their marriage, Tan wrote:

What is amazing about this story is not Liniang, but scholar Liu. There are many love-crazed women in this world like Du, who dreamed of love and died, but they do not return to life. [For they do not have] Liu, who laid out Du's portrait, called out to her, and worshipped her; who made love with her ghost and believed that it was her flesh and blood; who conspired with a nun to open her coffin and carried her corpse without fear; who traveled to Huaiyang to beg his father-in-law — he suffered it all with no regrets. This is truly amazing.[64]

The perfect love of Du would have been futile without Liu's reciprocation. To emphasize this reciprocity of love is to dismiss the stereotypical identification of females with the inner world of emotions and males with the outer world of principles.

Sanctity of Love, Sex, and Marriage

The idea of the reciprocity of *qing* in part accounted for the growing incidence of companionate marriage in the seventeenth century (see Chapter 5). The currency of companionate marriage perhaps explains the young women's high regard for the marriage institution itself. In the scene "Spectral Vows," after Liu and Du's ghost pledged their love and consummated it, Liu asks Du to reveal her identity. Du sighs: "This is my fear, sir scholar: 'betrothal makes wife, elopement only concubine.' I will tell my story when incense smoke has sealed our wedding pact." The two then exchange marital vows. Tan Ze noted: "Du's insistence on becoming a wife reveals the depth of her love. If she had been lax [about the vow], then their relationship would have been merely a brief love affair."[65] In applauding Du's respect for the marriage institution, these women asserted that *qing* is a respectable and, indeed, noble sentiment. Love is not disruptive or scandalous, as some critics of *The Peony Pavilion* had charged. Instead, it is the heart of matrimony.

Not only are romantic sentiments compatible with marriage, so too is sexual love. The love between Du and Liu is passionate and erotic; the play contains explicit references to sexual intercourse. When her ghost visits Liu at night, Du declares, "This body, 'a thousand gold pieces,' I offer you without hesitation. Do not disdain my love. My life's desire is fulfilled if I may share your pillow night by night." Comments on such scenes as this provide a rare glimpse into the views of young women on sex, a taboo subject normally discussed only covertly. On the scene "Union in the Shades" above, the young women wrote: "Theirs is purely a divine love, not carnal." Yet this divine love does not preclude carnal pleasures. On Du's earnest but shy and composed disposition as she enters Liu's chamber, they remarked: "She still behaves like a lady."[66] The pursuit of love — including sexual love — is fitting for a respectable woman.

This insistence that sex between devoted lovers is not lewd is further supported by the woman critics' defense of Tang Xianzu's explicit references to the sexual act. One very provocative scene describes Liu's foreplay with Du, before a knock at the door disrupts them and sends Du fleeing:

> Sleep now, while I
> cradle your swelling breast,
> guarding with this kerchief
> firm flesh now moist with sweat
> and slender curve of waist
> against the springtime's chill.

Chen Tong remarked: "These words depict the pleasures of the two lovers and convey their inseparable love to the extreme. They foreshadow the pains of subsequent separation."[67] In other words, plot development and dramatic effect demand explicitness. The fact that Chen, an unmarried young woman when she wrote this commentary, chose to comment on such a sex scene suggests a certain openness within the women's quarters to this subject. Of course, Chen wrote her commentary in private, with no intention of publishing the manuscript.

This openness and Chen's matter-of-fact tone suggest that these young women thought of sexual love as respectable. In another example, Du's maid inquires about the details of her mistress's lovemaking with Liu, pursuing the sensitive subject of virginity:

> How did you hide from lamp in lover's study?
> Where did you buy the wine to pledge your love?
> And when you took your pleasure
> was there no speck of blood in the breaching?

Fearing that moralists would condemn the playwright's words as lewd, Tan came to his defense: "These lascivious words refer to pleasures of a ghost, hence they sound elegant."[68]

To summarize, the three woman critics conceived of *qing* as a supreme principle in life, one with a transformative power that endowed the world of dreams and fantasies with a ring of reality. Furthermore, romantic love, one aspect of this *qing*, is a proper component of marriage. Qian Yi lamented: "Today, many fine marriages are delayed because people are picky on matters of family status and insist on amassing big dowries and trousseaus. When is this going to change?"[69] Love, not money or family advancement, is what marriage is about. As such, love is a worthwhile and respectable sentiment.

This vindication of *qing*, and, by extension, female talent, struck a sympathetic chord among other woman readers of the *Three Wives' Commentary*.[70] Lin Yining (1655–ca. 1730), a Hangzhou woman active in the female poetry club Banana Garden Seven, contributed a preface to the commentary. An accomplished poet and playwright herself, Lin found the critics' public exposition of love particularly laudable: "Women's talent is not supposed to be seen in the world. But now, the three wives have concentrated their outstanding talents in one family and produced this work in succession. This is a great enterprise that will last to eternity." Although hyperbole is common in prefaces, Lin's excitement is genuine, stemming from her agreement with the three women's appraisal of Du. Contending with some male critics' view that Du is unchaste, Lin wrote: "Thanks to the commentary of the three wives, Du Liniang's name is vindicated in public. She is within the bounds of propriety, and her elegant legacy lingers." Those who failed to see this plain truth, Lin added, were not worth talking to.[71]

These women's affirmation of the respectability of *qing* is similar to that of men of letters like Wu Ren, Hong Sheng, and Feng Menglong, but their approach is different. Whereas men engaged in philosophical arguments that sought to accommodate *qing* to both Confucian and Buddhist tenets, as we have seen above, women focused on the compatibility of love and marriage and of *qing* and talent. Male deliberations on the boundaries between emotion and moral principle, or between love and desire, were at best marginal concerns to female devotees of *qing*. In general, they were more likely to emphasize the unabashed expression of *qing* rather than its moderation. Even the three women's defense of matrimony has a subversive twist — Du and Liu had already consummated their love before they exchanged nuptial vows.

Phoenix and Crow: Resonances from Other Women

Scores of Ming and Qing women wrote commentaries on *The Peony Pavilion*. But unlike that of Chen, Tan, and Qian, these works were not published. Given the fragmentary nature of these accounts, it is hard to analyze their expositions of *qing* systematically; suffice it to note that they highlight aspects of the three women's commentary already discussed.

The late Ming woman critic, Yu Erniang, for example, resembled Chen Tong and Tan Ze in her devotion to literature and in her death at the tender age of sixteen. A native of Taicang, Jiangsu, Yu admired *The Peony Pavilion* because "one writes to express oneself. But most authors fail to express themselves fully. [Tang Xianzu's] 'Love is not love at its fullest if one who lives is unwilling to die for it, or if it cannot restore to life one who has so died' are truly words from the heart." Yu's words, in turn, are just as expressive and direct. In her commentary, she used the first-person pronoun: "I love to sleep, and whenever I sleep I would have dreams. In my dreams I see what I cannot see and hear what I cannot hear when awake. Liniang simply gets ahead of me in her dreams."[72] Yu's view of the authenticity of dreams echoes that of Chen, Tan, and Qian, and her statement on the purpose of writing epitomizes the personal author-reader relationship that lies at the heart of the cult of *qing*.

Another commentator was Cheng Qiong (ca. 1695–ca. 1719), a native of Shexian, Anhui. Like many other devotees of the play, she was a well-educated poet who died in her prime. A close friend of her husband's remarked that she excelled in calligraphy, painting, mathematics, and chess, had a quick mind, and was full of philosophical insights. Evidently, Cheng often discussed Chan Buddhism and literature with friends of her husband.[73] Mother of an infant son, she compiled a primer for his education when he turned four. When he died soon thereafter, Cheng burned the primer, sealed the ashes in his coffin, and shortly died from grief.[74]

Cheng's husband, Wu Zhensheng (1695–1769), was a well-to-do

scholar. Deeply shaken by her death, Wu called himself "the old widower" and wrote volumes in her memory. This passion and prolifigacy also marked their relationship in her lifetime. When Cheng fell sick and knew that she would die, she wrote a poem to bid Wu farewell:

> Romance and happiness are seldom equally shared,
> But unusually close, our lives and hearts are joined as one.
> I regret that this piece of clay will soon be shattered,
> Who can create another Madame Guan?[75]

Madame Guan refers to the Yuan calligrapher and painter Guan Dao-sheng (1262–1319). In a famous poem written for her husband, she compared a couple to two figurines shaped from one piece of dough. The conjugal bond is analogous to pulverizing the two figures, mixing the clay with water, and reshaping it into a new man and a new woman, so that "there is you in my clay, and me in yours."[76] In comparing herself to Guan, Cheng Qiong not only expressed her love for her husband but also conveyed her pride in her own talent.

Cheng's celebration of qing was no philosophical abstraction; it was intimately related to her experience of it in her marital life. One day, when Wu complained that he was suffering from too much qing, Cheng consoled him with a line by Tang Xianzu: "In all times, there is a world of law [fa] and a world of qing." She went on to argue that the latter is superior: "Talent is more lovable than riches; when it resonates with qing, our pleasure penetrates our soul."[77] This equation of talent and qing recalls the similar argument of Tan Ze and Qian Yi. Conversations like this suggest that the rapport between Cheng and Wu was built on an intellectual attraction. Their devotion to each other is in itself the best illustration of the mutual reinforcement of love and talent.

An enthusiast of The Peony Pavilion, Cheng Qiong watched it performed by the family troupe sponsored by a lineage elder and found the actress who played Du Liniang "the most seductive in the region." She was familiar with the Three Wives' Commentary, but found it lacking in explorations of hidden meanings and analogies. In her preface for an edition of the play that her husband annotated and published, Cheng did not divulge much of her interpretation.[78] She was said to have written a commentary of her own, entitled The Embroidered Peony (Xiu Mudan), in which she compared the different editions of the play and excised over 60 words from the original. Since this work was not published and is no longer extant, we have no access to the hidden meanings that she revealed. From fragments of it recorded by her husband's close friend Shi Zhenlin (1693–ca. 1779), however, Cheng appeared to be obsessed with the problem of an unequal marriage.

Like her fellow readers, Cheng saw in Du Liniang a perfect woman:

"Her looks most enchanting; her heart most tender; her vision most far-sighted; her wisdom most sagacious; her will most steadfast." These qualities were manifested in her insistence on a husband worthy of her beauty and talent. Referring to a line from the play "phoenix fated to follow crow," Cheng compared Du to a phoenix who preferred to pursue her ideal man in dreams rather than to marry a crow in real life. "I wish every woman was like me," Cheng was unabashed in identifying herself with Du, "and would rather die alongside the phoenix of my dream than to share a life with a mundane crow." Cheng herself was fortunate enough to have a worthwhile mate, but she realized that for the beautiful and talented, finding a perfect match was next to impossible. Hence Du's tenacity was all the more laudable.[79]

Although Cheng's celebration of love marriages echoes that of the *Three Wives' Commentary*, her concerns go beyond the latter's affirmation of the respectability of love and sanctity of marriage. In her sympathy for the phoenix who has to marry a crow, she was addressing a peculiar social problem that arose with the spread of woman's education. A talented woman often found her husband in an arranged marriage an unworthy intellectual companion. The problem was either so common or so novel that it caught the attention of writers and readers of popular literature. One of its variants, that of henpecked husbands and jealous wives, became a stock theme in Ming and Qing short stories and plays, as we will see in the discussion of Xiaoqing below. These stories were clearly inspired by real-life experiences. Several woman writers discussed in the later chapters married men so undistinguished that the latter's only claim to fame was as Ms. So-and-so's husband.

The dissatisfaction felt by such women was not couched in terms of an overt attack on the traditional marriage system. Instead, it propelled them to seek the company of other talented women, fostering the various types of networks that sprang from the inner chambers. At the same time, many mothers, all too aware of the unhappiness of overeducated daughters, became convinced that talent was a most unfortunate gift in a woman. The large number of female poets who died in their prime, discussed below, seemed to bear them out. The coming of age of the female reader was thus a mixed blessing to the women concerned: the sweet promises of nuptial bliss and female friendship were tinged with the dangers of disappointment, consumption, and fatality.

The Making of Xiaoqing Lore

These less happy aspects of the cult of *qing* were embodied in the lore of Xiaoqing (1595–1612), the most celebrated reader of *The Peony Pavilion*. Whereas talented young women — Chen Tong, Tan Ze, Qian Yi, Ye Xiaoluan, Yu Erniang, Cheng Qiong — saw in Du Liniang their alter egos and read the play as a metaphor of their own lives, frustrated men reacted with similar emotional intensity not to any character in the play but to the tragedy of Xiaoqing, an ill-fated concubine. Ellen Widmer summarizes the contrast between the appeal of the two heroines: "Du [Liniang]'s happier, healthier persona made her the right woman to triumph over nature and convention, while Xiaoqing's passive, ethereal beauty made her the right woman to fascinate readers by the way she died."[80]

Tang Xianzu probably did not anticipate that by investing Du Liniang with flesh and bone, he founded not only a literary industry but also a folk tradition of talented but ill-fated heroines. Widmer's study concentrates on the series of Xiaoqing biographies and plays written by these men as well as the interest taken by some woman poets in Xiaoqing.[81] My analysis focuses instead on the making of female readers into subjects of legends as well as the multiple and often contradictory meanings they were made to shoulder, notably the enchantment and fatality of love. In *The Peony Pavilion*, Du Liniang lives happily ever after as a proper wife; Xiaoqing's life was doomed from the start as a concubine. Underneath the reaction to their contrasting fates was a spectrum of views on the institution of marriage, women's nature, and women's appointed roles in society. In the final analysis, the lasting appeal of the Du Liniang–Xiaoqing stories was symptomatic of anxiety over a woman's proper place in family and society.

The life of Xiaoqing was a tragedy beyond belief. As told by her male biographers, Xiaoqing was one of the "thin horses" — girls sold as concubines — from Yangzhou. When she was fifteen, the son of a high official, Feng Yunjiang (1572–ca. 1661), bought her and brought her home to Hangzhou. Feng's wife, a jealous woman, moved Xiaoqing to a villa on West Lake and forbade Feng to see her. Xiaoqing found solace in writing poetry, painting, and the occasional company of a friend, Madame Yang. Madame Yang sought to persuade Xiaoqing to leave Feng, but she refused. Later, after Madame Yang followed her husband to a posting away from Hangzhou, Xiaoqing, lonely and depressed, became emaciated but decked herself out in ornate clothing and fresh makeup every day.[82] Before she died at the age of seventeen, she emulated the heroine of *The Peony Pavilion* by having her portrait drawn, then consecrating it by burning incense and offering a libation of wine. The jealous wife burned her manuscripts, but eleven poems and one letter to Madame Yang were saved.[83]

Within a decade of Xiaoqing's supposed death in 1612, she had become enshrined in popular imagination as the quintessential suffering heroine. Her story was first popularized in the form of biography and then in dramas and tales. The author of a preface to one of the many plays eulogizing her life wrote, "soon after Xiaoqing died, the whole world knew about her [because of the plays]."[84] Eventually, more than fifteen such plays appeared, reaching even an illiterate audience.[85] The same publishing boom and theater culture that magnified the appeal of Du Liniang also perpetuated the Xiaoqing lore. As writers vied to discover new meaning in an old tale, Xiaoqing was made to carry more symbolic weight than her short life and career could justify.

The Xiaoqing legend not only took shape on the pages of books but also was embodied in a paraphernalia of personal artifacts and public monuments. Her poems were copied and circulated, at first privately and then in published works; different versions of her biography surfaced; dramatists reworked her story into plays with increasing imagination; her portrait became a collector's item as painters vied to supply their own versions; a tombstone erected for her at West Lake inspired poetry from men and women as they visited the site or celebrated periodic renovations. The Xiaoqing lore could not only be read and seen but also cut up, possessed, and incorporated. The fascination with Xiaoqing was thus regenerated on the borderlines between material and literary cultures from the seventeenth to the eighteenth century. By the nineteenth century, her story, now fiction-cum-history, had secured a place in West Lake lore.[86]

The Xiaoqing legend was intertwined with that of Du Liniang from the start. To generations of reader-writers, male and female alike, the two shared a similar persona. This personal identification, one that conveniently glossed over the disparate statuses between wife and concubine, stemmed from one of Xiaoqing's poems.

> The sound of cold rain is unbearable through the lonely window,
> I light a lamp to leaf through *The Peony Pavilion*.
> Some in this world are even more stubborn in love than I,
> Xiaoqing is not the only heartbroken one.[87]

The "some in this world" refers to Du Liniang. Cited by many women readers at the time, this poem is a pictorial depiction of the world of meanings evoked by a woman reading fiction. Xiaoqing, like many other readers, identified emotionally with Du, the aspirant of true love. The gap between her own unrequited love and Du's fulfillment only served to make Du more enticing. To be sincere, to be "stubborn in love," became the highest virtue regardless of outcome. In her emphasis on sincerity and in her identification with fictional characters through reading, Xiaoqing epitomized the tenets of the cult of *qing*.

Xiaoqing's identification with Du Liniang was carried to an extreme in her obsession with her own portrait. According to two early biographies, Xiaoqing had her portrait drawn when she was ill. The artist had to try

The solitary Xiaoqing: in her quarters by West Lake, the dejected concubine reads *The Peony Pavilion* by a lamp (Lei Jizhi, *Tiaodeng ju*. First published 1627; reprinted—Zheng Zhenduo, *Zhongguo gudai mukehua xuanji*).

three times before she was satisfied. Then she consecrated it as a faithful replica of her own spirit and died.[88] This so resembled the scene in which Du Liniang drew her own portrait before dying that one biographer remarked that Xiaoqing, too, wished to be resurrected.[89] In accepting an unhappy marriage with a "crow," the young concubine seemed more passive than Du. Moreover, as a concubine, Xiaoqing had no realistic hope of the happy ending that Du enjoyed. Yet Xiaoqing derived comfort from her heroine, and modeled her death after hers.

The Xiaoqing story thus epitomizes the many tensions in the commercial world of seventeenth-century Jiangnan: the visibility of the literate woman, the enchantment of love, and the threat both pose to traditional ideals about marriage, motherhood, and womanhood. Given her poignant symbolic meanings, even if Xiaoqing had not been a real person, she might well have had to be invented. It was, in fact, the controversies surrounding her authenticity that illuminated in clearest relief the social tensions plaguing the world of her readers.

Suspicion of Female Literacy

The authenticity of Xiaoqing was called into question almost as soon as her biographies and poetry appeared. The suspicion that behind every published woman lurked a male ghost writer was quite common in the print culture of Jiangnan. Alongside the valuation of the serene female voice championed by some was a complex of attitudes toward female talent that was far less favorable. Some could not believe that women could truly be men's intellectual equals; others insisted that women's words, no matter how refined, should not be disclosed beyond the inner quarters. The tensions between these positive and negative assessments of a woman's literary worth were thus rooted in larger concerns with the attributes of womanhood and a woman's proper place in society.

Readers and commentators of *The Peony Pavilion* were frequent suspects. As we have seen, the *Three Wives' Commentary*, for example, was first privately circulated in the name of Wu Ren, the husband, out of Tan Ze's modesty. A reissue under the names of three women was met with disbelief. Wu Ren crafted a detailed defense of the women but admitted that he could not offer material proof. The original manuscripts of both Chen and Tan, he explained, had been lost to fire in two separate accidents. Tired of making endless apologies for the authenticity of the women's words, Wu became resigned to the fact that he could never persuade everybody: "Doubters will always find pretexts to doubt, but that will not stop believers from believing."[90]

An even fiercer debate raged over the authenticity of Xiaoqing. From the beginning, her identity was shrouded in mystery. In fact, the identity of everyone involved in the Xiaoqing story was obscured in the biographies and plays. Scholars in the twentieth century have argued that Xiaoqing's husband was the son of Feng Yunjiang, a resident of Hangzhou and a lifelong friend of art collector Wang Ranming.[91] Liu Rushi (1618–64), a famous courtesan whose career will be discussed in Chapter 7, visited Feng when she traveled to West Lake between 1638 and 1640. When Feng was 86 years old, Liu's husband, the poet and scholar Qian Qianyi (1582–1664), referred to him as "an old friend of fifty years." Feng also befriended the novelist Li Yu (1611–80), who discussed poetry with him.[92] These details, however, were not known to most readers of the Xiaoqing tale in Ming and Qing times. Her maiden name, Feng, coincidentally the same as her married name, was not given in Ming biographies; Feng Yunjiang was never identified in full.[93]

Friends of Feng Yunjiang were the ones who most vehemently argued that Xiaoqing was a fictitious character. Qian Qianyi, for example, wrote that Xiaoqing's biography and poetry had been made up by a certain scholar named Tan as a divertissement. The name Xiaoqing, Qian added, was invented by taking apart the two radicals that formed the word *qing*. Qian's theory was so popular in the seventeenth century that one scholar, Shi Yushan (1618–83), decided to investigate. A friend of Shi's who lived in Hangzhou and knew Feng Yunjiang's father verified that the story was true. A nineteenth-century rebuilder of Xiaoqing's tomb argued that Qian Qianyi had heeded requests from the family of Feng's wife to falsify records.[94] The twentieth-century scholar Chen Yinke points out that taking a concubine with the same surname is taboo according to the *Book of Rites*, but Feng Yunjiang had done just that. Chen argued that Qian was covering up for his friend's breach of the rites.[95]

Fictitious or not, the ready acceptance of Qian's theory in the seventeenth century reveals a common mistrust among men toward the literary accomplishments of women. Although many men condoned or even encouraged the writing of an occasional poem as a harmless pastime for respectable women, they balked at the thought of submitting such works to print. Even when women's words were published, they were often thought to be inferior to men's. The scholar-official Zhou Lianggong (1612–72) admonished women not to publish their verse because "it is rare that women can write poetry at all. Taking into consideration that the poet is female, editors do not have very high expectations. Therefore even unpolished works have found their way to the press." There is, however, a curious inconsistency between Zhou's words and deeds: his own concubine was a published song lyric poet.[96]

Even editors who promoted women's writings were not immune to this mistrust of female talent. Wu Hao, a Qing editor who included the works of many women in his anthology of Hangzhou verse, stated plainly that "the works of women should be judged by lower standards; we cannot be too picky."[97] No matter how far the woman poet has departed from her prescribed domestic roles, the assumption that her abilities and callings in life are to be distinct from those of the public man persisted. Through the debate on the literary worth of women's words and the propriety of their publication, the use of male standards was never challenged. A condescending attitude toward female talent is thus one manifestation of an entrenched belief in separate and unequal male and female spheres.

The powerful grip of this belief is evinced by the insistence that there was no place for the woman's voice in the public arena. Wu Ren, who helped his wife Qian Yi publish the *Three Wives' Commentary*, was ridiculed by a male scholar as "a simpleton who was so eager to promote his wives that he lost sight of propriety." The critic's reasons: "Women's words should go no further than the inner quarters. Even if [his] women manage to write, the husband should appreciate these works privately. How dare he publish them as if to boast to the world? Not to mention that some verses and dialogues in dramas are unfit for respectable women. These, in particular, should be kept strictly private."[98] This obsession with upholding the private/public or inner/outer boundary seemed almost wishful thinking, considering the extent to which the spread of women's cultural education had eroded such distinctions in real life.

These prevalent attitudes of condescension and disapproval help explain why as Xiaoqing's poems became critically acclaimed, doubts about their authenticity arose. Shi Yushan, the scholar who investigated the credibility of Qian Qianyi's theory, voiced concern that Xiaoqing's works might have been touched up by male writers. "Unfortunately," his friend in Hangzhou replied, "few poets around the West Lake are capable of such a job."[99]

Women were thus subjected to a blatantly conflicting message: suspicion of female talent on the one hand, valorization of women's voice on the other. They embraced the tensions and sought to negotiate the boundaries between inner/outer in a variety of ways. Some opted to publish their works, albeit in a man's name. Many continued to have volumes of collected works published and attached their names with pride. Others appeared to have internalized men's views that a woman's word should not go beyond her inner chambers. Their weariness can be gleaned from the glut of remarks found in Ming and Qing records of a sister or a neighbor who wrote for divertissement but burned the manuscript afterward, saying that poetry or writing was not a woman's calling.[100] Although some of these women had absorbed such values from their parents, others had to ward off pressure from husbands who disapproved of woman poets.[101] Often, however, it was the mother-in-law who issued prohibitions, lest writing distract the bride from her household duties.[102] Very often, women themselves internalized the restrictions imposed on their space and creativity.

Although many gifted women must have thus been silenced and many manuscripts burned, the claim of manuscript burnings was sometimes a literary trope — witness the large number of *published* works entitled "Scrawl Rescued from Fire" and the like. It is also important to stress that as common as the suspicion toward female talent was, it was by no means shared by all men. As noted earlier, many held a countervailing belief in the superiority of the female poetic voice. Tales of suppression and enforced silence, however potent they may be, do not detract from the fact that many daughters were nurtured in families supportive of their literary pursuits, where mothers, fathers, husbands, and/or mothers-in-law figured as teachers and companions in poetic adventures. The family dynamics in these households will be recounted in later chapters.

Male and female attitudes toward the spread of female literacy and its manifold public expressions were thus laden with contradictions. Yet it is important to emphasize that underneath the cacophony lies a common premise — the distinct constitution, hence the distinct poetic voice and literary purpose, of males and females. Those who argued that females should not publish, that their literature should be judged by separate (lower) standards, or that their verse serves as an exalted model for men were, in the final analysis, alike in perpetuating a belief that females and males are distinct in functions and abilities. All the contestations that surrounded the place of the female author and her authenticity, in the end, served to reinforce the cherished ideal of separate spheres.

The Fatality of Talent

A parallel process to the making of female readers into subjects of public lore is the apotheosis of young poets into domestic goddesses. Both processes were fed by the deep-seated doctrine of separate spheres and its relegation of females to an inner and serene realm. I discuss domestic goddesses, born posthumously of a fascination with female immortality, in Chapter 5; here I turn briefly to the morbid fascination with the death of teenage poets. Xiaoqing joined an array of teenage girls in seventeenth-century Jiangnan who became legendary after their untimely death, among them Chen Tong, Tan Ze, and Ye Xiaoluan. Other examples abound, as gleaned from mourning poems published by their parents. There is inconclusive evidence that some girls may have committed suicide

to escape marriage, but others are said to have died of illness. I will speculate on the causes of several untimely deaths in Chapter 5.

For its part, the public fascination with these deaths contributed to a
prevalent superstition that talented women were doomed. This belief in
the fatality of talent thrived on the fertile soil of enhanced opportunities
for women's education in real life, serving as yet another reminder of the
gap between social realities and beliefs. Yet just as fictional characters had
the power to influence life by shaping the reader's expectations, the belief
in fatality of talent may have been realized as self-fulfilling prophecy. It
was at the junction of fiction, belief, and reality that the Xiaoqing tale
joined those of Ye Xiaoluan and Yu Erniang, two other ill-fated readers of
The Peony Pavilion who exhibited the pathos of unfulfilled genius.

Although Ye Xiaoluan is a historical personage and the authenticity of
Xiaoqing is mired in controversy, some aspects of Ye's life are curiously
parallel to Xiaoqing's. Both devotees of *The Peony Pavilion*, for example,
were apotheosized after their untimely deaths.[103] In the early nineteenth
century, Ye Xiaoluan's poetry appeared in a collection of poetry by
women associated with West Lake.[104] Since Ye was a native of Wujiang
and had never been to Hangzhou, her appearance in the collection can
only be explained by the fact that her persona had posthumously merged
with Xiaoqing's. Furthermore, in a collection of works that commemorated the rebuilding of Xiaoqing's tomb, a female poet wrote, "The two
posthumous works, *Manuscripts Saved from Fire* and *Fragrance Reborn*
[of Xiaoqing and Ye Xiaoluan, respectively], might well be called heart-
rending."[105] The coupling indicates that the two lives had taken on the
same symbolic meaning. Since much of Xiaoqing's suffering stemmed
from her marriage whereas Ye Xiaoluan died without consummating hers,
the only common symbol they could have shared was that of the female
writer whose talent aroused the jealousy of heaven.

Similarly, the persona of Xiaoqing became conflated with that of another teenage girl, Yu Erniang, discussed above as author of a commentary on *The Peony Pavilion*. Much like the Xiaoqing lore but on a smaller
scale, the story of Yu Erniang was told and retold by scores of writers.
Eventually, the personae of the two avid readers of *The Peony Pavilion*
fused into one in the Xiaoqing plays. In a scene in *Shadows on Spring
Waves* (*Chunbo ying*), for example, an old woman tells Xiaoqing about
Yu Erniang. Xiaoqing, then sick in bed, empathizes: "A heartbroken one
meeting a heartbroken one; perhaps we shall walk the road to the underworld together." Xiaoqing even suggests that Yu's story be written for
songs performed by blind women so that more can hear it.[106] In another
play, *The Garden of Romance* (*Fengliu yuan*), Xiaoqing and Yu appear as
immortals in a heavenly garden, ruled by none other than Tang Xianzu.

Du Liniang and her lover Liu Mengmei are custodians of the garden register.[107]

The fusions of Xiaoqing and Ye Xiaoluan and of Xiaoqing and Yu Erniang underscore the popular pathos of talented people who die before reaching their full potential. Although indicative of a certain suspicion toward women's talent, this belief was often expressed by the same people who promoted women's education and published their writings. For example, after editing the posthumous manuscripts of his wife and two daughters for publication, Ye Shaoyuan (1589–1648), the father of Ye Xiaoluan, was so overcome by loneliness and grief that he wrote: "Talent brings affliction. If only [my wife] and my two daughters had not been so talented, and if only their talent had not been so polished, they would not have provoked the jealousy of heaven."[108] These bitter comments should not be taken at face value. They appeared, after all, in the preface of a volume published to immortalize the poetic legacy of his wife and daughters. Reference to the fatality of talent could thus be interpreted as a thinly veiled disguise for the exact opposite — a celebration of female talent.

Whether female talent is a blessing or a curse is hardly the real issue at stake in the popularity of the Xiaoqing lore. In the eyes of male readers, Xiaoqing was the latest in a long line of literary reincarnations of Qu Yuan (340–ca. 278 B.C.), a loyal minister of Chu and reputed author of the famous *Songs of Chu*. The poignancy of Xiaoqing–Ye Xiaoluan–Yu Erniang stemmed in large part from their incorporation into the Qu Yuan lore, an age-old forum for political discourses on loyalty and dissent.

The identification of Xiaoqing with Qu Yuan belonged to a long tradition of viewing the ruler-minister relationship in the allegorical terms of a marriage between husband and wife.[109] One biography has Xiaoqing comparing herself to the minister of Chu. To the biographer, her refusal to remarry was analogous to Qu's refusal to serve another ruler.[110] The author of a later biography went further in presenting Xiaoqing as a mouthpiece for both Qu's and her own predicament. In words that are clearly the voice of the author himself, Xiaoqing cries out, "Heaven will surely find use for the talent it endowed me with." Furthermore, Xiaoqing's literary endeavors are tinged with the promise of salvation and even immortality: "Heaven can destroy my body, but not my writings."[111] Xiaoqing was Qu Yuan in both her talent and her banishment.

In a later story of Xiaoqing that appeared in a popular collection of stories on wise and resourceful women, *The Book of Female Talents* (*Nü caizi shu*), the author made the identification of Xiaoqing with Qu Yuan even more explicit. Xiaoqing must have been Qu in her previous life, he wrote. Similarly, her husband Feng was the king of Chu who failed to appreciate Qu's talents and loyalty; the jealous wife was Minister Shang-

The talented Xiaoqing: the tragic heroine appears as Qu Yuan, the loyal minister of Chu, in *The Book of Female Talents*. Unable to find a true friend in this world, she looks in vain to her shadow in the water (first published ca. 1644–61; reprinted — Fu Xihua, *Zhongguo gudian wenxue*, p. 905).

guan, Qu Yuan's antithesis. The tragedy of Xiaoqing and Qu Yuan was that they tried, in vain, to find a true friend in this world.[112] Unrequited loyalty coupled with the futility of talent accounted for the poignancy of Xiaoqing–as–Qu Yuan, not the fatality of talent.

These authors empathized with Xiaoqing not because she was a woman victimized by an unfortunate marriage over which she had no control but because of her wasted talent and its lack of appreciation by those in power. To the extent that this identification of Xiaoqing with the banished minister resonated with the concerns of men in the public sphere, her story was divested of its specific gendered meanings. What mattered to her male readers was not her predicament as a woman, but the tragedy she shared with certain men. This bias is particularly evident in men's identification with Xiaoqing not only as a victim of an inept ruler but also as a victim of a jealous and spiteful wife.

Whereas the male and female expositions of *qing* in *The Peony Pavilion* differ only in emphasis, not in substance, readings of the Xiaoqing story are unmistakably gender specific. Women saw Xiaoqing primarily as a fellow reader of *The Peony Pavilion* and another alter ego of Du Liniang. Men, however, latched onto her image as a victim of the jealous wife, an image absent in *The Peony Pavilion*. In reading Xiaoqing as a metaphor for their own frustrations, male readers betrayed their anxieties over the fluid status system and the increasingly difficult ladder of success in Ming-Qing Jiangnan.

Xiaoqing as Victim of Jealous Wife

Jealous wives abound in Chinese history, yet they seem particularly potent in the urban culture of seventeenth-century Jiangnan, where the issue of female jealousy fascinated both popular writers and serious thinkers. Yenna Wu has shown that the theme of marital strife between shrewish wives and henpecked husbands reached the peak of its popularity in the seventeenth century, when it "developed from a stock situation in jokes and anecdotes into full-blown comedy and satire."[113] My contention is that this interest in female jealousy, of which the appeal of Xiaoqing as a hapless concubine is one facet, is indicative of a heightened concern with a larger issue — women's rightful place in family and society. "Jealous wife" was often a derogatory substitution for "assertive woman," and the popularity of Xiaoqing's image as the victim of jealousy signified mounting concern with strong and aggressive women in and out of the inner chambers.

In the Xiaoqing dramas, the portrayal of the heroine as a victim of jealousy was accompanied by two transformations not found in the earlier biographies. First, the wife appears not only as jealous but as spiteful, and the husband is transformed from a timid scholar to a stupid and vulgar man — the stereotypic henpecked husband. Second, as a victim of jealousy, Xiaoqing is rewarded with various forms of life after death.

The coupling of female jealousy with spite was expressed most succinctly by the author of *Jealousy-Curing Soup* (*Liaodu geng*): "Only those [women] who are spiteful are jealous; only those who are jealous are spiteful."[114] In *The Garden of Romance*, the husband is made to unwrap the wife's foot-bindings and fetch water to wash her feet, the ultimate symbol of subjugation and humiliation. The wife boasts of her ability to "strike him and curse him whenever I want."[115] In *Shadows on Spring Waves*, the wife takes comfort in the thought that even "men as strong as iron and stone are no match for women as wicked as snakes and scorpions."[116] In *Jealousy-Curing Soup*, the analogy is highlighted by the jealous wife sending poison to Xiaoqing's sickbed in the guise of medicine.[117]

Xiaoqing's benevolent friend, Madame Yang, is a contrast to the jealous wife and personifies the traditional notion of ideal womanhood. She is kind, an efficient household manager, and, most important, tolerant. She tells the jealous wife in *The Garden of Romance*: "The taking of concubines is natural to human nature. You should accept her to show the generosity of your spirit."[118] In *Jealousy-Curing Soup*, Madame Yang herself is eager to find a decent concubine for her husband, because the couple is childless. In the end, Madame Yang arranges to make Xiaoqing her husband's concubine. As a result, both give birth to a son; the jealous wife repents and everybody praises Madame Yang's virtue.[119]

As if to compensate for Xiaoqing's suffering in real life, all the Xiaoqing dramas reward her with miraculous happy endings. In *Shadows on Spring Waves*, she escapes the wheel of karma and becomes the disciple of a divine nun, the same nun who met Xiaoqing when she was nine and recommended illiteracy as her salvation.[120] Other dramatists portrayed Xiaoqing as an aspirant of true love. In matches preordained in heaven, she finally marries deserving men. Here, the Xiaoqing dramas merge with the genre of the "scholar-beauty romances."[121] Still other dramatists portrayed her as a fairy from heaven, who returns there after an interlude of earthly suffering.[122]

In all these dramas, the male author's sympathy clearly lies with Xiaoqing, and his condemnation of the jealous wife is unequivocal and total. To be sure, the stark contrast between the jealous wife and the henpecked husband on the one hand and the benevolent Madame Yang and Xiaoqing on the other may be overdrawn for dramatic effect. Moreover, depictions in drama do not necessarily represent the authors' views, let alone reality. They do, however, serve as indicators of common fears and shared stereo-

The ethereal Xiaoqing: in the fantastic ending of *Shadows on Spring Waves*, Xiaoqing attains eternal happiness. The divine nun comments: "People think that Xiaoqing is anguishing in the underworld; little do they know that you are wandering freely in the three mystical islands" (Xu Yejun, *Chunbo ying*, frontispiece).

types; they illuminate as well the lines of cleavage in a debate on the position of women in and out of the family. Enacted in the form of essays, jottings, vernacular stories, and dramas, this discourse on jealousy and concubinage is indicative of a sense of malaise felt by those who saw the gender hierarchy and familial order eroding. Disorder in the boudoir spelled disaster for harmony in the political realm. An overdose of *yin* power spilling out from the inner chambers was about to turn the world upside down.

Man, Wife, and Concubine: Discourse on Female Jealousy

The very visibility of women in the culture and society of Jiangnan struck many contemporary observers as menacing. Joanna Handlin-Smith argues that scholar-officials like Lü Kun were at once impressed and troubled by the strength of women participants in rebellions and cult movements in the late sixteenth and seventeenth centuries. They thus became conscious of the growing power of women and sought ways to cope with it.[123] Most indicative of this recognition is a plan of militia mobilization drawn up by the Huizhou literatus Jin Sheng (1598–1645) in which he recommended that women and girls be instructed in street fighting to defend themselves and their native place.[124] Although this plan, formulated in 1636, was never fully executed, it bespeaks the disarray in gender roles and social order. In this atmosphere of impending doom, the jealous wife stood as a metaphor for the powerful and assertive woman who threatened public order even as she was being called upon to defend it.

Signs of trouble were found at the core of family relations. The writer Li Yu made similar observations about women's power in the domestic realm. Li, who had many concubines and thus showed no sympathy for female jealousy, lamented:

In the past, the most that a jealous wife would do to subdue her husband was to force him to kneel, to forbid him to sleep, to have him hold the lamp or fetch water, or to strike him. But recently, there are jealous and ill-tempered women who lock themselves up and go on hunger strikes. Trying to shift their anger onto others, they make their family feel guilty by having them watch their dying acts. There is another type of jealous wife who no longer resorts to force or traps. She is tolerant and generous. Her husband, subdued by the power of her evenhandedness, volunteers to send the concubines away. Isn't it true that even within the inner chambers, there is always something new under the sun?[125]

The behavior of such "jealous and ill-tempered women" resembles the portrayal of the wife in the Xiaoqing dramas, suggesting that the coupling of jealousy and spite in these dramas was rooted in observations of actual behavior.[126]

Another indication of increasingly aggressive female behavior lies in the flood of teachings against it. Didactic literature for women in Ming and Qing times was vehement in its condemnation of jealousy. *The Book of Filial Piety for Women (Nü xiaojing)*, for example, taught that "there is no greater sin than jealousy" and reiterated the warning that jealousy was the first of seven reasons for a divorce.[127] Similarly, the *Instructions for the Inner Chambers* devoted one chapter to admonishing the wife to be kind to all her husband's concubines. "For female behavior is distinguished by its tolerance and discredited by its jealousy." If the wife did not suppress her jealousy, she endangered her place in the family hierarchy.[128] It is clear to us that such teachings, in pitting wife against concubines, were intended to serve the interest of the husband.

From the wife's perspective, the behavior men branded as "jealous" was often the last resort in a struggle to keep a wayward husband in check and to maintain control over household management. The legal system offered wives little protection from the intrusion of concubines. Nominally, the Ming statutes stipulated that commoner men could take a concubine only if they were over 40 and had no son. Offenders were to be punished by 40 lashes. This was, however, seldom enforced.[129]

In the statutes, concubines were condoned as potential bearers of sons who could rescue a dying family line. The same view was reflected in the compilation of genealogies. Some clans or lineages allowed concubines to be entered in the genealogy only if they bore children; some included them if they were brought in because the first wife was barren.[130] The character of Madame Yang, the ideal wife, in *Jealousy-Curing Soup*, personifies this position. Not being able to produce a son, she volunteers to travel to Yangzhou to procure a concubine for her husband.

Some men supported strict regulation of concubinage as specified in the legal codes to uphold harmony in the household. Their argument was that "if the number of concubines and maids is not regulated, sons and daughters would be born without proper order. Each woman would favor her own, resulting in differences [in treatment]. If not regulated by the rites, estrangement will arise. Many will neglect their filial duties; the unfilial will stir up dissension."[131] In other words, they saw controlled concubinage as essential to the maintenance of hierarchy in the family. This, like the condemnation of jealousy in the moral instruction books, reflects the interest of the male head of household.

However, such regulations were by and large ignored by men themselves in the seventeenth century, when concubinage was rampant in scholar-official and merchant families. Procreation had little to do with it. Concubines like Xiaoqing were bought as objects of pleasure or companions for male devotees of *qing*. The words of Li Yu are more useful than legal stipulations in explaining men's behavior in this regard:

Marrying a wife is like investing in an estate. Only the five grains should be planted in its fields, and only ramie and mulberry should be planted as trees. Any growth that simply looks good should be weeded and discarded, because one has to depend on it for subsistence, and the resources from the land are limited. Buying a concubine, however, is like nurturing a garden. Flowers that bear seeds and those that do not can be planted just the same. Trees that give shade and those that do not are just as good. For they are intended for pleasure. What is planted is for the ear and the eye, not for the mouth and belly.[132]

Against husbands who bought concubines for pleasure, wives had little recourse but their own wits. The increasingly assertive female behavior observed by writers like Li Yu was in part a reaction to rampant concubinage. Xie Zhaozhe, author of a sixteenth-century compendium of social customs, Five Miscellanies (Wuzazu), observed: "It is hard to meet even one beautiful woman these days, but households are flooded with jealous women. By the same token, gentlemen are few but mean people are many. In Jiangnan [female jealousy] is particularly severe in Xin'an; in Fujian it is worst in Pucheng. For [jealousy] is practiced in the household."[133] The author was a native of Fujian and had visited Xin'an and recounted tales of jealous women there.

Observers who reported the conspicuous presence of jealous wives in the sixteenth and seventeenth centuries alluded to larger historical circumstances, notably the social and moral upheavals engendered by the monetary economy, to account for this upsurge. This awareness that jealousy resulted from forces larger than the female psyche was often expressed in terms of a comparison between Ming-Qing society and that of the Southern and Northern Dynasties (A.D. 219–587), a period known as the heyday of jealous wives.[134] In both periods, these writers charged, assertive wives lorded it over their husband to advance the interests of their powerful natal family. The jealous wife was thus at once cause and symptom of social disorder and moral degeneracy.

The discussion of female jealousy in the Ming-Qing period, in fact, was couched in terms of an ancient lexicon codified in the Southern and Northern Dynasties period. For example, the title of the popular Xiaoqing play, Jealousy-Curing Soup, refers to a soup concocted from oriole meat for an empress of Southern Liang dynasty who was sick from jealousy. The potion reduced her jealousy by half but left spots on her face.[135]

The similarities between the debates on jealousy in the Northern and Southern Dynasties and Ming-Qing times are highlighted in a petition by an official in the Northern Wei court for the establishment of state-sanctioned concubinage. One passage adumbrates the arguments of Ming supporters of regulated concubinage: "People today have lost their sense of propriety. When fathers and mothers marry off their daughters, they teach them jealousy. When mothers-in-law and sisters meet, they encourage each other in envy. The subjugation of husbands becomes a female virtue; the ability to be jealous becomes women's work." The official saw jealousy as disrupting the rites governing the husband's relationship with his wife and concubines. The disruption, he feared, would lead to adultery and lewdness. To combat jealousy, he recommended a system of assigning a fixed number of concubines according to the husband's official rank.[136] This petition clearly saw jealousy as a weapon with which a wife could subdue her husband and protect her own family's interest.

In the Northern Wei as in Ming-Qing times, the jealous wife often acted in concert with her natal family. Strife between the husband and wife could thus spill out of the boudoir and become mired in family rivalries. The early Qing writer Chen Yuanlong (1652–1736) thus described the jealous wife: "In times of strife, she could always martial *her influential clan* against the husband; by plotting incessantly against him at home, she thwarted his amatory adventures and made for him a bed of thorns" (italics added).[137] As families became locked into competition for limited resources and prestige, women—as daughters and wives—were often powerful players despite their marginal positions in the official kinship system.

A twentieth-century scholar argues that two factors accounted for the widespread jealousy in the Northern and Southern Dynasties: a breakdown of the moral fabric due to political chaos and the system of ranking families according to their wealth and power. Daughters from wealthy families could lord it over their husbands.[138] Both conditions were also present in the commercialized areas in the seventeenth century. The author of *Five Miscellanies* affirmed the correlation between the degree of moral control in society and female assertiveness: "There were few jealous women in the Song, for both moral teachings and family instructions were strict then. In our [Ming] dynasty jealous women are too many to be counted."[139] The strife inherent in the man-wife-concubine triangle is thus symptomatic of the social transgressions at large that ensued from a monetarized economy.

In short, attitudes toward female jealousy were gender-specific. Male authors and readers sympathetic to Xiaoqing as a victim of a jealous wife were motivated by the same set of values upheld by men who bought concubines as objects of pleasure. Their condemnation of female jealousy converged with their defense of the power of the patriarch, often in the name of the "traditional moral order." It is therefore not surprising that male scholars who championed greater freedom for women in the eighteenth and nineteenth centuries took the side of jealous wives. For example, Yu Zhengxie (1775–1840), who also condemned footbinding, female

infanticide, and widow suicide, argued that jealousy was merely the natural response of wives to husbands who took concubines.[140]

Women's sympathy for the jealous wife, in turn, accounts for the cold
shoulder they turned to the Xiaoqing plays. Although many delighted in
reading Xiaoqing's verse and wrote poems in her memory, they did not
share men's condemnation of the jealous wife. Women failed to be moved
by the Xiaoqing plays because these works reflect the public concerns and
private fears of men. The dearth of women's comments on the plays contrasts sharply with their enthusiasm for Xiaoqing's poetry and their craze
for Du Liniang.

Whereas devotees to Du Liniang modeled their lives after hers, readers
of the Xiaoqing story used her as a negative example. A fourteen-year-old
peasant girl from the countryside west of Yangzhou city, for example, was
a maid in a wealthy household. She was taught how to read and write
poetry and gained a reputation as a talented woman in her neighborhood.
A rich merchant wanted to take her as a concubine. She refused, saying: "I
don't want to be another Xiaoqing." Her master then proposed to marry
her to a peasant. She refused as well, saying: "I can't be another Shuangqing." He Shuangqing allegedly was a peasant girl, and poems attributed
to her were circulated by literati men as a curiosity. The double burden of
working in the fields and writing proved too taxing, however, and she died
young from overwork. In the end, this Yangzhou peasant girl stayed single
and devoted her time to poetry until her death at the age of seventeen.[141]

Female readers of the Xiaoqing legend saw her as she really was — a
concubine bought and sold as property. They responded to her literary
image as a successor to Du Liniang, an aspirant of true love, only against
the stark reality of her marriage, one over which she had little control.
Male writers, on the other hand, transformed Xiaoqing's image as a pro-
ponent of true love into a purely romantic one. Furthermore, when they
portrayed her as a victim of female jealousy, they defended the system of
concubinage that was the root of Xiaoqing's misfortune.

The Cult of Qing and Gender Relations

In this chapter, I have analyzed the cult of *qing* in both its romantic and
its stark aspects and distinguished between the male and female readings
of the cult. I conclude with some general observations on the implications
of the cult for the gender system. Similar to the spread of moral precepts
and anthologies of women's verse, the cult of *qing* carried ambivalent
implications for gender relations and the lot of women. The rise of women
who read and wrote, and the cult of *qing* they helped perpetuate, created a
new space in which some women enjoyed augmented freedom and fulfill-

ment. These changes, however, did not challenge the basic premise of the gender system in the seventeenth century — the male/female distinction as a descriptive and prescriptive doctrine.

It is tempting to exaggerate the potential of the cult of *qing* as a gender equalizer. Narrowly focusing on romantic love, scholars have usually rendered *qing* as "love" and suggested that the idea of reciprocal love heralded a more symmetrical relationship between men and women. Although concrete examples of such golden couples abound, the overall impact of the cult on gender relations is not so straightforward. This ambiguity is partly due to the fact that the meaning of *qing* to a seventeenth-century reader was much broader than romantic love, encompassing friendship between people of the same sex and other human relationships.[142] Another difficulty is that the cult of *qing* was not a unified body of doctrine. Some writers upheld *qing* as an equalizer between the sexes; others celebrated it as the marker of more distinct male and female domains.

Emphasis on matters of the heart brought the concerns of men closer to the traditional prerogatives of women. As such catchwords as *qing* and *resonance* gained currency, more men came to value women as emotional companions, either inside or outside the bounds of arranged marriage. Hence the seventeenth century witnessed both a rising incidence of companionate marriages and an elevation of courtesans, brothel culture, and concubinage. Both were results of men's search for intimacy and emotional fulfillment. In this sense, the cult of *qing* enabled some women to lead fuller lives and was conducive to a new perception of women as intelligent beings and natural writers. In itself, however, it did not challenge gender stereotypes — woman as an emotional and temperamental sex. In fact, the cult of *qing* often reinforced the traditional identification of women with nature and the domestic, although these attributes were valued more highly than before.

The very definition of womanhood was debated and the existing understanding of sexual differences reconsidered, but the results were often new gender stereotypes or a reaffirmation of old ones. For example, Shi Chengjin (1659–ca. 1740), a prolific Yangzhou vernacular writer, opened one story with a popular saying: "Although man and woman are different, in love and desire they are the same" (*nannü suiyi, aiyu zetong*). That is, the search for emotional and physical gratification is basic human nature. *Qing*, in this sense, is a leveler between the two sexes. Shi, however, by no means implied that men and women are equal or identical. He went on to note: "Women are born with a nature like flowing water. Even when a young woman pairs up with a young man, her heart can still be seized by the seduction of someone romantic and handsome, let alone a young woman marrying an old man. He would not be able to please her, nor to satisfy her sexual desire."[143] The term *flowing water* refers to a woman's changeable nature, especially in sexual matters. Here, Shi echoed a popular view of women as insatiable, hence dangerous for the weak-willed man. Unlike many writers, however, Shi implied that a wife's sexual needs should be satisfied as much as possible.

The moral of this story is that an old man should never take young concubines, even if he enjoys the pleasure or wants a son. In a separate essay, Shi lectured on the evils of concubinage in general, calling it a "major, unforgivable sin." He reasoned that many wives are by nature jealous and have no stomach for sharing a husband with other women. Such wives, he observed, often starved and tortured the concubine, their henpecked husbands too meek to intervene. Shi reluctantly conceded that only if a man is without a son and his wife consents to it could he take a concubine.[144]

Shi's stance on marriage and concubinage appears to be more sympathetic to women than that upheld by male authors of the Xiaoqing lore examined above. In acknowledging that women are entitled to sexual fulfillment as much as men, Shi introduced an element of symmetry in gender relations. His argument against concubinage, too, was conducive to a more equal relationship between husband and wife. Yet ultimately, his view of women being intrinsically lustful served to reinforce gender stereotypes instead of challenging them. In spite of, or because of, a new emphasis on *qing*, the age-old persona of the femme fatale was all the more vivid in the eyes of some men — overly sentimental and oversexed, women still posed a constant threat to men of weak will.

Against this familiar image of the femme fatale, the image of Du Liniang is suggestive of new opportunities for women in the urban culture of seventeenth-century Jiangnan. The educated, sensuous, and truthful heroine of *The Peony Pavilion* personified the cult of *qing* fanned by the publishing industry and theater culture. She became the model and inspiration for countless women who saw in her hopes for their own futures. To them, love, talent, and virtue were all noble pursuits, perfectly compatible with a woman's conventional role as custodian of domesticity. Even the tragedy of Xiaoqing served to enhance the appeal of the romantic ideal of a love match, attractive exactly because of its unlikely attainability, in the young readers' eyes.

Part Two

WOMANHOOD

Margins of Domesticity

ENLARGING THE WOMAN'S SPHERE

W E HAVE SEEN HOW the changes unleashed by commercialization, commercial publishing, and the cult of *qing* had the ironic effect of accentuating male/female distinctions and hence of reinforcing the traditional doctrine of separate spheres (man : outer / woman : inner). This apparent resilience of the notion of gender distinction, however, says nothing about two sets of ideological changes that altered the woman : inner sphere itself.

The first set of changes stemmed from the spread of women's education and, as a result, the growing numbers of male-like women writers and professional artists. Their mobility and erudition were glaring reminders of the gulf between the principle of separate spheres and the actuality of gender disorder. The parameters of the woman's domain were subtly enlarged to close the gap. The second set of changes concerns attributes of womanhood. The man : outer / woman : inner construct remained viable only with significant modifications in the definitions of both the woman's sphere and womanhood itself. These adjustments alleviated the incongruity between theory and practice and realigned the gender system with socioeconomic realities. This chapter discusses the enlargement of the woman's place; the next chapter focuses on the redefinition of womanhood.

Classifying Women

As we have seen, the reading public's fascination with stories of Xiaoqing and shrewish wives betrayed anxieties over the erosion of a clearly defined place for women in family and society. Writers and readers were just as intrigued by signs of gender disorder in real life: cross-dressing women, girls raised as boys, women archery experts, and male embroidery masters, to name a few examples discussed in this book. To make sense of this gender confusion, a host of new labels for women appeared in both literati writings and popular literature in the sixteenth and seventeenth centuries. These new female markers, and the impulse to classify that produced them, are most indicative of a recognition of how far social realities had departed from the ideals of gender distinction.

During the Ming and Qing, the publishing industry purveyed stories and pictures of women in an unprecedented scale in the forms of moral instruction books and biographies. The enthusiasm of the reading public for stories about women is also evinced by a large body of almanacs, encyclopedias, and collectaneas that invented and reworked a growing repertoire of heroine tales. Particularly revealing of the confused status system and gender categories at the time are the novel ways in which these works described and classified women. The proper attributes of the new woman and a woman's place were first broached not in academic treatises but in these popular stories.

Deng Zhimo (fl. 1596), a man of letters who compiled a large number of stories on women from traditional sources, grouped the subjects of these tales into ten categories: woman martyrs (*lienü*), wise women (*xiannü*), talented women (*cainü*), feisty women (*hanfu*), beautiful women (*meinü*), soldiers' wives (*zhengfu*), prostitutes (*jinü*), singing girls (*geji*), dancing girls (*wuji*), and merchants' wives (*shangfu*). Some of these are traditional categories in which women are classified by morality or husband's occupation, but others are based on behavior or looks. The fusion of morality and entertainment discussed in Chapter 1 also infused the gender types by which women were perceived in popular minds.

Beauty (*mei*), in particular, became a common attribute of womanhood, even for respectable women. In a later chapter, Deng subsumed under the heading "worthy virtues" (*meide*, literally "beautiful virtues") categories such as "natural beauty" (*tianzi*) and "forbearance" (*duoliang*). In so doing, Deng expanded the meaning of beauty; both virtue and looks, or inner and outer qualities, could be described as beautiful.[1]

The growing attention to women's appearance is highlighted in another collection of stories modeled on Deng Zhimo's, which was apparently a commercial success. Attributed to the famous literatus Chen Jiru (1558–1639), it classifies women into seven categories: virtuous women (*jiefu*), talented women (*cainü*), beauties (*meinü*), ugly women (*choufu*), prostitutes (*jinü*), poor women (*pinnü*), and romantics (*liqing*).[2] The pairing of beauties / ugly women is indicative of the prevalent fascination with the looks of women. This fascination perhaps stemmed from a psychological need to distinguish the physical appearance of man and woman amid a time of confused status symbols and gender norms.

The perceived need for physically distinguishing the two sexes is gleaned from a late sixteenth-century encyclopedia compiled by a Yangzhou man, in which he contrasted "female beauty" and "female deportment" with "male beauty" and "male deportment." A section entitled "Labels for Women" gives more evidence of troubled times. In contrast to such conventional ideals as "quiet women" (*shunü, jingnü*) is a host of women who do not fit into old gender types:

Woman scholar (*nüshih*, literally "lady historian"; this word is spelled with an extra "h" on the end to distinguish it from *nüshi*, which is a different word in Chinese): woman conversant with the Classics
Man-like woman (*nüshi*): woman who does male deeds[3]
She-husband (*nü zhuangfu*): woman with the talents of a man
Good daughter–bad wife (*nüer bufu*): women who know the way of a daughter but not the way of a wife[4]

Some of these categories, especially those from story collections, were products of ancient literary conventions — soldiers' wives, for example — and may not represent new constructions of womanhood at the time of publication. But in a society populated by such women reader-writers as Xiaoqing and devotees of *The Peony Pavilion*, the proliferation of labels such as "woman scholar" or "talented woman" must have an unmistakable ring of authenticity.

The very obsession during the seventeenth century with classifying and naming women bespoke a need to create order out of gender confusion. These new markers themselves, however, were hardly adequate to reconstitute the gender order. The struggle to redefine a woman's place had to begin with larger contestations over the very meaning of domesticity, the traditional root of a woman's identity and raison d'être.

In but Not of the Family: Discourse of Domesticity

No one epitomized the possibilities and limitations of the new woman more than Huang Yuanjie (Jieling; ca. 1620–ca. 1669), whose life and career violated every definition of traditional womanhood expressed in the dictum of Thrice Following–Four Virtues.[5] Not only was Huang as educated as her male contemporaries and more gifted than most in poetry and painting, her public career also defied all existing schemes of classifying women. Huang Yuanjie was a professional artist and writer who remained the breadwinner of her family throughout her married life. With or without her husband and children, she roamed the towns of Jiangnan seeking employment and patrons. Wives of high officials, courtesans, and male scholars accorded her the same hospitality. Huang was as at home in the female world as in the male, in respectable circles as well as in the entertainment world. The agility with which she glided in and out of these disparate worlds bespeaks how permeable domestic boundaries had become.

Huang Yuanjie was born into a poor branch of an illustrious clan in Jiaxing, Zhejiang. Brought up under the wings of an elder brother who was an aspiring scholar and an elder sister who was a poet, Huang became acquainted with scholarship and literature at an early age. Her family was so poor that her sister had to become the concubine of the grandson of a former grand secretary. Zhang Pu (1602–41), one of the founders of the famous late Ming literati group Return [to Antiquity] Society (Fu she), allegedly wanted Yuanjie as a concubine, but she finally married a failed scholar, Yang Shigong, who was never able to support his wife, son, and daughter.[6]

Huang managed to make ends meet by teaching as well as selling poetry, painting, and calligraphy — no small feat for a woman in a competitive field dominated by men.[7] She had gained a reputation as a poet as early as the 1630's. During the turmoil of the Manchu conquest of the south in 1645, Huang was kidnapped by soldiers or hoodlums and may have been raped or sold to a brothel. Upon her release, she wandered around Wuxian and Jiangning in Jiangsu province and then went into hiding at the villa of a local gentry family in Jintan, Zhenjiang prefecture, in neighboring Zhejiang province. Later, she settled briefly by West Lake at Hangzhou, a haven for artists, courtesans, and their literati and merchant patrons. It was there, into the 1650's, that Huang was most productive as a painter. In the company of the leading male and female literary figures of her day, Huang's works fetched higher and higher prices. As her reputation reached the capital, Huang was invited there to tutor the daughter of an official, joining the ranks of an increasing number of "teachers of the inner chambers" (guishu shi), professional itinerant teachers. The deaths of her son and, shortly afterward, of her daughter interrupted Huang's tenure in the north; before a year passed she returned to Jiangnan. She soon fell ill and died while staying with the wife of a retired Manchu official in Nanjing. She left behind over a thousand poems.[8]

Although Huang Yuanjie's career, seen in the context of the dynastic transition, appears extraordinary, the forces that shaped her life were not. The extent of Huang's education and mobility suggests how obsolete the old gender norms had become in the seventeenth century. Given such erudite and publicly visible women as Huang, the age-old ideal of the domestic woman laboring incessantly for her family with her hands, not her mind, was sorely in need of revision. Moreover, the very meaning of domesticity itself, the seat of a woman's identity, was undergoing phenomenal changes in the face of larger social processes such as heightened lineage formation and privatization of cultural life. With the social and gender systems in flux, the position of women in family and society became an open-ended question, at once a symptom of disorder and the root of its cure. In addition, the nature of gender difference, a concern triggered in part by the cult of *qing*, became a burning issue as women's education and their earning power placed them squarely in traditionally male domains.

Struggling to make sense of these changes and to alleviate the distance between norms and reality, scholars and popular writers sought to reconsider or expand traditional definitions of woman's place and abilities. I analyze their deliberations in this chapter and the next; here it is important to highlight the glaring departure of actual practices from ideals by taking a closer look at two aspects of Huang Yuanjie's life: her inverted conjugal relations and her ambivalent social standing. Both are symptomatic of the changing shape and scope of domesticity in Huang's times.

Huang's conjugal life made a mockery of the Confucian dictum of Thrice Following, which described gender relations in an ideal world of perfect stability and harmony. Thrice Following demanded that a woman's social status and self-identity be defined by those of the man in each stage of her life cycle — father, husband, son. The myriad social changes in Ming-Qing Jiangnan, however, threw the status system for both sexes into disarray.[9] Educated women such as Huang Yuanjie acquired multiple identities, some irrelevant to their domestic roles (writer, painter), some derived from their liaisons with other women (teacher, friend). The husbands of such women stayed home or followed them around, but in either case his station in life was defined by hers.

A scene recounted by Yang Shigong, Huang's husband, of one of her many unaccompanied trips along the waterways of Jiangnan graphically illustrates this role reversal. A downpour had swollen the river that Yuanjie was trying to cross. Yang, standing by the riverbank to send her off, lost track of her whereabouts. As he glanced to the side, he caught sight of her crouching in a shabby post station, book cases and luggage scattered in a shed next door. Feeling sorry for her travail, Yang tried to retain a sense of humor: "Even if she had wanted to emulate Fufeng [Ban Zhao] in recording her eastward journey, she would not be in the mood to do so."[10] The normative conjugal relationship was reversed in the case of Yang and Huang. He was stationary, while *she* braved hardship on the road and strove to win a place in literary history.

Huang's mobility and extra-familial identities call into question another set of age-old attributes for women: respectable/mean, defined according to a woman's distance from the family system.[11] The family has always been a most important attribute of a woman's identity. Most women, be they from gentry, merchant, or commoner backgrounds, had no identities other than those prescribed by the male-centered kinship system — daughter, wife, daughter-in-law, and mother. They were socialized in the inner chambers of the women's quarters, and their social networks evolved around their families. As such they were "respectable" (*liang*) women, regardless of the bureaucratic rank of their husband or the size of their family holdings, if any.

Some commoner women spent at least part of their life cycle on the fringe or outside the family system, during which time they were called "mean" (*jian*). Prostitutes are notable examples. Standard didactic literature found the prostitute deplorable because of her rejection of familial ties. A Ming county magistrate pitied prostitutes who had to be "wives of ten thousand men when alive; ghosts without husbands when dead."[12] Prostitutes who quit to marry, thus re-entering the family system, were described as "turning to respectability" (*congliang*). Girls who were pawned to owners of theatrical troupes, adopted by madams in brothels, or sold as maids were regarded as having compromised their respectability.

Huang Yuanjie, who lived in the gray zone between the two, showed that the respectable/mean duality was by no means absolute. By the usual standards, her respectability should have been irreproachable. She was the daughter of a literati family, no matter how poor. Moreover, she had been betrothed to her husband since youth and stayed married to him throughout her life — she was neither a courtesan nor a concubine. Yet many of Huang's contemporaries consistently questioned her respectability. After all, she did not depend on the family system for subsistence, traveled frequently and widely, and was unabashed about her public profile — much like the courtesans she mingled with. Even before 1645, when her chastity may have been violated by kidnappers, Huang was a published author and led an itinerant life more akin to a courtesan's than to that of a respectable housewife.[13]

In the end, it was more Huang's career than her morality that made her male contemporaries uneasy. The highly public profile of a professional female artist forced them to reconsider the demarcation lines of domesticity and a woman's station in life. A friend of her brother's, for example, disapproved of the popularity of Huang's poems because they smacked of "colors of the wind and dust [pleasure quarters]." He implied that only respectable women could be worthwhile poets. Huang's brother, who was supportive of her writing career, opposed her friendship with Liu Rushi because of Liu's background as a courtesan. His message was that although the vigor of traveling and networking required of a professional artist is compatible with a respectable woman, she should nonetheless restrict her socializing to men and women of her own kind.[14] Both were concerned with Huang's ability to obliterate the boundaries between women from good families and entertainers from the pleasure quarters, but neither questioned the propriety of her literary pursuits per se.

Combating suspicion and outright slander, Yuanjie's male biographers — all prominent literary leaders of the day — defended her respectability by highlighting her heritage and faithfulness to her family. Wu Weiye (1609–71), a leading poet, dismissed the issue by labeling her a "daughter from a literati family" (*rujia nü*) at the outset. Shi Yushan, a contemporary of Yuanjie's, began by mentioning that "the Huangs have illustrious ancestors." He ended his account of Yuanjie's life by heaping praises on her feminine virtues: "Many women are distinguished by their talent [*cai*], but few have perfected their virtue [*wande*]. For those lacking in integrity [*yi*] always ended up being more popular. Li Qingzhao is not worth mentioning; even Zhu Shuzhen, who married a stupid husband, complained too much in her poetry." In contrast to these famed female poets from the Song dynasty, Yuanjie was endowed with both talent and virtue: "As a daughter from a family of heritage, Lady Huang found outlet for her true nature [*qing*] at the tip of her brush; she endured poverty and remained faithful to her [marital] contract unto death without a word of complaint. Thus she is a true lady [*nüshi*]."[15] Similarly, the leading official and poet Qian Qianyi called Huang "daughter of a literati [*ru*] family" and graced one of her poetry collections with a laudatory preface.[16]

Although Wu Weiye, Shi Yushan, and Qian Qianyi spoke highly of Yuanjie as a poet and approved of her career as a professional artist, it is significant that they chose to portray her as a good woman from a clean family who has duly fulfilled her wifely duties. There are two ways to assess such defenses on Huang's behalf. On a positive note, a woman's new identities (breadwinner, writer) were considered compatible with her traditional calling, just as feminine talent could embellish virtue. At the same time, however, whatever a woman's achievements in the literary and artistic worlds, she remained entrenched in her familial and domestic identities. That is to say, the possibilities of public ventures for educated women had the ironic effect of enhancing the normative relevance of domesticity. The meaning of domesticity, meanwhile, had become more encompassing, at least in the minds of such literary leaders as Wu, Shi, and Qian.

Huang Yuanjie herself reiterated her claims to respectability in terms of her familial loyalties. She began the preface to her own poetry collection, *Songs of the Detached Hermit* (*Liyin ge*, which can also be rendered *Detached and Concealed Songs*), with these words: "I was born into chaste gates, and I married an untitled scholar. My elder brother and sister have genteel tastes in literature and the arts, and I have aspired to be like them since young." On her career, she wrote: "Although I make a living from my brush and ink, my voice and shadow have not ventured beyond the hermit's gate." In proclaiming herself a "hermit," Yuanjie followed a convention of her day, popular among men of letters and courtesans. Resisting the corruption of the world with a pure and sincere heart, she could be in the world but not of it. Sympathetic to her friend's self-defense of respectability, the former courtesan Liu Rushi gave Huang the sobriquet Unblemished Lyricist (Wuxia Cishi).[17]

Like the leading literati who came to her defense, Huang chose to portray herself first and foremost as a woman who had fulfilled her obligations to her family. The definition of such obligations, however, was expanded to include a career in the public domain. Her other apology, that her "voice and shadow" remained firmly entrenched in the realm of domesticity, was obviously not meant to be taken literally, for both her poetic voice and actual person were in full public view. Huang Yuanjie was, in effect, dissociating her physical and social locations from the seat of her self-identity. In so doing, she opened a way for other women to combine domesticity with a career, literary achievements with feminine virtue, and respectability with sociability and mobility.

In negotiating the boundaries between respectable/mean, inner/outer, and private/public, Huang Yuanjie epitomized the possibilities and limits for a woman educated in the Confucian school of morality. She did not consciously reject the doctrine of separate spheres intended to keep a woman within bounds of domesticity; instead, her self-defense of respectability suggests that she took these categories seriously. Yet it did not stop her from pursuing her vocation and extra-familial sociabilities. Whatever the ambivalence she felt, Huang's physical and social mobilities are evidence of the fluidity of the gender system and the permeability of domestic boundaries in a commercialized society.

The disjuncture between the physical location of one's body and the psychological seat of one's identity illustrated by Huang Yuanjie was a significant means employed by many educated women to subvert their supposed domestic confinement. Later in the book, we will see how gentry wives created communities with other women across time and space without venturing out of their inner chambers. We will also encounter vicarious travelers in Chapter 6, women who roamed every corner of the empire by reading imaginatively. The same separation between one's bodily and psychological locations was noted by the literatus Zhong Xing who, as noted in Chapter 1, deemed women's poetry superior to men's because of women's innate serenity, a state of mind that ensued from their detachment from the physical materiality of the public men's world. The continued support of Huang Yuanjie and other women readers of domesticity and its implied doctrine of separate spheres was thus understandable in light of the profound reinvention of meaning within the domestic sphere itself.

Valorization of Women's Talent

The expanded meaning of domesticity was in part a result of the recognition and endorsement of female talent in public arenas. We have seen how men of letters and commercial publishers, convinced of the literary merits and marketability of women's poetry, vied to discover and anthologize verses by women. In addition to poetry anthologies, stories, and dramas purveyed by commercial publishers, local histories also became a forum for the valorization of women's literary talent. It was here that the demise of virtue as the sole criterion of signifying women was most evident.

Since the sixteenth century, gazetteers of various administrative units — most notably county, but also prefecture, province, and region — had proliferated, partly because it had become cheaper and easier to have them printed. The willingness of local elites to shoulder the work and often the cost under the supervision of state officials arose from a deep-seated desire to crystallize communal identities by glorifying their locale. The importance of female virtues to local identities is evinced by the inclusion of sections on woman martyrs and chaste widows alongside the names and deeds of local sons who excelled in scholarship, trade, art, or age. Most remarkably, however, women distinguished solely on the basis of literature also began to figure prominently in the emergent local identities in the Jiangnan region.

In the 1596 edition of the Xiushui county gazetteer, for example, a pair of poet friends, Lu Shengji and Sang Zhenbai, concluded a list of notable local women. Xiushui, part of Jiaxing prefecture in Zhejiang, is the native place of Huang Yuanjie. Flanked by the conventional sacrificial widowed mothers, daughters who cut their thighs to make medicinal soup, or wives who fought Japanese pirates to avoid rape, Lu and Sang stand out as testimony to a new standard by which women were signified — literature. The entry on Lu reads:

Lu Shengji (courtesy name Wenluan), granddaughter of Lu Guang, a prefect during the Tianshun period [1457–64]. Her father died when she was young, and her mother ordered Lu to marry Zhou Kai as wife. Lu was given to poetry by nature. Depressed and unhappy over marrying a man who failed to be her match, she poured her sorrows and frustration into her verse. Her poetry collection, *Scribbles by Wenluan* (*Wenluan cao*), was published and is known to the world.[18]

In the words of Cheng Qiong, Lu Shengji was a "phoenix who married a crow." Yet she remained a loyal wife, was an obedient daughter, and had a gentry pedigree — Lu was a respectable woman on all counts. She was eulogized in local history, however, not for her virtue but for her poetic talent. Her friend Sang, who fared better in her conjugal life, was similarly remembered as a published poet. In addition to their appearances in later versions of county and prefectural gazetteers, Lu and Sang also graced the pages of numerous Ming and Qing anthologies. Beside their own poetry collections, the verses they exchanged were widely circulated in separate volumes.[19] Lu and Sang were famous women in and beyond their native place, during their own lifetime and in posterity.

The valorization of female talent in local histories became more formalized and commonplace as time went on, in step with the quickening pace of public sponsorship of virtues. In the early Qing period, woman poets, often under the more conventional-sounding label "wise ladies" (*xianyuan*), appeared as a separate category in the county gazetteers of Hangzhou prefecture, an area with a particularly high concentration of women writers. They were considered on a par with filial daughters, chaste widows, and women martyrs.[20] In the nineteenth century, well-versed women often came to be called by the more direct name "talented lady" (*caiyuan*) as they grew in number and sophistication.[21]

The compilers of one such hagiography for Jiaxing county in Zhejiang confessed that previous historians of their native county had neglected talented women. Having combed genealogies and family histories to come up with a list so as not to be outdistanced by neighboring counties, they launched into a brief apology for valorizing woman's talent: "Cao Dagu completed the *Dynastic History of the Han*; Wei Xuanwen lectured on the *Offices of Zhou* [*Zhou guan*]. Their intention was not to boast of their talent and erudition." Cao, honorary name of Ban Zhao, completed the famed dynastic history on her dead brother's behalf and taught it to the most prominent scholars of her day, including the foremost Han commentator on the Confucian classics, Ma Rong (79–166). Wei Xuanwen is the honorary name of a woman née Song, an upper-class woman well versed in the Confucian classic *Offices of Zhou*. Written copies of this work had vanished in the protracted warfare following the collapse of the Jin dynasty in A.D. 316. She was summoned by the emperor Fujian (r. 357–85) of the short-lived Qin dynasty to lecture to 120 male scholars from behind a curtain.[22]

Having evoked the names of two women crucial to the transmission of the Confucian canonical tradition, the local historians went on: "In our native county, the womenfolk have pursued their traditional work as in ancient times. But occasionally they have also displayed a bit of literary flair. Our previous gazetteers have failed to take note of them. Now we follow the format in the prefectural gazetteer and include them after the section on virtuous women. These talented women are so well endowed by nature, how can their names be left out in history?"[23]

The existence of such a defense suggests that the valorization of women's talent on the pages of local history was not without its critics. The attention to talented women was deeply troubling to those who maintained that a woman's name should not be heard in public. Yet ironically, the same men and women distressed by the erosion of domestic boundaries also saw properly cultivated daughters as the key to buttress such demarcations. Given its nature, women's education was one of the most contested issues in seventeenth-century China and brought to the fore all the contradictions of a gender system in flux.[24]

Although the proportion of literate women to the population as a whole remained extremely small in the seventeenth century, the visibility of such erudite and mobile women as Huang Yuanjie lent the problem of women's education a larger-than-life urgency in the minds of her contemporaries. The point of contestation, however, was the proper balance between moral cultivation and cultural education, not the propriety of women's education itself.[25] The valorization of educated women in local histories is proof not only how well accepted education was but also how permeable the domestic boundaries had become in practice.

The permeability of domestic boundaries, a salient aspect of the confused gender order, was a direct result of the popularity of women's education. The educated woman traversed old domestic boundaries by assuming a public place in local history, as we have seen, and by pursuing a career, as in Huang Yuanjie's case. Yet if we examine more closely the positions of two kinds of "career women," itinerant teachers and professional artist-writers, we will see that their public careers and earning power did not undermine the premises of the prevalent gender system. To the contrary, the new and multiple roles assumed by the educated woman ultimately only served to reinforce the ideal of separate male/female spheres.

Itinerant Women Teachers

Both the currency of women's education and its double-edged nature are most evident in the rise of a class of professional women teachers in the seventeenth century in the wealthy regions of Jiangnan and around the capital. Known to their contemporaries by the name of "teachers of the inner chambers," these itinerant women made a living by teaching girls of elite households the classics, the art of poetry, and painting.[26] Huang Yuanjie was a famous example who was invited to Beijing, as was her friend, another professional writer, Wang Duanshu (Yuying; Yingranzi). Professional artists, too, sometimes were hired as teachers. Wen Shu (1594–1634), daughter of a Suzhou family of illustrious painters, became such a famous painter herself that other women sought her as a tutor.[27]

After their debut in the seventeenth century, professional teachers appeared more frequently by the early- and mid-eighteenth century. The libertine poet Yuan Mei (1716–97), for example, told of an "elder aunt" hired by a high official to live with and teach his two "daughters," who were in fact the official's concubines. Yuan referred to her as one who "went out [from her inner chambers and native place] to be a 'teacher of females' " (*chuwai wei nüfu*).[28]

These teachers of the inner chambers were daughters of literati families with a tradition of women's learning. For example, the family of Gui Maoyi (ca. 1762–ca. 1832), a famous poet from Changshu, published volumes of her verses, including a joint collection with her mother, also a poet. Gui traveled in Jiangsu and Zhejiang as a teacher and was remembered for her sojourns in Hangzhou. Another teacher of poetry and painting, Cao Jianbing, was a prolific writer in the high Qing period who published a joint poetry collection with her mother and grandmother. She also authored a Southern-style drama. Another eighteenth-century writer, Su Wanlan, was the wife of a poor teacher in Renhe, Zhejiang. She was so successful as a teacher that she eventually opened up her own "family school" (*jiashu*) for girls.[29] These teachers were often compared to the Han woman historian-teacher Ban Zhao. As spiritual descendants of the most revered woman scholar in the Confucian tradition, teachers of the inner chambers acquired an unassailable mantle of respectability.

Taken together, the lives of these learned women suggest a pattern of an emergent profession. Women's learning, especially poetry, was a family tradition. Many woman teachers were from learned but poor households in Jiangnan and had been educated by their mothers or grandmothers. In fact, it appears that teaching provided a means of livelihood for women from downwardly mobile gentry families who had lost out in the increasingly competitive examination system. As published poets or recognized painters, these women were in effect professional artists before their fame landed them jobs as teachers. Contrary to Confucian strictures of keeping a woman quiet and nameless, a woman's literary reputation could be an economic asset for her family.

The employers of tutors were high officials, and the students were their

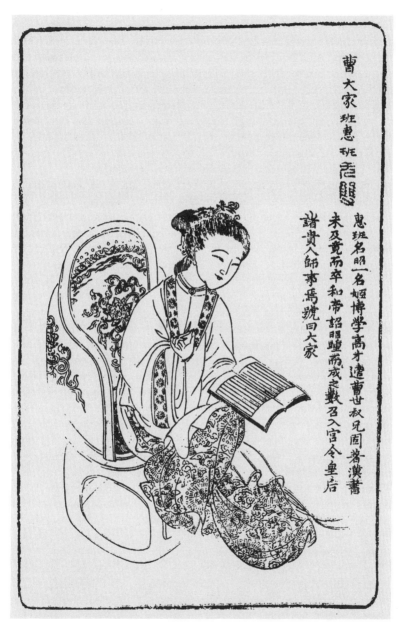

Cao Dagu, the quintessential teacher of the inner chambers. The Han dynasty scholar appears in the early Qing depiction as a young lady. With book in hand, she embodies the new womanhood: talented, virtuous, and beautiful (Jin Guliang, *Wushang pu*. First published ca. 1690–99; reprinted—Zheng Zhenduo, *Zhongguo gudai banhua congkan*, vol. 5).

daughters and concubines but seldom their wives. The pay for such short-term services could be substantial; the symbolic "thousand pieces of gold" was mentioned in several cases. The subject of instruction was sometimes basic literacy and painting, but most often the art of poetry. Since employment was meant to be short-term, these teachers had to move frequently. The verbs "coming and going" (*wanglai*) and "going in and out" (*churu*) often used to describe their trajectories testify to the itinerant nature of their work. Su Wanlan's "family school" was a rare exception and suggests a gradual institutionalization of women's education.

Being a teacher of the inner chambers was a most unlikely profession according to the ideal Confucian gender system. First, a woman's ability to make a living independent of her father and husband threatened to undermine the old dictum of Thrice Following. Second, employment as a teacher depended on one's fame as an accomplished artist. The very notion of fame for a woman, however, violated the ideal image of a quiet and cloistered woman. A woman's "name" was not supposed to be known outside her inner quarters. Third, the physical mobility of an itinerant teacher and her ability to trespass the boundary of her own quarters and that of her students' subverted the ideal of the female sphere as an enclosure. The so-called six hags — midwives, matchmakers, and the like — were stigmatized exactly because of their agility in penetrating such boundaries. Fourth, the overarching importance of poetry in the curriculum of gentry daughters was proof of the existence of a model of education in contention with the orthodox model of moral cultivation.

In spite of its potentially disruptive nature, the fact that teacher of the inner chambers was considered a respectable profession by the literati who wrote about it is a remarkable statement about the acceptance of women's cultural education, at least among some quarters in Jiangnan. As we will see later, this can be explained by a heightened desire for learned mothers in gentry families and the importance of such brides to a family's marriage strategy. At the same time, it is not hard to surmise from the lives of these teachers that many of the rigid gender norms no longer corresponded to the fluidity of social realities.

The ease with which itinerant teachers traversed domestic boundaries is remarkable, as is their ability to earn an income. Yet the job of educating girls was a natural extension of the sacrosanct duties of mothers in the domestic realm. And since itinerant teachers were housed in the women's quarters and had minimal contacts with men, they did not violate the integrity of the inner chambers. For these reasons, the rise of the profession of teacher of the inner chambers did more to reinforce the notion of separate spheres than to subvert it. In sustaining a woman-to-woman transmission of knowledge, these women can even be seen as the architects of a reconstituted woman's sphere, one in which cultural education figured prominently.

Professional Writer as Honorary Man

The mobilities of a second kind of "career women," professional writers, were harder to square with the intention of Confucian gender norms. The extraordinary career of Wang Duanshu demonstrates how professional writers faced a far more complicated set of negotiations between the domestic and public spheres, as well as between the male and female domains.

Wang Duanshu, who had eight brothers, hailed from a scholarly family in Shanyin, Shaoxing prefecture. Her father, Wang Siren (1575–1646, *jinshi* 1595), was famous as a writer of essays, a genre in vogue in late Ming times, and renowned for his incisive humor. Too old to join the loyalist resistance on the sea when the Qing army overran Shaoxing in 1646, Wang posted a sign "No Surrender!" on his door, refused to shave his head as ordered by the Manchus, retreated to the mountains, and starved himself to death.[30] Both Siren's literary legacy and his loyalist commitment had an indelible impact on his daughter.

Wang Duanshu's career and accomplishments as a writer were strikingly similar to Huang Yuanjie's. Educated by her father, whose bureaucratic career was interrupted by frequent retirements at home, Duanshu was well versed in history and the Classics. Like Huang Yuanjie, Duanshu was a master of the difficult Han genre of rhyme-prose (*fu*) as well as an accomplished painter. Wang, too, was a teacher of the inner chambers and was invited to Beijing to teach women in the imperial palace, an offer she turned down.[31] Both women wrote prefaces to the plays of Li Yu, one of their mutual friends. And both were better educated, more famous, and more employable than their husbands. Together, they constituted the prototype of a seventeenth-century woman of letters who earned a living from her literary and artistic talents.

The paths of the two women were so similar that they probably met while sojourning in Hangzhou in the early Qing period. Evidently they shared many friends, including Li Yu, through the poetry societies and other literati associations that flourished around West Lake, the center of art patronage networks.[32] Although there is no written evidence of a deeply felt friendship, the two talented women occasionally commented on each other's works. In a poem crafted upon reading a certain verse by Huang Yuanjie, Wang Duanshu praised the artistic finesse of her counterpart. It is noteworthy that Wang chose to do so by comparing Yuanjie to the famous calligrapher Wang Xizhi (321–79) and the Song master poet

Huang Tingjian (1045–1105).[33] Contrary to the gentry widow Shang Jinglan, who, as we will see, situated Huang Yuanjie primarily in a female genealogy, Wang Duanshu saw her friend, and perhaps herself as well, as a successor to male calligraphic and poetic geniuses.

Wang Duanshu was well aware that the lifestyle and concerns of a woman writer were more akin to those of the public man than of the domestic woman. Wang, an extremely prolific writer and poet, made her debut as a professional artist shortly after the Qing conquest.[34] The contestations surrounding her decision are indicative of the problematic position of the female professional artist in the eyes of her kin. Mao Qiling (1623–1716), a leading scholar from her native Shaoxing prefecture, described the occasion graphically: "When the chill and hunger became unbearable, Yuying [Duanshu] left her home with her husband, Ding [Shengzhao; b. 1621], who was pushing a cart. Desolate while on the road, they sold her calligraphy, painting, and writing for a living."[35] Mao made it clear that Wang's debut was necessitated by the family's poverty. While theirs was by no means the only gentry family impoverished by the devastating dynastic transition, the fact did not reflect well on the ability of the men in the household to provide for their family members.

Although the reactions of Ding's kinsmen were not known, Duanshu's brothers were a little embarrassed by her debut. Before Duanshu's departure, her brothers tried to dissuade her. She recorded their arguments in a long poem. Her brothers' objection: "Our father's name is well known throughout the four seas; how dare you [shame his name by] seeking shelter under strangers' roof? Your elder brothers will clothe you, and your younger brothers will supply your needs. Who are you going to depend on but us?" Duanshu rebuked: "Indeed, our father was a literary leader, but all that he left behind was pictures and books. Your sister is lazy and in poor health, with no aptitude for sewing and needlework." She pleaded that she could support herself by "plowing with my tongue," meaning teaching and writing.

Wang Duanshu proceeded to argue for the propriety of her public exposure: "Do not worry, brothers, Huang Chonggu was a famous woman in her days."[36] Huang, a talented woman who passed herself off as male for one year and distinguished herself as an official for the Shu kingdom (908–25), served as a respectable precedent for women who trespassed the public domain. The strict ideological boundary between her domestic sphere and his public sphere was in practice surmountable as long as the public woman recognized that with or without male garb, she could only function as a surrogate man. Citing the cross-dressing Huang Chonggu as her model, Wang Duanshu appeared to portray herself as exactly that.

Wang Duanshu's rebuttal silenced her brothers. "With utmost reluctance I picked the third as departure date," Duanshu continued, "and left home crying, books in hand." In having the final word, she did not forget to tease her brothers: "Now I'm all the more convinced that [this one line from] the *Songs* is right — 'Do not live by your brother's words.' "[37] In spite of their initial objections, Duanshu's brothers later supported her publishing ventures and contributed congratulatory prefaces. Instead of tarnishing her family's name, Wang Duanshu's success embellished the reputation of the Wangs. Although her father, Siren, had died before Duanshu's public career was launched, he had predicted that she alone had the talent to be his successor in a remark: "My eight sons together cannot add up to one daughter."[38] He clearly eyed her with pride as a surrogate son.

Women writers like Huang and Wang were perceived by their male relatives as performing a man's job. There is a degree of objective validity in this perception. In Wang Duanshu's case, she was merely following her father in selling writings and paintings for a living. Although all literati occasionally responded to requests for epitaphs or biographies from men and women who could afford to pay, Wang Siren depended on such remuneration as a regular source of income. Siren was said to be "addicted to money." According to one of his friends, "his face lights up whenever he sees money. On that day, his essays are particularly inspired. He earns much of his income by concocting hollow praises in epitaphs. But being extremely generous, he spends money freely on his kinsmen and affines, or on parties and feasts for friends. In no time [his hard-earned cash] disappears."[39] Besides an education, Duanshu was likely to have benefited from her father's many social connections. Writing for money was a family tradition initiated by Wang Siren; Duanshu, although a daughter, was merely his most talented heir.

Much more than a surrogate son, Duanshu acted as surrogate husband in literati circles, although her husband, Ding Shengzhao, was often by her side. Duanshu, for example, wrote memorials to the Southern Ming court on his behalf, seeking the rehabilitation of the name of his father, a Donglin martyr.[40] In fact, Wang wrote so many poems, letters, elegies, biographies, and epitaphs on her husband's behalf that an unknowing reader would suppose him an illiterate. She even sat in for him in a poetry contest sponsored by his poetry club. Apparently enjoying the role reversal, Wang wrote poems adopting a male voice, and in one of them she parodied the melodrama and clichés that plagued the works of lesser women.[41]

Not only was she skilled in genres favored by men and at ease with assuming a male voice, Wang Duanshu also excelled in subject matters traditionally considered masculine. Most outstanding in this regard is a series of biographies of Ming loyalist martyrs she authored in 1648 and

1649. It was customary for men to eulogize women who threw themselves into wells, leaped into rivers, or cursed soldiers to avoid rape; Duanshu followed this male convention in eulogizing nine such martyrs of chastity.[42] More exceptional, however, were accounts *she* wrote of six *men* who died for the fallen dynasty.

Duanshu thus described the circumstances that precipitated the production of these documents of loyalism: "After the tragic turmoil, we lost our livelihood and were sojourning in Meishan. I have no patience for women's work, but sought to relieve my pent up frustration by wielding my writing brush."[43] Although she could not state so explicitly, her "frustration" had more to do with the faltering loyalist cause than her personal economic plight. In the portraits of loyalist heroes she crafted, Duanshu consciously parted ways with official eulogies by men by focusing not on the family descent or public careers of these martyrs but on the events and inner struggles leading to their fatal decisions. She was interested in how they lived out their personal convictions in critical moments, not in loyalty as an abstract virtue. As a fellow loyalist, she was moved by sparks of the noble spirit from members of both sexes and all classes.

In recording martyrdom, Wang Duanshu displayed not just her political sympathies but also her skills as a storyteller. These vivid biographies, although short, read like novels; they are embellished by graphic descriptions of the setting and colloquial dialogues that highlight the character of the protagonist. A particularly poignant contrast with official eulogies is this moving account of a beggar from Nanjing:

Begging in the southern capital, the beggar learned in the middle of the fourth month in 1644 from rumors that the northern capital had fallen. He asked around but could not confirm the news. One day, upon spotting a scholarly-looking man by the Peach Leaf Pier, he seized his garments and asked: "Sir, what's the latest news from the northern capital?" The scholar replied: "Indeed, the mourning decree has arrived — the Chongzhen emperor hanged himself." Sighing and grieved, the beggar went to the market to buy a jug of wine, which cost about two *fen*. Having only seven *li* in his pocket, he pleaded: "Fill it up if you can; if not, just get me whatever it's worth." The shopkeeper handed him a full jug. The beggar downed it in one mouthful and started to run along the riverfront. People on the street thought him drunk and paid little attention. The beggar suddenly broke into tears, screaming: "So the Chongzhen emperor is really dead!" He beat his chest several dozen times and bowed to the north several dozen times, then leaped into the river and died.[44]

Wang Duanshu also wrote fifteen biographies of better-known loyalist officials, including Liu Zongzhou, Ni Yuanlu, Qi Biaojia, and her own father, Wang Siren. Of Siren's suicide by refusing to eat Qing dynasty grain, she remarked, "Counting his 73 years, I regret that they are too short. But [in light of the agonies that lasted] several dozen days [between the fall of Shaoxing and his martyrdom], I'm afraid they are already too long."[45] In the seventh month of 1646, two months before his suicide, Siren donated money for a loyalist force supporting the prince of Lu in which Ding Shengzhao, Duanshu's husband, served as an army-inspecting censor.[46] Although it is not known if Duanshu played a personal part in the resistance, her writings testify to the extent to which she identified with the loyalist cause. Although it was not unusual for women to harbor loyalist sympathies (see Chapter 7), extensive writings like Duanshu's were extremely rare.

In publicly disclosing her political convictions through writing, Wang Duanshu was exercising the prerogatives of the male scholar-official. Her admission ticket into the otherwise exclusive male literati club was her exceptional literary talent and vision. In a most unusual endorsement, 47 Zhejiang men of letters who signed themselves as "oath younger-brothers from the One-Autumn Society" (*Tongqiu she mengdi*) financed and oversaw the publication of Duanshu's 30-chapter collected works, *Red Chantings* (*Yinhong ji*). Among them were Zhang Dai, the famous drama aficionado, and two brothers from the Ding family.[47] Judging by the many poems she wrote for such occasions, Duanshu partook in their drinking parties and poetry contests. It is not clear, however, whether she was present as a dependent of her husband, or if she was accepted as a full-fledged member on her own. Occasionally the group would gather for parties in the pavilion of Wu Shan (ca. 1610–ca. 1671), a respected widow who sold her paintings for a living and led an active social life.[48] Theirs was a poetry club that thrived on the mixed talent and company of both sexes without causing any apparent embarrassment or scandal.

The men of letters Wang associated with looked upon her as a male in her talents and concerns even as they endorsed the gender inversion that this entailed. In his preface for one of Duanshu's collected works, for example, an uncle remarked with pride: "Our family has produced a famous scholar [*mingshi*]; it is a *she* who hails from the inner chambers." He explained that according to convention critics dismiss a male writer who wallows in sentimentality and tenderness for writing like a woman. By writing in bold strokes — like a masculine man — Duanshu has rescued the reputation of all womankind in history.[49] Intending to pay Duanshu the highest compliment by crowning her an honorary man, her uncle was in effect perpetuating not only the separation between the male domain and the female but also the superiority of the former.

As such, the premise of Wang's supporters was no different from that of her critics. Similar to those who questioned Huang Yuanjie's respectability, these critics do not seem to have set their views in writing, but the gist of their objections can be gleaned from the arguments of those men who came to the women's defense. A longtime friend of Duanshu's father, for example, rebuked that "you do not know Yingranzi [Wang Duanshu] if you describe her writings and personal character as unruly [*hutian hudi*]." He praised Duanshu's respectability as a man-like woman, who "did not take the examination but is endowed with the talents of those who do, is not supposed to care about the empire's rise and fall [*xingwang*] but is nonetheless deeply concerned." She thus deserved immortality in the company of famous men in history.[50]

Implied in this defense is that Wang Duanshu was subjected to personal attacks from critics who dismissed both her behavior and writing as "unruly." This indictment is inevitable if Duanshu were to be judged by the letter of moral precepts prescribing a life of silence and ignorance. What her defender was arguing, however, is that she be judged by the moral and intellectual requirements for a gentleman. By virtue of her superior talent and erudition, Wang Duanshu won an honorary place in the company of literati men. In other words, Wang's supporters and critics agreed that the norm for the majority if not all women was domesticity. Her defenders were merely arguing that exceptional women should be accorded preferential treatment as honorary men.

At first glance, professional women writers and artists may appear threatening to the prevailing gender arrangements. What more potent subversion of Thrice Following could there be than a female breadwinner? Yet as embarrassing as this phenomenon of gender inversion may have been to the woman's husband and brothers, it did not disrupt the premises of the gender system. In praising Wang Duanshu as a woman so extraordinary that she deserved to be an honorary man, her male supporters tacitly upheld a gender hierarchy that ascribed a higher value to maleness, characterized by high cultural attainment, concern for public affairs, and literary disclosure of heroic sentiments. Although individual women thus gained liberties normally not allowed to members of their sex without jeopardizing their respectability, the overall asymmetry of the gender system was maintained and even strengthened.

Phoenix and Crow: Role Reversals

The conjugal relations of a woman with such a male-like writing career are by nature problematic. The marriage between Wang Duanshu and Ding Shengzhao was arranged by their fathers, as was customary in scholar-official families. Soon after Shengzhao's birth, his father begged Wang Siren for a name and the hand of Siren's daughter, Duanshu. A native of Beijing, Shengzhao grew up to be a recalcitrant boy about whom his father-in-law had this to say: "He loved to play and despised his father's books. His mother would break into tears in his face and refuse to eat."[51] Being a concubine from a peasant family, Shengzhao's mother had to resort to desperate tactics to discipline her son. After Shengzhao's father died at the hands of eunuch Wei Zhongxian, Siren thought it snobbish to back out from the betrothal. Around 1636, when the bride and groom were barely fifteen, Duanshu traveled to Beijing to begin her new life.[52]

Shengzhao mended his ways somewhat but was never much of a scholar. Benefactor of a special inherited degree (*engong*), he received an empty appointment in 1639, which he "sneered at." Between 1643 and 1644, the couple returned to Zhejiang, where they stayed through the Qing conquest.[53] In the spring of 1644, Duanshu dipped into her own pockets to buy Shengzhao a concubine. Although it is not clear who initiated the idea, the two became too intimate for Duanshu's comfort, and she recorded her outrage in a poem. The concubine, née Chen, bore a son and a daughter during her eight years with the Dings before her untimely death. Duanshu wrote a mourning poem on her husband's behalf.[54] They appear to be the only children born to the couple.

The concubine episode is a graphic illustration of a reversed power asymmetry between husband and wife. Without Duanshu's consent and money, Shengzhao would not have been able to procure a concubine. Such is the extent of his passivity that he did not even craft a mourning poem of his own when the concubine died. Exceeding her husband in talent, earning power, and fame, Duanshu made decisions on domestic affairs and, after 1645, on the location and durations of their sojourns. Duanshu did not repudiate the Thrice Following dictum, yet the de facto role reversal is clear — it was her husband who followed her about, and it was her station in life that defined the couple's status. Ding Shengzhao was not a "crow" in its classic sense; he was well versed enough to hold his own in the company of men of letters. Yet he knew he was no match for his exceptionally gifted wife.

Ding openly acknowledged the role reversal in his household — she was the scholar and breadwinner and he, the inner helpmeet. Of Duanshu he wrote: "My wife is by nature addicted to history books and skilled in brush and ink. She sneers at the usual 'womanly work.' " Referring to their itinerant conjugal life, he compared themselves to a pair of soaring wild duck and wild geese, but adding that "my wife encourages and magnifies me."[55] The imagery of soaring birds conveyed his pride in Duanshu's achievements and the mobility she brought about. In choosing the verb that means "to encourage and magnify" (*xu*), he suggested that he saw Duanshu as a teacher and benefactor.

Ding contented himself with the same go-between role that Huang

Yuanjie's husband played in promoting the name and works of his wife. On her behalf, for example, he visited the famous poet Mao Qiling, showing him manuscripts of Duanshu's poetry collection, and begged him to contribute a preface to the published version. To another friend, Ding brought a copy of *Red Chantings* and asked for an afterword. Apparently Duanshu knew both of them personally; she did not depend on Ding's social networks.[56] His intermediary function is thus different from the usual roles husbands and fathers played in circulating women's verse (discussed in later chapters). Since gentry wives and daughters had limited extra-familial connections of their own, they had to rely on the male head of household as the family's representative to the outside world. Ding and Huang Yuanjie's husband, in contrast, were sheer deputies of their wives.

Although the true feelings of the overshadowed husband were not revealed, Ding expressed overt satisfaction with his conjugal life: "It is worth noting that in marrying my wife I also gained a friend." Despite the superficial resemblance to companionate couples in the use of the word *friend*, however, the Wang-Ding union may not be as intimate as Ding would have his readers believe. For all her "singing in harmony" with her female friends, brothers, and relatives, few extant poems were composed for or with Ding Shengzhao.[57] The only time he figured in her works is when she wrote poems, essays, pacts, epitaphs, and memorials on his behalf. They seem less a companionate couple than a traditional match, with she acting as the husband and he, the wife.

Women Writing: Crafting a New Sociocultural Space

Wang Duanshu was so agile in crossing boundaries and yet so at ease in a world of her own that she could adopt a multiplicity of voices in her writing. Some of her poems are autobiographical, the one on traveling to her wedding in Beijing mentioned above is an example; many others were composed in the persona of her husband. There are also poems crafted in a male voice lamenting the futility of pursuing wealth and power. Most astonishing, however, are poems she wrote on behalf of other women to herself. Deliberately distancing her voice from her real self, she playfully composed a poem in her reclusive mode on behalf of a visiting friend and one in the person of her sister-in-law who, according to the poem, was overcome with thoughts for Duanshu on an autumn night. Duanshu also imagined herself a reader of her *Red Chantings* and an admirer of her own portrait.[58] The lines between male and female, or between self and others, were temporarily obliterated in the creative process of writing.

The freedom with which Wang Duanshu shifted in and out of her own persona to playfully assume other identities is emblematic of the new social space that a professional woman writer occupied in the seventeenth century. Without defecting from her traditional roles of mother and wife, she found a niche in the public sphere, supported her family, and gave full rein to her "man-like" concerns and sentiments in writing. The popularity of her works suggests the extent to which the publishing boom that began in the sixteenth century and the new author-reader relationship that ensued altered the milieu in which an educated woman formulated her personhood and expressed herself. In this floating world, professional and amateur woman writers celebrated their enhanced visibility and repertoire with growing versatility and eloquence.

Although the social conditions that nurtured the professional woman writer had been brewing since the sixteenth century, Wang's debut was occasioned by the economic deprivation suffered by many Jiangnan gentry families on the heels of the Manchu conquest. Both she and Huang Yuanjie were renowned poets and painters before the fall of the Ming and may have received occasional gratuities for their works. Yet explicit references to their making a living as a writer and painter did not appear until after the dynastic transition, which left their families without a viable means of livelihood. In eking out a living, Huang and Wang were merely substitute husbands; as such they remained firmly under the dictates of familial morality. Their apparent violation of the ideal quiet woman was overlooked, interpreted as an expedient measure to ensure the survival of the family. In the name of loyalty to family and allegiance to Thrice Following, professional writers in fact turned the ideal prescription of separate spheres on its head.

This new space was not crafted without extreme psychological stress. The very real possibility of eventual public disclosure of her private thoughts was at once exhilarating and worrisome. After all, being a published author was a far cry from being a mere private teacher of sons and daughters. No doubt, many women were so afraid of being branded a seeker after fame that their manuscripts never saw the light of day. For the handful of women determined to brave this competitive public world of publication and patronage, life was an uphill battle against the condescending attitude of even their male editors.

Huang Yuanjie, who wrote a preface and commentary for one of Li Yu's plays, constantly had to defend herself from accusations that her paintings, calligraphy, and poetry were plagiarized.[59] Similarly, the authenticity of the verses of Xiaoqing, as we saw in Chapter 2, was questioned by men who thought them too good to have been written by a woman. Even against such odds, women like Huang Yuanjie and Wang Duanshu managed to preserve their respectability while eking out a living as writer, painter, and teacher. In the sense that they, not their husbands, were the breadwinners of the family, they were truly professional artists.

This emergence of publicly recognized women writers coincided with an expansion of their repertoire into public matters, as Wang Duanshu's portraits of Ming loyalists so amply demonstrate. In taking up genres and subject matters previously reserved for men, they enlarged the possibilities for women and helped bridge the gap between what was perceived as the man's domain and the woman's domain.

The three aspects of this new space opened up by professional writers — freedom of movement, expanded repertoire, widespread but by no means unanimous respectability — were also evident, albeit in less concentrated forms, in the lives and works of amateur writers. Gentry wives, too, began to tread unfamiliar territories without jeopardizing their good name in the late sixteenth century. The model for both amateur and professional writers, in fact, lies in a mid-Ming gentry wife, Zou Saizhen (fl. early sixteenth century), who enjoyed a surge of popularity in seventeenth-century anthologies.

Her father, husband, and later, son and son-in-law were all *jinshi*s; Zou Saizhen enjoyed an impeccable cultural pedigree. A learned poet and essayist, Zou is said to be the first Ming woman to have published her collected works in a separate volume under her own name. Cao Xuequan (1574–1646), a famous poet-official who contributed a preface to *Collected Works from the Hall of Meridian Dreams* (see Chapter 5), cited Zou's story at length to suggest that she was the forerunner of Shen Yixiu, Ye Xiaoluan, and the other gifted Shen and Ye women featured in the family anthology.[60]

Zou Saizhen, widowed after forty-odd years of a happy marriage, survived all her children and a younger brother. Similar to Shang Jinglan and other woman writers who came after her (see Chapter 6), Zou's respectability was enhanced by her old age and widowhood. So revered was she that she was crowned an honorary man and commonly referred to as Pu Shiqi. "Shiqi," meaning "a scholar's equal," is her sobriquet; "Pu" is her husband's surname. This appears to be a rare example of a learned woman becoming widely known by her husband's family name, and that of her father's being forsaken or forgotten.[61]

Befitting her male-sounding and male-meaning name, Pu Shiqi excelled in genres and repertoire traditionally associated with the public men. She authored, for example, an account of her father's deeds (*xingzhuang*) and funeral odes for her husband and son.[62] The leading seventeenth-century literary critic Qian Qianyi remarked of Pu and a gentry friend of hers: "They were in fact great scholars of the [Confucian] *Dao* [*Daoxue suru*] in the female quarters; these women should not be judged solely by their verse and prose." Another man of letters followed this line of praise: "With her virtue and talent, if Saizhen were to be enlisted in the ranks of scholar-gentry, she would surely emerge as a literary leader and an extraordinary man."[63] Similar to defenders of Wang Duanshu, in arguing that a learned woman should be judged by male standards, these admirers of Pu Shiqi were in effect upholding values that deemed man superior.

Pu Shiqi established a respectable precedent for gentrywomen being educated like a man, writing like one, and being praised as one. The breadth of these women's concerns, which informed their expanded repertoire of subject matters, was in part rooted in their enhanced physical mobility. Pu led a mobile life due to the frequent transfers of her husband. We will encounter many more examples of gentrywomen travelers in the later chapters: a late Ming magistrate's wife, Wang Fengxian, who authored a travelogue; a Suzhou wife, Xu Yuan (1560–1620), who crafted poems on tribal attacks in Yunnan. Their writings, similar to Pu Shiqi's, are graphic illustrations of the link between opportunities to travel and expansion of the writer's repertoire.

Physical mobility, however, is not a prerequisite for the development of broad literary visions. Even women who did not venture out of their homes—the armchair travelers—made known their views on national politics and military affairs. Gu Ruopu (1592–ca. 1681), a prolific writer, virtuous widow, and matriarch whose niece founded the Banana Garden Five poetry society, for example, was a prolific essayist on statecraft and economics.[64] The import of her impressive literary vision and male-like concerns to the Hangzhou women she inspired are discussed in Chapter 6.

Famous women writers like Ban Zhao, Li Qingzhao, and Guan Daosheng have, of course, been recognized throughout Chinese history. Some of them, too—such as Ban Zhao—attained fame and respectability as surrogate son and brother. The novelty in the debut of women writers in the seventeenth century lay not only in their sheer numbers but also in the reversal of roles and status between woman and man. In the cases of Huang Yuanjie and Wang Duanshu, it was the wife who merited a separate entry in biographies and her husband or brothers who went down in history as her dependents. There were, as well, frequent expressions of regret that a certain gifted woman had married a stupid husband. In the careers of these exceptional women, one sees the genesis not of a new order but of a familiar world turned upside down.

Revered as honorary men in real life, Pu Shiqi, Huang Yuanjie, and Wang Duanshu could well have been the inspiration behind a glut of verses, dramas, and stories featuring woman scholars, warriors, or officials in the Ming-Qing period. The drama *Woman Principal Graduate* (*Nü zhuangyuan*) by Xu Wei (1521–93) is the most famous example of this genre, but some lesser-known works were authored by women.[65] This popularity of literary images of man-like women influenced the self-perceptions and expectations of readers in real life. We have seen how Wang

Duanshu cited the example of Huang Chonggu to persuade her brothers that public life could be the calling of learned women. To Wang, Huang Chonggu's forays into officialdom as a woman in disguise revealed the fluidity of gender boundaries and the freedom women could enjoy in extending their domestic existence into public domains.

Yet the proliferation of male-looking heroines wielding swords or the examinee's brush in stories and dramas also sent a contradictory message to female readers. Instead of challenging the ideology of separate spheres by mixing and redefining gender roles, these heroines encouraged their female readers to aspire to be more like men. No one wrote a play called *Male Daughter-in-Law* admonishing men to emulate the sacrificial house-wife. Not only were male concerns in the public domain deemed superior, the theoretical separateness of male and female worlds was reinforced.

In other words, the gender inversions heralded by publicly visible women writers were by and large temporary transgressions that served to perpetuate the prevailing official gender ideology. For this reason, they were condoned or even welcomed as fiction and in real life.

Inspired by the popularity of the woman principal graduate in litera-ture, some gentry families actually raised and educated their daughters as boys. One such girl, Yu Qiren (b. 1639), was a granddaughter of a *jinshi* from Yutian, Fujian province. Raised by her sonless widowed mother as a son, Qiren was clothed in male attire from infancy, unlike Jiwen, her elder sister by two years who apparently wore female garb. Her mother, née Chen, hailed from a family of scholars and had a brother with a *jinshi* degree. Although she could have coached Qiren and Jiren, the serious mother chose to hire tutors to provide a formal education. Both sisters were well versed in classical learning, poetry, and painting—traditional arts of the male literati increasingly mastered by learned daughters, as we have seen throughout this book. In 1650, when Qiren was twelve by Chinese count, she began to receive guests as male head of the household, befriending visiting scholars and students and gaining a reputation as a prodigy.

Yu Qiren functioned so well in the literati's social and intellectual world that her mother toyed with the idea of having her recommended to the provincial examiner. Madame Chen was said to have abandoned her ambition only when someone reminded her that for all of Qiren's erudi-tion and male garb, she was not a male: "Although Huang Chonggu was a principal graduate, what good did it do? It makes more sense to emulate Ban [Zhao], who, having mastered books that could fill a hundred castles, could stand face-to-face with any scholar in the realm." That is to say, instead of playing the futile game of trying to gain entrance into men's public world as a (disguised) man, Qiren had better assume her female identity, which in effect allowed her just as much room to pursue her studies. Her mother was convinced by this logic and within the same year, she sealed a betrothal agreement with a local gentry family. Although Qiren no longer received guests and mingled with men of letters, she remained clothed in male robes. At a tender age, Yu Qiren had her poetry collection published, and a number of poems she crafted on social occasions as a surrogate man were anthologized.[66]

Whereas Yu Qiren was intentionally raised by her mother as a son, another early Qing gentry daughter, Xu Deyin, fancied herself a boy although she was reared as a girl. Daughter of a prominent family from Qiantong, Hangzhou, Deyin received a man-like education in the Classics, history, literature, and poetry. Her father, Xu Xuling (*jinshi* 1655), recalled that when Deyin was barely several years old, whenever scholar-official friends of her grandfather's came to visit she would take off all her earrings and hair ornaments, fold the lapel of her robe in a man's style, and greet the guests, making deep bows like a man. Her grandfather and his friends were as delighted by her company as she was with theirs, and she often joined their poetry parties.

Her grandfather complimented Deyin by referring to the story of Han Yu's prodigal son. Han Yu (768–824), a Tang dynasty literary giant, fathered an ignorant son. Not familiar with the term "*jin-gen* [literally 'gold-root'] chariot," an ancient vehicle that transported imperial passengers, the son misread it "*jin-yin* chariot," literally "gold-and-silver chariot." Xu Deyin's grandfather sighed: "If [Han Yu] had you as his son, then there would have been no misreading of *jin-gen*. What a shame that you are a girl!" He was thus implying that although Deyin was as good as a son in carrying on the family's tradition of learning, since she was a girl she had to content herself with the traditional female roles. Indeed, Deyin later married a scholar-official, became a chaste widow, and persevered in bringing up her son.[67]

Similar to the ambivalent meanings of the literary image of the woman principal graduate, these examples of gender inversion in real life were laden with contradictory messages. On the one hand, their eventual assumption of female identities and roles bespoke the wisdom of the words of Xu Deyin's grandfather. No matter how erudite and male-looking some daughters were, the gulf between being male and female, in part inscribed in biology, in part perpetuated by a powerful ideology, was formidable. Females could not be males forever except in disguise. Yet on the other hand, the ease with which these girls reverted back to their female identity was indicative of the casualness with which temporary transgressions of gender boundaries were regarded. With or without male attire, in concerns, activities, and self-perceptions, exceptional individual women had begun to blur the centuries-old boundary between inner and outer and between the male and female spheres.

In spite of, or because of, these temporary transgressions, the premise of separate spheres remained intact. As long as women strove to become man-like, to the point of holding the male scholar-official as their role model, the ideological and functional asymmetry in the gender system remained unchallenged. The new space crafted by women writing and struggling to extend the boundaries of femininity ultimately served as a safety valve, preempting and diffusing criticisms from the most educated members of the female population.

Yet as salient as the resilience of the notion of separate spheres is the de facto recognition of an enlarged female sphere from within this formulation. A woman's place is no longer confined to the kitchen or the loom; in serving and providing for her family, she may be allowed to traverse waterways, sell her writings and paintings, move into gentry households as a tutor, and mingle with literati men. Although the actual number of these extraordinary "career women" is small, their examples inspired countless domestic women to brave new terrains in person and in writing. This enlarged woman's sphere, similar to the new sociocultural space opened up by the woman writer, was crafted not by repudiating the old domestic boundaries but by pushing and stretching them to new limits. A similar process was at work in enlarging the traditional definitions of womanhood.

Talent, Virtue, and Beauty

REWRITING WOMANHOOD

W E HAVE SEEN THAT under the facade of the persistent ideal of separate spheres, both the boundaries of domesticity and the woman's sphere were extended. This chapter examines the closely related process of rewriting womanhood, which was often couched as a debate over the content and goals of women's education. The social changes behind this debate, the ideals of womanhood being contested, and educated women's own definitions of femininity are the focus of this chapter. Women's education was conducted on three levels: socialization, which involves inculcation of norms and values by manipulating a woman's living quarters and body; cultural education, the acquisition of reading and writing skills and general cultural literacy; and moral education, the cultivation of feminine virtues. The proper balance between the three was the single most important issue in the contestations over womanhood.

In concrete terms, the new womanhood was fashioned by juggling three attributes: virtue (*de*), talent (*cai*), and beauty (*mei*). As will be shown in this chapter, the valorization of women poets in anthologies and local histories, as much as the presence of highly articulate reader-writers in real life, signaled the rising importance of talent as an attribute for women. This accent on female talent was also facilitated by larger social processes that pushed the family onto the center stage of cultural production and learning. The new womanhood represents a hollowing out of the age-old Confucian Four Virtues (womanly speech, womanly virtue, womanly deportment, and womanly work), although rhetorically the new and the old formulations are strikingly similar.

The Centripetal Woman

These four Confucian attributes describe an idealized centripetal woman, whose trajectories are diametrically opposed to those of an ideal man. The Confucian vision of social order is predicated on the centrifugal extension of a man's moral perfection. A set of ordered priorities describes the various fields of action for him, as expressed in a famous passage from the *Great Learning*:

Things being investigated, knowledge became complete. Their knowledge being complete, their thoughts were sincere. Their thoughts being sincere, their hearts were then rectified. Their hearts being rectified, their persons were cultivated. Their persons being cultivated, their families were regulated. Their families being regulated, their states were rightly governed. Their states being rightly governed, the whole kingdom was made tranquil and happy. From the Son of Heaven down to the mass of the people, all must consider the cultivation of the person the root of *everything besides*. [Italics added][1]

That is to say, a man was responsible for keeping order in the family, local community, government, and the world at large; his private morality was the root of public good. Although a gentleman was not to seek after vanities, fame and immortality awaited those who achieved this expansionary enterprise. A woman, too, was to be incessant in her moral cultivation. Her contribution, however, stopped at the "ordered household." A woman's field of action was to be confined to the domestic and the private; her orientation in life was centripetal.

The Confucian ideology reinforced a gender hierarchy with its doctrine of separate spheres. It is curious, however, that the task of guarding the inner/outer and male/female boundaries fell primarily on the women. One of the most frequent admonitions in conduct books for women was to maintain strict boundaries. Some authors drew from such Confucian classics as the *Book of Rites* to justify this distinction; others, like this scholar-official from Yangzhou, were more concerned with giving practical advice: "Men and women should not sit together or use the same hangers, towels, or combs." A woman should not venture outside her quarters without good reason; when she had to, she should cover her face with a scarf. The point of all this was obvious: "The purpose of strict demarcation between the inner and the outer is to prevent disorder." Such admonitions, in fact, had first been penned by the Song Confucianist Sima Guang (1019–86) and were reiterated verbatim in precepts and household instructions.[2]

Although the dualities woman/man and inner/outer were presented as absolute and fixed entities, in practice the lines were not so neatly drawn. Even normative formulations did not consign the ideal woman to a static and cloistered existence. In Chinese, the concept of "inner" (*nei*) encompasses the meaning of "domestic" or "private" in English, but these terms are not identical. Inner/outer is a relational category that describes a series of nested hierarchies whose boundary changes with context. A woman, for example, is the "inner helpmate" of her husband, the "outer person," but the couple and their children constitute the inner vis-à-vis his extended family. The entire lineage, in turn, is the inner unit against the outside community. Moreover, the ambiguity of such Chinese terms for common descent groups as *jia*, *zu*, and *zong* means that the boundary of the "we group" can be redrawn as circumstances change.[3] This ambiguity allows individuals much room for maneuvering between ideal norm and actual behavior. In fact, exactly because of its inherent conceptual ambiguity, the distinction between inner/outer or woman/man had to be accentuated physically and visually by compartmentalizing living quarters, differentiating attire, and binding the women's feet.

A woman was taught her place ideologically, a lesson encapsulated in the famous dictum of Four Virtues. First mentioned in the *Book of Rites*, the Four Virtues were popularized by Ban Zhao in her *Precepts for Women*, one of the most popular didactic works in Chinese history. Ban Zhao first explained the Four Virtues in the negative, as if to caution against overexertion: " 'Womanly virtue' does not mean that she has to excel in talent and wisdom; 'womanly speech' does not mean she has to be argumentative; 'womanly deportment' does not necessarily mean glamour and beauty; 'womanly work' does not mean that she has to vie in skill." Ban then explained in positive terms how a woman should behave; among other things, she should cultivate a sense of shame, offend nobody in speech, take regular baths, and devote herself to spinning, weaving, and preparing food and wine.[4] In contrast to a man's expansionary arenas, a woman's calling lay at the stove and the spinning wheel and loom; her orientation was to be inward, and she herself was to be modest in personality, appearance, behavior, and movement.

This centripetal ideal of womanhood was reinforced by the structure of her daily surroundings, particularly the layout of houses, and the restructuring of her body, notably through footbinding. Gender inequalities, observes Pierre Bourdieu, are taught to children through gestures and postures, as well as through the organization of the space they occupy.[5] The spatial organization of Ming-Qing houses, too, embodied the Confucian ideal of a humble, quiet, and domestic woman. The courtyard house, the norm among Han Chinese, was in itself a reflection of the Confucian insistence on separating inner from outer, as well as the centrality of family life. "Its basic feature is that the rooms open out to the privacy of interior space and present their blank backs to the outside world. Within and without are clearly defined. . . . Inside the enclosure . . . human relations and feelings can rise to a high and even uncomfortable level of warmth."[6]

An idealized depiction of the doctrine of separate spheres in elite households, with the man studying and the women cooking. Although their domestic spaces adjoin, the male and female worlds are functionally and spatially distinct (Qian Gu, "A Section of Crane Forest and Jade Dew: Calligraphy and Painting." Original in National Palace Museum, Taibei. Reproduction courtesy of Arts–Special Collections, University of California, Los Angeles).

The composition of the housing compound reminded an individual of his or her place in a nested hierarchy of social universes — stem family, extended family, branch, lineage. Individual bedrooms clustered around a living room (*tang*), where a small family gathered for meals. The family socialized with other families living in the same compound in an adjoining open courtyard (*yuanzi* in Beijing; *tianjing* in Huizhou). The ancestral hall (*citang*), a concrete expression of agnatic solidarity, was often adjacent to the courtyard. The smaller *tang* can be called an "inner living room" and the courtyard an "outer living room." A team of Japanese architects who surveyed commoner houses in China, many of which have survived from Ming-Qing times, has concluded that this living arrangement reflects the "Confucian patriarchal social order" and its ideal of familism.[7] The further delineation of interior space into inner and outer, however, suggests that inner/outer are relative categories whose meaning changes with context.[8]

Space allocation inside the housing compound taught a woman her place in the world. The kitchen, one context in which she could realize the virtue of "womanly work," was hidden away in a shaded area where sunshine from the open courtyard could not reach. Bedrooms and living rooms, in contrast, basked in sunlight.[9] Moreover, in Ming-Qing gentry households, the rooms farther away from the front door were designated the female quarters (*guikun*). The term appears in a late sixteenth-century sample contract for real estate transactions, which includes a checklist of various components of what appears to be a sizable housing compound.[10] Alvaro Semedo (1585–1658), a Portuguese Jesuit missionary who sojourned in Shanghai, Yangzhou, and other Jiangnan cities, found a most apt analogy for the women's quarters — a sanctuary. If an unknowing guest (probably the missionary himself) ventured near it by mistake, warnings of "There are women inside!" warded him off. He also observed that female chambers never had windows that opened on the street.[11] At work, a woman's place was damp and shaded; at rest, her quarters were to be sheltered and inward-looking.

Footbinding as Socialization

The spatial organization that embodied the inner/outer and male/female distinctions was reinforced by footbinding, a restructuring of the woman's body itself. Footbinding has been construed as the most graphic symbol of the restriction and victimization that women suffered in the male-centered Chinese family system. The title of an article by a cultural anthropologist sums up the verdict of Western observers and Chinese reformers since the late nineteenth century: "Bound Feet, Hobbled Lives:

Women in Old China."[12] This characterization is not wrong, but it leaves out the complex motives and feelings of the mothers and daughters involved. Part of the problem is that footbinding has become the categorical attribute of Chinese women's oppression by a savage and patriarchal "old" China; their individual voices and class differences submerged by a common history of denial. "Old China" appears timeless, its women faceless and generic; each is thus deprived of a history. Later in this chapter, we will see how educated women in the seventeenth century viewed their own bodies and their feet. The pride they felt, tinged with a secret delight, defies simple dichotomies of men-against-women, or victims-versus-agents. In the following chapters we will see that bound feet did not prevent women from traveling and forming long-distance social networks — a far cry from leading hobbled lives. Here, however, our concern lies with footbinding as a means of socialization and the values it is supposed to transmit.

It is natural for modern-day reformers to consider footbinding a men's conspiracy to keep women crippled and submissive, but this is an anachronistic view that finds no support in the historical records. Legend has it that one of the first women who bound her feet was Yaoniang, a dancer in the court of the Southern Tang ruler Li Yu (r. 961–75).[13] Casual documentary references suggest that the practice was gradually adopted by respectable daughters during the Song, especially after the late twelfth century. The Neo-Confucian philosopher Zhu Xi (1130–1200) was supposed to have promoted the custom when he served as prefect in southern Fujian. His alleged purpose was to teach the unruly locals the virtue of segregating women from men.[14]

Although this story cannot be substantiated, there is a degree of historical truth in the coupling of footbinding with the doctrine of separate spheres. Patricia Ebrey has argued that the spread of footbinding in the Song stemmed from the scholar-gentry's insecurity with blurred boundaries — between the two sexes and between the Han Chinese and peoples from the steppes. The desire for wives and courtesans with small feet was necessitated by new notions of masculinity: "If the ideal man among the upper class was relatively subdued and refined, he might seem too effeminate unless women came to be even more delicate, reticent, and stationary."[15] In other words, the impetus for the spread of footbinding was rooted in larger concerns of defining nationhood and gender values and was not directed against women per se.

Anxieties concerning blurred sexual and racial boundaries peaked around the Ming-Qing transition. The worst fears of the Song Neo-Confucians seemed to have materialized. The growing visibility and mobility of women in a relatively open society threatened to erase gender distinctions. In addition, the threat and eventual success of the Manchu conquest, its haircutting edict, and its later short-lived prohibition of foot-binding fostered a hysterical atmosphere full of sexual overtones. The enforced shaving of men's foreheads, in particular, was seen as an assault on men's virility, a savagery matched only by the raping of their women, and incited suicidal loyalist resistance in some Jiangnan cities.[16] Although no one openly advocated footbinding, the very establishment of the Man-chu dynasty created a need to re-emphasize the differences between "we" and "they" and between "he" and "she." The ban on footbinding, thus doomed from the start, was rescinded in 1668, four years after its pro-mulgation.[17]

By the seventeenth century, footbinding had become an accepted prac-tice among girls raised in Jiangnan cities. The development of a host of female-exclusive rituals rendered it an even more effective tool of social-ization. Begun around the age of six, the "age of reason" for sons, foot-binding prepared a girl physically and psychologically for her future role as wife and a dependent family member. The age when girls started to have their feet bound coincided with the age when boys moved out of the women's quarters to enroll in lineage schools or begin instruction with private tutors.[18] From that age on, sexual differences were accentuated; not only were children taught that the two sexes differed constitutionally and occupied distinct stations in life, but they were also taught to look different. Through footbinding, the doctrine of separate spheres was en-graved onto the bodies of female children.

The ritual of footbinding, an exclusively female affair, reinforced the ideal and practice of separate male/female domains. Long before the bind-ing started, a girl's mother would prepare the various implements needed. Besides alum, an astringent, these were either implements already in use in the women's world — scissors, nail clippers, needle, and thread — or made for the occasion by the elder women in the house. A sample checklist reads: a bandage ten centimeters wide and ten meters long, lightly starched and free of wrinkles; five pairs of cloth shoes with flat bottoms; three pairs of cloth slippers for bed; several pairs of tight socks.[19] Although the size and quantity of paraphernalia might vary from family to family, the prepara-tion was always meticulous and the instructions, specific. It is noteworthy that the materials needed for footbinding were themselves products of "womanly work" (*nügong*) — weaving, sewing, needlework. By using them, a girl would soon be taught to master these skills.

A central event in the domestic women's culture, the process of foot-binding was often launched with a prayer to the gods. A Ming household almanac printed in Fujian stipulated rules for picking auspicious days to inaugurate this rite of passage.[20] In Suzhou, binding customarily started on the twenty-fourth day of the eighth month, when the Tiny-Foot

Maiden (Xiaojiao Guniang), the deity in charge of footbinding, enjoyed offerings from her devotees. On that day, girls shaped rice balls from glutinous rice and red beans, praying that their bones would be just as soft. Offerings to the stove god were also made. The date was chosen in part for practical reasons: it was more pleasant for a girl to start binding in the cool of autumn. Both the starting date and rituals varied from area to area. In some regions, mother and daughter also made sacrifices to Guanyin, the omnipotent protector of women. Before binding was to start, a mother would sew and embroider a tiny pair of shoes and place it on top of an incense burner in front of a Guanyin statue.[21]

These female-exclusive rituals and the beliefs behind them help explain the longevity and spread of the custom. For all its erotic appeal to men, without the cooperation of the women concerned, footbinding could not have been perpetuated for a millennium. In defining the mother-daughter tie in a private space barred to men, in venerating the fruits of women's handiwork, and in the centrality of female-exclusive religious rituals, footbinding embodied the essential features of a women's culture documented by the writings of the women themselves (to be recounted in the following chapters). Throughout a woman's life, fascination with the foot continued to be a central motif in her interaction with other women. Women exchanged poems eulogizing small feet; mementos such as embroidered shoes were as widely used as poems in cementing female friendships.

In this lies the ambivalent nature of a woman's self-identity and women's culture in seventeenth-century China. On a negative note, women seemed to have accepted without question a philosophical and ethical tradition predicated on their confinement. In the seventeenth century, they had yet to question the premise of that tradition, nor did they raise objections in a concerted voice. On a positive note, they managed to create a meaningful and colorful world of their own within the constraints of their historical time and space. Every ferry ride taken by Huang Yuanjie on the waterways of Jiangnan, every prayer whispered to Guanyin, and every poem inscribed onto a friend's heart tell a story of the negotiations women made with the necessities of human existence.

Both the enduring strength of the Confucian tradition and the Herculean achievements of individual women have to be recognized in this study of women's education. The combination of ideological teaching, manipulation of living space, and bodily restructuring added up to a powerful apparatus inculcating the Confucian notions of ideal womanhood in countless women. Even before the reconstitution of Confucian orthodoxy in the eighteenth century, when the state made the canonization of female chastity a top priority, this apparatus was firmly in place. We have to appreciate its pervasiveness and effectiveness in the supposedly permissive era of the late Ming and in the face of dynastic transition in order to comprehend the contours of private and social life for both sexes in the seventeenth century. At the same time, however, we should bear in mind that education was a dubious enterprise involving human agency; there were inevitable gaps between intention and result, or between norms and behavior. A woman's view of her life had its own logic and rhythm that might or might not conform to the Confucian ideal of separate spheres and the centripetal woman.

Return to Family: "Privatization" of Chinese Life

The ideals of centrifugal man and centripetal woman were thrown into confusion by the currents of social change unleashed by the monetary economy and commercial printing in the sixteenth and seventeenth centuries. These changes were most clearly manifested in the shifting parameters of domesticity and the contents of family life. Owing to their different orientations, however, men and women experienced the changes differently. Whereas the ideal of centripetal women masked rising incidences of female transgression of the public domain, the centrifugal orientation of men was increasingly countered by an inward turn in emotional, religious, and social lives. The family emerged as the central field of action where the trajectories of these men and women intersected.

In particular, the enlarged and reconstituted family domain was the site where the new woman — talented, virtuous, and beautiful — thrived. This reconstitution of the family domain is a composite phenomenon with private and social dimensions: an emotional valuation of domestic life, emergence of the family as a repository of learning, heightened lineage formation, and the growing importance of well-groomed brides in the elite family's cultural capital. Not only the subjective definitions of domesticity but also the actual functions of the family as a social, political, and cultural institution were undergoing profound changes. All these developments had a direct bearing on a woman's everyday life and abstract definitions of womanhood.

Before we discuss the changing context and content of an elite woman's life, it is important to clarify the meanings of "family" and "private." In using "family" I allude to the connotations of *jiazu*, a deliberately ambiguous term that embodies the often conflicting orientations of the family as a ritualistic and as an economic unit. In English it encompasses the household, the lineage, and the clan.[22] Similarly, the word *private* is also used in intentionally ambiguous ways. In English scholarly literature, "private" and "domestic" are often used interchangeably to designate a realm clearly separated from the so-called public sphere. This dichotomized conceptualization, never apt in Chinese society, was invalidated even further by changes in the seventeenth century, when the meanings of "private" and "public" were undergoing major transformations.

These transformations were not just rhetorical; they involved social changes that augmented the political, economic, and cultural positions of the family in society. These changes, as disparate as they may seem, all bespeak the interpenetration of the private and public: first, public men increasingly sought solace in domestic life as a haven of rest; second, the family assumed a host of previously public functions; third, the early Qing state deemed lineage organizations, by virtue of the familial virtues they embodied, the quintessential public institution. As a result of these changes, the domestic unit increasingly took on public functions and significance. Above all else, this interpenetration means that the demarcation lines between private, domestic, and public were not fixed; they had to be drawn according to context.

The first development, the veneration of domestic life as a haven of rest, was inspired by political upheavals and sustained by economic affluence. One practical ramification of this was the cultivation of hobbies and tastes in gentry homes — the valuation of leisure itself. We have seen the craze among newly rich readers for guides to genteel tastes; the gentlemen themselves were no less enthusiastic. Disenchanted with the thought of serving a corrupt court or alien rulers, many well-to-do scholars shunned political appointments in favor of domestic pleasures: sipping tea while playing a game of chess, meditating or unrolling a scroll while being enveloped in clouds of exotic incense. Other private pleasures were found in open spaces: flower-viewing parties, outings to local sights, poetry parties under the moon. Poems and diaries recording these events, as we will see later, reveal that wives, concubines, and even children often participated, as did close friends. The women also organized trips and parties of their own. With or without their men, gentrywomen were just as eager to enjoy the delights embedded in the rhythms of domestic life and afforded by their families' wealth.

One result of this introspection on the part of wealthy public men was a boom in the decorative arts and utilitarian objects such as furniture, as well as an elevation in the status of the craftsmen who produced them. James C. Y. Watt has attributed this boom to the money economy:

The demand for contemporary works of art reflected both consumer affluence and the success of market forces. Under the stimulus of free competition among independent producers, the quality of many types of decorative art reached a rarely attained level, and certain art forms made their appearance or were popularized for the first time. Hardwood furniture and carvings in wood, bamboo, soapstone, rhinoceros horn, and, of course, jade . . . became extremely popular.

The result of this boom, Watt continued, was blurred demarcation lines between the artist and the craftsman:

While most literati would not have gone as far as the reactionary officials at court, who petitioned for the revocation of the imperial order conferring official rank on craftsmen who rendered exceptional service, some, like Wang Shizhen, felt uneasy about distinguished and prosperous craftsmen and manufacturers socializing with the gentry. On the other hand, the dramatist and painter Xu Wei (1521–93) wrote a poem in praise of the jade carver Lu Zigang, and Li Rihua was friendly with potters.

Gender lines were also blurred to some extent.

Fashion, then as now, was closely linked with decoration. Late Ming decoration was colorful, and one of the most conspicuous aspects of fashion at the time was the colorful robes worn by men and women alike. A contemporary writer remarked that "in the districts of the southeast, the students and the rich and scholarly families all wore red and purple clothes like women."[23]

A certain degree of status and gender disorder was perceived to be an integral part of the popularity of decorative arts, inspired in part by a valuation of leisure and everyday pleasures.

To be sure, there is nothing new about fin-de-siècle retreats into private life; these have recurred throughout history whenever public life is in shambles. The novelty of the seventeenth century, however, lies in the craze in the very notion of taste itself that was fanned by the publishing boom and buoyed by the money economy. Self-appointed connoisseurs of taste made a fortune by authoring books and essays on tea, wine, cuisine, musical instruments, and other pleasures of everyday life. More was being promoted than taste, however: namely, a new lighthearted attitude toward life and the mundane pleasures it offered. The leading connoisseur Li Yu encapsulated the spirit of the age in a famous book, *Casual Expressions of Idle Feelings* (*Xianqing ouji*), published in 1671. Li had an opinion on everything from the proper way to prepare crabs to the right time to have sex and instructed readers in the arts of play production, the training of concubines, architecture, furniture, food and drink, flowers and trees, and so on.[24] The same commercial publishers who fanned the cult of *qing* also popularized a cult of private pleasures, to be shared with loved ones in a domestic setting.

At the same time that men disillusioned with public life retreated to domesticity as a haven of rest, the family emerged as a locus of a multitude of social and cultural activities. Family-based publishing and drama troupes exemplify this trend. In addition, craftsmen of refined goods—silversmiths, cabinetmakers—often took up residence in a patron's house to manufacture their wares.[25] In the education of boys and girls, too, the family assumed a pivotal role as competition for success grew keener. These developments bear witness to a privatization of Chinese cultural life, most pronounced in urban gentry and merchant families, as the family assumed a host of functions previously found in the public arena or handled by nonprivate agents.

The most prominent aspect of this trend was the family's emergence as a repository of knowledge and learning. This accompanied an increase in the importance and variety of the family's cultural capital, of which printed books constituted a prevalent form. The late Ming publishing boom created a fad in book collecting, enabling individual families to build impressive libraries. The most famous ones—the Tianyi Pavilion of the Ningbo Fans and the Tansheng Hall of the Shaoxing Qis—stood as monuments to the owner family's erudition and wealth, as well as the sophistication of its locale. The Qi family boasted a collection of close to 9,000 titles and 90,000 volumes; even less endowed bibliophiles could amass a library half that size.[26] A poignant expression of this trend toward privatized learning can be found in the lineage-based schools of New Text Confucianist scholarship in eighteenth- and nineteenth-century Changzhou analyzed by Benjamin Elman.[27]

This emergence of the family as a repository of scholastic knowledge greatly enhanced women's chances of receiving an education in the Classics, philosophy, and history. All the most prolific women poets and writers of the seventeenth century benefited from the cultural resources of their families. Later in the eighteenth century, a handful of daughters were even schooled in science, mathematics, and other subjects previously considered irrelevant to a woman's vocation or beyond her intellectual means. A Nanjing woman, Wang Zhenyi (1768–97), for example, read her grandfather's books and learned astronomy and calendrical science from him. She discussed geometry in letters to her sister and left treatises on such subjects as lunar eclipses and the globe-shaped earth.[28]

Although knowledge of astronomy was rare, poetry writing was an extremely popular form of cultural capital. Timothy Brook notes that in Ningbo, poetry clubs figured as an important means of network-building for the gentrymen, and that this and other forms of cultural expertise amassed by less than 50 upper gentry families enabled them to dominate Yin county for centuries. Supplementing landholding and other means of economic domination, mastery of cultural expertise created "a mantle of exclusiveness in which the elite wrapped itself."[29] As we will see, women's poetry clubs, publication of female family members' collected works, and well-groomed daughters became crucial components of this mantle for gentry households in Jiangnan after the late sixteenth century. The import of women's learning is accentuated when the privatized family is considered in its larger context of increasingly fierce competition for power and resources in local society.

The Private as Public: Strategies of Lineage Formation

Just as important as the internal changes in family life were changes in the family's context or social position. Most notably, gentry elders increasingly sought to incorporate their kin into common descent groups. Much of the impetus stemmed from a need to reconstitute a stable local society out of the ruins created first by the intrusion of money into human relations and later by the political trauma of the Manchu conquest. In the fluid and violent society of seventeenth-century Jiangnan, the common descent group and the civil service were the two foremost time-honored institutions providing a sense of community and continuity.

Hence the landlord-literati in both Jiading and Changzhou, as Jerry Dennerline and Benjamin Elman show in separate studies, vied to form corporate estates and strengthen the ritual and educational functions of the lineage, fostering an identification of lineage interest with public functions.[30] In the process of stabilizing local society, the common descent group consolidated itself as a territorial entity. In her study of corporate lands owned by lineage organizations, Chinese historian Zhang Yan found a phenomenal increase in both the pace and size of acquisition in the Ming-Qing period. This growth in lineage economic prowess was particularly prevalent in Jiangnan and the southern provinces of Guangdong and Fujian.[31]

A similar process of lineage development was at work in the peripheral areas. Ueda Makoto, in his study of lineage formation in the mountainous areas of Zhejiang, shows that heightened landlordism and class stratification strengthened lineage formation in the late Ming and early Qing. Ostensibly emphasizing a common identity and shared interests between rich and poor members, lineages softened the blow of a potentially explosive polarization. The projects sponsored by lineages served as a limited channel for returning wealth and resources to the less privileged.[32] In other words, lineage formation was one means of creating stability and security in an increasingly stratified and competitive society.

Marriage alliances were an important strategy for a lineage struggling to establish itself or to maintain its hegemony in local society. In areas with a tradition of strong lineages—Ningbo, Jiaxing, Tongcheng, Huizhou, for example—the leading families had long adopted a strategy of marrying only among themselves. Zhang Ying (1638–1708), an early Qing grand secretary from a prominent family in Tongcheng, took great pride in his mother's distinguished pedigree.[33] Marriage ties supplemented the manipulation of cultural capital described above by maintaining exclusive elite networks.

In peripheral areas with a less entrenched power structure, marriage alliances were an even more potent tool for the upwardly mobile families. In a study of the rise to prominence of a migrant lineage on the eastern Sichuan frontier from the mid-eighteenth to twentieth century, Yamada Masaru shows that the Tus followed a different marriage strategy in each of the three stages of their ascendance. Initially, they intermarried with other migrant lineages of the same province of origin, Hubei, as theirs. Then, in the early nineteenth century, the Tus pursued ties with powerful families originally from the Hu-Guang area, thus expanding their own trading networks. In the last stage, the six major branches (*fang*) of the Tus launched a concerted effort to cultivate affinal ties with the established local notables, a sign of their own newly acquired prominence.[34]

Yamada's study is instructive in highlighting the crucial role of women, both as daughters and brides, in a lineage's efforts to define and establish itself in local society. Although it is difficult to duplicate Yamada's finely textured study for earlier periods, it is clear that the marriage alliance was a conscious strategy for both established and aspiring families in the seventeenth century.[35] The importance of affinal ties to family mobility explains families' willingness to invest in the education of daughters. Both cultural and moral education increased a daughter's cachet as wife, making her the pride of both paternal and marital family. Well-groomed brides were a conspicuous form of cultural capital.

The social dynamics conducive to lineage formation were reinforced by the state. To purge what it considered the subversive influence of literati societies that had flourished in the late Ming, the early Qing state encouraged a return to the family. As vertical institutions encompassing members from different generations and social classes, kinship organizations were deemed useful in fostering respect for hierarchy among the populace. The family as a social institution had a double persona: in the eyes of its members it established the boundary of an inner circle; in the eyes of the state, however, it was the very embodiment of public (*gong*) virtues. In contrast, the state branded horizontal groups built on extra-familial ties "private," with the negative connotations of "selfish" (*si*).[36] This enshrinement of the family as the proprietor of public virtues, as well as its emergence as a repository of culture and learning, reconstituted the meaning of public/private in the seventeenth century. The family had become the stage where private and public intersected. The meaning of domesticity, correspondingly, was enlarged and magnified.

From the perspectives of the women concerned, the elevation of family life and kinship organizations changed the milieu in which a woman operated. The inward turn taken by men brought them closer to the traditional arena and prerogatives of women, thus creating new patterns of gender interaction. One mode of such new patterns — companionate marriage — will be examined in the next chapter. Moreover, in their very living quarters, women from prominent lineages gained access to the world of scholarship and drama performances previously reserved for the public man. The privatization of Chinese cultural life thus served to enlarge a gentrywoman's horizons without her having to step out of her home.

At the same time, the exemplary value of feminine virtues could bring her recognition far beyond her inner quarters. A diligent, frugal, and chaste woman was publicly recognized as a symbol of the family's moral uprightness, just as her chastity arch guarding the village entrance bespoke the honor of her community.[37] Supplementing canonization by the state, lineage organizations also devised their own incentives to promote chaste widowhood. The Fans of Suzhou, for example, awarded rice to widows who stayed single for a mere three years, a requirement much more lenient than that of the state. The Wangs of Kunshan, for their part, subsidized young widows with both rice and cash, a reward extended to both secondary wives and Wang daughters who married out.[38] The active interest of lineages in promoting female virtues highlighted the symbolic weight attached to a woman's name in the public standing of her family. A woman's morality was never simply a private affair.

Thus women assumed a pivotal symbolic role at the crossroads where the family met the state and where private and public morality intersected. Women's education, whatever its proper content, emerged as the missing link to anchor the world. The three arguments for women's education that emerged in the seventeenth century have to be understood in the context of this return to the family as a locus of social and personal life as well as the recognition of women's contributions to it. The first and most-often cited justification referred to her role as moral guardian, which demanded an education that cultivated her motherly and wifely virtues. Second, her poetic and artistic achievements translated into cultural capital for the family — hence the support of a cultural and literary education for daughters. Third, men's search for emotional solace in private life prompted them to desire companionate wives. In other words, women's education, both moral and cultural, could increase her value in the marriage market, to the benefit of herself and her kin. Men who spoke up for women's education or who quietly taught their wives and daughters subscribed to one or more of these arguments. As the domestic sphere was reconstituted to embrace public values and functions, the traditional preserve of women took on entirely new meanings both to them and to society at large.

Women's Education for Motherhood

Women's roles as mother and guardian of the inner sphere provided the strongest justification for a renewed interest in their moral education in the late Ming period. Motherhood, the seed of good governance and peace in the realm, was a time-honored tenet of the Confucian ethical tradition.[39] Liu Xiang's *Biographies of Exemplary Women*, the archetype of didactic literature for women, opened with fourteen stories of exemplary mothers, followed by tales of women who were sagacious, wise, chaste, self-sacrificing, and eloquent. All were intended as contrasts to a trail of femmes fatales at the end of the book.[40] Both the primacy of motherly virtue and the pitfalls of its degeneration were thus amply clear in the structure of the *Biographies*. This message seemed particularly apt in Ming and Qing times. One scholar summed up the vital connection between motherhood and the restoration of social order: "Rebels and bandits descended from heaven, but were given birth to by women." He proceeded to write a precept urging women to forsake luxurious habits and cultivate virtue so as to be rearers of good sons.[41]

Although the logic behind women's education in the name of motherhood is straightforward, the exact meanings of "moral education" and "feminine virtue" were controversial issues in the seventeenth century, in part because of an uneasy co-existence in the Confucian tradition of two potentially incompatible visions of women's education. Although there was no disagreement that women's education was, ultimately, training for motherhood, the proper proportion of moral to literary education was constantly debated. The famous story of Mencius' mother epitomizes the importance of a mother's morality to her son's scholastic success. She was said to have moved three times to shield her son from bad influences in the neighborhood. When he still ran off from school, she cut the web of her loom to teach him the perils of abandoning one's vocation halfway.[42] This story celebrates her moral acumen, not her erudition. There was a strong tendency throughout history to define the good mother exclusively in terms of her virtues, not her talents.

In reality, in Song and Yuan times it was widely recognized that mothers well versed in the Classics could enhance a son's examination success. A widowed mother's supervision of her son's education figured so prominently in biographies of prominent men that it became almost a literary convention. In the Yuan period, for example, scholar-officials often credited their first teachers — mothers — who recited to them such Classics as the *Analects*, *Mencius*, and *Book of Filial Piety*.[43] This oral transmission was particularly crucial in times of political turmoil, when collections of books were often scattered or destroyed. The Ming state formally recognized women's contribution to men's education by conferring honorary titles on wives and mothers of scholar-officials.[44] Hence alongside the model of Mencius' mother, there is a strong undercurrent in the Confucian tradition sanctioning the cultural education of woman, in preparation to become a son's first teacher. The mother's role in the oral transmission of the Classics won her a niche, albeit indirect, in the Confucian canonical tradition.[45] Although both are predicated on the assumption that a woman's raison d'être is motherhood, there is an obvious tension between the vision of an illiterate mother teaching by moral example and that of a learned mother drilling her son in the rudimentary Classics.

This tension is partly rooted in the intrinsically ambivalent position of women in Chinese family and society. From the male point of view, women's education was, like their procreative power, double-edged. A woman's ability to procreate gave her power in the family, but her ability to disrupt boundaries between the inner and outer made her dangerous.[46] Similarly, although wise mothers with rudimentary literary skills were needed to oversee the education of sons, women who learned to read and write might become so unruly as to venture out of the inner chambers, thus violating the very rationale of women's education and the norm of the centripetal woman.

The seventeenth-century discussion of the attributes of womanhood represented a flare-up of these tensions inherent in the Confucian tradition. But more fundamental changes were at stake as well: not only the agenda but also the assumptions of women's education had changed. In the face of women's growing visibility in Chinese cultural life — as readers, audience, authors — within and outside the family, the pressing issue was no longer "what if women were literate?" but "how are we to construct new concepts of womanhood that can accommodate old values to that reality?" Motherhood ceased to be the only justification for women's moral and cultural nurturance and the undivided source of their self-esteem. The pivotal importance of motherhood was not denied; rather, it was reinforced as a woman's motherly duties came to be seen as compatible with her callings as wife and poet.

The new womanhood was forged not by denying the conventional Thrice Following–Four Virtues formula, but by subtly reinterpreting the meaning of these attributes. In an earlier article I show how one of the four virtues, "womanly speech," underwent a metamorphosis to mean not only the spoken word but also the written word, a change that justified the emergence of women writers. A woman's niche was enlarged to encompass both the kitchen and the scholar's studio.[47] Later, we will see that the meanings of "womanly deportment" and "womanly work" were similarly reinterpreted during the seventeenth century.

Talent, Virtue, and Beauty

The proper balance of talent, virtue, and beauty was deliberated openly in essays, jottings, and vernacular stories in the seventeenth century. The anxieties that accompanied this process of constructing a new womanhood were betrayed by the currency of the dictum "For a woman, to be virtuous is to be untalented" in the seventeenth century.[48] This saying should not be taken at its face value; it did not signify heightened subjugation of women in Ming-Qing times but, rather, anxieties over the erosion of social and gender boundaries. As is clear from the case of Xiaoqing, even those who bemoaned the fatal nature of talent continued to promote women's education. Talent and virtue were widely seen as compatible attributes of womanhood among the Jiangnan reading public and scholar-official households.[49]

The story of an overindulgent husband from the Three Kingdoms period (220–65) became the peg for a discussion of fitting "beauty" into the emergent "talent-virtue" formula. Preserved in primers for primary education, both the plot and the moral of the Xun Fengqian story were familiar to men and women in Ming-Qing times. Son of an official in the state of Wei, Xun married a daughter of Cao Hong (d. 232) and was apparently deeply in love with her. One winter, she lay sick with a high fever. Xun went out to the courtyard, froze himself, returned to her bed, and pressed his chilled body next to hers to relieve her temperature. She died, and so shortly did he.[50] Although readers might find Xun's devotion admirable and the scene of two bodies pressed against each other provocative, his attachment to his wife was the kind of sentiment most subversive of the Confucian ideal of familism. For this reason Xun was remembered in official history as a laughable, weak-willed man.

Xun Fengqian was also supposed to have declared: "Neither talent or virtue is relevant to a woman. She should be signified primarily by her beauty [se, 'colors' or 'appearance']." This remark complicated the implications of Xun's story enormously. "Beauty" in this context referred not only to a woman's looks but also to her sex appeal. Read out of context, Xun's line undermined the moral of the story. In denying that virtues signify a woman, Xun negated the premise of Confucian womanhood. In sanctioning physical attraction between man and wife, he could be seen as subverting Confucian familism itself.

This intriguing ambiguity as well as the currency of the categories of talent, virtue, and beauty rendered Xun Fengqian a frequently quoted ancient in the late sixteenth and seventeenth centuries. Xie Zhaozhe, author of the famous compendium *Five Miscellanies*, called Xun's saying "words of wisdom for all time." The gravamen of Xie's complaint was what he perceived as an inverted gender system in his times: "A woman's beauty should be [her foremost trait], just as talent is a man's. Nowadays, people ignore woman's beauty and harp upon her talent. Does it mean that man will have to be assessed by his beauty? What kind of a world would it be if [homosexual men such as] Longyang and Mizi [xia] were ranked higher than You and Xia [Confucius' disciples]?"

What Xie opposed was omitting beauty as an attribute for womanhood; he by no means implied that women should not have talent. "Women should be known by their beauty [*se*], and then by their acumen [*hui*]. But they are no better than puppets if they are dull-witted and lacking in literary flair." He made it clear that beauty means both looks and literary talent: "The streets are full of women with a face, but those who can write are as few as the morning stars." He then heaped praises on a handful of woman poets in history — Zhuo Wenjun (ca. 179–117 B.C.), Ban Jieyu (ca. 48–5 B.C.), Yu Xuanji, Li Qingzhao — and mourned others whose names had been lost to history.[51] To Xie, poets figured as the fairest of women.

Ye Shaoyuan, devoted husband of the gentry poet Shen Yixiu, mused over the secret of her attraction to him after her untimely death by engaging in an imaginary dialogue with Xun Fengqian. Disagreeing with Xun's saying, Ye told himself that "I miss Wanjun [Yixiu] not because of her beauty." Yet beauty was certainly part of her allure. "But being graceful on the outside and wise on the inside, she surely is most elegant, enchanting, and deeply inspiring [*yaren fengzhi*]." Significantly, the last expression was originally used to describe elegant verse from the *Book of Songs* and was associated with the famous fourth-century A.D. woman poet Xie Daoyun.[52] Yixiu's persona as a poet made her look beautiful in her husband's eyes. In the next chapter, we will see that the companionate marriage between the two was also permeated by a physical intimacy reminiscent of the devotion of Xun Fengqian to his wife.

Ye Shaoyuan also regarded his daughter Xiaoluan as unsurpassed according to the "talent-virtue-beauty" formula. After editing her posthumous works, Shaoyuan was so overcome by grief that he began to immortalize her: "Consider the famous ladies in history — Zhuo Wenjun has no virtue; Zuo Fen is short on looks; Xun Fengqian's wife lacks talent. [For Xiaoluan] to have all three, how could she have avoided heaven's jealousy?"[53]

Ye Shaoyuan and Xie Zhaozhe, both scholar-officials, were in fact arguing that (1) beauty was an important trait for woman and (2) intelligence and poetic talent were indispensable components of beauty. A woman's looks could not be separated from her inner qualities, which might include innate genius but were more often the results of moral cultivation and cultural education.

This confluence of talent, virtue, and beauty was also evident in a new image of heroines in Ming-Qing vernacular novels. The scholar protagonist in *The Jade Tender Pear* (*Yujiaoli*), for example, outlined his ideal woman thus: "She who has talent but no beauty cannot count as a belle [*jiaren*]. Neither can she who has beauty but no talent. Even if she has both but lacks a resonance of *qing* with me, she cannot count as *my* belle."[54] That this new image of woman represented a subtle subversion of the Confucian Four Virtues was evident in the description of such a belle in another story. "A wide, square forehead like a cicada's and dark, thick eyebrows like a moth; lips like apricots and cheeks like peaches — that's womanly deportment. But if she is too aloof, taciturn, and does not have an enchanting smile, then she falls short of glamour." Contrary to Ban Zhao's admonition, "womanly deportment" did mean glamour to many men.

Also at stake here was a conflation of female virtue and talent: "Sewing, embroidery, spinning, and weaving — that's 'womanly work.' But if she does not read books and cannot compose a verse or two, then she is short on skills." The author went on to argue that a woman who stayed in her quarters and whose heart did not stir in the romantic springtime might be considered to have womanly virtue but in fact was a mere puppet.[55] This picture of an enchanting and intelligent beauty bears a marked resemblance to Du Liniang, the heroine of *The Peony Pavilion*, who became the alter ego of many respectable daughters.

Hence in men's eyes beauty was a defining trait of the new woman. Although this was nothing new in the pleasure quarters inhabited by courtesans and writers of vernacular stories, it is significant that even such gentlemen as Ye Shaoyuan appreciated it in his wife and sought to enlarge its meaning to encompass both talent and virtue. Ironically, this new emphasis on feminine beauty may have been a result of a deeply felt need to restore a certain balance in the gender system by making women, now reading the Classics, publishing books, and taking up other "manly" tasks, *look* more like women. Such blurred gender distinctions evidently troubled Xie Zhaozhe. As suggested above, the very maintenance of the Confucian social hierarchy was predicated on a visual distinction between the two sexes; the anxiety about blurred boundaries could be one explanation for the spread of footbinding in this age.

Whereas the expansion of the meaning of womanly deportment to include poetic talent served to justify and encourage women's expanding horizons, the imperative of visually distinguishing the sexes could have the opposite effect of perpetuating old gender stereotypes and restricting women's field of action. This ambivalence was more pronounced in the views of beauty, talent, and virtue held by the women themselves.

Talent and Virtue in Women's Eyes

In women's eyes, Confucian ethics was rife with inconsistencies and conflicting demands. In discussing chaste widowhood, for example, Mark Elvin has pointed out that the moral demand for a widow to remain chaste often conflicted with the economic interests of her husband's kinsmen and could contradict the wishes of her parents.[56] This tension was partly due to conflicting loyalties arising out of woman's multiple roles as wife, kin, and daughter, and partly due to the frequent incongruity between moral law and human emotions. Despite the specificity of behavioral rules, how a woman acted in a given situation was often a matter of expediency that involved conscious choices. Although this modicum of freedom enabled an individual woman to negotiate a space of her own within the formal dualities of inner/outer and public/private, the uncertainty also generated considerable psychological pressure.

The norms of women's education were just as riddled with conflicting signals. We have seen that the Confucian tradition embodied two different visions of women's education and, ultimately, of womanhood. On the one hand, the model of Mencius' mother taught the virtue of moral steadfastness. When reinforced by admonitions that a woman should not learn too many words and should stay away from poetry at all cost, Mencius' mother could become the model ignorant woman. On the other hand, the recognition accorded mother-teachers versed in the Classics encouraged women to be cultured and learned. Many educated women themselves saw no conflict between poetic talent and virtue. For every mother who taught her daughters to celebrate feminine virtue by poetry, however, there was an equally stubborn illiterate woman who did not stray from the prescriptions of the first model.

The defense of women's education by Hangzhou matriarch and poet Gu Ruopu suggests that the model of the talented and virtuous woman was encountering resistance within the female quarters at the same time it was gaining acceptance in the learned society at large. Illiterate women were often the strongest defenders of the old womanhood—the ignorant woman—that was in fact being shunned by many educated men in the Jiangnan cities. In response to one such old woman who criticized Gu's hiring a teacher for the girls in her family, Gu Ruopu wrote a poem outlining the arguments on both sides.

Since first the Primal Forces were discrete
and human relations engendered thus complete,
men must be the arbiters of Right
and in the home all virtuous women Chaste.
But if we fail to take up poetry and prose,
how shall we our natural gifts dispose?
An elder woman ridiculed me for this:
"You do not practice true and wifely ways,
engaging teachers to instruct the girls,
as if they sought to win the world's regard.
They put aside our normal women's work
and waste their efforts to recite and learn."

In other words, the old woman regarded the acquisition of literacy, let alone the ability to write poetry and prose, an unnecessary distraction from a woman's true calling — being a good wife diligent in needlework, spinning, and weaving, the traditional womanly work. Gu Ruopu, however, argued that female virtue was too important to society to have its interpretation left to men:

Ban Zhao wrote the *Precepts for Women*,
that we might know the code of proper conduct.
I feel ashamed of my stupidity,
unable to correct my faults,
yet I pity those today who cultivate
appearances; they're only pretty dresses.
Not treating moral training seriously
will visit shame upon the family name.
Bring girls together, let them study,
teach them to distinguish right and wrong.
Ask them to investigate essentials —
the Four Virtues, the Three Obediences —
make the ancient ways their standard.[57]

In justifying women's education in the name of motherhood and family honor, Gu was following a strategy used by men. In using a classical lexicon but expanding the meaning of feminine virtue and womanly work to include poetic talent, Gu was a forceful advocate of the new image of woman. Both Gu and the elder woman considered themselves true Confucian daughters, and their disagreement is a graphic reminder that the conflicting Confucian images of ideal womanhood were at once a source of flexibility and tension.

It is thus not surprising that the self-perceptions of women writers in the seventeenth century were rife with conflicts and tensions, although these women did not seem to perceive of them as such. With historian's hindsight, such tensions are most discernible in three areas: their affirmation of motherhood and moral education; their portrayals of their own bodies, especially bound feet; and their views on the boundaries between the prescribed male and female domains. As the educated and virtuous women entered male preserves, they chose to re-emphasize their identities as women and to celebrate their femininity.

A major component of the educated women's self-definition was undeniably female virtue itself. Their affirmation of moral education was unequivocal; they recognized all too well the enormous power that the Confucian tradition gave the woman as the domestic guardian. Hence women reacted to the prevailing social and moral crisis with a crusading fervor. The project of rebuilding the family was not a public man's job; many wives and mothers realized that they alone could set the public and private realms straight by being vigilant in the inner chambers. Yet unlike the ignorant woman that Gu Ruopu rebuked, they saw poetry and learning as indispensable elements of moral renewal.

Their tacit acceptance of an implied seclusion within the domestic realm has to be weighed against the satisfaction women derived from both the augmented importance of domesticity and their own role in it. The glorification of moral womanhood, especially motherhood, endowed private responsibilities with public and political significance. In women's eyes, espousing the sanctity of motherhood and its attendant doctrine of separate spheres meant the very opposite of confinement: it was their most natural way of contributing to the world. The ideal woman was centripetal in disposition, but the power of her virtues radiated from the inner chambers to change the world.[58]

The pride and satisfaction stemming from an awareness of a pivotal role in upholding the Confucian social and gender system can be gleaned from the poetry of Fang Weiyi (1585–1668), daughter of a leading gentry family in Tongcheng, Anhui. Widowed at seventeen, Fang Weiyi returned to her natal household and remained single for the remaining 66 years of her life. Her virtue was boosted by the chaste widowhood of a younger sister, Weize, and the martyrdom of an elder sister, Mengshi, who asked a maid to drown her in a pond when her husband died defending the city of Ji'nan from the Manchus in 1640.[59] Spared from the chores of raising children and household duties, Weiyi and Weize dedicated their lives to writing poetry, annotating books, and educating boys and girls in the family. For eight years Weiyi raised and educated her young nephew Fang Yizhi (1611–71), who grew up to become a prominent Confucian thinker.[60]

For a widowed niece whom she had taught poetry, Weiyi once wrote a poem that ended with these words of admonition:

> Be steadfast like a rock.
> When your son completes his studies,

Your day of honor and glory will come.
Your unyielding integrity will shine in history,
Generations will emulate your motherly virtue.[61]

Not only did Fang Weiyi see herself as moral guardian in her capacity as a teacher of girls, she and Weize compiled an anthology of poetry by women, evidently for didactic purposes, divided into sections featuring the "uprights" and the "perverts."[62]

To some modern observers, the enthusiasm with which such educated women as Fang Weiyi, Fang Weize, and Gu Ruopu took to the task of guarding Confucian morality is evidence of the depth of their "victimization" — they seem oblivious that the very subject of their defense, the very source of their pride, the very seat of their identity, is a male-centered system that assigns woman an inferior place. This reading is valid if we can judge seventeenth-century individuals by twentieth-century standards. The fact that there was no viable alternative to the Confucian system in the seventeenth century is a sign more of the system's strength than of stupidity or failure on the part of its defenders. Without understanding the pride of the women and recognizing the rewards they reaped, we cannot comprehend the linchpin of the gender system in Ming-Qing China — the active support of gentrywomen and the prize they thus claimed.

Inner and Outer Beauty

A second component of the educated women's self-definition was a feminine appearance, most notably bound feet. In an age of confused gender norms and blurred boundaries, the women themselves became more concerned with their visual distinctions from men. Women who cultivated their looks at the expense of virtue, those whom Gu Ruopu dismissed as mere "pretty dresses," were frowned upon. Yet educated women agreed with men such as Ye Shaoyuan and Xie Zhaozhe who saw appearance or beauty as an expression of admirable inner qualities. The old attribute of womanly deportment does not begin to describe the manifestations of female beauty these women embraced.

In their inner chambers, mothers, daughters, and friends were not at all shy about discussing their bodies and looks; fragments of these conversations can be gleaned from the verses they exchanged and the essays they wrote. Shen Yixiu, the beloved wife of Ye Shaoyuan, mused over one such tender moment after her favorite third daughter, Ye Xiaoluan, died at the age of sixteen:

When you were thirteen, I took you to visit your uncle and he wrote you a poem praising your beauty. You were displeased[, saying that beauty does not distinguish a woman]. One early morning, I stood by your bed and saw you, face unwashed and hair uncombed, charming and graceful beyond belief. I teased you: "You didn't like it when others said you're beautiful. But look at you, so pretty even ungroomed! Even I find you irresistible; what will your future husband have to say?"

Shen Yixiu went on to describe how Xiaoluan would hide away in her study within the women's quarters all day, absorbed in calligraphy, literature, and the zither.[63] Unfortunately, Xiaoluan died five days before her wedding and never set eyes on her future husband. The perfect harmony of her beauty and talent constituted the portrait of Xiaoluan engraved on the heart of her mother.

Neither father nor mother was hesitant in adoring the beauty of their daughter. To Shen Yixiu, Xiaoluan's beauty was more dazzling than a plum blossom but not as overbearing as a crabapple flower; she struck a golden balance between "air from the forest" (*linxia zhifeng*) and "decency of the inner chambers" (*guifang zhixiu*).[64] "Air from the forest" refers to the nonchalant and carefree disposition of a woman artist. The connotation of open space and freedom is in direct contrast to the confinement implied in "inner chambers." First associated with the fourth-century gentrywoman poet Xie Daoyun, the phrase was often used to describe erudite courtesans in late Ming times. Shen Yixiu, however, found it an entirely respectable characterization for her talented daughter.

Comparison with Xie Daoyuan befits Xiaoluan's image of herself, who, as shown in Chapter 2, admired Du Liniang as if she were a friend. While unabashed about her poetic talent, the gentry girl was always eager to make a statement on the distinction between outer and inner beauty. The summer before Xiaoluan's death, Yixiu had several soft silk skirts tailored for Xiaoluan, but the pleats remained neatly folded and the garments untouched. Ye Shaoyuan sometimes teased his daughter by saying that she had looks that could topple empires. Xiaoluan would mildly rebuke him: "Why would a woman pride herself on having a face that can bring down a kingdom? Father, do not call your daughter such."[65] Denouncing the femme fatale, Xiaoluan eyed the attention on a woman's outward beauty with suspicion.

Notwithstanding her disclaimer that beauty did not signify a woman, Ye Xiaoluan wrote a series of nine poems on a woman's features and bodily parts — hair, eyebrows, eyes, lips, arms, waist, feet, and the full body — concluded by one on the Double Seven Festival. Imitating the "linked-pearl" format devised by a male writer, Liu Xiaochuo (481–539), Xiaoluan composed these verses as a poetic exercise several months before her sudden death. The lines that flowed from her brush, however, vividly convey a teenage girl's fascination with the enchantment of the female body. The one entitled "Feet" reads:

> They say lotuses blossom as she moves her feet,
> But they can't be seen underneath her skirt.
> Her jade toes so tiny and slender,
> Imprinting her fragrant name as she pauses.
> Her pure chiffon skirt swirls in a dance,
> Steadfast as the new moon.[66]
> Her light silk garment sways in soft, flowing motions,
> As she kicks her jade hook halfway up.
> [Consort Yang] left her stocking behind at Mawei,
> Adding to the remorse of the Tang emperor;[67]
> At the banks of River Luo the goddess treads elegantly,[68]
> Bringing sadness to Cao Zhi.[69]

Although full of historical allusions, Xiaoluan's verse is infused with an unspoken delight that a sixteen-year-old girl, months before her wedding, found in her own small feet. This delight, entirely dignified, has a sensuous quality that recalls the discussion on the bedroom scene by the three young commentators of *The Peony Pavilion*.

In "The Full Body," Xiaoluan contemplated the connections between inner and outer beauty:

> They say as her shadow falls onto the pond,
> Even waves are stirred by her picturesque countenance.
> As she moves her steps toward the curtain,
> The god of spring is startled that flowers have lost their
>   fragrance.
> Beauty fills a beholder like a feast,
> As no adornment of makeup can.
> Frowns are all the more enchanting,
> Without the ornament of powder and rouge.
> As lotus clouds her two cheeks,
> Her smile reveals bewitching dimples.
> The plum blossom opens into five petals,
> Its pure beauty is embraced inside.[70]

Here Xiaoluan celebrates the natural beauty of a tender-aged girl, emphasizing that her charm has nothing to do with artificial embellishments. This view of feminine beauty as an expression of an inner moral strength and intelligence is in agreement with that of her father's and mother's. The reference in the last couplet to plum petals states this view directly and is also mildly erotic in its suggestive power.

Xiaoluan showed her scribbles to her mother Shen Yixiu, who was so pleased that she took up her brush and responded with a similar linked-pearl series, with the disclaimer: "Yet my daughter has the genius of an immortal; mine pales by comparison." It is no accident that both mother and daughter found the subject matter of the series so enticing. Although laid down by an ancient man and coded in established allusions, the subjects of feminine beauty and the Double Seven Festival, a female-exclusive event honoring the Weaving Maid and women's handiwork, are both central to the poets' identities as women.[71]

Footbinding: A Woman-to-Woman Tradition

Shen Yixiu did not leave accounts of the footbinding ceremonies of her three daughters, nor did any of the seventeenth-century gentry mothers. Many of the practices and rituals of women's culture were transmitted orally, which accounts for a glaring hiatus in written descriptions of a crucial rite of passage in a woman's life. The verses they exchanged, although laden with poetic conventions, provide a glimpse into the central place occupied by feet and shoes in gentrywomen's definitions of self and in their interactions with relatives and friends. Our present understanding of footbinding is based on four sources, all written by men: missionary accounts, literati studies of the custom's origins, erotica, and abolition literature, which sometimes include interviews with women. These sources naturally perpetuate our current reading of footbinding as a man-to-woman story. The other half of the picture, footbinding as a woman-to-woman story, has to be sought in the voices of the women themselves, both the binder and the bound.

In response to her daughter's poem on feet, Shen Yixiu crafted this verse:

> They say she leaves her footprint on the green moss lightly,
> Only as she stands alone, lost in thought.
> He hears the tinkling of jade ornaments from afar,
> Only because she shifts her bound feet slightly.
> The slender, slender feet, creating lotuses at every step,
> The Duke of Donghun cannot but be indulgent.[72]
> The slim, slim socks as they move,
> Inspire the pity of Cao Zhi in his verse.
> As spring befalls the emperor's garden,
> The fallen petals make a fitting companion.
> As she walks the treasure house in the moon,
> The fragrant greens become more lovely.[73]

Less cluttered with historical allusions, Shen Yixiu's poem also lacks the sensuousness that permeates her pubescent daughter's. Yet even with her reserved tone, Shen's description of slight movements of the bound feet, vibrations that unite the beauty and her lover, is provocative. Using historical figures as poetic allusions, mother and daughter can indulge in small talk on seduction and other sex-related subjects while still sounding respectable.

Other gentrywomen were sometimes more direct. Xu Yuan, a gentry wife from Suzhou, wrote a series of poems for the courtesans and singing girls she befriended. The subject matter of Xu's poetry and her female intimacies will be taken up in Chapter 7; here I focus on the prominence of small feet in her portrayals of feminine beauty. Teasing a singing girl named Sanli (Three Beauties), for example, Xu composed this verse:

> You tender and bewitching girl, skin smoother than jade,
> Fragrance wafts from every step the lotus makes.
> Slender waist can hardly withstand the morning breeze,
> Why not build a jade terrace and hide her in mansions of gold?[74]

Lofty "jade terraces" and "mansions of gold," the dwelling places of goddesses, were common terms for the abodes of mistresses. Besides singing girls, Xu Yuan also befriended a highly talented courtesan, Xue Susu (1598–1637), an accomplished painter who counted horseriding among her many hobbies.[75] Before praising Susu's man-like talents and concerns in a series of poems dedicated to her, Xu Yuan set the scene by highlighting the feminine grace produced by the movement of her bound feet:

> Lotus blossoms as she moves her pair of arches,
> Her tiny waist, just a hand's breadth, is light enough to dance on
>   a palm.
> Leaning coyly against the east wind,
> Her pure color and misty daintiness fill the moon.[76]

Some of these poets may have been merely imitating poetic conventions or practicing the use of allusions when they crafted these verses on the arched feet. Yet the very recurrence of the theme of small feet suggests the importance that feet and, by extension, shoes, assumed in the boudoir life of gentrywomen. Many female friendships, in fact, were sealed by the exchange of shoes as mementos. For example, a gentry wife, Madame Ma, sent this poem back to a friend who just made her a pair of shoes:

> Tiny petals of golden lotus falling into the Jade Pond,
> Imagining you, embroidering in the inner chambers.
> Your skillful handiwork laboriously sent from afar,
> Dare I tread onto balconies wet with dew?[77]

The future bride, too, had to make a pair of shoes to present to her mother-in-law.[78] This practice was common in seventeenth-century Hangzhou, as evinced by the pair of shoes made by the young bride Chen Tong for the mother of Wu Ren, her betrothed (see Chapter 2 for the story of Wu buying this pair of shoes).

To a modern critic, the gentrywomen's enchantment with bound feet, to the point of defining their femininity by it and devising rituals around it, is a profound statement of their victimization. However valid this critique is from hindsight, it does not accord with the self-perceptions of these women. When they appreciated their bound feet, these gentrywomen were, in fact, celebrating three elements crucial to their identities as women: their agency as individuals, their gentility as members of the leisure class, and their handiwork as women. That a pair of nicely shaped small feet represented the triumph of individual willpower and effort was expressed in a common saying: "A plain face is given by heaven, but poorly bound feet are a sign of laziness."[79] It was, in fact, the most important aspect of a woman's beauty that she could have control over.

In the seventeenth century, a pair of bound feet was also a statement of a woman's class background or her privileged upbringing. Hence it was said that the extraordinary courtesan Liu Rushi, who wore the robe of a literatus on her first visit to her future husband, Qian Qianyi, made certain that her tiny feet protruded from beneath the robe. Liu also commissioned a famous craftsman to make the soles of her shoes.[80] In so doing, Liu was distinguishing herself from less well groomed prostitutes. Well-appointed small feet were the female equivalent of the mandarin's silk robe and his refined disposition; both were emblems of a privileged class. This sentiment is most evident in a poem by Hu Shilan, a Qing gentry poet from Zhili who fell upon hard times in mid-life and had to make a living as an itinerant teacher. She reminisced:

> Remember those bygone days in the depth of my inner chambers,
> Fragrant pieces of jade adorned my tender skin.
> My little maid stood by me under canopy of flowers,
> So that my tiny shoes wouldn't slip on mosses so green.
> Little did I know that in mid-life I would have to roam around,
> Braving the scorching sun and furious storms.[81]

To Hu, her bound feet were the most graphic reminder of the happiness of her privileged childhood. A pair of well-bound feet adorned by delicate shoes was at once a statement of feminine beauty and class distinction.

Most of the implements needed for footbinding were either made by the women themselves or were tools already in use for the traditional "womanly work." The bound foot itself was women's handiwork. The exchange of embroidered shoes was thus a most fitting ritual marking a central event and defining trait in these women's lives. These women had done the best they could in creating meaning and dignity from within the space allotted to them. To mourn their ignorance or to condemn a system that repressed them without recognizing their pride and satisfaction is to ignore the most essential feature of the women's lives and of the gender system in seventeenth-century China.

Womanly Work: From Necessity to Art

The agility of women in transcending the given limitations of life is most clearly demonstrated by their subtle reinterpretations of the traditional virtue of "womanly work." In the seventeenth century, women's handiwork took on somewhat contradictory new meanings — as art and commodity. With new interpretations infused into each of the Four Virtues, a woman's life acquired new meanings that the continued use of old labels failed to convey. Unlike the overhauling of womanly speech to mean written word or the enlargement of womanly virtue to encompass talent, however, the content of womanly work did not change. Instead, the same chores acquired new subjective meanings for the women involved. Needlework was no longer a woman's only calling; its purpose was no longer to supply family members with garments, shoes, and bedding. Embroidery, in particular, was transmuted into a self-chosen means of expressing individual creativity.[82] This availability of choice, at least for gentry-women, made a world of difference — between the realm of necessity and the realm of freedom.

Ni Renji (1607–85), a virtuous widow from Pujiang, Zhejiang, was one of the many artists instrumental in transforming embroidery from mere traditional women's work to a highly polished art form, admired and collected by men and women. Her embroidered paintings were not only expressions of her inner spirit as an artist but also articulations of the aspirations of other women. As such, they were prized by art collectors and were valorized as her family's most precious cultural capital.[83]

Daughter of a *jinshi*, Ni Renji married Wu Zhiyi, grandson of a famous pirate-subduing general from Yiwu, in 1624. Like her gentry sisters from the same period, Renji owed her sophisticated education to the cultural resources of her family. Renji was widowed two years into her marriage; her perseverance eventually won her a chastity arch in 1673. Like the Tongcheng poet-teacher Fang Weiyi, widowhood in an affluent household provided her the leisure and freedom to develop her skills and vision as artist. Although she had her verse collections published and was eulogized in local histories as a poet and traditional painter, Ni Renji was most noted for paintings made with needle and thread.[84] In a poem, she described her insights into gaining control over her medium:

> The needle has a spirit [*shen*],
> Apart from its outward traces.
> Not fingers nor silk filaments,
> But by a graceful power, a painting is done.[85]

Ni Renji "painted" landscapes, figures, and sutras. Her self-awareness as a woman artist is evident from her subjects and the process of her production. She once embroidered a section from the *Heart Sutra*, a treatise on bodhisattvahood popular among women. In 1649, she embroidered a portrait of the Bodhisattva Guanyin, whom women worshipped as their protector, using the hair of a devotee, née Wu, as thread. Although also practiced by men, copying sutras and painting portraits of Guanyin were common acts of devotion among pious women. Ni turned this routine into a highly personal and expressive form of art, both for her and for her fellow Guanyin devotee.[86]

The weaving of minute strands of hair into an image of Guanyin was a most fitting monument to the birth of a women's culture. It marked Ni's celebration of her skills and talent, her ties with another woman, and their common devotion to a deity who looked after the well-being of womenfolk. Without dropping a stitch, Ni Renji and other artist-embroiderers had turned the virtue of womanly work on its head.

Other women in Ni's time also labored to develop needlework into an art form. For example, both the courtesan-archer Xue Susu and courtesan-turned-concubine Dong Xiaowan (1624–51) were renowned for their artistry.[87] Yet most notable were the dwellers of the Dew Fragrance Garden of Shanghai, the housing compound of the late Ming literatus Gu Mingshi (*jinshi* 1559). For the Gu wives, daughters, and concubines, embroidery was a family tradition and its most valuable cultural capital. Née Miao, concubine of Mingshi's son Huikai, so excelled in the art that she became the founder of a female school of art, the Gu-Family Embroidery (*Guxiu*).[88] Marsha Weidner has written of the seriousness these women brought to their art: "They approached embroidery as members of her husband's social circle did painting, by looking to the ancients and copying famous works of the Song and Yuan dynasties."[89] Han Ximeng, wife of Gu Mingshi's grandson, Shouqian, so respected the Song-Yuan masters that she embroidered a set of eight album leaves modeled after their masterpieces in 1634.

The leading male painters of the day recognized both the skill and artistic judgment of these women. The famous painter Dong Qichang, a teacher of Gu Shouqian, was so impressed by Han Ximeng's album leaves that he inquired from Shouqian the secret of his wife's art. The answer: "In the sharp cold of winter, steamy heat of summer, windy darkness or rainy gloom, [she] does not dare to undertake it, [but] often when the sky is clear, the sun unclouded, the birds happy and the flowers fragrant, she absorbs the vitality of life before her eyes and stitches [it] into fine silk from Suzhou." Dong Qichang was so dazzled that he thought her art "beyond human capability."[90] About twenty embroidered paintings by Han, per-

The art of the Gu Family Embroidery at its finest: the Queen Mother of the West, the highest Daoist goddess, surges through the clouds with her talented attendant in full colors. Some scholars attribute this work to Han Ximeng (*Guoli gugong bowuyuan*, plates 24, 25).

haps the most famous of the Gu family embroidery artists, are still extant in Chinese museums. So sought after were the works of the Gu women that an entire family industry was later established on their labor.[91]

The elevation of embroidery to a respectable art form in the hands of these women has two curious implications for the gender system in the late sixteenth to seventeenth centuries. First, to some extent this quintessential attribute of female virtue was devoid of gender specificity. A number of men, notably scholar-officials skilled in martial arts, took up embroidery as part of the amateur ideal for a gentleman, no different from chess, musical instruments, or painting. One of these masters, Lei Fu (*jinshi* 1616), was a provincial administration commissioner in charge of troop training in Yangzhou. Another wizard, Wan Shouqi (1603–52), was a knight-errant poet and famous hero of the Ming loyalist movement.[92]

The interest of these martial arts and weaponry experts in so-called womanly work is most telling of the lightheartedness with which a certain degree of gender role reversal was regarded. Contrary to the official obsession with boundaries and separate spheres, such playful transgressions were found all over society: men excelling in needlework, women devoted to scholarship and literature, husbands sending their wife off to seek employment, women donning men's robes. Seen in this light, the Ming-Qing gender system was more flexible in practice than what the official ideology would have one believe.

More important than the interest taken by men, the transmutation of needlework into an art has significant implications for the construction of womanhood. In much the same way as the elevation of poetic talent, the development of embroidery-as-art as an attribute of gentry womanhood represents a hollowing out of the original meaning of the Confucian womanly work. It is thus no accident that not only were embroidery artists accomplished poets, they also chose to represent their identities as artist in the form of verse. Literature and art had come to distinguish a woman as much as her morality; cultural education and moral cultivation were firmly established as twin gateways to a new womanhood.

Yet inherent in this process was the divorce of artistic creation from economic production. The hollowing out of womanly work was predicated on a bifurcation of women into economic producers and cultural producers.[93] Only well-to-do women enjoyed the family resources and leisure to embroider paintings for personal edification and religious devotion. Even as needlework was divorced from household production for the gentry artists, it became a means of subsistence for lower-class daughters. Someone had to make the garments, shoes, and bedding for these families, after all. Relying on the services of seamstresses, some housewives shunned needlework altogether.

Hence that observant arbiter of taste Li Yu lamented that many women in his day "pursue only men's skills, and sneer at women's work. They see weaving and sewing as mean labor and consider needle and thread their worst enemies. They would even hire old women and poor daughters to make their three-inch arch shoes for them."[94] In a commercialized economy, the freedom accorded some women to engage in "manly" tasks, most notably scholarship and writing, as well as artistic pursuits, was predicated on the hired hands of lower-class women. Although this book is concerned primarily with the culture of privileged women, the fact that women were more divided by class than they were unified by gender in seventeenth-century China should not be forgotten.

The injection of new meanings into the old Four Virtues of womanly speech, womanly deportment, womanly virtue, and womanly work described in this chapter testifies to the central paradox that characterized the gender system in seventeenth-century China: the resilience of old norms in the face of new socioeconomic realities was possible only with a subtle revamping of the meaning of the normative demands. The strength of the system lies in its adaptability and flexibility; the hollowing out of its traditional precepts, at the same time, can be viewed as a sign of its vulnerability. The glass is half-empty and half-full — the observer's perspective and values alone determine the verdict.

Gentrywomen felt this ambivalence just as keenly. In their eyes, the seventeenth century was at once a time of heightened ideological control and augmented social freedom. Underneath the surface of a revival of familism and popularization of old gender norms lay the gestation of a new womanhood, one more in line with the opportunities offered by the urban society, most notably the widening channels of women's education. This change was almost imperceptible; for this very reason it was most effective in undermining the restrictive old boundaries. The educated women were still at home, but the content of domestic life had changed; they reiterated their allegiance to Four Virtues, but only because they could breathe new meanings into the old labels.

Through these subtle changes in part effected by women themselves, the gender system managed to harness the continued support of the most educated of the womenfolk. To understand more fully the reasons for their satisfaction, we will have to turn to the richness of the women's culture they crafted and the communities of friends they enjoyed.

Part Three

WOMEN'S CULTURE

5

Domestic Communities

MALE AND FEMALE DOMAINS

A S THE PREVIOUS CHAPTERS have made clear, notions of gender distinctions and separate male/female spheres endured in the face of socioeconomic changes. Although the parameters of domesticity and womanhood were enlarged, the deep-seated belief that men and women were constituted differently retained its hold on members of both sexes. It is against this background of the entrenched notion of distinction that a limited practice of gender equalization — companionate marriage — must be understood. It was limited because despite the substantive satisfactions it brought the individuals concerned, it effected no formal changes in the marriage institution, nor did it realign the gender-based division of domestic labor. Ultimately, the romantic image of a "golden couple" merely served to mask the persistence of formal power disparities and functional distinctions between husband and wife in the Chinese family.

By "companionate marriage" I refer to a union between an intellectually compatible couple who treat each other with mutual respect and affection. A focus on individual compatibility and emotional needs, however, was the very concern that the Confucian familial system sought to discourage. Matrimony was never simply an affair of two individuals in imperial China. Husband-wife relationships in Jiangnan gentry households are explicable only against the background of active lineage formation and reconstitution of local communal order. As long as affine alliances remained the linchpin of elite family strategies for local dominance, conjugal bliss came only as a joyful surprise after the fact, one that neither bride nor groom could control.

Although companionate marriages did not effect lasting changes in the area of equalized gender relations, more important developments were brewing in an entirely different arena — intimacies between women within the inner female domain. Under the stricture of separate male/female spheres within the household, conjugal life was at best one of the many constituents of the housewife's emotional and social universe. Female companions, as we will see, were a most conspicuous presence in the inner chambers. Moreover, the presence of a critical mass of educated women in the same neighborhood, together with heightened opportunities for exchanging letters and manuscripts with those from afar, facilitated the proliferation of women's communities in seventeenth-century Jiangnan. Often taking the form of informal poetry clubs, these communities provided an occasion for women from the same or different families to gather for fun or more serious ventures. Thus inhabiting expansionary social spaces, these women were a far cry from the cloistered creatures of official rhetoric.

This chapter examines the content and the context of the domestic existence of gentry wives and daughters in seventeenth-century Jiangnan, both as they viewed it and as we might understand them in the larger context of kinship and marriage alliances. Our story begins with their marital relations and ends with the women's crafting of a culture of their own in step with the rhythm of everyday life. Both the weft and warp of the domestic woman's world — male-female intimacies and exclusive female sociabilities — had a life of their own but they also intersected at significant junctures.

Wanted: An Inner Helpmate

With the rise of women's education and the currency of a new womanhood, connubial relationships became increasingly problematic. Most telling of the enhanced cultural levels of gentry wives was the recurrence of two patterns of conjugal relations — companionate marriage, in which man and wife were compatible, albeit seldom equal; and the "phoenix-crow" dyad, whereby the wife excelled in talent and achievements. Neither represented a new form of marriage, since they were relationships that lasted for the lifetime of the individuals concerned. Moreover, both involved the elevation of a woman's cultural level to a plane equal to or even surpassing that of her husband; the man was not called upon to take charge of the kitchen or the loom. As such, these unconventional marital relations exposed the asymmetry in the old gender system without changing it.

The popularity of companionate marriage in seventeenth-century Jiangnan was, ironically, rooted in a heightened gender-based division of domestic labor. The duties of a housewife in an elite household, if taken seriously, were taxing and time-consuming. Companionate marriage brought no change in the multiple roles that a domestic woman was to assume — model mother, filial daughter-in-law, and industrious household manager. The cultural skills required to perform these tasks satisfactorily, however, became more complicated. Hence the popularity of household almanacs discussed in Chapter 1, guidebooks that combined practical and moral instructions to make the housewife's chores more manageable.

For a landowning family, managing the household budget was a considerable feat: records had to be kept, rents collected, and a large array of expenditures paid out.[1] Counting domestic servants, the size of a household could easily reach 20 or 30 people; the housewife's traditional calling of running the kitchen could be a logistical nightmare. In addition, it was increasingly common for the gentry mother not only to supervise but to personally provide an elementary education to her children. It thus became amply clear that without at least rudimentary literacy and arithmetic skills, a bride could hardly fulfill her traditional roles adequately. This recognition, combined with growing attention to matters of the heart inspired by the cult of *qing*, prompted a new ideal of the respectable housewife: an inner helpmeet who was at once an adept manager and her husband's soul mate. She was the domestic incarnation of the new woman — talented, virtuous, and beautiful.

Befitting the currency of women's education and valorization of female talent, the most salient symbol of this conjugal relationship was the practice of husband and wife jointly composing or exchanging verses in the same rhyme scale, known in Chinese as "singing in harmony" (*changhe*). Also popular between friends of the same sex, this exchange epitomizes the two essential features of companionate marriage: the pride of place given to personal resonance, and female talent as a limited gender leveler.

Emotional and artistic resonance had long been what men sought in the company of courtesans. The desirability of companionate wives in the marriage market supplemented, instead of displacing, the demand for soul mates in the pleasure quarters. Even as the late Ming flowering of courtesan culture (see Chapter 7) promoted the talented beauty ideal both within and without domesticity, the dynamics of urban families also rendered it possible, indeed desirable, to have cultured wives.

Shi Chengjin, a Yangzhou writer and publisher of popular and didactic literature, highlighted the appeal of educated brides in his marital choice. Since Shi's wife, née Zhou (1674–1732), was fifteen years his junior, she was probably a second wife. As a result, he appeared to be free to make his own selection. Shi had heard of her attractions even before they met: "She was well known throughout our neighborhood. . . . Studied with a tutor at six [*sui*]; she could recite whatever she read. When she was about thirteen to fourteen [*sui*], she already acted like an adult, being restrained in her words and laughter." Most important of all was her reputation for

intelligence: "Besides womanly work, she was also proficient in the Classics, literature, calligraphy, and arithmetic; choice verses poured from her mouth. Everybody praised her as a talented girl [*cainü*]. I heard about her and asked for her hand." They married when she was fifteen.[2]

From this short description one can imagine the kind of attention that an educated girl of marriageable age received in urban neighborhood gossip. Lady Zhou's reputation for precocity turned out to be no exaggeration. Mother of two sons and three daughters, she served her in-laws, educated the children, took charge of Shi's family estate, and handled all domestic financial transactions. With her at the helm of household, Shi could devote his energy to his writing and publishing ventures. Calling her a "helpmeet" (*neizhu*), "good companion" (*liangban*), and "fairest mate" (*jia'ou*), Shi credited her with his career success. In his writing, Shi consulted her whenever an issue related to matters in the female quarters arose. "I defer to her opinion," he said. Their nuptial life of over four decades was documented, in the typical fashion of the day, by verses they exchanged. Shi preserved them as cherished possessions at the time of her death, but apparently they were never published.[3]

The companionate relationship between Shi and Zhou was predicated on her education, which rendered her an intellectual companion and effective household manager. Yet no matter how much singing in harmony there was at home, she remained an *inner* helpmate and was never called upon to partake in his world in a public capacity. The grateful husband was no doubt sincere in the rhetoric of gender equalization, expressed in such terms as "good companion" and "fairest mate." Yet in the end companionate marriage served to reinforce the doctrine of separate spheres. Similarly, the emphasis on compatibility between husband and wife had the ironic effect of accentuating the demarcation of gender roles in family and society.

Companionate Marriage: A Literary Ideal

The cult of *qing*, the publishing boom, women's education, and the "talent-virtue-beauty" ideal all contributed to the currency of companionate marriages in seventeenth-century Jiangnan. Although many real-life couples did not live happily ever after, the pages of Ming-Qing novels and dramas were inundated with romantic and idealized portrayals of

---

(*Opposite*) The romantic ideal of a companionate couple: in private quarters surrounded by a lush garden, books, flower arrangements, and incense, the couple enjoys emotional intimacy and intellectual resonance (Wang Zhideng, ed., *Wusao ji*. Preface dated 1614; reprinted — Chang Bide, p. 160).

love matches. The new ideal woman had to be paired off with a scholar who understood her needs and who could hold his own in a poetry contest with her. In the same way that girls regarded the enchanting Du Liniang as their alter ego, romance and conjugal bliss had also become the aspirations of respectable female readers.

Portrayals of companionate marriage in Ming-Qing literature are too numerous to be recounted here, but one poignant scene from Li Yu's play *Ideal Love Matches* (*Yizhong yuan*) conveys the essential element of the romantic ideal in novels and dramas: female literary talent as an equalizer in conjugal relations. Although the plot is fictional, all four protagonists in this play were famous personalities in the actual artistic and literary world. In the play, two eminent late Ming literati, Dong Qichang and Chen Jiru, ended up marrying the female forgers of their paintings. The two women, Lin Tiansu and Yang Yunyou, were famous painters in real life, whose social relations among the artistic community in Hangzhou will be discussed in Chapter 7. The play contains a scene in which Lin, disguised as a man, goes through a fake wedding with Yang.

"He" says to the bride: "My dear, you and I are true friends sharing resonance through literature [*wenzi zhiji*], not just your ordinary couple off the street. We should cut through the theatrics of the wedding ceremony and get to the heart of it. Share a few drinks; have a little intimate chat—don't be shy." The author summed up the case: "Talent seals a marriage; dexterity works as matchmaker [*cai zuohe, ji weimei*]."

At this point, Huang Yuanjie, invited by Li Yu to comment on the play, could hardly contain her excitement. Allegedly an ugly woman, Huang, as we recall, married a crow. Her marginal comments on these lines are at once her endorsement of Li Yu's craft and the ideal love match itself: "I have never heard of such nuptial scenes before. The plot development is innovative and the lyrics, enticing. What a delight it is to watch a drama of this sort!"[4]

Playwrights and novelists did not invent the romantic ideal of a scholarly husband paired with a cultured wife. The literary images in vogue in the seventeenth century were derivatives of a prototype featuring the famous Song poet Li Qingzhao (b. 1084) and her husband Zhao Mingcheng, a specialist on inscriptions on ancient stone and bronze wares. The picture of their domestic bliss, as the two immersed themselves in collections of books and art objects, was more touching than fiction because of its reality. The disintegration of their family fortunes due to the fall of the Northern Song dynasty added to the allure of these tender moments described by Li, in a famous preface she wrote for his work:

We had the finest paper and the most complete collection of paintings and calligraphy in our house. After dinner, we would retreat to our Guilai Hall, heat up water for tea, and finger through piles of books and histories. [We had a little contest] — name an event, then name the book title, chapter, page, line. The winner can have a sip of tea as reward. When both were right, we lifted up our cups and broke into laughter; sometimes [we got so excited that] the tea spilled all over our laps.[5]

Li Qingzhao and Zhao Mingcheng, perhaps the most famous companionate couple in Chinese history, continued to inspire less fortunate women in the seventeenth century. Wu Bai (d. 1660), a Hangzhou woman widowed at eighteen without consummating her marriage, vicariously basked in marital bliss by reading about the couple's domestic intimacies. In a letter, Wu told her sister of the pleasure she derived from reciting the above account by Li Qingzhao: "It makes the flower of my heart blossom and cleanses my lungs and intestines."[6]

In presenting marriage as a matter of individual compatibility and happiness, the romantic literary image of the companionate couple promised hope to girls whose future was still an unknown and solace to wives whose fantasies were irrevocably dashed. But this exclusive focus on the personal dimension masked a basic truth about marriage as far as elite families were concerned: as the linchpin of alliance building, it was hardly a matter of individual choice. In fact, this lack of control was the very factor that made the literary ideal of romantic love and companionate marriage so appealing. The tragedy of Xiaoqing, who could not choose her mate, must not have been too far from the minds of women who fantasized about a different destiny.

Martyrs of Love

The pervasiveness of this romantic connubial ideal, one facet of the cult of *qing*, suggests a new reading of the chaste widow cult. In the eyes of local officials and the state, widows who committed suicide exemplified sacrificial loyalty, a key virtue that upheld the Confucian social and gender hierarchy. An alternative reading, plausible in some cases, is that these women were martyrs of love, following their husbands to the grave to honor nuptial vows or memories of a romance that could never be replicated.

The validity of this alternative reading hinges on personal motives, a dimension that is intentionally omitted from the hagiographic literature. If we penetrate the heavy didactic rhetoric, however, the emotional intensity of some suicide accounts is striking and the passionate devotion between husband and wife unmistakable. It is perhaps no accident that the Ming-Qing period, a time when love suicides were all the rage in novels and dramas, also witnessed the height of a chaste widow cult.[7] Moreover, the sporadic but revealing appearances in local histories, poetry anthologies, and even genealogies of the love-crazed widow devastated by her husband's death suggest that love suicides occurred in real life as well as in fiction.

For example, a prefectural gazetteer of Suzhou preserves the story of Qin Shu, widow of a certain He Shugao. Qin, a late Ming woman, was canonized by Censor Qi Biaojia as "Virtuous Martyr of the Inner Chambers" (*guizhong yilie*). On their nuptial night, Qin and He "sang in harmony," each composing poems in 25 rhymes. They also made an explicit vow using an antique mirror that they would die together. Although details of their domestic life are not known, such nuptial ritual is a mimicry of the ideal of companionate couple taken directly from dramas and novels.

In 1642, He died in an epidemic. Qin broke the mirror into two, buried one half with He and wore the other half on her body. Before she starved herself to death, she composed this verse:

> Our love is constant in life as in death,
> My heart now longs for the other world.
> Vowing to be wedded for three lives,
> We are reunited today with the mirror.[8]

Although Qin was likely to have subscribed to the Confucian dictum of "a good woman does not serve two husbands," she chose to couch her suicide strictly in terms of love, codified in a private pledge known only to the couple.

The official promoters of the Confucian creed sanctioned wifely devotion, a prerequisite for the virtue of chastity. The sheer emotional intensity of devotion exhibited by some wives, so fixated on conjugal concerns, could undermine the very intent of the moral system, however. For the widow, this tension between human emotions and the moral imperative was no less relevant; they were equally potent forces propelling her to her fateful decision. In another example of a love-crazed widow, the persuasive mix of superstition, Confucian morality, and the cult of love is most evident: Wang Yuezhuang (1521–38), a woman from Haiyan, a county in Jiaxing, Zhejiang, married Xiang Sheng at the tender age of fifteen. Xiang died in a year, leaving her a handkerchief on his deathbed while saying: "Don't forget me. Seeing this will be like having me around."

Wang was devastated. She moved her bed next to his coffin and resisted her mother-in-law's pressure to remarry. Gazing into a mirror, she murmured: "People say that a woman with a long neck will bring down three husbands. How dare I marry again, with this long neck?" Repeatedly she tried to hang herself, but was saved every time. For a year she did not touch meat and tried to alleviate her grief by busying herself with needlework. One day she was so overcome by loneliness that she composed this poem:

> A solitary lamp lighting an empty chamber in vain,
> Every cricket echo from the four walls breaks my heart.
> Yet I have no complaint for the sorrow I see,
> having burned deadly incense in my past life.

Blaming her lost love on bad karma, she made up her mind to die. Having bathed and changed her clothes, she composed a poem outlining her resolution. She then succeeded in hanging herself, clinching her husband's kerchief in one hand.[9]

This alternative explanation for widow suicide, that of heartfelt love for a deceased husband, does not detract from the persuasion of moral teachings exhorting widows to remain chaste. In fact, the prevalent ideal of the companionate couple could well be an impetus for the chaste widow cult. Without a cult of conjugal love, it would be harder to explain the apparent enthusiasm with which some widows embraced an ideology that was predicated on the denial of their emotional and sexual needs.

Golden Boy and Jade Maiden: Personal Intimacy

Since gentrywomen were the first beneficiaries of education, they figured most prominently in the flood of accounts of golden couples from seventeenth-century Jiangnan. Although we use "companionate couple" to describe them, the term carries a different nuance in its Chinese context. The English usage of "companionate marriage" presumes marriage to be a private matter between two individuals. In Chinese, the label "golden boy–jade maiden" (*jintong yunü*) is a tribute not only to the couple's individual resonance but also to the comparable status of their families. Both the individual subjective and the familial objective dimensions are important to our understanding of the dynamics between a companionate couple. This section focuses on the emotional life and domestic division of labor of one such couple; the larger context of family strategies is treated in the next section.

Shen Yixiu (1590–1635) and Ye Shaoyuan (1589–1648), parents of the teenage poet Ye Xiaoluan and eleven other children, were just such a perfect match.[10] Both hailing from distinguished families in Wujiang, Shen and Ye were also compatible at the individual level, sharing interests in poetry, Buddhism, and children. Born into a family of scholars and dramatists, Shen was taught reading and writing when she was three or four by some "women in the family," probably her aunts. Henceforth Shen pursued her studies with keen interest, devouring volumes of the Classics and histories.[11] This early love of reading developed into a lifelong devotion to poetry writing; her collected works contain more than 700 poems documenting every facet of her domestic and emotional life.[12] Besides keeping up with her interest in history, Shen also delved into Sanskrit sutras later in life. Such well-groomed intelligence rendered Yixiu an engaging wife and an excellent mother-teacher.

For his part, Ye followed a conventional albeit undistinguished scholar-official career, gaining the *jinshi* degree in 1625 at the age of 36. He served briefly as instructor in the Nanjing military school (1627) and in the National University in Beijing (1628), followed by two years as a secretary in the Ministry of Works (1628–30). Disenchanted by the rampant corruption of public life, Ye took leave and returned to Wujiang in 1631, where he enjoyed a brief year of conjugal bliss while discharging his duties as a local gentry. A series of illnesses plagued the family, however, claiming the lives of two daughters, two sons, his mother, and, finally, Yixiu in 1635. Much of Ye's writing—prose, verse, and journal—mentioned his public life only in passing; nor did he preserve letters, epitaphs, or elegies he wrote as an official. Instead, his extant writings are in the main records of the domestic concerns he shared with his wife and children, graphic illustrations of the return to private life that characterized this period.[13]

Although their relationship later warmed up, Yixiu found little consolation from Ye Shaoyuan when she first entered his house. The young bride seldom returned to her maternal family, although they lived nearby in the same county, for she had no one to return to. Her mother had already died, her father was often away, and the aunt who raised her had left.[14] Like almost every young bride, Yixiu started as a lonesome stranger in her new home.

Not only was Shaoyuan preoccupied with his studies, he was often away from home. Soon after the wedding banquet, Shaoyuan returned to the house of his adopted father, Yuan Huang, to concentrate on his studies. In the six years that followed, before he started his examination circuit at Kunshan, he was either studying in the homes of mentors and friends or at home with his cousin. Even during the odd months when he did stay home, Shaoyuan was not allowed to sleep in Yixiu's chambers without explicit permission from his mother; mostly he spent the night in his study. Their first child, a daughter, was not born until five years after the wedding.[15]

Yixiu's relationship with her mother-in-law, née Feng, was stormy at times. Yixiu's brother Shen Zizheng described Madame Feng as a difficult woman whom Yixiu had to serve with self-restraint and a low voice. Even Ye concurred that his mother demanded that Yixiu wait upon her all the time. A widowed mother with an only son, Madame Feng guarded her son's studies with a vengeance. Fearing that Yixiu's hobby, poetry writing, would distract her from household duties and hinder Shaoyuan's examination success, Madame Feng forbade Yixiu to write, which drove her to tears late at night. Judging from the size of Yixiu's collection, however, this ban must have been rescinded later. The young couple found room to share brief moments of intimacy, as she sat by him and copied his examination essays in her elegant hand.[16]

The frequent absence of the degree aspirant did not improve with the launching of his bureaucratic career. Yixiu followed Shaoyuan briefly to Nanjing for his new post, but stayed home with the children when he left for the capital. Although the couple spent only sporadic time together until his early retirement in 1631, Shen's affection for Ye can be gleaned from the tenderness she expressed in poems she wrote to send him off to the examinations and, later, on official duties (and, perhaps, from the large number of children she happily bore). Each of these poems is a snapshot of their growing intimacy. In 1628, for example, Shaoyuan left for Beijing to take up a post, Yixiu pitied him for toiling too much. On another occasion, one autumn day Yixiu was overwhelmed by loneliness when a letter she was expecting from Shaoyuan in Beijing did not arrive; when it did arrive with a verse, Yixiu crafted responses in the same rhyme scheme. On a stormy night, Yixiu could not sleep; so she rose to sew a robe for Shaoyuan while composing four poems expressing her contentment.[17]

Ye Shaoyuan more than reciprocated his wife's affection. Soon after Shen's death at age 46, Ye expressed his love in explicit terms as he crafted an elegy that was, unlike conventional works in the genre, sentimental and poignant: "There are problems that one cannot discuss with friends, only with one's wife. Now I walk into the room and there is nobody to talk to." He missed Yixiu, for "by propriety we were man and wife; in intimacy we were also friends."[18] Only a few months after Yixiu's death, Shaoyuan had already crafted over 120 poems dedicated to her memory.[19]

Ye Shaoyuan's memory of his connubial life was full of sexual innuendoes: "*Qing* is what life is all about. As a couple gets intimate, their love grows out of the emotions they share. When the moon shines into the golden canopy, one would not see a lone husband; when a jade hairpin drops onto the pillow, one seldom finds the wife alone." Sexual pleasure was, in turn, reinforced by intellectual companionship. Ye went on: "You were my companion in moonlight parties; a close friend in flower festivals. We delighted in the art of gardening and amused ourselves by discussing history. Ours was definitely not a mismatch."[20] To honor the memory of Yixiu, Ye Shaoyuan never remarried.

To her husband, the enchantment of Yixiu stemmed from her blend of talent, beauty, and virtue — the new ideal woman — as discussed in the preceding chapter. Shaoyuan repeatedly compared himself to Xun Feng-qian, who, as we have seen, was chastised by orthodox historians for his emotional attachment to his wife. To Shaoyuan, however, Xun was a friend who alone understood his profound loss.[21] A spirit medium told Ye that in a past life he had been the Song poet Qin Guan (1049–1100), famous for his love lyrics, and that Yixiu was the reincarnation of Qin's wife.[22] This revelation of the legendary ancestry of their romance comforted Shaoyuan, who apparently believed in it with all sincerity. Conjugal love, expressed in harmony of poetic talents, was elevated into a principle that transcended the life and death of individuals.

The compatibility of Ye Shaoyuan and Shen Yixiu shows that companionate marriage embodied two contrasting implications for male-female interactions. Whereas the notion of inner helpmate accentuated the division between his and her domains, husband-wife intimacy mitigated against this separation. Later, we will also see that as far as the wife was concerned, her identity as woman was forged, on the one hand, *despite* such mediations and, on the other, *because of* the currency of notions of compatibility between the two sexes.[23]

Gendered Division of Household Responsibilities

Despite their intellectual and emotional compatibility, husband and wife assumed divergent household responsibilities. In Yixiu's case, the Confucian ideal of separate spheres was a given fact of life mandated by her husband's public career; a scholar-official simply had agendas other than remaining at home and taking care of domestic chores. Ye Shaoyuan's year-by-year journal shows that for the twenty years between his marriage and the attainment of the metropolitan degree, he sojourned in the residences of senior scholars five times, for durations of at least several months; and he traveled to Kunshan, Jiangyin, and Nanjing to take the examinations twelve times, each trip lasting from two weeks to three months. For the trip to the capital for the metropolitan examination, he was away from home for seven months.[24]

Although he delighted in coaching his children as his schedule permitted, Ye Shaoyuan's main domestic responsibility appears to have been the arrangement of his daughters' marriages; his journal records the names of friends who approached him for the hand of each of his four daughters, which he personally granted.[25] Betrothal agreement, a most crucial family alliance strategy, was too rife with public significance to be left in women's hands, although mothers often served consultative roles. In contrast to the attention he gave to his daughters, Ye made no mention of the betrothal of his sons.

Yixiu's domestic tasks included educating the children, which she attended to personally, and managing the domestic treasury. Although details of household finances are scarce, Yixiu clearly wielded the "power of the key" to the domestic bursary after she had passed the young bride stage. Two years after their marriage, Shaoyuan wanted to help a close friend who was in danger of losing the roof above his head. Not daring to ask his mother, he consulted with Yixiu in private, who sold part of her dowry for 40 ounces of silver to help defray the cost of a house.[26] This incident shows that Shaoyuan's mother was then still in charge, and that Yixiu brought a sizable dowry with her, the usual humble disclaimer notwithstanding.

Whatever was left seemed to have dissipated through the years. Two later references to Yixiu's selling her dowry, couched in conventional terms of "jewelry and garments," were recorded in Shaoyuan's journal: In 1626, for 40 ounces; again in 1629, for 27 ounces.[27] Upon Yixiu's death, Shaoyuan opened the bursar's chest, not knowing how much was there, for "all monetary transactions were being handled by my wife." He found piles of pawnshop receipts mixed with bundles of poems; the household had no cash other than spare change.[28]

The housewife's financial prerogatives were limited to the household level, the "inner" in relative terms; Ye Shaoyuan handled dealings, more appropriately called disputes, with the other units of the family and with the public world at large. The Yes were a prominent landowning family, but Shaoyuan belonged to a minor branch, weakened all the more by his father's untimely death. Members of the primary branch (*zhangfang*), whom Shaoyuan had no qualms in calling a "ruthless clan, fierce lineage" (*qiangzong hanzu*), were relentless in their aggrandizement. In 1601, when Shaoyuan was twelve and barely two years after his father's death, these clansmen plotted to encroach upon the weaker branch's property. Ye's adopted father, Yuan Huang, came to their defense, but encountered malicious slander. The father of Shaoyuan's then-fiancée Yixiu, although commanding local respect, was away from home. Finally, the local magistrate intervened and saved Shaoyuan's branch from bankruptcy.[29]

Another dispute flared up in 1623, shortly before Shaoyuan attained his metropolitan degree. Clansmen from the primary branch criticized Shaoyuan for sparing expenses on the secondary burial site of an elder couple in the family; although Shaoyuan was backed by many allies, the dispute highlighted his own precarious position both within and without the family.[30]

Besides his own clansmen, Shaoyuan had his share of troubles with tenants. In 1620, he confronted an old tenant who defaulted on his rent payment on a plot of land that the Yes had long owned. The tenant, according to Ye, turned the case around and accused Shaoyuan of swallowing his family property, a common grievance in the Yangzi Delta. The magistrate who took up the case blackmailed Ye, trying to squeeze a large bribe out of him. A prominent local gentry, former Grand Secretary Zhou Daodeng (d. 1632/33), interceded on Ye's behalf and rescued him.[31]

Hence Shaoyuan and Yixiu formally observed the female : inner / male : outer division of labor. Although mitigated in practice by informal consultations, this distinction between male and female responsibilities and the frequent physical absence of the husband constituted basic facts in the gentry wife's emotional life. As a result, relationships with other women — daughters, cousins, friends — figured prominently in her everyday existence, partly by necessity. As we will see, these women turned their social isolation from men into a celebration of women's culture. For all its relative isolation and separation, however, a woman's world was never completely independent from that of men. In shaping her outlook and in providing a window to the world at large, husband and male kinsmen played a crucial role in a woman's emotional and social life. Although husband-wife intimacy was stigmatized by the Confucian family, a view internalized by Yixiu's mother-in-law, its paramount importance to the individuals concerned is amply clear in the story of Shaoyuan and Yixiu.

Family Alliances: Adoption and Marriage

The currency of the golden boy–jade maiden ideal highlights the increasing attention paid to female talent in bride selection among Jiangnan gentry families. Its implication for individual happiness, however, is doubtful indeed, especially when seen against the larger context of alliances between elite families. Ye and Shen were merely lucky that their family's choice turned out to be someone they could learn to love.

The betrothal pact between Shaoyuan and Yixiu, sealed when he was nine and she a year younger, was a small cog in a long-standing alliance between two of the five most distinguished Wujiang families.[32] The Yes had multiplied and prospered on the northern shore of Lake Fen in the southern part of Wujiang, south of Suzhou city, since the fourteenth century. Locals nicknamed the strip of land by the lake where the main division (pai) congregated the Ye Family Belt (Yejia dai).[33] Ye Shaoyuan's immediate family alone had produced four successive generations of jinshi-ranked officials before him. Although not the best endowed branch, as we have seen, Shaoyuan's father passed onto him over 1,000 mu of land, which later dwindled to less than 200 in Shaoyuan's hands.[34]

To maintain their local prominence, the Yes cast their nets widely in marriage and adoption alliances. Shaoyuan's father, a jinshi, married a daughter of the Feng family from Pinghu, a county in Jiaxing prefecture,

Zhejiang province, over 100 *li* away. The benefit of long-distance affinal ties was evident in 1608, when incessant rains for four months washed out much of the year's harvest in Wujiang. A sister of Shaoyuan's mother sent the Ye kinsmen 50 *shi* of relief grain.[35]

The Yes were particularly close to the Yuans, notables in Jiashan, Zhejiang, on the opposite shore of Lake Fen. The provincial boundary did not deter personal friendship and affinal ties — the two families lived only fifteen *li* apart in actual distance. When Shaoyuan was four months old, he was adopted out to Yuan Huang after a brief illness as a talismanic measure. Yuan, a scholar famous as the popularizer of ledgers of merit and demerit, was a longtime friend of Shaoyuan's father, the two having studied together and captured the *jinshi* degree in the same year.[36] When Shaoyuan was three, Yuan Huang was sent to Korea as a military councillor; Shaoyuan then moved back to Jiashan with Yuan's wife. He returned to the Ye family after his betrothal agreement with Shen Yixiu, upon which he received the name "Shaoyuan," meaning "continuing the Yuan tradition," from his father by birth.[37] Ye Shaoyuan remained close to Yuan Huang's son, Tianqi (1581–1627); the two studied together and passed the metropolitan examination the same year.[38] The auspicious friendship between their fathers was re-enacted 40 years later.

When Ye Shaoyuan's mother suggested that he be adopted out as an apotropaic measure, she mentioned that such was the custom of Suzhou. Superstition aside, short-term adoption also created lasting family alliances with ritualistic and economic consequences. Although Ye Shaoyuan eventually returned to his paternal home without changing his family name, he called himself Yuan's "male heir" (*si'nan*) in a work by Yuan he helped edit.[39] Upon the death of his mother, Yuan Tianqi insisted that Shaoyuan, his adopted brother, be given 100 *mu* of land from the family holdings, for they had incurred a debt of several hundred ounces in gifts from Shaoyuan's mother. Shaoyuan declined on the pretext that as someone with a different surname, he could not inherit the Yuan family fortune.[40] Whatever the outcome of the negotiation, fictive kinship legitimated a limited transfer of family property, couched in terms of gifts.

Adoption for the more conventional purpose of continuing the family line is also evident in the Ye family. The second son of Shaoyuan and Yixiu, who died in 1635 without an heir and whose fiancée was later canonized as a chaste widow, posthumously adopted a son of his brother's. Since this officially designated heir (*sizi*) was also a Ye, a name change was not necessary.[41] But even changes of surname could in some cases be reversed in the next generation. One of Shaoyuan's cousins, descendant of the same grandfather, changed his name when adopted out to the Wus, another prominent Wujiang family. His son, however, reverted to Ye.[42]

Examples of short-term adoptions without name changes can also be found in the Shen family. Yixiu's brother Zinan was raised by a Shen elder in his grandfather's generation.[43] Adoption appears to be a strategy that was widely used, and flexibly, among the Wujiang elite families to supplement marriage alliances, or simply to enhance a son's educational opportunities.

Ye Shaoyuan's allegiances make it amply clear that for a gentryman, kinship and friendship ties, whatever their emotional meaning for the individual concerned, were first and foremost integral elements of the family's strategy to protect and perpetuate itself. The same was all the more true for connubial ties.

Similar to the Yes, the Shens were a longtime Wujiang gentry family, with four generations of *jinshi* before Yixiu's. Yixiu's father, a vice commissioner in Shandong, was one of three sons who captured the highest metropolitan degree. Literature was a particularly important form of cultural capital for the family; Yixiu's uncle was the famous dramatist Shen Jing (1553–1610), founder of the Wujiang school of drama. Considered an equal, albeit a rival, of Tang Xianzu by their contemporaries, Shen Jing counted among his many students the novelist Feng Menglong. Six younger brothers of Yixiu achieved literary fame in their own right. One of them, Shen Zizheng (1591–1641), whom Yixiu was particularly close to, was hailed as the successor to Shen Jing. All six brothers were mentioned in local gazetteers.[44] In the eyes of local historians, a companionate marriage was most appropriate indeed between these two illustrious families.

Ye Shaoyuan and Shen Yixiu served both families well by virtue of the large number of children they raised, allowing diversified alliance-building. Yet they did not woo such other Wujiang notables as the Wu, Zhou, Pan, Pang, and another, unrelated Shen lineage, all of whom had marital ties with the larger Ye or Shen families.[45] Instead, Shaoyuan married his sons and daughters either to children of his friends or descendants of Yixiu's own family. Their eldest daughter, Wanwan (1610–33), was promised to Yuan Tianqi's third son soon after she was born, capping an already close Yuan-Ye relationship forged by two generations of *tongxue* (those who studied under the same scholar), *tongnian* (those who passed the examination in the same year), and adoptive kinship ties. A second daughter, Xiaowan (1613–ca. 1660), married a grandson of Shen Jing, her maternal cousin, in another Shen-Ye union.[46] The third son of Shaoyuan and Yixiu married a daughter of Yixiu's brother, perpetuating the Ye-Shen union. Marriages between maternal cousins, within the "five mourning grades" (*wufu*) of close relatives, appear to have been customary.[47]

Male adoption and marriage alliance were the two foremost means used by the gentry families of Wujiang to perpetuate their local status.

Their importance to these families can be gleaned from the involvement of the male household heads in such decisions. From this perspective, friendship, kinship, and marital ties were instruments that served the interest of the family as a corporate unit. The popularity of companionate marriages signified the heightened attention paid to the bride's educational level at a time when local elite families were jockeying for dominance in an increasingly competitive environment.

Unhappy Endings

The misfortune that befell the eldest daughter of Shaoyuan and Yixiu, Ye Wanwan, was a warning to those who idealized companionate marriage as personal romance without due attention to the familial context. Completely ignored by her husband for seven years, Wanwan was so distressed that she died prematurely at the age of 22. When Shaoyuan betrothed her to the third son of Yuan Tianqi, his best friend, he thought it a match made in heaven. "You were our first-born daughter; we loved you more than a boy," he recalled. Even Shaoyuan's mother, who waited for five years for her first grandchild, was delighted. Both she and Yixiu would wake up to tend her at night at her slightest stir.

Within one year of Wanwan's birth, Yuan Tianqi came with a betrothal request, which Ye granted. "As the proverb goes, 'two families intimate for generations are brought closer by a betrothal [*shizhi qiya, fudi Pan-Yang*].'" He had in mind the familial definition of companionate marriage, assuming that Wanwan's best interest was served by such an auspicious union.[48] In terms of history and prestige, the Yes were a more prominent local lineage. The Yuans, a relatively marginal elite family lacking in civil service degrees, were in a sense "marrying up," although they apparently were wealthier. Yuan Huang and Tianqi were the only *jinshi* in their respective generations. When Ye Shaoyuan mourned Yuan Tianqi's untimely death in 1627, he lamented that "your family is on the verge of full-blown prosperity, but suddenly a feeling of exhaustion creeps in."[49] At the time of the matrimonial promise, however, the Yes' established name and the Yuans' ascending fortune seemed most compatible.

The betrothal was much celebrated in the local communities, as Ye recalled: "Everybody boasted of your [Wanwan's] prosperity and was envious of your good fortunes."[50] The optimism was based on more than superstition. With the history of the two families' intimacy dating back to her grandfather's generation, Wanwan was all the more likely to be mother of a prosperous household blessed with successful husband and sons.

Wanwan's good fortune turned into a mockery as her betrothed took

no interest in her. At Yuan Tianqi's incessant request, the wedding ceremony took place in 1626, when Yuan was posted as county magistrate in
faraway Gaoyao, Guangdong province. One year later, Wanwan was to
travel with the young Yuan to the south to be united with his father. Before
they even left the borders of Zhejiang, he became homesick and turned
back. Shaoyuan chided: "Does he have no feelings for his parents?"[51] This
is the only specific mentioning of the husband's misdeeds in Wanwan's
lifetime, for Shaoyuan was not disposed to air dirty laundry implicating
his best friend, nor would Wanwan and Yixiu want to embarrass Shaoyuan.[52] Shaoyuan regretted that an ideal match turned sour but blamed it
on fate and bad geomancy.[53]

Shaoyuan called Wanwan's seven years with Yuan an "empty marriage," which nibbled at her health and spirit. She, too, once fantasized
about romance and conjugal bliss. Her unrequited love is conveyed in
"Thoughts on Viewing Spring Flowers":

> Many lament the passing of spring;
> Many await its return with their loved ones.
> The passing, the return, I am indifferent,
> My heart tied in knots to no benefit.
> I can't ask the flowers about my sorrow,
> Crying alone on the garden steps.
> The god of spring lets his flowers burst into flames,
> This god, his passion is too hot.
> But the one who views the flowers,
> Her perfume stays as pure as ice crystals.[54]

During her seven years of marriage, especially after 1628, Wanwan
often returned home to seek solace from her mother and sisters. In one of
their bed chambers, the three sisters would stay up all night, fantasizing
about buying a mountain and retiring as hermits. Wanwan apparently
was obsessed with the plan and would break into tears whenever she was
reminded that she had no means of implementing it. No matter how
unrealistic, her "mountain addiction" provided a modicum of hope to an
otherwise bleak life, hence her mother and sisters were only too happy to
indulge her.[55] This close contact maintained by mother and daughters and
the emotional support they provided each other were important elements
in a woman's domestic life and the germ of the women's culture discussed
below.

Witnessing firsthand their sister's unhappy marriage must have been
instructive to Xiaowan and Xiaoluan. The perils of an arranged marriage
that did not work were crystal clear to these teenage girls, a sobering
contrast to the romantic ideal purveyed in such dramas as *The Peony*

Pavilion, which the sisters loved to read. Unlike Du Liniang, gentry girls like them could not choose their prince at will. Influenced by her sister, Xiaowan's own disillusionment with marriage can be gleaned from her autobiographical drama, *Dream of the Mandarin Ducks* (*Yuanyang meng*). Written when Xiaowan was 23, four years after the deaths of Xiaoluan and Wanwan, the Northern-style drama featured herself and her two sisters. The "mandarin ducks" in the title does not allude to romance between man and woman, as its usage usually connotes, but refers to a poem attributed to the Han general Su Wu, bidding farewell to his brother: "We used to be as close as a pair of mandarin ducks, / Now we drift as far apart as the Shen and Shang stars."[56] Instead of mourning the elusiveness of romance, the playwright focused instead on the ethereal love between siblings.

Ye Xiaowan cast the three intimate sisters as sworn brothers, none of them married. In a blissful encounter, the three indulge in wine, poetry, and philosophy, sharing aspirations of becoming recluses. After the sudden death of the youngest brother, the eldest also dies of grief. The author's alter ego, Hui Baifang, dreams that the departed are reborn as Daoist immortals and seeks enlightenment from the Daoist master Lü Chunyang. Lü says to him: "You think you had a dream, as if the rest of the time you were not in a dream." Thus awakened to life's illusory nature, Hui too becomes an immortal. In the Daoist magical mountain of Zhongnan, the three brothers are ultimately reunited.[57]

To the extent that this drama is autobiographical, it provides a window on Xiaowan's sentiments. Although couched in Daoist terms of detachment, evinced by the obvious reference to Wanwan's "mountain addiction," the drama is in fact a celebration of the love that united the three Ye sisters in real life, a *qing* that transcends life and death. Xiaowan's decision to cast them as males could be a veiled statement of her dissatisfaction with the lot of women, particularly their lack of control over their marital destiny. It is noteworthy that the brothers' freedom from conjugal duties not only deepens their love for each other but is also a prerequisite for their immortality. Read against the stark reality of her sister's unhappy marriage, Ye Xiaowan's play can be taken as a woman's renunciation of marriage in favor of sibling solidarity and religious deliverance.[58]

Domestic Religion

Xiaowan's interest in Daoism and Chan Buddhism was a family tradition. Religious devotion and dream interpretation were dominant motifs in Yixiu's rapport with her daughters. One day late in 1632, when Wanwan had barely finished composing a poem celebrating her sister Xiaoluan's imminent wedding, a maid arrived with the news of Xiaoluan's sudden death. Wanwan collapsed soon after returning to her mother's house and died 70 days after Xiaoluan. Several days before her demise, Wanwan had a series of dreams. In the first one, she found herself in magical mountains and grottoes and worried that this was an omen of her death. Yixiu comforted her: "No, the Bodhisattva [Guanyin] is known as the compassionate deliverer; I've sent someone to offer prayers on your behalf, that's why you found yourself in paradise."

Before Wanwan breathed her last, Yixiu recited to her a chant:

> The four elements are illusions,
> Why be attached?
> Focus on Our Buddha,
> You will have no worries.[59]

Wanwan sat up, pressed her palms together, let out a cry, broke into a sweat all over her body, and faded away. Her parents were convinced that she became an enlightened being. Shaoyuan thought it probable that she was the reincarnation of Princess Yongxing of the Southern Tang (934–58) who, before her death at the age of 23, prayed to the Buddha: "May I be reborn, for many lives to come, not into a being with feelings [youqing zhiwu, sattva]." Yixiu pawned Wanwan's clothes to hire more monks and nuns to offer prayers to that end.[60] Shattered by the death of both daughters, Yixiu became increasingly obsessed with death and rebirth near her own life's end.

A cousin of Yixiu's, a Daoist nun, thus summarized the emotional journey of Yixiu: "In its extreme, qing gives rise to [the realization that] the nature of phenomena lacks real substance."[61] The cult of love, easily dashed, for neither mother nor daughter had control over her marital destiny, embodied the seed of its negation — a Buddhist renunciation of qing. Although Yixiu's own marriage turned out to be fulfilling, she gravitated to the renunciation of qing toward her life's end.

Religious piety was a dominant motif in gentrywomen's domestic life; Yixiu and the women in her family constituted merely one of many examples from seventeenth-century Jiangnan. Some acts of devotion were personalized statements of the women's artistic refinement — we have seen that Fang Weiyi and Ni Renji painted or embroidered portraits of the Bodhisattva Guanyin with great finesse. Daily devotion also fostered communities of women, as sisters gathered to study the sutras, or as mother interpreted a daughter's dreams and recited chants. These rituals and religious sentiments are termed "domestic religion" in the sense that they were embedded in everyday life in the inner chambers and were integral to the women's worldviews and self-identities.[62]

These women's search for piety at home and in the immediacy of daily life was part of the rise of a lay Buddhist movement in late Ming China. In her study of Chu Hong, one of the leaders of this revitalization project, Chün-fang Yü characterizes this syncretic movement as one that "emphasized recitation of the Buddha's name, nonkilling, and compassion both for one's fellow human beings and for animals." These simple demands secured the lasting popularity of the lay movement from the late Ming through the Qing.[63] The domestic domain eclipsed the monastic order as the site of religious practice for males and females; this is yet another facet of the privatization of Chinese life that imparted myriad meanings and functions to the domestic terrain.

Shen Yixiu was a typical practitioner of this lay syncretic movement. Her interest was in part intellectual; she was particularly attracted to the esotericism and speculations of the Chan and Tiantai sects. But even more important were domestic practices. Before her children barely learned how to speak, Yixiu impressed upon them the virtues of freeing captive animals. In her later years she used her authority as household manager to impose her piety on her family by maintaining a strict vegetarian kitchen. Since anything that moved, even shellfish, was forbidden, Ye Shaoyuan had to forgo the delicious lake crabs, for which the Yangzi Delta is famous. Yet apparently he did not refrain from such delicacies outside his home.[64]

Other women expressed their religiosity in highly ritualistic ways. Cheng Qiong, who, as mentioned in Chapter 2, wrote a commentary to *The Peony Pavilion* to reconcile the celebration of *qing* with its Buddhist renunciation, enacted elaborate rituals when she fell ill. In the family's private living room, she lit Korean stone lanterns, draped herself in her husband's meditation robe, and said prayers to the third daughter of Miaozhuang Wang, another name for Guanyin. At her side she asked her favorite female Daoist adept to ring a little green bell.[65] Theatrics seems to have a strong appeal to some women. We have already seen how Qian Yi, another commentator on the drama, set up an altar in her garden and made offerings to Du Liniang.

As serious as these female devotees were, there were no icons or belief systems unique to them. Just as Guanyin was not a goddess solely for women, domestic religion often involved husbands, although it was particularly meaningful to the women themselves. Shen Yixiu, Cheng Qiong, and Qian Yi all discussed Buddhist doctrines with their husbands. Women's religiosity, be it manifested in practice, rituals, or doctrine, benefited from the introspection that characterized the inner world of men in the seventeenth century. The merging of Confucian tenets with those of Buddhism and Daoism, rampant in the philosophical world at large, enriched the religious life of women by sanctioning religious piety and discussions of metaphysics in the domestic setting.

Even with the participation of men, however, domestic religion touched the heart of women's identities as women. To some believers, at least, domestic religion affirmed the superior spiritual prowess of woman, leading to a more positive assessment of the female sex. Like arguments for the superiority of the female poet by virtue of her serenity, however, this veneration was predicated on perceived male-female distinctions. One indication of a widespread recognition of female spirituality was the popular belief in the desirability of being born (and reborn) a woman, promoted by a Suzhou spirit medium, Madame Chen, who called herself the Tiantai master Lezi. Lezi and her daughter, Xizi, attracted a large following among gentrymen and gentrywomen in Suzhou. Shen Yixiu had kept frequent contact and correspondence with her; the bereaved Ye Shaoyuan implored her to convey news from his deceased wife and daughters.[66] Believers, including such literati as Ye Shaoyuan and Qian Qianyi, were convinced that she was a thousand-year-old adept reincarnated into the body of a woman to beseech the world to seek deliverance from transmigration. In the Suzhou area, after Ye Xiaoluan's death, believers reported séances in which the gods spoke through Lezi and other women mediums. Women, said the gods, were endowed with a special spiritual sensitivity; they should seek to become immortals in their womanly bodies after death.[67]

Lezi taught that in the afterworld she had founded the Hall of No Leaves (Wuye tang), a realm reserved for women where they could complete their spiritual exercises and prepare to ascend to paradise. Lezi told the bereaved Ye that both Yixiu and Wanwan had been admitted into her hall, together with over 30 other woman devotees, served by an entourage of women attendants. Wanwan was a particularly insistent believer who, in her previous life as a male scholar, had beseeched the Bodhisattva Guanyin that she be reborn a woman gifted with literary talent.[68] The valorization of women's spirituality was thus bound up with celebration of their talent.

The Making of Domestic Goddesses

Not only were domestic women true believers, many were regarded as immortals by their kinsmen and became recipients of family worship after death. Men were key figures in the making of female domestic deities. In late Ming times, signs betraying an official fear of women's religious power, ranging from edicts outlawing "lewd" sects with large female followings to Confucian precepts admonishing housewives to shun superstitions, were widely evident. At the same time, however, many scholar-officials and men of letters openly endorsed the spiritual prowess of women, as the large and public male following of Lezi and Tan Yangzi, another spiritual female, attests.[69] In private homes as well, husbands and fathers unabashedly promoted the religiosity of their female kin, to the point of deifying them after death.

The Yangzhou writer Shi Chengjin, for example, ascribed to his wife, née Zhou, natural and supernatural faith. A "born believer in the Buddha," not only did she chant sutras incessantly, she was conversant with their meaning and contents. One day shortly after lunch, she gathered her daughters and daughters-in-law for an informal lesson. With a book in hand, she started to recount tales of the kings of brightness (*mingwang, vidyārāja*), a class of deities with furious appearances who are destroyers of evil spirits in esoteric Buddhism. All of a sudden, she wiped her eyes with her hands, saying: "Having chanted all those sutras with my heart, now a messenger is here to take me to the Buddha; I have to go." She dropped her book, sat up, closed her eyes, and passed away. Shi clearly believed in the authenticity of her last vision.[70] Instead of chastising her daily devotion, he exhorted his readers to worship the Buddha with the same single-mindedness as she had.

Ye Shaoyuan concurred that women were more attuned to the spiritual world. Not only did he encourage Yixiu to keep company with Lezi and other Buddhist and Daoist adepts, he sought their help to recall his dead daughter, Xiaoluan, whom he believed was a reincarnated immortal. Neither parent thought that Xiaoluan had really died. Seven days after her demise, her body was light and tender, but her flesh remained firm. Before the coffin was sealed, Yixiu wrote Xiaoluan's name on the body's right arm so that in afterlife, they could recognize each other by the vermilion mark. Yixiu then laid an embroidered portrait of Guanyin on her, together with two sutras that Yixiu had handcopied as acts of devotion — the *Chant of the God of Infinite Compassion* and the *Diamond Sutra*.[71]

Partly out of grief and partly out of his own belief in the afterlife, Shaoyuan began to prepare for Xiaoluan's return. He and Yixiu redecorated her bedroom as a family shrine, consecrating a Guanyin statue and Buddhist sutras on a table. Meditating in the room, he called out to his daughter: "If you want to come back and play, how about if I burn incense in your room and boil water for tea?" He also invited her to appear and speak to him in his dreams.[72] After her fifth brother claimed to have seen her amid magical mountains and grottoes in a dream, Shaoyuan became all the more convinced that Xiaoluan was a celestial being who had descended upon his family for an earthly sojourn.[73]

Belief in rebirth and communication with the dead, derived from the

Buddhist tenet of reincarnation, was extremely popular among late Ming literati. Dreams were channels whereby the living communicated with the spiritual world; to men and women alike dreams were not merely symbols but authentic experiences that constituted part of reality.[74] We have seen how Qian Yi and her husband Wu Ren had a supernatural experience of "sharing a dream"; both took it seriously as a sign of their resonance. Domestic intimacy and visions in the bedroom could thus take on transcendental significance. "Mundane" domestic life was far from mundane.

Ye Shaoyuan sought the help of spirit mediums to communicate with Xiaoluan.[75] In these séances, Xiaoluan's various appearances as the Yes' domestic goddess were all extensions of her real-life persona as talented beauty. In 1636, Lezi conducted a séance in which she disclosed that Xiaoluan had been a female librarian in the Moon Palace (*Yuefu shishu nü*) in her immediate past life. Later in 1642, another medium claimed that Xiaoluan was the reincarnation of Cao Dagu, honorary name of the Han scholar-teacher Ban Zhao and model of all latter-day erudite women.[76]

Hence Xiaoluan was remembered as the custodian of secular and mystical knowledge, a most fitting image for an ill-fated young woman born into a family that valorized female talent. Her poetry collection, including verses she dictated in séances, was widely anthologized.[77] Woman painters treasured Xiaoluan's paintings and modeled their works after hers; poets harmonized with Xiaoluan's verses. As late as the nineteenth century, men and women still claimed to see her in séances.[78] Through the circulation of her writings and paintings, the domestic goddess lived on in public imagination.

The Ye Xiaoluan lore acquired multifarious and sometimes conflicting meanings as time went on. In Chapter 2, we saw how Xiaoluan was identified with the concubine Xiaoqing, both being ill-fated literary geniuses. Yet this fatalism, seemingly dismissive of women's talent, coexisted with a fantastic celebration of its immortality. In another facet of Xiaoluan's legacy, she, Du Liniang, and Tan Yangzi were all valorized as female deities. Du, resurrected in Tang Xianzu's famous drama, was merged in popular imagination with the other two young gentrywomen, both believed to be immortals with an active life after death.[79] Deified by men, Ye Xiaoluan became the inspiration and model for women poets for centuries to come. Resurrected or not, she attained true immortality in their hearts and minds.

A World of Her Own: Domestic Poetry Club

The discussions of companionate marriage and domestic religion thus far have focused largely on the connectedness between his and her worlds.

At the same time, we have seen that with or without an acquired emotional intimacy, husband and wife in a gentry household occupied separate spheres of responsibility, a functional distinction reinforced by spatial separation of the female quarters and the frequent traveling the husband's public career entailed. Separate spheres encouraged the flowering of a women's culture in the inner chambers, a culture that was separate but not separatist.

In women's eyes, their lives were punctuated by a logic and rhythm of their own, expressed in literature and religious rituals, to which men were not privy. Only by exploring the meanings of these female-exclusive sociabilities to the women concerned can we appreciate the significance of the overarching contexts of their existence: in male-centered formal kinship and power structures, whatever independence that women could claim was derivative.

Shen Yixiu presided over an informal community of women that gathered for parties and outings and exchanged verses. An example of the "domestic" type of female networks, this poetry club evolved around women from two families—the Shen and the Ye. This dependence on kinship and affinal ties can be interpreted in both positive and negative light: Yixiu had to choose her friends from among the women thrown together by family alliances in which she had little say; the membership of her poetry club was, in this sense, constrained. Yet, as we have seen, these were in fact wide-ranging networks, encompassing the entire spectrum of notables in Wujiang and its neighboring Jiashan. From this perspective, kin and affinal ties were not restrictive; rather, they were conducive to the expansion of female networks.

Shen Yixiu and her daughters, as we have seen, were highly educated; literature and scholarship were the Shens' and the Yes' foremost cultural capital. Hailed as "talented ladies" (*mingyuan*), their poetry collections were featured prominently in Wujiang and Suzhou local histories, in a separate section devoted to women writers under the category "Literature and the Arts."[80] The vitality and prolifigacy of the domestic poetry club of Shen Yixiu were evident in the large body of poems they produced.

Central to the group was Yixiu, her three elder daughters, and her cousin and best friend, Zhang Qianqian. Other members, as can be gleaned from the dedications of poems, included relatives from primarily the Shen family — Yixiu's sisters, sisters-in-law, cousins, nieces, aunts, and "lineage aunts" (*zugu*)—a group of about fifteen women (see Fig. 1). Praising the tradition of literary pursuits of the Shen ladies, the leading literatus Qian Qianyi wrote: "Therefore, all the aunts and sisters gave up scissors and rules [seamstresses' implements] to work on prose and poetry; they abandoned needlework to devote time to the art of the brush."

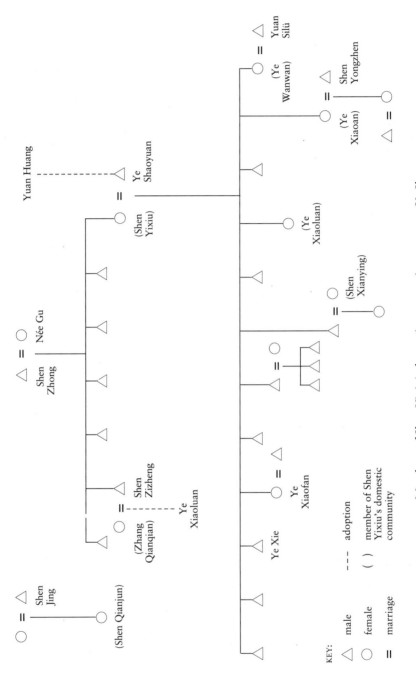

FIG. 1 Members of Shen Yixiu's domestic community. SOURCES: Ye Shaoyuan, *Wumengtang quanji*, *passim*; Ye Xie; Okuzaki, "Soshūfu Gokōken."

KEY:

△ male

○ female

= marriage

- - - adoption

( ) member of Shen Yixiu's domestic community

Besides the works of Yixiu and her daughters, Qian also selected 25 eulogistic poems by their relatives and friends for inclusion in his poetry anthology.[81]

The composition of Yixiu's informal female network shows marked disparities with the official, male-centered kin and affinal affiliations outlined earlier. First, there was an overwhelming representation of women born or married into the Shen family, at the expense of the Yes. Yixiu's daughters and daughters-in-law, of course, were exceptions. Although a few members cannot be identified, the named ones—presumably those whom Yixiu was closest to—were mostly Shen women. The primary reason for this is the exceptional fame of the Shens as a literary family and hence an abnormally high proportion of female poets. It was also facilitated by the physical proximity between the Shens and the Yes. Although Yixiu seldom visited her own paternal home, she kept in touch with her female relatives. Ye Shaoyuan's estrangement from the powerful branch of his family and the fact that he did not have brothers also contributed to a paucity of Ye women who mattered in Yixiu's social and emotional life.

A second disparity between the male and female versions of community is the absence of Yuan women in Yixiu's group, except for her daughter Wanwan, who married a Yuan. Although Ye Shaoyuan and Yuan Tianqi were adoptive brothers and best friends who spent much time together, there is no record of friendship between their wives, or between Yixiu and any of the Yuan women.[82]

A third noteworthy feature of Yixiu's community is the prominence of maids, who were dubious, at best inferior, members of the family system in men's eyes. These young girls, known as either "maids" (*binü*) or "personal attendants" (*shinü*), were present at most of the women's gatherings and were, naturally, companions in the inner chambers. Yixiu and her daughters developed a rapport with some of them. For a maid who died at age eleven, Yixiu composed a moving poem. Xiaoluan's attendant, Hongyu, often mentioned in Xiaoluan's poems, picked flowers, urged her to take naps, and learned to compose a few verses. When Xiaoluan returned in a séance after her death, she first wrote a poem conveying her thoughts for parents, then she asked to see Hongyu, "saying" that "I miss her." Aged seventeen upon Xiaoluan's death, Hongyu was later sent home by Shaoyuan and married a scholar as concubine.[83]

Shen Yixiu's attendant, Suichun, created a stir in the inner chambers when she turned fifteen. The pubescent girl became coy, developed a figure, and wandered the quarters starry-eyed. The three daughters composed rounds of poems teasing her, amazed at how bewitching her glance and slender waist had become. Intrigued and delighted by the emergent charm of the feminine body, these girls were obviously having fun. The sentiment recalls their fascination with the small feet discussed in the preceding chapter. Even Yixiu chimed in. Besides harmonizing with her daughters' verses, she composed one teasing Shaoyuan, warning him that Suichun appeared to be infatuated with him.[84]

Although Ye Shaoyuan was not privy to these pleasures in the female quarters, he was quite fond of his wife's sociability and humor: "She did not wear jewelry or heavy makeup but instead would attend women's parties in simple attire and hairdo. But she was very humorous, she enjoyed jokes, and she could really drink."[85] Evidently, Ye was not invited to these parties. Although there is no record of guest lists or other details of these "women's parties" (funü yanhui), judging from paintings they differed little from gatherings of male literati of the day—drinking, joking, games, playing musical instruments, viewing flowers, and the inevitable round of poetry writing.[86]

In a set of poems, Shen Yixiu described, with a touch of humor, the looks and personalities of five of her friends—cousin Zhang Qianqian, sister-in-law née Zhou (wife of Yixiu's younger brother, Shen Zibing), her sixth younger sister, a Madame Wang, and a cousin surnamed Qi.[87] The cordial tone of these poems together with the existence of other poems documenting their friendship suggest that these women were in frequent contact and were emotionally close. In addition, a certain "lineage aunt," who taught Yixiu's daughter Xiaoluan to play the zither, was also a frequent visitor to Yixiu's quarters.[88]

Tender moments in the boudoir evolved around the mother-daughter axis. Among her children, Shen Yixiu was closest to the three elder daughters—Wanwan, Xiaowan, and Xiaoluan—each three years apart. Of the 727 poems in Yixiu's collected works, 92 were written with or in the memory of her three daughters.[89] In one entitled "Teaching Embroidery to My Daughter in Early Summer," Yixiu wrote that the education of her daughter reminded her of her own coming of age.

> Remember at age thirteen,
> I first learned embroidery leaning on my bed.
> Unaware of the worries springtime would bring,
> I delighted in flowers soon to blossom.
> At fifteen I played the flute,
> Willow catkins clinging to my sleeves.
> Trying a swing with friends,
> We frolicked in shadows of grass and flowers.
> I started to paint my eyebrows when sixteen,
> In springtime I painted them long and slender.
> So blows the spring wind for twenty years,
> Through those long and speechless empty days.
> Time flows and renews,

> But my morning dreams are the same as ever.
> Only that all the roses have wilted,
> In this season of sadness.[90]

As she advanced into her mid-thirties, Yixiu was keenly aware of the need to transmit women's culture from one generation to the next. Later, the death of two daughters prompted her to contemplate not only a temporal but also a spatial transmission of women's legacy.

Friendship and Kinship: Negotiated Intimacies

Learning embroidery, sharing wine, daydreaming about retiring to the mountains, teasing a maid — these female-exclusive routines and activities in the inner chambers were deeply meaningful to the women concerned. Even as we recognize a certain autonomy of this women's culture and the agency of women in its creation, however, it is clear that they did not make their female world as they pleased. Even seemingly innocent friendships between individual women were results of negotiations with the family, kinship, and power systems at large, as the friendship between Shen Yixiu and Zhang Qianqian attests.

When Yixiu was seven, her mother died. Her father invited a sister who had married into a Zhang family to look after the children.[91] The daughter she brought with her, Zhang Qianqian, became Yixiu's favorite cousin, and the two remained best friends for life. Yixiu's intimacy with Qianqian is instructive of the multilayered ties that often bound women in such domestic groups: paternal cousins by birth, they grew up together as sisters. Moreover, Qianqian married Yixiu's brother, and hence was also a sister-in-law. In addition, she adopted Yixiu's daughter and reared her for nine years, giving her the same education in poetry as Yixiu would have done.

The intimacies between Yixiu and Qianqian, documented by 28 poems and a detailed account written by Yixiu, illustrate the opportunities and restrictions inherent in this kind of women's network rooted in family ties. Although familial relationships provided a natural milieu for contact, the practices of patrilineality and virilocal marriage in the Chinese family meant that women could not choose where they lived. As a result, physical separation between close friends was almost inevitable during certain stages of their lives. The following collection of vignettes of the lifelong friendship between Yixiu and Qianqian shows just how frequent these partings could be:

1597–1605: Qianqian, age three, was brought by her mother to Yixiu's house. The two cousins grew up together, until Yixiu was married out.

1605–1610: Yixiu became a bride in the Ye family and Qianqian was brought back to her father's house; the two did not see each other for five years.

1610: Qianqian married Yixiu's brother Zizheng; Yixiu returned to her maternal home for the wedding. Yixiu's eyes lit up upon seeing Qianqian — she had matured into a woman glowing with feminine charm. "When the ancients said a woman is both beautiful and glamorous, this must be what they meant," Yixiu mused. They stayed up at night to chat with two to three other female companions; spent several days together.

1613: Yixiu visited home and saw Qianqian briefly.

1616: Yixiu's third daughter, Xiaoluan, was adopted by Shen Zizheng and Qianqian.

1617: Yixiu's father retired to his native place; Yixiu visited home several times. Qianqian had put on weight, her body looking fuller and her skin, tender as ever. Yixiu and other Shen sisters teased and nicknamed her "Consort Yang," the Tang femme fatale renowned for her voluptuous beauty. They then teased Yixiu, asking her to write a poem for Qianqian that could compare to the immortal lines that the famous Tang poet Li Po wrote for Consort Yang. Yixiu fought back: "I'm no Li Po, but I'm fit to carry his ink slab."

1618: When Yixiu's husband was taking his examination in Nanjing, Yixiu and Qianqian stole away to a lake for two days. "At night we parked the pleasure boat and brought out the wine," recalled Yixiu. "We talked about our past and our dreams in life and had a great time." According to Yixiu, Qianqian could really hold her wine.

1622: Yixiu visited home for her father's funeral and saw Qianqian for several days.

1625: In 1624, Qianqian's husband had left home to find employment as a private military adviser on the northern frontier and was never to see her again; Qianqian fell ill and Xiaoluan returned to Yixiu's in 1625.

1626: Yixiu invited Qianqian to stay with her for several months. They wrote poetry together. On a certain evening, the two broke into tears while drinking and talking about the "snobbish ways of the world" and the departed Zizheng. They ended up composing poems for each other. Yixiu's read, "With a bottle of wine we lament how long sorrows can last. / Gazing at each other, we, a brokenhearted pair."

1627: Yixiu, Xiaoluan, and Qianqian were invited to stay at Shen Zibing's house for a few days. Then Yixiu went to Nanjing with her husband for his new appointment and was away from home when news of Qianqian's death arrived.[92]

These partings and reunions were often determined by the decisions or whereabouts of fathers and husbands. In this sense, the formal kinship structure, shaped ostensibly by men and the public world, limited the options available to individual women. Yet personal friendship and fictive kin ties were intimacies over which women had their own say. Although they could not choose to be at the same place at the same time, the friendship between Yixiu and Qianqian was maintained by the exchange of poems and was no less intense for the arbitrary constraints placed on it. Cousins by birth and sisters-in-law by the choice of their fathers, these two women chose to cement their friendship by the adoption of a daughter, with the consent of their husbands.

In a temporary arrangement that superficially resembles Ye Shaoyuan's adoption to Yuan Huang, Yixiu's third daughter, Xiaoluan, was adopted by Shen Zizheng and Zhang Qianqian. Xiaoluan left her parent's household when she was barely six months and did not return until she was nine. After four of her own children had died in infancy, Qianqian was eager to raise a daughter; Xiaoluan did not change her name and since she was female, the question of inheritance was irrelevant. Ye Shaoyuan referred to Shen Zizheng as Xiaoluan's "rearing maternal uncle" (*yujiu*) and to Qianqian by her old relation of "maternal aunt" (*jinmu*).[93] The adoption of Xiaoluan was primarily a means whereby a pair of best friends commemorated their intimacy. Unlike male adoptions, the reasons for female adoptions were personal and emotional and did not involve the family as a corporate unit.

For the women's community, adoption intensified the bonds between members by creating an additional layer of fictive kin ties. By pursuing adoption for her daughter and personal friendship with her cousin, Yixiu sought to graft a women's tradition onto the family system in unofficial but significant ways. Moreover, in extending her community far beyond the circle of local gentry families, she created a space for women's networks alongside the male-controlled webs of family alliances.

Family Deaths: Crisis and Transitions

Ironically, death was often the occasion by which the women's networks expanded. Death in the family was an experience common to so many women that it brought together those who had never met.[94] The exchange of poems commemorated such newly formed ties and these poems, if published, drew in yet another circle. Alongside the tender sweetness of boudoir life, death and parting constituted a dominant theme in the literature of women's culture.

A death in the family is, of course, not an experience unique to the female sex. The public writings of scholar-officials are full of epitaphs and elegies for friends and acquaintances. Yet the sheer number of emotional elegiac poems written by Ming and Qing women and their highly personal tone suggest that women were particularly sensitive to truncations in family life. Whereas men tended to conceive of the family as an unbroken line of descent from one generation to the next, women focused instead on the interruptions and the moments of crisis in each individual life.

Even allowing for women's sensitivity to tragedies and transitions, the frequency with which death descended upon the families of woman poets in Ming-Qing Jiangnan is extraordinary. In the case of Shen Yixiu, she lost her best friend Zhang Qianqian in 1627, one daughter in 1632, and another in 1633. In the span of a mere three years, between 1632 and 1635, six members of the immediate family went to the grave, including Yixiu herself, who died in 1635.

Teenage girl poets seem particularly vulnerable. A cursory look among Yixiu's acquaintances yields several examples: Zhou Yifen, daughter of the notable Wujiang Zhou family who lived three houses away from Yixiu's, was a painter and poet who died in her late teens or early twenties. Shen Renlan, a gentrywoman poet in Jiaxing (unrelated to Yixiu), lost her daughter Huang Shuanghui who, like Xiaoluan, was a young poet of some repute. She died in 1626 at the age of fifteen. A similar fate befell Renlan's daughter-in-law.[95] The belief that a woman long on talent is short on fortune, which, as we have seen, was popular among men and women in the seventeenth century, does seem to have some factual validity.

Some explanations for these frequent deaths, no matter how speculative, are needed before we examine the implications of death to the women's communities. Although her parents believed that Wanwan died from pent-up frustration from an unhappy marriage, she and Xiaoluan may have succumbed to an epidemic, given the suddenness and proximity of their deaths. The local gazetteers, however, failed to record the outbreak of an epidemic in 1632. Frederic Wakeman has identified the period 1626–40 as the beginning of the "Maunder minimum," characterized by frequent famines, plagues of locusts, and smallpox. Two major epidemics broke out in China in 1586–89 and 1639–44.[96] The two young women in their teens, and their four-year-old brother as well, were perhaps victims of this wave of epidemics and general deterioration of health.

Shen Yixiu and her second son succumbed to a "lung disease" that was almost certainly tuberculosis. Ye Shaoyuan recorded in his journal how his son began to cough a large amount of blood in early 1633; his wife soon followed suit. In the following year Yixiu's health deteriorated to the point where she was often bedridden. Soon after the "lung disease" took the life of her son, in mid-1635 Yixiu started to cough much blood "just like her son." Five months later she passed away.[97] The frequent diseases and deaths that struck Shen Yixiu and the families of other gentrywomen are more understandable in light of the fact that the average life span in seventeenth-century China was probably half today's figure.[98]

Besides physiological explanations, there could be psychological factors as well. The fragmentary nature of documentary evidence renders any psychological explanation speculative. But the large number of teenage deaths shortly before and after the consummation of marriage suggests that this is a most vulnerable period in a woman's life, a hypothesis borne out by Margery Wolf's research in modern Taiwan.[99] In addition, in her study of madness in Qing China, Vivien Ng notes that "young women, particularly those on the verge of marriage, seemed to be especially susceptible to the lecherous attention of malevolent spirits, and they often became temporarily insane as a result." Ng's observations are based entirely on anecdotal history.[100]

The connection between prenuptial anxieties and spirit possession is more directly borne out by an edict issued by Tang Bin, governor of Jiangnan, in 1686. Seeking to stamp out the cult of Wutong, the God of Money, who was widely believed to be a debaucher of women, Tang disclosed that every year, local magistrates reported several dozen cases of spirit possession. "Young women with outstanding beauty, when suffering from chills or fevers, often claim that 'Wutong is going to marry me as wife.' They see delusions in which they have sexual relations with the god, and then become emaciated and die." In his study of Wutong, Richard von Glahn has argued that feigning union with Wutong was a culturally accepted strategy employed by women to avoid sleeping with their betrothed husbands or to escape conjugal obligations altogether.[101]

Although this attribution of intention to brides-to-be is probable, it is difficult to substantiate. From our study of teenage poets thus far, however, this much is clear: these women had heightened romantic sensitivities, were brought up on a steady diet of idealized love matches and were made all too aware of the fragility of their hopes by watching the mismatches suffered by elder sisters, mother, or aunts. Since they would not see their groom until the wedding day, the period leading up to that day was naturally plagued by anxieties. Some may have become so depressed by the prospect of serving mean mothers-in-law or unworthy husbands that they took their own lives; some may have succumbed to illness because of stress.

Ye Xiaoluan's demise came five days before her wedding, in the tenth month, after a 25-day-long illness. Yet for that entire lunar year, Xiaoluan's poems had been full of premonitions. In an unfinished one, for example, she wrote:

> In dreams there are mountains as refuge from the world,
> When awake I find no wine to drown my sorrow.
> In life freedom and leisure are hardest to come by.

The first line clearly recalls Wanwan's "mountain addiction." In another grim verse, Xiaoluan adopted the voice of someone at the end of life's travails and invited her sisters to join her:

> I pity that my sideburns are full of gray,
> And sigh that this floating life is a hurried hundred years.
> One day we will find the great Way together,
> And lose ourselves in idle talks of metaphysics under a thatch.[102]

Both Yixiu and Shaoyuan thought this fatalism a bad omen at the time, but became convinced after the fact that it was positive proof that Xiaoluan was an immortal, since she had long tried to prepare her parents for her imminent return to paradise. An equally plausible reading is that Xiaoluan, reluctant to follow the footsteps of her unhappy sister Wanwan, had become infatuated with the Daoist-Buddhist ideal of resignation and transcendence championed by Wanwan and Yixiu. These factors weakened her immunity and her will to survive the disease that claimed her prodigious life.

Extending the Community: Eulogies and Publication

Frequent family deaths alerted Shen Yixiu to the fragility of the women's legacy. Besides writing mourning poetry, she plunged into two publishing projects for the three years between the passing away of her two daughters and her own death. Her private sorrows transmuted into a burning public and historical mission, Yixiu was intent on preserving and transmitting women's words across time and distance. In collecting, printing, and distributing manuscripts, she relied on the financial and logistical support of her male kinsmen. The evolution of Shen Yixiu's informal poetry club into a "public" community of women would not have been possible without the interest taken by her husband and the extra-familial networks he provided. Men's kinship and public connections facilitated the expansion of female social relationships.

The first project was editing the manuscripts left by Xiaoluan and Wanwan. The blocks for Xiaoluan's were readied for printing within 100 days of her death, suggesting a sense of urgency and seriousness of purpose.[103] By 1634, both volumes were published and distributed to women poets in Jiangnan whom Yixiu had admired. The verses struck many sympathetic chords. One of them, Shen Renlan, whose similar tragedies are noted above, wrote back: "Upon reading Xiaoluan's poems I could not help but miss my own dead daughter Shuanghui. The pain was unbearable. I tried to follow the rhymes of the mourning poems composed by her sisters Wanwan and Xiaowan, but I became so choked with tears that the words did not come."[104]

TABLE 3
The Extended Women's Community of Shen Yixiu

Name	Place of origin	Relationship with Yixiu	Face-to-face meetings
Shen Renlan	Jiaxing	friend	no
Huang Yuanzhen	Jiaxing	friend	no
Huang Yuanjie	Jiaxing	friend	no
Wu Shan	Nanjing	friend	no
Wang Hui	Suzhou	son-in-law's sister	no
Madame Shen	Wujiang	cousin	yes
Zhou Lanxiu[a]	Wujiang	niece	probably yes
Shen Zhiyao	Wujiang	younger sister	yes
Shen Xianying	Wujiang	niece	yes
Shen Huaman	Wujiang	niece	yes
Shen Huiduan	Wujiang	niece	no
Shen Qianjun	Wujiang	cousin	probably yes
Zhang Ruixian	Kunshan	not clear	probably not
Yan Qiongqiong	Wujiang	niece	probably yes
Huang Dezhen[a]	Jiaxing	friend	no

SOURCE: Ye Shaoyuan, *Tonglian xuxie, passim.*

[a]Zhou Lanxiu, whose mother was a Shen daughter related to Yixiu, was also Huang Dezhen's sister-in-law, both having married into the Sun family of Pinghu (cf. Sun family tree in Pan, *Jiaxing de wangzu,* p. 66).

Shen Renlan's eulogistic poems, together with those of fourteen relatives and friends, were later published by Ye Shaoyuan in a volume entitled *Legacy from Toiletry and Writing Brush (Tonglian xuxie)*. An analysis of the relationship between these women and Shen Yixiu as well as the channels through which they came into contact reveals a two-tiered pattern in the expansion of women's communities. For relatives, Yixiu only had to mobilize members of her existing informal poetry club, or whatever was left of it. This resulted in a similar overrepresentation of Shen women (see Table 3). For friends, namely those with no recognized kin ties, she needed to mobilize the public networks of men, who, for their own reasons, were often eager to assist such cross-fertilization.

Male intermediaries were crucial in recruiting the five friends represented, including the itinerant teacher, writer, and painter Huang Yuanjie. The way Huang Yuanjie came into contact with the Ye women's poetry illustrated the indispensable role played by male kin in the forging of "social" and "public" women's networks. In 1633, Ye Shaoyuan was paying a courtesy visit to an examiner Fang in Zuili, 70 *li* southwest of the seat of Jiaxing, where he ran into a relative, Feng Maoyuan (*juren* 1615). Addressed by Shaoyuan as "cousin," Feng was a maternal nephew of Shaoyuan's mother, who, as mentioned above, hailed from the prominent Feng family in Pinghu, Jiaxing prefecture. Feng Maoyuan was also a relative of Huang Yuanjie's, another native of Jiaxing. Feng called on examiner Fang to recommend Yuanjie's brother Huang Xiangsan to him. Upon reading Xiangsan's writings, Ye Shaoyuan put in his good word too. Huang later captured the highest rank in that examination.[105] Through Feng, a mutual kinsman, the poetry of Ye Xiaoluan and Wanwan was sent to the Huang family.

Later, Huang Xiangsan called on Ye Shaoyuan to express his gratitude, bringing the elegiac poems of his two sisters, Yuanjie and Yuanzhen, as a gift. Ye felt honored; not only did he print them in the *Legacy* collection, he also carefully stored away the originals.[106] At the time, Huang Yuanjie enjoyed a considerable reputation as a poet and painter in the Jiangnan artist community. The use of *her* poetry as memento in the forging of *male* networks suggests the currency of a new author-reader relationship, one in which women writers and readers played conspicuous roles. Feng Mao-yuan kept up his role as an intermediary between the Yes and the Huangs. Over a decade later, in 1648, he brought Ye Shaoyuan a copy of Yuanjie's poetry collection, *Songs of the Detached Hermit*.[107]

All the friends who sent Yixiu poems, including Huang Yuanjie, had never met Yixiu personally (and, in fact, never did). Yet Huang felt for the misfortune of Yixiu as she was stirred by the pessimism and resignation expressed in Xiaoluan's poems. Reflecting on her own poverty-stricken life, she developed a sense of empathy, although she had never met the three women from Wujiang. One of the twenty poems she wrote in response reads:

> Deep is the night, thick as willow branches,
> The beautiful soul, now vanished, can never be called back.
> If only she had met Huang Jieling [Yuanjie] in the bygone days,
> Her moaning and sorrow would have found some relief.[108]

Although Shen Yixiu died too soon to follow up on these newly formed ties, the emotional intensity in the eulogistic poems by Shen Renlan and Huang Yuanjie suggests that literate women developed friendships through sympathetic readings of each other's writings. That they lived in different cities with no face-to-face interaction was of secondary importance to the concerns they shared as women in general and as mothers in particular. In other words, women's networks expanded through dissemination of the word without a corresponding increase in physical mobility. In a society where most women could not choose where to live, literary and textual transmissions enabled the forging of regional women's cultures.

Besides editing her daughters' posthumous poems and soliciting responses from Jiangnan gentrywomen, Shen Yixiu embarked on a second project to preserve women's words for posterity. Asking help from her husband, she reasoned:

Although our daughters have died, fortunately the world does not lack talented women who can write. It's a shame that most of their works are not being passed on. Take Yuan Lüzhen, for example. She came from such a big gentry family in our city. It's pure luck that you once lodged in her family and found her manuscripts tucked away in a corner. We've kept them for ten years, and the world still hasn't heard about her. I once also heard that in Wuxing there's a woman named Wu who managed to publish her works. When I tried to locate them, I found that she had died and the volumes were no longer extant. Would you help me collect all of the unpublished writings by women scattered in this world? I'd love to edit them when I have the time. In ten or twenty years we can publish them. Wouldn't that be nice? But some women writers are already well known, and I don't want to waste energy on them.[109]

The result, although incomplete, was *Her Meditations (Yirensi)*, a collection of 241 poems by 46 female poets edited by Shen Yixiu, with short commentaries, and published by her husband after her death.[110]

The organization of *Her Meditations* reveals that locating and preserving women's writings were the editor's central concerns. Unlike most other contemporary anthologies, its four sections are divided by the availability of the sources — published works; unpublished handwritten manuscripts; poems passed on by word of mouth; and those cited by other writers in their published works. The contents reflect both the centrality of women's culture in the lives of the authors and the editor's awareness of it. Of the 241 poems in the collection, 83 were dedicated to other women friends, sisters, daughters, or other female relatives. In contrast, only 7 were written for men. Some of the 46 poets featured were related to each other as mother, daughter, or cousin. The poetry of Wang Fengxian, a widowed gentrywoman, and her two daughters conveys a story of close emotional ties truncated by untimely deaths of both daughters. Shen Yixiu noted tersely: "extremely similar to our family."[111]

Through reading each other's works, women poets realized that they were not alone in mourning their loved ones. As poets and sympathetic readers, they perpetuated not only the cult of *qing*, but also their own poetic legacies.

Posthumous Legacies: Power of the Printed Word

Family publication was the last joint project of Shen Yixiu and Ye Shaoyuan, the companionate couple. The division of labor between them was typical of family publishing ventures in Jiangnan. A woman might take full responsibility for editing and collating the manuscripts of other women, or she might collaborate with her husband. But when it came to cutting the blocks and making the financial arrangements, it was the husband's or the son's job. Haggling with printers and book merchants was still not womanly work. In addition, men's extra-familial networks and their use of women's manuscripts to cement male ties also facilitated the dissemination of the women's word.

Nothing is known of the specific arrangements or expenses incurred in the Ye family publishing ventures. As a leading literary family, the Shens were experienced in family publishing; Ye Shaoyuan may have obtained introductions to craftsmen from them.[112] Ye was well versed in the procedures of government publishing himself. During his tenure as an instructor at the National University in Beijing, he used the blocks stored there to print personal copies for a large number of acquaintances as a favor; twenty-some ounces of silver sufficed for two copies of such monumental works as the *Thirteen Classics* or the *Twenty-one Official Histories*.[113]

One year after Yixiu's death, in 1636, Ye Shaoyuan compiled her works, combined them with eight other works of sons and daughters of the Ye family, and issued them as *Collected Works from the Hall of Meridian Dreams* (*Wumengtang quanji*), named after a hall in the Ye family mansion.[114] New titles were added following the death of a son in 1640 and another séance in 1642, and several later printings were made.[115] In 1646, during the turmoil of the Manchu conquest, the Ye mansion was raided, and at least some of the woodblocks were destroyed.[116] Although there is no record of the number of copies originally printed, the commercial presses immediately reprinted portions of it or included selections in anthologies. Particularly popular were the verses by women. Before the end of the Ming dynasty, the poetry collections of Yixiu, Xiaoluan, and Wanwan as well as Yixiu's *Meditations* had appeared in separate volumes.[117] Ironically, by the time these testaments to a once-domestic women's culture were made public, the group's formal life had came to an abrupt end.

One unintended result of Shen Yixiu's awareness of the communicative power of the printed word and her efforts to preserve women's writings was the creation of a large body of materials documenting her own life cycle. These records — preserved in poetry, biography, and more — reveal that Yixiu was a family-oriented person, devoted to her husband and children even while she was burdened by her duties of serving her mother-in-law and managing the household. Besides a brief trip to Nanjing where her husband was to take up a new post, she never traveled beyond her native Wujiang. Like many gentrywomen of her day, her physical mobility was restricted. Her social life, in turn, centered on female relatives from her maternal and husband's families — aunts, cousins, sisters-in-law, daughters, and nieces — in patterns regulated by the dictates of the patriarchal family.

Although proximity of residence and frequent contact created strong emotional bonds, such women's networks were unstable, their membership changing with the departure of a woman following her husband or father. Physical separation and distance, however, did not sever or weaken these networks. On the contrary, the common experiences of parting and, ultimately, of death were so strong that they brought together women who had no family ties or who had never met. To the extent that the exchange of poems and other forms of writings commemorated these expanded networks, the spread of literacy and printing facilities in the seventeenth century worked, however indirectly, to enlarge the communities of women in Jiangnan.

Engraved onto woodblocks and inscribed in black and white, the legacy of domestic women's communities and their private intimacies acquired a transcendental significance. One-and-a-half centuries after Shen Yixiu's death, the muses in her family had become celebrities in their native Suzhou prefecture. When Ren Zhaolin (fl. 1776–1823), a man of letters whose wife, Zhang Yunzi (b. 1756), headed a "public" poetry club, wanted to adduce proof of the illustrious heritage of his native Suzhou, he invoked the name of Shen Yixiu and mentioned her daughters.[118] Ren was probably also the one who named the poetry club after the ancient name of Suzhou — "Ten Wuzhong Poets." Women poets joined the ranks of chaste widows and virtuous martyrs as symbols of communal honor and local pride.

So natural was this equation of talent with virtue to some members of the literati that in describing poets they employed the very language and conventions used by gazetteer writers to celebrate local chaste widows. Zhang Yunzi, the acknowledged leader of Ten Wuzhong Poets, for example, was introduced by her nephew in these terms: "Many women have been known by their poetry in history. But *our* Suzhou, on the shores of Lake Tai and other waters and bordered by the East and West Dongting mountains, is particularly adorned by an auspicious aura. Even among women, those skilled in rhymes and rhythms are too numerous to hail from one family" (italics added).[119]

From Shen Yixiu and Ye Xiaoluan to Zhang Yunzi — in the course of over a hundred years the legacy of a literate women's culture had become a visible icon in the public realms of communal pride and local history. Born out of the intimacies in the inner chambers, this women's culture had transcended time and space and whatever constraints that the male-centered kinship structure may have inflicted. Shen Yixiu, who labored so hard in her last years to preserve and transmit the women's legacy, would have been pleased.

This transcendence was all the more remarkable in light of Shen Yixiu's domestic and stationary existence. Shen was a model domestic woman who strayed neither from her inner chambers nor from the norms of womanhood as taught to her. As submissive daughter-in-law, devoted wife, industrious household manager, and responsible mother, she can be said to have lived up to her calling even by the strictest standards. Except for a sojourn in Nanjing and outings with women friends, Shen did not venture out of her quarters physically. It is significant that even for such a quintessential domestic woman, life was far from being a predetermined course marked by isolation and confinement. As far as Shen was concerned, separate male/female spheres by no means implied cloistering from either the concerns of men or the company of other women.

To Shen Yixiu, the doctrine of separate spheres meant first and foremost a functional differentiation between his and her domestic duties, which she seemed to have accepted without question. In spite of this functional separation, Shen's intellectual and emotional worlds showed a remarkable degree of interpenetration between the male and female domains. She was equally avid in discussing literature and Buddhism with her husband as she was with other females. Although she developed emotional ties with her daughters and friends in the absence of male company, as she contemplated publication projects to preserve their poetic legacy she enlisted the help of her husband and his kin-based networks. The domestic woman's world was often separate from that of man's, but it was not separatist.

In her relatively stationary existence Shen Yixiu was typical of most respectable housewives. Yet a growing number also found that to fulfill their familial calling, they had to travel away from home or be active in the public arena. These gentrywomen's mobility, extensive social networks, and the breadth of their literary visions are the subject of the next chapter.

Social and Public Communities

GENEALOGIES ACROSS TIME AND SPACE

CHEN YIXIU'S "DOMESTIC" poetry club, the most common form of women's community, remained hidden in the domestic realm for most of its life span. Other gentry poets navigated the social and public arenas more openly — by traveling outside home or by becoming such well-known writers that they overshadowed their male kin. In this chapter, I examine the communities formed by these women writers in realms that radiated from, but extended far beyond, the domestic. Not only were the domestic/public boundaries extremely fluid, but the roles a woman could assume were also quite wide-ranging.

The gentry poets portrayed in this chapter — travelers, matriarchs, and members of "social" and "public" poetry clubs — expanded the "domestic" women's communities across three kinds of boundaries: geographical, temporal, and social. Without defying the demands of Thrice Following, these prolific and serious-minded women ventured into male domains of literature, public visibility, and responsibility. Each in her own way demonstrated that a woman's familial calling could be reconciled with her new vocation as writer. By constructing genealogies of learned women, they even sought to graft a tradition of literate women's culture onto the male-centered kinship system.

On the Road

Geographical confines were the least troublesome boundaries that gentry poets negotiated. Traveling was indeed quite common for women from scholar-official families in seventeenth-century Jiangnan. Whether a local excursion or a trek across provinces, traveling was not perceived as a violation of the domestic woman's propriety. As the itinerant artist Huang Yuanjie argued, the virtues of domesticity and purity depended more upon

a woman's moral intentions — her subjective will — than the physical location of her body.

It was especially common for daughters and wives to accompany bureaucrats to their distant postings. Bound feet may have slowed long-distance trips, yet gentrywomen, who rode in palanquins, carts, and boats, eagerly took to the road with a sense of obligation and adventure. By serving fathers or husbands in transit and in faraway posts, they were complying with the literal meaning of Thrice *Following*. This compliance, translated into opportunities to explore new horizons, brought joy and new knowledge to the traveler, not to mention the envy of friends they left behind.

Wang Fengxian, wife of a magistrate of Yichun, Jiangxi province, was one such gentrywoman. In the early winter of 1600, Wang oversaw the packing of their belongings and readied her family — husband Zhang Benjia, two daughters, and an infant son — for the two-month river trip back home to Jiangnan. After a three-year stint at this outpost in mountainous western Jiangxi, the magistrate and his family boarded a river barge for the eastward journey home. Wang Fengxian, a well-educated poet, kept a travel diary. What interested her most was neither the logistics of traveling nor the famous sights on the way, but the minute pleasures and moments of revelation on the road.

The journey itself was slow and taxing. It took the family three weeks to make its way downstream on the Gan River system, passing by the city walls of Nanchang, to the shores of Lake Poyang, the largest lake in the country. There they changed onto an upstream course via the Xin River, sailing to the Jiangxi-Zhejiang border. This last leg of the Jiangxi journey was rougher than usual, since the water level was too low for their vessel. "We found and moved into a smaller barge to spend the night," wrote Wang. "Consider this cabin roomy only if you stand on your knees. If you stand up straight, your hair gets caught in the roof; if you lie down straight, your feet hit the board. It is hard to wash up. All I could do is to tie my hair up with a kerchief and sit hunched up all day. The discomfort is too much for words."[1]

But the gentry wife prided herself on her endurance: "By nature, I am affected by neither travail nor comfort. So I manage to shrug off the ordeal with a long laugh." Furthermore, poetry provided a much-welcomed di-

---

(*Opposite*) Modes of traveling by class and gender: late Ming prints typically depict the woman traveler in a horse-drawn cart, the man on horseback, and the attendants on foot. Gentrywomen also rode in carts pulled by men, palanquins, and boats; peasant women walked (*Xixiang ji*. Late Ming edition; reprinted — Chang Bide, pp. 234–35).

version. Watching her infant son blowing a reed, Wang urged her two elder daughters to join her in composing four-line poems teasing him. When they finally docked and hurried to rest in an inn, Wang fell ill and was kept up all night. To pass the time, she again set her thoughts to verse.[2] The key role played by reciting and composing verses in the everyday life of women and in bringing mother and daughters together, as we have seen in such domestic women as Shen Yixiu and her daughters, is just as evident here.

Like Yixiu, Wang Fengxian attended to her daughters' literary education personally. She had them recite the three genres of Tang poetry and taught them such historical and poetic classics as the *Zuo Chronicles* and *Book of Songs*, together with samples from the *Songs of Chu* and *Selections of Refined Literature* (*Wenxuan*), a model anthology compiled by the Southern Dynasties prince Xiao Tong (501–31). Both daughters were prolific poets who died in their prime.[3] As noted earlier, Shen Yixiu, struck by the similar tragedies that befell the two families, included works by Wang and her daughters in *Her Meditations*.[4]

Wang Fengxian's younger brother endorsed not only his sister's erudition but also the female tradition of learning she initiated with unrestrained enthusiasm. In a preface to Wang's published poetry collection, *Scribbles Rescued from Fire* (*Fenyu cao*), he wrote: "Fortunately, the precarious thread of our family learning is preserved in history by the work of one famous lady."[5] Another brother placed first in the county examination, but Fengxian was the most prolific and well-known writer in her family.

After their brief respite at the inn, Wang and her family crossed the Jiangxi border, rode to the nearest port on the Qu River in Zhejiang and continued to head east by boat. Wang Fengxian's spirit picked up as they sailed through the cliffs cut by the Fuchun River, an area rich in legends and ancient history. Gazing at the roaring rapids, the gentry poet became nostalgic about Wu Zixu (d. 484 B.C.), a famous minister of the Spring and Autumn period who ended his life in the area. A native of Chu, Zixu fled to the rival kingdom of Wu when the Chu ruler murdered Zixu's father and brother. He succeeded in aiding the Wu king's conquest of Chu. The Wu king, however, mistrusted Zixu and forced him to commit suicide when the latter advised against accepting the surrender of Wu's archenemy, Yue. As Zixu had feared, Yue staged a comeback on the brink of extinction and eliminated Wu. "Thinking of Wu Zixu," wrote Wang Fengxian, "I cannot hold back my rage and regret [for inept rulers]. I compose a short verse and throw it into the river as consecration."[6]

As virile sentiments that betray a burning concern for the fate of one's country, "rage and regret" (*fenhen*) are hardly appropriate for a refined lady. Yet this is not the only time that Wang Fengxian exhibited "manly" concerns. Having read *A Book for the Burning* (*Fenshu*), the battle call of the eclectic thinker-teacher Li Zhi (1527–1602), she was unabashed in her approval of Li's radical critique of the Confucian tradition, which included his affirmation of human bodily desires and the propriety of women's education. In a poem she praised Li's writings: "Every character is chiseled, a model for the world; / Every word is medicine, serving as my teacher."[7] In spite of her heroic sentimentalism and admiration for the works of Li Zhi, Wang Fengxian did not think of herself as overstepping the prescribed boundaries for women. In her personal life, Wang was exemplary in her adherence to the requirements of feminine virtues.

Wang's husband died soon after their return to Jiangnan, and she followed the course for a respectable widow, managing family affairs while coaching her son for the examination for over three decades. Both daughters died in the course of Wang's long widowhood. Pouring her remorse into poetry, Wang was said to have burned most of her verses, telling her brother that "literature is not the woman's way [*fudao wuwen*]; let me commit them to fire." Her brother argued: "I disagree. Most of the 300 *Songs* were from women's hands. . . . The compiler of the *Songs* included them in the Guofeng section, the fountainhead of moral persuasion." He went on to point out that his sister was beyond reproach in her conduct as daughter, wife, and mother, and hence her words were "exemplars for the inner quarters." He was responsible for the publication of her poetry collection.[8]

No matter how far it took her from her boudoir, Wang's trip to and from western Jiangxi was one expression of her faithfulness to the dictum of Thrice Following—she had to serve her husband at home, in transit, and in sojourn. Many gentrywomen took similar journeys. This lack of control over place of residence, as discussed in the preceding chapter, resulted in many truncated friendships and an overwhelming sense of transition and emotional interruption. From the point of view of the official kin structure, gentry wives and daughters played their roles well by following their men's footsteps. Their outward journey was merely an extension of their domestic calling.

Although the women would not have disputed this, they also welcomed a chance to venture from their familiar environment. Experiences on the road often left an indelible mark. At the conclusion of her journey, Wang Fengxian looked back: "We passed through many counties. At times we toiled and seemed to have come to a dead end, lost in thought for the rise and fall of history. At times the sun was warm and the wind gentle, the waves sparkling and the moon serene. All the delights in our hearts, the depth of our vision, the gains and losses, the repetitions and variations, I cannot bear to forget any of them."[9] For Wang, her eastward journey was a metaphor for the vicissitudes of life itself.

The woman travelers rarely left travelogues like Wang Fengxian's. Huang Yuanjie, the itinerant teacher and writer, seemed to prefer dwelling on the pleasures of reunion than on the tribulations of the road. In spite of the paucity of firsthand travel accounts, it is clear that many women in the seventeenth century took to the road for three reasons. First, wives, daughters, and daughters-in-law followed the bureaucratic transfers of fathers and husbands. While Shen Yixiu, for example, sojourned in Nanjing, her daughter was on her way to Guangdong. Be it a move "up" to metropolitan centers or "down" to the distant periphery, these women retained full respectability in spite of the new terrains they traversed.

Second, women traveled for pleasure. Despite the stipulation that a good woman never ventured from the inner chambers, many ladies stole to the mountains for retreats with their families, visited local sights with other women, or took pleasure boat rides on the lakes and waterways of Jiangnan. Shen Yixiu and best friend Zhang Qianqian, for example, went boating and drinking on a lake; records of such outings abound in the poetry of gentrywomen. This small group of privileged women enjoyed the leisure and means to partake in the late Ming travel boom. These trips, too, were considered entirely within the bounds of respectability. It is clear that there existed a gap between the ideal of a cloistered woman and a degree of de facto acceptance of her mobility and visibility, however circumscribed such freedoms were.

The mobility of a third kind of woman traveler was more unconventional. Professional writers and artists led an itinerant existence, as we have seen in the examples of Huang Yuanjie and Wang Duanshu. Similarly, courtesans lacked permanent homes; they traversed provinces and regions seeking patrons, inspiration, or simply adventure. Their transitory lives and their contributions to the travel boom are examined in the next chapter.

Armchair Travelers

Despite its growing popularity, traveling was still a privilege and chancy undertaking for the majority of women. For every woman who took to the road, there were many more vicarious travelers at home. Through the long-distance correspondence that women maintained with relatives and friends, the impact of the travel boom reverberated in the inner chambers. In the same way that dreaming about "mountains" eased the pains of an unhappy marriage for Ye Wanwan, armchair traveling through reading the many letters and poems the traveler sent home provided escape for the unfortunate women left behind.

Wu Bai (d. ca. 1660), a Hangzhou woman widowed at eighteen without consummating her marriage, was consigned to a lifelong cloistered existence. One of her two sisters apparently married an official whose career took her to the heart of Zhejiang and the Yangzi Gorges. Green with envy, Wu Bai seized upon every opportunity to learn about her trips and to maintain a tenuous link with the outside world through letters. One to her sister reads:

I read your letter to brother, in which you wrote: "The Three Gorges, for a stretch of several hundred *li*, are bounded by cliffs as stiff as a standing screen and summits as piercing as a sword. . . . " It is my sister's heavenly destiny that brought you there. How envious I am, how envious! Some ancient said that it was the regret of his life not to have been to Yizhou, having visited all of the other eight *zhou*s. What does my sister think of this? If you wouldn't mind sending me some pictures, then your younger sister, widowed in her quarters, can indulge herself as an armchair traveler.[10]

Wu Bai's longing to overcome her confinement, at least psychologically, was expressed in another letter to her sister. "I have heard that for the hundred and some *li* where the Fuchun River joins the Tong River, the water is an azure blue. So you have feasted your eyes on this? What joy, what joy! I take it that you don't miss the twin peaks and twelve bridges of our native place? But don't forget to come home someday."[11] Her knowledge of geography and her plea for pictures bespoke both her boredom and her eagerness to break out of her isolation. An avid reader, Wu delved not only into geography but also into poetry and herbal medicine.[12]

For Wu Bai, writing alleviated the monotony of her daily life, and vicarious traveling, like reading literature, enabled her to partake in a larger and more eventful world. Before Wu's death after five years of widowhood, she immersed herself in these activities while maintaining a frequent correspondence with her father and two sisters. Having been warned by her father that poetry was not a woman's calling, Wu wrote this reply: "With due respect to your teaching that poetry writing is not a woman's calling, do you suppose that your daughter didn't know it?" Yet Wu went on to defend her addiction in much the same way as did Fang Weiyi, the respected Tongcheng widow.

"Your daughter seems to be destined by heaven [*tianyuan*] in the way of poetry," Wu could barely disguise her pride in her poetic talent. "Whenever I feel sick, with no relief for my pent-up frustrations, chanting a verse in the most nonchalant way will surely dispel all my headaches and sorrows." Poetry for her, Wu emphasized, was purely diversion. "If I had to tax my brain and rack my mind over it, that would mean poetry made me sicker; then I would have burned my brush and thrown away my ink long ago. Need I wait for your admonition now?"[13] Wu accepted that her unfortunate widowhood was ordained by heaven but insisted that so was her poetic talent.

To the isolated and cloistered widow, writing poetry and letters *was* armchair traveling. Although Wu did not state so explicitly, she hinted that her loneliness and domestic confinement would have been unbearable without these outlets. Along with the popular belief that talent caused a woman's downfall was an equally persuasive argument that poetic talent could help safeguard chaste widowhood. Without such outlets, it would have been more difficult for women to live up to the strenuous demands of widowhood and the domestic woman ideal. Thanks to these vicarious vehicles for transcending her isolation, Wu Bai adhered steadfastly to the Thrice Following, and her name was cloaked in unquestionable respectability.

It is thus no accident that many of the outstanding women writers in seventeenth-century Jiangnan were virtuous widows—Wang Fengxian, Fang Weiyi, and Zou Saizhen are discussed above; Shang Jinglan and Gu Ruopu, below. Their extraordinary output can be attributed to their freedom from conjugal duties and their desperate need for literature as an emotional and psychological outlet. They also constituted a most famous and respected kind of woman writer. Their unquestionable respectability was rooted in three factors: class, for their families were well enough off to support their livelihood; virtue, exemplified by their proper conduct as chaste widows; and age, longevity being an unequivocal sign of heaven's approval of their ways. With the firm support and blessing of their families and communities, these virtuous widows served as useful reminders that premature death was not the only destiny for women endowed with poetic talent.

Shang Jinglan and the "Social" Community

For Shang Jinglan (1605–ca. 1676), widow of the famous Ming loyalist martyr Qi Biaojia (1602–45), a three-decade long widowhood allowed for a cherished freedom and respected space within the realm of domesticity. She taught her daughters and daughters-in-law poetry, "singing in harmony" with them, and contributed prefaces to works by other women. Their poetry club differed from the one in Shen Yixiu's family in that it was a "social" form of community. Friends from outside the family, most notably Huang Yuanjie, were as active as female relatives. Shang Jinglan's community of poetic women thus operated in a wider geographical space than did domestic communities. It also inhabited multiple social locations that encompassed male/female and domestic/public domains. Shang's broad horizons and the high respect in which she was held enabled her to negotiate the geographical and social boundaries of her women's community with ease and grace.

Although Shang Jinglan's upbringing was similar to Shen Yixiu's, their life cycle patterns and social relations differed as a result of the divergent career paths of their husbands. Daughter of a minister of works from Guiji, part of Shaoxing prefecture in Zhejiang, she received a classical education at home and was a famed gentry poet by the time she married Qi Biaojia from the neighboring county of Shanyin. Presiding over a large family of dramatists and scholars, Qi's father was a bibliophile whose Tansheng Hall collection was as famous as that of the Fan family's Tianyi Pavilion in Ningbo.[14] Biaojia, a majestically handsome man, passed the provincial examination when he was sixteen and became a *jinshi* when only twenty. The marriage between Shang Jinglan and Qi Biaojia in 1620 was hailed as the union of a golden couple, and like Ye Shaoyuan and Shen Yixiu, they stayed faithful and loving until death.

Qi Biaojia's long and prominent bureaucratic career had a major impact on his family life and Shang Jinglan's physical mobility. During their 25 years of marriage, Qi Biaojia served in Fujian for seven years and in Beijing for six. Jinglan accompanied him to both posts and, except when Qi was traveling on official duties, spent most of these years with her husband. Between 1635 and 1642, Qi retired from bureaucratic life and the family returned to Shanyin for a period marked by a tranquil family life and a busy social schedule, with Qi as community and lineage leader.[15] In other words, Shang Jinglan did not experience the frequent absence of a degree aspirant and a tight family budget that characterized most of Shen Yixiu's life. In addition, the traveling and sojourning outside her native place broadened her perspectives (she traveled from Shanyin to Beijing in 1632 to meet up with Qi, arriving in a single horse-drawn cart) and brought her friends beyond the immediate circle of aunts, sisters-in-law, and cousins.

Female friends and relatives were crucial to Shang Jinglan in all stages of her life, for although she and her husband seldom lived apart, they often led separate daily lives. This was partly due to demands of the times and Qi's importance as a gentry-official and partly due to temperament. Qi Biaojia's diary, meticulously kept almost every day of his adult life, was filled with accounts of court intrigues and social dislocation during the last years of the Ming dynasty. As a judge in Fujian and later a supreme commander in Suzhou-Songjiang, Qi was preoccupied with relieving local people from soaring rice prices, hoarding, inflation, and famine. As a retired gentryman at home, he built charitable kitchens and schools, managed lineage land, ransomed women sold into brothels, and mobilized community efforts for plague relief.[16] When taking a rest from public duties, Qi, a drama aficionado, often watched performances in friends' homes until dawn.

Shang Jinglan had her own circle of friends and in the main led a social life separate from her husband's. One entry in Qi Biaojia's diary conveys the separate rhythms of their daily lives: "My wife invited several sisters and friends to chat; I sat there bored for a whole morning before I went out to review some drama scripts at a friend's." Or, on another day: "My wife and her sisters threw a birthday party for my mother in the garden while I wrote letters inquiring about the siege of the capital."[17] The contrast between the tranquillity of the women's world and the imminent collapse of a dynasty is striking. Yet for all the apparent gap between her daily activities and his, Qi's frequent mentions of "my wife" and her whereabouts suggest an emotional resonance that united the couple despite the functional separation of his and her domains.

The experience of travel and the possession of her own social networks prepared Shang Jinglan for life as a respected matriarch for over 31 years after Qi Biaojia's martyrdom in 1645. But separate social spheres did not mean that Qi and Shang led disjointed lives. Jinglan shared her husband's devotion to garden designing and book collecting. Amid accounts of famines and tenant revolts, Qi's diaries for the years 1635–37 record some restful moments in the couple's family life. After Qi returned to Shanyin from Beijing in 1635, he often took Jinglan for pleasure boat rides and sightseeing trips.[18] At least several times a month, the two would steal away to the hills, where Qi was building his own mountain retreat called the Yu Villa. Sometimes they brought their two sons and the family would spend a few days reading together while supervising the building crew. After construction was completed in 1636, Qi and Shang often held parties there. On Shang's birthday that year, for example, three Chan Buddhist monks and a group of friends gathered to celebrate, lighting lanterns as entertainment.[19]

The political commitment of her husband and two sons in the last days of the Ming dynasty shattered Shang Jinglan's tranquil family life. In 1642, Qi Biaojia returned to office in Beijing. After the fall of the capital, he strove to keep order in the Yangzhou area while balancing competing factions in the Nanjing court. After Nanjing and Hangzhou fell in 1645, Qi fasted for three days and then drowned himself in a pond.[20] His sons Lisun (b. 1627) and Bansun (b. 1632) joined the loyalist cause and gave refuge to many outlawed resisters on their family estate. Both were seized after the loyalist plot failed. Lisun bribed his way home but died not long afterward; Bansun was exiled to the northwest and spent twenty years there before he escaped to Jiangnan in 1667 and became a monk.[21] Although no record of Shang Jinglan's direct participation in her husband's and sons' loyalist action exists, she paid a dear price and, when order returned to Jiangnan, lived the life of a sonless widow.

During Shang Jinglan's seventy-odd years, she gave birth to four daughters and three sons and witnessed the death of all her sons and one daughter. Her poetry, therefore, conveyed the same agony over the passing away of children and close relatives as Shen Yixiu's.[22] But unlike Yixiu, Jinglan's life was marked by a large family of daughters, daughters-in-law, and grandsons and wide social networks. The communities of women she built around her were closely knit and long-lasting. The artistic and political accomplishments of her male kinsmen in the Qi and Shang families, her husband's martyrdom in particular, enhanced her reputation as a virtuous widow and head of the Qi household. Perhaps as a result, her fame as a poet also rose in the early Qing; her contemporaries remarked that her poems were even better than her husband's.[23] Other gentrywoman poets in Jiangnan paid her visits when they were in the Shaoxing area, and much laughter was heard in the Yu Villa.

Members of the women's communities around Shang Jinglan were of two equally important kinds: those related to her by blood and those who were not. To the former group belonged Shang's four daughters, two daughters-in-law, sisters, nieces, and other "women in the family." Jinglan taught her daughters—Deyuan, Deqiong, Deqian, and the second daughter, Mrs. Zhu, whose name is not given in records—the art of poetry from the time they were young. Since all married into local families, they lived close enough to take part in the various activities organized by their mother and her friends. The two daughters-in-law, Zhang Dehui and Zhu Derong, came from high official families and were similarly well versed in the formal requirements of poetry. The gathering of so many poets in one family seemed propitious; many early Qing writers made remarks such as "Madame Shang, widowed at 42 [*sui*], brought up her two sons, three daughters, and two daughters-in-law. They have set many a grapevine and many a flower to verse. Those walking through Plum Grove thought that they saw the twelve celestial attendants." Plum Grove (*Meishi*) was an area in Shanyin where the Qi family clustered. "Celestial attendants" (*yaotai*) refers to talented girls serving the Queen Mother of the West.[24]

Friends of Shang Jinglan played as important a role as her family members and relatives in the women's community in Plum Grove. Unlike Shen Yixiu's group, visits of friends from the neighborhood or afar or the arrival of their poems were routine to Shang's community. Often her friends

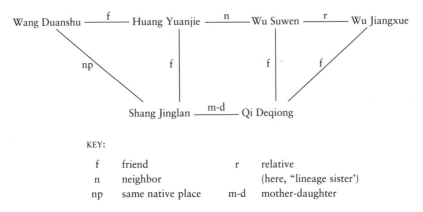

FIG. 2   An example of the friendship network centered on Shang Jinglan and Qi Deqiong

copied poems received from Jinglan and passed them on to a neighbor, sister, or friend. This brought about another exchange of poems, and a new friendship was sealed. This process was similar to that experienced by Shen Yixiu's group after the death of her two daughters in that the exchange of poetry initiated and signified new ties. A closer look into one such friendship network around Shang Jinglan reveals that similar to the mediating role of Shen Yixiu's male relatives in introducing her to new friends, mutual male friends and neighborhood relationships contributed to the growth of the "social" type of female networks. Both cases demonstrate how gentrywomen in seventeenth-century Jiangnan built their own friendship networks on existing forms of social relations, notably kinship, neighborhood, and native-place ties (see Fig. 2).

Huang Yuanjie, the itinerant poet and teacher who befriended Shen Yixiu in 1633, visited Shang Jinglan around 1654. Although this was probably their first meeting, the two may have long known each other through several mutual friends.[25] They quickly developed a rapport, and Shang invited Huang to stay. The company of a writer as accomplished as Huang excited and inspired the entire group that gathered around Shang Jinglan. The large body of poems they composed with or for Huang Yuanjie during her yearlong stay in Plum Grove was later handcopied by Huang's daughter and published.[26]

These poems documented not only the friendship that developed between Huang Yuanjie and the Qi women but also the day-to-day activities of their women's community. Outings to the Qi's country home, the Yu Villa, and to that designed by his father, the Mi Villa, were their favorite. The women left many poems describing how they made rubbings of stone stelae, picked peaches, viewed jasmine and plum blossoms, or stole away on a rainy day to the library in the villas. The whole group was once invited to a lantern party by a certain Madame Wu who lived nearby. Festivals or the mere passing of the seasons were occasions for gatherings; so were the comings and goings of friends.[27]

In a poem entitled "For Huang Yuanjie, Teacher of the Inner Chambers," Shang expressed her admiration for her friend's erudition by comparing her to other illustrious writers in history:

> For ten years I have lived behind closed doors in Penglai,[28]
> Not expecting to set eyes on her dress pretty as the clouds.
> Her genius follows that of Ban Zhao,
> The elegance of her style matches Zuo Shi.
> In calligraphy she vies with Youfu in all eight styles,
> In the genre of rhyme-prose she writes like Sima Xiangru.
> As I hold her arm today and feel our harmony,
> I begin to see she is indeed the Xue Tao of our day.[29]

In Shang Jinglan's depictions, Huang Yuanjie negotiated the borders between male/female and private/public domains with extreme ease. By deeming Huang as good as a man, Sima Xiangru, but also a woman writer in her own right, Shang alluded to the androgynous freedom Huang enjoyed as a writer-teacher. Shang also called attention to the fluidity of Huang's social locations; she was as at home in the genteel abode of Ban Zhao as she was in the courtesan quarters of Xue Tao.

More significantly, as a tribute by one woman poet to another, this poem documents Shang Jinglan's construction of a genealogy of women writers. Except for Sima Xiangru, all the names she invoked were female. By comparing Huang to three of the most accomplished woman writers in the history of Chinese literature — Ban Zhao, Zuo Fen, and Xue Tao, Shang conveyed a sense of an unbroken tradition of erudite women that had begun centuries earlier and culminated in her own times. The making of a literate women's history extended the horizons of the poet in time, just as actual or vicarious traveling projected her trajectory in space. This extension temporally and spatially defied her supposedly secluded and centripetal existence.[30]

Indeed, Shang Jinglan's own life is an eloquent statement of the public influence that a widowed poet could exert. To begin with, her adherence to the moral and sexual strictures of chaste widowhood did not prevent her from leading an active social life. She traveled to the mountains at will, hosted drinking parties, and invited Huang Yuanjie, whose reputation, as we have seen, was questioned in some quarters, to be a house guest for one year. Her own unblemished name, however, became all the more laudable and appeared to have enhanced Huang's respectability.

Shang's apparent social freedoms were afforded by her long widowhood and family background: widows blessed with property, offspring, and old age commanded familial authority and communal respect. Shang Jinglan made good use of these sanctioned freedoms to build an enduring women's community around her and to extend its borders across space, time, and social location.

Women's Communities as Icons of Localism

Seriousness of purpose alone does not explain the expansive scope of Shang Jinglan's socializing and her respectable name. The fame of Shang Jinglan's community and of the Banana Garden poets, discussed below, was bound up with the localism of their native places, Shaoxing and Hangzhou, respectively. In the context of surges of localism in seventeenth-century Jiangnan, many men appeared to be willing to put the propriety question aside as they paraded the talents of daughters from their own families and native places.

Wang Siren, father of the professional writer Wang Duanshu, conveyed his discomfort with how far such veneration had gone: "Lately, in Jiangsu and Zhejiang, whenever a lady scribbles a verse, people seize upon it as if it were the sound of jade. The fame of women in the inner chambers can even surpass that of men."[31] As mentioned earlier, female talent was valorized in local gazetteers and became a criterion along with moral steadfastness for the enshrinement of a woman's name in history. Shen Yixiu and her daughters, too, by the eighteenth century had become entrenched symbols of the sophistication of their native Suzhou prefecture. The frequency of such valorizations seems to signal a conscious rivalry among the major Jiangnan urban centers.

Suzhou, a major contestant for the laurels, counted among its ranks a pair of close friends, Xu Yuan and Lu Qingzi, who maintained their friendship over distance through poetry. They were said to be renowned as the Two Masters from Suzhou.[32] When Xu Yuan's verses, *Shuttling Chants* (*Luowei yin*), were published by her husband in 1613, a distant uncle lamented in the preface that women's poetry had prospered in the early Ming but since declined. That is, "until the recent century when in *our* [italics added] Suzhou, there appears Madame Fan," or Xu Yuan.[33]

Hangzhou, too, had its share of illustrious poets. In the 1630's, a native son recited an entire genealogy when he prefaced the works of his elder sister, Gu Ruopu. This exultation, too, followed the gazetteer convention:

Recently many women have produced writings. To focus on *our* [italics added] Hangzhou, in the past decades we have had Yuyan, daughter of Mr. Tian [Yiheng] Ziyi, and her "Posthumous Scrawls from Yushulou"; Jingfang, daughter of Mr. Yu Changru, and her *Posthumous Songs from Jingyuan*. As for those still alive, we have the calligraphy of Zhang Qiongru, the paintings of Liang Mengzhao, and the poetry of Zhang Siyin. Feminine and graceful, these works all leave a fragrant legacy. Indeed, as Mr. Ma said, "The meandering waters of the Qiantang River and the grandeur of the mountains cannot be monopolized by the male literati."[34]

Such collective invocation of the woman writer's name and works created a space for women not only to read and write privately but also to do so publicly and in the company of other women. This surge of familial and local pride thus facilitated the "social" and "public" forms of women's communities.

The irony is that for all their agility through space and time, social and public communities of women were also implicated in contests of localism. In other words, the most dynamic and visible communities were inherently the most fragmented. The women themselves were often relentless in drawing boundaries between "we" and "they." Fang Mengshi (d. 1640), a poet from Tongcheng, Anhui, wrote a letter to her sister Fang Weiyi denigrating Xu Yuan, the pride of Suzhou: "She barely learned how to read, her verses are slapdash, full of pettiness and platitudes. There are in fact no talented [women] in this world, so people have to invent them and call her as such. Now I know that Suzhou people are vain and vulgar, and I don't mean just the men."[35] The literatus Qian Qianyi, most impressed by Mengshi's own erudition and eloquence, chimed in with a lame defense of Xu Yuan, who hailed from the same prefecture as he: "Madame [Fang] has gone too far in slandering *our* [italics added] Suzhou. Granted, the Suzhou people are asking for it. I know it in my heart but dare not say it out loud."[36]

Fang Mengshi's revulsion at Xu Yuan might stem from their different tastes in poetry. As we will see in the next chapter, Xu frequently used colloquialisms and delighted in unconventional subjects such as tribal attacks on the borders of Yunnan. Fang might even have questioned the morality of Xu, who, by all accounts a respectable lady, befriended singing girls and wrote verses for them. But the fact that Fang chose to couch her loathing in native-place terms suggests that women were not immune to the regionalism and localism of seventeenth-century Jiangnan.

Sentiments like Fang Mengshi's were seeds of discord to women's culture as well. Although further research on women from the lower classes and different regions is needed to ascertain the possibilities of a common women's culture in seventeenth-century China, suffice it to note here that among gentrywomen writers in Jiangnan, identity as woman was often subservient to familial and communal loyalties. From this perspective, the space carved out by women writers was not extraneous to existing hierarchies; rather, it belonged to the larger process whereby distinctions were created and redefined in society. I will elaborate on the implications of this in the next chapter.

Public Community: The Banana Garden Poets

The seminal example of a women's community's prominence in the identity of its native place is the Banana Garden poetry club of Hangzhou. The reputation of this early Qing community soared so high that it acquired a formal name — Banana Garden Seven — with the visibility of a public institution on the cultural landscape of Hangzhou. In the sections that follow, I examine the familial and public identities of its members, the legacy of the women's culture they created, and the multiple connections between this culture and other forms of social organization, most notably the male-centered official kinship system.

Local sons and daughters of Qing Hangzhou had no lack of famous sites, scholar-officials, and heroes to remember their hometown by, but the women of the Banana Garden held a special place in their collective memory. In the second half of the seventeenth century, a group of gentrywomen gathered regularly in their villas to drink, compose poetry, and exchange paintings — activities no different from what their literati fathers and husbands would have done if the Qing government had not cracked down on the poetry clubs as hotbeds of loyalist resistance. The women, however, enjoyed a reprieve from both the political and moral authorities. The Banana Garden Five, as the most renowned five members were known collectively, became a fixture on the Hangzhou cultural landscape. Later, with the departure of two members, the remaining three invited four relatives and friends to form the Banana Garden Seven, a "public" women's community. My discussion here focuses on this latter group of seven. Occasionally, I use "women of the Banana Garden" to refer to all nine poets and their associates.[37]

The word *public* describes two characteristics of the Banana Garden Seven poetry club: its physical visibility in public and the literary fame of its members. A favorite pastime of the Banana Garden women was poetry parties on pleasure boats that navigated the scenic waters of West Lake. Contrary to Confucian precepts prescribing anonymity, quietude, and domesticity, the public presence of these woman poets by no means detracted from their social standing and respectability. To the people of Hangzhou, the sophisticated style and erudite taste they brought to the lake bespoke their distinguished pedigree. A native son noted the contrast between these refined ladies and their vulgar sisters:

At the time, Hangzhou people had extravagant habits. In the warm and clear spring, pleasure boats with brocade curtains swarmed the waters; sightseers on the lake rivaled those on the shore in gaudery. All were decked out in bright earrings, feather-shaped jades, and silk chiffon dresses with pearly tails, showing off [their fashion] to each other. Chai [Jingyi] Jixian alone would paddle a small boat with

最恨無情芳
草路隆些闌舍
墨名西東

A woman skirts the shores of West Lake in a palanquin to attend festivities (Zhou Ji, *Xihu erji*. Late Ming edition; reprinted — Nagasawa, *Mindai sōzubon zuroku*, p. 44).

Feng [Xian] Youling, Qian [Fenglun] Yunyi, Lin [Yining] Yaqing, and Gu Qiji [Si], all high-class ladies [*dajia*, literally "great families"]. In plain dresses of raw silk and hair gathered into a single bun, these ladies passed around the writing brush and shared sheaves of paper. The pleasure-seeking women [*younü*] in neighboring boats beheld them and lowered their heads, feeling embarrassed that they were no match.[38]

Chai, Feng, Qian, Lin, and Gu were daughters of local notable families who constituted the core of the Banana Garden poetry club. The contrast between them and the other women in this stylized depiction smacks of the disdain with which oldtime gentry families regarded the nouveaux riches. In the eyes of the established elites, well-educated and presentable daughters constituted one hallmark of gentility. Neither the cloistered maiden nor the showy powdered-face was to be an apt model.

Not only were these women at ease in their outings, but they were also unintimidated by what other women regarded as a conflict between literary fame and moral respectability. Showing no such signs of agony or self-doubt as burning their manuscripts, they seemed to have taken the late Ming deliberations on writing as a woman's calling for granted. To them, writing was such a natural and honorable undertaking for women that it needed no apology or constant justification. At least four of the Banana Garden women had their collected works published in their lifetime, with prefaces and commentaries written by the other poetry club members. As can be gleaned from extant fragments of such works, these women commented on national affairs, their lives as women, their dedication to literature, and their friendship. Although these concerns resembled those of writers from domestic poetry clubs, the public standing of the Banana Garden poets gave their writings a tone of unapologetic confidence.

The fellowship of women across generations created an environment conducive to their self-confidence, serious literary purpose, and public concerns. The Banana Garden poets were descendants — physical in some cases, spiritual and philosophical in others — of an extraordinary Hangzhou matriarch, Gu Ruopu. The founder of the Banana Garden poetry club, Gu Yurui, was Ruopu's niece.[39] During Ruopu's long and prolific life of over 90 years, she served as role model and teacher to Yurui and many younger poets. Although she was not a formal member of the Banana Garden poetry clubs, under her tutelage these women constructed a literature-based women's culture that stood as the crowning achievement of a spectrum that included domestic and social networks.

The women of the Banana Garden crafted a historical space for themselves — across generations and against the current of time, they established a genealogy of women writers traceable to a female progenitor, Gu

Ruopu. This women's tradition was significant in its spatial dimensions as well. In public domains — be it the waterways of Hangzhou, the world of publishing, or the pages of local history — these women forged a group identity that transcended familial ties. Although in their familial lives these women might have shouldered father's or husband's responsibilities, in their own Banana Garden they gathered as women and as writers. They inhabited a space that straddled the domestic and the public not as substitutes for men but as bona fide women.

Gu Ruopu the Mother-Teacher: Education as Living Faith

The women of the Banana Garden came together through the mediation of three principles of social organization: kin and affinal relations, neighborhood, and male poetry clubs. Opportunities for social interaction, however, would not have automatically brought about the formation of networks if the women had not wanted to sustain contact and give it an institutional expression. Gu Ruopu's quarters provided them such a rallying point. They constituted, in this sense, a truly voluntary women's association under the tutelage of an extraordinary role model.

Gu Ruopu the mother-teacher played a leadership role not only among the women but also within her marital family, the Huangs, during most of her adult life. A virtuous widow for over 60 years, she outlived the Huang patriarchs and assumed the status of a matriarch. A local gazetteer published soon after her death honored Gu by issuing her biography under her own name, not that of her father or husband, and eulogized her unusual contributions to the kinship system, including the establishment of sacrificial fields: "Concerned that the lineage laws [*zongfa*] had fallen into disarray, Gu personally compiled the Huang genealogy and set up sacrificial fields to provide for ritual functions. For her entire life she aspired to emulate Fan Zhongyan's charitable estates but did not have the means. She said: 'My descendants will fulfill my dream.' "[40] Gu Ruopu was no rebel in acquiring the power and esteem denied to most women. In a sense, she was merely exercising the prerogatives of a lineage elder. At the same time, we have to recognize her as a woman who lived out the traditional calling of serving her family to the fullest.

For Gu, her lifelong commitment was that of a mother-teacher. Daughter of a notable Hangzhou gentry family, Ruopu married Huang Maowu, the eldest son of a local family of comparable standing, in 1606. Gu and Huang, an examination candidate, shared some tender moments during their thirteen years together, which produced two sons and two daughters. In 1619, Huang Maowu passed away after a long illness without attaining a degree. His father, Huang Ruheng (1558–1626; *jinshi* 1598), lamented that his son "showed promise, but lacked time, outstanding writings, and laudable deeds to distinguish himself."[41] In other words, Maowu died without any substantive accomplishments short of the sons he fathered; Ruheng pinned his hopes on the young widow and her two sons.

Huang Ruheng, a firm believer in the virtues of educated mothers, saw in Ruopu the missing link in the transmission of scholarship through the male line of descent in his family. A notable literary figure in Hangzhou and a friend of the dramatist Tang Xianzu, Huang was advanced in age when his son died.[42] He then sought to impart his literary expertise to his daughter-in-law. He reasoned: "My two infant grandsons have shown promising beginnings; my daughter-in-law is agile with ideas and schooled in literary composition. She would make a good mother, raising and teaching the two boys. Through them, my son will live on."[43]

Gu Ruopu had received a literary education in her youth and was "singing in harmony" with her husband as a young bride. But her father-in-law gave her a man's literary education by leading her systematically through the *Book of Changes*, *Book of Songs*, the Daoist classic *Zhuangzi*, *Songs of Chu*, and prose from the Qin-Han masters. Ruopu was a most enthusiastic student. "Everyday Ruopu would wait for Ruheng in the living room," recorded a local history. "Before Ruheng emerged, she would stand as still as a screen, holding her books." Huang Ruheng was pleased both with her intelligence as a surrogate son and her filial piety as a daughter-in-law. Before a roomful of guests feasting on the food and wine prepared by Ruopu, he handed her the highest praise: "[Seeing her,] it seems as though my son is still alive."[44]

The young widow took to the task of mother-teacher seriously. For her elder son she had a "study-boat" built. Docked at a hidden corner on West Lake, the boat provided a refuge from the noise and distraction of home.[45] In the daytime Gu hired tutors to instruct the boys, while she went over the library holdings left by her husband systematically. She reported to her younger brother that in due time she devoured the *Four Books*, chronological histories, works on Ming history, and political treatises. In the evening she would sit the boys down and explain to them what she herself had learned that day. Often they carried on deep into the night. A new intellectual world opened up in front of Gu. "I so delighted in it that I did not think of getting tired [*cui*]," she admitted.[46] Both sons grew up to be men of letters, but neither captured any examination honors.

It was on the women of her family that the impact of Gu's educational vision was more strongly felt. Convinced that the ability to read and comprehend books was crucial to a woman's moral training, she hired teachers to instruct the girls in her family reading and writing. When an old woman chided her, Gu wrote a long poem defending her belief in women's literary education (cited above). Although many Jiangnan mothers who taught their daughters or nieces at home believed in the compatibility of female virtue and literary education, as we have seen in the examples of Shen Yixiu and Fang Weiyi, Gu Ruopu went one step further in arguing that a literary education was essential to the pursuit of virtue; without it, a woman could not be a good wife and mother.

The goal of women's education was not simply to internalize women's prescribed roles. To Gu Ruopu, the teacher-disciple relationship was a means for establishing and renewing meaningful connections with other women on a daily basis. For example, she engaged her daughter-in-law Ding Yuru in readings of Tang poetry and discussions of national politics. Evidently convinced by Gu's arguments for reviving the military colony system (*tuntian*), Ding debated the issues with her husband over cups of wine.[47]

Gu's tutelage was equally felt by women from the generation after Ding's. Years after Ding died, Yao Lingze, young bride of one of Gu's grandsons, became another devoted student. Yao lived next to Gu's quarters. For years she waited on Gu daily, often holding books in hand, fulfilling her filial duties while inquiring about the meaning of words. The two were seen engrossed in discussions early in the morning; other times they were still going strong at night.[48] The image of Yao, an eager student besieging an elder with books in her hands, is reminiscent of the young Gu Ruopu.

Gu imparted her learning and vision to kinswomen so remote that they were ritually insignificant according to kin rules constructed around the patrilineal line. In the women's eyes, kinship ties, be they maternal or affinal, provided a context out of which they forged personal relationships meaningful to them. For example, Lin Yining, a core member of the Banana Garden community, was the daughter-in-law of Gu Ruopu's niece, Gu Yurui. Yurui brought the young bride to the attention of Ruopu. Yining, then fifteen years old, won the admiration of the ailing Ruopu and became one of the last beneficiaries of her personal guidance. Lin grew up to be a gentry writer and painter well known in her native Hangzhou and throughout Jiangnan. Her first volume of collected works was published in 1697 when she was in her early forties.

A prolific writer of *shi* poetry, song lyrics, prose, Yuan song-verse (*sanqu*), and drama, Lin Yining won a rare recognition in her husband's genealogy. Unlike the usual bride who was mentioned only in passing as née so-and-so, Lin's official name (Yining) and courtesy name (Yaqing), together with the titles of her works, were recorded before the names of her sons.[49] Lin, one of the few seventeenth-century women dramatists, had a wide social network beyond the Banana Garden. We have already seen that she contributed a preface to the *Three Wives' Commentary*.

As practiced by Gu Ruopu, women's education is comparable to the true Confucian education prescribed for men by the Tang Confucian re-vivalist Han Yu and such Song Neo-Confucian thinkers as Zhu Xi, who viewed the Confucian tradition as a living faith that each individual has to affirm through a lifelong process of learning and teaching.[50] Although one cannot find explicit quotations of the Neo-Confucian canons in Gu Ruo-pu's extant writings to justify women's education, her relationship with many of the Banana Garden poets was characterized by a teaching-learn-ing exchange that was no different from the one Zhu Xi envisioned for male patriarchs.

Whereas the Neo-Confucian philosophers envisioned an unbroken chain of sages carrying the torch of the Way from one generation of men to the next, the women in Gu's orbit forged a fellowship of women along both vertical and horizontal ties. The kinship structure was a given in their lives — they could not choose their kin or evade their filial duties, but the community of women was a voluntary creation. Like-minded women, who may or may not have hailed from the same family, gathered in the Banana Garden to teach and to learn from each other. In this sense, educa-tion supplanted kinship as the most important organizational principle of the women's culture.

Female Connections: Kin, Neighbors, and Friends

As paramount as the teacher-learner tie was to the women's voluntary association, they were not averse to utilizing pre-existing affinities — kin-ship, neighborhood, male poetry clubs. Of these three, kinship ties were most important. Two of the four key members of the Banana Garden poetry clubs, Lin Yining and Qian Fenglun, were related to Gu Ruopu's natal family by marriage (see Fig. 3). Lin married Qian Zhaoxiu (1652–1711; *jinshi* 1691), whose mother, Gu Yurui, was Ruopu's niece and founder of Banana Garden Five. Qian Fenglun was Zhaoxiu's sister and married Ruopu's grandson. A third member of Banana Garden Seven, Gu Qiji, was the sister of Lin's sister-in-law and a remote relative of Ruopu.[51] The Gus, Qians and Lins, all prominent Hangzhou gentry families, had forged marriage alliances for generations, making a precise account of kin and affinal relationships difficult. Suffice it to note that Lin Yining, Qian Fenglun, and Gu Qiji were all third-generation kinswomen of Gu Ruo-pu's.

Besides kinship, the convenience of living nearby also facilitated inter-action between unrelated women. Two of the other four backbone mem-bers, Chai Jingyi and her daughter-in-law Zhu Rouze, were neighbors of Lin Yining's. Chai became intimate friends with Lin, Qian Fenglun, and Gu Qiji, as the frequent poems they exchanged attest. An accomplished

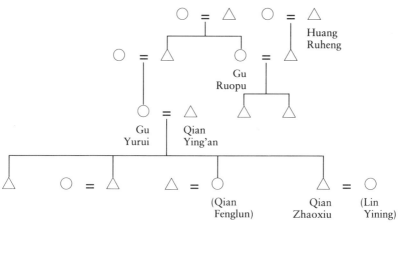

FIG. 3   The Gu, Qian, and Lin family trees. SOURCES: *Wulin Qianshi zongpu*; Hu Wenkai, *Lidai funü, passim.*

painter and prolific poet, Chai was a popular "gentry poet" featured in the anthologies of women's works issued by commercial publishers. Daughter of a *juren*, Chai hailed from a respectable literati family, but her pedigree was not as distinguished as that of the Gu women. Qian Fenglun and Lin Yining's husband were direct descendants of Qian Liu (852–932), founder of the Wuyue Kingdom (907–78), a state that encompassed Jiangsu and Zhejiang in the Five Dynasties period. Moreover, both were daughters of *jinshi*s. Despite her slight inferiority in social status measured by the ranks of patriarchs, Chai was recognized by her woman friends as their leader (*jijiu*) on the strength of her literary and artistic talent.[52] Many of Jingyi's anthologized poems document her friendship with the Banana

Garden women—she teased them, partied with them, sent them off on trips, wrote them verses as letters, and composed poems on their portraits. The popularity and respectability of her works were conducive to the public acclaim that the Banana Garden Five and Banana Garden Seven enjoyed.[53]

Besides kinship and neighborhood ties, male literati networks also played a part in female friendship. The other two members of Banana Garden Seven, Zhang Chayun (Hao) and Mao Anfang (Ti), were related to each other through their male relatives—Chayun's brother and An-fang's father both belonged to the acclaimed late Ming literati poetry club known as the Ten Poets of Hangzhou (Xiling Shizi). We do not know how they came to befriend the Banana Garden women. Chayun and Anfang might have been introduced to Chai Jingyi first, since her father was a friend of the Ten Poets. Both appeared to be short-term members of the poetry club. Zhang Chayun died at age 24. Her posthumous works so moved Shang Jinglan that she wrote a preface.[54] Mao Anfang was the daughter of the famous Hangzhou poet Mao Xianshu (1620–88). When she was in her teens, she asked him to teach her the secrets of his art. He chided, "Poetry is not your business." She disagreed and learned her art well. In fact, not only did he not oppose her writing poetry, he even contributed a preface to her published work. Mao Anfang's friendship with the Banana Garden women, too, was truncated by her death at around age 40.[55]

No matter how brief Zhang's and Mao's association with the Banana Garden women was, the literary prestige of their male kinsmen helped promote the name of the women's poetry club. The gentry standing of their families, similar to the royal pedigree of the Qians, ensured that the women's literary fame did not detract from their respectability. However entrenched the belief that a virtuous woman is an ignorant one or that poetry is not a woman's calling, the morality of the Banana Garden women was never questioned. Renowned on the pages of local histories, genealogies, and anthologies as "gentry" (guixiu) poets, they were the pride of their families and native places. Talent and virtue, as well as fame and respectability, were compatible for women born into the right families and circumstances.

While utilizing maternal and affinal kinship ties, neighborhood proximity, and male poetry societies in creating a women's community, the Banana Garden poets imposed a new logic on these pre-existing forms of social organization. Bound by a commitment to teach and to learn, they came together in their gardens and on the pages of each other's manuscripts with new identities—as writer and as woman. Their writings reveal what each of these identities meant to them.

Poetry: My God and My Son

Although, unlike such professional writers as Huang Yuanjie, these gentry poets did not have to peddle their talents and names for a living, their vision and commitment were no less serious. Literature vindicated their individual existence while giving them an identity in a larger community that transcended familial loyalties and time. Some constructed the community by recreating a woman-to-woman literary history; others played a part in a man-woman-man transmission of scholastic and artistic family traditions.

Mao Anfang epitomized the extreme sense of self-vindication felt by dedicated women poets. Approaching 40 and still without a son, Anfang once attended a women's party. Her sister-in-law presented her a herb believed to be conducive to the conception of male fetus (*yi'nan cao*) and suggested: "If you compose a poem about the herb, perhaps it will bring good luck." Anfang believed in the power of the poetic word not as talisman, however, but as the very essence of life. To her well-intentioned but misguided relative she answered: "Poetry is my god and spirit [*shenming*]; I give birth to sons through the act of writing."[56] Biological procreation perpetuated the male line of descent; literary creation vindicated the woman writer's existence as an individual and opened a gateway to immortality.

Mao Anfang's individualistic vision is not anti–patrilineal family in intent. Her statement implies that motherhood need not be a woman's only goal in life. But if Mao had had biological sons, she probably would have seen her mission as poet as compatible with that as mother. Her friends in the Banana Garden lived comfortably with their literary and familial callings without seeing a conflict between the two priorities.

Chai Jingyi wrote poetry to instruct and to encourage her daughter-in-law, Zhu Rouze. Similar to the Tongcheng widow Fang Weiyi, Chai found verse an effective medium for teaching female virtues. To Zhu the young bride she wrote:

> Stopping by your fragrant quarters,
> I watch you trying on new makeup.
> Your hairdo should stay small,
> Your spring outfit need not be long.
> Through sickness, stay diligent in weaving and embroidery,
> Although poor, do not forget to practice your verse.
> I am pleased by your industry,
> Seeing you by the well and the mortar.[57]

Modesty in fashion and hairstyle, as we have seen, distinguished these gentrywomen from their vulgar counterparts on West Lake. It is also noteworthy that to Chai Jingyi, wielding the brush is an integral part of female virtues; to neglect to practice poetry composition is a transgression as serious as moral laxness.

Poetry served motherhood as a means of education for both girls and boys. Chai Jingyi wrote poems to exhort her sons to be upright in times of national crisis.[58] This was a widespread practice among educated Jiangnan mothers, but more significant was Chai's crucial role in initiating her sons into a supposedly man-to-man poetic tradition. In response to their queries on her poetic vision, she outlined her own reading of what constituted the authentic heritage in the history of Chinese poetry:

> The Four [early Tang] Masters broke the ground of correct
>   beginnings,
> Gao [Xi], Cen [Can] and their followers are each able in their
>   own ways.
> The ornate style burns off its last glow, returning to true simplicity,
> Li Po should be second to Tu Fu.

In another poem, she taught that one can come to grasp the essence of Chinese poetry by living in it day and night, and by reciting the *Book of Songs* and *Songs of Chu*. She referred to what Confucius considered the persuasion of the *Book of Songs* — "mild and gentle, sincere and good" (*wenrou dunhou*) — and asked her sons to take the *Songs* as their teacher.[59]

Besides poetry, Chai Jingyi also taught her sons how to play the zither (*guqin*), an art acquired from her father who was a master of this musical instrument. When Jingyi was ten, her father Chai Shiyao (*juren* 1618) gave her a zither and initiated her into the world of music, an art she cherished for life. She handcopied scores for the instrument and a work prefaced by her father and taught them to her sons, the Shen brothers.[60] Chai Jingyi, as mother, became a link in the transfer of a musical tradition from the Chai patriarch to sons of the Shen family.

In contrast, Gu Ruopu filled the gap in the transmission of scholarship from one Huang patriarch to the next. We have seen how Gu received personal instruction from her father-in-law upon the death of her husband and studied her husband's books in order to teach her sons. Learned mothers like her thus constituted a crucial link in the perpetuation of family learning.

The written word was Gu Ruopu's favorite medium of education and discussion. The poem she crafted to argue for the virtues of a literary education for women is cited above, and in the preface to her own collected works she made a passionate appeal that writing was a woman's calling. Despite her claim she wrote only for diversion, many of her poems, essays, and letters were clearly written with a specific audience and educational purpose in mind. In 1632, having decided to divide the Huang family property and to establish independent households for her two sons, she wrote them an open letter. In this well-known example of Gu's polemical writing, she outlined her vision of the kinship system, reiterated her dedication to it, and offered advice on practical living to her sons.

The letter opens with a brief account of her marriage and the death of her husband thirteen years later. Gu highlighted the official view of the family as an unbroken line of male descent in recounting his last words: "Don't waste money on my funeral; teach our sons well so they can inherit the fragrance of [my family's] books; serve grandfather well to make up for my unfilial sins." The verbs "to inherit" (*ji*) and "to make up for" (*xu*) carry strong connotations of continuing a line. Gu then related how she lived in fear and trembling as a young widow and mother lest the enterprise initiated by her husband's ancestors come to a halt. The emphasis here is on vertical lines of descent and succession of the male tradition.

In the crucial section that follows, Gu introduced a woman's perspective in justifying family division. Although people held up nine generations under one roof as an ideal goal, she reasoned, these theorists paid scant attention to the social dynamics within such a large group of people. Focusing on practicalities, Gu observed that each family member is born with idiosyncrasies. "The differences and similarities in people's feelings [*renqing*] can take so many forms, how can I expect to always get what I want?" Moreover, when people have been together for too long, they get on each other's nerves. "Therefore those who are apart want to be together; those who are together want to split up." In other words, in light of human nature, a big family is not necessarily a desirable goal. In her case, Gu felt sure that her two sons would be well provided for in separate households, for her two daughters-in-law were wise, frugal, and respectful of the ancestors' rules.[61]

Gu's letter is a telling statement on how a gentry mother and virtuous widow regarded the kinship system and its ideology. Her message should be understood on two levels. Undeniably, the letter is a strong affirmation of the male-centered family, with its emphasis on patrilineality. Although Gu was sincere, if not earnest, in her dedication to this official ideology, it is misleading to infer that Gu embraced an ideology that discriminated against females. Her letter goes beyond the official kinship ideology in emphasizing how crucial women are to family survival. If she had not acted at the untimely death of her husband, the man-to-man transmission of knowledge would have been interrupted. Without the wisdom and frugality of her daughters-in-law at the helm of each of the divided households, the family tradition would be precarious. Gu was alerting her readers to the fact that the family could not run without the moral and intellectual guidance of its women. Despite their lack of formal power in a male-dominated structure, women — as mothers, wives, and matriarchs — were indispensable. In Gu Ruopu's eyes, and as we can affirm from her own position in the Huang family, women were hardly outsiders to the family system.

Although scholars have studied the importance of family and kinship in the formation of artistic and philosophical schools, they have not paid enough attention to the complicated roles played by learned daughters and mothers in the transmission of knowledge within a family, or from one family to another. The examples of Gu Ruopu and Chai Jingyi illustrate that women's education, justified on the grounds of motherhood, had a significant impact not only on the women's self-perception but also on the entire patrilineal family. Such mother-teachers as Gu and Chai made a powerful difference to their sons' careers and the transmission of family traditions. The power that originated from the women's private quarters thus shaped the course of the family's public existence. The women's perspective is unmistakable, for example, in Gu Ruopu's argument for family division based on her understanding of human feelings.

Hidden Dragon or Crowing Hen: The Man-Like Woman

The feminine perspectives articulated by the Banana Garden poets have to be assessed in the context of their man-like accomplishments and sentiments. They were better educated than most men, let alone women, in the empire; they had opportunities to write, to publish, and to become famous; they enjoyed considerable freedom in their familial and social lives. Indeed, in their educational background and concerns they were akin more to male literati — their fathers and husbands — than to the model domestic woman. Gu Ruopu, as we recall, was schooled in the examination curriculum and debated national policy issues with her daughter-in-law. The latter's stepmother, too, was said to have written a passionate indictment of Li Zicheng, the peasant rebel who invaded Beijing and brought down the Ming dynasty.[62] Chai Jingyi, upon visiting the ancient battlegrounds of the woman warrior Liang Hongyu, expressed her admiration for Liang's heroism in a poem.[63] Like Wang Duanshu, who wrote unabashedly of her loyalist sympathies, these women did not think that dedication to domestic duties precluded a concern for public affairs and the well-being of their country.

If judged according to the doctrine of separate spheres (man : outer / woman : inner), the concerns of these women would have to be considered unwomanly. Yet throughout this book, I have noted the permeability of the private/public boundary in practice. Here, too, the best way to situate and to understand the Banana Garden women is not to ask Were they woman-like or man-like? Were they rebels or victims of domestic confinement? Instead, we should appreciate their words and deeds as illustrative of a limited degree of tolerance for expanding or rewriting the boundaries of gender roles. In their self-perceptions and education these women showed a remarkable ability to cross boundaries without feeling the need to articulate or justify their actions.

The breadth of the emotional and intellectual concerns of the Banana Garden women was rooted in two factors: having men as teachers and having each other as friends. With the examples of Shen Yixiu and Ye Xiaoluan, we have emphasized the importance of the mother-daughter bond in education and the transmission of women's culture. Some of the Banana Garden women — Qian Fenglun and Lin Yining, for example — were educated by their mothers. But many were significantly influenced by the knowledge and art of their fathers. Of the nine core members of the two Banana Garden societies, at least three inherited their fathers' learning. The incidences of companionate marriage were also extremely high — six out of nine published poetry they composed with husbands.

Apart from interactions with men, the concerns and self-perceptions of these highly educated women were also shaped by the public women's community they created. We have seen, in the section on Gu Ruopu's view of education as a living faith, many examples of one woman teaching another. The company of like-minded painters and poets encouraged the Banana Garden women to hone their artistic vision and skills. A hallmark of their seriousness can be found in Qian Fenglun's volume of poetry, *Works from the Pavilion of Antique Fragrance (Guxianglou ji)*. Although it was customary for relatives and friends to contribute polite prefaces, Chai Jingyi and Feng Youling (Xian) together with Qian's two brothers and two other women friends wrote critical commentaries on Qian's work.[64]

Brought up reading men's books but supported by a wide women's network, these women were not unambivalent about their identities as women. Chai Jingyi and Lin Yining represent two poles. Lin Yining was unabashed in stating a wish to be a man. In the preface to one of her volumes of poetry, she recounted how she had been educated by her mother in her youth and had learned the stories of the exemplary women well. Yet she was especially attracted by the Confucian canonical tradition. "My wish is to be a major Confucian scholar [*daru*], not a Ban [Zhao] or Zuo [Fen]," said Lin, referring to the two famous erudite women whom others emulated.[65] Instead of becoming a Confucian scholar, however, in her adult life she settled for the more conventional roles of a wife-mother and writer-painter. Although her prolific and acclaimed writing career was hardly ordinary, Lin remained painfully aware that her achievements would have been greater had she been a man.

Gu Ruopu, whose modesty was more akin to Chai Jingyi's despite her extraordinary words and deeds, would have disagreed with Lin's boldness. Gu described her motive for writing as "voicing my natural feelings and complaints," not to gain fame. This same justification dotted the essays of men of letters who argued for the propriety of women writing. Gu added a rhetorical question: "How dare I pretend to emulate such ancient women as Ban and Zuo, so as to bring laughter upon myself?"[66] The disagreement between Lin and Gu, however, is more one of posture than of substance. Whether Gu was emulating Ban and Zuo mattered less than her actual output and erudition. By claiming to be modest, however, she avoided controversy and gained room to pursue her heart's desire.

Chai Jingyi shared Gu Ruopu's modesty. In a poem to her daughter-in-law, Zhu Rouze, she passed on these words of wisdom:

> Be a hidden dragon, do not act,
> The hen who crows brings shame upon herself.
> Take heed, my daughter of the inner chambers,
> Be gentle and docile, and you'll have no worries.[67]

"Hidden dragon, do not act" is a quotation from the *qian* hexagram of the *Book of Changes*. The first of six stages of transformation in the natural or human world, the hidden dragon will in due time leap up, fly, and exceed limits. Although the *qian* hexagram is identified with the *yang* or male principle, Chai Jingyi appropriated this male symbol to affirm a woman's power in passivity. At first glance, Chai seems in this poem to have accepted the norm of a docile woman without reservation. Yet between the lines, her message is the same as Gu's: Be modest, so that you can be left alone. Chai did not teach her daughter-in-law to forsake her outstanding abilities; she merely advises her to hide them.

The achievements of the Banana Garden community of women, however, were by no means modest or hidden from public view. In the gray area between the women's self-perceptions and the postures they presented to the world, in between their private ambitions and public modesty, lies the true story of their lives. With the same agility in navigating boundaries, they eked out an existence between the official kinship system and the unofficial women's culture.

Women's Culture and the Kinship System

A Chinese woman, in the eyes of the male-centered official kinship system, led a transient and subservient existence. An outsider to her natal and marital families, she had to be controlled by such dictums as Thrice Following–Four Virtues, or she would threaten the stability of the male descent line. From the perspective of the women's culture, however, individual women were connected to each other in ways that defied time and physical distance. A woman was a member of a female line of descent that included kinswomen but was constructed on a logic different from that of kinship. She took the officially prescribed roles of wife and mother most seriously, but she also found solace in the company of neighbors and friends from afar.

The relationship between the women's culture described in this book and the official kinship structure is fraught with ambiguities. On the one hand, women's culture was by no means hostile to kinship. The women themselves saw no conflict between their familial roles (mother, wife) and extra-familial identities (friend, neighbor, writer), and they drew on the kinship system to recruit members for their own networks. The extreme example of Gu Ruopu the matriarch shows how some women derived power and self-esteem from serving that system.

On the other hand, the construction of a female line of descent and a space beyond domesticity contradicts the official kinship ideology. Since neither men nor women in the seventeenth century conceived of this contradiction as a direct or conscious affront, historians are free to draw conclusions as to how "subversive" this women-created space was. My own view is that given the strength and vitality of the kinship ideology in the seventeenth century, the women's culture has to be seen primarily as part of that structure rather than as its antithesis. The articulation of women's culture created a new space for women outside official kinship without directly challenging it. This space made life palatable and meaningful for the women, who in turn played a vital role as mother-teachers in the reproduction of the kinship system.

Yet women were not mere accomplices. The public presence of such women's networks as the Banana Garden poetry clubs highlights the gap between the idealized view of women in the kinship system and the life they actually experienced. The official kinship treatises — genealogies and household instructions — described and prescribed a hierarchical and gender-differentiated family structure. This was a fragmented world comprehensible in terms of distinct spheres clearly marked by boundaries — inner/outer, senior/junior, male/female.

In contrast, the educated gentrywomen saw life in the inner chambers as being permeated by *qing*, an emotive connectedness. As we have seen, this awareness of being part of a whole can take many forms. Cheng Qiong and other devotees of *The Peony Pavilion* expressed it in theatrics — exaggerated sentiments embodied in stylized domestic rituals. Shen

Yixiu and others strove to collect and publish verses by women. The Banana Garden poets gave the women's extra-familial network an institutional expression and public presence.

These women were fully schooled in the boundaries prescribed by the official kinship system within which they were supposed to operate. Yet having fulfilled their wifely and motherly duties, the gentry poets were allowed an unofficial sphere of freedom in which they found companionship and intellectual fulfillment. This gap between ideology from men's eyes and reality as experienced by women helps explain why the most educated group of women in seventeenth-century China did not openly challenge an ideology that relegated them to a nominally cloistered and subservient existence.

Transitory Communities

COURTESAN, WIFE, AND PROFESSIONAL ARTIST

THE WOMEN STUDIED IN the preceding chapters were wives, daughters, or relatives of scholar-officials. By birth or marriage, they had access to the privileges enjoyed by the men who staffed the imperial bureaucracy or served as leaders in local communities. In other words, by adhering to Thrice Following — by following the social station of father, husband, or son — these women became vicarious members of the elite. It is hardly surprising that they were among the first in the female population to receive a sophisticated education and to gain access to channels of self-expression.

This chapter focuses on a different group of women — courtesans and singing girls — who honed essentially the same poetic and artistic skills as gentry daughters, although to a different end and far outside the gentrywomen's privileged homes. Ascending to the apex of a highly stratified public entertainment world, courtesans followed a different rhythm from that punctuated by the demand of Thrice Following and its implied domesticity. By examining their upbringing, intimacies with each other, liaisons with men, and, perhaps most surprisingly, their friendship with gentrywomen, I will argue in this chapter that there existed common forces, which I will speak of in terms of gender, that structured the lives of both gentrywomen and courtesans.

Individual wives and female entertainers may have eyed each other with suspicion and jealousy, but from our analytical perspective they appear to have shared a certain gendered position. When the lives of gentry wives and women from the pleasure quarters are viewed from the perspective of gender and their training to serve the same group of men, the apparent gap in their social status and moral standing becomes much narrower. The competition between wife and concubine-to-be was all the fiercer because of their membership in the same cultural world of male elites and their common gendered position. Moreover, the transitory lives of the women portrayed in this chapter will demonstrate that female social markers — wife, concubine, professional artist, singing girl, and courtesan — were seldom permanent. A woman traveled from one station to another through life's many stages, especially in traumatic times of dynastic transitions.

It was their shared literary acumen and transitory lifestyles that brought some of the empire's most expressive and physically mobile women together to form a transitory community. These communities, often forged outside familial contexts, were more encompassing and multivalent than any of the "domestic," "social," or "public" varieties examined thus far. In this chapter, I will describe how an unlikely cohort of gentry wives, professional writers, and female entertainers befriended each other in private villas, on the shores of West Lake in Hangzhou, or through the exchange of letters, manuscripts, and paintings across distance. Yet the very dynamic and inclusive nature of these communities meant that they were also fragmented and unstable. With no anchor in everyday family life or kinship structures, these fleeting liaisons were neither institutionalized nor transmitted across generations.

The same irony that informed a woman's life at the individual level was thus also at work on the community level: wife and entertainer were positioned to "follow" the same group of male elites, hence they were as united by their gendered position as they were divided by their competition. Similarly, the transitory extra-familial networks that women from different walks of life forged were both cohesive and divisive. In other words, community and fragmentation were two sides of the same coin. This twin deployment of "women-as-same" and "women-as-different" is, I would argue, the very operating principle of the Confucian gender system.

The Floating World of Courtesans and Singing Girls

The gendered position of the Chinese courtesan is similar to that of other women on one level and vastly different on another. The highly refined courtesans stood at the apex of a system of traffic in women that included various grades of prostitution and the training and selling of girls as concubines and maids. Although courtesans and singing girls occupied opposite poles in the highly stratified pleasure quarters, they shared a fundamental gendered position in imperial China: the social station of a woman was defined by that of the men in her life. The same principle, Thrice Following, governed the social station of the respectable wife as well. Although the majority of women were neither gentry wives nor courtesans, each in her own way aspired to better her lot by "following" a man, be it by marriage or informal sexual favors. With the notable exception of females who claimed religious or spiritual powers, for most daughters, the best shot at respectability was to become the legal wife of a commoner; the closest they could approach centers of power was to serve as a maid or concubine in a gentry household. Most women were thus constituted as woman in relation to men.

Yet even as the courtesan aspired to "follow" her men, she inhabited ambivalent multiple social and gendered positions unimaginable for other women. To understand why, it is necessary to clarify the meaning of the label *courtesan* in the context of Chinese political culture, economic life, and social customs. The English word *courtesan* is at best an approximate rendition of what a Chinese in the seventeenth century would call a *mingji* (literally, "famous prostitute"). The Renaissance courtesan, whose name derived from *cortigiana*, the feminine form of *cortigiano* (courtier) in Italian, was often the mistress of a king or nobleman. In contrast, imperial princes and noblemen played at best marginal political roles in seventeenth-century China; nor were courtesans directly tied to court life. Although the most accomplished ones served a clientele of high-ranking scholar-officials, both their ascendance in the entertainment world and the prosperity of that world were possible only with the surplus generated by the monetary economy of Jiangnan. The seventeenth-century Chinese courtesan hailed from the same socioeconomic milieu that produced the commercial print culture examined in Chapter 1.

As companions of male elites, both European and Chinese courtesans were distinguished by their mastery of his art. Ann Rosalind Jones's description of the Renaissance courtesan is also applicable to China: "Singing, making music and witty conversation, familiarity with classical and modern literature — these were the accomplishments of the courtier, and they were also the accomplishments that distinguished the *cortigiana onesta* from the less well-paid prostitute."[1] This similarity was a product more of the nature of the trade — a woman dependent on men's patronage for a living had to cater to their taste — than of comparable historical situations.

It is also tempting to compare Chinese courtesans to the salonnières of seventeenth-century France; both were public women who arbitrated literary and artistic tastes. But their differences are more glaring: the French women were daughters of wealthy holders of the highest professional offices; Chinese courtesans invariably hailed from humble families. According to Carolyn Lougee, salonnières married husbands from older and higher families than their own; such hypergamy constituted true social mobility and brought about a fundamental shift in the French social structure.[2] The few celebrated cases of Chinese courtesans marrying leading scholar-officials, in contrast, remained isolated examples of individual mobility.

The Chinese courtesan had more in common with the Japanese *tayū*, first-class courtesans who presided over a hierarchy of licensed quarters in the urban centers of Kyoto, Osaka, and Edo in the seventeenth century. Like her Chinese counterpart, the *tayū* was distinguished by her accomplishments in arts and literature, not by the sexual favors she might choose to render. The famous *tayū* Yachiyo, for example, frequently invited scholars to lecture on such great works as the *Tale of Genji* at her house in Shimabara, the entertainment district in Kyoto. Not only was Yachiyo a master of musical instruments, singing, and tea ceremony, she was so skilled in calligraphy that her Yachiyo style became a model for other courtesans. One of her poems was anthologized in a collection published shortly after she left the trade in 1658 at the age of 24.[3] The career and talents of Yachiyo resembled those of Liu Rushi and Wang Wei, her contemporaries in the Jiangnan urban culture, whose lives and works are examined below.

Although both the Chinese and Japanese courtesans were products and expressions of an emergent urban culture sustained by economic prosperity, there were salient differences in the political worlds they inhabited and the legitimacy of that urban culture. Similarities in the courtesan's allure and skills masked the diverse backgrounds of her clientele in the two countries and a more fundamental difference in the nature of political system that this represents. The Japanese scholar Teruoka Yasutaka has identified a shift in the *tayū*'s patrons in the mid-seventeenth century that ensued from the rise of nouveau riche merchants at the expense of the impoverished samurai: "From the early 1600's until the second half of seventeenth century, guests of the licensed quarters who sought audience with *tayū* were mostly from high society, with good education and manners. In Kyoto, they were aristocrats or well-established merchants; in Edo, daimyo or senior Bakufu retainers. From the 1650s and 1660s, however, nouveau riche townsmen gradually replaced these more sophisticated customers as patrons." This decline in the social status of the clientele, ironically, ushered in the golden age of high courtesan culture, when the pleasure quarters were the very site of urbanity. This golden age, which lasted from the mid-1660's to turn of the century, paralleled a 40-year economic boom (1660–1700). The eventual decline of the high standards and luster of the *tayū* houses, however, was due to direct political pressure from the Bakufu. In 1695, when the Bakufu imposed harsh control measures on merchants, two opulent courtesan houses were forced out of business.[4]

In other words, Japanese courtesan culture owed its rise to the affluence generated by urban merchants and manufacturers, and its decline resulted from political measures that sought to curb the merchants' control of economic life. The changing composition of the *tayūs'* clientele was thus rooted in the rigid legal and social barriers separating the Japanese merchants from samurai-bureaucrats, hallmark of the Tokugawa political system.

Herein lies the crucial difference between the world of the Japanese courtesan and that of her Chinese counterpart. Although Chinese courtesan culture was also sustained by the wealth generated in urban centers, scholar-officials continued to constitute the primary clientele until the eighteenth century. They were able to do so because scholar-officials did not shun commercial enterprises as the Japanese samurai did. The space between politics and economics, as well as between businessmen and bureaucrats, was much less demarcated in Ming-Qing China. It was on the borderline of these worlds that the Chinese courtesan eked out her varied existence.

Chinese courtesan culture had served various integrative functions since its codification in the Tang dynasty. From the start, the entertainment world was part of the so-called general culture and literary history. The contributions of courtesans and singing girls to the development of the genre of lyrical song verse (*ci*) were particularly prominent. According to Kang-i Sun Chang, courtesans and musicians from the palace Music Office (Jiaofang) had to flee the capital and were scattered throughout the country after the An Lushan rebellion (755). This was instrumental in the flourishing of entertainment halls, Jiangnan urban culture, and the popularity of song lyrics following the mid-Tang period.[5] Marsha Wagner, in turn, emphasizes the integrative function of late Tang courtesan quarters, "in which the integration of men and women, of aristocrats and commoners, is reflected in the merging of elite and popular literary styles."[6]

Through the ages, as the courtesan culture attained its special place in society and political culture, it acquired three characteristics: its indispensable role in the public life of scholar-officials; the primacy of music and poetry as the vocabulary of social interaction and the recognition of women as artistic creators; and the permeability of its boundary with the domestic world. Specifically, the entertainment house provided a space where examination candidates were initiated into the tastes and manners of the power elite, where new songs and tunes were rehearsed, and where women could be procured as secondary wives or household singing girls.[7] In other words, the Chinese courtesan served an indispensable integrative function in society, bringing together the public and private lives of the male elites, as well as the oral and visual arts favored by the urban commoner and the scholar-gentry's literary tradition.

This courtesan culture blossomed in the late Ming period; both its visibility and respectability peaked at this time. The late imperial courtesans surpassed their medieval counterparts in numbers and the amount of economic resources at their and their clients' disposal. Some courtesans became so well educated that they were hailed as equals of literati men. The famous example of Liu Rushi, the driving force and model for her lover Chen Zilong's efforts to revive the genre of song lyrics, bespeaks the literary and artistic import of the late Ming courtesan.[8] Even more significant was the shift in the physical location of the interaction between literati and courtesan cultures: it became customary for female entertainers to appear as guests in parties held at literati homes. There is some indication that the more sophisticated of these women were invited not just as entertainers but as artistic equals.[9] The woman-artist, a most unlikely figure in the official repertoire of ideal women, shuttled physically and figuratively between the male-public and female-domestic worlds.

Thus in late Ming times, the scholar's domestic hall and private garden, as much as the entertainer's house, emerged as a new arena for interactions between private/public, man/woman, and, as we will see, woman/woman.[10] The intimacies between gentry wives, courtesans, and singing girls, discussed below, represent an intrusion of courtesan culture into the domestic realm. This intrusion, yet another facet of the privatization of Chinese life in which the domestic realm took on new cultural and productive functions, was enabled by the inherently ambivalent location of courtesan culture in elite society. The intensity and frequency with which it occurred in late Ming Jiangnan, however, testifies to the permeability of domestic and familial boundaries in a society in flux.

Both the cultural aura of courtesans and their literary prominence declined in the early Qing period. By 1673, the Qing court had formally ended the centuries-long tradition of maintaining official prostitutes in the capital and the provinces. Although the pleasure industry continued to flourish in the private sector under the nominal supervision of civilian authorities, it had lost much of its late Ming luster. Courtesans who survived the fall, however, continued to write, paint, and congregate in villas on West Lake in the early Qing period.[11] The fortunate ones migrated to their next station in life: concubine and wife.

Wife and Entertainers: Tensions Between "Gender" and "Class"

Extra-familial communities — the literary and affective intimacies between wives and entertainers — were possible in part because men construed their members to be the same — as woman. Yet for this very reason these liaisons were inherently fragmented and divisive. The tensions between commonalities and divisions constituted an integral part of the gender system that these women were in.

The commonalities were rooted in Confucian ethics and expressed, in part, in the curriculum of cultural education for women. I argued earlier that domestic women and entertainers were defined by the same ethical standards embodied in the formulation of Thrice Following. That is to say, although gentry wives, concubines, courtesans, and singing girls hailed from different social worlds and were separated by deep power disparaties, they served and were expected to remain loyal to the same group of privileged men. As such, they moved in the same cultural universe as these men; the fine arts cultivated by the amateur gentleman — zither, chess, calligraphy, and painting — also distinguished his lady companion both in his own home and in the entertainer's house.

Similarly, the apparent moral gulf between wife and courtesan was far from insurmountable. In theory and in practice, both the "good" domestic woman and the "bad" public seductress could attain virtue through loyalty to a man. Hence in Tang and Ming vernacular stories, the courtesan heroine typically appears as a sagacious and faithful lover. A courtesan is "chaste" by virtue of her pure intentions and moral tenacity.[12] In the traumatic late Ming and early Qing times, courtesans and respectable women alike had ample opportunities to emulate these heroines in real life as loyalists and martyrs.

According to Confucian ideology, political loyalty is a natural extension of personal loyalty. One curious consequence of the intensified chastity cult in the late imperial times was to make loyalism a natural imperative for women. It is no accident that during the Ming-Qing transition, many women shamed their male companions by becoming actively involved in loyalist resistance — committing public suicide in protest, serving as scouts and liaisons for the loyalist troops and navy, or actually taking up arms and riding into battle.[13] We have seen that Wang Duanshu, the professional writer, publicized her loyalist sentiments in a series of biographies of men who died resisting the Qing. Many courtesans, too, were unabashed sympathizers of the Southern Ming court-in-exile. Liu Rushi's clandestine assistance of the organizers of insurrections, as we will see, was the most famous example.

When women took the ethical demand of loyalty to their men (one meaning of Thrice Following) seriously, they created for themselves the possibility not only of political participation as loyalists but also of a new way of being evaluated morally as gendered individuals rather than merely as members of a certain clan or status group. The gulf separating courtesan from gentry wife was secondary to their shared position as "woman" defined relative to "man." In this sense, "woman" constitutes a social category analytically distinct from class or status, although they intersect in practice. According to official ideology, what signified an individual woman and vindicated her existence was her willingness to follow the social station of her man, whatever it happened to be, and to remain loyal to him.

In spite of, or perhaps because of, this common gendered position of the entertainer and wife, legal boundaries marking off the inner chambers from the pleasure quarters persisted from the Tang dynasty to the Qing. This insistence was in part a reflection of the men's view of the distinct functions served by the wife and singing girl. In the eyes of male patrons, women from the pleasure quarters were the antitheses of their wives. Wives and female entertainers occupied separate spheres in the lives of these men, each serving different aspects of their essential needs—familial, procreative, and managerial for the wife; social, intellectual, and sensuous for the entertainer. In addition, since business and political deals were often forged over banquet tables in the pleasure quarters, courtesans were involved in the public world of men in which the wife had no direct place. The distinction was obliterated when a courtesan became a concubine or even wife, but the functional incongruity between the two kinds of women remains unequivocal from the perspective of the male-centered kinship system.

This insistence on clear nominal boundaries can also be interpreted as a way to contain and neutralize the inherently ambivalent, hence potentially disruptive, social position of the pleasure woman. Commonly raised by a "foster mother," an aging courtesan, in the entertainment quarters, the courtesan lived in two worlds, within and without the family system, but belonged to neither. Although she might opt to retire and marry eventually, for the years she was in the trade she remained an outsider to the official kinship structure. As such, she was the odd one that violated the norm, the undomestic woman who was *not* raised in the inner chambers and was *not* destined to be mother and guardian of inner morality. Yet her ambivalent existence was condoned because she satisfied the very men committed to safeguarding the sanctified boundaries of domestic morality.

The same ambivalence is evident in the courtesan's agility in straddling the seemingly incompatible worlds of the private woman and the public man. Embodiment of both feminine charms and literati refinement, she made a mockery of the supposedly distinct male and female spheres in the ideal world of Confucian precepts. Her feminine physique, epitomized by her meticulously bound and perfumed small feet, was just as appealing as her mastery of the gentleman's arts and her conversance with affairs of the state.[14] In her personal connections as well, the courtesan inhabited the heart of the social universe of the most influential men in the empire — examination candidates, scholar-officials, men of letters, wealthy merchants. She personified the woman at her most charming and the man at his most public. Yet just as was her marginality in the male-centered official kinship system, this gender ambiguity was condoned and even welcomed because it gratified the men who sought relief from public and domestic responsibilities.

The nominal wife-entertainer boundary was eroded not only by pleasure-seeking men but also by powerful forces unleashed by the monetary economy. The contempt voiced by gentry wives for songs from the pleasure quarters was in fact a sign that the boundaries between the two worlds had been breached. Another sign was the domestic women's imitation of fashion trends from the pleasure quarters. For example, Ming gentrywomen used folding fans, once exclusive to prostitutes, although they did not give up their traditional round fans.[15] More significant than fashion were the personal contacts between women from the two worlds: gentry wives befriended courtesans by exchanging poems and paintings; wives invited singing girls to parties in private villas. I discuss concrete examples of these liaisons below.

As powerful as these forces of community were the seeds of discord and division. My emphasis here on the commonalities among gentry wives, courtesans, and singing girls stems from an attempt to highlight the validity of gender as a category for historical analysis. This emphasis, however, has to be seen with its corollary: the status distinctions and power disparaties that separated women. All women are subjected to contradictory formations within the categories of gender and of class. As Peter Stallybrass has put it so well, writing of early modern England: "To emphasize gender is to construct woman-as-the-same: women are constituted as a single category, set over against the category of men. To emphasize class is to differentiate *between* women, dividing them into distinct social groups." In the case of China, an emphasis on gender would lead us to focus on the shared identities and concerns between gentry wives and courtesans; an emphasis on class, in turn, would lead us to highlight the gulf in economic power, position in the kinship structure, and social status. Stallybrass also points out that to construe women only by class division serves the ruling elite's interest in perpetuating the existing power alignments.

Insofar as women are differentiated, those in the dominant social classes are allocated privileges they can confer (status, wealth). In societies where heterosexuality and marriage are prescribed, those privileges can only be conferred back on *men*, so the differentiation of women simultaneously establishes or reinforces the differentiation of men. The deployment of women into different classes, then, is in the interests of the ruling elite, because it helps to perpetuate and to naturalize class structure.[16]

Implied in the dictum of Thrice Following is exactly this formulation of women within the categories of gender and class. In its claims of universal application to women from all classes and status groups, this dictum opened the way for the construction of women-as-same (gender). At the same time, its exact purpose was the deployment of women into different classes. By demanding that every woman assume the social station of her father, husband, or son, the dictum, at least in intention, reinforced the differentiation of men and the predominant position of the elites.

The degree of success of this deployment in reproducing the class structure in seventeenth-century China cannot be assessed without a study of gender relations among the lower classes; hence it lies outside the scope of this book. What I am arguing here, however, is that the dictum of Thrice Following was the key to the perpetuation of the gender system. Contrary to current assumptions, adherence to Thrice Following did not always mean restriction and self-denial for the women concerned. Many women, in fact, found privileges and a range of freedoms in "following" men, although they may or may not have been aware that such freedoms were, ultimately, circumscribed.

By focusing on gentry wives and courtesans, the most privileged women by virtue of their pivotal positions in the private lives of the male elite, we can begin to understand how compliance — by legal marriage or sexual services — benefited a small number of women. Much like the civil service examination, which promised wealth and power to all men but in reality rewarded only a few, Thrice Following lured all women into supporting the prevailing gender arrangements by promising them a share in the privileges of elite males, although those who made it to the top remained a minority indeed. The result was a gender system so flexible and resilient that intimacies between women only served to reinforce its appeal.

In this light, the social and cultural achievements of the famous courtesans who appear later in this chapter should not be overly romanticized. The operation of procuring and educating girls from humble backgrounds, the system that was at once the courtesans' ladder of success and the curse of many others, has to be understood for what it was: a mechanism pitting one woman against another in competition for men's attention. This competition was essential to the reproduction of the gender system. At the lower ranks, the forces of division, of deploying women-as-different, were unleashed in the most brutal ways.

Grooming a "Thin Horse"

There existed a clear gradation in the traffic in women, although all women were, to some extent, treated as property. Sue Gronewold, who has studied prostitution in nineteenth- and twentieth-century China, argues that "the sale of women for prostitution was only an extreme form of the general trade in women which included the adoption of daughters and future daughters-in-law, and the purchase of servants and brides."[17] As we have seen, a woman's value in these various transactions was determined by a combination of talent, virtue, and beauty, and educated brides were important to the alliance-building strategies of gentry families. In this section, we investigate another application by focusing on the traffic in concubines, maids, and prostitutes, who were bought and sold with an undisguised price tag.[18]

Whereas the value of gentry brides was primarily a function of her talent and virtue, beauty and talent were overriding emphases in the market for prostitutes, concubines, and maids. This is evinced by the business and local cultures of Yangzhou, the national center for the procurement of beautiful girls in late Ming times.[19] Xie Zhaozhe, author of the famous compendium of Ming customs and social life, *Five Miscellanies*, attributed the pivotal position of Yangzhou to the abundance of its waterways, which nurtured natural beauties.[20] He was right in crediting the waterways, albeit for the wrong reason. The central location of Yangzhou in the Ming tribute-grain system, commanding the confluence of the Grand Canal and the Yangzi River, made it an ideal center for the salt trade and the traffic in women. Xie went on to describe the shrewd business sense of Yangzhou residents: "The people of Yangzhou have long treated [their beautiful women] as precious merchandise. Merchants bought young girls from everywhere. They dressed up the girls and taught them crafts such as calligraphy, drinking games, zither, and chess, expecting a handsome return. The girls are called 'thin horses.' Having spent a long time together, they are like real parents and daughters."[21]

The name *thin horse* came from a poem by the Tang poet Bo Juyi, in which he lamented the speed at which the ownership of young prostitutes changed hands.[22] By late Ming times it had become a term reserved for girls sold on the Yangzhou market. In a passage called "The Thin Horses of Yangzhou," the late Ming writer and drama aficionado Zhang Dai described with satire and humor the manner in which the transaction was conducted:

Do not let anybody know you want to buy a concubine. Otherwise, the female procurers [yapo] will flock to your door like flies. The earliest one will arrive at dawn to "kidnap" you to look at her girls. The latecomers all trail behind. . . . In one house there are always five or six girls to show. When one procurer gets tired, others take over. After four or five days, or after seeing the sixtieth girl, with the same white face and red dress, everyone looks the same.

The buyer sealed the transaction by sticking a hairpin into the hair of the girl he picked. The owner of the thin horse would then produce a price list, stating the number of bolts of silk and cloth, gold flowers, and the amount of bride price needed. If the buyer agreed on the price, the wedding ceremony would proceed with no time wasted.

Before you return home, an orchestra bearing the ceremonial wine will be waiting at your door. In a flash those bringing the wedding cakes arrive. The orchestra leads them away. From a few blocks away, sedan chairs, lanterns, torches, candles, and ceremonial gear appear with musicians and ceremonial assistants. Then comes the cook bringing the entire banquet complete with vegetables, fruits, dishes, candies, and utensils. Without being ordered, the procession will usher you to pick up the girl. . . . Before noon they will finish staging the whole ceremony, ask for their tip, and hurry on to some other house.[23]

Zhang Dai may have exaggerated the speed of the wedding ceremony, but his description conveys the efficiency with which the business of selling women was run as well as the size of the enterprise. Each procurer's house had at least five or six marketable girls, with probably more in training. The army of orchestra players, musicians, sedan-chair bearers, cooks, and porters available must have numbered close to a hundred. It is not clear, however, whether each house had its own team or whether they were subcontracted. Although there is no record of the total number of procurer houses in Yangzhou at the time, the business of selling women must have been a considerable part of the city's predominantly service-oriented economy.

In reality as well as in popular perception, the traffic in girls was part of the commercialized economy and culture of Yangzhou. A stereotypical image of decadent Yangzhou, born in the first commercial boom it experienced in the Sui and Tang dynasties, resurfaced in the sixteenth century. When writers eulogized Yangzhou, they spoke of the natives' willful neglect of agriculture as well as streets dotted with shops, luxury goods, and, invariably, beautiful women. In an early Qing gazetteer, for example, a poet reiterated an age-old convention in portraying the decadent Yangzhou:

Guangling [Yangzhou] daughters are as numerous as clouds.
. . . .

They are born not to weave and spin,
But to learn songs and dances.
Powerful men converge in front of their gardens,
Big merchants gather at their gates.
. . . .
At age thirteen or fourteen they are ready,
Who cares if he is old if he has gold.[24]

The connections among merchant culture, money, music, and prostitution are amply clear.

One result of this thriving market in girls was the prevalence of foot-binding. A Qing observer noted, "The practice of footbinding is more widespread in Yangzhou than in other places. Even coolies, servants, seamstresses, the poor, the old, and the weak have tiny feet and cramped toes."[25] As late as the twentieth century, the most sought-after prostitutes in Shanghai were said to have "Suzhou faces, Yangzhou feet."[26] Catering to the men they were intended to serve, women groomed for the market regarded the size and shape of their feet as the hallmark of their person-hood. The elaborate female-exclusive rituals honoring the Tiny-Foot Maiden or the Bodhisattva Guanyin that launched the binding procedure for gentry girls were just as central to the coming of age of the thin horses.

The late Ming man of letters Tan Youxia (1586–1637) outlined a set of apparently well-accepted criteria in selecting personal attendants in a let-ter to his younger brother: "I am looking for two maids to answer to my needs. Around here people are country bumpkins; please [pick them and] bring them down on the same boat with you when you come. For each one I am willing to spend 20 to 30 ounces of silver. But she should have a face that is not repulsive. Her height should be taller than Cold Jade by one-and-a-half feet [*chi*]. Her fingers cannot be [as fat and dumb as] ham-mers." Having dispensed with what to avoid in terms of face and ap-pearance, Tan went to the heart of the matter: "Her feet should be smaller than those of a Suzhou boat-woman's by a foot. Also, she has to be a virgin [*nüshen*]; not yet twelve [*sui*] but at least ten would be a perfect age."[27] It is clear that his priority was the size of bound feet, the sexual connotations of which were suggested by his preference for virginity. Tan was a member of the Return [to Antiquity] Society (Fu she) and, as we will see, companion of the famous courtesan Wang Wei.

We have examined footbinding from two angles: as a socialization device inscribing the Confucian ideal of a centripetal woman and as a central event in the development of a women's culture in the boudoir. A third dimension — as a means women employed to cater to the erotic fantasies of men — is evident in the prominent place that the golden lotus assumed in culture of the pleasure quarters. The incongruity between this use of footbinding and its moralistic use as an educational device is hardly surprising, for it highlights the conflicting demands that men placed on women — as moral guardians and sex objects. Footbinding served the goals of safeguarding a woman's purity while accentuating her sensuousness, both of which rendered her desirable in men's eyes. In her purity she symbolized the Confucian man's ideal of a harmonious world governed by moral principles; in her erotic appeal she spoke to his carnal desire. In this sense, the "good" and "bad" women, signified by one combination of the talent-virtue-beauty formula or another, were competing for the same group of educated and affluent men. Hence it is no accident that in the seventeenth century courtesans, concubines, and gentry wives were the women who routinely had their feet bound.

Yet footbinding alone was no guarantee of success at a time when poetic talent figured prominently in definitions of womanhood. The Yangzhou thin horses received a literary and artistic education to enhance their market value not only in procurers' houses but in commoner households as well. Early Qing sojourners in Yangzhou observed how common it was for parents to have their daughters learn music and dance.[28] In a city where transactions in women were essential to the economy and culture, the selling of daughters was not, as often described by moralistic magistrates, a desperate act by families on the verge of starvation. Instead, it was the reaping of a long-term investment by enterprising families.

The commercialized Jiangnan area offered daughters from humble families opportunities for education and employment both within and without the family system. Girls growing up in procurer houses, drama troupes, or brothels and those brought up by their parents but earmarked for the entertainment world received an education different in intent from that of gentry daughters, but the curricula overlapped in some areas. The daughters of gentry poet Shen Yixiu, for example, started to recite poems around four, acquired literacy around nine, learned the art of poetry and needlework in their early teens, and took up painting and musical instruments as their interest and time allowed. Mothers, aunts, or professional teachers of the inner chamber acted as instructors. By comparison, the education of commoner daughters to prepare them for life as an entertainer or concubine was less systematic and more functional, with a curriculum skewed toward songs, stories, and drama. Madams of brothels, procurer houses, or drama troupes, often called "foster mothers," were the teachers.

Li Yu, the famed connoisseur, explained in great detail his program for the training of concubines. Although nominally concubines were members of the family system, especially if they managed to bear sons, they were more akin to female entertainers in the way they were brought into the household and in the sexual services they rendered.[29] In fact, male writers in the seventeenth century preferred the term *buying a concubine* (*mai qie*) to *marrying* (*qu*). Therefore, Li's program can be taken as an ideal representation of education for women in the various grades of establishments in the entertainment world. Singing girls and prostitutes from lower-class houses received only fragments of such elaborate training, but first-class courtesans could vie with Li Yu in literary and artistic accomplishments.

Li Yu believed that cultivation of talent was as important as the cultivation of beauty. For him talent consisted of four skills: the abilities to write literature, to play musical instruments, to sing and dance, and to do needlework. The first three were listed in descending order of importance; the fourth was considered so basic that it needed no explanation.[30] The development of literary skills had to begin with the recognition of characters and the acquisition of basic literacy. Li advised that vernacular stories made perfect textbooks because the stories were already familiar.[31] Then, those women good at songs could be taught the art of writing song lyrics. Those wanting to learn poetry should begin by reading and reciting poems. As for musical instruments, the most suitable one was the zither. Finally, training in singing and dancing consisted of three parts: the search for a suitable role, correction of native dialects, and development of a stage presence. These contrast with the norm of "naturalness" governing behavior in the women's quarters. Such training should not aim solely at performing drama on stage, although the primary demand came from that quarter.[32]

This training program differed from that of gentrywomen in its emphasis on stage performance and its use of vernacular stories as the gateway to literacy. But the same ultimate goal, the cultivation of talented beauties, lay at the heart of both kinds of education. Moreover, the definition of "talent" for women intended for roles within and outside the family system was the same — it was borrowed from the definition of a cultivated gentleman. Li Yu, in explaining the importance of literary skills to the education of a concubine, wrote, "those who call themselves cultivated ladies [*guixiu*, literally "lady in the inner chambers"] cannot lack any one of the four arts: calligraphy, painting, zither, and chess. But some priorities have to be established. They should start with the basics, and go on to other skills as their natural talents allow. If they excel in any one of these arts they will gain fame as gifted women [*cainü*]."[33] In Li Yu's description, a woman can better her station in life if she applies herself to the arts of the cultivated gentleman.

What Li Yu failed to mention is that for daughters from both gentry and more humble origins, education constituted a ladder of success only in conjunction with the marriage market. No matter how erudite and refined, a woman could not be considered successful until she had landed an eligible gentleman. The educational goal of producing talented beauties, therefore, masks the principle of competition built into the institutions of women's education and marriage. For all the disparaties between the wife and the thin horse, however, they did find themselves face-to-face in the same gentryman's villa.

Wife, Courtesan, and Singing Girl on a Friendship-Love Continuum

The tensions between commonality and division, or between construing women by gender and by class, were brought into the open in the liaisons between gentry wives and courtesans and singing girls. The nature of these instances of female companionship hovers between the two poles of platonic and sensual on a friendship-love continuum. This continuum, in turn, is part of the larger discourse of love, sex, and beauty already examined in the discussions above of Shen Yixiu, her daughters, and the commentators on *The Peony Pavilion*. In an age when the boundaries between various forms of affection, or between "emotional" and "physical" love, were blurred, whether some of these liaisons can be called "lesbianism" is not an appropriate question. Instead, it is important to emphasize the wide range and multiple nature of intimacies that women pursued in the boudoir and the freedom that gentry wives apparently enjoyed in gliding along the love-friendship continuum.[34]

One gentry wife who unabashedly pursued intimacies with singing girls, courtesans, and other wives was Xu Yuan, whose respectable family background stood in curious juxtaposition with the bold tone and unconventional subject matter of her verse. Daughter of a Suzhou scholar family, she received a literary and moral education from a female instructor and was said to be conversant with such didactic works as the *Instructions for the Inner Quarters* (*Neize*). Her husband, Fan Yunlin (1558–1641), served as secretary in the Ministry of War, a job that took him to the riotous border regions of the empire. When off duty, however, Fan was at the core of Suzhou literati society, entertaining leading scholar-officials of the day, viewing drama performances, and financing printing projects.[35] Xu and Fan apparently enjoyed a cordial relationship, exchanging verse frequently. She also accompanied him on most of his missions to the southwestern border. On the surface, they appear to be a typical couple from the gentry society of late Ming Jiangnan.

Yet for all the conventional education she received, Xu Yuan was not the conventional gentry wife. Her voluminous poetic works are eclectic and ironic, dotted with such incongruities as using vulgar colloquial expressions to convey lofty moral ideals or allowing poems she wrote for prostitutes and Daoist adepts to be published right after a traditional lament for her deceased parents. It is clear that Xu thrived on contradictions. On the one hand, she seems to have accepted the ideal norms for women taught in the didactic literature. The title of her twelve-*juan* poetry collection, *Shuttling Chants* (*Luowei yin*, which could also be rendered "Cricket chants"), refers to the repetitive sound of the spool carrying the woof thread back and forth between the warp threads. Not only did she compare herself to a weaving maid, the vocation of the ideal housewife, but exhortations to Confucian virtues were a common theme in her poems. In one, for example, she admonished an orphaned younger sister to devote herself to the pursuit of feminine virtues; in another, she appeared as a filial daughter, remembering her parents in terms of her mother's loyalty to the household and her father's loyalty to the emperor. In addition, Xu Yuan authored funerary epitaphs and biographies for a number of women, in which she highlighted their adherence to the traditional virtues.

Perhaps to some extent these exhortations were merely a literary trope. Yet Xu seemed to have internalized at least part of the moral teachings, as was evident in a poem she addressed to the wives of her younger brothers. Following a family crisis (probably the death of her parents), Xu issued a stern warning to her sisters-in-law to take their wifely duties seriously: supervise the wet nurses, guide their sons in their studies, punish whoever dares to disobey.[36] Already over 50 when her poetry collection was published, Xu at times appeared to take on the moral authority of a matriarch, admonishing her juniors to be steadfast in walking the path of virtue.

On the other hand, Xu Yuan seemed to have flaunted her defiance of norms of decency not only by composing frequent poems for courtesans and singing girls but also by including them in her published collection. Most notable was a series of five regulated verse she crafted for the famous Suzhou courtesan-painter Xue Susu, in which she compared the talented Xue to the Hangzhou courtesan Su Xiaoxiao (fl. fifth century) and three other historic figures surnamed Xue: the Tang courtesan-poet Xue Tao (768–831); a Wei court lady from the Three Kingdoms period, Xue Lingyun (fl. 220–26); and a Commander Xue, probably a reference to the famous Tang general Xue Rengui (614–83), who was remembered in history and popular legend as an expert archer.[37] Each of these three Xues stood for aspects of Xue Susu's extraordinary life. Xue Tao alluded to Susu's courtesan background and erudition; Xue Lingyun, a woman who could sew in the dark and was revered as "god of the needle" (*zhenshen*), referred to Susu's magical fingers and wrists as a painter; General Xue, for his part, symbolized Susu's renowned finesse as a horseback archer and her interest in military affairs. In addition, Xu Yuan expressed her admiration for Xue Susu's bound feet: "Lotuses blossom as you move your pair of arches, / Your tiny waist, just a handful, is light enough to dance on a palm."[38]

Xu Yuan most probably came into contact with Xue Susu through her husband. Fan Yunlin had admired Xue's talents since her courtesan days, as evinced by a colophon he attached to a painting "Flowers" that Xue crafted in 1615: "Once during the time when Sujun [Susu] was in the 'blue building' [brothel], from even a Tiger Hill [excursion] boat did I espy half her face, and then I realized that she was not just another pretty powdered [face]. I obtained from a friend an ink-orchid fan by her. It was like having obtained a precious jade; to this day I store it away as a treasure."[39] Xue Susu was an extraordinary woman, accomplished in both the civil and military arts. A witness to her flair as an archer described her movement while galloping on horseback, crossbow in hand: "Or she puts a ball on the ground at a distance, and while her body is turned and her arms are crossed backward, she hits the one on the ground with another ball. She never misses one such shot in a hundred."[40] It was understandable that the unconventional Xu Yuan would admire such a colorful and talented character, although the details of their relationship are not known.

Xu Yuan also socialized with less renowned singing girls. In a verse dedicated to one "Anqing the Singing Girl" (geji Anqing), for example, Xu wrote: "I was sojourning on a lake one day in spring when Anqing came by and presented me with a gift of 'Spring Songs.' Her pure voice echoes like the whistle of light breeze in a flute; all those seated were delighted."[41] It was customary for late Ming literati to invite courtesans to parties in their homes, as mentioned above. The wives of these men evidently found it not improper to follow suit.

The presence of singing girls in Xu's quarters was quite common. In another series of five poems, "Written in Jest for Sanli the Singing Girl," Xu Yuan focused exclusively on the girl's body.[42] The appeal of the feminine body to Xu Yuan was just as evident in some of her other poems. Once she was so taken by the charm of a woman who sat in a boat moored next to hers that she composed three poems. Although in classical poetry the word *meiren* (literally, "beauty") was a symbol for the upright gentleman, in Xu Yuan's hands the literal meaning of the word was restored. Appearing frequently in her poetry, it clearly refers to the beautiful women she encountered and admired.[43]

Before we further discuss the intimacies between Xu, the singing girls, and Xu's friend Lu Qingzi, it is important to situate these verses in the larger context of Xu's works and her reputation. Xu seemed to be more aware of the inherently disruptive nature of a writing woman than other educated women of her day. Unlike such writers as Gu Ruopu, Xu never explicitly defended the rightfulness of the undertaking, but neither did she recoil from controversies. In reply to a Songjiang man who beseeched her, through her husband as intermediary, to author a biography eulogizing his widowed mother, Xu laughed: "Are you not seeking directions from the blind, asking for my words from *outside* the inner chambers to describe her virtues of docility *inside* the inner chambers?" (italics added)[44] That is to say, Xu assumed that writing is by definition a public act but saw no reason why women should refrain from it. Her demurral notwithstanding, Xu did heed the request and wrote a long biography heaping praises on the widow's industry and dedication. It is important to note that by "words from outside the inner chambers" Xu was referring to the act of writing itself, not to women making a living from writing. Unlike such professional writers as Huang Yuanjie and Wang Duanshu, Xu was well provided for by her affluent husband, who also financed the publication of her *Shuttling Chants*.

Since Xu considered writing itself a controversial public act, she did not see why women should limit themselves to the conventional repertoire of prudent themes. The suggestive verses she composed for singing girls are as remote from the usual musings of gentry wives as are several poems on traveling and sojourning on the southwestern border. Following her husband, assigned to coordinate defenses in Yunnan province, Xu left a trail of verses on signposts of her journey to the frontier: a postal station here, a highway there. Although the details are not clear, she appeared to have sojourned in a southern Yunnan town, since she later bade farewell to a Madame Ma she befriended there, together with Mister Ma's concubine.[45] These vestiges of life on the road may remind us of those of magistrate's wife Wang Fengxian discussed in the preceding chapter, but Xu Yuan's keen eye for the extraordinary sets her apart from most other gentry poets. In a long poem, for example, she detailed an unsuccessful tribal attack on the border town. Her description of the rebel leader: "The green-eyed barbarian chief, full of vainglory, / Gigantic fists; big nose; face covered with beard."[46] Her disdain for the tribal people clearly reflects that of the Han generals.

Although Xu Yuan's socializing with singing girls may seem less shocking in light of her consistent defiance of conventional themes and norms of modesty, more problematic is the enormous popularity of her works. As noted earlier, Xu's reputation was the subject of a controversy: native sons valorized her as the pride of Suzhou, but a woman poet from Tongcheng, Fang Mengshi, attacked her viciously. In spite of Fang's fury, Xu's works were widely read both in Suzhou and elsewhere, and many major seventeenth-century anthologies devoted space to her verse and prose. Her name and the titles of her two poetry collections were enshrined in successive editions of local gazetteers.[47] The reservations of her critics, either about her literary merits or her scandalous deeds, did not seem to prevent respectable men and women from admiring the refreshing boldness of her works. It was, in fact, scholar-officials from the Suzhou establishment who first vied to admire and circulate her works. Commercial publishers followed suit to capitalize on this explosion of interest.[48]

Xu Yuan's friendship with courtesans and singing girls, as documented by her poetry, attracted no overt comment from her respectable readers. Although explicit references to another woman's bewitching waist or swaying steps may have been considered in bad taste, attraction between women itself was acceptable in the gender system of seventeenth-century China.[49] More examples of such attraction can be found in Xu Yuan's intimacies with her friend Lu Qingzi.

Like Xu Yuan, Lu Qingzi was a gentry wife who delighted in composing verse for singing girls and whose works were laden with references to the feminine body. Lu, too, hailed from the moneyed and cultured society of Suzhou. Her father, Lu Shidao (1517–80), served briefly as secretary of the Ministry of Rites but spent most of his life as an amateur painter. He was a disciple and collaborator of the foremost Suzhou master, Wen Zhengming (1470–1559).[50] Lu Qingzi married a man who led an equally idyllic life, Zhao Yiguang (1559–1625), a descendant of the Song imperial family. Zhao fancied himself a recluse but often busied himself with entertaining powerful and learned friends. He was also involved in a number of publishing projects, including his own works and those of his wife. The publication of both of Qingzi's collected works, *Building a Hermitage* (*Kaopan ji*) and *Magical Herbs* (*Xuanzhi ji*), was financed by her husband, as in Xu Yuan's case.[51]

Xu and Lu were widely known as close friends who exchanged poetry. The two may have influenced each other, for Lu's corpus of verse and prose exhibits the same juxtaposition of pious eulogies of virtuous women with suggestive verses composed for young and beautiful women of dubious origins. Lu's social net was cast wider than Xu's; recipients of her poetry included a prostitute-turned-nun, lay Buddhist devotees, maids, a large number of concubines and singing girls, and the usual circle of gentry wives and chaste widows. Although less so than Xu, Lu also dabbled in unconventional themes for domestic women. In one entitled "Drought," for example, she expressed her worries for exhausted farmers toiling to battle a late summer dry spell.[52] Yet just like Xu, Lu seemed to have accepted without question the propriety of the Thrice Following dictum. Moved by the martyrdom of a young widow, Lu crafted a long poem that opened with the couplet: "The male body is promised to his country, / The chaste woman wills to follow her husband."[53] This is a classic statement of the ideal Confucian norm of separate spheres.

Perhaps Lu embraced this normative division between the male and female spheres not to highlight women's cloistering and submission but to defend the sanctity of the female world of love and sentimentality from the interference of men. As long as women fulfilled their familial duties, the predominant norms did not prohibit them from seeking pleasure in each other's company. Lu Qingzi, like Xu Yuan, kept company with singing girls, as her poems for "prostitutes" (*ji*) testified. One of them was named Wang the Fourth (Wang Si).[54] In addition, Lu called a number of women who frequented her parties by their surnames followed by the term "beauty" (*meiren*) instead of the usual "madame" or "sister," an uncommon usage that was also Xu Yuan's. Lu's poems to them, most probably singing girls or concubines, are fixated on their bodily charms: slender waist, rosy cheeks, trembling steps, flowing hair. A typical poem, to "Beauty Feng," reads:

> The goddess sings shyly in her melodic voice,
> The beauty has a face to topple a wall.
> Her slender waist dances, vying with willow catkins
>   for softness,
> Her charm glitters, as bright as the moon.
> Burning burning, her colors only flowers can match,
> Tender tender, so light she can dance on a palm.
> The orioles, the swallows, they utter not a word,
> Only the descending eagle, stirring from the clouds.[55]

Such seductive language was not simply a literary trope, nor was it reserved for women from the entertainment quarters. Even poems Lu composed for several filial and chaste women were dotted with descriptions of their fair appearance or tender age.[56] The same is true for those dedicated to Xu Yuan and other respectable wives who were gentry friends of Lu's. In a pair of poems crafted separately for Xu and a Madame Mao (née Zhou) but using a parallel structure, Lu hinted at the two attractions that all her female companions held for her: literary resonance and feminine beauty. In the one for Xu, Lu wrote:

> Our love [*qing*] was already deep when together,
> Our parting brings sadness to my heart.
> If you ask why I became so involved,
> It's for all our resonance.

The one for Madame Mao, in turn, highlights another aspect of female charm:

> I don't know you well although we've met,
> Now that you're gone I miss you more.
> If you ask why I became so involved,
> It's for your fairest color.[57]

Both the enchantments of poetic resonance and beauty (color) were in fact combined in Xu Yuan.

Lu Qingzi expressed her longing for Xu in highly expressive and sensual terms. When Xu went on a trip to Wuhu in Anhui province, Lu sighed:

> Fragrance swirls around my gate,
> Inanimate objects stir up my deep longing.
> I love and adore [wanlian] that tender beauty,
> Her jade face as fair as raw white silk.[58]

These are not written in the repertoire of language used in farewells between casual friends. The same intensity of physical longing is evident in the ten poems written on the eve of Xu's travel to faraway Yunnan. In one, Lu lamented:

> Your face is a dazzling crimson,
> My hair, a desolate white.
> I want to pursue the pleasure of my lifetime,
> But the vehicles crowding the road cannot bring me there.[59]

Although Lu's exact dates are unknown, judging from her husband's years she was about the same age as Xu. Hence her contrast of Xu's youthfulness with her own fatigued looks is likely to signify her emotional distress at parting instead of a gap in biological age.

Lu's explicit use of such seductive expressions as "to love and adore" and "pleasure of a lifetime" is suggestive of her erotic feelings for Xu Yuan.[60] Although such unabashed language was rare in the written works of other women, the subject of love and sex may well have been a conversational routine in the inner chambers. We have seen in Chapter 2 that the three young commentators on *The Peony Pavilion* were forthright in their discussions of the sanctity of love, sex, and marriage. In the private exchanges between gentry wife Shen Yixiu and her daughter, too, issues of physical beauty and sexual attraction were not shunned, as shown in Chapter 4.

Seen against these earlier examples of a discourse on beauty, love, and sex in the boudoir, the spectrum of love and friendship pursued by Xu Yuan and Lu Qingzi was hardly surprising. In a society that upheld the doctrine of separate spheres as the ideal, women were left with much leeway to pursue affective bonds of their own without men's interference.

However circumscribed this freedom turned out to be, its heartfelt meaning to the women concerned cannot be denied.

To recapitulate the argument so far, the gentrywomen's culture, born of emotional, literary, and physical intimacies, was an expression of women's agility in exploring the cracks between the idealized theory of separate spheres and the everyday realities of the inner chambers. In eking out a space of their own, these women created the possibility of an emphasis on gender (women-as-same) that overlaid the divisive categories of familial loyalty and class. This emphasis on the commonality of women was given only weak and fragmented expressions in the seventeenth century, in the form of such poetry clubs as the Banana Garden Seven or individual bonds between wives and singing girls.

This emergence of female gender as one of the principles of social organization and definition of personhood co-existed with divisive forces within the women's communities. The disagreement between Fang Mengshi and Xu Yuan, mired in a contest for pride of locale, also stemmed from their different interpretations of the constitution of the voice of a moral woman. In the context of the intimacies pursued by Xu and Lu Qingzi, a third seed of dissent is brought out in clear relief: jealousy in the competition for men's and each other's favors.

Lu Qingzi was keenly aware of the divisiveness of the possessive lover. In a tender poem crafted for Maiden Wu, a young concubine who was not yet fifteen (*sui*), Lu lamented: "Her elder sister [first wife], eager to love [her husband], is envious of the affection Wu receives."[61] Similarly, she was full of sympathy for a maid-concubine who, presumably the loser in a contest for love, was forced to leave the household.[62] After Lu's own son died in infancy, her husband procured a concubine, but it is not clear if the unfortunate girl was from Lu's own household. In any case, Lu amply demonstrated her ability to put down women she felt threatened by. In a series of three poems entitled "Taunting a Shaman," she warned of the deceit of a female relative of her husband who might have exerted too much religious power in the inner chambers:

> The "goddess" speaks forceful words, turning lies into truth,
> She beholds others with eyes of scorn.
> No need to beg the Weaving Maid to teach you real tricks,
> Just learn the lute and you can play god.[63]

If the secluded lives of gentry wives were rife with both love and discord, the same tensions were all the more powerful in the lives of courtesans. In the sections that follow, we explore how the same themes of love and deceit, freedom and dependence, power and futility, were sketched out on a different canvas by examining the worlds of two courtesans, Liu

Rushi and Wang Wei. As glaring as these common themes, however, are the differences between gentry wife and female entertainer. By highlighting such differences with respect to life cycle, self-perceptions, residence pattern, and social networks, we will come to understand that the gender system allowed women the possibilities for a considerable range of movement and fulfillment, but only in terms of trade-offs: agility in the male domain came at the price of heightened dependence on men; freedom and pleasure in the female domain, in turn, entailed an acceptance of exclusion from a host of public activities.

Liu Rushi: The Self-Naming Courtesan

These conflicting forces are highlighted in the life of Liu Rushi (1618–64), one of the most accomplished courtesans in late Ming Jiangnan. Her life was so unusual and her deeds so daring that her many biographers seem compelled to treat her either with admiration or contempt.[64] For an entertainer, hers was the quintessential success story: reared as a concubine and later sold to a brothel, Liu quickly rose through the ranks of the entertainment quarters. At the zenith of her courtesan career, she participated in the thriving literary and political associations in Jiangnan, mingling with the most acclaimed poets and politicians of the day. When Liu was 22, she courted and won the hand of a scholar-official 36 years her senior, Qian Qianyi (1582–1664). Qian's legal wife, née Chen, was still alive, but Qian married Liu with the ceremony proper for a first wife and treated her as such.[65] Twenty-three years later, when Qian died an old man, a bitter property dispute broke out with Qian's clansmen. To protect the interests of her daughter and son-in-law, Liu committed suicide at the age of 46.[66] Although Liu was by all accounts an independent and daring woman, ironically it was in her liaisons with men, Thrice Following in its figurative sense, that she realized her subjectivity as a woman. (See Table 4 for a summary of Liu's activities as a courtesan.)

Kang-i Sun Chang's book on Chen Zilong treats Liu's career as a poet; here the focus is on her self-perceptions and socializing as a courtesan. The opportunities to travel widely and to associate with many men during her formative years allowed Liu to develop an expansionary worldview and a sense of self that was alien to a woman reared in the inner chambers. Yet for all her daring deeds and freedom of movement, the courtesan was even more dependent on men's favors for survival and well-being than were gentry wives. The inner domestic space allowed to gentrywomen by the doctrine of separate spheres was denied to women raised in the public entertainment world.

When contrasted, the wife and the courtesan thus reveal an irony on

TABLE 4
Liu Rushi's Training and Career as Courtesan

Year	Age	Location	Event
1618	0	Jiaxing	Born
?	?	Wujiang	Sold to a Zhou household as concubine; taught by the master (p. 48)
1631/32	13/14	Suzhou?	Expelled from the Zhou household; sold to a brothel (pp. 52, 82, 117)
1632–35	14–17	Songjiang, Suzhou	"Period of initiation"
1632–34			Affairs with suitors (pp. 68, 105–6, 121)
1634		Jiading	Visited Jiading to broaden network (pp. 83, 328)
1635		Songjiang	Lived with Chen Zilong; associated with the Ji Society (pp. 105–6, 235, 277, 1105)
1635–40	17–22	Songjiang	"Period of maturity"
1635–36		Wujiang	Left Chen Zilong; moved to Wujiang to take over courtesan house (pp. 57–59, 119, 325, 328)
1636		Jiading	Second visit to Jiading (pp. 83, 328)
1638–40		Hangzhou	Sojourns at the West Lake (pp. 377, 384)
1640		Jiaxing, Wujiang, Songjiang	Recovered from illness in Jiaxing; traveled to Wujiang; stopped over in Hangzhou; returned to Songjiang (pp. 83, 433, 439)
1640, Eleventh month	22	Yushan (Changshu)	Visited and proposed to Qian Qianyi at his home (pp. 226, 343)
1640, Twelfth month	22	Yushan	Moved in with Qian Qianyi (pp. 518–19)
1641, summer	23	Yushan	Married Qian Qianyi (p. 650)

SOURCE: Chen Yinke, page references given in parentheses.

which the workings of the gender system hinged: those women with the greatest physical mobility were also the most dependent on men; those whose movement was most restricted were the freest to voice and pursue their desires within their circumscribed world.[67] From this analytical perspective, all women are subjected to a certain freedom-dependence nexus. The exact balance between the two and the specific forms that it took, however, varied by social station and by the life cycle.

In particular, Liu Rushi's freedom in naming herself is emblematic of the fragmentary and uncertain nature of her existence in the public entertainment world. The domestic daughter dutifully progressed from one clearly defined stage in her life cycle to the next — daughter, bride / daughter-in-law, mother, mother-in-law — all named with reference to her expected contributions to the male-centered kinship system. In contrast, since the female entertainer occupied no formal place in the official kinship system, her life cycle followed no fixed, linear pattern. Age and experience held no promise for advancement inside or outside the recurrent cycle of maid-concubine, prostitute, courtesan, and mistress; nor was she confined to only one identity at any given point in time.

As if to impose a certain order on her transitory life and shifting identities, Liu Rushi assigned herself a multitude of names as she journeyed through the many transitions of her early life. Nothing is known about Liu Rushi's parents and family background, except that she was *not* born into a Liu family, nor was Rushi her given name. During the first 23 years of her life, Liu Rushi changed her name, or took on new names, at least six times.[68] As she began to gain fame as a courtesan in her late teens, she abandoned her original family name of Yang and henceforth called herself Liu. Once she married Qian Qianyi, Liu seems to have stopped adopting new names. Although existing materials do not allow exact dating of her name changes, they do suggest that each was related to a critical event in her life.

Rubie Watson, an anthropologist who has studied naming practices in a Hong Kong village, concludes that "the process of naming marks important social transitions for Chinese men; the more names a man has the more socialized and also, in a sense, the more individuated he becomes. By contrast, married women in rural China are essentially nameless."[69] Like the adult men that Watson has studied, Liu Rushi changed her name to mark the transitions in her life. Chen Yinke argued that her given name at birth was Yunjuan (cloud beauty), a common name for girls born into commoner households in Zhejiang. When she was sold from the Zhou household to a brothel at the age of thirteen or fourteen, she changed Yunjuan to Yinglian (shadowed pity). In the next two or three years, during the period of her initiation into brothel life, she took another name, Ai (love).[70] At this early stage she kept her family name of Yang and was known to men who frequented the pleasure quarters as Yang Ai.

The surname change from Yang to Liu symbolized a more radical break with the past and the patrilineal family system, a break that gentrywomen seldom made. The exact date of the change is not known, but sometime between 1636 and 1638 the rising star of the Suzhou pleasure quarters came to call herself Liu Yin.[71] She had just ended a love affair with Chen Zilong, editor of the important anthology of practical statecraft, *Collection of Essays on Statecraft from the Ming Dynasty* (*Huangming jingshi wenbian*), and later a Ming loyalist.[72] Even before the publication of her first poetry collection in 1638, Liu was gaining a reputation as a calligrapher and poet among the leading Jiangnan literati circles. Her choice of names, however, indicated the profound ambivalence she felt at the height of her glamorous career.

Liu alludes to her courtesan background, and *yin* literally means to hide or to conceal. In a letter to a friend, Liu wrote, "All I want to do is to retreat [from public life]."[73] Curiously, the name was popular among courtesans and professional artists — the very women who hid neither their presence, their works, nor their name from public view — in seventeenth-century Jiangnan. Huang Yuanjie, for example, called her poetry collection *Liyin* (to detach and conceal or the detached hermit). Several other courtesans contemporary to Liu and Huang also chose *yin* as part of their names.[74] This apparent contradiction of public women favoring a name that means concealment is explicable only as a playful reinterpretation of a story from the *Biographies of Exemplary Women*, a classical didactic work. Far from its literal meaning of resignation or retreat, *yin* was turned on its head and made into an affirmation of these women's acclaimed talents.

One of the exemplars in the *Biographies of Exemplary Women* was a virtuous wife who lectured her husband, a corrupt official, on the virtue of concealment: "In the Southern Mountain," she said, "there was a black leopard. For seven days it hid itself in the fog and rain without coming down for food. By so doing, it hoped to make its fur plush and its markings bright. It hid itself to avoid calamities."[75] The black leopard, fog, and the Southern Mountain were all part of the lexicon associated with the recluse. Whatever moral the story was intended to convey, it came to be used to admonish women to stay modest, quiet, and cloistered. Courtesans like Liu Rushi, however, punned on "markings" and turned the moral on its head. For "markings" (*wenzhang* or *wencai*) can mean either the patterns on an animal's fur or the lines crafted by a writer and their flair.[76] In other words, in calling themselves *yin*, courtesans and professional writers were not necessarily championing a lifestyle of resignation. On the contrary, through a parody of the didactic *Biographies of Exemplary Women*, they were celebrating their education and literary talents.

To some, the tension between a respite from public life and the pursuit of literary excellence was reconcilable. In the second half of the 1630's, both were very much on Liu Rushi's mind.[77] Two collections of her poetry were published; one in 1638 by her former lover Chen Zilong, another in 1639 by her friend and mentor Wang Ranming (1577–1655). Wang, a wealthy patron of the arts whose pivotal role in the Hangzhou artist communities is discussed below, also published a collection of her letters in 1641.[78] Even as Liu's company and works were being sought by patrons far and near, however, Liu herself was becoming anxious over the prospects of finding a husband. She was twenty years old (21 *sui* by Chinese count) in 1638, already beyond the marriage age of daughters of respectable families. For two years she was constantly on the road, pursuing new relationships or running away from old suitors. Wang Ranming helped by providing introductions and shelter. Wang also suggested Qian Qianyi, a literary leader and retired high-ranking official, as a possible candidate. Liu visited him, then 59 years old, at his home in 1640, and they were married the following year. Qian gave her a new name, Hedong (East of the river).[79] This, together with Rushi and Wowen Jushi, both alluding to a common opening line in Buddhist sutras, were the names she used until she took her own life 23 years later.

Courtesans like Liu Rushi took great liberties in assigning themselves new given names or even family names. For these women, a change of name was an act of individuation and self-expression, one that often marked a significant transition in life. Yet for all the courtesan's agility, her eagerness to land a respectable husband betrayed the precariousness of her existence. When Liu Rushi married Qian Qianyi and was named by him, she became, at least symbolically and nominally, entrenched in the world of domesticity and male-centered kinship that was all too familiar to gentry wives.

Courtesans in the Public World of Men

Much like her self-named identities and representations, the social relations of Liu Rushi were also shaped by the contradictory forces of freedom and dependence. In her associations with male friends, Liu appeared to be keenly aware of her freedom in trespassing gender boundaries. In all her letters to her patron-friend Wang Ranming, for example, she referred to herself as "younger brother" (*di*) or the contradictory but revealing "female younger brother" (*nü di*).[80] Her self-representation as a man-like woman was also evident in her dress. Liu often appeared at parties wearing men's clothes; even after her marriage to Qian Qianyi, she made courtesy calls on behalf of Qian in robes like those worn by members of the literati. This earned her the nickname "Confucian gentleman" (*rushi*, also a pun on her name Rushi).[81] As the many examples of cross-dressing gentry daughters receiving guests discussed in the preceding chapter show, this practice was by no means initiated by Liu. Yet more unusual was the extent to which Liu's personal and artistic styles matched her male attire. Most female artists favored dainty strokes; Liu's calligraphy and paintings, however, were acclaimed for their bold, cursive style. Not only was she outspoken on political issues, she thrived on discussions of military strategies. Liu's hero was the female general Liang Hongyu, who repelled an invading army in the Song dynasty. Liu aspired to be like Liang and was called Liang Hongyu by some of her male friends.[82]

Liu did not, however, present herself to her male friends and clients as an androgynous *person*; her identity was firmly based on her self-representations as an androgynous *woman*. In daring to be man-like in concerns and looks, Liu did not forget that her femininity was her ultimate attraction. Among women the courtesan was freest to negotiate and even to violate gender norms and roles; yet at the same time she was committed to accentuating her feminine identity. This ambivalence was best expressed in Liu's pride in the small size of her bound feet. Even when dressed in men's robes, she made sure that her tiny feet protruded from the garments.[83]

Bound feet did not hamper Liu's physical mobility, however. It was in her transitory lifestyle that the courtesan was at once freest in her movement and most dependent on male patronage. The life of a courtesan in late Ming Jiangnan involved constant traveling and sojourning, for the ability to build connections and to penetrate male gentry networks was the mark of success in the trade. Between 1631 and 1641, the duration of Liu Rushi's courtesan career, she rarely lived in one place for more than a year. Songjiang, where she first built up her reputation and connections through her association with Chen Zilong between 1632 and 1635, remained a home base to which she returned after long trips or sojourns. Otherwise she had brief stays in the city of Suzhou, visited the loyalist network in Jiading, toured Hangzhou for parties and friends, moved to Wujiang to look after her foster mother's establishment, and retreated to Jiaxing, her native place, to recuperate from some nagging illness. These cities and towns formed a ring of about 300 kilometers in circumference in the most prosperous region of the Lower Yangzi. Navigating the crisscrossing waterways of Jiangnan by boat, Liu was often invited to take a hurried rest in the mansions of patrons and friends. Whereas gentry wives accompanied husbands on their bureaucratic travels, courtesans and professional writers endured the travails of journey as a necessary condition of their jobs. On the road, these women were by and large dependent on men for introductions, expenses, and shelter, although occasionally patrons' wives also extended them hospitality.[84]

The reward for this heightened dependence was an expansion of terrains that few domestic women could experience firsthand. The lives of such gentrywomen as Shen Yixiu and Shang Jinglan evolved around their families; the number of non–family members in the poetry clubs they formed was directly proportional to the extent of their forays outside their native county. Both the domestic and social variants of women's communities were relatively stable (insofar as they were buttressed by the written word) and had a long lifespan. Another characteristic was their relatively separate existence from the social networks of their male kin. In contrast, members of women's communities in the entertainment quarters were not related by blood, although they often addressed each other by kin terms. These extra-familial networks constitute a variation of public communities. Unlike the public poetry clubs of gentrywomen, however, membership in courtesan networks was fluid and short-lived.[85] Above all, these networks were so enmeshed in male networks that it is impossible to account for the activities of one without the other.

Liu Rushi's agility in moving in and out of a large array of male circles widened both her perspective and her social network. Their impressive scope was aptly summed up by Chen Yinke: "Almost all of the famous scholars Liu Rushi associated with, directly or indirectly, appear in the prefaces and introduction of [*Collection of Essays on Statecraft from the Ming Dynasty*]. Among them, the most obvious ones are the chief editor Chen Zilong and the proofreader Qian Qianyi, Liu's mate during the second half of her life."[86] We concentrate here on two aspects of Liu's liaisons with these leading literati of her day to demonstrate her ironic dependence on the male domain—the pivotal role played by men in her personal and political orientations, and the lack of clear boundaries between her male and female networks.

Contrary to the experience of gentry daughters in the inner chambers, male teachers were more instrumental in Liu's education and the shaping of her outlook than females. First among them was Zhou Daodeng, a retired grand secretary in Wujiang, who purchased Liu as a maid-concubine when she was a young girl. Liu's wit and intelligence won Zhou's favor. Sitting her on his lap, he often taught her literature. Zhou was Liu's first teacher, initiating her into basic literacy and the appreciation of poetry and the novel.[87] For gentry daughters, this role was usually fulfilled by mothers, although sometimes the father shared the responsibility at an early stage.

Intimacies with men since youth were clearly conducive to Liu's male-like style and concerns. When Liu made her debut as a courtesan, she had brief relationships with two men, both close friends of Chen Zilong. One, Li Cunwo (1603–45), had a lasting impact on Liu's love of calligraphy and the abandoned style of her brush strokes.[88] Above all, Chen Zilong, with whom she was closely related for three years, imparted a political idealism and brought her into the circles of the Return [to Antiquity] Society and Ji Society members, both being literati associations dedicated to political and literary reforms. The borrowed house in Songjiang in which Chen and Liu lived together in 1635 was within walking distance of the Southern Villa, the compound in which Chen and his Ji Society friends studied, wrote poetry, and lamented the degenerate state of politics over flasks of wine.[89] Although Liu held her own in these parties and was by no means considered inferior, if not for sustained contacts with such an impressive entourage of men in the vanguard of the political and literary reform movements, her political acumen, chivalry, and loyalist activism would have taken more subdued forms.

Although it was not unusual for gentrywomen to discuss and be concerned with national affairs, as we have seen in the example of Gu Ruopu, they were seldom as deeply committed to political activism as Liu. After marrying Liu, Qian Qianyi remarked with admiration that "my sick wife, idle in the house, nevertheless still worries about her country" and "the lady in the inner chambers fixes her heart on the universe's chessboard [national affairs]."[90] During the moral and political turmoil that engulfed the empire in 1644, Liu Rushi threw herself into the loyalist resistance movement, a cause for which her former lover Chen Zilong was martyred in 1647.

Liu's efforts to persuade Qian Qianyi to commit suicide after the fall of Nanjing in 1645 are well known, as is Qian's decision to surrender instead. Facing a dilemma between personal loyalty to husband and political loyalty to the Ming court in exile, Liu opted for instilling a change of heart in Qian. Although details of her loyalist involvement remained extremely obscure, Chen Yinke argues that not only did Liu aid clandestine plotters of Ming restoration in the late 1640's and 1650's, but she also convinced Qian to join her. Chen has reconstructed several examples of their loyalist activities from Qian's later poetry. In 1650, Liu and Qian hosted the visit of famous loyalist Huang Zongxi (1609–95); shortly after this Qian set off to Jinhua, Zhejiang, to persuade a Qing commander to defect. Before the 1654 and 1659 Yangzi forays by Koxinga, a loyalist naval commander based on Taiwan, Qian and Liu helped drum up support on land, coordinating sympathizers under the guise of poetry parties. Liu even contributed funds to one leader who later died in battle.[91] Although these attempts turned out to be futile in the end, Liu Rushi demonstrated that conjugal loyalty was not the prerogative of gentry wives, nor was political loyalty the exclusive concern of public men.

It is no accident that many of the foremost late Ming courtesans were involved in the loyalist resistance.[92] Their wide social networks, which spanned diverse literati groups, their marginal existence, and their itinerant lifestyle made them ideal scouts, messengers, and fundraisers. There is also a deeper structural reason for the courtesans' activism. As mentioned earlier, the extension of domestic loyalty to political loyalism was inherent in Confucian ethics, and this extension facilitated the loyalist sentiments of a number of gentrywomen schooled in the virtue of chastity. Although hardly exemplars of chastity in its strictest sense, courtesans as members of society were subjected to the same overarching demands of loyalty. The personal rapport they developed with loyalist men, in fact, encouraged them to approach the loyalty-loyalism continuum from the other way around — commitment to national political ideals predated commitment to any individual man. In the eyes of the loyalist men, so strong was the association of courtesan with loyalism that, as Kang-i Sun Chang has pointed out, "after the fall of the Ming, the courtesan became metaphor for the loyalist poets' vision of themselves."[93]

Such is the irony of the courtesan's life: embedded in the world of public men, she could ride horses, traverse mountains, and partake in national affairs *as a woman*. She did not have to justify her male-like deeds as those of an honorary man. Yet in return for this agility in the male domain, the courtesan sustained only fragmented networks with other women. Not only was the woman freest in her movements most dependent on male favors, she was also the most isolated from other members of her sex.

Transitory Communities of Sojourning Women

On the rare occasions when courtesans and other marginal women gathered, however, they did so in style. To socialize they did not scribble a verse to make a date with a cousin, nor did they stop by a neighbor's for a drink; instead, they brought their entourage to West Lake in Hangzhou, the artists' community par excellence. As traveling became a necessity for merchants and a fad among the leisure class in the second half of the Ming dynasty, Hangzhou, a historic and scenic city, attracted visitors from all over the empire. In Ming-Qing times, Hangzhou was a busy inland river port that was a major sericulture center with a considerable shipbuilding industry. In addition, its high-quality printing industry and well-heeled art patronage networks enticed aspiring artists, writers, courtesans, and tourists who simply wanted a piece of the action, to visit or to sojourn.[94] The lake itself and the mansions, inns, and restaurants on the lakeshore constituted a physical public space for the educated and commercial elites, sites where people hailing from different places mingled. The most publicly active women — courtesans and professional artists — forged legendary friendship ties on the lake. When Liu Rushi's frequent travels first took her to Hangzhou in the autumn of 1638, she found communities of men and women in which she was much at home.

No one who needed introductions or money in Hangzhou could afford not to call on Wang Ranming, a salt merchant from Xin'an, home of the famous Anhui merchants. Wang was a wealthy patron of the arts known for his lavish parties and well-placed connections. His flower boat on West Lake, "Garden Without a Mooring," was graced with the calligraphy and often with the company of the foremost artists of the day — Chen Jiru, Dong Qichang, and Li Yu, to name a few.[95] Liu Rushi first called on him in

Public space in motion: on the edges of water and land, West Lake near Hangzhou provided fleeting meeting grounds between nature and civilization, legends and mundane life, residents and travelers, women and men (*Mingshan tu*, modeled on Jiajing period prints but first published in its present form ca. 1633; reprinted — He Lezhi, p. 15).

1638, and the two, 41 years apart in age, quickly became good friends. In the next two years Liu sent him 30 letters, which he published in 1641. In one of them Liu wrote: "Ji Shuye said that the most precious thing between [two] people is a free interchange of their nature. Whenever I came across these words, I couldn't help but sigh. Now as I regard your [friendship] toward me, I come to realize how true they are."[96] Ji Shuye is the famous writer and zither player Ji Kang (223–62), a member of the Seven Sages of the Bamboo Grove.

Through Wang Ranming, Liu Rushi came into contact with courtesans equal to herself in fame and talent. For all that they had in common, however, because of their sojourning lifestyle their friendship could not have been sustained without their mutual male friends. Wang Ranming, for example, in his frequent traveling brought news of one woman to another. He once sent the works of one woman painter to Liu Rushi, asking for the latter's comments. Liu, seemingly impressed, asked to read her poems as well. Similarly, before the blocks for Liu's letters were cut, Wang sent them to Lin Tiansu (fl. 1620–42), a Fujian courtesan-painter to whom he was particularly close, and asked her to write a preface.[97] Although both the domestic and social types of women's community benefited from occasional introductions by male relatives, extra-familial communities of sojourning women could not be sustained without a male mediator.

The lure of West Lake and patrons like Wang were also instrumental in bringing courtesans and professional female artists together. Besides Huang Yuanjie, another respectable wife who eked out a living by being a painter on the lake was Wu Shan.[98] Wu was another extraordinary woman who straddled seemingly incompatible worlds. A native of Dangtu, Anhui, Wu Shan married a scholar, Bian Lin. Stricken by some unknown difficulties, the family roamed around for seven years, between 1631 and 1638, without a permanent home. During these years, Wu cultivated a wide social network and perhaps even began to sell her works. In 1635, when she was sojourning in Nanjing, Wu came across the poetry collection, *Fragrance Reborn*, of the ill-fated Ye Xiaoluan, the daughter of Shen Yixiu. Eager to introduce herself to Ye's father Shaoyuan, she sent a messenger to him bearing a fan, a eulogistic poem, and a letter signed Wild Woman from Guxi (Guxi Yenü).[99] Guxi refers to her native place, Dangtu. Both her bold sobriquet and direct communication with a male stranger without a formal introduction were alien to the habits of gentry wives and suggest that Wu was already functioning in the public domain as a woman artist.

Wu Shan moved to West Lake immediately after the Manchu conquest, as the turmoils of dynastic transition drove her family into dire straits. In 1647, she "attached" herself (*fu*) to the former courtesan Gu Mei, concubine of Gong Dingzi (1615–73), an official who surrendered first to peasant rebel Li Zicheng and then to the Qing. Although not drawing a fixed salary, being a companion of ex-courtesans entailed monetary rewards and excellent opportunities for network building. Huang Yuanjie, as we will see, was also invited by Qian Qianyi to be Liu Rushi's companion. Wu Shan accompanied Gu, then renamed Xu Zhizhu, to Hangzhou and nearby scenic spots, becoming even more prolific and publicly visible. She and at least one of her two daughters frequented parties on Wang Ranming's pleasure boat, and the poetry of both mother and daughter was widely circulated in the Jiangnan area. Wu had become a professional writer so well known and deserving of support that the local magistrates of Hangzhou were said to have donated part of their salaries to her.[100]

Most probably through Wang Ranming, Wu Shan befriended Huang Yuanjie, a woman with whom she had much in common. Wu was said to have so admired her fellow professional artist that she invited Huang to stay with her for several months. Her farewell poem to Huang was also a description of herself: "A knapsackful of calligraphy and paintings; a bagful of poems, / Filled with waters and valleys here, there, and everywhere."[101] The economic necessity of peddling works of art and the drudgery of constant traveling are here given a lighthearted twist; in the embrace of constantly changing landscapes the itinerant life of the woman artist seemed almost liberating.[102]

Like Wu Shan, Huang Yuanjie found respite on West Lake from her transitory life. When Huang sojourned there, she was the next-door neighbor of retired courtesan Xue Susu, the horseback archer, and they entertained each other with calligraphy and paintings.[103] One male scholar described her life as a professional artist on the lake: "Huang Yuanjie, a native of Jiaxing, has a soaring reputation as a poet. She often travels in a light boat, carrying her brushes, between Wu and Yue. I once saw her living in a rented place by a bridge in Xiling [Hangzhou], selling her poetry and painting by a small pavilion. She would stop once she made enough to live on."[104]

Another sojourner who graced Wang Ranming's flower boat on the lake was Wang Wei (Xiuwei; ca. 1600–1647), a Yangzhou courtesan who was a friend of Liu Rushi. In one of the parties she met and befriended Lin Tiansu, then visiting from Fujian, and the two courtesans celebrated their chance meeting with poems and paintings. Without the lure of West Lake and Wang's hospitality, the paths of these two women, who lived thousands of miles apart and who were always on the move, might not have crossed. A description of Wang Wei's lifestyle by one of her friends is almost identical to that of Huang Yuanjie cited above: "Wang Wei often travels in a light boat, carrying her books, between the five lakes."[105] The coincidence may stem from a conventional cliché, or it may suggest that women travelers like Huang and Wang were part of a larger trend. However small their number relative to the growing population of itinerant men, women were essential participants in the travel boom that mesmerized China in the sixteenth and seventeenth centuries.

Wang Wei, the Soaring Eagle

Wang Wei, a courtesan who more than any other women contributed to the traveling boom, was a native of Yangzhou, home of the thin horses. Her father's death when she was only six is said to have precipitated her apprenticeship in the entertainment quarters. Her rise in that world was as meteoric as that of Liu Rushi, as was the breadth of her socializing and the inevitability of her decision to marry, and will not be recounted here.[106]

Instead, aspects of Wang Wei's life and poetry will be used in this section to embellish four themes already developed in this book: the mobility of women; the overriding importance of literature and poetry to the emergent woman writer; the prevalence of *qing* and new attributes of womanhood; and the friendship between courtesans and gentry wives.

Traveling was for Wang Wei an expression of individual freedom, much like the self-naming practices and cross-dressing habits of Liu Rushi. In contrast to gentry wives such as Wang Fengxian who accompanied their husband on his travels or other courtesans who roamed the waterways in search of patrons, Wang Wei enjoyed traveling for its own sake. Describing herself as "by nature addicted to mountains and waters," she would have traversed them even if she had not been required to do so by her profession. Wang Wei wrote travelogues when she toured Hunan, and several of her poetry collections bear titles related to traveling, such as *Poems from Wandering* (*Yuanyou pian*), *Distant Existence* (*Wanzai pian*), and *Scrawl in Anticipation of Mountains* (*Qishan cao*).[107]

In a pair of poems meaningfully entitled "The First Step," Wang captured the lure of traveling with this couplet: "My eyes and ears delight in new discoveries, / As old sights blur into a haze." In another: "Every traveler takes in what she sees, / Others hear of her experience only from a distance."[108] Traveling is thus an act of constant renewal, addictive because of the never-ending promise of yet another discovery. And, as an authentic experience known only to the traveler herself, it is also an expression and fulfillment of her individuality.

Wang Wei was such a famous traveler that she was credited with the editorship of an anthology of travelogues entitled *Records of Famous Mountains* (*Mingshan ji*). Although the anthology appeared to be a project of more commercial than literary value, Wang Wei's preface is a moving statement of the meaning of physical freedom to a woman who could no longer enjoy it. She began by recalling her youthful adventures: venturing into Hunan by boat to pay respects to the Buddha in the Jiuhua mountains; ascending the Yellow Crane Pavilion in Wuhan; viewing the waterfall on Lu Mountain in Jiangxi. Her mood turned pensive as she recounted that at the time of writing, she was sick and housebound on West Lake. "By nature I belong to the wilderness; I grew up to be as unrestrained as a soaring eagle. Little did I know that such a fate would befall me."[109]

Yet like numerous women who never had a chance to venture out of their inner chambers, Wang Wei found solace in vicarious traveling through literature. In her serene Hangzhou quarters surrounded by pine trees, bamboo groves, plum blossoms, and crabapple trees, the soaring eagle toyed with the idea that freedom has more to do with one's state of mind than with the location of one's body. Upon losing herself in the travelogues of bygone and contemporary writers, she found that "they all narrate happenings in time and express feelings through [descriptions of] scenery. Demons and spirits are the writer's servants; dragons and krakens can be made to soar or sink. The way of literature is preserved in transformations." The magical power of a writer's brush brought Wang Wei, as reader and author, temporary relief, but failed to quench her longing for the direct experience of the wilderness. At the end of her preface, she remarked grimly: "I lay myself down; I can no longer wander."[110]

Being housebound was an existential ordeal for Wang Wei, for it signified the confinement of the entire female population. In a preface to her own poetry collection, she expressed an awareness of her limitations as a woman: "Not being born a man, I cannot right all wrongs that prevail under heaven; instead I work within the confines of one room."[111] Although her courtesan's life could hardly be said to be physically "confined within one room," it took a woman as free to travel and as exposed to the public world of men as Wang Wei to verbalize the female predicament in unequivocal terms.

Wang's efforts to create meaning from within that confinement echoed those of other women who might not have been as conscious of their female predicament: religious devotions and poetry as expressions of her innermost self. She spelled out the meaning of poetry to her: "During the time left from my devotions and sutra reciting, every word and every chant that came upon me, be it in remembrance of flowers in rain or longing for waters and mountains, arose from inspirational gusto [*xing*] and ended as expressions of my heart [*ji yi*]."[112] To the extent that even casual and unadorned words constituted true poetry as long as they arose from the poet's heart, even the housebound lady had something to contribute to literature and could connect with the world at large without setting foot out of her inner chambers.

Wang Wei's affirmation of poetry as the site of both the creation and expression of a woman's subjectivity brings a sense of closure to several major themes of this book: talent as a new attribute of womanhood, the centrality of poetry to an emergent women's culture, and the primacy of *qing* in leveling barriers. All these themes were exemplified by Wang Wei's friendship with a gentry wife, Xiang Lanzhen, whom Wang consistently called by her courtesy name topped by her husband's family name, as Madame Huang Mengwan. Xiang, a native of Jiaxing, was a prolific poet with two published poetry collections; another volume appeared posthumously. Xiang married the *juren* son of a major literati family famed for housing several published woman poets under one roof. She was also remembered as a stern mother who supervised the studies of her son, an

imperial student.[113] In other words, Xiang Lanzhen was a respectable gentrywoman and irreproachable in her duties as wife and mother. She was, at the same time, serious about her poetic pursuits. In her last words to her husband, she declared that "I have no regrets in this world but this wish: may my name be appended to those of other lady-poets [*guixiu*] by virtue of my insignificant scribbles."[114] Similar to the perceptions of so many women discussed in this book, poetry figured at once as Xiang's seat of identity and her gateway to immortality.

Although the circumstances of their meeting are not known, Xiang and Wang Wei became friends while living in an unidentified site surrounded by lakes and mountains. Impressed by Xiang's erudition, Wang sought her company in drinking parties and outings to temples, as testified to by a poem she crafted in response to one that Xiang sent. Her fondness for Xiang was later expressed in a eulogistic poem replete with Chan Buddhist overtones:

> A pebble in an autumn dike,
> Who can see through it as our previous, present, and future lives?
> Her perceptive mind was not fated to live as long as the pine,
> But her plum soul will shine as bright as the moon.
> Words on bamboo leaves and white silk fill her toiletry chest,
> Even casual scribbles turned into sounds of pure jade.

These two lines paid tribute to Xiang's poetic legacy and contrasted it with the impermanence of life alluded to in earlier lines. Yet most telling of Wang's own devotion to the cult of *qing* was the last couplet of the poem:

> I think your husband, now in mourning like Xun Fengqian before,
> Can never deny the true love he feels for you.[115]

The story of Xun's devotion to his wife has been noted in the context of a discourse of talent, virtue, and beauty. It is also useful to note that Wang's own poetic talent was vindicated by her close friend and traveling companion Tan Youxia with a reference to Xun Fengqian. In his preface for Wang's *Scrawl in Anticipation of Mountains*, Tan wrote: "Xun Feng-

---

(*Opposite, top*) The Jinhua mountains in Hunan. (*Bottom*) The Lu mountains in Jiangxi. The housebound Wang Wei recalled her youthful ventures into these mountains in her preface to *Records of Famous Mountains*. Produced in the golden age of Chinese woodblock prints, these are fine examples of the incorporation of landscape painting techniques into woodblock printing. Recarved and reanthologized in China and Japan, these popular prints are probably the same ones that appear in the collection of travelogues that Wang was said to have edited (*Mingshan tu*, modeled on Jiajing period prints but first published in their present form ca. 1633; reprinted — He Lezhi, pp. 6, 29).

qian said, 'Neither talent nor virtue is relevant to a woman. She should be signified primarily by her beauty.' These are words of the uninformed. For a person [as distinguished] as Wang, with poetry [as gifted] as hers, why would beauty matter at all?"[116] For Tan Youxia, Wang Wei's enchantment was rooted in her poetic and artistic talent. Indeed, very few woman of her day lived up to the new womanhood better than Wang Wei.

Wang's allusion to Xun Fengqian in her eulogy for Xiang Lanzhen, in turn, signals her deep attachments to *qing* and poetry. The allusion is a tribute to the love that bound Xiang and her husband through life and death, the same love immortalized in *The Peony Pavilion*. As she paid tribute to this conjugal love and her own love for Xiang, Wang Wei brought together all the conflicting elements of the cult of *qing*. In opening the poem with Chan allusions, Wang recalled the attempts made by male scholars to reconcile *qing* with its Buddhist renunciation. Yet the very fact that her friendship with and remembrance of a gentry wife were mediated by their shared love of poetry brought the power of verse, *qing*, and female friendship into a seamless closed circle.

Gender: A Category of Social Organization

An account of intimacies between Liu Rushi and Huang Yuanjie can serve as a summary statement of the relevance of gender, or an awareness of women-as-same, to women in seventeenth-century China. The friendship between the ex-courtesan and professional artist, sealed by their shared love of the amateur gentleman's art, is also indicative of the transitory nature of communities of women who were marginal to the family system.

It is not known when the two first met. In 1643, on the occasion of the completion of Liu's new home, which also housed Qian Qianyi's collection of rare books and antiques, Huang was invited to be Liu's guest and companion. She stayed with Liu and Qian from the winter of that year to at least the summer of 1644, exchanging paintings and poetry with Liu.[117] Analyzing a landscape that Huang painted for Liu in 1651 and that was mounted on the same scroll as one of Liu's works, James Cahill has speculated that their friendship might have influenced the styles of both artists.[118] As in the case of Wu Shan serving as ex-courtesan Gu Mei's travel mate, Huang's companionship entailed monetary remuneration. In a poem dedicated to Liu, Huang thanked her for being "generous in gold," implying that Liu had supported her livelihood. Yet the luxury of being able to spend everyday moments together was the best reward: "We looked into the mirror together, waited for the moon to rise together, and played the zither [*zheng*] together."[119]

Huang Yuanjie's visit was cut short by the fall of the Ming capital of Beijing. In late 1644, Liu and Qian left for Nanjing, where Qian was to serve as minister of rites in the Southern Ming court. Huang followed them and reached Nanjing in early 1645, where she celebrated a second Spring festival in their mansion.[120] The Spring festival was a time of family reunion in China. The fact that Huang spent two consecutive New Years with Liu Rushi and Qian Qianyi instead of with her own family suggests that she lived outside the dictates of the family system.

That such physical contact and artistic rapport between Liu Rushi and Huang Yuanjie was possible at all is significant. As noted above, the issue of Huang's respectability became controversial because she occupied an ambivalent space between the domestic world of faithful wives and the public world of literati men. Huang's friendship with the ex-courtesan Liu allows us to examine her ambivalent position in its full context. Huang Yuanjie was a member of all three types of women's community described in this book—Shen Yixiu's domestic, Shang Jinglan's social, and Liu Rushi's transitory public community. Equally at home in all three, Huang exemplified a new order in the making. The ethical distinction between respectability and meanness and the concomitant subjugation of an individual to the dictates of the family system were in certain rare but significant cases nullified by a sense of shared womanhood.[121] The common ground between Huang Yuanjie and Shen Yixiu, Shang Jinglan, or Liu Rushi was not the social status of their husband but their common dedication to literature and the resonance they felt as women. The liaisons between Xu Yuan, Lu Qingzi, and singing girls were another form of association between women from different stations in life, constituted less by shared love of literature than by their sensual attraction for each other.

It would be farfetched to argue that women's communities in seventeenth-century Jiangnan were social equalizers. Their members were, after all, few in number and tended to hail from the same cultural milieu. They do, however, highlight the crucial importance of literacy and education in the creation of a women's culture structured by a raison d'être distinct from other markers of social organization and distinction. The ability to read and write allowed these women to keep in touch despite physical separation, to relate to women from different social backgrounds, to broaden their networks and concerns beyond the inner chambers, and, when the need arose, to make a living to provide for husbands and children. The fact that most women in seventeenth-century China could neither read nor write does not detract from the importance of literacy for those who could. It is no accident that Shen Yixiu, Liu Rushi, Wang Duanshu, and other women in their times devoted time and effort to collect, edit, and publish the works of other women.[122] These efforts, together with those of the teachers of the inner chambers, served to enlarge the women's culture and to transmit it from one generation to the next.

The development of the different forms of women's communities described in this book signified the emergence of female gender as a category of social organization and self-identity. Through reading and writing, women from different age groups and families formed an array of networks, ranging from the formal, lasting, and visible to the private, transitory, and invisible. These women — mothers, daughters, distant relatives, friends, and neighbors — were brought together by a voluntary bond of womanhood superimposed on other principles of association such as kinship. That many of these women's communities did not disband with the death of individual members but were reconstituted by precedent-minded women in posterity demonstrates that female gender had become one of the principles of social organization. Networks of literate women similar to the ones examined in this book, in fact, persisted into the nineteenth century.

Voluntary bonds between women occupied an ambiguous position in the Confucian view of family and society. On the one hand, they are neither an overt element in the official kinship structure nor one of the five cardinal relationships. On the other hand, the official ideologies never explicitly prohibited them as long as they did not interfere with the workings of male-centered structures. In the cracks between the morally laudable and the permissible, literate women quietly created their own expansionary space, a circumscribed world that was nonetheless punctuated by freedom and fulfillment in women's eyes.

The power and integrity of the space opened up by this women's culture hinged on continued compliance; it thrived as long as it did not pose a fundamental threat to the official gender system. We do not know if educated women were consciously aware of this trade-off, but the de facto freedoms they enjoyed may explain their lack of incentive to topple the prevailing system built on the dictum of Thrice Following. In this light, the resilience of the seventeenth-century gender system depended not on its repressive ability to silence women but on the exact opposite — the opportunities it allowed for diversity and plurality of expression. However circumscribed they appear in hindsight, educated women seized upon these opportunities as the gateway to personal fulfillment and greater gender equality.

This, then, is the ultimate paradox of so-called Confucian patriarchy: it is at once more powerful and less powerful than the Western feminist and Chinese modernist discourses assume it to be. In the face of sweeping socioeconomic changes brought about by commercialization in the late

Ming period, the prevailing gender system was able to perpetuate itself by allocating a new social space for women to write, publish, and build communities. Yet the female gender was always being mediated by other divisive categories. The dual principles of constituting women-as-same (gender) and women-as-different (class) worked to contain through empowerment. The transitory communities of courtesans and professional artists and the fleeting intimacies between wives and singing girls demonstrate most graphically the tensions inherent in this dual construction of womanhood.

Epilogue

The seventeenth century constitutes an unusual historical moment, riddled with paradoxes. Political history witnessed one traumatic jolt after
another: Ming palace scandals, corruption, class wars, a brutal conquest,
the drawn-out Qing pacification and consolidation. At the same time,
social history surged on, as books and goods changed hands, the gentry
family became a center of learning and cultural production, and educated
women built communities in and out of the family. The monetary economy called every value and practice into question; old boundaries marking the domestic realm, gender distinctions, and the place of woman in
society no longer seemed so unequivocal.

Yet the more things changed in society, the more strangely familiar they
became. Commercial printing, which made books more accessible, heralded new ideas about *qing* and womanhood, but these changes merely
expanded the traditional elite instead of undermining its literature-based
power and authority. Literate women's culture extended the domestic
woman's trajectory through time and space, but she became all the more
committed to domestic values and her own role in the family as a result.
Concepts of womanhood were contested, and the new, more embracing
formulation that emerged gave sanction to women's intellectual and
moral pursuits. The end result was that the twin premises of the gender
system — Thrice Following and separate spheres — were realigned with socioeconomic realities. The labels did not change, but their meanings were
revamped; underneath the familiar rubrics both the content and context
of everyday life in elite households were transformed.

Many things have been omitted from this narrative, some deliberately,
some reluctantly. The imperial state, for one, hardly figures in the analysis. Social dynamics in seventeenth-century Jiangnan had a life of their
own, one that the imperial state was unwilling or unable to interfere in.
With the consolidation of the high Qing state in the eighteenth century,
society no longer was left alone. As Susan Mann shows in her forthcoming

Women in Eighteenth-Century China: Gender and Culture in the Lower Yangzi Region, the active interest taken by the state in women and family and the flourishing of evidential scholarship in the high Qing period created new discourses of marriage and female morality. Both had a direct bearing on how women from the various classes were to live.

Reluctantly left out of this book are the majority of the Chinese population—people who toiled instead of writing poetry, people who did not live in Jiangnan. It is undeniably true that this book focuses on a tiny and highly atypical group of men and women. Most history books do. But their story is significant, I believe, in showing us the dynamic aspects of Chinese tradition and the possibilities for historical change. Although the Confucian tradition upholds stability and self-perpetuation as its highest goals, in practice it is neither stagnant, "super-stable," nor cyclical. The resilience of cherished dictums masks the substantial changes in meaning and realities of life that transpired.

This inherent gap between ideology and practice is most evident in the area of gender relations. Boiled down to its basics, the central thesis of this book is that gender relations constitute the most essential, volatile, and dynamic aspect of Confucian tradition. Contrary to the popular perception that gender relations belong to the feudal backwaters, my contention is that they constitute the most enabling aspect of Chinese tradition. The contestations over the meaning of modernity today would be more meaningful if tradition were being re-imagined as a series of trade-offs, and both its strengths and weaknesses were being confronted seriously.

If Chinese modernity cannot be defined as the negation of tradition, then the unusual historical moment we have witnessed—the seventeenth century—is instructive in showing how tradition can be harnessed to further untraditional goals, and how women can be incorporated into new ways of imagining national and local communities. In these ways, the "teachers of the inner chambers" still have much to teach the Chinese nation today.

REFERENCE MATTER

Notes

For complete author names, titles, and publication data for the works cited here in short form, see the Works Cited, pp. 351–77.

Introduction

1. For an excellent description of the birth of Chinese women's history as a field of study, see Du Fangqin, "Qishi nianlai."

2. Xu Tianxiao, p. 2.

3. For an analysis of this as part of a larger rendition of "China-as-woman," see Chow, pp. 5–9, 14, 141–42. Hershatter also shows that the predominant representation of prostitutes in twentieth-century Shanghai was that of victim-sundered-from-natal-family. She argues that this image of the victimized prostitute "tells us much about the gendered language of political crisis in Republican China" (p. 1119).

4. For an English translation of "The New Year's Sacrifice," see Lu Hsün, 1: 150–73.

5. Chen Dongyuan, pp. 18–20.

6. For a classic statement of this position, see Soong.

7. Mohanty, p. 74.

8. Du Fangqin, *Nüxing guannian*, pp. 13, 378. For the "four thick ropes" in Mao's report, see Ono, pp. 148–49. I thank Kathryn Bernhardt for calling my attention to this. For another example, see Li Xiaojiang, esp. pp. 145–49, for her enthusiastic endorsement of the May Fourth women's liberation movement as an integral part of the Marxist New Democratic revolution.

9. For representative works of this revisionist scholarship, see K. Johnson; Andors; and Wolf.

10. See, e.g., the chapter, "Principles and Contradictions of the Confucian Patriarchal Order," in Stacey, pp. 15–65. Stacey makes occasional references to changes in the Song or late Ming times, but her treatment of "Confucian patriarchy" is basically ahistorical.

11. My early thinking on the victimization/agency issue benefited greatly from Atkinson, especially her critique of the "woman as victim" and "woman as agent" dichotomy and her argument for a "bifocal" approach.

12. Tierney, p. 153.

13. Scott, pp. 42–43.

14. For this "sexual re-imagining of the political realm," see Lewis, pp. 67–80.

15. *Li Chi*, 1: 441 (in section on suburban sacrifices, "Kiao Theh Sang" [Chiao-te-sheng in Wade-Giles, Jiao te sheng in *pinyin*]). Another reference to *sancong* can be found in "Hwan" I [Hun i in Wade-Giles, Hun yi in *pinyin*], or section on the meaning of the marriage ceremony, in ibid., 2: 432–34.

16. For references to *cong* in *Neixun*, see Yamazaki, pp. 217–18.

17. Du Fangqin, *Nüxing guannian*, p. 57. See also pp. 165–66. Similarly, Chen Dongyuan (pp. 48–49) has written that a wife's submission to husband was so complete that "her only recourse was to be his plaything [*wanwu*] forever."

18. For a further development of this argument contrasting the legal and ethical demands of female submission with examples of henpecked husbands in literature and real life, see Yuasa, pp. 134–37.

19. Chung, pp. 88–89; Chung goes on to point out that the ideal roles of good daughters, wives, and mothers were extended to allow palace women to wield functional and even political power.

20. For elite women's property rights in the Song, see Ebrey, "Women in the Kinship System." Ebrey's argument that women's enjoyment of property rights was greatest under the Song is by no means shared by all scholars. Jennifer Holmgren (pp. 12–13), for example, argues that in late imperial times, customary law continued to accord rights in her dowry to the widow when she left her husband's family.

21. Holmgren (pp. 4–14, 20–22) argues that for economic reasons widow fidelity had been the norm of the poorer classes since the second century, and that Ming law encouraged the spread of this norm to the elites. But I do not think that she has proved her innovative argument. For the chastity cult, see Elvin, "Female Virtue"; and Mann, "Widow."

22. For an attempt to link the consolidation of patriarchy since the tenth century to women's exploitation in the so-called petty capitalist mode of production, see Gates.

23. For a summary of "power of the key" from both literary sources and anthropological fieldwork, see Cheng; "*Kinbeibai* to Kagi," in Niida; and McDermott.

24. The lack of accurate demographic data makes it extremely difficult to determine female literacy rates in the seventeenth century. One indication of rising literacy rates is the proliferation of woman writers — 242 in the Ming and 3,667 in the Qing — who appeared in the encyclopedia of Chinese woman writers by Hu Wenkai (*Lidai funü zhuzuo kao*; figures supplied by Paul Ropp and his student Lu Yun). For a later period, Evelyn Rawski (*Education*, p. 140) estimates that "information from the mid- to late nineteenth century suggests that 30–45% of the men and 2–10% of the women in China knew how to read and write."

25. Joseph McDermott (p. 14), in his study of the power of wives over household finances in nineteenth-century China, makes a similar plea for turning away from "what women could not do" to "what they actually did." For an analysis of the shortcomings of the "domination-resistance" conception of power, see Abu-Lughod.

26. Foucault, pp. 94, 99.

27. Bourdieu, *Outline*, p. 41.

28. Ebrey, "Women, Marriage and the Family," pp. 197–223.

29. For the reaction of such Ming scholars as Lü Kun, Tang Shunzhi, and Li Zhi to the growing visibility of literate women see Handlin-Smith's classic study, "Lü Kun's New Audience"; see also her *Action in Late Ming Thought*.

30. "Doubled Vision of Feminist Theory," in Kelly, p. 57.

31. Bourdieu, *Logic*, p. 55. For "habitus" and "embodiment," see idem, *Outline*, pp. 72–95.

32. "Introduction" and "Toward a Unified Analysis of Gender and Kinship," in Collier and Yanagisako, pp. 1–50.

33. Dorinne Kondo (p. 299), an anthropologist who studied power and gender in the Japanese workplace, has also noted that "words like 'resistance' and 'accommodation' truly seem inadequate, for apparent resistance is constantly mitigated by collusion and compromise at different levels of consciousness, just as accommodation may have unexpectedly subversive effects." Compare Robertson's (pp. 65, 82) use of the concept of negotiation.

34. Lerner, p. 242.

35. For the exchange of letters among gentry women in Ming-Qing China, see Widmer, "Epistolary World."

36. Smith-Rosenberg, p. 312. In this study of love letters exchanged between female friends over a long period of time, Smith-Rosenberg concludes that the intense and platonic bonds between these women testifies to the emergence of a separate female culture in Victorian America.

37. Kenneth Ch'en, pp. 288–89.

38. For sutra-reading groups, see Handlin-Smith, "Lü Kun's New Audience," p. 28, although what is rendered "the classics" there should read "sutras" (both being *jing* in Chinese). Candida Xu (1607–80), granddaughter of the famous Ming Christian scholar Xu Guangqi, gathered with fellow Christian women to study the Bible and to make handiwork for their church in Songjiang (Pfister, pp. 307–8). I am grateful to Dr. Theodore N. Foss for this reference.

39. I identified these three forms of women's communities as familial, intra-familial, and extra-familial in my dissertation. I thank Richard von Glahn for suggesting the terminology of domestic, social, and public.

40. I refer to the eighteenth-century French usage of *souvenir* here, meaning both memory and common object (Orest Ranum, "The Refuges of Intimacy," in Chartier, *Passions*, p. 232).

41. Recent research on women's literature written in a "women's script" (*nüshu*) in Jiangyong county, Hunan, however, suggests that even as these rural women broke with Confucian tradition by inventing an alternative script, they betrayed their adherence to it in the importance they attached to the written word. There is a flood of anthologies and documents on *nüshu*. For an analysis, see Silber. Although local legend has it that a Song woman invented the script, the earliest extant document could not have dated before 1900.

42. De Bary, "Individualism and Humanitarianism."

43. The debates on the nature of Chinese commercialization and its departure from Western-style capitalism can only be mentioned in passing here. Mark Elvin

has spoken of a "high-level equilibrium trap" in *Pattern of the Chinese Past*. Philip Huang has described the Chinese experience as "involutionary commercialization," one that left small family subsistence farming intact. For a summary of the debates on the nature of this commercialization, see "Introduction," in Huang.

44. For a brief summary, see Rawski, "Economic and Social Foundations."

45. For an explication of the geological foundation of Jiangnan, see Umitsu Masatomo, "Chūgoku Kōnan deruta no chikei keisei to shichin no ritchi," in Mori, *Kōnan deruta shichin*, pp. 27–56.

46. Scholars have not agreed on, however, the effect of this commercialization on relations of production in the peasant household economy. For a short overview of the economic transformation of Jiangnan in the early and mid-Qing, see Naquin and Rawski, pp. 147–58. For the peasant household economy, see Philip Huang; and Rawski, *Agricultural Change*. For a detailed survey of sub-county-level production and marketing centers (*shi* and *zhen*) in the Yangzi Delta, see Fan.

47. Honig, pp. 20–35.

48. Zhou Zhenhe, p. 15. For the invasion of Wu dialects into five Jiangbei counties, see Zhou Zhenhe and You, pp. 44; and Honig, p. 25. One example of the rivalry among variants of the Wu dialect is Songjiang prefecture. In the Ming, the Jiaxing tongue was most prestigious; in the Qing, the Suzhou tongue took over; the early twentieth century saw the rise of Shanghai dialect (Zhou Zhenhe and You, pp. 67–68).

49. Spence and Wills, p. xvii. For a view of both a systemic crisis in the seventeenth century and the success of the Manchu dynasty to reconstruct the old imperial system despite the rupture, see Wakeman, *Great Enterprise*.

50. See, e.g., Guoli zhongyang daxue.

51. Miyazaki, pp. 1–11.

52. Rowe, *Hankow, 1796–1889*; and idem, *Hankow, 1796–1895*. For Rowe's further characterization of China's early-modern society by its valuation of human feelings and the individual as well as a limited form of egalitarianism, see "Women and the Family."

53. Ropp, *Dissent*.

54. Clunas, pp. 4–7. Although I appreciate Clunas's intention of situating Chinese history in a larger comparative framework, I do not find his designation of "early modern" convincing or meaningful. His perceptive analysis alone serves that purpose admirably.

55. In her study of printing in early modern France, Natalie Davis argues that although the spread of printing facilitated new controls on popular thought, its more formidable results were a richer urban culture and a breaking down of the monopolies of knowledge (see "Printing and the People," in Davis). Similarly, Roger Chartier (*Cultural Uses of Print*, p. 238) writes: "The circulation of books on a scale hitherto unknown has effects that might seem contradictory. On the one hand, it encouraged the inculcation of new disciplines, whether they involved the faith, civil behavior, or trade technologies. On the other hand, it broke down mental barriers by enabling people to escape the repetitiousness of a restricted daily life by grasping information or throwing themselves into fiction." On a more theoretical level, he warns of the fallacies of treating "popular culture," or that of

any social class, and the culture imposed by the church or state as distinct and antagonistic entities (pp. 3–11). This insight is relevant to Chinese society as well.

56. In a posthumously published article, Joseph Fletcher ("Integrative History") tried to avoid using the West as the reference point in the study of Asian history. Focusing on East and Central Asia in the sixteenth to eighteenth centuries, he argued that China, the Middle East, Central Asia, and India shared an "early modern history" characterized by seven traits, most notably population growth, proliferation of regional cities, rise of the urban classes, and quickened pace of change. These definitions of "early modernity," however, still bear the smirch of the Eurocentric definition to my mind.

Chapter 1

1. For a similar argument that middle-class women in eighteenth-century England were also avid members of the emergent reading public because of the leisure at their disposal, see Ian Watt, p. 44.

2. Wakeman, "Seventeenth-Century Crisis," p. 3.

3. The relationship between commercialization, class formation, and social order in Ming-Qing Jiangnan has preoccupied generations of Japanese scholars. For an introduction to this tradition, see the chapters by Oyama Masaaki, Tanaka Masatoshi, Tsurumi Naohiro, and Shigeta Atsushi in Grove and Daniels. Mainstream Japanese scholarship, exemplified by Oyama and Shigeta, sees in the seventeenth century a consolidation of a feudal system of dominance by the local gentry (*kyōshin*) over the so-called *kyōdōtai* community. For a contending view focusing on the collapse of such a structure of dominance in the same period, see Hamashima; and Mori, "Minmatsu no shakaikankei." A recent generation of scholars, shunning such terms as *feudalism*, had produced finely textured studies of the local gentry and local society. For an innovative attempt to reconcile the two positions, see Kishimoto, "Min-Shin jidai no kyōshin." None of these scholars deals with the status of women. Taking the experiences of women into account, my views on the issues of status system and local control are closest to Kishimoto's. For a fascinating study of how commercialization affected the social value of women's work as textile producers from 1000 to 1800, see Bray.

4. In his classic study of Jiading during the Ming-Qing transition, Jerry Dennerline elucidates the effects of commercialization on social networks, ideology, and leadership structure; see especially the introduction and chap. 3. For rural-urban migration in seventeenth-century Songjiang and the fluid social system that ensued, see Kishimoto, "Chihō shakai to 'seron' "; see also Liu Zhiqin.

5. Kishimoto, "*Rekinenki*," pp. 71–72. For vagabonds and gangsters in seventeenth-century Jiangnan, see Ueda, "Kōnan no toshi no 'burai.' " The Qing state encouraged vertical groupings but considered horizontal groupings such as literati societies subversive.

6. Ueda has attempted to show that overlapping and shifting circuits were first established in local society in the mid-Ming, consolidated in the late Ming, and peaked around the turn of the nineteenth century; see "Mura ni sayō suru jiryoku."

7. For the demise of village chief and tax chief, see Kishimoto, "Chihō shakai to 'seron,' " p. 131; and Dennerline, p. 70.

8. For the county as a social unit fostered by absentee landlordism, see Ueda, "Chiiki to sōzoku," pp. 146–51. For the county as the context for marriage alliances in Tongcheng, Anhui, see Beattie, pp. 51–52.

9. For an extant guide to brothels and gambling dens, see Shen Hongyu. For merchant guidebooks, see Brook, "Guides for Vexed Travellers."

10. The lack of major technological innovations in Ming printing has led scholars to downplay its importance. In a revisionist attempt, recent Japanese scholars have argued that the Jiajing period was the watershed in Chinese printing, when printed, not handcopied, books became readily available to people outside the traditional literati class; see Inoue; and Ōki, "Shuppan bunka."

11. Due to its lower overhead costs, woodblock printing was the dominant means of book production in the seventeenth and eighteenth centuries. Genealogies, which had been printed by movable type since the late Ming, were an exception. The repetition of names minimized the number of pieces of type needed. For books printed by movable type in the Ming-Qing period, see Zhang Xiumin, *Yinshua shi*, pp. 678–729.

12. K. T. Wu, pp. 203–4; Tsien, pp. 172–75.

13. Inoue, pp. 418–22. Ōki ("Shuppan bunka," pp. 74–98) calls them the "newly literate strata" and the "new middle strata." They were also the target readership of vernacular novels. For Ōki's debate on this issue with Isobe Akira, see Ōki, "Hakuwa shōsetsu." Isobe ("*Saiyūki* no shutaiteki juyōsō") argues that Chinese social structure was polarized into two classes—the "powerholders" and the "ruled"—and that readership of such novels as *Journey to the West* was restricted to the former.

14. Craig Clunas (pp. 36–39, 46) has made an interesting distinction between manuals of refined tastes and the household almanacs consumed by petty rural landowners. This distinction is less salient for my level of analysis here.

15. In a study of eighteenth-century English periodicals, Kathryn Shevelow (p. 10) emphasizes that the values and representations of a class can predate its socioeconomic existence: "We can use the notion of 'middle class' to designate a particular representation of cultural values, beliefs, and practices that existed prior to, or simply apart from, their eventual conceptual coalescence into a social category." Compare Armstrong, pp. 63–66.

16. Ye Shusheng, p. 220.

17. K. T. Wu, p. 223.

18. Sakai, p. 89.

19. This and other wage information is from Nakayama, pp. 96–97. The statute book with sample prices is entitled *Yuzhi Da-Ming lüli zhaoni zheyu zhinan* (Zhang Xiumin, *Lunwen ji,* p. 148). For a study of food and condiment prices gleaned from Ming novels and jottings, see Yang Yongan, 1: 151–90. See also Clunas, pp. 128–32, 177–81.

20. Han Xiduo and Wang, p. 3. For a survey of Ming bureaus involved in *guanke* and titles of books produced, see Li Zhizhong, pp. 217–44; for the early Qing, see pp. 285–304. Li (p. 214) observes that the first Ming emperor, Taizu (r.

1368–99), sent books of poetry and novels to his princes to distract them from political intrigues. In 1639, Qing Taizong printed a Manchu translation of the novel *Romance of the Three Kingdoms* (p. 285). For a list of officially and commercially produced editions of this novel, see Zhang Xiumin, *Yinshua shi*, p. 466.

21. Inoue, pp. 422–27; Tsien, p. 178.

22. For examples of *jiake* being sold in bookstores, see Inoue, p. 427.

23. Famous examples include Mao Jin and Zang Maoxun (1550–1620); see Ōki, "Shuppan bunka," pp. 36–38, 77–79; and Xu Shuofang, pp. 294–97.

24. Rawski, "Economic and Social Foundations," pp. 17–28.

25. Ōki, "Shuppan bunka," pp. 30–31.

26. Xu Peiji, p. 220.

27. Xiao, "Jianyang Yushi," pt. 1, pp. 243–45; pt. 2, pp. 198–99.

28. For the use of lineage ties by Huizhou and Shanxi merchants in recruiting employees, see Yu Ying-shih, pp. 566–69.

29. For a study of 31 of the Huang brothers and 46 of their extant works, see Zhang Xiumin, *Lunwen ji*, pp. 171–79. Zhang slightly modified his tables in a later work (*Yinshua shi*, pp. 503–7). For patterns of the Huangs' migration to Hangzhou, Nanjing, and Suzhou, see Ōki, "Shuppan bunka," pp. 61–71.

30. For the Liu family, see Fang Yanshou.

31. For Yu Xiangdou, see Zhang Xiumin, *Lunwen ji*, pp. 162–70; and Xiao, "Jianyang Yushi," pt. 2, pp. 195–219. For a discussion of the new division of labor among woodblock cutters, see Ōki, "Shuppan bunka," pp. 50–53.

32. One such book merchant was Tao Zhengxiang (1732–97), owner of a famous bookshop in Beijing. He made so much money by his aggressive pricing policy that other merchants dealing in paintings and calligraphy followed suit. For his epitaph, see Sun, 1.35ab. Part of this epitaph is cited in Yu Yingshi, pp. 572–73.

33. Cf. Yu Yingshi, p. 576; Rawski, "Research Themes," pp. 97–98.

34. The composite name "gentry-merchant" (*shen-shang*) epitomizes the dual preoccupation and sources of power of these families. For examples of several such families from Jiangsu and Zhejiang, see Lai Huimin, "Mingmo-Qingchu shizu de xingcheng yu xingshuai," in Guoli zhongyang daxue, pp. 381–82. For Chinese merchants' lack of independence from the scholar-officials, see Yu Yingshi; and Ho, "Salt Merchants."

35. For the growth of regional pride in Huizhou, see Zurndorfer, chap. 6.

36. Zhang Xiumin, *Lunwen ji*, p. 174; Ji, p. 216; Xiao, "Yu Xiangdou," p. 206.

37. K. T. Wu, pp. 254–55; Inoue, p. 419.

38. *Jiajing Jianyang xianzhi*, 3.6, cited in Zhang Xiumin, *Lunwen ji*, p. 162. For early Qing poems describing the market, see Xiao, "Jianyang Yushi," pt. 1, p. 244.

39. *Shu jian*, 3a, in Tu.

40. These guides were part of the Ming revival of *xiaopin*, or short essays, as a genre. For essays on the latest "what-to-do's" in such hobbies as incense burning and tea tasting, see Cao, pp. 238–41. For an analysis of these manuals of taste in a discourse of things-in-motion, see Clunas.

41. The classic on tea is Lu Yu's *Cha jing*. It was reprinted, together with Song and Ming treatises on tea, in a popular anthology, *Cha shu*, ed. Yu Zheng (1612). This anthology was so successful that Yu, a connoisseur of tea himself, later issued a reprint bearing the same title with additional essays. Both copies are in the Naikaku bunko. Clunas (p. 28) argues that given the frequent anthologizing, the entire body of Ming connoisseurship literature can be thought of as a single text.

42. *Shu jian*, 5a, in Tu.

43. Yuan Hongdao, 5a–8b. There is a Japanese copy of this treatise on flower arrangement, printed in 1882. Fang Kebin's encyclopedia, *Guang baichuan xuehai*, in which Yuan's work can be found, includes a wealth of treatises on hobbies ranging from orchids, gold fish, and fruit trees to the more traditional chess, tea, wine, and stationery. For the contents of another anthology, *Eight Discourses on the Art of Living*, see Clunas, p. 18. For an analysis of this late Ming "glorification of obsession," see Zeitlin, "Petrified Heart"; and idem, *Historian of the Strange*, chap. 3.

44. This famous drama set in the Ming-Qing transition was completed in 1699. The book merchant's monologue cited here is taken from K'ung, pp. 212–13. I have made minor changes in romanization, spelling, and translation of official titles to make them consistent with the usages in this book.

45. Mote and Chu, p. 169.

46. Zhang Xiumin, *Yinshua shi*, pp. 519–21.

47. K. T. Wu, "Ming Printing," pp. 203–10; Zhang Xiumin (*Yinshua shi*, p. 499) distinguishes four schools of illustration: Beijing, Nanjing, Jianyang, and Huizhou. For a short summary of Ming woodblock illustration, see Carlitz, pp. 120–21.

48. "Fanli," *Mudanting huanhun ji* (Hangzhou, 1625), cited in Zhang Xiumin, *Yinshua shi*, p. 498.

49. Xiao, "Jianyang Yushi," pt. 1, pp. 231–38; pt. 3, pp. 239–40, 247n6. Many scholars date this work to 1063 according to its preface, but Xiao argues that the preface date cannot be taken as printing date. The more convincing Yuan dating derives from Xiao's research on genealogies of the Yu family. For Liu Xiang's *Lienü zhuan*, see Shimomi, *Ryū Kyō "Retsujoden."*

50. Wu Guofu, "Xu," in Wang Duanshu, *Yinhong ji*, *xu* 2ab, 3b–4b. Wu further argued that Wang, who was concerned with national affairs, was an exception that proved the rule. In her unusual patriotic fervor and personal integrity, Wang was in fact writing as an honorary man, according to Wu. This attitude was thus condescending toward women. For the career of Wang Duanshu and her patriotism, as expressed in her commitment to Ming loyalism, see Chapter 3 below.

51. Xu Yejun [Shijun], "Guige xumu," in Wang Qi, *Chidu xinyu, chubian*, 24.*mu* 1a.

52. For a comprehensive analysis of the ideal norms for mothers and wives prescribed in the Confucian precepts, see the introduction to Yamazaki.

53. See M. Theresa Kelleher, "The *Nü ssu-shu*, or, Four Books for Women," paper presented at the Neo-Confucian Seminar, Columbia University, Apr. 3, 1987. For a history of paintings derived from one of these precepts, see Julia

Murray's "Didactic Art for Women: The *Ladies' Classic of Filial Piety*," in Weidner, *Flowering in the Shadows*, pp. 27–53.

54. For Ban Zhao's biography and translations of a selection of her writings, see Swann, *Pan Chao*. For an annotated edition of the *Nüjie* and a list of its reprints in the Ming-Qing period, see Yamazaki, pp. 75–106.

55. Ko, "Pursuing Talent and Virtue," pp. 20, 28–32. See also Chapter 3 below for the arguments of these defenders of women's literary and cultural education.

56. For a complete list of female instruction books in use in Ming-Qing times, see Yamazaki, pp. 31–45. Information on the number of copies printed, however, is not available. See also Carlitz, p. 123, for a tradition of books of precepts written by women.

57. Wei, p. 117; Zhang Xiumin, *Lunwen ji*, pp. 178–79; Xu Peiji, p. 230; Han Xiduo and Wang, pp. 20, 126.

58. Ye Shusheng, p. 223; Zhang Xiumin, *Lunwen ji*, pp. 178–79.

59. Carlitz, p. 135n41; see also pp. 124–25 for a partial list of *Lienü zhuan* and *Guifan* published in the late sixteenth and seventeenth centuries.

60. For one fictionalized *Lienü zhuan*, see Youlongzi.

61. Von Glahn, p. 694.

62. Carlitz, pp. 134–35, 139–40; see also pp. 132–33 for an analysis of the possible motives of the compilers of four illustrated books of precepts.

63. Gu Zijun, "Yu Chen Jinshui," in Wang Qi, *Chidu xinyu, erbian*, 12.16ab.

64. Carlitz, p. 128.

65. Zhang Luping.

66. "Nü lunyu," *juanshou* 1a, in Chishang ke. Although the 1595 edition cited here is better printed than the 1592 one, it is laden with mistakes. Due to a binding error, chaps. 7–9 of *Nü lunyu* are missing from the earlier edition; chaps. 10–12, together with the last line of chap. 9, in turn, are missing from the later edition. Both copies in the Naikaku bunko.

67. It is possible that Chishang ke was fooled by Song Ruozhao's modesty. Unwilling to claim authorship of *Nü lunyu* herself, she attributed it to Ban Zhao. In fact, another precept written by a Tang woman, *Nü xiaojing*, was also attributed to Ban. In both cases, however, the identity of the true authors was well known (Wang Xiang, "Lunyu xu," 1b, in idem, *Nü sishu jizhu*).

68. Carlitz, p. 138.

69. For a list of the published and unpublished works by 23 female dramatists, see Xu Fuming, *Yuan Ming Qing xiqu*, pp. 270–72.

70. After compiling this table, I came across an excellent study of many of these titles by Kang-i Sun Chang. Readers interested in anthologizing strategies should consult her "Guide to Ming-Ch'ing Anthologies."

71. Cao, chap. 4 *passim*.

72. Stephen Owen, "Poetry in the Chinese Tradition," in Ropp, *Heritage of China*, pp. 295–96.

73. Chang, "Guide to Ming-Ch'ing Anthologies," p. 141; for the relations between the cult of love and the late Ming revival of song lyrics, see Chang, *Ch'en Tzu-lung*.

74. "*Gujin Mingyuan shigui* xu," 1a–3a, in Zhong.

75. Ibid., 3b–5a.

76. "Fanli," 1b, in Xu Shumin and Qian. See "Fanli," 2b–3a, for the list of sponsors and financiers. Some were well-known scholars and promoters of women's poetry, but the names of commercial publishers are also included.

77. "Xu," 1a, and "Fanli," 2ab, in Hu Baoyi. Harvard-Yenching has this edition and another that was prefaced 1716 (under Baoyi's given name, Hu Xiaosi) which is the same except for the date. Hu included a large number of poems by his wife, Gu Kezhen, but did not acknowledge her role in editing.

78. "Fanli," 3b, in Deng Hanyi. The sequel (*erji*), preface dated 1678, is boxed together with the first volume (*chuji*) in the Naikaku bunko.

79. This trend of diversified representation continued through the seventeenth and eighteenth centuries. Women from peripheral areas were particularly well represented in a nineteenth-century anthology, *Guochao guixiu zhengshi ji*, compiled by a woman, Yun Zhu (1771–1833). For the controversy surrounding the authenticity of one peasant poet, He Shuangqing, see Ropp, "Shi Zhenlin and the Poetess Shuangqing."

80. Hu Wenkai, *Lidai funü*, pp. 542–43. For Liang Ying's biography and some of her poems, see also Wu Hao, 30.30b–31b; and Yun, 12.16b.

81. Shi Zhenlin, *Xiqing sanji*, 1.21, 60.

82. Ropp, "Seeds of Change"; idem, *Dissent*, pp. 120–51.

83. Furth, "Patriarch's Legacy." Furth also terms this "bohemian counterculture" the culture of a "floating world." Her usage, however, differs slightly from mine.

Chapter 2

1. Waltner, "Not Becoming a Heroine." Waltner supports her case by a study of a fictional character reading another fictional character. Kang-i Sun Chang (*Ch'en Tzu-lung*, p. 63) shows that the late Ming courtesan Liu Rushi "was always trying to find metaphysical equivalents to her life in the female images she read in contemporary drama and fiction."

2. Charlotte Furth first made this observation of the structural link between *The Peony Pavilion* and the Xiaoqing plays in her "Poetry and Women's Culture," p. 5.

3. The play *Mudanting* was based on an earlier *huaben* (vernacular story), *Du Liniang muse huanhun*, that appeared in the early sixteenth century. For the text of this *huaben*, see Xu Fuming, *"Mudanting" yanjiu ziliao*, pp. 12–19.

4. This authentic edition was the so-called Yuming tang *dingben* (Tang Xianzu, *Sanfu heping Mudanting*, "Xu" 2ab; hereinafter cited by title only).

5. Ibid., 1a.

6. For the friendship between Hong Sheng and Wu Ren, see Chen Wannai, pp. 244–46. For Wu Ren and Mao Xianshu as neighbors in the Wu Shan district, see Zhu Peng, comp., *Wu Shan yishi shi*, 13b, in Ding Bing, *Wulin zhanggu congbian*, vol. 2. Mao Xianshu's daughter, Anfang, was a member of Banana Garden Seven, a women's poetry club discussed in Chapter 6.

7. *Sanfu heping Mudanting,* "Xu" 1b–2a.

8. Hong Zhize, *"Huanhun ji ba,"* in *Sanfu heping Mudanting,* "Ba" 3a.

9. *Sanfu heping Mudanting,* "Xu" 2ab; see also Wu Ren, *"Sanfu ping Mudanting* zaji," in *Xiangyan congshu,* 1: 4.1b.

10. For a convenient summary of the circumstances of the production of the three women's commentary, see Wang Yongjian.

11. Chang, *Ch'en Tzu-lung,* p. 11.

12. Hirose, "Mindai denki no bungaku."

13. There are two excellent compilations of remarks on the play primarily by men: Xu Fuming, *"Mudanting" yanjiu ziliao,* pp. 81–138; and Mao Xiaotong, 2: 845–1060. For contemporary accounts of performances of the play in Ming-Qing times, see Xu Fuming, *"Mudanting" yanjiu ziliao,* pp. 139–212.

14. Zang Maoxun (1550–1620), publisher of one of these illustrated editions of the *Mudanting,* himself wrote a revised version of the play (see Xu Shuofang, p. 294; Hirose, "Zō Bōjun," pp. 71–86). One of the earliest editions of the play was produced in the Wanli reign (1573–1620). The same woodblocks were still in use in the mid-1640's and were later purchased by a Huizhou book merchant to produce the Huaide tang edition, the most popular version now extant (appendix to Tang Xianzu, *Mudanting,* pp. 275–76). According to Evelyn Rawski ("Economic and Social Foundations," p. 20), a woodblock carved of the standard wood could print 16,000–26,000 copies. For a list of 26 Ming, Qing, and modern editions of the play, see Mao Xiaotong, 2: 1421–24. At least 19 were printed between the Wanli and Qianlong years (1736–95), although it is not clear if all are extant.

15. Information on these versions that Chen Tong collated can be found in an untitled passage by her. It appeared after Wu Ren, *"Huanhun ji* xu," 2a–3a, in *Sanfu heping Mudanting.* For the reference to Wuxing book market, see notes by Tan Ze, also untitled, in ibid., 3ab.

16. Almost all the foremost dramatists of Tang Xianzu's day reworked *The Peony Pavilion.* Chief among them is Shen Jing (1553–1610), founder of a contending Wujiang school of drama (Xu Shuofang, preface to Tang Xianzu, *Mudanting,* p. i). Another famous example is Feng Menglong (1574–ca. 1645), writer of popular stories and compiler of *Qingshi* (Anatomy of love).

17. Xu Shuofang, p. 51. The Yihuang area in Jiangxi was the stronghold of Haiyan tunes originally from Jiaxing, Zhejiang. The enormous popularity of Tang's dramas contributed to the flowering of an indigenous Jiangxi Yihuang tune (Wang Anqi, pp. 275–81).

18. When performed in popular venues, the dialogue and tunes of the drama were adopted to suit pedestrian tastes. For references to the staging of *The Peony Pavilion,* see Wang Anqi, pp. 186, 189, 196, 197.

19. Xu Fuming, *"Mudanting" yanjiu ziliao,* pp. 140–54; Tang Xianzu, *Peony Pavilion,* p. xiv.

20. Some scholars argue against rendering the Chinese term *xiqu* ("music-drama") as "opera," for the former were written by men of letters whereas operas were composed by musicians (Xu Shuofang, p. 74). Although this distinction is valid, I find it appropriate to call music-dramas that were performed on stage "operas."

21. The Yuan was the golden age of the Northern-style drama (*zaju*). The later years of Yuan also saw the emergence of a Southern style called *chuanqi*, which flourished in the Ming. The Northern style was the elite form, whereas Southern dramas were often inspired by folk songs (Mackerras, pp. 13–15; Strassberg, "Authentic Self," pp. 70–73). In the fifteenth and sixteenth centuries, Southern drama flowered into a variety of regional tunes. Scholars identified four broad categories—Yuyao, Haiyan, Geyang, and Kunshan—although there were a lot more local varieties. Constant cross-fertilization also makes strict demarcation difficult. Kunshan, a literati style, originated in Suzhou. It spread to the North in the Qing and became a significant element of Beijing opera. It is hard to identify individual works with a particular style, since all major works were adopted for a host of local tunes and dialects. For a study of the evolution of the various regional styles of Ming Southern drama, see Wang Anqi, p. 273–306.

22. Wang Anqi, pp. 79–87. I am indebted to Wang for her exhaustive study of both the social and artistic aspects of the Ming theater. For accounts of Qing male troupes, see Hinsch, pp. 152–56. For Ming-Qing all-female troupes, see Hu Ji and Liu.

23. Zhang Dai, p. 75.

24. Based on a fifteen-year study, Tanaka Issei ("Kōnan chihōgeki no henshitsu") argues that in the sixteenth and seventeenth centuries, local drama in Jiangnan completed a process of polarization into two modes—lineage (elegant) and market (popular)—that became the norm throughout the country.

25. For his arguments on the three kinds of professional troupes, see Tanaka, "Ming-Ch'ing Local Drama," pp. 143–47. Tanaka has also argued that the Southern drama that flourished in Ming times, *chuanqi*, was an elite genre favored only by the well-educated. The late Ming, however, saw a revival of popular local drama as peasants renewed their resistance to the authority of officials and landlords (p. 160). I do not see the *chuanqi* as an exclusively elitist form, although the language is usually refined. Many *chuanqi* dramas, in fact, championed romantic love, a theme that Tanaka considers "popular." Episodes from such *chuanqi* dramas as *The Peony Pavilion* were performed in the villages and market towns; its protagonist Du Liniang was a legendary name. Tanaka furnishes one piece of support for this (p. 148*n*20).

26. For family troupes, see Wang Anqi, pp. 94–113. For literati and commercial theater in early Qing Yangzhou, see Strassberg, *World of K'ung Shang-jen*, pp. 127–33.

27. Guests sometimes brought their own troupes to parties. For references to respectable women watching opera from behind a screen, see Wang Anqi, pp. 160–61.

28. The play, *Yanzi jian*, was published under the name of Yuan Dacheng, the infamous Ming minister who surrendered to the Manchus. For Yuan Lizhen, see Tan Zhengbi, *Wenxue shenghuo*, pp. 271–76.

29. One of the operas performed was on the infamous Ming eunuch Wei Zhongxian and a loyal martyr Yang Lian. The popular version cast Yang in a negative light. Although Zhang Dai had changed it before he staged it, the audience was not aware of it at first and hissed when Yang appeared on stage (Wang Anqi, pp. 111–12).

30. Performances at temple fairs were often organized by professional promoters with ties to secret societies (Tanaka, "Ming-Ch'ing Local Drama," p. 146). Wang Anqi (pp. 130–37) confirms the involvement of the underworld, but notes that local notables who were drama enthusiasts could also serve as organizers. Called *huishou* (heads of fair), they were in charge of collecting money from the villagers to help defray costs. Wang considered these performances an expression of community spirit. For performances commemorating annual festivals, see Xu Fuming, *Yuan Ming Qing xiqu*, pp. 246–55.

31. Tang Xianzu, *Peony Pavilion*, ix.

32. Hsia, p. 276. See also Strassberg, "Authentic Self," pp. 73–78.

33. For a summary of Wang Gen's life and thoughts, as well as an introduction to the Taizhou school, see de Bary, "Individualism and Humanitarianism," pp. 157–78; and Shimada, pp. 246–48.

34. Handlin-Smith, *Action in Late Ming Thought*, p. 46; see pp. 41–54 for background on Luo Rufang. For the relationship between Tang Xianzu and Luo, see Xu Shuofang, pp. 14–19.

35. Hsia, pp. 250, 276–79. For the influence of the Taizhou school on dramatists of the Suzhou school, see Geng. Flourishing in the late Ming and early Qing, the Suzhou school produced popular dramas promoting the cult of *qing*.

36. Meng Fanshu.

37. Hong Sheng, p. 1.

38. Wu Ren, marginal comments on Scene 50, cited in Chen Wannai, pp. 107–8.

39. Wu Ren, "Huo wen," 4b, 6a, in *Sanfu heping Mudanting*.

40. Most scholars from the PRC see Tang Xianzu as an unabashed idealist who used the cult of *qing* to declare war on Neo-Confucianism (*lixue*). To them, Tang's notion of *qing* is always at odds with *li* (principle). See, e.g., Yang Tianshi. I take exception to this view and find the arguments of Xu Shuofang (pp. 14–27) more convincing. Xu sees Tang as being caught between a philosophical commitment to *li* and an emotional commitment to drama and *qing*. The confrontation between *qing* and *li* is the central theme of *Mudanting*, but in his own life Tang sought to find a meeting ground between the two, however futile such efforts turned out to be.

41. Feng Menglong, pp. 1–2. For Feng's publishing activities, see Ōki, "Shuppan bunka," pp. 143–58. For an English translation of *Qingshi*, see Mowry, which also contains an excellent introduction to the literary environment that produced this anthology of love stories as well as to its authorship.

42. Ōki, "Fū Muryū *Sangen*." On Feng's exposition of love in his *Sanyan* story collection, see Han Lifan; see also Zeitlin, "Petrified Heart," pp. 7–16.

43. Hanan, *Chinese Vernacular Story*, pp. 79, 96–97, 221n13.

44. Goyama, pp. 445–46, 449n14. The name of the scholar is Xu Rundi (fl. 1796–1820); for a discussion of his views, see Yuasa, pp. 164–65. Kang-i Sun Chang (*Ch'en Tzu-lung*, pp. 9–10) points out that for Ming loyalists, love for one's country was no different from love for a woman. For a similar argument by a Suzhou man of letters, Wei Yong (fl. 1643–54), see Cao, p. 186.

45. For Rousseau and *La Nouvelle Heloïse*, see Darnton. I am grateful to Harold Kahn for this reference.

46. The story of a certain lovestruck woman from Neijiang was first recorded by a Qing scholar of drama, Jiao Xun (p. 37). Some scholars, however, have doubted its credibility (Xu Fuming, *"Mudanting" yanjiu ziliao*, pp. 214–15; see also pp. 215–16 for the story of another female reader who fell in love with Tang Xianzu).

47. Xu Fuming, *Yuan Ming Qing xiqu*, p. 104.

48. Xu Fuming, *"Mudanting" yanjiu ziliao*, pp. 217–18.

49. Cheng Qiong, "Pi *Caizi Mudanting* xu," in Mao Xiaotong, 2: 920.

50. Ye Xiaoluan, p. 13. After Xiaoluan died, her father likened her to a fairy from the moon, a synonym for a talented young lady poet. See Chapter 5 for the domestic lives of Ye Xiaoluan, her mother, and her sisters.

51. Qian Yi, "*Huanhun ji* jishi," 1ab, in *Sanfu heping Mudanting*. Qian Yi's portrait of Du Liniang was included in the first published edition of the commentary. See Xu Fuming, *"Mudanting" yanjiu ziliao*, p. 221.

52. This is perhaps the most famous scene of the play. See Tang Xianzu, *Peony Pavilion*, pp. 42–53.

53. Qian Yi, "*Huanhun ji* jishi," 1b–2a, in *Sanfu heping Mudanting*.

54. Wu Ren, "Huo wen," 7ab, in *Sanfu heping Mudanting*.

55. Mao Xiaotong, 2: 883–84; Xu Fuming, *Yuan Ming Qing xiqu*, pp. 104, 118*n*2.

56. This belief that *qing* and *wen* were one and the same was also popular among men. See Meng Fangshu, p. 50; and Mao Xiaotong, 2: 948.

57. English translation in Tang Xianzu, *Peony Pavilion*, p. 1; Chen's and Qian's comments in *Sanfu heping Mudanting, shang* 1a.

58. Tang Xianzu, *Peony Pavilion*, pp. 68–69. The "sixteen years" in quote refers to Du's age by Chinese count.

59. *Sanfu heping Mudanting, shang* 40b, *xia* 15b–16a. The term *wusheng zhai* is from Chen's comments on Tang Xianzu's preface, the manifesto of cult of *qing* cited above (*yuanxu* 1a, in ibid.).

60. *Sanfu heping Mudanting, shang* 2b. Significantly, the word *zhen* also means a portrait. The scene in which Du drew a self-portrait is called "Xie zhen" (sketching a likeness) in Chinese.

61. "The reopening of a dream world" is my translation, from Tang Xianzu, *Mudanting*, p. 174. For Tan's comments, see *Sanfu heping Mudanting, xia* 15b.

62. My English translation, from Tang Xianzu, *Mudanting*, p. 159. Birch's translation of this line does not include the word "talent" that triggered Tan's and Qian's comments; see *Sanfu heping Mudanting, xia* 3a.

63. Tang Xianzu, *Peony Pavilion*, p. 26; *Sanfu heping Mudanting, shang* 15a. Another late Ming woman who commented on the play echoed this vindication of female talent: "Education benefits a woman even after her death" (Huang Shusu, "*Mudan ji* ping," cited in Xu Fuming, *"Mudanting" yanjiu ziliao*, p. 88).

64. *Sanfu heping Mudanting, xia* 78b. For these actions of Liu, see *Peony Pavilion*, Scenes 26, 28, 35, 53.

65. Tang Xianzu, *Peony Pavilion*, p. 186; *Sanfu heping Mudanting, xia* 4b.

66. Tang Xianzu, *Peony Pavilion*, p. 164; *Sanfu heping Mudanting, shang* 92a–93b.

67. Tang Xianzu, *Peony Pavilion*, pp. 173–74; *Sanfu heping Mudanting, shang* 101a.

68. Tang Xianzu, *Peony Pavilion*, p. 319; *Sanfu heping Mudanting, xia* 84b.

69. *Sanfu heping Mudanting, shang* 27b.

70. The *Sanfu heping Mudanting* was a popular work that was reissued by commercial publishers. For two of these editions, see Mao Xiaotong, 2: 1423.

71. Lin Yining, "*Huanhun ji* tixu," 2b, in *Sanfu heping Mudanting*.

72. Tang Xianzu himself wrote two poems lamenting Yu Erniang's death. The scholar who first recorded her story was a friend of Tang's, attesting to its credibility (Jiao, pp. 37–38; Xu Fuming, "*Mudanting" yanjiu ziliao*, pp. 213–14). Yu's story was recounted by two women who wrote prefaces for the *Three Wives' Commentary* (Li Shu, "*Huanhun ji* ba," 1ab; Gu [Qiji] Si, "*Huanhun ji* ba," 2b).

73. Shi Zhenlin, *Xiqing sanji*, 4: 48. Shi (1693–ca. 1779), Cheng Qiong's husband and another friend, Cao Zhenting (1697–1773) were close friends. All three were natives of Shexian and traveled to Beijing together in 1736 for the metropolitan examination. Both Shi and Cao apparently knew Cheng well, calling her by her assumed name of Andingjun (the tranquil one).

74. For the preface of the primer, see Shi Zhenlin, 1: 67–69.

75. Ibid., 1: 65–66. For the love between Wu and Cheng, see also Liu Xuan.

76. Guan Daosheng's husband was the famous calligrapher Zhao Mengfu. For a brief account of their marriage, see Ma and Zhou, pp. 253–58. For Guan's poem, see p. 256. The marriage of Guan and Zhao, as well as that of Song poet Li Qingzhao and husband Zhao Mingcheng, was often invoked in the Ming-Qing times as an example of a companionate marriage between a man of letters and a talented wife.

77. Shi Zhenlin, 4: 48.

78. Cheng Qiong, "Pi *Caizi Mudanting* xu," in Mao Xiaotong, 2: 919–21; see also pp. 916–17 for Wu Zhensheng's own preface. The work itself is no longer extant.

79. Shi Zhenling, 4: 49–50. The object "woman" in Cheng's appeal is omitted in the original; I infer from Cheng's use of the word *jia* (a woman marrying a husband) that she was addressing other women. For the line "phoenix fated to follow crow," see Tang Xianzu, *Peony Pavilion*, p. 161.

80. Widmer, "Xiaoqing's Literary Legacy," p. 128.

81. Ibid., pp. 111–55. See also Ko, "Social History," chap. 4.

82. Madame Yang is said to have been the wife of a scholar from Qiantang, Yang Yuanyin (*jinshi* 1595) (Pan, pt. 2, pp. 12–13).

83. This brief life story is compiled from the three earliest Xiaoqing biographies. I refer those interested in textual matters of the Xiaoqing "story complex" to Ko, "Social History," pp. 126–31; Widmer, "Xiaoqing's Literary Legacy," pp. 114–19; and Yagisawa, "Shōseiden no shiryō." Yagisawa has laboriously studied the dating of these three biographies and compared them to nine others composed later. The name "Feng Yunjiang" does not appear in any of these stories. For a discussion of Xiaoqing's literary corpus, see Widmer, "Xiaoqing's Literary Legacy," p. 113.

84. Zhuo Keyue, preface to *Chunbo ying* and *Qing shengwen*, cited in Pan,

"Xiaoqing kaozheng," pt. 2, p. 15. Xu Yejun's *Chunbo ying*, first published in the late Ming, is one of the three most frequently staged and critically acclaimed Xiaoqing plays. The other two are Zhu Jingfan, *Fengliu yuan* (preface dated 1629) and Wu Bing, *Liaodu geng* (first published in Chongzhen reign, 1628–44).

85. I have counted a total of sixteen, including one play written in the early Republican era. Some are no longer extant. For lists of titles and authors, see Xu Fuming, *Yuan Ming Qing xiqu*, pp. 311–12; Pan, "Xiaoqing kaozheng," pt. 2, p. 14; Yagisawa, "Fū Shōsei densetsu," pt. 2, p. 78. For an introduction to the major Xiaoqing plays, see Ōtsuka.

86. For a crude Freudian analysis of the Xiaoqing biographies, concluding that she suffered from narcissism because she was sexually and mentally repressed, see Pan, *Xiaoqing zhi fenxi*.

87. Chen Wenshu, *Xihu sannüshi zhuan*, p. 18. This volume contains a popular collection of Xiaoqing's extant works.

88. Jianjian Jushi, 12.3b–4a; Zhi Ruzeng, 39b–40a.

89. Zhi Ruzeng, 40a.

90. Wu Ren, "Huo wen," 6b–8a, in *Sanfu heping Mudanting*.

91. For Feng Yunjiang's identity, see Chen Yinke, pp. 368, 448–49; and Pan, "Feng Xiaoqing kao," p. 1709. Feng's year of birth is deduced from a poem by Qian Qianyi celebrating his 79th birthday (80 *sui* by Chinese count) written in 1654 (Chen Yinke, p. 368). For Wang Ranming and his friendship with Liu Rushi and Huang Yuanjie, see Chapters 3 and 7 of this book.

92. Chen Yinke, pp. 448–49; Pan, "Xiaoqing kaozheng," pt. 1, p. 19.

93. For scholars who have argued that Xiaoqing's surname is Feng, see Yagisawa, "Shōsei den no shiryō," pp. 75–78; and Pan, "Xiaoqing kaozhang ," pt. 1, p. 18.

94. For the texts of Qian Qianyi's argument, Shi Yushan's investigation, and Chen Wenshu's rebuttal, see Chen Wenshu, *Lanyin ji*, renamed *Xihu sannüshi zhuan* in a convenient modern edition, pp. 8–9.

95. Chen Yinke, p. 448. For both sides of the argument, see Widmer, pp. 128–30. I agree with her conclusion that the available evidence is inconclusive and that "instead of pursuing this issue further, it is more fruitful to probe the doubts about Xiaoqing's existence, and to see why they persisted for so long" (p. 130).

96. Zhou Lianggong, *Shuying*, 1.1, 24. His concubine also compiled a book of quotations of Ming elite women (Hu Wenkai, *Lidai funü*, p. 251).

97. Commentary under "Gu Ruopu," in Wu Hao, 30.1a.

98. Xu Fuming, *Yuan Ming Qing xiqu*, p. 267.

99. Chen Wenshu, *Xihu sannüshi zhuan*, p. 8. Forged works attributed to Xiaoqing did exist. For one of these fabrications, "Complete Works of Feng Xiaoqing," see Pan, "Shu Feng Xiaoqing quanji hou."

100. To cite two examples, see "Zhenxian zhuan," in Shi Zhenlin, *Huayang san'gao*, pp. 11–12; Yun, entry on Liu Shi, 8.15ab. Even the prolific poet Fang Weiyi was said to have burned her more morbid poems, but many survived and were published (Hu Wenkai, *Lidai funü*, p. 82).

101. Widmer ("Epistolary World," pp. 7, 28) describes the ambivalent stance of some men who on the one hand published writings by women but on the other pro-

hibited their own daughters from learning poetry. For an example of a husband who forbade his wife to write poetry, see Liu Yunfen, *xinji*, p. 36, entry on Yonghu nüzi.

102. The mother-in-law of Shen Yixiu was an example (Ye Shaoyuan, "Wang-shi Shen anren zhuan," appendix to Shen Yixiu, *Lichui ji*, p. 151).

103. Xiaoqing was identified with various immortals in dramas featuring her pathos. Moreover, one nineteenth-century female poet recalled that at her birth her mother had a vision of Xiaoqing appearing with Guanyin, the goddess of mercy, holding a double-headed lotus (Chen Wenshu, *Xihu sannüshi zhuan*, p. 55). In the nineteenth century Xiaoqing was even offered sacrifices on the day of the Cold Food (*hanshi*) Festival in Hangzhou (ibid., p. 59; no cooking was done on *hanshi* in remembrance of a loyal minister, Jie Zhitui, who was burned to death in the Spring and Autumn period). Xiaoqing's link to Jie Zhitui may have been fostered by a seventeenth-century parody of the classic story, attributing Jie's death to his jealous wife. (For a description of the parody, see Hanan, *Chinese Vernacular Story*, p. 205.) The same process of posthumous deification is found in Ye Xiaoluan's case (see Chapter 5).

104. Chen Wenshu, *Xiling guiyong*, 8.6a.

105. Chen Wenshu, *Xihu sannüshi zhuan*, p. 52.

106. Xu Yejun, 14ab.

107. Zhu Jingfan, 9ab, 11a. The idea of Xiaoqing becoming an immortal in a heavenly garden presided over by Tang Xianzu resurfaces in a later Xiaoqing drama called *Wanhua ting* (Pavilion of ten thousand flowers) by Lang Yufu. Yagi-sawa ("Fū Shōsei densetsu," pt. 2, pp. 86–88) argues that in this drama Xiaoqing is made a commander of erotic desires.

108. "Xu," Ye Shaoyuan, *Wumengtang quanji, shang*, pp. 3–4.

109. For the use of this sexual allegory by the Jin poet Cao Zhi (192–232), see Roy. For the Qu Yuan lore and its changing significance through the centuries, see Schneider.

110. Zhi, 36ab.

111. Zhu Jingfan, 1a, 2a.

112. Yuanhu yanshui sanren, p. 1.

113. Yenna Wu, "Inversion of Marital Hierarchy," p. 363; she develops this theme further in *Chinese Virago*. Patrick Hanan (*Chinese Vernacular Story*, pp. 172, 241*n*28) also calls female jealousy "a fearfully overworked theme in seventeenth century fiction and drama" and an obsession of the comic writers of the time.

114. Wu Bing, 1.43a.

115. Zhu Jingfan, 1.5b.

116. Xu Yejun, 6a.

117. Wu Bing, 2.19a–20a.

118. Zhu Jingfan, 1.7a.

119. Wu Bing, 1.15a, 2.34a–36a.

120. Xu Yejun, 22b–23a.

121. In *The Garden of Romance* (Zhu Jingfan, 1.18b), Xiaoqing marries a failed examination candidate who compares himself to Qu Yuan, an interesting twist to the image of Xiaoqing as a rejected minister discussed above. In another play, *Xihu xue*, written by an anonymous author in the mid-Qing, Xiaoqing marries the magistrate of Hangzhou, who indicts the jealous wife (Pan, "Xiaoqing kaozheng," pt. 2, p. 15).

122. Zhang Dao's Southern-style drama *Meihua meng* is an example.

123. Handlin-Smith, "Lü K'un's New Audience," pp. 27, 36.

124. Jerry Dennerline, "Hsu Tu and the Lesson of Nanking: Political Integration and the Local Defense in Chiang-nan, 1634–1645," in Spence and Wills, p. 110.

125. Li Yu (*Xianqing ouji*, 1.18ab, in *Li Yu quanji*, vol. 5) added that these were not fictitious but real occurrences and that he hoped writers of dramas would make use of them to embellish their works.

126. Yenna Wu ("Inversion of Marital Hierarchy," p. 366) argues that jealous wives made frequent appearances in Ming lawsuits.

127. Cited in Yamazaki, pp. 364–65. The seven reasons for divorcing a wife were first listed in *Lienü zhuan*.

128. Yamazaki, pp. 225–26. For the emphasis on suppressing jealousy in these instruction books, see Fujikawa.

129. The age limit of 40 is by Chinese count (*Ming huidian*, cited in Chen Dongyuan, p. 207).

130. Taga, p. 5.

131. Xu Sanchong, "Jiaze," in Chen Dongyuan, pp. 207–8.

132. Li Yu, *Xianqing ouji*, 3.45b, in *Li Yu quanji*, vol. 5.

133. Xie Zhaozhe, p. 211.

134. For an excellent treatment of the relationship between female jealousy and the changing position of women in the Northern Dynasties, see Yamamoto.

135. Yu Zhengxie (p. 495) opened his essay defending female jealousy with tales of jealous women in the dynastic histories, including a petition for regulated concubinage in the *Wei shu* (discussed below). Xie Zhaozhe (pp. 212–15) also devoted a long section to the deeds of jealous women throughout the dynasties. The original recipe for oriole soup can be found in the *Shanhai jing* (The classic of mountains and seas), a fanciful geographical work.

136. Petition by Yuan Xiaoyou, "Zongshi zhuan," *Wei Shu*, cited in Chen Dongyuan, pp. 71–73; and also in Yu Zhengxie, p. 495.

137. Levy, *Warm-Soft Village*, p. 30.

138. Chen Dongyuan, pp. 73–74. Yamamoto Noriko (pp. 89, 93, 101, *et passim*) also raises the point of daughters from powerful families lording it over their husbands, but she further argues that the jealousy exhibited by the Northern Wei women was intensified by the sinification process of the Northern Wei people.

139. Xie Zhaozhe, p. 214.

140. Yu Zhengxie (p. 497 *et passim*) argues: "The way of husband and wife is to become one. If the husband takes a concubine and the wife is not jealous, she must be indifferent. Indifference destroys the way of the family." Yu further distinguished between jealousy as a natural response and violent behavior using jealousy as a pretext. The latter should be punished by law, but the former was actually a superior virtue for women. See Ropp, "Seeds of Change," pp. 15–16, for a discussion of the same text; my translation of the quote is based on his.

141. All but one poem allegedly by this peasant girl from Yangzhou has been lost. For her story and that of He Shuangqing, see Lei and Lei, 4.4b, 9b.

142. In her excellent study of the cult of *qing*, Kang-i Sun Chang (*Ch'en Tzu-*

lung, p. 18) argues that romantic love and patriotism became two sides of the same coin, and that "the courtesan has become a mediator between love and loyalism." Although I agree with her thesis, I do not think that the cult can be attributed entirely to courtesan culture. As I will show later, changing relationships in literati households were just as important.

143. "Lao zuonie" (story no. 19), in Shi Chengjin, *lihan* (group 3), *ce* 8, 47a–55a. For Shi and this collection of stories, see Hanan, *Chinese Vernacular Story*, pp. 209–10. The saying "Although man and woman are different, in love and desire they are the same" also appeared in a sixteenth-century almanac (Yu Xiang-dou, 21.1a).

144. "Quqie nabi lun," *Tong tianle*, in Shi Chengjin, *lihan*, *ce* 15, 31b–32a.

Chapter 3

1. Deng Zhimo, *juan* 4–5.

2. Chen Jiru, *juan* 6.

3. There are various ways to translate *nüshi*. *Shi* generally means scholar, both degree-holder and commoner, but can also refer to men in general (Ho, *Ladder*, p. 35; *Ciyuan*, p. 346). Hence *nüshi* can be rendered "woman scholar" or "manlike woman." An additional complication is that a usage of *nüshi* current both in the seventeenth century and today is simply "lady" or "respectable woman." Hence Shi Yushan referred to Huang Yuanjie as *nüshi*, and Huang was called *shinü* in the title of her poetry collection (see note 13 to this chapter).

4. Huang Yizheng, 8.24b–25a. This monumental dictionary of 46 *juan* classifies words current at the time of compilation.

5. Huang Yuanjie's years of birth and death are educated guesses; neither can be verified with certainty. My estimate of her birth year is based on the following: (1) allegedly Zhang Pu, who died in 1641, asked for Huang's hand one year before his death (Chen Yinke, pp. 19–20); (2) Huang had gained a reputation as a poet by 1633, when her brother brought her verse as a memento to Ye Shaoyuan. She could not have been too young. Her year of death, in turn, is deduced from (1) Shi Yushan wrote that Huang died in the villa of Tong Guoqi in Nanjing, who retired there in 1661. Hence Huang could not have died before 1661; (2) Mao Qiling mentioned in 1669 that Huang's daughter had passed away. According to Shi Yushan's biography, Huang's death followed her daughter's closely. Hence Huang could not have died after 1669.

6. Chen Yinke, pp. 19–20. In addition, Yuanjie's first cousin (*congzi*) Huang Dezhen was also a well-known poet. Dezhen was mistaken in some accounts for Yuanjie's "sister." For the family's poverty and the marriage of Yuanjie's sister as concubine, see Chen Yinke, p. 475; and Hu Wenkai, *Lidai funü*, p. 663.

7. Female painters who contributed to the income of their families were not uncommon in Ming-Qing Jiangnan; many of them were from families of professional painters (Weidner, "Women in the History," p. 14; Laing, p. 32).

8. For biographies of Huang Yuanjie, see "Huangshi Jieling xiaozhuan," in Shi Yushan,, 17.13a–14a, and Ruan, 40.19a–20a. For a convenient collection of these and many of the most cited accounts of Huang's life, see Wang Qishu, 14.5b–

8a. For Huang's career as a painter, see Weidner, "Ladies of the Lake." The retired Manchu official is Tong Guoqi, who returned to Nanjing in 1661 and headed a salon in his villa; his wife, née Qian, was a Christian known to missionaries as Madame Agathe (Chen Yinke, pp. 964–81; Okamoto Sae).

9. For the fluidity of the status system in Ming-Qing society, see Ho, *Ladder*, pp. 53–91. Susan Mann ("Grooming," p. 206) argues that the high Qing period was also a time of fluid social boundaries. The root cause—commercialization—was similar to that in the seventeenth century, but a series of imperial edicts that began in 1723 abolishing the debased (*jian*) people as a hereditary class was also a powerful impetus.

10. "Huang Jieling *Yueyoucao* tici," in Mao Qiling, *tici* 13a–14a. "Fufeng" refers to Ban Zhao's native place. She composed the "Traveling Eastward" rhyme-prose while journeying with her son from Loyang, the capital, to his post in Chenliu, in A.D. 113 (Swann, *Pan Chao*, pp. 113–30).

11. In the eyes of the state, *jian* (debased) refers to a hereditary status of certain occupational and regional groups; *liang* (respectable) people are those who are not *jian*. Philip Kuhn (pp. 21–23) points out that many of the "unfree" groups traced their origins to punishment by the state or defeat in warfare. In other words, as a legal category applicable to both sexes, *liang/jian* derived its meaning from the state or actions in the public sphere. I argue here that in reference to a woman's status in popular usage *liang/jian* acquires a different meaning, based on her relationship with the family system.

12. This is a popular saying quoted by a magistrate on the application filed by a prostitute for a license to quit her trade (*congliang zhizhao*) and to marry; reprinted in a Ming collection of edicts, [*Ke*]*falin zhaotianzhu*, 4.1a–1b. The case was from Le'an county, but it is not clear whether this is the one in Shandong or in Jiangxi.

13. In 1643, Huang sent her husband to visit Qian Qianyi, a leading literatus, to ask for a preface to grace her poetry collection, *Shinü Huang Jieling ji*. This practice was common among male writers who had to build a reputation and sell books. Later, in the winter of that year, Qian and his wife Liu Rushi invited Huang to stay in their newly built library and living quarters. Her husband did not travel with her (Chen Yinke, pp. 287, 483, 818, 847, 863).

14. Ruan, 40.19a.

15. Wu Weiye, *Meicun jiazang gao, juan* 58, cited in Chen Yinke, p. 18; Shi Yushan, 17.13a, 14a.

16. Chen Yinke, p. 483. Qian Qianyi's preface for Huang is in his *Muzhai chuxue ji*, 33.29b–31b.

17. Huang also compared herself to the Han woman scholar-teacher Ban Zhao, who was often summoned in the Ming-Qing times to justify women's education from within the Confucian tradition ("*Liyin ge* xu", in Xu Shumin and Qian, *yueji* 2.21b–22a). The collection itself is no longer extant. The name Wuxia Cishi appears in an inscription by Liu on a fan Huang painted (Chen Yinke, p. 487). See Chapter 7 for further discussions of "hermit" and "concealment" (*yin*) as favorite names of courtesans.

18. *Xiushui xianzhi* (1596), 6.40ab.

19. The collection of verses Lu and Sang exchanged is *Zuili erji changhe*. For Sang's biography, see Hu Wenkai, *Lidai funü*, pp. 148–49; for Lu's, see ibid., p. 172.

20. In the *Qiantang xianzhi* (preface dated 1718), for example, seven categories of women were valorized: empress/consort, wise lady, filial daughter, chaste daughter, woman martyr, chaste widow, long-lived mother (*juan* 28–29). In the *Renhe xianzhi* (1686) there are five: chaste widow, virtuous daughter, filial daughter, filial wife, wise lady (*juan* 20).

21. For a particularly well researched list of woman poets with good biographies, see *Jiaxing fuzhi* (1866), *juan* 79.

22. The *Zhou guan* is another name for *Zhou li* (*Rites of Zhou*). In his treatise on women's education, *Fuxue*, the Qing scholar Zhang Xuecheng cited these two examples of women assuming a pivotal role in the oral transmission of the Confucian canon. Zhang cautioned that, however, these are exceptional cases in emergency situations (*Fuxue*, p. 241, in Gao Jianhua, vol. 2; Mann, " 'Fuxue,' " pp. 45–46).

23. *Jiaxing xianzhi* (1892), 29.35a.

24. Susan Mann ("Grooming," pp. 204–22 *passim*) shows that a similar obsession with a woman's status provoked a "conversation" on wifely duties and purity of the marriage market in the eighteenth century.

25. Ko, "Pursuing Talent and Virtue," pp. 9–10. The percentage of educated women in the entire population was negligible. Evelyn Rawski (*Education and Popular Literacy*, p. 140) estimates that "information from the mid- and late nineteenth centuries suggests that . . . 2–10% of the women in China knew how to read and write." There is, however, no quantitative evidence for this claim.

26. R. H. Van Gulik (p.66) mentions that in Ming times, nuns also served as teachers in female quarters by teaching girls reading, writing, and feminine skills.

27. On Wen Shu, see Laing, pp. 32–33.

28. Yuan Mei, p. 24.

29. For Gui Maoyi, see Hu Wenkai, *Lidai funü*, pp. 784–85; Shi Shuyi, 6.3ab; Chen Wenshu, *Xihu guiyong*, 14.1a. One of her published works is *Xiuyu xucao*. The joint collection with her mother, Li Xinjing, was entitled *Eryu cao* and published in 1771 (Hu Wenkai, *Lidai funü*, p. 785). On Cao Jianbing, see Hu Wenkai, *Lidai funü*, p. 540; Yun, 5.11b–12a; and Zhang Zengyuan. For Su Wanlan, see Hu Wenkai, *Lidai funü*, pp. 798–99; and Yun, 10.15a.

30. For brief biographies of Wang Siren, see Jiang Jinde, "Qianyan," in Wang Siren, *Wenfan xiaopin*, pp. 1–8; and Ren Yuan, "Qianyan," in Wang Siren, *Wang Jizhong shizhong*, pp. 1–3. For Wang Duanshu, see also Widmer, "Epistolary World," pp. 10–11; Hanan, *Li Yu*, pp. 18, 215n31.

31. The offer allegedly was made during the Shunzhi reign (1644–61) (Gu Dunrou, p. 180). This sounds curious, given the loyalist affiliations of Wang and her family.

32. Wang Ranming, patron and friend of Huang Yuanjie, mentioned that he saw Huang and Wang Duanshu on West Lake at around the same time (Chen Yinke, p. 369). Li Yu lived in Hangzhou from around 1650 to 1657 (Gu Dunrou, p. 180 *et passim*; Huang Lizhen, pp. 8–9).

33. "Du Yuanhu Huang Yuanjie shi," in Wang Duanshu, 8.12b. See also her "Ti Huang Jieling hua," in Yun, 2.19ab.

34. Wang's collected works, *Yinhong ji*, contains many genres besides poetry (see below). In addition, she published four poetry collections; an anthology of women's verse; an anthology of women's essays; a history of emperors and empresses from previous dynasties; and what appear to be another collected works and another historical study. Only *Yinhong ji* and the anthology of women's verse, *Mingyuan shiwei*, are extant. Fragments of her poetic works are preserved in anthologies. For a list of titles, see Hu Wenkai, *Lidai funü*, pp. 248–49.

35. "Guixiu Wang Yuying *Liuqie ji* xu," in Mao Qiling, *xu* 7.7a–8a.

36. "Chumen nan," in Wang Duanshu, *Yinhong ji*, 2.1b–2a.

37. Ibid.

38. Ruan, 40.5a.

39. Tao Yuanzao, *Quan Zhe shihua*, *juan* 35, cited in Cao, p. 86.

40. Wang Duanshu, *Yinhong ji*, 19.1b–6a. Duanshu's father-in-law was Ding Qianxue (*jinshi* 1619). It is not known if the two memorials, both dated 1647, were actually submitted to the Southern Ming court.

41. Ibid., 9.4b–5a, 10.3a, *et passim*.

42. Ibid., 23.1a–9a. Four of these martyrs were explicitly stated to be natives of Guiji; hence it is likely that Wang Duanshu learned of their deeds by word of mouth.

43. Ibid., 20.9a–b. A seventh biography, that of a friend who sojourned in Guiji, was added later (20.9b). The first six were also published in *Shigui shu*, a collection of loyalist writings compiled by Zhang Dai, a personal friend of Duanshu and her husband's (20.9b). For an excellent study of Wang Duanshu as a loyalist writer, see Widmer, "Ming Loyalism and the Woman Writer."

44. "Jinling qigai zhuan," in Wang Duanshu, *Yinhong ji*, 20.8a–b.

45. Wang Duanshu, *Yinhong ji*, 21.9ab. The next *juan* contains eight more loyalists' biographies. Shaoxing fell in the fourth month of 1646; Wang Siren retreated to the mountains and committed suicide in the ninth month.

46. The involvement of Wang Siren and Ding Shengzhao in the loyalist resistance is mentioned in Ding's memorial to the Southern Ming, actually written by Duanshu, dated the second day of the second month, 1647; see "Zouwei chenqi dangyan shi," in ibid., 19.1b–3a. This and the other memorial that Duanshu wrote are dated "xx *yuannian*" (the first year of xx); from context it can be surmised that "xx" refers to Yongli, the reign name of the prince of Lu inaugurated in 1647.

47. For a complete list of these 47 names and the preface they contributed, see "Ke *Yinhong ji* xiaoyin," 1a–2b, in Wang Duanshu, *Yinhong ji*, *juan* 1. This is the fifth preface in the first *juan*; each preface is paginated separately. Several items in *Yinhong ji* are dated 1650. Although none of the prefaces is dated, Ding Shengzhao mentioned in his that the works document Duanshu's "seventeen years' mourning for her country" (Ding, "Xu," 2a, in ibid., *juan* 1). It is thus likely that this work was published in the early 1660's. Mao Qiling recalled that when he first read *Yinhong ji*, Wang Siren was still alive. Since Siren died in 1646, Mao had either read an earlier handcopied edition or suffered from a lapse of memory ("Guixiu Wang Yuying *Liuqie ji* xu," in Mao Qiling, 7.7a–8a). Ellen Widmer ("Xiaoqing's Literary Legacy," p. 135) dates this collection to 1651. According to

Ding, the title *Yinhong* alludes to the fall of the Ming, "red" being an allusion to the suicide of the last Ming emperor.

48. For the many poems Duanshu composed to match Wu Shan's, see Wang Duanshu, *Yinhong ji*, 9.12a–b, 14a–b, 15a, 15b; 10.9b–10a. In one she explicitly referred to "all the men" who gathered at Wu's pavilion (9.15b). For Wu Shan and other women who sold paintings for a living, see Laing, pp. 88–91. Wang Duanshu also wrote many poems for her "oath elder sisters" (*mengzi*). It is not known if they were wives of the society's members or if they were themselves members (Wang Duanshu, *Yinhong ji*, 11.1b, 13.4b, 15.1b).

49. Wang Shaomei, "Xu," 1b–2a, in Wang Duanshu, *Yinhong ji*, *juan* 1, first preface.

50. Wu Guofu, "Xu," 3a–4b, in ibid., second preface.

51. "Zeng ruren Dingmu Lishi muzhiming," in Wang Siren, *Wenfan xiaopin*, p. 480.

52. Both the age of fifteen and the year 1636 are deduced from a poem that Wang Duanshu wrote for the occasion, which reads: "At sixteen [*sui*] I left the female quarters, / To marry in Beijing afar" ("Beiqu," in Wang Duanshu, *Yinhong ji*, 2.3a–b). Both Duanshu and her husband were born in 1621.

53. There is a slight inconsistency in the records regarding the exact year of their return south. In his memorial, Ding wrote that "in the second month of 1643, I accompanied my mother's coffin back to Zhejiang" ("Zouwei chenqi dangyan shi," in Wang Duanshu, *Yinhong ji*, 19.1a). In Ding's preface to *Yinhong ji*, however, he stated that he brought the family south after the suicide of the Chongzhen emperor, which did not happen until the third month of 1644 ("Xu," 1b). The earlier date seems more likely. In the wake of the Manchu conquest of Jiangnan, it was difficult and dangerous to make the trip south.

54. Wang Duanshu, *Yinhong ji*, 9.16a, 4.14b–15a.

55. Ding, "Xu," 1a, 2a, in ibid.

56. Mao Qiling, "Guixiu Wang Yuying *Liuqie ji* xu," 8a; Xing Xizhen, "Ba," 1b; both in Wang Duanshu, *Yinhong ji*.

57. One rare exception is a poem Wang wrote with Ding as they sat up one night writing poems about a painted round fan (Zou, Yuying 28a–29b). Ding's quote is from "Xu," 2a, in Wang Duanshu, *Yinhong ji*.

58. Wang Duanshu, *Yinhong ji*, 10.4b–5a, 11.9b, 27.1ab. See Robertson for a discussion of the problematic position of the feminine poetic voice in a masculinized tradition.

59. For Huang Yuanjie's complaint and her preface, written about 1655, see Hanan, *Li Yu*, pp. 16–17.

60. Cao Xuequan, "*Wumengtang ji* xu," p. 1, in Ye Shaoyuan, *Wumengtang quanji*. Zou Saizhen's work, *Shizhai ji*, contained two *juan* of verse and one *juan* of prose. It is no longer extant, but is mentioned in *Siku tiyao* (Hu Wenkai, *Lidai funü*, pp. 189–90).

61. A group of Hangzhou poets, the Banana Garden Seven, occasionally signed their works by their husband's last name. For example, Chai Jingyi, whose husband was a Shen, sometimes signed her works "Shen Jingyi." Her friend Feng Xian (*zi* Youling), who married a Qian, also used a compound name, Qian-Feng Xian (Hu

Wenkai, *Lidai funü*, p. 396). They differ from Pu Shiqi in that these adoptions of the husband's surname were temporary and did not involve a new given name. The use of compound names is still common among Chinese women today.

62. For the former, see ibid., p. 189; for the latter, "Jifu Pugong wen," is reprinted in Zhao Shijie, 11.10a–11b. Her long funeral ode for a son, "Ji Longer wen," follows (11.12a–15a).

63. Qian, *Liechao shiji*, *runji* 4.7b; comments after "Jifu Pugong wen," in Zhao Shijie, 11.11b.

64. Gu Ruopu's essays were collected in *juan* 5 and 6 of her *Woyuexuan ji*, published in 1651. Hu Wenkai (*Lidai funü*, pp. 206–8) evidently saw a copy of this very rare work. Glimpses of Gu's ideas on military colonies can be found in a letter, "Yu Zhang furen," in Wang Qi, *chubian* 2.7b–8a.

65. Xu Fuming, *Yuan Ming Qing xiqu*, p. 273. For the general theme of biology and gender ambiguity, see Furth, "Androgynous Males and Deficient Females." For gender crossing in the works of Pu Songling, see Zeitlin, *Historian of the Strange*, chap. 4.

66. The information on Yu Qiren here is based on her biography in Zhou Zhibiao, 7.15a–16a. A shorter version can be found in Liu Yunfen, *erji*, *zuli* 13. See also Hu Wenkai, *Lidai funü*, p. 296. Her poetry collection was no longer extant but 26 poems, many crafted on social occasions with other men of letters, were anthologized in Zhou Zhibiao, *juan* 7. Five others appeared in Liu Yunfen, pp. 89–90.

67. Xu Xuling's preface to Deyin's poetry collection was reprinted in Wang Qishu, 4.9ab. The collection was first published in 1705, and a sequel followed in 1752. For Xu Deyin and her works, see also Yun, 6.2b–4b, 11.4b; Wu Hao, 30.8a; Hu Wenkai, *Lidai funü*, p. 475. In her adulthood Xu became a prolific and respected poet. She was so famous that fellow Hangzhou poet Lin Yining invited Xu to join the Banana Garden poetry club. Some correspondence was exchanged, but Xu never became a full-fledged member. Xu and Lin did not meet until over a decade later, in 1705, when both their husbands were sojourning in Beijing. Lin was so impressed by Xu's poetry that she arranged for its publication (Wang Qishu, 4.9a).

Chapter 4

1. "The Great Learning," in *Four Books*, p. 7.

2. Shi Jinchen, "Yuanti ji," in Chen Hongmou, *juan xia* 9ab. For the doctrine of separate spheres formulated by Sima Guang and Cheng Yi (1033–1107), see Ebrey, "Women, Money and Class," pp. 641–44.

3. For the conceptual ambiguity of Chinese kinship terminology, see J. Watson, and the comments by Denis Twitchett that follow (p. 623).

4. Cited in Yamazaki, pp. 93–95.

5. My use of "centripetal" to describe the ideal Chinese female orientation was inspired by Bourdieu (*Outline*, p. 92): "The opposition between the *centrifugal*, male orientation and the *centripetal*, female orientation . . . is the true principle of the organization of domestic space, is doubtless also the basis of the relationship of

each of the sexes to their 'psyche,' that is, to their bodies and more precisely to their sexuality." Bourdieu has explained further the links between feminine virtues, bodily orientations, and female domestic space in *Logic*, pp. 66–79.

6. Tuan, pp. 107, 124.

7. Mogi et al., pp. 216–17; 232–34. Interestingly, in contrast to this scheme of individual–family (*jia*)–lineage (*zu*), the Hakka circular compound is constructed on the basis of individual–*zu*, reflecting a diluted sense of family loyalty among the Hakka people (p. 236). Although the dating of extant houses, on which most studies of spatial organization are based, cannot be too exact, scholars are agreed that their structures have not changed much since the Ming-Qing times.

8. Bourdieu (*Outline*, p. 110) remarks of this relational and fluid nature of dualities: "The house, for example, is globally defined as female, damp, etc., when considered from the outside, from the male point of view. . . . But it can be divided into a male-female part and a female-female part when it ceases to be seen by reference to a universe of practice coextensive with *the* universe, and is treated instead as a universe . . . in its own right, which for the women it indeed is, especially in winter." For descriptions of inner and outer living rooms in seventeenth-century Yangzhou, see Yazawa, pp. 26–27.

9. In Jiangnan, *sanhe yuan* compounds (buildings on three sides of an open courtyard) are most common. The shaded kitchen is also called the "dark room" (*anjian*) and quarters exposed to sunlight, "bright rooms" (*mingjian*) (Asakawa, pp. 101–2; Mogi et al., pp. 218–19).

10. For the contract, see Yu Xiangdou, 17.1b.

11. Alvaro Semedo, *Imperio de la China*, cited in Yazawa, pp. 27–29. This book was written in 1621 and first published in Madrid in 1624 (Grove and Daniels, p. 76n153).

12. Greenhalgh. Greenhalgh's thesis is that "once footbinding was established . . . its perpetuation became bound up with that of the family system in a vicious, self-repetitive cycle: the family system demanded footbound wives to do its domestic and reproductive tasks; and footbound wives, physically constrained from doing otherwise, reinforced the power structures which strengthened the system" (p. 15). I take exception to this argument because it is built on an erroneous premise: that a woman's domestic labor has no economic value. Women were indispensable laborers in the cotton and silk industries in Ming-Qing Jiangnan.

13. Okamoto Ryūzō, pp. 55–58. The Southern Tang was a regional kingdom in the Five Dynasties–Ten Kingdoms period of disunity before the Song reunification.

14. Levy, *Footbinding*, p. 44; Jia, 8b.

15. Ebrey, "Women, Marriage and the Family," p. 221; see also pp. 216–21. For Ebrey's argument that modern-day charges of Neo-Confucianism as "misogynist" are often exaggerated and historically misinformed, see "Women, Money and Class," especially pp. 613–21.

16. Wakeman, "Localism and Loyalism," pp. 58–60. For a study of the development of the haircutting policy from the 1610's to 1645, see Chen Shengxi.

17. As early as 1636 and 1638, the Manchu leader Abahai (Hung Taiji) issued edicts prohibiting footbinding (Chen Shengxi, p. 71). Curiously, this ban on footbinding went almost unnoticed in the eighteenth century (Zhao Yi, p. 656).

18. Greenhalgh, p. 18*n*11. The age at which this separation occurred varied from three to six.

19. Okamoto Ryūzō, p. 18.

20. The almanac is *Tongshu leiju keze daquan*, mentioned in Zhang Xiumin, *Zhongguo yinshua shi*, p. 243. The starting day was often linked to the number five (*wu*), a homophone of another character meaning "to stop growing" (Levy, *Footbinding*, pp. 56, 308*n*63).

21. For the Tiny-Foot Maiden, see Okamoto Ryūzō, p. 22; Hu Pu'an, *xiabian*, p. 164; Levy, *Footbinding*, pp. 57, 232. In Hunan, late in the eighth month was also the time for girls to have their ears pieced (Hu Pu'an, p. 334). For offerings to Guanyin, see Levy, *Footbinding*, p. 57.

22. On the conceptual fluidity of Chinese kinship terms and problems of rendering them into English, see J. Watson; "Introduction," in Ebrey and Watson. For the conflicting orientations of the family as *zong* and *jia*, see Ebrey, "Conceptions of the Family," pp. 225–26.

23. J. Watt, p. 9.

24. Li Yu, *Xianqing ouji*, in *Li Yu quanji*, vol. 5. The translation *Casual Expressions of Idle Feelings* is Patrick Hanan's (*Li Yu*, pp. 28, 224*n*113). On this book, see ibid., pp. 59–75. Hanan argues that the phrase "idle feelings" sometimes means aesthetic contemplation (p. 69). For examples of other connoisseurs of taste and their publications, see Cao, pp. 238–41.

25. Clunas, p. 67.

26. Inoue, pp. 420–21. For the building of the Qis' famous Tansheng tang collection, see Terada. For the collections of bibliophiles in Hangzhou, see Swann, "Seven Intimate Library Owners."

27. Elman, *Classicism, Politics, and Kinship*.

28. On Wang Zhenyi, see Xu Wenxu; and Liu Yongcong, p. 324.

29. Brook, "Gentry of Ningbo," pp. 35–43.

30. Dennerline, pp. 98–120; Elman, *Classicism, Politics, and Kinship*, pp. 15–35.

31. Zhang Yan, pp. 19–21, 38–54. Timothy Brook ("Funerary Ritual," pp. 465–99) argues that the dominance of the agnatic lineage in the sixteenth and seventeenth centuries accounts for a shift from Buddhist funerary rituals to Neo-Confucian rites.

32. Ueda, "Chiiki to sōzoku."

33. Beattie, p. 41; see also pp. 51–52, 128 for marriage alliances among the Tongcheng elite families. For Ningbo, see Brook, "Gentry of Ningbo," pp. 27–29, 39–40. Lai Huimin (in Guoli zhongyang daxue, pp. 394–96) also notes the geographically widespread marriage alliance circles of the Jiangsu and Zhejiang gentry families she studied.

34. Yamada also argues that lineage formation was a crucial element in the forging of institutionalized "circuits" of social relationships that stabilizes a local society. This argument is based on the earlier works of Ueda Makoto (see, e.g., Ueda's "Chiiki to sōzoku" and "Shūken gyōsei to chiiki erito").

35. For marriage alliances between the Chuang and Liu families of Changzhou from the Ming–Qing transition to the eighteenth century, see Elman, *Classicism, Politics, and Kinship*, pp. 42, 57–73. Elman (p. 71) points out that women were

"important participants in affinal relations between lineages." For marriage strategies of Wuxi elites, see Dennerline, "Marriage, Adoption and Charity in the Development of Lineages in Wu-hsi from Sung to Ch'ing," in Ebrey and Watson, pp. 170–209.

36. Elman, *Classicism, Politics, and Kinship*, pp. 32–35; Kishimoto, "Chihō shakai to 'seron,' " pp. 135–39.

37. The works of Susan Mann have explored the relationship between a woman's private virtues and her position in society at large. For chaste widows as a symbol of family and community honor, see "Widows." For respectable wives as a symbol of family and class honor, see "Grooming." These pioneer works are instrumental to my thinking on the overlappings between the private and public discussed here.

38. *Fanshi jiacheng, juan* 15, and *Langye Wangshi pulue, juan* 10, both cited in Taga, *Sōfu no kenkyū*, pp. 516, 565.

39. Shimomi Takao ("Jukyō shakai to boseigenri") has argued that motherhood is in fact the founding principle of Confucian social order, and that ideally all male-female relations are extensions of the mother-son tie.

40. Chapter 1 of the *Lienü zhuan*, on exemplary mothers, is the only one featuring fourteen women. All the remaining six chapters featured fifteen. This inconsistency prompted some commentators to add a fifteenth mother. I follow the *Sibu congkan* edition in leaving it out (Shimomi, pp. 252–54).

41. "*Nüjing* xu," in Xia Shufang, *xu xia* 8.8a–11b. The book of precepts he wrote is *Nüjing* (n.p., 1608). For the frequent mentions of widowed mothers' supervising a son's studies in Ming-Qing biographies, see Ho, *Ladder*, pp. 88–89.

42. Mencius' mother appeared as the eleventh in the "Exemplary Mother" section of Liu Xiang's *Lienü zhuan*. For an annotated version of this story, see Shimomi, *Ryū Kyō "Retsujoden,"* pp. 219–36. For an English translation, see O'Hara, pp. 39–42.

43. Makino.

44. R. Huang, p. 193.

45. See the Introduction to this book for Ban Zhao and Wei Xuanwen, the two women who figured as crucial transmitters of the Confucian canonical tradition.

46. For this notion of dangerous power of women, see Emily Ahern, "The Power and Pollution of Chinese Women," in Wolf and Witke, pp. 193–214.

47. Ko, "Pursuing Talent and Virtue," pp. 19–22, 29–30.

48. Although the origins of this dictum have often been dated to the Song, it, and several variations of it, did not appear until the seventeenth century (Chen Dongyuan, pp. 188–93).

49. Ko, "Pursuing Talent and Virtue," pp. 9–10; Liu Yongcong.

50. The story of Xun Fengqian first appeared in the "Indulgence" section of *Shishuo xinyu*, a famous collection of anecdotes on scholar-officials from the second to fourth century by Liu Yiqing (403–44) (Morohashi, 9: 635–36, or pp. 9989–90). Cao Hong was a first cousin of the famous warlord Cao Cao (155–220).

51. Xie Zhaozhe, pp. 217–18, 221.

52. Ye Shaoyuan, "*Lichui ji* fu," in Shen Yixiu, *Lichui ji*, p. 156. For *yaren fengzhi*, see *Ciyuan*, p. 1798.

53. Ye Shaoyuan, remarks attached to "Fenhu shiji," in Ye Xiaoluan, p. 43. Zhuo Wenjun, widowed daughter of a Han merchant, eloped with the famous writer Sima Xiangru (179–117 B.C.). Zuo Fen (d. 300), talented sister of the Jin writer Zuo Si, was selected to be an imperial concubine. The emperor, however, was said to shun her because of her uninviting looks but often summoned her to compose essays and eulogies.

54. Yiqiu sanren, 5.3a. On new heroines in Ming-Qing novels, see also Zhao Xingqin.

55. Yuanhu yanshui sanren, p. 71.

56. Elvin, pp. 142–48.

57. Gu Ruopu, 2.1b–2a. Unpublished English translation by Maureen Robertson (used by permission). See also Robertson (pp. 79–80) for Gu's arguments in support of women's writing.

58. Susan Mann (" 'Fuxue' ") calls this extension "the unfolding of the [woman's] Dao" and analyzes its import in a nineteenth-century debate on women's learning.

59. Hu Wenkai, *Lidai funü*, p.85.

60. Peterson, pp. 21–22.

61. Cited in Yi, 1.69b.

62. Yun, 1.17b–18a. It is not known if the Fangs' anthology, *Gonggui shishi*, and a companion volume of essays by women, are extant.

63. "Jinü Qiongzhang zhuan," in Shen Yixiu, *Lichui ji, xia*, pp. 129–30.

64. Ibid., p. 129. Both *linxia zhifeng* and *guifang zhixiu* derive from the *Shishuo xinyu*.

65. Ibid.

66. Yaoniang, one of the first women to bind her feet, was a court dancer. Her feet were said to be shaped like the new moon (Okamoto Ryūzō, pp. 55–58).

67. Consort Yang Guifei (719–59) is said to have left behind a three-inch shoe at Mawei, where she was killed. Although this was a fabrication and Yang, like most Tang women, probably had natural feet, bound feet were integral to her image as femme fatale. For accounts of Yang's shoe and stocking, see Levy, *Footbinding*, p. 38; and Okamoto Ryūzō, p. 64.

68. Cao Zhi (192–232) was author of the famous "Rhapsody of the Goddess of River Luo." Although poetic convention accorded the goddess the power to tread on water without getting her socks wet, she was not associated with footbinding. For changes in images of the goddess, see Schafer, pp. 90–91, 112–16.

69. "Yanti lianzhu," in Ye Xiaoluan, pp. 38–40. This series of poems was widely reprinted in Ming-Qing anthologies and collectanea. See, e.g., Wang Zhao and Zhang Chao, 2d *ji*, 36.2b–3a; Gao, 5: 28–29; and *Xiangyan congshu*, 1: 3.4a–6b.

70. Ye Xiaoluan, p. 40.

71. Shen Yixiu, *Lichui ji*, p. 118. For the Double Seven Festival, an event celebrated by women from all classes throughout China, see Mann, "Women's Work and the Household Economy," pp. 4–9.

72. The Duke of Donghun refers to Xiao Baojuan, emperor of Southern Qi (r. 499–501). According to legend, he built golden lotus pedestals in his garden and

had his favorite Consort Pan walk on them. Xiao was so indulgent that he was assassinated by a rival. Consort Pan hence figured as a famous femme fatale.

73. Shen Yixiu, *Lichui ji*, p. 119. Ye Shaoyuan also dabbled in this poetic exercise. But his linked-pearl series (ibid., pp. 119–21) contrasts sharply with those of his wife and daughter in its detached academic tone.

74. Xu Yuan, 8.4b.

75. For reproductions of four of Xue Susu's paintings and a brief introduction to her life, see *Views from Jade Terrace*, pp. 82–88.

76. Xu Yuan, 8.22b–23a.

77. Ma Ruren, "Xie jixie," in *Mingyuan shigui chao*, n.p. [48b].

78. Howard Levy (*Footbinding*, p. 271) reports that for the Taiwanese women (mostly born in the 1890's) he interviewed, "shoes and binding clothes were essential parts of the dowry." The bride also had to make her mother-in-law and sometimes every women in her husband's family a pair of shoes.

79. This saying was familiar to a daughter of a peddler in Shandong in the 1870's (Pruitt, p. 22).

80. Chen Yinke, p. 270; Huaipu jushi, 7a.

81. Yun, 9.5b–6a.

82. The same has been said of the meaning of needlework to Tanchun, a daughter of Jia Zheng's in the novel *Story of the Stone*: "Needlework, in other words, is for Tanchun strictly a means of personal expression, a skill over which she exercises full control and which she puts to use only when her spirit moves her" (Wong Kam-ming, "Point of View and Feminism: Images of Women in *Hongloumeng*," in Gerstlacher, p. 69).

83. A portrait of the Bodhisattva Guanyin that Ni embroidered with hair was a family treasure for 300 years and was still extant in the 1950's. Another one is said to be extant in Japan (Hong Liang, p. 21).

84. One of her poetry collections, *Ningxiang ge shiji*, was first published in 1664. For Ni Renji's life and poetry, see Wang Qishu, 1.12b–13b; Hu Wenkai, *Lidai funü*, pp. 136–37; and Tong Shuyu, *Yutai huashi*, 1.28a–b, in *Xiangyan congshu*, vol. 10.

85. Cited in Hong Liang, p. 21. The absence of needle traces is the hallmark of a good embroidered painting.

86. Ibid., p. 22*n9*. For the Bodhisattva Guanyin as a favorite subject of woman painters, see *Views from Jade Terrace*, pp. 22–23, 70–72.

87. For the embroidery skills of Xue Susu and Dong Xiaowan, see Zhu Peichu, pp. 62–63, 67.

88. *Ciyuan*, p. 1581. See also Gu Zhangsi, *Tufeng lu* (preface dated 1798), 6.18b–19a, in Nagazawa, vol. 1. The name "née Miao," absent in many sources, is cited in Lin, p. 23.

89. Weidner, "Women in the History," p. 22. Weidner has shown that embroidery, besides being an art in itself, also provided the basic training for many woman painters. For Han Ximeng and her album leaves, see Zhu Peichu, pp. 62–66.

90. Translation by Marsha Weidner ("Women in the History," p. 22). For the Chinese original, see Zhu Peichu, pp. 64–65. One sign of a rising attention to

women's handiwork is the popularity of *Nügong yuzhi* (n.p., preface dated 1625), attributed to a woman called "Longfu nüshi." It is widely reproduced in such collectanea as the *Shuofu*. The first chapter contains anecdotes on such implements as iron, scissors, mirror, and ruler; the second contains poems written in a woman's voice. Some scholars have argued that it is actually authored by a man. In either case, both the emphasis on "women's work" and its coupling with women's poetry are indicative of currents of the day.

91. See Xu Weinan (pp. 8–17) for a list of the extant works. The commoditization of the Gu women's handiwork began in the late Ming as the family's fortunes dwindled. At about the same time, Gu Lanyu, a great-grand-daughter of Gu Mingshi, began to teach embroidery to women outside her family (Lin, p. 24; Zhu Peichu, p. 67). By the Qianlong period, more than half of the embroiderers hired by the Gu family were men (Xu Weinan, p. 4).

92. For short biographies of these and other male embroiderers, see Zhu Qiqian, 28b–30a. This work is divided into four sections: textile, embroidery, needlework, and miscellaneous. The "embroidery" section features about a hundred embroiderers, mostly women.

93. The commoditization of this art, in turn, resulted in a new synthesis between art and business as far as the women who produced for the market were concerned. I plan to take up this issue in a separate study on the Gu family embroidery business. On Qing policies promoting women's household handiwork, see Mann, "Household Handicrafts and State Policy."

94. Li Yu, *Xianqing ouji*, 3.46a, in *Li Yu quanji*, vol. 5.

Chapter 5

1. For the central role of housewives in the management of family finances in the late nineteenth century, see McDermott. Although documentary evidence of the same caliber is not available for the period studied here, fragmented references in novels and private writings suggest that wives in gentry households exercised similar prerogatives in the seventeenth century.

2. "Wangsheng qishi zhuan," *Yuhua xiang*, 16a, in Shi Chengjin, *lihan, ce* 15.

3. Ibid., 16a–b, 17b.

4. *Yizhong yuan*, pp. 3424–25, in Li Yu, vol. 8. For the plot of *Ideal Love Matches*, see Hanan, *Li Yu*, pp. 169–75.

5. Li Qingzhao, "*Jinshilu* xu," in Zhao Shijie, 3.13ab.

6. Wu Bai, "Jizi shu," cited in Ma and Zhou, p. 228. Many of Wu's letters were published in *Chidu xinyu*, but this one is in neither the *chubian* or *erbian*.

7. For love suicides in Ming–Qing literature, see Goyama, pp. 421–49.

8. *Tongzhi Suzhou fuzhi*, 127.17ab. A "reunified broken mirror" (*pojing chongyuan*) is a famous proverb referring to a couple reunited after a temporary separation. The proverb derives from the story of Xu Deyan, of the Chen dynasty (557–89), and his wife, Princess Lechang. After their separation in warfare, they were brought together by the poem inscribed on the back of her half of the mirror (*Ciyuan*, p. 1217).

9. Tian Yiheng, 4.7ab.

10. According to the *Wujiang xianzhi* (1684), they had "sixteen children" (35.16b). I have been able to identify only eight boys and four girls by name. Most probably the rest did not survive past the first birthday (cf. Yagisawa, "Yō Shōgan," p. 90). Even if the lower count of twelve is used, Yixiu gave birth at an average interval of 2.4 years during her married life of 29 years.

11. Shen Zizheng, "*Lichui ji xu*," in Shen Yixiu, *Lichui ji*, pp. 1–2.

12. This collection, *Lichui ji*, was published by Shen's husband after her death. It is readily available as part of Ye Shaoyuan's *Wumengtang quanji* and was also widely anthologized. For the publication of this collection, see below.

13. Ye Shaoyuan took the tonsure in 1645 as a form of passive resistance to the Manchu regime. Partly for this reason and partly for the fact that his writings were mostly private in nature, most of them were not published until the nineteenth century, although fragments of his essays and poetry are found in *Wumengtang quanji*, the family anthology he edited and published. For Ye's life, see his autobiography, *Zizhuan nianpu*; and biography in Goodrich and Fang, pp. 1576–79.

14. "Biaomei Zhang Qianqian zhuan," in Shen Yixiu, *Lichui ji*, pp. 131–32.

15. Ye Shaoyuan , *Zizhuan nianpu*, pp. 6–9; "Wangshi Shen anren zhuan," appendix to Shen Yixiu, *Lichui ji*, p. 151.

16. Shen Zizheng, "*Lichui ji xu*"; and Ye Shaoyuan, "Wangshi Shen anren zhuan," in Shen Yixiu, *Lichui ji*, pp. 1, 151–52, respectively.

17. Shen Yixiu, *Lichui ji*, pp. 5–6, 33, 36, 69, 114–15.

18. Ye Shaoyuan, "Bairi ji Shen anren wen," in ibid., pp. 147–48.

19. These and eulogies for Shaoyuan's mother and children were published in *Wumengtang quanji*, under the title *Qinzhai yuan*. For those dedicated to Yixiu, see Ye Shaoyuan, *Qinzhai yuan*, pp. 5–15.

20. Ye, "Bairi ji Shen anren wen," in Shen Yixiu, *Lichui ji*, pp. 144–45.

21. For Shaoyuan's comparing himself to Xun Fengqian, see Ye Shaoyuan, *Qinzhai yuan*, pp. 8, 16, 31; idem, *Nianpu xu*, p. 39; and idem, *Nianpu bieji*, p. 81.

22. Ye Shaoyuan, *Nianpu bieji*, p. 90; idem, *Xu yaowen*, p. 11. In dismissing the two maids of his daughter Xiaoluan at her death, Ye consciously emulated Qin Guan (*Nianpu bieji*, p. 81).

23. For a late eighteenth-century example of a companionate couple, see Ropp, "Between Two Worlds." Ropp (pp. 117–18) makes the argument similar to mine that the intensive bonds between husband and wife did not preclude intimate, even passionate friendship between the wife and her female friends.

24. Ye Shaoyuan, *Zizhuan nianpu, passim*.

25. Ibid., pp. 8, 10, 17, 19.

26. Ibid., pp. 6–7; "Bairi ji Shen anren wen"; and "Wangshi Shen anren zhuan," in Shen Yixiu, *Lichui ji*, pp. 146, 152, respectively.

27. Ye Shaoyuan, *Zizhuan nianpu*, pp. 17, 19.

28. Ibid., p. 33.

29. Ye Shaoyuan used the term *qiangzong hanzu* at least twice. For one such usage, together with a brief account of the dispute, see ibid., pp. 4–5. See also "Wangshi Shen anren zhuan," in Shen Yixiu, *Lichui ji*, p. 151.

30. Ye Shaoyuan, *Zizhuan nianpu*, p. 14.

31. Ibid., p. 12. According to Chen Yinke, the famous courtesan Liu Rushi was Zhou Daodeng's maid before she joined the pleasure quarters (cf. Chapter 7).

32. Yixiu lost her mother when she was seven. She reacted with composure and maturity, even starting to share some household duties. An uncle, thus convinced that she would make a good bride, sealed a betrothal agreement with Ye Shaoyuan's father, a close friend (Ye Shaoyuan, "Wangshi Shen anren zhuan"; and "Bairi ji Shen anren wen," in Shen Yixiu, *Lichui ji*, pp. 151, 146, respectively).

33. "Shou chongsaoshi Shiruren qishi jizhi Junqian wushi xu," in Ye Xie, 12.1a–2b. Ye Xie (1627–1703, *jinshi* 1670) was the longest-surviving and most successful son of Shaoyuan and Yixiu.

34. For a Ye family tree, see Okuzaki, "Soshūfu Gokōken," p. 437. The size of landholdings, originally given in *qing* (1 *qing* = 100 *mu*), is from Shaoyuan's biography in *Wujiang xianzhi* (1684), 35.16b. Since the chief editor of this gazetteer was Shaoyuan's son, Xie, the figures should be reliable. The dwindling fortune was a result of his lackluster bureaucratic career, large immediate family, and lack of concern for money matters. Between 1639 and 1643 alone, Ye Shaoyuan sold about 100 *mu* of land to finance travel expenses for his sons, a dowry for a fourth daughter, and family funerals (Ye Shaoyuan, *Nianpu xu*, pp. 42–45, 48, 51).

35. Ye Shaoyuan, *Zizhuan nianpu*, p. 7. The large household that Shaoyuan had to support consumed ten *shi* of rice every month (Ye Shaoyuan, *Nianpu xu*, p. 45).

36. All four of Shaoyuan's elder brothers died in infancy. For his own illness and adoption, see Ye Shaoyuan, *Zizhuan nianpu*, pp. 1–2. Yuan Huang came from a family of distinguished physicians, which placed them on the fringes of local elite society. For the family background of Yuan Huang, see Brokaw, pp. 64–75.

37. The betrothal pact was sealed by Shaoyuan's father in 1598, one year before his death (Ye Shaoyuan, *Zizhuan nianpu*, pp. 3–4). In 1605, Yuan Huang acted as Shaoyuan's surrogate father, crafting a formal request for marriage on his behalf. The Yes were eager to consummate the betrothal because Shaoyuan's grandmother was critically ill. Yuan also wrote a personal letter to Yixiu's uncle, urging him to see to it that Yixiu's father granted his permission for an immediate wedding. The ceremony took place two months before the grandmother passed away. For the two letters by Yuan, see Yuan Huang, 4.27ab, 10.18b–19b.

38. Ye Shaoyuan, *Zizhuan nianpu*, pp. 7, 14–16.

39. Cited in Okuzaki, *Kyōshin jinushi*, p. 180.

40. Ye Shaoyuan, *Zizhuan nianpu*, p. 8. See Waltner, *Getting an Heir* (pp. 98, 112) for adoptions with name changes and those without.

41. Shaoyuan's second son, Ye Shicheng (1618–35), died while taking his examination for entrance to the local school (Ye Shaoyuan, *Zizhuan nianpu*, p. 32). For his fiancée, née Gu (1618–72), see appendix to Ye Shicheng, pp. 28–32; *Wujiang xianzhi* (1684), 40.13b; and *Wujiang xianzhi* (1747), 35.24b–25a. The adoption is mentioned in *Wujiang xianzhi* (1684), 40.13b. The heir, Ye Shuchong (*jinshi* 1676), was the son of Ye Shirong (1619–40), Shaoyuan and Yixiu's third son. Okuzaki ("Soshūfu Gokōken," p. 436) is wrong in identifying him as the son of their second daughter, Xiaowan.

42. Okuzaki, "Soshūfu Gokōken," pp. 431, 436, 438.

43. Ibid., p. 436. This short-term adoption is not mentioned in Shen Zinan's biography in *Wujiang xianzhi* (1747), 32.29ab.

44. *Wujiang xianzhi* (1747), 32.27b–29b. On Shen Zizheng, see Fu Xihua, *Mingdai zaju*, p. 172. On Shen Jing, see Fu Xihua, *Mingdai chuanqi*, pp. 70–72. For the Shen family tree, see Okuzaki, *Kyōshin jinushi*, appendix p. 57; and Okuzaki, "Soshūfu Gokōken," p. 433.

45. For marriage networks of these families, see Okuzaki, "Soshūfu Gokōken," pp. 425–40. A late nineteenth-century anti-Manchu activist, Chen Qubing, wrote an interesting history of the five major Wujiang families as part of his efforts to glorify late Ming local history. The Shens and Yes were two of them (Chen Qubing, *Wushizhi*, pp. 301–4).

46. Cf. Ye Shaoyuan, *Zizhuan nianpu*, pp. 8, 10; Yagisawa, "Yō Shōgan," p. 87.

47. For a description and a diagram of the five mourning grades, see Feng Hanyi, pp. 38–43.

48. Ye Shaoyuan, "Ji zhangnü Zhaoqi wen," appendix to Ye Wanwan, p. 33; Ye Shaoyuan, *Zizhuan nianpu*, p. 8. For the Yuan family trees, see Okuzaki, *Kyōshin jinushi*, pp. 88–91.

49. Ye Shaoyuan, "Ji zhangnü Zhaoqi wen," in Ye Wanwan, p. 34. The Yuans had been barred from taking the examination for three generations in the fifteenth century; hence they turned to medicine (Brokaw, pp. 64–66, 74–75; Okuzaki, *Kyōshin jinushi*, pp. 181–82).

50. Ye Shaoyuan, "Ji zhangnü Zhaoqi wen," in Ye Wanwan, p. 33.

51. Ibid.; Ye Shaoyuan, *Zizhuan nianpu*, p. 17. For Shen Yixiu's reluctance to send Wanwan off to Guangdong, see the six poems she composed for the occasion (Shen Yixiu, *Lichui ji*, pp. 63–64).

52. Apparently there were more grievances after her death. Wanwan was buried by her own parents. Three years after her death, Ye Shaoyuan decried that her husband, Yuan Silü, had not once visited her burial site at her parent's home, nor had he sent any offerings of wine, paper money, or chants ("Zhaoqi sanzhou jiwen," in Ye Shaoyuan, *Tonglian xuxue, xia*, pp. 17–18). The husband's name, Silü, is mentioned by Okuzaki; neither Ye Shaoyuan nor Shen Yixiu referred to him by name. Finally, in 1642, the husband followed the demands of propriety and moved her remains to the Yuan burial site (Ye Shaoyuan, *Nianpu xu*, p. 49). In the seventh month of 1645, before the Manchu army reached Wujiang, Yuan Silü's house was burned down by the raging troops of a rival local gentry. He sought assistance from Ye, shortly before Ye took the tonsure (Ye Shaoyuan, *Nianpu xu*, p. 58; Okuzaki, *Kyōshin jinushi*, pp. 182–83, 301). The two kept in touch. In 1648, Yuan Silü paid a brief visit to Ye (Ye Shaoyuan, *Jiaxing rizhu*, p. 230).

53. In 1626, the year of Wanwan's wedding and Xiaoluan's betrothal, Ye Shaoyuan transferred his father's remains to a second burial site. With hindsight, he regretted that the dragon was obscured at the new site and water flowed straight through; hence both daughters met tragic ends (Ye Shaoyuan, *Zizhuan nianpu*, p. 17).

54. Ye Wanwan, p. 1; Zheng Guangyi, *Cainü shige*, pp. 1402–4.

55. Ye Shaoyuan, "Ji zhangnü Zhaoqi wen," in Ye Wanwan, p. 35. Shen Yixiu (*Lichui ji*, p. 40) also mentioned Wanwan's frustration at not being able to buy a mountain in the seventh poem she wrote upon Wanwan's death.

56. For a convenient edition of this drama, see Ye Shaoyuan, *Wumengtang quanji, shang*. For background on this drama, see Yagisawa, "Yō Shōgan," pp. 85–98. Yagisawa examined a Ming edition of the drama in the private collection of Nagasawa Kikuya, which contains a preface by Shen Zizheng not found in the *Wumengtang quanji* edition. The preface is dated 1636, probably the same year when the drama was written (pp. 95–96). For the excerpt from the Su Wu poem, see p. 95.

57. Ye Xiaowan, p. 15.

58. Ye Xiaowan was betrothed to her maternal cousin, Shen Yongzhen, in 1629 (Ye Shaoyuan, *Zizhuan nianpu*, p. 20). Little is known about her marital life. The fact that none of her extant poems mentions him probably means that the match was less than cordial. Xiaowan's posthumous poetry collection, *Cunyu cao*, was handed by her son-in-law to her brother, Ye Xie, who published it as part of *Wumengtang shichao* and appended to his own *Siqi ji*. These are grim verses, often dedicated to her sisters and other Shen women.

59. The term *four elements* (*catvāri mahābhūtāni*) refers to earth, water, fire, and wind. A similar chant by Yixiu is included in her poetry collection, *Lichui ji*, p. 117. Xiaoluan and Wanwan died in the same lunar year, but by the Gregorian calendar Xiaoluan died in 1632 and Wanwan, in January 1633.

60. Ye Shaoyuan, "Ji zhangnü Zhaoqi wen," in Ye Wanwan, pp. 35–36; Shen Yixiu, *Lichui ji*, p. 41.

61. Shen Darong, daughter of Shen Jing, was Yixiu's cousin, but they addressed each other as "sister" (cf. Okuzaki, *Kyōshin jinushi*, p. 433). She contributed a preface to Yixiu's posthumous poetry collection ("Ye furen yiji xu," in Shen Yixiu, *Lichui ji*, pp. 7–9).

62. My use of the term *domestic religion* was inspired by Barbara Myerhoff's study of the domestic lives of Jewish women in *Number Our Days*. Chün-fang Yü (pers. comm.) has also spoken of a new religious ideal and practice in Ming-Qing China, one that she called "domesticated spirituality." I am grateful to Professor Yü for sharing her expert knowledge of late Ming Buddhism with me.

63. Chün-fang Yü, pp. 227–28.

64. Ye Shaoyuan, "Wangshi Shen anren zhuan," in Shen Yixiu, *Lichui ji*, pp. 152–53.

65. Shi Zhenlin, 1.66.

66. Yixiu often composed poems for Lezi and other adepts; see, e.g., *Lichui ji*, pp. 9, 46, 71. In 1635, five months before Yixiu's death, her eighth son fell ill; Yixiu sent another son, Shirong (1619–40) to seek instructions from Lezi. Lezi predicted a series of deaths in the family and suggested the remedy of painting a portrait of the Bodhisattva Cundi (Zhunti), another name for Guanyin, and chanting to it every morning and night. This worship lapsed after Yixiu died; Shaoyuan believed this to be the cause of Shirong's death five years later (Ye Shaoyuan, *Nianpu bieji*, p. 86; idem, *Zizhuan nianpu*, p. 34).

67. Ye Shaoyuan, *Xu yaowen*, p. 9; Qian, *Liechao shiji, runji* 4.54b–55a. Ye

referred to Lezi by the honorific "Legong" (Old Master Le). Qian Qianyi authored a long apology for Lezi, recounting some of the séances. Qian openly admitted that he was a believer and defended Lezi's fortune-telling as a means she employed to attract the nonbelieving masses to her true message of salvation ("Tiantai Le fashi lingyi ji," in Qian, *Muzhai chuxue ji*, 43.12a–16b).

68. Ye Shaoyuan, *Xu yaowen*, pp. 10–11; Qian, *Liechao shiji, runji* 4.49a–50a (entry on Ye Xiaoluan). Qian explained that the leafless branch implied by the name Hall of No Leaves signified purity and truth.

69. For Tan Yangzi, see Waltner, "Visionary and Bureaucrat"; and idem, "Learning from a Woman."

70. "Wangsheng qishi zhuan," in Shi Chengjin, 16b–17a.

71. Ye Shaoyuan, "Ji wangnü Xiaoluan wen," in appendix to Ye Xiaoluan, pp. 59–60; Shen Zizheng, "Ji shengnü Qiongzhang wen," appendix to Ye Xiaoluan, p. 53. Shen Zizheng wrote that he heard that Yixiu, upon writing Xiaoluan's name in vermilion, beseeched her to seek rebirth as a boy into his household. Both Yixiu and Shaoyuan, however, failed to mention this in their accounts, and the desire to be reborn a boy does not accord with their belief in Lezi's Hall of No Leaves mentioned above.

72. Ye Shaoyuan, "Yuandan zaigao wangnü Xiaoluan wen," in appendix to Ye Xiaoluan, pp. 61–62.

73. Ye Shaoyuan, "Ji wangnü Xiaoluan wen," in appendix to Ye Xiaoluan, p. 59.

74. Men were firm believers in the authenticity of dreams. Shen Zizheng was in Huizhou when Ye Xiaoluan died and hence did not receive the news until later. Four days after Xiaoluan's death, Zizheng dreamed of her, and they discussed poetry. She even dictated verses to him. Afterward, when he learned of her death, he became convinced that Xiaoluan was an immortal, and that it was her detached soul who appeared in his dreams (Shen Zizheng, "Ji shengnü Qiongzhang wen," in appendix to Ye Xiaoluan, pp. 52–53).

75. The first took place in 1634 in the Suzhou home of one of his nephews, Yan Sheng. Yan had a servant who claimed to be a messenger from the underworld. Details of this meeting are recounted in Ye Shaoyuan, *Yaowen*, pp. 1–7. Yixiu was not present, but Shaoyuan told her all about it upon returning home (cf. Ye Shaoyuan, *Zizhuan nianpu*, p. 31).

76. Ye Shaoyuan, *Xu yaowen*, p. 11; idem, *Qionghua jing*, p. 2. Lezi told Shaoyuan that since Xiaoluan was already an immortal, she did not have to go through exercises in the Hall of No Leaves, where Yixiu and Wanwan were.

77. See, e.g., Qian, *Liechao shiji, runji* 4.50b–51a, which includes fourteen poems by Xiaoluan, three of which were dictated in dreams or séances.

78. Ma Quan (b. ca. 1690), a Changshu woman, entitled one of her paintings "Flowers and Insects After Ye Xiaoluan." For her long inscriptions describing her amazement with the sophistication of Xiaoluan's techniques, see *Views from Jade Terrace*, p. 135. For women writing poetry for Ye Xiaoluan, see Yun, 14.12a, 19.5a. One of the nineteenth-century men who saw Xiaoluan in séances is Wang Shoumai, who in 1856 published an account of these séances and of an ink slab allegedly belonging to Xiaoluan. The account is entitled *Yanyuan zalu* (cited in

Goodrich and Fang, p. 1579; cf. *Views from Jade Terrace*, pp. 135–36). A twentieth-century bibliophile and descendant of Ye Xiaoluan, Ye Dehui, compiled a volume that included accounts of her séances taken from *Wumengtang quanji* and poems by visitors to her tomb (see *Nüshi Shuxiang ge yilu*).

79. Many in the seventeenth century speculated that Tang Xianzu's portrayal of Du Liniang was based on the life of Tan Yangzi (Jiao, pp. 35–36). A long discussion of Tan Yangzi is attached to the *Sanfu heping Mudanting*, but these women did not think that Tan was the inspiration behind the creation of Du ("*Huanhun ji* fulu," 1a–2a, in Tang Xianzu, *Sanfu heping Mudanting, shang*). For the identification of Xiaoluan with Du Liniang, see Chapter 2.

80. See, e.g., *Tongzhi Suzhou fuzhi*, 139.1a–2a.

81. Qian, *Liechao shiji, runji* 4.51ab. Although published under Qian Qianyi's name, the comments on women poets in the *Liechao shiji* were attributed to his wife, Liu Rushi.

82. Yuan Tianqi's wife visited the Yes in 1632 with her twelve-year-old daughter to mourn the death of Wanwan, her daughter-in-law (Ye Shaoyuan, *Nianpu bieji*, p. 78). Yet there is no mention of Yixiu's contact with her.

83. Shen Yixiu, *Lichui ji*, p. 109; Ye Xiaoluan, pp. 7, 12, 25. On Xiaoluan's séance, see Ye Shaoyuan, *Xu yaowen*, p. 12. On Hongyu's departure, see Ye Shaoyuan, *Zizhuan nianpu*, p. 36.

84. For poems teasing Yixiu's attendant Suichun, see Ye Xiaoluan, p. 22; Ye Wanwan, pp. 19–20; and Shen Yixiu, *Lichui ji*, pp. 86–87, 97.

85. Ye Shaoyuan, "Wangshi Shen anren zhuan," in Shen Yixiu, *Lichui ji*, p. 155.

86. One such painting is entitled "Shinü chunxi tu" (The scene of maids in honor playing in spring), a Qing work depicting 83 women holding an outdoor party. Some are dressed in male attire. Reproduced in Han-Ajia bunka kōryū sentā, p. 91; captions on p. 115.

87. Shen Yixiu, *Lichui ji*, pp. 9–10. Yixiu's younger sister, Zhiyao, married an unworthy husband who indulged in gambling. Zhiyao was so distressed that she committed suicide in 1644 when she was in her thirties (Ye Shaoyuan, *Nianpu bieji*, p. 94).

88. See, e.g., Shen Yixiu, *Lichui ji*, p. 8. The exact relationship of the "lineage aunt" is unclear. She was probably a distant relative of the same generational rank as Yixiu's father.

89. Shen Yixiu's husband, Ye Shaoyuan, ranked second, with 54 poems (Shen Yixiu, *Lichui ji, passim*). See also Ko, "Pursuing Talent and Virtue," p. 27; for the education of Yixiu's daughters and the mother-daughter bond it engendered, see pp. 22–28.

90. Shen Yixiu, *Lichui ji*, p. 2. The ages of "thirteen" and "sixteen" in this poem refer to ages by Chinese count, or *sui*.

91. Although Shen Yixiu had eight brothers and at least two sisters, her mother, née Gu, gave birth to only Yixiu and Zizheng (Shen Zizheng, "Ji shengnü Qiongzhang wen," in appendix to Ye Xiaoluan, p. 50).

92. Reconstructed from "Biaomei Zhang Qianqian zhuan," in Shen Yixiu, *Lichui ji*, pp. 131–34.

93. Ye Shaoyuan, *Zizhuan nianpu*, p. 10. Here, Ye Shaoyuan wrote that Xiaoluan was sent to her adoptive parent's when she was "four months old." This is probably wrong, as all other accounts say "six months." See, e.g., "Jinü Qiongzhang zhuan," in Shen Yixiu, *Lichui ji*, p. 128; Shen Zizheng, "Ji shengnü Qiongzhang wen," appendix to Ye Xiaoluan, p. 50.

94. Irving Lo (pp. 44–45) has pointed out that Chinese women poets produced many elegies written on the deaths of family members. Lo also mentions an eighteenth-century poetess, Xi Peilan, who lost two sons and a brother on three successive days. Xi's tragedy was similar to Shen Yixiu's.

95. "Zhou Yifen shixu," in Shen Yixiu, *Lichui ji*, pp. 127–28; Ye Shaoyuan, *Tonglian xuxue*, p. 1. For Shen Renlan's family tree, see Pan, *Jiaxing de wangzu*, p. 41.

96. Wakeman, "Seventeenth-Century Crisis," pp. 5–6; Dunstan, pp. 9–10, 16–18.

97. Ye Shaoyuan, *Zizhuan nianpu*, pp. 30–33; idem, "Bairi ji Shen anren wen"; and idem, "Wangshi Shen anren zhuan," in Shen Yixiu, *Lichui ji*, pp. 146, 149, 155, respectively.

98. Michael Marmé (p. 43) estimates the life expectancy of birth cohorts in Suzhou, 1680–1829, to be 36.76 for women and 33.68 for men.

99. Relating a woman's life cycle to the anxieties she experiences, Margery Wolf argues that marriage is one of these stressful transitions. In particular, she points out that young brides are prone to suicide ("Women and Suicide in China," in Wolf and Witke, pp. 111–41).

100. Ng, p. 58.

101. "Qinghui yinsi shu," in Tang Bin, 1.67b–68a. Tang Bin's edict is also discussed in von Glahn; see pp. 699, 701, for his arguments on female strategies. Ye Shaoyuan (*Jiaxing rizhu*, p. 228) reported a case of spirit possession of one of Wutong's attendants in Suzhou in 1648. The possessed woman had been married for several months.

102. Ye Xiaoluan, pp. 9, 22; see also pp. 2, 15, 30, 32, 33. In addition to death, Xiaoluan seems obsessed with dreams. In 1631, she wrote a fantastic essay about a recluse called Zhumengzi ("one who cooks dreams"). One night, from the window of his cloistered room he sees two beauties in the garden outside, pouring their hearts' sorrow out to each other in heavenly songs. When Zhumengzi seeks them, they disappear into banana groves; hence he thinks they must be banana spirits ("Jiaochuang yeji," in Ye Xiaoluan, p. 41).

103. At the time of the lunar New Year celebration of 1633, Ye Shaoyuan mentioned to Xiaoluan that the cutting of the blocks was finished and that he would make an offering of a printed copy to her ("Yuandan zaigao wangnü Xiaoluan wen," in appendix to Ye Xiaoluan, p. 62).

104. Ye Shaoyuan, *Tonglian xuxue, shang*, p. 1.

105. Ye Shaoyuan, *Nianpu bieji*, p. 78; idem, *Zizhuan nianpu*, pp. 31–32.

106. Huang Yuanjie mentioned that in 1634 her brother showed her printed copies of Xiaoluan's and Wanwan's poetry, saying that Feng Maoyuan wanted her to write elegies in response (Huang Yuanjie, "Du Ye Qiongzhang yiji," in Ye Shaouyuan, *Tonglian xuxue, shang*, p. 7). Most probably the poems of Huang

Dezhen, Yuanjie's first cousin, were also brought to Ye Shaoyuan via the same channel.

107. Ye Shaoyuan, *Jiaxing rizhu*, p. 241. Feng Maoyuan took good care of Ye Shaoyuan in his old age, often bringing him money, rice, wine, and food and kept him company (ibid., pp. 210, 219, 222, 224–26, 229, 244–46). Ye passed away in Feng's mansion in Pinghu. Feng continued to send yearly allotments of cash and rice to needy widows and children in Shaoyuan's family ("Feng xiaolian Jianshan zhuan," in Ye Xie, 18.1a–2b).

108. Ye Shaoyuan, *Tonglian xuxie, shang,* p. 6.

109. "Bayu," in Ye Shaoyuan, *Wumengtang quanji,* p. 1.

110. Shen Yixiu, *Yirensi.* For consistency I quote from the *Wumengtang quanji* edition.

111. Ibid., p. 13. For a frequently anthologized poem that Wang wrote in the memory of her daughter, see Zheng Guangyi, pp. 1365–66.

112. For a reference to the Shen's family publishing, see Ōki, "Shuppan bunka," p. 79.

113. Ye Shaoyuan, *Zizhuan nianpu,* p. 19.

114. The Wumengtang was situated to the east of the living quarters of Wanwan and Xiaoluan (Ye Shaoyuan, *Nianpu bieji,* p. 88).

115. For the nine original titles, see Ye Shaoyuan, *Zizhuan nianpu,* p. 37, where Ye mentioned that the works of a son, Shirong, were added later. Zheng Zhenduo, a modern collector, mentions another 1636 edition with twelve titles. The most glaring difference is the addition of Ye Xiaowan's drama *Yuanyang meng,* which was prefaced "autumn 1636" (Yagisawa, "Yō Shōgan," p. 96). Since Ye's *Nianpu* discloses that the original edition was issued in the ninth month of 1636 and that it only has nine titles, it is likely that this longer 1636 edition is a later reprint. In the Naikaku bunko, there is a Ming edition of *Wumengtang shizhong,* with ten titles. The *Wumengtang quanji* that I cite in this book is a composite reprint based on the original 1636 edition, with all the later additions. For individual titles and a summary of the differences between the various Ming editions, see Yagisawa, "Yō Shōgan," pp. 92–94; and Goodrich and Fang, p. 1578.

116. Ye Shaoyuan, *Jiaxing rizhu,* pp. 135–36.

117. Both the Library of Congress and Naikaku bunko have Ming editions of *Yirensi.* The former's copy is boxed with *Qiyan'ai,* eulogies of Yixiu by her children; the latter's copy is boxed with *Qinzhai yuan,* a collection of Shaoyuan's eulogies for his mother, wife, and children. In addition, Ye Xie—Shaoyuan and Yixiu's son—published *Wumengtang shicao sizhong* under the name of his study, Erqi caotang (Yang Shengxin, p. 71).

118. Ren Zhaolin, "Xiuyuji xu," in Shen Xiang, *Feicui ji,* 1a, in Ren and Zhang. This collection is made up of the works of the Ten Wuzhong Poets, each with its title and pagination. There is also a culminative pagination, but it is fraught with inconsistencies. I cite the former here. For an analysis of this poetry club, see Ko, "Lady-Scholar."

119. Song Guangping, "Ba," in Zhang Yunzi, *Chaoshengge ji,* 16ab, in Ren and Zhang.

Chapter 6

1. Wang Fengxian, 5.20a–27a. For Wang Fengxian, see Hu Wenkai, *Lidai funü*, pp. 90–92.

2. Wang Fengxian, 5.23b.

3. The eldest daughter, Zhang Yinyuan, died at the age of 27 *sui*. She was said to have been warned of her own demise, when a god revealed to her in a dream that she was the librarian of the Jade Emperor, the highest god in the Daoist pantheon, and had been sent for an earthly sojourn of three times nine years (Shi Shuyi, 1.17b). Both the belief in the reality of dreams and Yinyuan's celestial identity recall the Ye Xiaoluan lore. Poems by Yinyuan and her younger sister Yinqing are widely anthologized; see, e.g., Zhou Zhibiao, 5.15a–19b; Zhong Xing, 31.1a–10b.

4. Shen Yixiu, *Yirensi*, pp. 11–14.

5. Wang Naiqin, "*Fenyu cao* xu," in Zhou Zhibiao, 5.28a–29a. *Fenyu cao* is no longer extant in its entirety, but fragments are preserved in numerous anthologies. Zhou Zhibiao provides the most complete selection.

6. Wang Fengxian, 5.25a. For the life and legend of Wu Zixu, see D. Johnson.

7. Wang Fengxian, "Du Li Zhuowu *Fenshu* yijue," in Zhou Zhibiao, 5.12b.

8. Wang Xianji, "*Fenyu cao* xu," in Zhou Zhibiao, 5.30b–31a. This preface is reprinted in Hu Wenkai, *Lidai funü*, pp. 91–92. Evidently Wang had a cordial relationship with her husband; several of her extant poems are testaments to their "singing in harmony." See, e.g., Zhou Zhibiao, 5.1b–3a.

9. Wang Fengxian, 5.27a. Compare Robertson, pp. 87–88.

10. Wu Bai, "Ji Maojiazi," in Wang Qi, *chubian* 8.11b–12a.

11. Ibid., 6.10b–11a.

12. Wu was particularly interested in women's poetry; she had her own opinion on such poets as Zhuo Wenjun and Su Hui, alleged writer of a famous circular poem. See, e.g., Wang Qi, *chubian* 4.10a, 24.4a, *erbian* 13.7b. Wu, a chaste widow herself, was full of admiration for Zhuo Wenjun, a widow who remarried a famous writer (ibid., *chubian* 24.4a). For her reading of the *Bencao* (Materia medica), see ibid., 24.5b.

13. Wu Bai, "Yufu shu," in Wang Qi, *chubian* 23.15a.

14. Qi Biaojia, a bibliophile himself, continued to build up his father's collection (Terada, pp. 541–45).

15. "Qi Zhongmin gong nianpu," in Qi Biaojia, *Riji, passim*.

16. Qi Biaojia, *Riji, passim*.

17. "Qibei rongyan," in Qi Biaojia, *Riji*, 3.14 entry; "Jucun shibi," in ibid., 8.24 entry.

18. "Guinan kuailu," in Qi Biaojia, *Riji*, 6.12, 6.14, 6.15 entries and *passim*. Qi served as an investigating censor in Beijing from 1631 to 1633.

19. "Jucun shibi," in Qi Biaojia, *Riji*, 10.8 entry. For the garden-building project, see Handlin-Smith, "Gardens."

20. Shang Jinglan was expected to follow suit according to one interpretation of Thrice Following. She did not. Thirty years later, in her reminiscence she cited

the need to look after her young children as her reason. See Shang Jinglan, Preface to *Qinlou yigao*, in Qi Biaojia, *Ji*, p. 289.

21. From biographies of Qi in Qi Biaojia, *Ji*, pp. 1–4, 232–41.

22. See, e.g., Shang's preface to her daughter's posthumous works, in Qi Biaojia, *Ji*, appendix, p. 297.

23. Qi Biaojia, *Ji*, prologue, p.3.

24. Zhu Yizun, *Jingzhiju shihua*, cited in Hu Wenkai, *Lidai funü*, p. 156. Shang's second daughter, Mrs. Zhu, is not mentioned in this and some of the other accounts. One possible explanation is that she died young, but there is no evidence. For the Queen Mother of the West, a Daoist deity favored by female devotees, see Cahill. In Tang poetry as in that of the Ming and Qing, the Queen Mother's attendants set a standard for female beauty, sexuality, and talent.

25. One such male friend was Wang Ranming, a patron of arts in Hangzhou. Qi Biaojia took Shang Jinglan to visit Wang on several occasions in 1635 ("Guinan kuailu," Qi Biaojia, *Riji, passim*). For Wang's role in fostering networks between courtesans and professional woman artists, see Chapter 7.

26. This collection is no longer extant, but an afterword by Mao Qiling is preserved in his collected works ("*Meishi changhe shigao* shuhou," in Mao Qiling, *shuhou* 5ab). The dating of Huang Yuanjie's visit is based on circumstantial evidence. From Mao's afterword, we learn that Huang returned to Jiaxing in 1658, and her husband asked Mao Qiling to compile Yuanjie's poems for publication. From a poem by Qi Deqian (Xiangjun), Shang Jinglan's daughter, we also learn that Huang Yuanjie stayed in their house for one year. In addition, Widmer ("Epistolary World," p. 13) suggests that Wang Ranming, who died in 1654, supplied the boat for Yuanjie's travel and may have accompanied her. Therefore, I estimate that her visit took place around 1654.

27. Qi Deqiong, *Weifen ji*, in Qi Biaojia, *Ji, passim*.

28. "Penglai" is a magical island in Chinese mythology. Shang Jinglan used it to describe her semi-reclusive and carefree life in Meishi.

29. "Zeng guishushi Huang Yuanjie," in Shang, p. 274. Each of the writers to whom Shang compared Huang conveys one aspect of Huang's life. Xue Tao was a learned ninth-century courtesan famous for her poetry (Hu Wenkai, *Lidai funü*, pp. 33–36). By comparing Huang to a courtesan, Shang was probably alluding to Huang's dubious history of being kidnapped and possibly sold to a brothel. Sima Xiangru (179–118 B.C.) was the most acclaimed writer of rhyme-prose (*fu*). Huang Yuanjie was skilled in this difficult genre, which flourished in Han times. "Youfu," literally "young woman." From context it is clear that she was a calligrapher, just like Huang, but I cannot trace her name or identity. "Zuo Shi" simply means "someone named Zuo." Shang did not specify whether it refers to the Han writer Zuo Si or his equally talented sister Zuo Fen. I think Zuo Fen is more likely, for two reasons: Zuo Fen was, like Huang, said to be a rather ugly woman, and the comparison is consistent with Shang's practice of comparing Huang to other female writers in the same poem.

30. Similarly, female painters in Ming-Qing times saw themselves as part of a larger tradition of female painters from early times (Weidner, "Women in the History," pp. 17, 21).

31. "*Zhongshan xian* xu," in Wang Siren, *Wang Jizhong shizhong*, p. 79.

32. Hu Wenkai, *Lidai funü*, p. 144. For selections from Lu's collected works, which included a good sampling of verses exchanged between Xu Yuan and Lu Qingzi, see Zhou Zhibiao, *juan* 8. See Chapter 7 for the friendship between Xu and Lu.

33. Qian Xiyan, "Fan Furen *Luowei yin* xu," in Xu Yuan, 2b.

34. Gu Ruoqun, "*Woyuexuan gao* xu," in Gu Ruopu, 5a. "Mr. Ma" refers to Ma Yuandiao, whose preface appears on 2a–3b.

35. Fang Mengshi, "Du Xu Yuan shi yu mei Weiyi," in Wang Qi, *erbian* 24.3ab.

36. Qian, *Liechao shiji, runji* 4.49a. For Qian's praises of Fang Mengshi, see ibid., 4.19ab.

37. Banana Garden Five and Banana Garden Seven denote the most active or famous members of these poetry clubs. Other women known to be active were not formerly included (Morohashi, p. 10258, or 9: 904). A comment by Xu Shumin in his and Qian Yue's anthology, *Zhongxiang ci* (*liji* 39a), suggests that the Banana Garden Seven was well known by 1688, when the anthology was published. I have been unable to locate the Banana Garden, supposedly a private garden on West Lake. It is never mentioned in extant poems by the members, nor did it appear in Ming-Qing guides to Hangzhou. One place in which the poets often gathered was the Gu family garden, Yuanpu (Plot of hope).

38. Wu Hao, 30.10b–11a. *Younü* could refer specifically to prostitutes or courtesans, but since respectable daughters also went boating on the lake, its more general meaning of "pleasure-seeking women" seems more appropriate here (cf. Morohashi, p. 11651, or 11: 109).

39. Although Gu Yurui was said to be the founder of the poetry club, she was not formerly included in the Banana Garden Five. For Gu Yurui, see Hu Wenkai, *Lidai funü*, p. 800; and Shi Shuyi, 2.23b. The preface by Qian Yinguang, a loyalist monk, to Gu's collected works, *Yizhengtang ji*, is reprinted in Xu Shumin and Qian, *liji* 37ab.

40. *Renhe xianzhi*, 20.51b. Another example of a woman's acquiring lineage land is that of Madame Qian of Changzhou, Suzhou prefecture, who instructed her son to procure a 130-*mu* charitable estate (Zhang Yan, p. 73).

41. Huang Ruheng, 15.6a. See Robertson (pp. 90–95) for a discussion of the series of seven poems that Gu crafted for her deceased husband.

42. For his frequent correspondence with Tang Xianzu, see Huang Ruheng, 24.42b–43a; 25.8a, 19a, 36a–37a, 43a–43b. He also wrote a eulogy for Tang (20.3b–4b).

43. Ibid., 15.9a; see also 31.12b. Huang Ruheng had nine children altogether (see 15.9a).

44. *Renhe xianzhi*, 20.51b.

45. Gu Ruopu's poem commemorating the construction of the study-boat was widely anthologized (see Gu Ruopu, *juan* 3; and Cai, 3 *jia* 14a).

46. Gu Ruopu, "Yu di," in Wang Qi, *chubian* 23.6b–7a. *Cui* can also mean obsession or disease.

47. For Gu Ruopu's arguments on *tuntian* and on her educating Ding, see "Yu

Zhang furen," in Wang Qi, *chubian* 2.7b–8a. For Ding Yuru debating her husband, see Chen Wenshu, 8.4ab.

48. Yao Lingze's living quarters, and her poetry volume, were named *Banyue lou* ("Half-moon pavilion"). It is obviously named after Gu Ruopu's *Woyuexuan* ("Moon slumber pavilion"). Yao died in her thirties, and her works were published posthumously as appendix to Gu's *Woyuexuan gao*. See *Renhe xianzhi* 20.51b–52a; and Wu Hao, 30.18a.

49. "Haichang leshan pai," in *Wulin Qianshi zongpu*, 3b. This genealogy, however, attributed Lin's drama *Furong xia* to her husband. Although it is no longer extant, scholars have understood it to be Lin's work (Xu Fuming, *Yuan Ming Qing xiqu*, p. 270). For biographical materials on Lin Yining, see Hu Wenkai, *Lidai funü*, pp. 396, 543; and Li Ruizhi, *gui sheng* 13b. Selections of her poetry can be found in Yun, 4.2a–3a; Cai, *yi* 28b–31b; and Wu Hao, 30.15a–16a.

50. See Han Yu, "Discourse on Teachers (*Shih-shuo*)," in de Bary et al., 1: 374–75.

51. For Qian Fenglun, see Hu Wenkai, *Lidai funü*, p. 757; Yun, 4.6a; and Wu Hao, 30.17a. For selections of her poetry, see Cai, *yi* 18a–20b; and Wu Hao, 30.17b. Yun Zhu (4.6) was wrong in stating that Qian was the wife of Gu's great grandson; Gu herself wrote that "she married my second grandson at age sixteen [*sui*]" (Hu Wenkai, *Lidai funü*, p. 757). For Gu Qiji, see Hu Wenkai, *Lidai funü*, p. 802; and Yun, 4.7ab. For her poetry, see Wu Hao, 30.16b.

52. The Wuyue Kingdom, with its capital in Hangzhou, remained the source of local pride in the Ming-Qing period. The Qian family naturally highlighted their royal pedigree in their genealogy, *Wulin Qianshi zongpu*. *Jijiu* (libationer) was originally the name of a post in the Han bureaucracy occupied by an elder in charge of education (Morohashi, pp. 8607–8, or 8: 471–2; Hucker, p. 130). In late Ming times it was frequently used to denote the male leader of a poetic group or school. Chai Jingyi was said to have been elected the *nüshi jijiu* ("woman leader"); see Yun, 4.3b.

53. For biographies of Chai Jingyi, see Hu Wenkai, *Lidai funü*, pp. 434–35; and Li Ruizhi, *gui sheng* 15a. For her works, see Yun, 4.3b–5a; Cai, *jia* 39a–40b; Wu Hao, 30.10b–12b; and Hu Baoyi, 1.1b–5a, 2.1a–4b, 3.3a, 4.2a–3b, 6.1b–4a. For Zhu Rouze, see Hu Wenkai, *Lidai funü*, p. 278; and Li Ruizhi, *gui sheng* 16b. For her poems, see Yun, 6.9a–10b; and Hu Baoyi, 1.12a–b, 2.11a, 3.8b–10a, 4.13b–14a. For Chai's son and Zhu's husband, Shen Yongji, see Wu Hao, 10.18a.

54. For Zhang Chayun, see Hu Wenkai, *Lidai funü*, p. 514; Yun, 4.8a–b; Shi Shuyi, 2.26b; and Wu Hao, 30.20a–b. For her poems, see Hu Baoyi, 3.6a; and Chen Yigang, *guimen* 8b.

55. For Mao Anfang, see Hu Wenkai, *Lidai funü*, p. 229; and Wu Hao, 30.13ab. Apparently she died shortly after her fortieth (*sui*) birthday; her husband wrote a poem commemorating the birthday. Both Qian Fenglun and Gu Qiji wrote eulogistic poems for Mao (Wu Hao, 30.16b, 17b).

56. Wu Hao, 30.13ab; cf. Yun, 4.8b.

57. Wu Hao, 30.12b.

58. Yun, 4.4a.

59. Hu Baoyi, 6.3b–4a. My translation of *wenrou dunhou* follows James Legge's (*Li Chi*, 2: 255).

60. Wu Hao, 30.10b; Hu Baoyi, 1.2a.

61. Gu Ruopu, "Shi zhuer," in Wang Qi, *chubian* 23.1a–2b; also in Zhou Lianggong, *Laigutang mingxian chidu*, pp. 243–44. We do not know the conflicts that led to the family division, nor is there information on the details of property division. I deduce from the active voice Gu used throughout the letter that she was instrumental in the decision.

62. Ding Yuru's stepmother, Zhang Siyin, was a famous Hangzhou poet (Chen Wenshu, *Xiling guiyong*, 8.4ab).

63. Hu Baoyi, 6.3a.

64. Hu Wenkai, *Lidai funü*, p. 757. Mao Jike (1633–1708), a famous Zhejiang poet, also contributed a preface. Mao mentioned that Qian Fenglun's brother, Zhaoxiu (Lin Yining's husband) and their neighbors were preparing Fenglun's manuscripts for publication in 1683. The result, *Guxianglou ji*, was a collection of Fenglun's verse crafted over a span of four decades. This preface is reprinted in Wang Qishu, 2.15a–b.

65. Cited in Wu Hao, 30.15a.

66. Gu Ruopu, "Yu di," in Wang Qi, *chubian* 23.7a.

67. Yun, 4.4b–5a. See Yip, pp. 157–59, for a discussion of the *qian* hexagram and the six stages of the dragon's transformation. Maureen Robertson (pers. comm.) sees the hidden dragon's transformation as a revelation about the worth and power of the individual.

Chapter 7

1. Ann Rosalind Jones, "City Women and Their Audiences: Louise Labé and Veronica Franco," in Ferguson et al., p. 304. My statement on the Italian origins of the English word *courtesan* is also taken from ibid.

2. Lougee, pp. 113–70. Lougee has also argued that by initiating newly risen groups into the tastes and manners of nobility culture, the salons served to reinforce the aristocratic social structure (pp. 212–13). For individual portraits of scores of salonnières, see Mason. For the French salon as an extension of the institutionalized court and its ambivalent position in the emergent bourgeois public sphere, see Landes, pp. 22–28.

3. Teruoka, p. 11.

4. Ibid., pp. 16, 19.

5. Chang, *Chinese Tz'u Poetry*, pp. 9–10. For a summary of the worlds of Tang public and private prostitutes, see Kishibe, pp. 197–227. For a portrayal of Tang courtesan culture through the life of one of its most famous courtesan-poets, Xue Tao, see Jeanne Larsen, "Introduction," in Xue, pp. xi–xxi.

6. Wagner, p. 91; see also pp. 81–91 for a summary of the four basic groups of female entertainers and a general discussion of Tang courtesan culture. For a similar argument about the origins of *ci* poetry, see Wang Shunu, pp. 100–103.

7. For a description of how candidates who gathered in Nanjing for the tri-

ennial provincial examination were socialized in the city's famous entertainment district along the Qinhuai River, see Peterson, pp. 25–27, 141–44. See also the descriptions of the Four Lords, four leading literati-poets active in the political and entertainment worlds of Nanjing, in Wakeman, *Great Enterprise*, pp. 136–45, 359–61.

8. For the contribution of Liu Rushi to the revival of song lyrics, see Chang, *Ch'en Tzu-lung*. For a summary of the literary and artistic talents of other Ming courtesans, see Wang Shunu, pp. 220–23, 230–41.

9. J. Watt, p. 7.

10. Due to space limitations, I cannot treat the meanings of rituals and nomenclature in the seventeenth-century entertainment districts here. For an excellent introduction, see Levy, *Mist and Flowers*. The Chinese original of this account, together with all the other major works in this genre, are reprinted in a convenient twenty-volume collectanea, *Xiangyan congshu*.

11. Wang Shunu, pp. 198–205, 261–65. Kang-i Sun Chang (*Chen Tz'u-lung*, pp. 119–20) argues that despite the fall of the Ming, courtesan-poets continued to be active in the early Qing. But by the eighteenth century, "courtesans were virtually excluded from the world of refined letters."

12. In contrast, Japanese courtesans (*tayū*) appeared in literature most often as goddesses of sex and poetry, an image intertwined with that of the fertility goddess (Saeki, pp. 82–100).

13. For these loyalist women warriors, see Ko, "Complicity of Women," pp. 480–85.

14. Footbinding had been a hallmark of courtesan culture since the late Song (Wang Shunu, pp. 248–52).

15. Lu Yong, *juan* 5, pp. 52–53. Folding fans were first introduced to China as tribute from Korea.

16. Peter Stallybrass, "Patriarchal Territories: The Body Enclosed," in Ferguson et al., p. 133.

17. Gronewold, p. 37.

18. The question of the price of women, in the context of general price fluctuations in the seventeenth century, needs further study. Preliminary investigations from Ming novels suggest that a well-groomed daughter could fetch a considerable sum. Comments in the late Ming novel *Jinpingmei*, for example, suggests that selling a daughter as a maid generated more cash than a shop assistant earned in six months. With it the family could buy enough rice for a year. See *Jinpingmei*, chapters 25, 49, 59; Dongguo xiansheng, p. 189.

19. The reputation of Yangzhou women as beautiful was the result of a long history of imperial patronage. The tradition of procuring women from Yangzhou for pleasure was started by Sui Yang-ti, the builder of the Grand Canal, in the early seventh century. Besides supplying his own harem, he also offered Yangzhou widows and virgins to his soldiers as wives. See Yao, 2.35b. The practice was followed by generations of emperors after him. In 1519, for example, the Zhengde emperor raided the city for virgins and widows. Yangzhou families with daughters at home scrambled for single men before the emperor's entourage arrived (ibid., 6.19b; Mao Qiling, "Wuzong waiji," *Xiangyan congshu*, vol. 11, 2.11a).

20. Xie Zhaozhe, pp. 210–11.

21. Ibid., 8.7a.

22. The poem reads, "Don't feed a thin horse, / Don't teach a young prostitute. / The results are obvious, / Watch if you don't believe — / Once the horse is fat it runs, / Once the girl grows up she sings and dances. / In three to five years, / They change owners. / Who's happier and who has toiled, / The new owner or the old? / Do listen and take heed, / And write down what I've said" (quoted in Chen Dongyuan, p. 210).

23. Zhang Dai, pp. 76–77. For a vivid fictional account of the grooming of "thin horses," see Ding Yaokang, pp. 522–23. I thank Professor David Ralston for bringing this to my attention.

24. Shi Runzhang, "Guangling nüer hang," in *Yangzhou fuzhi, yiwen* 31.15ab. The ages of "thirteen or fourteen" are by Chinese count. For other examples, see *Jiajing Weiyang zhi*, 11.22b–23a, 37.3ab; and *Yangzhou fuzhi, yiwen* 31.23ab. Even genealogies of local families follow suit: see *Jiangdu Yangshuxiang Sunshi zupu, juan* 1, *zhuan* section. Yangzhou's decadent image lasted into the twentieth century. A gazetteer published in 1938 states that middle-class families in Yangzhou often hired eighteen- or nineteen year-old girls to wait on the man of the house (Wang Peitang, p. 473).

25. "Fanmen qiyulu," in *Xiangyan congshu*, 6: 1.7a.

26. Zhonghua tushu jicheng bianji suo, p. 143.

27. Wang Qi, *chubian* 13.2b.

28. The famous poet Zheng Xie (1693–1765) furnished many examples. One reads: "In a thousand households [of Yangzhou] daughters are raised by teaching them how to sing, / Within ten *li* flowers are planted instead of crops" (Zheng Xie, p. 5).

29. The careers of about 70 courtesans recorded in a Yuan biography, *Qinglou ji*, illustrate that the thin line dividing the concubine and the prostitute was often illusory. Van Gulik (p. 252), who studied the biographies, concluded, "Some singing girls were bought as concubines by wealthy men, then left them to join a private theatrical troupe owned by another man, and finally married their master or drifted back to their original profession. Others became Taoist nuns and roamed all over the larger cities of the empire, earning their living now as actresses, then as prostitutes, to end in misery, or in the harem of a Chinese or Mongol official."

30. Li Yu, *Xianqing ouji*, in *Li Yu quanji*, 5: 3.46a.

31. Hanan (*Chinese Vernacular Story*, pp. 10–11) discusses this point in the context of the wide readership enjoyed by vernacular stories.

32. Li Yu, *Xianqing ouji*, in *Li Yu quanji*, 5: 3.47b–50a, 52a, 57a–58a, 60b–61a.

33. Ibid., 3.51a.

34. The notion of a friendship-love continuum is taken from Smith-Rosenberg, pp. 311–42.

35. For details of these activities of Fan Yunlin, see Zhang Huijian, pp. 363, 372, 406, 457, 473. Xu Yuan's upbringing and education are mentioned in prefaces to her poetry collection. See, e.g., "Xuzi Fan furen shi xu"; and "Fan furen *Luowei yin* xu," 4a, in Xu Yuan, 2ab, 4a, respectively.

36. Xu Yuan, 2.1b–2a; 3.18b–19b, 29a–30a; 11.3a–9a, 17a–20b; 12.5a–6b.

37. For Xue Susu's paintings, see *Views from Jade Terrace*, pp. 82–88. Xue Susu herself used a seal *Nü jiaoshu* (Female collator) on one of her paintings, which was first used by Xue Tao. This suggests that Susu identified herself with Xue Tao with pride (ibid., p.86).

38. "Zeng Xue Susu wu shou," in Xu Yuan, 8.22a–23b.

39. Fan Yunlin also wrote the title of the painting. For this colophon, translated by Irving Lo, and a reproduction of the painting, see *Views from Jade Terrace*, pp. 84–85.

40. For Xue Susu's life and works, see Tseng; my translation of descriptions of Xue's archery skills is based on ibid., pp. 202–3.

41. "Zeng geji Anqing," in Xu Yuan, 3.31b–32a.

42. "Xizeng geji Sanli wushou," in Xu Yuan, 8.4a–5a. For a translation of one of these poems, see Chapter 4.

43. Xu Yuan, 8.45b–46a, 50ab.

44. Xu Yuan, 11.3a. This biography is anthologized in Zhao Shijie, 3.35a–40a.

45. Although none of the poems is dated, these trips to the frontier were likely made in the last decade of the sixteenth century, since Fan Yunlin was appointed secretary of the Ministry of War in 1595 (Xu Yuan, 5.3a, 6a; 8.42a–43b).

46. Ibid., 3.12b–13a. For other poems on military affairs on the border, some written when she was no longer there, see ibid., 5.4ab, 6.5ab, 8.41b–42a; see also Zheng Guangyi, pp. 1311–12.

47. The different representations of Xu Yuan in these anthologies would make an interesting study for a separate article. Qian Qianyi and Liu Rushi, for example, were extremely terse, including only two conventional poems using the voice of a palace woman in their *Liechao shiji*. At the opposite end is Zhong Xing, who, in his *Mingyuan shigui*, devoted an entire chapter to Xu and another to her friend Lu Qingzi (*juan* 32, 33). Only two other poets were so privileged, one being the courtesan Wang Wei, who will be discussed later in this chapter. For several examples of Xu's prose, see the popular anthology by the commercial printer Zhao Shijie (8.42ab, 9.14a). For an example of citations of Xu's works in local gazetteers, see the "Literature" (*yiwen*) section in *Suzhou fuzhi*, 139.1b.

48. That scholar-officials took the lead in popularizing Xu's works was disclosed by Qian Qianyi and Liu Rushi in their entry on Xu in the *Liechao shiji* (*runji* 4.44b). They found the literary merits of Xu's verse wanting. Xu's friend Lu Qingzhi fared slightly better (ibid., 4.8ab).

49. The famous example of a ménage à trois in Shen Fu's autobiographical novel, *Fusheng liuji*, provides additional support that a homoerotic liaison between wife and singing girl was accepted and even welcomed by men. For a discussion, see Ropp, "Between Two Worlds." For a brief introduction to lesbianism in imperial China, see Hinsch, pp. 173–78. I take exception, however, to Hinsch's contention that "lesbianism never inspired a sustained literary tradition such as that associated with male homosexuality, and the scattered mentions of lesbianism that remain are unrelated" (p. 174).

50. Zhang Huijian, pp. 164, 219, 220, 237, 241, 243, 321. Lu Qingzi's

daughter-in-law, Wen Shu (1595–1634), was a descendant of Wen Zhengming. Wen Shu became a famous painter and sold her works after Zhao Yiguang's death to make ends meet (*Views from Jade Terrace*, pp. 31–33, 88–91).

51. Zhang Huijian, pp. 259, 378, 398, 440, 444, 457, 460, 474. See also *Wuxian zhi*, 79.52b, 54a, for other works by Zhao. The title of Lu's collection, *Kaopan ji*, was borrowed from a line in the *Book of Songs*. My translation of "building a hermitage" follows its conventional interpretation. Chen Shih-Hsiang ("*Shih-ching*," pp. 22–23) has argued that the word "*pan*" either "means 'joy' or signifies dance."

52. "Han," in Lu Qingzi, *Xuanzhi ji*, 1 *shang* 2b–3a.

53. "Bi jiefu," in Lu Qingzi, *Kaopan ji*, 4.11b–12a. See the poem on 1.1b for the same theme. This poetic collection also circulated in Japan, as testified by an Edo period copy also housed in the Naikaku bunko.

54. Lu Qingzi, *Xuanzhi ji*, 3.5a, 9a.

55. Lu Qingzi, "Zeng Feng meiren," in Zhong, 32.16a. For other poems to *meiren*, see Lu Qingzi, *Xuanzhi ji*, 2.15ab, 18b–19a; 3.7a; 4.1ab.

56. Lu Qingzi, *Kaopan ji*, 2.2ab, 6b–7a; 4.10b–12a; 5.8a, 15ab.

57. Lu Qingzi, *Xuanzhi ji*, 1 *shang* 5a, 6a. Also in Zhong, 32.17b–18a.

58. "Ji Fan furen Wuhu," in Lu Qingzi, *Kaopan ji*, 2.5a. Only the middle half of the poem is translated here.

59. "Song Fan furen congyi you Diannan," in Lu Qingzi, *Xuanzhi ji*, 1 *shang* 4b.

60. Whether Xu's feelings for Lu were just as strong is less certain. Kang-i Sun Chang (pers. comm.) suggests that Lu's poems for Xu are highly "expressive," whereas Xu's poems for Lu are often merely "descriptive." For the notion of "description-expression" as a spectrum of poetic elements, see Chang, *Six Dynasties Poetry*.

61. "Zeng Feng guancha rujun Wuji," in Lu Qingzi, *Xuanzhi ji*, 2.8a; also in Zhong, 32.10a–11a.

62. "Qie boming," in Lu Qingzi, *Kaopan ji*, 3.8a–9a; also in Zhong, 32.6ab; and Liu Yunfen, pp. 47–48. See Lu Qingzi, *Kaopan ji*, 5.17b–18a for another poem on the same theme.

63. "Chao nüwu," in Lu Qingzi, *Xuanzhi ji*, 3.30a.

64. The most complete biography of Liu Rushi is the three-volume *Liu Rushi biezhuan* by Chen Yinke, the famous historian of the Tang. Chen's unique historiographical method, based on his extensive knowledge of poetry and classical allusions, was particularly well suited to the subject matter here. The result was a brilliant and original biography that illuminated many aspects of Liu's life glossed over or misrepresented by other biographers. My study of Liu's life is heavily indebted to this work. A convenient collection of conventional accounts of Liu's life is Huaipu jushi, which contains 56 accounts of or references to Liu Rushi's life, without comments. Other biographies can be found as citations in Chen Yinke. On Chen Yinke's poetry-based historiographical method, see Wang Rongzu, pp. 344–46. For a summary in English of Liu's life, see Chang, *Ch'en Tzu-lung*, pp. 19–37.

65. Madame Chen, in fact, continued to live in the same household until she

died in 1658. One of Liu's courtesan friends, Wang Wei, also married in a ceremony accorded to first wives. Some former Ming officials chose to have their
consorts instead of first wives honored by the Qing court (Chen Yinke, pp. 639–
42).

66. For a brief English description of the property dispute, see Hummel, pp.
529–30. For a detailed account, see Chen Yinke, pp. 1206–17. Included in these
pages are Liu's last words and appeals by Liu's daughter and son-in-law.

67. Furth states this irony eloquently in her "Poetry and Women's Culture,"
pp. 1–3.

68. Contemporary materials are murky on the issue of Liu Rushi's original and
adopted names. Because of her illicit associations with various politically powerful
men, her biographers obscured or fabricated her identity and other aspects of her
life. Chen Yinke was the first scholar who paid special attention to Liu Rushi's
names and drew on his extensive knowledge of the Classics and poetic allusions to
reconstruct a chronology of her name changes. My analysis would not have been
possible without Chen's work.

69. R. Watson, p. 619.

70. That Liu Rushi's original given name was Yunjuan is merely an educated
guess based on poetic allusions (Chen Yinke, pp. 28, 31). The name Yinglian, in
turn, may signify Liu's sympathy for Xiaoqing, who was obsessed with her own
shadow. Liu's choice of the name Ai, as Chen Yinke (p. 33) suggests, may be
related to a courtesan in the Northern Song dynasty, Yang Aiai. It is likely that
both names used in this early period, "shadowed pity" and "love," are related to
the sentiments befitting an adolescent girl's initiation into a world of love and love
games. See Shen Qiu, "Hedongjun zhuan," in Huaipu jushi, 1ab, for evidence that
she used the name Yang Ai in 1636.

71. Chen Yinke, pp. 32, 35, 214, 334.

72. Chen Yinke (pp. 105–6) reasons that Liu and Chen lived together in the
spring and early summer of 1635, after which Liu decided to leave Chen because
his first wife and family objected to her marrying Chen even as a concubine. On the
slandering of Liu Rushi by Chen Zilong's friends, see Zhuang.

73. The origin of the association of the name *liu* with courtesanship is the
legendary character Zhang Tailiu, a Tang dynasty concubine (Chen Yinke, pp. 32,
35, 334). For Liu's letter, see Wang Xiuqin and Hu, p. 104.

74. Chen Yinke, p. 34.

75. Liu Xiang, p. 47.

76. For the double meaning of *wenzhang* or *wencai*, see *Peiwen yunfu*, p. 630;
and Morohashi, 11: 969.

77. Another indication of her desire to retreat and hide was her growing interest in Buddhism. Two names she started to use in the late 1630's were Rushi and
Wowen jushi, both taken from the phrase "rushi wowen" ("I heard it said") that
introduces many Buddhist sutras. The entry on Qian Qianyi in Hummel (p. 149) is
wrong in stating that Qian gave her the two names, for Liu signed her works with
them before meeting Qian in 1640.

78. Hu Wenkai, *Lidai funü*, pp. 430–32; Chen Yinke, pp. 335–36, 571.

79. This period of Liu Rushi's life before her marriage is documented by her

letters to Wang Ranming, reprinted in Wang Xiuqin and Hu, pp. 103–10. For the name "Hedong," see Chen Yinke, pp. 32, 525–27.

80. Wang Xiuqin and Hu, *passim*. This practice was not uncommon among courtesans of her day. The Nanjing courtesan Gu Mei (1619–64), for example, was referred to as "elder brother Mei" (*Mei xiong*) by her male friends (Meng Sen, pp. 107–8).

81. Liu's passing herself off as a man when she first visited Qian Qianyi at his home is a legendary scene. The Qing painter Yu Qiushi painted a portrait of the scene, with Liu wearing a turban and a man's robe. For an account of the visit and descriptions of Liu's attire, see Huaipu jushi, 1b; and Chen Yinke, pp. 270, 343, 375.

82. For Liu's calligraphy, see Chen Yinke, p. 66. For Liu's admiration for Liang Hongyu, see ibid., pp. 166, 664, 751. Liu was not alone in her interest in military affairs. As mentioned above, Xue Susu was an accomplished equestrian and archer.

83. Chen Yinke, p. 270. Another indication of the care and pride Liu took in her bound feet is that she once had a renowned craftsman make the soles of her shoes (Huaipu jushi, 7a).

84. For example, the Yangzhou courtesan Wang Wei befriended the wife of Wang Ranming, as evinced by one of Wang Wei's poems dedicated to Madame Wang (Qian, *Liechao shiji, runji* 4.64b–65a). Huang Yuanjie, too, was invited by the wife of Tong Guoqi, a high-ranking Manchu official, to stay with her. For a summary of the owners and names of the houses where Liu Rushi stayed on her travels, see Chen Yinke, p. 561.

85. Sisterhoods did exist in the pleasure quarters in late Ming Jiangnan. In early to mid-seventeenth-century Nanjing, for example, as many as 20 or 30 courtesans would call each other "handkerchief sisters" (*shuopa zimei*). The group ritual, called a "box party" (*hezi hui*), centered on a game they started on the fifteenth day of the first month, at the tail end of the New Year celebrations. The well-adorned women piled delicacies and fruits in boxes, vying with each other for the most exotic selection. The game was an excuse to hold drinking parties that lasted a month. With the decline of the Nanjing pleasure quarters, such parties could no longer be found (Zhou Lianggong, *Shuying*, p. 10). The Qing poet Zhu Yizun (1629–1709) made a similar reference to the "handkerchief sisters" in the Nanjing quarters and traced them to the last quarter of the fifteenth century (Lo, p. 43). Prostitutes from the same brothel in modern China also call each other "sister" and often form sisterhoods (Gronewold, pp. 9, 15; Tsung, pp. 351–52).

86. Chen Yinke, p. 296. For the rise of practical statecraft in the seventeenth century, which replaced the previous emphasis on moral cultivation in Confucian discourse, see Elman, *Philosophy to Philology*, pp. 53–56.

87. Chen Yinke, p. 48. Chen (pp. 58–59) suggested that Liu might first have been sold to a brothel before she was purchased by Zhou, which means the foster mother in the brothel was her first teacher. But there is no concrete evidence for this.

88. Ibid., p. 74.

89. The Nan Yuan was also where Chen Zilong later compiled the *Huangming*

jingshi wenbian in 1638 and edited Xu Guangqi's *Nongzheng quanshu* in 1639 (ibid., pp. 276–77). On Chen Zilong's compilation work, see Zhu Dongrun, pp. 119–22.

90. Cited in Chen Yinke, pp. 282–83.

91. Qian and Liu might also have been involved in the aborted rebellion of Huang Yuqi, a loyalist from Jiangyin, in 1648. In any case, Qian was arrested by the Qing authorities for his alleged involvement, but was freed by the efforts of Liu. My discussion of their loyalist activities here is based on Chen Yinke, pp. 1011–97; and Hu Wenkai, "Liu Rushi nianpu," p. 43. For Koxinga's campaigns in the Jiangnan region, see Struve, pp. 180–93.

92. The Yangzhou courtesan Wang Wei was eulogized in an official Qing hagiography seeking to promote loyalism as an abstract creed (Xu Zi, 60.8a). Another example was Gu Mei, a leading courtesan in Nanjing. During the Manchu invasion, she saved one of the loyalists, the knight-errant Yan Ermei, by hiding him in her room (Meng Sen, pp. 129–30). For other examples of loyalist courtesans, see Chang, *Ch'en Tzu-lung*, pp. 16–17.

93. Chang, *Ch'en Tzu-lung*, p. 17.

94. The volume of overseas trade, which had made Hangzhou famous in the Song-Yuan times, dwindled after the sixteenth century. For an excellent study of the history of Hangzhou as a port and development of its manufacturing industries from the Spring and Autumn period to the Qing, see Wu Zhenhua. For the local culture and society in late imperial Hangzhou, see Hangzhou lishi congbian bianji weiyuanhui.

95. For Wang Ranming as a salt merchant, see Widmer, "Epistolary World," p. 13; and Handlin-Smith, "Gardens," pp. 71–72. For a study of Anhui merchants as art patrons in the seventeenth century, precursors of the famous Yangzhou merchants in the eighteenth century, see Chin and Hsu, pp. 19–24).

96. Wang Xiuqin and Hu, p. 104. The collection published by Wang contained 31 letters. The first 30 were sent to him before late 1640 and the last one, sent in spring of the following year, was added as appendix (Chen Yinke, p. 371).

97. Letter of Liu to Wang, in Wang Xiuqin and Hu, p. 105. For the text of Lin Tiansu's preface to Liu Rushi's collection of letters, see Chen Yinke, pp. 368–71. For Lin Tiansu (Xue)'s paintings, see *Views from Jade Terrace*, pp. 95–96.

98. Unless otherwise noted, details of Wu Shan's life discussed in the following sections are taken from Deng Hanyi, 12.16ab. Deng was a personal friend of Wu's husband. See also 12.19b–20a for Wu's elder daughter, Bian Xuanwen. For a list of Wu Shan's works, see Hu Wenkai, *Lidai funü*, p. 298.

99. Ye Shaoyuan, *Nianpu bieji*, pp. 79–80. Wu's poem was published by Ye Shaoyuan in *Tonglian xuxue, shang*, pp. 9–10.

100. Deng Hanyi, 12.16ab. Examples of Wu Shan's socializing with Wang Ranming and other men abound. In 1649, Wu and her elder daughter, Bian Xuanwen, composed rounds of poetry with monks and men of letters on Wang Ranming's "Garden Without a Mooring." These poems were compiled by one of the men, Shen Yichen, as *Hufang shi*; reprinted in Ding Bing, *Wulin zhanggu congbian*, 22: 6774–81.

101. This famous poem is widely anthologized. See, e.g., Deng Hanyi, 12.18b;

and Chen Yigang, *guimen* 2a. For Wu's invitation to Huang Yuanjie, see "Huang-shi Jieling xiaozhuan," in Shi Yushan, 17.13a.

102. Wu Shan ended her itinerant life when her elder daughter married an official, Liu Jundu, who served her as his mother. Shortly before the marriage, Wu's husband died. The young wife died at the age of 33, and Liu married Wu's second daughter. Wu continued to write and publish, and lived to over 60 (Deng Hanyi, 12.16b, 19a). The ease with which she reverted to a gentrywoman's life supports my argument that the boundary between "public" and "domestic" women was neither absolute nor clear-cut.

103. Yun, *fulu* 16b.

104. Chen Weisong, *Furen ji*, in *Xiangyan congshu*, 1: 2.24b. The landlord of Huang Yuanjie's "rented place" was none other than her friend and patron, Wang Ranming (Ruan, 40.19ab).

105. Zhong, 36.1a. This is the most famous biography of Wang Wei, written by her friend Zhong Xing as an introduction to a collection of her poems. Reprinted in Hu Wenkai, *Lidai funü*, p. 88. For Wang Wei's parting poem to Lin Tiansu, see Zhong, 36.22a. Wang Wei's dates (ca. 1600–1647) were suggested by Kang-i Sun Chang ("Guide to Ming-Ch'ing Anthologies," p. 133).

106. For Wang Wei's two marriages, friendship with Liu Rushi, and other episodes of her life, see Chen Yinke, pp. 427, 431–33.

107. Hu Wenkai, *Lidai funü*, pp. 88–90. Chen Jiru commented on one of her travelogues, entitled *Chuyou gao*, which is no longer extant (ibid., p. 88).

108. Wang Wei, "Qibu," in Zhong, 36.1ab.

109. Wang Wei, "Xiao yin," 1ab, in *Mingshan jixuan*. According to Qian Qianyi (*Liechao shiji, runji* 4.63a), Wang Wei was the editor of this anthology, entitled *Mingshan ji*, numbering several hundred *juan*. This work appears to be no longer extant in its entirety. An abridged version in the Gest Library, *Mingshan jixuan*, also credits Wang Wei as editor. I cannot ascertain the extent of Wang's involvement in both projects. The latter was printed in part from the blocks of an earlier work, the 46-*juan Tianxia mingshan shenggai ji* (1633). For a textual history of this earlier work and its illustrations, see the introduction to He Lezhi.

110. Wang Wei, "Xiao yin," 1b, in *Mingshan jixuan*.

111. Wang Wei, preface to "Yueguan shi," cited in Qian, *Liechao shiji, runji* 4.62b–63a; also in Hu Wenkai, *Lidai funü*, p. 88.

112. Wang Wei, preface to "Yueguan shi," cited in Qian, *Liechao shiji, runji* 4.62b–63a; also in Hu Wenkai, *Lidai funü*, p. 88.

113. The other published poets from the Huang family included Shen Renlan and Huang Shude. For brief biographies of them and Xiang Lanzhen, see Qian, *Liechao shiji, runji* 4.45a–46a; see Pan, *Jiaxing de wangzu*, p. 66, for a family tree. For Shen Renlan's contributions to Shen Yixiu's publication project, see Chapter 5 of this book. Xiang was also a friend of Lu Qingzi, who contributed a preface to one of her poetry collections, *Caiyun cao*. This preface is anthologized in Zhao Shijie, *juan* 4; also reprinted in Hu Wenkai, *Lidai funü*, p. 176. Lu wrote a poem for Xiang (see Lu Qingzi, *Xuanzhi ji*, 2.14a–15a, and Xiang also crafted one for Lu (Qian, *Liechao shiji, runji* 4.46a). It is not clear, however, if Lu and Xiang ever met face-to-face.

114. Cited in Qian, *Liechao shiji, runji* 4.45b.

115. Wang Wei, "Ku Huang funren Mengwan," in Qian, *Liechao shiji, runji* 4.58b–59a. For her earlier poem in response to one sent by Xiang, see 4.64a. I am grateful to Kang-i Sun Chang and her graduate student Chi-hung Yim for suggesting the translation of the last two lines of this poem.

116. "*Qishan cao* xiaoyin," in Tan Youxia, p. 159.

117. Chen Yinke, pp. 287, 483, 818.

118. James Cahill, "The Painting of Liu Yin," in Weidner, *Flowering in the Shadows*, pp. 115–16.

119. Xu Shumin and Qian, *yueji* 2.22b.

120. Chen Yinke, pp. 847, 863.

121. Ellen Laing (pp. 34–35) discusses the same "leveling factor" in the context of female painters. A female painter from the gentry class and one from the commercial class produced paintings using the same image of a solitary woman in a peony garden.

122. Liu Rushi helped edit the section on women poets in Qian Qianyi's 81-volume compilation, *Liechao shiji*, published in 1649. The entries on these women were said to have been written by Liu (Chen Yinke, pp. 983–84).

Works Cited

Abu-Lughod, Lila. "The Romance of Resistance: Tracing Transformations of Power Through Bedouin Women." *American Ethnologist* 17 (1990): 41–55.

Andors, Phyllis. *The Unfinished Liberation of Chinese Women, 1949–1980.* Bloomington: University of Indiana Press, 1983.

Armstrong, Nancy. *Desire and Domestic Fiction: A Political History of the Novel.* New York: Oxford University Press, 1987.

Asakawa Shigeo 浅川滋男. "Tsoke no minzokushi: Kose chihō no kamado to dai-dokoro" "灶間"の民族誌: 江浙地方のカマドと台所 (Ethnography of the stove: stoves and kitchens in Jiangsu and Zhejiang). *Kikan jinruigaku* 季刊人類学 18, no. 3 (1987): 60–125.

Atkinson, Jane Monnig. "Anthropology." *Signs* 8 (1982): 236–58.

Beattie, Hilary. *Land and Lineage in China.* Cambridge, Eng.: Cambridge University Press, 1979.

Bourdieu, Pierre. *The Logic of Practice.* Trans. Richard Nice. Stanford: Stanford University Press, 1990.

———. *Outline of a Theory of Practice.* Trans. Richard Nice. Cambridge, Eng.: Cambridge University Press, 1977.

Bray, Francesca. *Fabrics of Power: Technology and Ideology in Late Imperial China.* In preparation.

Brokaw, Cynthia. *The Ledgers of Merit and Demerit: Social Change and Moral Order in Late Imperial China.* Princeton: Princeton University Press, 1991.

Brook, Timothy. "Family Continuity and Cultural Hegemony: The Gentry of Ningbo, 1368–1949." In Joseph Esherick and Mary Rankin, eds., *Chinese Local Elites and Patterns of Dominance.* Berkeley: University of California Press, 1990.

———. "Funerary Ritual and the Building of Lineages in Late Imperial China." *Harvard Journal of Asiatic Studies* 49 (1989): 465–99.

———. "Guides for Vexed Travellers: Route Books in the Ming and Qing." *Ch'ing-shih wen-t'i* 4, no. 5 (June 1981): 32–76.

Cahill, Suzanne E. *Transcendence and Divine Passion: The Queen Mother of the West in Medieval China.* Stanford: Stanford University Press, 1993.

Cai Dianqi 蔡殿齊, comp. *Guochao guige shichao* 國朝閨閣詩鈔 (Poetry of refined ladies from the reigning dynasty). 10 vols. N.p., 1844.

Cao Shujuan 曹淑娟. *Wan-Ming xingling xiaopin yanjiu* 晚明性靈小品研究 (A

study of essays of natural expression in the late Ming). Taibei: Wenjin chubanshe, 1988.

Carlitz, Katherine. "The Social Uses of Female Virtue in Late Ming Editions of
Lienü Zhuan." *Late Imperial China* 12, no. 2 (Dec. 1991): 117–52.

Chang Bide 昌彼得, comp. *Mingdai banhuaxuan chuji* 明代版畫選初輯 (Selected
Ming wood engravings, first compilation). 2 vols. Taibei: Guoli zhongyang
tushuguan, 1969.

Chang, Kang-i Sun. *The Evolution of Chinese Tz'u Poetry: From Late T'ang to
Northern Sung.* Princeton: Princeton University Press, 1980.

———. "A Guide to Ming-Ch'ing Anthologies of Female Poetry and Their Selection Strategies." *Gest Library Journal* 5, no. 2 (Winter 1992): 119–60.

———. *The Late-Ming Poet Ch'en Tzu-lung: Crises of Love and Loyalism.* New
Haven: Yale University Press, 1991.

———. *Six Dynasties Poetry.* Princeton: Princeton University Press, 1986.

Chartier, Roger. *The Cultural Uses of Print in Early Modern France.* Trans.
Lydia G. Cochrane. Princeton: Princeton University Press, 1987.

Chartier, Roger, ed. *Passions of the Renaissance.* Vol. 3 of Philippe Aries and
Georges Duby, eds., *A History of Private Life.* Cambridge, Mass.: Harvard
University Press, 1989.

Chen Dongyuan 陳東原. *Zhongguo funü shenghuo shi* 中國婦女生活史 (A history
of the lives of Chinese women). Shanghai: Shangwu yinshuguan, 1928. Reprinted—Taibei: Shangwu, 1981.

Chen Hongmou 陳宏謀. *Jiaonü yigui* 教女遺規 (Bequeathed precepts for female
education). In idem, *Wuzhong yigui* 五種遺規 (Five bequeathed precepts). Taibei: Dezhi chubanshe, 1961.

Chen Jiru 陳繼儒, comp. *Caimei gushi* 采眉故事 (Stories of the colored eyebrows).
Nanjing: Sanduozhai, 1771.

Chen, Kenneth K. S. *The Chinese Transformation of Buddhism.* Princeton:
Princeton University Press, 1973.

Chen Qubing 陳去病. *Wushizhi* 五石脂 (Five-colored medicinal stone). First serial-
ized 1909. Reprinted—Suzhou bowuguan 苏州博物馆 et al., ed., *Danwu biji;
Wucheng riji; Wushizhi* 丹午笔记, 吴城日记, 五石脂 (Jottings by [Gu] Dan Wu;
Suzhou diary; Five-colored medicinal stone). Suzhou: Jiangsu guji chubanshe,
1985.

Chen Shengxi 陳生玺. "Qingchu tifaling de shishi yu Hanzu dizhujieji de paixi
douzheng" 清初剃发令的实施与汉族地主阶级的派系斗爭 (Execution of the hair-
cutting edict in the early Qing and factional strife within the Han landlord
class). *Lishi yanjiu* 历史研究 4 (1985): 67–77.

Chen Shih-Hsiang. "The Shih-ching: Its Generic Significance in Chinese Literary
History and Poetics." In Cyril Birch, ed., *Studies in Chinese Literary Genres.*
Berkeley: University of California Press, 1974.

Chen Wannai 陳萬鼐. *Hong Sheng yanjiu* 洪昇研究 (A study of Hong Sheng). Taibei: Xuesheng shuju, 1970.

Chen Wenshu 陳文述 [Yidao jushi 頤道居士], comp. *Xihu sannüshi zhuan* 西湖三
女士傳 (Stories of three West Lake lady scholars). First published as *Lanyin
ji* 蘭因集 (Karmic orchids). Reprinted—Hangzhou: Liuyi shuju, 1928.

———. *Xiling guiyong* 西泠閨詠 (Chantings by refined ladies on West Lake). In

Ding Bing 丁丙, comp., *Wulin zhanggu congbian* 武林掌故叢編 (Collectanea of legends from Hangzhou), vol. 9. Qiantang: Dingshi Jiahuitang, 1883. Reprinted—Taibei: Jinghua shuju, 1967.

Chen Yigang 陳以剛, comp. *Guochao shipin* 國朝詩品 (Tastes of poetry from the reigning dynasty). 22 *juan*. Dihua shuwu, 1734. Copy in the Library of Congress.

Chen Yinke 陳寅恪. *Liu Rushi biezhuan* 柳如是別傳 (Unofficial biography of Liu Rushi). 3 vols. Shanghai: Shanghai guji chubanshe, 1980.

Cheng Bilian 城壁連. *Woguo zhufu zhi diwei ji qi yaoshiquan* 我國主婦之地位暨其鑰匙權 (The position of housewives in our country and their power of the key). N.p., 1963. Copy in the Hoover Institution.

Chin, Sandi, and Hsu Cheng-chi (Ginger). "Anhui Merchant Culture and Patronage." In James Cahill, ed., *Shadows of Mt. Huang: Chinese Painting and Printing of the Anhui School*. Berkeley: University Art Museum, 1981.

Chishang ke 池上客, comp. *Mingyuan ji'nang* 名媛璣囊 (Pouch of pearls from famous ladies). 4 *juan*. Preface dated 1595. Copy in the Naikaku bunko.

Chow, Rey. *Woman and Chinese Modernity: The Politics of Reading Between West and East*. Minneapolis: University of Minnesota Press, 1991.

Chung, Priscilla Ching. *Palace Women in the Northern Sung, 960–1126*. Leiden: E. J. Brill, 1981.

Ciyuan 辭源 (Origins of words). Hong Kong: Shangwu, 1987.

Clunas, Craig. *Superfluous Things: Material Culture and Social Status in Early Modern China*. Urbana: University of Illinois Press, 1991.

Collier, Jane Fishburne, and Sylvia Junko Yanagisako, eds. *Gender and Kinship: Essays Toward a Unified Analysis*. Stanford: Stanford University Press, 1987.

Darnton, Robert. "Readers Respond to Rousseau: The Fabrication of Romantic Sensitivity." In idem, *The Great Cat Massacre and Other Episodes in French Cultural History*. New York: Vintage Books, 1985.

Davis, Natalie Zemon. *Society and Culture in Early Modern France*. Stanford: Stanford University Press, 1975.

de Bary, Wm. Theodore. "Individualism and Humanitarianism in Late Ming Thought." In Wm. Theodore de Bary et al., *Self and Society in Ming Thought*. New York: Columbia University Press, 1970.

de Bary, Wm. Theodore, Wing-tsit Chan, and Burton Watson, comps. *Sources of Chinese Tradition*. 2 vols. New York: Columbia University Press, 1970.

Deng Hanyi 鄧漢儀. *Shiguan* 詩觀 (Perspectives on poetry). N.p., 1672. Copy in the Naikaku bunko.

Deng Zhimo 鄧志謨, comp. *Huangmei gushi* 黃眉故事 (Stories of the yellow eyebrows). N.p., preface 1616; reprinted 1742.

Dennerline, Jerry. *The Chia-ting Loyalists: Confucian Leadership and Social Change in Seventeenth-Century China*. New Haven: Yale University Press, 1981.

Ding Bing 丁丙, comp. *Wulin wangzhe yizhu* 武林往哲遺著 (Works of the bygone sages from Hangzhou). 64 titles. Qiantang: Dingshi Jiahuitang, 1898–1900.

———. *Wulin zhanggu congbian* 武林掌故叢編 (Collectanea of legends from Hangzhou). 26 vols. Qiantang: Dingshi Jiahuitang, 1883. Reprinted—Taibei: Jinghua shuju, 1967.

Ding Yaokang 丁耀元. *Xu Jingpingmei* 續金瓶梅 (Sequel to *Jingpingmei*). In *Jing-pingmei xushu sanzhong* 金瓶梅續書三种 (Three sequels to *Jingpingmei*). Re-printed—Ji'nan: Qilu shushe, 1988.

Dongguo xiansheng 東郭先生. *Xianhua Jinpingmei* 閑話金瓶梅 (Random talks on *Jingpingmei*). Taibei: Shishi chubanshe, 1978.

Du Fangqin 杜芳琴. *Nüxing guannian de yanbian* 女性观念的衍变 (Evolution in the concept of "woman"). He'nan: He'nan renmin chubanshe, 1988.

———. "Qishi nianlai guonei funüshi yanjiu zongshu, 1919–1989" 七十年來国内妇女史研究綜述, 1919–1989 (An overview of the study of women's history in China in the past seventy years, 1919–1989). Unpublished paper, 1990.

Dunstan, Helen. "The Late Ming Epidemics: A Preliminary Survey." *Ch'ing-shih wen-t'i* 3, no. 3 (Nov. 1975): 1–59.

Ebrey, Patricia. "Conceptions of the Family in the Song Dynasty." *Journal of Asian Studies* 43 (1984): 219–45.

———. "Women in the Kinship System of the Southern Sung Upper Class." In Richard W. Guisso and Stanley Johannesen, eds., *Women in China: Current Directions in Historical Scholarship*. Youngstown, N.Y.: Philo Press, 1981.

———. "Women, Marriage and the Family in Chinese History." In Paul Ropp, ed., *Heritage of China: Contemporary Perspectives on Chinese Civilization*. Berkeley: University of California Press, 1990.

———. "Women, Money and Class: Ssu-ma Kuang and Sung Neo-Confucian Views on Women." In Academia Sinica, Institute of History and Philology, ed., *Papers on Society and Culture of Early Modern China*. Taibei: Academia Sinica, 1992.

Ebrey, Patricia, and James Watson, eds. *Kinship Organization in Late Imperial China, 1000–1940*. Berkeley: University of California Press, 1986.

Elman, Benjamin. *Classicism, Politics, and Kinship: The Ch'ang-chou School of New Text Confucianism in Late Imperial China*. Berkeley: University of California Press, 1990.

———. *From Philosophy to Philology: Intellectual and Social Aspects of Change in Late Imperial China*. Cambridge, Mass.: Harvard University, Council on East Asian Studies, 1984.

Elvin, Mark. "Female Virtue and the State in China." *Past and Present* 104 (Aug. 1984): 111–52.

———. *The Pattern of the Chinese Past*. Stanford: Stanford University Press, 1973.

Fan Shuzhi 樊树志. *Ming-Qing Jiangnan shizhen tanwei* 明清江南市鎮探微 (A close-up study of Jiangnan towns in the Ming-Qing period). Shanghai: Fudan daxue chubanshe, 1990.

Fang Yanshou 方彥寿. "Jianyang Liushi keshu kao" 建阳刘氏刻书考 (A study of the Liu family publishers in Jianyang). 2 pts. *Wenxian* 文献 36 (Feb. 1988): 196–228; 37 (Mar. 1988): 217–29.

Feng, Han-yi. *The Chinese Kinship System*. Cambridge, Mass.: Harvard University Press, 1967.

Feng Menglong 馮夢龍. *Qingshi* 情史 (Anatomy of love). Reprinted—Changsha: Yuelu shushe, 1986.

Ferguson, Margaret, Maureen Quilligan, and Nancy Vickers, eds. *Rewriting the*

Renaissance: The Discourses of Sexual Difference in Early Modern Europe. Chicago: University of Chicago Press, 1986.

Fletcher, Joseph. "Integrative History: Parallels and Interconnections in the Early Modern Period, 1500–1800." *Journal of Turkish History* 9, no. 1 (1985): 37–57.

Foucault, Michel. *An Introduction.* Trans. Robert Hurley. Vol. 1 of *The History of Sexuality.* New York: Vintage Books, 1980.

The Four Books. Trans. James Legge. Reprinted—Taibei: Culture Book Company, 1990.

Fu Xihua 傅惜華. *Mingdai chuanqi quanmu* 明代傳奇全目 (Complete catalog of Ming Southern-style dramas). Shanghai: Renmin wenxue chubanshe, 1959.

———. *Mingdai zaju quanmu* 明代雜劇全目 (Complete catalog of Ming Northern-style dramas). Shanghai: Renmin wenxue chubanshe, 1958.

Fu Xihua, comp. *Zhongguo gudian wenxue banhua xuanji* 中国古典文学版画选集 (Selected wood regravings from classical Chinese literature). 2 vols. Shanghai: Shanghai renmin meishu chubanshe, 1981.

Fujikawa Masakazu 藤川正数. Review of Yamazaki Jun'ichi 山崎純一, *Kyōiku kara mita Chūgoku joseishi shiryō no kenkyū* 教育から見た中国女性史資料の研究. *Ōbirin daigaku Chūgoku bungaku ronsō* 桜美林大学中国文学論叢 13 (Mar. 1987): 239–40.

Furth, Charlotte. "Androgynous Males and Deficient Females: Biology and Gender Boundaries in Sixteenth- and Seventeenth-Century China." *Late Imperial China* 9, no. 2 (Dec. 1988): 1–31.

———. "The Patriarch's Legacy: Household Instructions and the Transmission of Orthodox Values." In Kwang-ching Liu, ed., *Orthodoxy in Late Imperial China.* Berkeley: University of California Press, 1990.

———. "Poetry and Women's Culture in Late Imperial China: Editor's Introduction." *Late Imperial China* 13, no. 1 (June 1992): 1–8.

Gao Jianhua 高劍華, comp. *Hongxiu tianxiang shi congshu* 紅袖添香室叢書 (Collectanea from the Red Sleeve Enhanced Fragrance Studio). 5 vols. Shanghai: Qunxueshe, 1936.

Gates, Hill. "The Commoditization of Chinese Women." *Signs* 14 (1989): 799–832.

Geng Boming 耿百鳴. "Lun Suzhoupai xiju di funüguan he aiqingguan" 论苏州派戏剧的妇女观和愛情观 (The concepts of "woman" and "love" in dramas from the Suzhou school). *Huadong shifan daxue xuebao: Zhexue shehuikexue ban* 华东师范大学学报(哲学社会科學版) 5 (1985): 39–43.

Gerstlacher, Anna, ed. *Women and Literature in China.* Bochum, Ger.: Brockmeyer, 1985.

Goodrich, L. Carrington, and Fang Chaoying, eds. *Dictionary of Ming Biography, 1368–1644.* 2 vols. New York: Columbia University Press, 1976.

Goyama Kiwamu 合山究. "Ming-Shin jidai ni okeru jōshi to sono bungaku" 明清時代における情死とその文学 (Love suicides in the Ming-Qing period and their depictions in literature). In *Itō Sōhei kyōju taikankinen Chūgoku bungaku ronsō* 伊藤漱平教授退官記念中国文学論集 (Essays on Chinese literature: volume commemorating the retirement of Professor Itō Sōhei). Tokyo: Kyūko shoin, 1986.

Greenhalgh, Susan. "Bound Feet, Hobbled Lives: Women in Old China." *Frontiers* 2, no. 1 (Spring 1977): 7–21.

Gronewold, Sue. "Beautiful Merchandise: Prostitution in China, 1860–1936." *Women & History*, no. 1 (1982): 1–114.

Grove, Linda, and Christian Daniels, eds. *State and Society in China: Japanese Perspectives on Ming-Qing Social and Economic History.* Tokyo: University of Tokyo Press, 1984.

Gu Dunrou 顧敦鍒. "Li Liweng pengbeikao" 李笠翁朋輩考 (A study of Li Yu's social networks). In idem, *Wenyuan chanyou* 文苑闡幽 (Probings in the literary garden). Taizhong: Tunghai daxue, 1969.

Gu Ruopu 顧若璞. *Woyuexuan gao* 臥月軒稿 (Manuscripts from the Moon Slumber Pavilion). No. 58 of Ding Bing 丁丙, comp., *Wulin wangzhe yizhu* 武林往哲遺著 (Works of the bygone sages from Hangzhou). Qiantang: Dingshi Jiahuitang, 1898–1900.

Gui Maoyi 歸懋儀. *Xiuyu xucao* 繡餘續草 (More scribbles in time left from embroidery). Shanghai: Lishi, 1832. Copy in the Harvard-Yenching Library.

Guoli gugong bowuyuan: cixiu 國立故宮博物院: 刺繡 (Embroidery in the collection of National Palace Museum). Tokyo: Gakken, 1970; reprinted—1982.

Guoli zhongyang daxue gongtong xueke 國立中央大學共同學科 (National Central University, Common Program), ed. *Ming-Qing zhiji Zhongguo wenhua de zhuanbian yu yanxu* 明清之際中國文化的轉變與延續 (Changes and continuities of Chinese culture during the Ming-Qing transition). Taibei: Wenshizhe chubanshe, 1991.

Hamashima Atsutoshi 浜島敦俊. *Mindai Kōnan nōson shakai no kenkyū* 明代江南農村社會の研究 (A study of rural society in Ming Jiangnan). Tokyo: Tōkyō daigaku shuppankai, 1982.

Han Lifan 韓黎范. "Jie nannü zhi zhenqing, fa mingjiao zhi weiyao" 借男女之真情, 发名教之伪药 (True love between man and woman exposes Confucian moralism as faked medicine). In *Ming-Qing xiaoshuo luncong* 明清小说论丛 (Studies in Ming-Qing fiction), vol. 1. Shenyang: Chunfang wenyi chubanshe, 1984.

Han Xiduo 韩锡铎 and Wang Qingyuan 王清原, eds. *Xiaoshuo shufang lu* 小說书坊录 (Information on stories and their publishers). Shenyang: Chunfang wenyi chubanshe, 1987.

Han-Ajia bunka kōryū sentā 汎亞細亞文化交流センター (Center for Pan-Asian cultural exchange), ed. *Chūgoku rekidai joseizō ten zuroku* 中国歴代女性像展図録 (Representations of Chinese women through the dynasties: an exhibition catalog). Tokyo: Han-Ajia bunka kōryū sentā, 1987.

Hanan, Patrick. *The Chinese Vernacular Story.* Cambridge, Mass.: Harvard University Press, 1981.

———. *The Invention of Li Yü.* Cambridge, Mass.: Harvard University Press, 1988.

Handlin-Smith, Joanna. *Action in Late Ming Thought: The Reorientation of Lü K'un and Other Scholar-Officials.* Berkeley: University of California Press, 1983.

———. "Gardens in Ch'i Piao Chia's Social World: Wealth and Values in Late Ming Kiangnan." *Journal of Asian Studies* 51 (1992): 55–81.

Handlin[-Smith], Joanna. "Lü Kun's New Audience: The Influence of Women's Literacy on Sixteenth-Century Thought." In Margery Wolf and Roxane Witke, eds., *Women in Chinese Society*. Stanford: Stanford University Press, 1975.

Hangzhou lishi congbian bianji weiyuanhui 杭州历史丛编编辑委員会, ed. *Yuan-Ming-Qing mingcheng Hangzhou* 元明清名城杭州 (Hangzhou, a renowned city in the Yuan, Ming, and Qing dynasties). Zhejiang: Zhejiang renmin chubanshe, 1990.

He Lezhi 何乐之, ed. *Mingkan mingshantu banhuaji* 明刊名山图版画集 (Pictures of famous mountains: A collection of Ming woodblock prints). Shanghai: Renmin meishu chubanshe, 1958.

Hershatter, Gail. "Sex Work and Social Order: Prostitutes, Their Families, and the State in Twentieth-Century Shanghai." In *Family Process and Political Process in Modern Chinese History*, pt. 2. 2 vols. Taibei: Academia Sinica, Institute of Modern History, 1992.

Hinsch, Bret. *Passions of the Cut Sleeve: The Male Homosexual Tradition in China*. Berkeley: University of California Press, 1990.

Hirose Reiko 広瀬玲子. "Mindai denki no bungaku: Tō Kenso no gikyoku ni okeru shinri hyōgen o chūshin toshite" 明代伝奇の文学: 湯顕祖の戯曲における心理表現を中心として (Ming Southern-style drama as literature: psychological expressions in the plays of Tang Xianzu). *Tōyō bunka* 東洋文化 71 (Dec. 1990): 55–90.

———. "Zō Bōjun ni yoru *Botantei kankonki* no kaihen ni tsuite" 臧懋循による牡丹亭還魂記の改編について (Zang Maoxun's revision of *The Peony Pavilion*). *Tōhōgaku* 東方學 81 (1991): 71–86.

Ho, Ping-t'i. *The Ladder of Success in Imperial China: Aspects of Social Mobility, 1368–1911*. New York: Columbia University Press, 1962.

———. "The Salt Merchants of Yang-chou: A Study of Commercial Capitalism in Eighteenth-Century China." *Harvard Journal of Asiatic Studies* 17 (1954): 130–68.

Holmgren, Jennifer. "The Economic Foundations of Virtue: Widow-Remarriage in Early and Modern China." *Australian Journal of Chinese Affairs* 13 (1985): 1–27.

Hong Liang 洪亮. "Ming nüshiren Ni Renji de cixiu he faxiu" 明女诗人倪仁吉的刺绣和发绣 (Embroidery in thread and in hair by Ni Renji, a Ming dynasty woman poet). *Wenwu cankao ziliao* 文物參考資料 9 (1958): 21–22.

Hong Sheng 洪昇. *Changsheng dian* 長生殿 (Palace of eternal youth). 1688. Reprinted—Beijing: Renmin wenxue chubanshe, 1980.

Honig, Emily. *Creating Chinese Ethnicity: Subei People in Shanghai, 1850–1980*. New Haven: Yale University Press, 1992.

Hsia, C. T. "Time and the Human Condition in the Plays of T'ang Hsien-tsu." In Wm. Theodore de Bary et al., *Self and Society in Ming Thought*. New York: Columbia University Press, 1970.

Hu Baoyi 胡抱一, comp. *Benchao mingyuan shichao* 本朝名媛詩鈔 (Poems of renowned ladies from the present dynasty). N.p., preface 1766. Copy in the Naikaku bunko.

Hu Ji 胡忌 and Liu Zhizhong 刘致中. "Lun jiaban nüxi" 论家班女戏 (On domestic female drama troupes). *Xiju yishu* 戏剧艺术, no. 4, *zong* 24 (Nov. 1983): 60–68.

Hu Pu'an 胡朴安, comp. *Zhonghua quanguo fengsuzhi* 中华全国风俗志 (Local customs in China). 2 vols. Hebei: Hebei Renmin chubanshe, 1986.

Hu Wenkai 胡文楷. *Lidai funü zhuzuo kao* 歷代婦女著作考 (An examination of women's writing through the dynasties). Shanghai: Shanghai guji chubanshe, 1985.

———. "Liu Rushi nianpu" 柳如是年譜 (A year-by-year account of Liu Rushi). *Dongfang zazhi* 東方雜誌 43, no. 3 (1947): 37–47.

Huaipu jushi 懷圃居士, ed. *Liu Rushi shiji* 柳如是事輯 (The life and deeds of Liu Rushi). Beiping: Wenzi tongmengshe, 1930.

Huang Lizhen 黃麗貞. *Li Yu yanjiu* 李漁研究 (A study of Li Yu). Taibei: Chunwenxue chubanshe, 1974.

Huang, Philip. *The Peasant Family and Rural Development in the Yangzi Delta, 1350–1988.* Stanford: Stanford University Press, 1990.

Huang, Ray. *1587: A Year of No Significance.* New Haven: Yale University Press, 1981.

Huang Ruheng 黃汝亨. *Yulin ji* 寓林集 (Collection from dwelling in the woods). N.p., 1624. Copy in the Naikaku bunko.

Huang Yizheng 黃一正, comp. *Shiwu ganzhu* 事物紺珠 (Names of things on memory beads). N.p., prefaced 1591. Copy in the Library of Congress.

Hucker, Charles O. *A Dictionary of Official Titles in Imperial China.* Stanford: Stanford University Press, 1985.

Hummel, Arthur, ed. *Eminent Chinese of the Ch'ing Period.* 2 vols. Washington, D.C.: U.S. Government Printing Office, 1943–44.

Inoue Susumu 井上進. "Zōsho to dokusho" 藏書と讀書 (Book collection and readership). *Tōhō gakuhō* 東方學報 62 (Mar. 1990): 409–45.

Isobe Akira 磯部彰. "Minmatsu ni okeru *Saiyūki* no shutaiteki juyōsō ni kansuru kenkyū" 明末における「西遊記」の主体的受容層に関する研究 (A study of the primary audience of *Journey to the West* in the late Ming period). *Shūkan Tōyōgaku* 集刊東洋學 44 (Oct. 1980): 50–63.

Ji Shuying 冀叔英. "Tantan Mingkeben ji kegong" 談談明刻本及刻工 (Ming editions and woodblock carvers). *Wenxian* 文献, no. 7 (Mar. 1981): 211–31.

Jia Shen 賈伸. *Zhonghua funü chanzu kao* 中華婦女纏足考 (A study of footbinding among Chinese women). Beijing: Cixiang gongchang, 1925.

Jiajing Weiyang zhi 嘉靖維揚志 (Gazetteer of Yangzhou compiled in the Jiajing period). Preface dated 1542. Reprinted—Shanghai guji shudian, 1981.

Jiangdu Yangshuxiang Sunshi zupu 江都楊墅巷孫氏族譜 (Genealogy of the Sun family of Yangshuxiang, Jiangdu). 1868. Copy in the Tōyō bunko.

Jianjian Jushi 戔戔居士. "Xiaoqing zhuan" 小青傳 (Biography of Xiaoqing). In Qinhuai yuke 秦淮寓客, *Luchuang nüshi* 綠窗女史 (Lady scholars from the green window). Ming edition. Copy in the Library of Congress.

Jiao Xun 焦循. *Ju shuo* 劇說 (Discourses on drama). Vol. 2, no. 9, of *Zhongguo wenxue cankao ziliao xiao congshu* 中國文學參考資料小叢書 (Pocket-size collectanea of references in Chinese literature). Shanghai: Gudian wenxue chubanshe, 1957.

Jiaxing fuzhi 嘉興府志 (Gazetteer of Jiaxing prefecture). 1866.

Jiaxing xianzhi 嘉興縣志 (Gazetteer of Jiaxing county). 1892.

Johnson, David. "Epic and History in Early China: The Matter of Wu Tzu-hsü." *Journal of Asian Studies* 40 (1981): 255–71.

Johnson, David, Andrew Nathan, and Evelyn Rawski, eds. *Popular Culture in Late Imperial China*. Berkeley: University of California Press, 1985.

Johnson, Kay Ann. *Women, the Family and Peasant Revolution in China*. Chicago: University of Chicago Press, 1983.

[*Ke*]*falin zhaotianzhu* [刻]法林照天燭 (Candles that shine unto heaven in the forest of law). N.p., Ming edition. Copy in the Library of Congress.

Kelly, Joan. *Women, History and Theory: The Essays of Joan Kelly*. Chicago: University of Chicago Press, 1984.

Kishibe Shigeo 岸辺成雄, ed. *Jukkyō shakai no joseitachi* 儒教社會の女性たち (Women in Confucian society). Tokyo: Hyōron sha, 1977.

Kishimoto Mio 岸本美緒. "Minmatsu Shinsho no chihō shakai to 'seron'" 明末清初の地方社会と「世論」(Local society and public opinion in the late Ming and early Qing). *Rekishikagu kenkyū* 歴史學研究 573 (Oct. 1987): 131–40.

———. "Min-Shin jidai no kyōshin" 明清時代の郷紳 (The local gentry in the Ming-Qing period). In *Ken'i to kenryoku* 権威と権力 (Authority and power). Vol. 7 of *Shirizu sekkaishi e no toi* シリーズ世界史への問い (In search of world history series). Tokyo: Iwanami shoten, 1990.

———. "*Rekinenki* ni miru Shinsho chihō shakai no seikatsu" 「歴年記」に見る清初地方社会の生活 (Portraits of early Qing local life as seen from the *Linian ji*). *Shigaku zasshi* 史學雜誌 95, no. 6 (June 1986): 53–77.

Ko, Dorothy. "The Complicity of Women in the Qing Good Woman Cult." In *Family Process and Political Process in Modern Chinese History*, pt. 1. 2 vols. Taibei: Academia Sinica, Institute of Modern History, 1992.

———. "Lady-Scholar at the Door: The Practice of Gender Relations in Eighteenth-Century Suzhou." In John Hay, ed. *Boundaries in China*. London: Reaktion Books, forthcoming.

———. "Pursuing Talent and Virtue: Education and Women's Culture in Seventeenth- and Eighteenth-Century China." *Late Imperial China* 13, no. 1 (June 1992): 9–39.

———. "Toward a Social History of Women in Seventeenth-Century China." Ph.D. dissertation, Stanford University, 1989.

Kondo, Dorinne. *Crafting Selves: Power, Gender, and Discourses of Identity in a Japanese Workplace*. Chicago: University of Chicago Press, 1990.

Kuhn, Philip. "Chinese Views of Social Classification." In James Watson, ed., *Class and Social Stratification in Post-Revolutionary China*. Cambridge, Eng.: Cambridge University Press, 1984.

K'ung, Shang-jen. *The Peach Blossom Fan*. Trans. Chen Shih-Hsiang and Harold Acton. Berkeley: University of California Press, 1976.

Laing, Ellen Johnston. "Wives, Daughters, and Lovers: Three Ming Dynasty Women Painters." In *Views from Jade Terrace: Chinese Women Artists, 1300–1912*. Indianapolis: Indianapolis Museum of Art; New York: Rizzoli, 1988.

Landes, Joan B. *Women and the Public Sphere in the Age of the French Revolution*. Ithaca: Cornell University Press, 1988.

Lei Jin 雷瑨 and Lei Jian 雷瑊, eds. *Guixiu cihua* 閨秀詞話 (Lady song-lyric poets). Shanghai: Saoye shanfang, 1916.

Lerner, Gerda. *The Creation of Patriarchy*. Oxford: Oxford University Press, 1986.

Levy, Howard. *Chinese Footbinding: The History of a Curious Erotic Custom*. New York: Bell, 1967. Reprinted—Taibei: Southern Materials Center, 1984.

Levy, Howard, trans. *A Feast of Mist and Flowers: The Gay Quarters of Nanking at the End of the Ming (Pan-ch'iao tsa-chi, by Yu Huai)*. Yokohama: Privately printed, 1966.

———. *Warm-Soft Village*. Tokyo: Dai Nippon, 1964.

Lewis, Mark Edward. *Sanctioned Violence in Early China*. Albany: State University of New York Press, 1990.

Li Chi: Book of Rites. 2 vols. Trans. James Legge. Oxford University Press, 1885. Reprinted—New Hyde Park, N.Y.: University Books, 1967.

Li Ruizhi 李濬之. *Qing huajia shishi* 清畫家詩史 (Poetic biographies of Qing painters). N.p., 1930.

Li Xiaojiang 李小江. *Xiawa de tansuo* 夏娃的探索 (The gropings of Eve). He'nan: He'nan renmin chubanshe, 1988.

Li Yu 李漁. *Li Yu quanji* 李漁全集 (Complete works). 15 vols. Ed. Helmut Martin. Taibei: Chengwen chubanshe, 1970.

Li Zhizhong 李致忠. *Lidai keshu kaoshu* 历代刻书考述 (An examination of printing in the previous dynasties). Chengdu: Bashu shushe, 1990.

Lin Xidan 林錫旦. *Suxiu manhua* 苏绣漫话 (Random chats on Suzhou embroidery). Jiangsu: Renmin chubanshe, 1981.

Liu Xiang 劉向. *Lienü zhuan* 列女傳 (Biographies of exemplary women). Shanghai: Shangwu, 1936.

Liu Xuan 刘宣. "Guanyu 'xinjian Xu Fangqing daowangshi' di zhiyi" 关于"新見许芳卿悼亡诗"的质疑 (Queries about the so-called newly discovered poems by Xu Fangqing for her deceased husband). *Wenxian* 文献 26 (Apr. 1985): 193–210.

Liu Yongcong 刘咏聪. "Qingdai qianqi guanyu nüxing yingfou you 'cai' zhi taolun" 清代前期关于女性应否有"才"之讨论 (Debates on whether women should have talent or not in the first half of the Qing dyansty). *Zhonghua wenshi luncong* 中华文史论丛 45 (1989): 315–43.

Liu Yunfen 劉雲份, comp. *Mingyuan shigui Cuilouji* 名媛詩歸翠樓集 (The Jade Pavilion collection of women's verse). 1673. Reprinted—Vol. 1, no. 24, of *Zhongguo wenxue zhenben congshu* 中國文學珍本叢書 (Collectanea of gems of Chinese literature). Shanghai: Beiye shanfang, 1936.

Liu Zhiqin 刘志琴. "Wan Ming chengshi fengshang chutan" 晚明城市风尚初探 (A preliminary study of late-Ming urban culture). *Zhongguo wenhua yanjiu jikan* 中國文化研究集刊 1 (1984): 190–208.

Lo, Irving Yucheng. "Daughters of the Muses of China." In *Views from Jade Terrace: Chinese Women Artists, 1300–1912*. Indianapolis: Indianapolis Museum of Art; New York: Rizzoli, 1988.

Lougee, Carolyn C. *Le Paradis des Femmes: Women, Salons, and Social Stratification in Seventeenth-Century France.* Princeton: Princeton University Press, 1976.

Lu Chang 陸昶, comp. *Lichao mingyuan shici* 歷朝名媛詩詞 (Poetry and song lyrics by renowned ladies from the past dynasties). 12 *juan*. N.p., 1773. Copy in the Library of Congress.

Lu Hsün [Lu Xun]. *The Selected Works of Lu Hsün,* 4 vols. Trans. Yang Hsien-i and Gladys Yang. Beijing: Foreign Languages Press, 1957–59.

Lu Qingzi 陸卿子. *Kaopan ji* 考槃集 (Building a hermitage). N.p., 1600. Copy in the Naikaku bunko.

———. *Xuanzhi ji* 玄芝集 (Magical herbs). N.p., preface 1610. Copy in the Naikaku bunko.

Lu Shengji 陸聖姬 and Sang Zhenbai 桑貞白. *Zuili erji changhe* 攜李二姬倡和 (Harmonized poems by two ladies from Xieli). N.p., Ming edition. Copy in the Naikaku bunko.

Lu Yong 陸容. *Shu Yuan zaji* 菽園雜記 (Random notes from Shu Yuan). Reprinted—Beijing: Zhonghua shuju, 1985.

Ma Zhaozheng 马兆政 and Zhou Feitong 周苇棠. *Zhongguo gudai funü mingren* 中国古代妇女名人 (Famous women from China's past). Beijing: Zhongguo funü chubanshe, 1988.

Mackerras, Colin. *The Chinese Theatre in Modern Times: From 1840 to the Present Day.* Amherst: University of Massachusetts Press, 1975.

Makino Shuji 牧野修二. "Gendai no jugaku kyōiku" 元代の儒學教育 (Confucian education in the Yuan dynasty). *Tōyōshi kenkyū* 東洋史研究 37, no. 4 (Mar. 1979): 59–63.

Mann, Susan. "'Fuxue' (Women's Learning) by Zhang Xuecheng (1738–1801): China's First History of Women's Culture." *Late Imperial China* 13, no. 1 (June 1992): 40–56.

———. "Grooming a Daughter for Marriage: Brides and Wives in the Mid-Ch'ing Period." In Rubie Watson and Patricia Ebrey, eds., *Marriage and Inequality in Chinese Society.* Berkeley: University of California Press, 1991.

———. "Household Handicrafts and State Policy in Qing Times." In Jane Kate Leonard and John R. Watt, eds., *To Achieve Security and Wealth: The Qing Imperial State and the Economy, 1644–1911.* Ithaca: Cornell University, East Asia Program, 1992.

———. "Widows in the Kinship, Class, and Community Structures of Qing Dynasty China." *Journal of Asian Studies* 46 (1987): 37–56.

———. "Women's Work and the Household Economy." Paper presented at the Eighth Berkshire Conference on the History of Women, Rutgers, The State University of New Jersey, June 8–10, 1990.

Mao Qiling 毛奇齡. *Xihe heji* 西河合集 (Combined collected works of Mao Xihe [Qiling]). 1720 edition.

Mao Xiaotong 毛效同, comp. *Tang Xianzu yanjiu ziliao huibian* 湯顯祖研究資料彙編 (Source materials for the study of Tang Xianzu). 2 vols. Shanghai: Shanghai guji chubanshe, 1986.

Marmé, Michael. "Population and Possibility in Ming (1368–1644) Suzhou: A Quantified Model." *Ming Studies* 12 (Spring 1981): 29–64.

Mason, Amelia Gere. *The Women of the French Salons.* New York: Century, 1891.

McDermott, Joseph. "The Chinese Domestic Bursar." *Asian Cultural Studies,* special issue (1990): 13–30.

Mei Dingzuo 梅鼎祚 [Yusheng 禹生; Yujin 禹金], comp. *Qingni lianhuaji* 青泥蓮花記 (Lotus in dark mud). 13 *juan.* N.p., ca. 1600, Reprinted—*Ming-Qing wenyan xiaoshuo xuankan* 明清文言小說选刊 (Selected reprints of classical fiction from the Ming and Qing dynasties). He'nan: Zhengzhou guji chubanshe, 1988.

Meng Fanshu 孟繁樹. "Lun *Changsheng dian* zhong di qing" 论「長生殿」中的情 (*Qing* in the *Palace of Eternal Youth*). *Yangzhou shiyuan xuebao: shehui kexue ban* 揚州师院学报(社会科学版) 1, *zong* 54 (Mar. 1984): 50–56.

Meng Sen 孟森. "Hengbo furen kao" 橫波夫人考 (A study of Madame Hengbo [Gu Mei]). *Xinshi congkan, wai yi zhong* 心史丛刊, 外一种 (Collected essays of Meng Sen, and one miscellaneous title). Changsha: Yuelu shushe, 1986.

Mingyuan shigui chao 名媛詩歸鈔 (Copy of poetry from renowned ladies). N.p., n.d. Handwritten copy in the Tōyō bunko.

Miyazaki Ichisada 宮崎市定. "Minmatsu-Shinsho to iu jidai" 明末清初という時代 (The late Ming–early Qing period). In Shibuya kuritsu Shōtō bijutsukan 渋谷区立松濤美術館 (Shōtō Museum, Shibuya-ward), ed., *Chūgoku no kaiga: Minmatsu-Shinsho* 中國の絵画: 明末清初 (Chinese paintings from the late Ming–early Qing period). Tokyo: Shōtō bijitsukan, 1991.

Mogi Keiichirō 茂木計一郎, Inaji Toshirō 稲次敏郎, and Katayama Kazutoshi 片山和俊. *Chūgoku minkyo no kūkan o saguru* 中國民居の空間を探る (Space in Chinese vernacular architecture). Tokyo: Kenchiku shiryō kenkyūsha, 1991.

Mohanty, Chandra Talpade. "Under Western Eyes: Feminist Scholarship and Colonial Discourses." In idem, Ann Russo, and Lourdes Torres, eds., *Third World Women and the Politics of Feminism.* Bloomington: Indiana University Press, 1991.

Mori Masao 森正夫. "Minmatsu no shakaikankei ni okeru chitsujo no hendō ni tsuite" 明末の社会関係における秩序の変動について (Changes in the hierarchies of social relations in the late Ming period). *Nagoya daigaku bungakubu sanjisshūnen kinen ronshū* 名古屋大学文学部三十週年記念論集 (1979): 135–59.

Mori Masao, ed. *Kōnan deruta shichin kenkyū* 江南デルタ市鎮研究 (A study of townships in the Jiangnan delta). Nagoya: Nagoya daigaku shuppankai, 1992.

Morohashi Tetsuji 諸橋轍次. *Daikanwa jiten* 大漢和辭典 (Chinese-Japanese dictionary). Tokyo: Taishukan, 1955. Reprinted—1971.

Mote, Frederick W., and Hung-lam Chu. *Calligraphy and the East Asian Book.* Ed. Howard L. Goodman. Boston: Shambhala, 1989.

Mowry, Hua-yuan Li. *Chinese Love Stories from "Ch'ing-shih."* Hamden, Conn.: Archon Books, 1983.

Myerhoff, Barbara. *Number Our Days*. New York: Simon & Schuster, 1978.

Nagasawa Kikuya 長澤規矩也, ed. *Mindai sōzubon zuroku* 明代插図本図錄 (Pictures from Ming illustrated books). Tokyo: Nihon shoshi gakkai, 1962.

———. *Min-Shin zokugo jisetsu shūsei* 明清俗語辞説集成 (Collections of Ming and Qing colloquialisms). 2 vols. Tokyo: Kyūko shoin, 1974.

Nakayama [Kishimoto] Mio 中山美緒. "Shindai zenki Kōnan no bukka dōkō" 清代前期江南の物価動向 (The secular trend of commodity prices in Jiangnan in the first half of the Qing period). *Tōyōshi kenkyū* 東洋史研究 37, no. 4 (Mar. 1979): 77–106.

Naquin, Susan, and Evelyn Rawski. *Chinese Society in the Eighteenth Century*. New Haven: Yale University Press, 1987.

Ng, Vivien. *Madness in Late Imperial China: From Illness to Deviance*. Norman: University of Oklahoma Press, 1990.

Niida Noboru 仁井田陞. *Chūgoku no dentō to kakumei 2: Niida Noboru shū* 中国の伝統と革命: 仁井田陞集 (The tradition and revolution of China: collected works of Niida Noboru). Tokyo: Heibunsha, 1974.

O'Hara, Albert. *The Position of Woman in Early China*. Reprinted—Taipei: Mei Ya Publications, 1971.

Okamoto Ryūzō 岡本隆三. *Tensoku monogatari* 纏足物語 (The footbinding story). Tokyo: Tōhō shoten, 1986.

Okamoto Sae 岡本さえ. "Tō Kokuki to Shinsho Kōnan" 佟国器と清初江南 (Tong Guoqi and early Qing Jiangnan). *Tōyōbunka kenkyūjo kiyō* 東洋文化研究所紀要 106 (Mar. 1988): 95–162.

Ōki Yasushi 大木康. "Fū Muryū *Sangen* no hensan ito ni tsuite (zoku): 'Shinjō' yori mita ichi sokumen" 馮夢龍「三言」の編纂意圖について(續): 眞情より見た一側面 (The editorial intention of Feng Menglong's *Sanyan*: from the vantage point of sincere love). In *Itō Sōhei kyōju taikankinen Chūgoku bungaku ronsō* 伊藤漱平教授退官記念中國文学論集 (Essays on Chinese literature: volume commemorating the retirement of Professor Itō Sōhei). Tokyo: Kyūko shoin, 1986.

———. "Minmatsu Kōnan ni okeru shuppan bunka no kenkyū" 明末江南における出版文化の研究 (A study of the print culture in late Ming Jiangnan). *Hiroshima daigaku bungakubu kiyō* 広島大学文学部紀要 50, special issue no. 1 (Jan. 1991): 1–176.

———. "Minmatsu ni okeru hakuwa shōsetsu no sakusha to dokusha ni tsuite: Isobe Akira shi no shosetsu ni yosete" 明末における白話小說の作者と読者について: 磯部彰氏の所説に寄せて (Authorship and readership of late Ming vernacular fiction: in light of Mr. Isobe Akira's arguments). *Mindaishi kenkyū* 明代史研究 12 (1984): 1–15.

Okuzaki Hiroshi 奥崎裕司. *Chūgoku kyōshin jinushi no kenkyū* 中國鄉紳地主の研究 (Studies in Chinese local gentry-landlords). Tokyo: Kyūko shoin, 1978.

———. "Soshūfu Gokōken no kyōshin Goshi no kakei" 蘇州府吳江県の鄉紳吳氏の家系 (Genealogies of the Wu family, a local gentry family in Wujiang, Suzhou prefecture). In *Sakai Tadao sensei kokishukuga kinen no kai* 酒井忠夫先生古稀祝賀記念の会 (Committee to commemorate the seventieth birthday of Professor Sakai Tadao), ed., *Rekishi ni okeru minshū to bunka* 歴史における民衆と文化 (People and culture in history). Tokyo: Kokusho kankōkai, 1982.

Ono Kazuko. *Chinese Women in a Century of Revolution, 1850–1950*. Ed. Joshua A. Fogel. Stanford: Stanford University Press, 1989.

Ōtsuka Hidetaka 大塚秀高. "Kunai bungaku no nagare: Shōseiden o ronjite Ri Gyo ni oyobu" 懼內文学の流れ: 小青伝を論じて李漁に及ぶ (The literary tradition of henpecked husbands: a discussion of the Xiaoqing story with a brief reference to Li Yu). *Saitama daigaku kiyō, Kyōyō gakubu* 埼玉大学紀要, 教養学部 25 (1989): 82–108.

Pan Guangdan 潘光旦. "Feng Xiaoqing kao" 馮小青考 (Study of Feng Xiaoqing). *Funü zazhi* 婦女雜誌 10 (1924): 1706–17.

———. *Ming-Qing liangdai Jiaxing de wangzu* 明清兩代嘉興的望族 (Notable families in Jiaxing in the Ming and Qing dynasties). 1947. Reprinted—Shanghai: Shanghai shudian, 1991.

———. "Shu Feng Xiaoqing quanji hou" 書馮小青全集後 (Afterword to the collected works of Feng Xiaoqing). 2 pts. *Renjianshi* 人間世 29 (1935): 19–22; 30 (1935): 19–21.

———. "Xiaoqing kaozheng bulu" 小青考証補錄 (Supplementary notes on the study of Xiaoqing). 2 pts. *Renjianshi* 人間世 1, no. 2 (1934): 18–21; 1, no. 3 (1934): 11–15.

———. *Xiaoqing zhi fenxi* 小青之分析 (Analyzing Xiaoqing). Shanghai: Xinyue shudian, 1927.

Peiwen yunfu 佩文韻府 (The Peiwen [emperor Kangxi's studio] dictionary of rhymes). Ca. 1713. Reprinted—Taibei: Shangwu, 1966.

Peterson, Willard. *Bitter Gourd: Fang I-chih and the Impetus for Intellectual Change*. New Haven: Yale University Press, 1979.

Pfister, Louis, S. J. *Notices biographiques et bibliographiques sur les Jesuites de Chine*. 1932. Reprinted—Nendeln, Liechtenstein: Kraus-Thomson, 1971.

Pruitt, Ida. *A Daughter of Han*. Stanford: Stanford University Press, 1967.

Qi Biaojia 祁彪佳. *Qi Biaojia ji* 祁彪佳集 (Collected works). 1835. Reprinted—Beijing: Zhonghua shuju, 1960.

———. *Qi Zhongmin gong riji* 祁忠敏公日記 (Diaries of Qi Biaojia, posthumous title Zhongmin). Yuanshan tang, n.d.; reprinted—Shaoxing: Shaoxing xiuzhi weiyuanhui, 1937.

Qi Deqiong 祁德琼. *Weifen ji* 未焚集 (Collection yet to be committed to the fire). In *Qi Biaojia ji* (Collected works of Qi Biaojia). Beijing: Zhonghua shuju, 1960.

Qian Qianyi 錢謙益. *Muzhai Chuxue ji* 牧齋初學集 (Work of rudimentary learning by Qian Muzhai [Qianyi]). 1641. In *Sibu congkan* 四部叢刊, *ce* 32, *han* 4. Shanghai: Shangwu, 1929.

Qian Qianyi, ed. *Liechao shiji* 列朝詩集 (Poetry from the dynasties). 81 *juan*. 1652. Reprinted—Shanghai: Guoguang yinshuashuo, 1910.

Qiantang xianzhi 錢塘縣志 (Gazetteer of Qiantang county). Preface 1718.

Rawski, Evelyn. *Agricultural Change and the Peasant Economy of South China*. Cambridge, Mass.: Harvard University Press, 1972.

———. "Economic and Social Foundation of Late Imperial Culture." In David Johnson et al., eds., *Popular Culture in Late Imperial China.* Berkeley: University of California Press, 1985.

———. *Education and Popular Literacy in Ch'ing China.* Ann Arbor: University of Michigan Press, 1979.

———. "Research Themes in Ming-Qing Socioeconomic History: The State of the Field." *Journal of Asian Studies* 50 (1991): 84–111.

Ren Zhaolin 任兆麟 and Zhang Yunzi 張允滋, comps. *Wuzhong nüshi shichao* 吳中女士詩鈔 (Poetry of Suzhou ladies). N.p., 1789.

Renhe xianzhi 仁和縣志 (Gazetter of Renhe county). 1686.

Robertson, Maureen. "Voicing the Feminine: Constructions of the Gendered Subject in Lyric Poetry by Women of Medieval and Late Imperial China." *Late Imperial China* 13, no. 1 (June 1992): 63–110.

Ropp, Paul. "Between Two Worlds: Women in Shen Fu's *Six Chapters of a Floating Life.*" In Anna Gerstlacher, ed., *Women and Literature in China.* Bochum, Ger.: Brockmeyer, 1985.

———. *Dissent in Early Modern China: "Ju-lin Wai-shih" and Ch'ing Social Criticism.* Ann Arbor: University of Michigan Press, 1981.

———. "The Seeds of Change: Reflections on the Condition of Women in the Early and Mid Ch'ing." *Signs* 2 (1976): 5–23.

———. "Shi Zhenlin and the Poetess Shuangqing: Gender, Class, and Literary Talent in an Eighteenth-Century Memoir." Paper presented at the "Engendering China" conference, Harvard and Wellesley Universities, Feb. 7–9, 1992.

Ropp, Paul, ed. *Heritage of China: Contemporary Perspectives on Chinese Civilization.* Berkeley: University of California Press, 1990.

Rowe, William. *Hankow: Commerce and Society in a Chinese City, 1796–1889.* Stanford: Stanford University Press, 1984.

———. *Hankow: Conflict and Community in a Chinese City, 1796–1895.* Stanford: Stanford University Press, 1989.

———. "Women and the Family in Mid-Qing Social Thought: The Case of Chen Hongmou." *Late Imperial China* 13, no. 2 (Dec. 1992): 1–41.

Roy, David T. "The Theme of the Neglected Wife in the Poetry of Ts'ao Chih." *Journal of Asian Studies* 19 (1959): 25–31.

Ruan Yuan 阮元. *Liang Zhe youxuan lu* 兩浙輶軒錄 (Light vehicle in Liang Zhe), 40 *juan.* Zhejiangju, 1890.

Schafer, Edward. *The Divine Woman.* San Francisco: North Point, 1980.

Saeki Junko 佐伯順子. *Yūjo no bunkashi* 遊女の文化史 (A cultural history of courtesans). Tokyo: Chūōkōron sha, 1987.

Sakai Tadao 酒井忠夫. "Mindai no nichiyō ruisho to shomin kyōiku" 明代の日用類書と庶民教育 (Household almanacs and popular education in the Ming). In Hayashi Tomoharu 林友春, ed., *Kinsei Chūgoku kyōiku shi kenkyū* 近世中國教育史研究 (Studies of the history of education in modern China). Tokyo: Kokudo sha, 1958.

Schneider, Laurence. *A Madman of Ch'u: The Chinese Myth of Loyalty and Dissent.* Berkeley: University of California Press, 1980.

Scott, Joan Wallach. *Gender and the Politics of History*. New York: Columbia University Press, 1988.

Shang Jinglan 商景蘭. *Jinnang ji* 錦囊集 (Works from the brocaded pouch). In *Qi Biaojia ji* (Collected works of Qi Biaojia). 1835. Reprinted—Beijing: Zhonghua shuju, 1960.

Shao Fan 邵飄, comp. *Lidai mingyuan zayong* 歷代名媛雜詠 (Miscellaneous chantings by renowned ladies from the past dynasties). 3 *juan*. N.p., 1792. Copy in the Harvard-Yenching Library.

Shen Hongyu 沈弘宇. *Piaodu jiguan* 嫖睹機関 (A guide to the trapdoors of brothels and gambling dens). 2 *juan*. N.p.: Deju tang, n.d. Microfilm copy in the Gest Library.

Shen Yixiu 沈宜修. *Lichui ji* 鸝吹集 (Oriole tunes). In Ye Shaoyuan, ed., *Wumengtang quanji, shang* 午夢堂全集, 上 (Complete works from the Hall of Meridian Dreams). Shanghai: Beiye shanfang, 1935.

Shen Yixiu, ed. *Yirensi* 伊人思 (Her meditations). Preface dated 1636. Copies in the Library of Congress and Naikaku bunko. In Ye Shaoyuan, ed., *Wumengtang quanji, xia* 午夢堂全集, 下 (Complete works from the Hall of Meridian Dreams). Shanghai: Beiye shanfang, 1935.

Shevelow, Kathryn. *Women and Print Culture: The Construction of Femininity in the Early Periodical*. London: Routledge, 1989.

Shi Chengjin 石成金. *Chuanjia bao* 傳家宝 (Family treasures). Yangzhou, 1739.

Shi Shuyi 施淑儀. *Qingdai guige shiren zhenglüe* 清代閨閣詩人徵略 (Brief biographies of refined lady poets from the Qing dynasty). 1922. Reprinted—Shanghai: Shanghai shudian, 1987.

Shi Yushan 施愚山. *Yushan xiansheng wenji* 愚山先生文集 (Collected essays). In *Shi Yushan quan ji* 施愚山全集 (Complete works of Shi Yushan). N.p., 1747.

Shi Zhenlin 史震林. *Huayang san'gao* 華陽散稿 (Loose drafts from Huayang). Vol. 1, no. 9, of *Zhongguo wenxue zhenben congshu* 中國文學珍本叢書 (Collectanea of gems of Chinese literature). Shanghai: Beiye shanfang, 1935.

———. *Xiqing sanji* 西青散記 (Random notes from Xiqing). 1737. Reprinted—Beijing: Zhongguo shudian, 1987.

Shimada Kenji 島田虔次. *Chūgoku ni okeru kindai shii no zasetsu* 中國における近代思維の挫折 (The crushing of modern thoughts in China). Tokyo: Chikuma shobō, 1949.

Shimomi Takao 下見隆雄. *Ryū Kyō "Retsujoden" no kenkyū* 劉向「列女傳」の研究 (A study of Liu Xiang's *Biographies of Exemplary Women*). Tokyo: Tōkai daigaku shuppankai, 1989.

———. "Ryū Kyō *Retsujoden* yori miru jukyō shakai to boseigenri" 劉向「列女傳」より見る儒教社会と母性原理 (The mother-principle in Confucian society as seen from Liu Xiang's *Biographies of Exemplary Women*). *Hiroshima daigaku bungakubu kiyō* 広島大学文学部紀要 50 (Mar. 1991): 1–21.

Silber, Cathy. "From Daughter to Daughter-in-law in the Women's Script of Southern Hunan." In Christina Gilmartin, Gail Hershatter, Lisa Rofel, and Tyrene White, eds., *Engendering China: Women, Culture, and the State*. Cambridge, Mass.: Harvard University Press, 1994.

Smith-Rosenberg, Carroll. "The Female World of Love and Ritual." In Nancy F.

Cott and Elizabeth H. Pleck, eds., *A Heritage of Her Own: Toward a New Social History of American Women*. New York: Simon & Schuster, 1979.

Soong Ching-ling. "Women's Liberation." In Marilyn Young, ed., *Women in China: Studies in Social Change and Feminism*. Ann Arbor: University of Michigan, Center for Chinese Studies, 1973.

Spence, Jonathan, and John Wills, Jr., eds. *From Ming to Ch'ing: Conquest, Region and Continuity in Seventeenth-Century China*. New Haven: Yale University Press, 1979.

Stacey, Judith. *Patriarchy and Socialist Revolution in China*. Berkeley: University of California Press, 1983.

Strassberg, Richard. "The Authentic Self in Seventeenth Century Chinese Drama." *Tamkang Review* 8, no. 2 (Oct. 1977): 61–100.

———. *The World of K'ung Shang-jen: A Man of Letters in Early Ch'ing China*. New York: Columbia University Press, 1983.

Struve, Lynn. *The Southern Ming, 1644–1662*. New Haven: Yale University Press, 1984.

Sun Xingyan 孫星衍. *Wusongyuan wen'gao* 五松園文稿 (Essays drafted in the Five Pine Villa). In idem, comp., *Dainange congshu* 岱南閣叢書 (Collectanea from the Dainan Pavilion). Ca. 1796–1820.

Suzhou fuzhi 蘇州府志 (Gazetteer of Suzhou prefecture). 1883.

Swann, Nancy Lee. *Pan Chao: Foremost Woman Scholar of China*. 1932. Reprinted—New York: Russell & Russell, 1960.

———. "Seven Intimate Library Owners." *Harvard Journal of Asiatic Studies* 1 (1936): 363–90.

Taga Akigorō 多賀秋五郎. *Sōfu no kenkyū* 宗譜の研究 (A study of genealogies). Tokyo: Tōyō bunko, 1960.

Tan Youxia 譚友夏 [Yuanchun 元春]. *Tan Youxia heji* 譚友夏合集 (Combined collected works of Tan Youxia). Vol. 1, no. 8, of *Zhongguo wenxue zhenpan congshu* (Collectanea of gems in Chinese literature). Shanghai: Shanghai zazhi gongshi, 1935.

Tan Zhengbi 譚正璧. *Zhongguo nüxing di wenxue shenghuo* 中國女性的文學生活 (The literary lives of Chinese women). Taibei: Zhuangyan chubanshe, 1982.

———. *Zhongguo nüxing wenxue shihua* 中國女性文學史話 (A history of Chinese women's literature). Tianjin: Baihua wenyi chubanshe, 1984.

Tanaka Issei 田仲一成. "Jūgo-roku seiki o chūshin to suru Kōnan chihōgeki no henshitsu ni tsuite (vi)" 十五～六世紀を中心とする江南地方劇の変質について (The transformed nature of Jiangnan local dramas in the fifteenth and sixteenth centuries, pt. 6). *Tōyōbunka kenkyūjo kiyō* 東洋文化研究所紀要 102 (Jan. 1987): 229–309.

———. "The Social and Historical Context of Ming-Ch'ing Local Drama." In David Johnson, Andrew Nathan, and Evelyn Rawski, eds., *Popular Culture in Late Imperial China*. Berkeley: University of California Press, 1985.

Tang Bin 湯斌. *Tangzi yishu* 湯子遺書 (Posthumous works of Master Tang). In Wu Yuanbing 吳元炳, ed., *Sanxian zhengshu* 三賢政書 (Political writings by the three sages). 1879. Reprinted—Taibei: Xuesheng shuju, 1976.

Tang Xianzu 湯顯祖. *Mudanting* 牡丹亭 (*The Peony Pavilion*). Beijing: Renmin wenxue chubanshe, 1978.

———. *The Peony Pavilion*. Trans. Cyril Birch. Bloomington: Indiana University Press, 1980.

———. *Wu Wushan sanfu heping Mudanting huanhunji* 吳吳山三婦合評牡丹亭還魂記 (*The Peony Pavilion*: Commentary edition by Wu Wushan's three wives). [Commentary by Chen Tong and Qian Yi.] Mengyuan *cangban*, 1694. Copy in University of Tokyo, Tōyō bunka kenkyūjo.

Terada Takanobu 寺田隆信. "Shōkō Kishi no 'Tanseidō' ni tsuite" 紹興祁氏の「澹生堂」について (The Tanshengtang library collection of the Qis in Shaoxing). In *Tōhō gakkai sōritsu yonjisshūnen kinen Tōhōgaku ronshū* 東方学会創立四十週年記念東方学論集 (Essays on Oriental studies: volume commemorating the fortieth anniversary of the Oriental Society). Tokyo, 1987.

Teruoka Yasutaka. "The Pleasure Quarters and Tokugawa Culture." In C. Andrew Gerstle, ed. *Eighteenth Century Japan*. Sydney: Allen & Unwin, 1989.

Tian Yiheng 田藝蘅, comp. *Shinüshi* 詩女史 (Lady-scholars of poetry). 14 *juan*. Preface dated 1557. Copy in the Naikaku bunko.

T'ien, Ju-kang. *Male Anxiety and Female Chastity: A Comparative Study of Chinese Ethical Values in Ming-Ch'ing Times*. Leiden: E. J. Brill, 1988.

Tierney, Helen, ed. *Women's Studies Encyclopedia*. New York: Peter Bedrick Books, 1991.

Tongzhi Suzhou fuzhi 同治蘇州府志 (Gazetteer of Suzhou prefecture compiled in the Tongzhi period). 1883.

Tseng Yu-ho. "Hsueh Wu and Her Orchids in the Collection of the Honolulu Academy of Arts." *Arts Asiatiques* 2 (1955): 197–208.

Tsien Tsuen-Hsuin. *Paper and Printing*. Vol. 5, pt. 1, of Joseph Needham, ed., *Science and Civilization in China*. Cambridge, Eng.: Cambridge University Press, 1985.

Tsung, Shiu-kuen Fan. "Moms, Nuns, and Hookers: Extrafamilial Alternatives for Village Women in Taiwan." Ph.D. dissertation, University of California, San Diego, Department of Anthropology, 1978.

Tu Long 屠隆. *Kaopan yushi* 考槃餘事 (Trivial concerns of a recluse). In Feng Kebin 馮可賓, ed., *Guang baichuan xuehai* 廣百川學海 (An ocean of learning from a hundred wide streams). N.p., Ming edition. Copy in the Naikaku bunko.

Tuan, Yi-Fu. *Space and Place: The Perspective of Experience*. Minneapolis: University of Minnesota Press, 1977.

Ueda Makoto 上田信. "Chiiki to sōzoku: Sekkō-shō sankanbu" 地域と宗族: 浙江省山間部 (Place and lineage in the mountainous regions of Zhejiang). *Tōyō bunka kenkyūjo kiyō* 東洋文化研究所紀要 94 (Mar. 1984): 115–60.

———. "Minmatsu-Shinsho Kōnan no toshi no 'burai' o meguru shakai kankei" 明末清初江南の都市の「無賴」をめぐる社会関係 (The social relations of vagabonds in late Ming–early Qing Jiangnan cities). *Shigaku zasshi* 史学雑誌 90, no. 11 (Nov. 1981): 1–35.

———. "Min-Shinki Settō ni okeru shūken gyōsei to chiiki erito" 明清期浙東における州縣行政と地域エリード (County administration and local elites in eastern Zhejiang in the Ming-Qing period). *Tōyōshi kenkyū* 東洋史研究 46, no. 3 (1987): 71–96.

———. "Mura ni sayō suru jiryoku ni tsuite" 村に作用する磁力について (Magnetic forces at work in a village). 2 pts. *Chūgoku kenkyū geppō* 中國研究月報 455 (Jan. 1986): 1–14; 456 (Feb. 1986): 1–20.

Van Gulik, R. H. *Sexual Life in Ancient China.* Leiden: E. J. Brill, 1974.

Views from Jade Terrace: Chinese Women Artists, 1300–1912. Indianapolis: Indianapolis Museum of Art; New York: Rizzoli, 1988.

Von Glahn, Richard. "The Enchantment of Wealth: The God Wutong in the Social History of Jiangnan." *Harvard Journal of Asiatic Studies* 51 (1991): 651–714.

Wagner, Marsha. *The Lotus Boat: The Origins of Chinese Tz'u Poetry in T'ang Popular Culture.* New York: Columbia University Press, 1984.

Wakeman, Frederic, Jr. "China and the Seventeenth-Century Crisis." *Late Imperial China* 7, no. 1 (June 1986): 7–26.

———. *The Great Enterprise: The Manchu Reconstruction of Imperial Order in Seventeenth-Century China.* 2 vols. Berkeley: University of California Press, 1985.

———. "Localism and Loyalism During the Ch'ing Conquest of Chiang-nan: The Tragedy of Chiang-yin." In idem and Carolyn Grant, eds., *Conflict and Control in Late Imperial China.* Berkeley: University of California Press, 1975.

Waltner, Ann. *Getting an Heir: Adoption and the Construction of Kinship in Late Imperial China.* Honolulu: University of Hawaii Press, 1990.

———. "Learning from a Woman: Ming Literati Responses to Tanyangzi." *International Journal of Social Education* 6, no. 1 (1991): 42–59.

———. "On Not Becoming a Heroine: Lin Dai-yu and Cui Ying-ying." *Signs* 15 (1989): 61–78.

———. "Visionary and Bureaucrat in the Late Ming: T'an-yang-tzu and Wang Shih-chen." *Late Imperial China* 8, no. 1 (June 1987): 105–33.

Wang Anqi 王安祈. *Mingdai chuanqi zhi juchang jiqi yishu* 明代傳奇之劇場及其藝術 (The theater and art of Ming Southern-style drama). Taibei: Xuesheng shuju, 1986.

Wang Duanshu 王端淑. *Yinhong ji* 吟紅集 (Red chantings). Qing edition. Copy in the Naikaku bunko.

Wang Duanshu, comp. *Mingyuan shiwei* 名媛詩緯 (Longitudinal canon of poetry by renowned ladies). 40 *juan*. N.p., 1667. Microfilm copy in the Yale University Library.

Wang Fengxian 王鳳嫻. "Donggui jishi" 東歸紀事 (Records on the eastward return journey). In Zhou Zhibiao 周之標, comp., *Nüzhong qi caizi lanke erji* 女中七才子蘭咳二集 (Second collection of orchid gurglings by seven talented scholars among women). Suzhou: Baohong tang, preface 1650.

Wang Peitang 王培棠. *Jiangsu sheng xiangtu zhi* 江蘇省鄉土誌 (Gazetteer of local customs in Jiangsu province). Changsha: Shangwu, 1938.

Wang Qi 汪淇, comp. *Chidu xinyu* 尺牘新語 (New sayings from letters), *chubian*; *erbian*. N.p., 1663–67. Copy in the Naikaku bunko.

Wang Qishu 汪啟淑, comp. *Xiefang ji* 擷芳集 (Collection of picked fragrances). 80 *juan*. Feihong tang, 1773. Incomplete copy in the National Diet Library, Japan.

Wang Rongzu 汪榮祖. "Rushi jian xianü de Hedongjun" 儒士兼俠女的河東君 (Hedongjun [Liu Rushi]: scholar-cum-female knight errant). *Mingshi yanjiu zhuankan* 明史研究專刊 5 (Dec. 1982): 339–48.

Wang Siren 王思任. *Wang Jizhong shizhong* 王季重十种 (Ten works by Wang Jizhong [Siren]). Ca. 1935. Reprinted—Hangzhou: Zhejiang guji chubanshe, 1987.

———. *Wenfan xiaopin* 文飯小品 (Literature as rice). 1661. Reprinted—Changsha: Yuelu shushe, 1989.

Wang Shunu 王書奴. *Zhongguo changji shi* 中國娼妓史 (A history of Chinese prostitution). Preface 1933. Reprinted—Shanghai: Shanghai Sanlian shudian, 1988.

Wang Wei 王微, ed. *Mingshan jixuan* 名山記選 (Selected records of famous mountains). 20 *juan*. N.p., Chongzhen edition. Incomplete copy in the Gest Library.

Wang Xiang 王相. *Nü sishu jizhu* 女四書集注 (Combined annotated edition of the *Four Books for Women*). N.p.: Shuye tang, 1795.

Wang Xiuqin 王秀琴 and Hu Wenkai 胡文楷, comps. *Lidai mingyuan shujian* 歷代名媛書簡 (Letters by renowned ladies through the dynasties). Changsha: Shangwu, 1941.

Wang Yongjian 王永健. "Lun Wu Wushan sanfu hepingben *Mudanting* jiqi piyu" 论吴山三妇合評本牡丹亭及其批語 (On the "Three Women's Commentary" to *The Peony Pavilion*). *Nanjing daxue xuebao: zhexue shehui kexue* 南京大学学报, 哲学社会科学 no. 4 (1980): 18–26.

Wang Zhuo 王晫 and Zhang Chao 張潮, eds. *Tanji congshu* 檀几叢書 (Collectanea from the sandalwood table). 50 *juan*. Preface 1695. Copy in the Naikaku bunko.

Watson, James. "Chinese Kinship Reconsidered: Anthropological Perspectives on Historical Research." *China Quarterly* 82 (Dec. 1982): 589–622.

Watson, Rubie. "The Named and the Nameless: Gender and Person in Chinese Society." *American Ethnologist* 13 (1986): 619–31.

Watson, Rubie, and Patricia Ebrey, eds. *Marriage and Inequality in Chinese Society*. Berkeley: University of California Press, 1991.

Watt, Ian. *The Rise of the Novel: Studies in Defoe, Richardson and Fielding*. Berkeley: University of California Press, 1964.

Watt, James C. Y. "The Literati Environment." In Chu-tsing Li and James Watt, eds., *The Chinese Scholar's Studio: Artistic Life in the Late Ming Period*. New York: Asia Society Galleries, 1987.

Wei Yinru 魏隱儒. *Zhongguo guji yinshua shi* 中国古代印刷史 (A history of traditional book publishing). Beijing: Yinshua gongye chubanshe, 1988.

Weidner, Marsha. "Ladies of the Lake: The Seventeenth Century Landscape Painters Lin Hsueh, Yang Hui-lin, and Huang Yuan-chieh." Unpublished paper.

———. "Women in the History of Chinese Painting." In *Views from Jade Terrace: Chinese Women Artists, 1300–1912*. Indianapolis: Indianapolis Museum of Art; New York: Rizzoli, 1988.

Weidner, Marsha, ed. *Flowering in the Shadows: Women in the History of Chinese and Japanese Painting.* Honolulu: University of Hawaii Press, 1990.

Widmer, Ellen. "The Epistolary World of Female Talent in Seventeenth-Century China." *Late Imperial China* 10, no. 2 (Dec. 1989): 1–43.

———. "Ming Loyalism and the Woman Writer: From Wang Duanshu (1621–1701?) to Wang Duan (1793–1839)." Paper presented at the Women and Literature in Ming-Qing China conference, Yale University, June 23–26, 1993.

———. "Xiaoqing's Literary Legacy and the Place of the Woman Writer in Late Imperial China." *Late Imperial China* 13, no. 1 (June 1992): 111–55.

Wolf, Margery. *Revolution Postponed: Women in Contemporary China.* Stanford: Stanford University Press, 1985.

Wolf, Margery, and Roxane Witke, eds. *Women in Chinese Society.* Stanford: Stanford University Press, 1975.

Wu Bing 吳炳. *Liaodu geng* 療妒羹 (Jealousy-curing soup). First published in Chongzhen reign, 1628–44. Reprinted—Vol. 3, no. 15, of Guben xiqu congkan biankan weiyuanhui 古本戲曲叢刊編刊委員会 (Editorial committee of collectanea of dramas in their ancient editions), ed., *Guben xiqu congkan* 古本戲曲叢刊 (Collectanea of dramas in their ancient editions). Beijing: Zhonghua shuju, 1957.

Wu Hao 吳顥, comp. *Guochao Hangjun shiji* 國朝杭郡詩輯 (Collected Hangzhou poems from the reigning dynasty). 32 *juan.* Qiantang: Dingshi, 1874. Copy in the Library of Congress.

Wu Jiangxue 吳絳雪. *Xu Liefu shichao* 徐烈婦詩鈔 (Poetry of the martyred Madame Xu [Wu Jiangxue, 1650–74]). Preface dated 1852.

Wu, K. T. "Ming Printing and Printers." *Harvard Journal of Asiatic Studies* 7 (1943): 203–60.

Wu Zhenhua 吳振华. *Hangzhou gugang shi* 杭州古港史 (History of Hangzhou as a port). Beijing: Renmin jiaotong chubanshe, 1989.

Wu, Yenna. *The Chinese Virago: A Literary Theme.* Cambridge, Mass.: Harvard University, Council on East Asian Studies, forthcoming.

———. "The Inversion of Marital Hierarchy: Shrewish Wives and Henpecked Husbands in Seventeenth-Century Chinese Literature." *Harvard Journal of Asiatic Studies* 48 (1988): 363–82.

Wujiang xianzhi 吳江縣志 (Gazetteer of Wujiang county). 1684.

Wujiang xianzhi 吳江縣志 (Gazetteer of Wujiang county). 1747.

Wulin Qianshi zongpu 武林錢氏宗譜 (Genealogy of the Qian family in Wulin [Hangzhou]). Copy in the National Diet Library, Japan.

Wuxian zhi 吳縣志 (Gazetteer of Wu county). 1933.

Xia Shufang 夏樹芳. *Xiaohe ji* 消喝集 (Thirst-quenching collection). N.p., preface 1628.

Xiangyan congshu 香豔叢書 (Collectanea of the fragrant and the beautiful). 20 vols. Shanghai: Guoxue fulun she, 1914.

Xiao Dongfa 肖东发. "Jianyang Yushi keshu kaolue" 建阳余氏刻书考略 (A brief study of the Yu family publishers in Jianyang). 3 pts. *Wenxian* 文献 21 (June 1984?): 230–47; 22 (Dec. 1984): 195–219; 23 (Jan. 1985): 236–50.

———. "Mingdai xiaoshuojia keshujia Yu Xiangdou" 明代小说家、刻书家余象斗 (Yu Xiangdou, a Ming novelist and publisher). In *Ming-Qing xiaoshuo lun-*

cong 明清小说论丛 (Studies in Ming-Qing fiction), vol. 4. Shenyang: Chunfang wenyi chubanshe, 1986.

Xie Zhaozhe 謝肇淛. *Wuzazu* 五雜组 (Five Miscellanies). Ming edition. Reprinted—Beijing: Zhonghua shuju, 1959.

Xiushui xianzhi 秀水縣志 (Gazetteer of Xiushui county). 1596.

Xu Fuming 徐扶明. *"Mudanting" yanjiu ziliao kaoshi* 牡丹亭研究資料考釋 (An examination of source materials for the study of *The Peony Pavilion*). Shanghai: Shanghai guji chubanshe, 1987.

———. *Yuan Ming Qing xiqu tansuo* 元明清戏曲探索 (Studies of dramas from the Yuan, Ming, and Qing dynasties). Hangzhou: Zhejiang guji chubanshe, 1986.

Xu Peiji 许培基. "Suzhou di keshu yu cangshu" 苏州的刻书与藏书 (Publishing and book-collecting in Suzhou). *Wenxian* 26 (Apr. 1985): 211–37.

Xu Shumin 徐樹敏 and Qian Yue 錢岳, comps. *Zhongxiang ci* 衆香詞 (Song lyrics from the fragrant crowd). 6 vols. N.p., ca. 1690. Reprinted—Shanghai: Dadong shuju, 1934.

Xu Shuofang 徐朔方. *Lun Tang Xianzu ji qita* 论湯顯祖及其他 (On Tang Xianzu and others). Shanghai: Shanghai guji chubanshe, 1983.

Xu Tianxiao 徐天嘯. *Shenzhou nüzi xinshi* 神州女子新史 (A new history of women of the Divine Land). Shanghai: Shenzhou tushuju, 1913. Reprinted—Taibei: Shihuo chubanshe, 1988.

Xu Weinan 徐蔚南. *Guxiu kao* 顧繡考 (A study of Gu Family Embroidery). Shanghai: Zhonghua shuju, 1937.

Xu Wenxu 徐文緒. "Qingdai nüxuezhe Wang Zhenyi he tade *Defengting chuji*" 清代女学者王貞仪和她的「德凤亭初集」 (Wang Zhenyi, a Qing woman scholar, and her *Works from the Defeng Pavilion*). *Wenxian* 文献 3 (1980): 211–14.

Xu Yejun 徐野君 [Shijun 士俊]. *Chunbo ying* 春波影 (Shadows on spring wave). 1625. Reprinted—No. 83 of *Songfenshi congkan* 誦芬室叢刊 (Collectanea from the Fragrance-Reciting Studio). N.p., 1916–22.

Xu Yuan 徐媛. *Luowei yin* 絡緯吟 (Shuttling chants). Qiyuan tang, 1613. Facsimile copy in the Tōyō Bunko. The Naikaku bunko has a 1630 edition.

Xu Zi 徐鼐. *Xiaotian jizhuan* 小腆紀傳 (Biographies of Southern Ming loyalists). 65 *juan*. Nanjing: Liuhe Xushi, 1887–88.

Xue Tao. *Brocade River Poems: Selected Works of the Tang Dynasty Courtesan Xue Tao*. Trans. Jeanne Larsen. Princeton: Princeton University Press, 1987.

Yagisawa Hajime 八木澤元. "Fū Shōsei densetsu to sono gikyoku" 馮小青伝 説と其戲曲 (The Feng Xiaoqing legend and dramas). 2 pts. *Kangakkai zasshi* 漢学会雑誌 4, no. 3 (1936): 81–91; 5, no. 2 (1937): 72–89.

———. "Mindai joryū gekisakka Yō Shōgan ni tsuite" 明代女流劇作家葉小紈 について (Ye Xiaowan, a Ming dynasty woman dramatist). *Tōhōgaku* 東方学 5 (1982): 85–98.

———. "Shōsei den no shiryō" 小青伝の資料 (Materials on the Xiaoqing biographies). *Shūkan Tōyōgaku* 集刊東洋学 6 (Sept. 1961): 64–78.

Yamada Masaru 山田賢. "Shindai no chiiki shakai to ijū sōzoku" 清代の地域 社会と移住宗族 (Local society and migrant lineages in the Qing dynasty). *Shakai keizai shigaku* 社会経済史学 55, no. 4 (1989): 72–89.

Yamamoto Noriko 山本徳子. "Hokuchōkei fujin no toki ni tsuite: Hokugi o chūshin toshite" 北朝系婦人の妬忌について:北魏を中心として (The jealousy of

Northern Dynasty women, with a focus on the Northern Wei). *Ritsumeikan bungaku* 立命館文学 270 (Dec. 1967): 78–104.

Yamazaki Junichi 山崎純一. *Kyōiku kara mita Chūgoku joseishi shiryō no kenkyū* 教育から見た中国女性史資料の研究 (A documentary study of Chinese women's history as seen from education). Tokyo: Meiji shoin, 1986.

Yang Shengxin 杨绳信. *Zhongguo banke zonglu* 中国版刻综录 (Combined listings of Chinese books printed by woodblock). Shaanxi: Renmin chubanshe, 1987.

Yang Tianshi 杨天石. "Wan Ming wenxue lilun zhong di 'qingzhen shuo'" 晚明文学理论中的「情真说」 (The discourse of "true love and sincerity" in late Ming literary theory). *Guangming ribao* 光明日报, Sept. 5, 1965.

Yang Yongan 楊永安. *Mingshi guankui zagao* 明史管窺雜稿 (Miscellaneous essays on Ming history). 2 vols. Hong Kong: Xianfeng chubanshe, 1987.

Yangzhou fuzhi 揚州府志 (Gazetteer of Yangzhou prefecture). 1685.

Yao Wentian 姚文田. *Guangling shilue* 廣陵事略 (Historical ancedotes of Yang-zhou). N.p., 1812.

Yazawa Toshihiko 矢沢利彦. *Seiyōjin no mita 16–18 seiki no Chūgoku josei* 西洋人の見た十六～十八世紀の中国女性 (Chinese women in the sixteenth to eighteenth centuries in the eyes of Westerners). Tokyo: Tōhō shoten, 1990.

Ye Dehui 葉德輝. *Nüshi Shuxiang ge yilu* 女士疏香閣遺錄 (Posthumous records from the Pavilion of Floral Fragrance). In Ye Qizhuo 葉啟倬, ed., *Xiyuan xiansheng quanshu* 郁園先生全書 (Complete works of Mr. Xiyuan [Ye Dehui]). Changsha, 1935.

Ye Shaoyuan 葉紹袁. *Jiaxing rizhu* 甲行日注 (Daily accounts from 1645 to 1648). In *Ye Tianliao sizhong* 葉天寮四種 (Four works by Ye Tianliao [Shaoyuan]). Shanghai: Beiye shanfang, 1935–36.

———. *Nianpu bieji* 年譜別記 (Supplement to year-by-year account). In *Ye Tianliao sizhong* (Four works by Ye Tianliao [Shaoyuan]). Shanghai: Beiye shanfang, 1935–36.

———. *Nianpu xu* 年譜續 (Sequel to year-by-year account). In *Ye Tianliao sizhong* (Four works by Ye Tianliao [Shaoyuan]). Shanghai: Beiye shanfang, 1935–36.

———. *Qinzhai yuan* 秦齋怨 (Elegies from the Qin Studio). In *Wumengtang quanji, xia* (Complete works from the Hall of Meridian Dreams). Shanghai: Beiye shanfang, 1935.

———. *Qionghua jing* 瓊花鏡 (Mirror of jeweled flowers). In *Wumengtang quanji, xia* (Complete works from the Hall of Meridian Dreams). Shanghai: Beiye shanfang, 1935.

———. *Yaowen; Xu yaowen* 窈聞, 續窈聞 (News from the abyss; sequel). In *Wumengtang quanji, shang* (Complete works from the Hall of Meridian Dreams). Shanghai: Beiye shanfang, 1935.

———. *Ye Tianliao sizhong* 葉天寮四種 (Four works by Ye Tianliao [Shaoyuan]). Vol. 1, no. 35, of *Zhongguo wenxue zhenben congshu* (Collectanea of gems of Chinese literature). Shanghai: Beiye shanfang, 1935–36.

———. *Zizhuan nianpu* 自撰年譜 (Self-compiled year-by-year account). In *Ye Tianliao sizhong* (Four works by Ye Tianliao [Shaoyuan]). Shanghai: Beiye shanfang, 1935–36.

Ye Shaoyuan, ed. *Tonglian xuxie* 彤奩續些 (Legacies from toiletry and writing brush). In *Wumengtang quanji, xia* (Complete works from the Hall of Meridian Dreams). Shanghai: Beiye shanfang, 1935.

———. *Wumengtang quanji* 年夢堂全集 (Complete works from the Hall of Meridian Dreams). 2 vols. (*shang, xia*). Preface dated 1636. Reprinted—Vol. 1, no. 49, of *Zhongguo wenxue zhenben congshu* (Collectanea of gems of Chinese literature). Shanghai: Beiye shanfang, 1935.

Ye Shicheng 葉世俌. *Baimin cao; fu* 百旻草, 附 (Draft of a hundred sorrows, with appendixes). In Ye Shaoyuan, ed., *Wumengtang quanji, xia* (Complete works from the Hall of Meridian Dreams). Shanghai: Beiye shanfang, 1935.

Ye Shusheng 叶树声. "Mingdai Nan-Zhili Jiangnan diqu siren keshu gaishu" 明代南直隶江南地区私人刻书概述 (A brief study of private printing in the Southern Zhili and Jiangnan regions in the Ming dynasty). *Wenxian* 32 (Feb. 1987): 213–29.

Ye Wanwan 葉紈紈. *Chouyan* 愁言 (Melancholy words). In Ye Shaoyuan, ed., *Wumengtang quanji, shang* (Complete works from the Hall of Meridian Dreams). Shanghai: Beiye shanfang, 1935.

Ye Xiaoluan 葉小鸞. *Fansheng xiang* 返生香 (Fragrance reborn). In Ye Shaoyuan, ed., *Wumengtang quanji, shang* (Complete works from the Hall of Meridian Dreams). Shanghai: Beiye shanfang, 1935.

Ye Xiaowan 葉小紈. *Yuanyang meng* 鴛鴦夢 (Dream of the Mandarin ducks). In Ye Shaoyuan, ed., *Wumengtang quanji, shang* (Complete works from the Hall of Meridian Dreams). Shanghai: Beiye shanfang, 1935.

Ye Xie 葉燮. *Siqi ji* 巳畦集 (Collected works from the morning fields). Erqi caotang, 1684. Copy in the Naikaku bunko.

Yi Zongtun 易宗涒. *Lidai mingyuan chipu* 歷代名媛齒譜 (Deeds of renowned ladies through the dynasties arranged by age). Cishitang, 1795.

Yip Wai-lim. *Diffusion of Distances: Dialogues Between Chinese and Western Poetics*. Berkeley: University of California Press, 1993.

Yiqiu sanren 奠秋散人. *Yujiaoli xiaozhuan* 玉嬌梨小傳 (The story of Jade Tender Pear). N.p., Kangxi edition (1662–1722).

Yu Xiangdou 余象斗, comp. *Santai wanyong zhengzong* 三台萬用正宗 (The authentic Santai encyclopedia of ten thousand uses). Fujian: Yushi Shuangfang tang, 1599.

Yu Ying-shih 余英時. "Zhongguo jinshi zongjiao lunli yu shangren jingshen" 中國近世宗教倫理與商人精神 (Religious ethics and merchant spirit in early modern China). In *Shi yu Zhongguo wenhua* 士與中國文化 (Scholar-officials and Chinese culture). Shanghai: Renmin chubanshe, 1987.

Yu Zhengxie 俞正燮. "Du fei nüren ede lun" 妒非女人惡德論 (Female jealousy is not a bad virtue). In *Guisi leigao* 癸巳類稿 (Manuscripts compiled in the year Guisi [1833]). Reprinted—Shanghai: Shangwu, 1957.

Yü, Chün-fang. *The Renewal of Buddhism in China: Chu-Hung and the Late Ming Synthesis*. New York: Columbia University Press, 1981.

Yuan Hongdao 袁宏道. *Ping shi* 瓶史 (Vase annals). In Feng Kebin, ed., *Guang baichuan xuehai* (An ocean of learning from a hundred wide streams). N.p., Ming edition. Copy in the Naikaku bunko.

Yuan Huang 袁黃. *Lianghang zhai wenji* 兩行齋文集 (Collected essays from the Lianghang Studio). N.p., 1624. Copy in the Naikaku bunko.

Yuan Mei 袁枚. *Suiyuan shihua* 隨園詩話 (Talks on poetry by Suiyuan [Yuan Mei]). Reprinted—Beijing: Renmin wenxue chubanshe, 1960.

Yuanhu yanshui sanren 鴛湖烟水散人. *Nücaizi shu* 女才子書 (The book of female talents). Preface dated 1659. Reprinted—Shenyang: Chunfeng wenyi chubanshe, 1983.

Yuasa Yukihiko 湯浅幸孫. *Chūgoku rinri shisō no kenkyū* 中國倫理思想の研究 (A study of Chinese ethical thoughts). Kyoto: Dōhō sha, 1981.

Yun Zhu 惲珠, comp. *Guochao guixiu zhengshi ji* 國朝閨秀正始集 (Correct beginnings: poetry by ladies from the reigning dynasty). 20 *juan*. Hongxiang guan, 1831–36. Copy in the Library of Congress.

Zeitlin, Judith T. *Historian of the Strange: Pu Songling and the Chinese Classical Tale*. Stanford: Stanford University Press, 1992.

———. "The Petrified Heart: Obsession in Chinese Literature, Art, and Medicine." *Late Imperial China* 12, no. 1 (June 1991): 1–26.

Zhang Dai 張岱. *Tao'an mengyi* 陶庵夢憶 (Dreamy reminiscence from Tao'an). Completed ca. 1646; first published in Qianlong period. Reprinted—Taibei: Jinfeng chuban, 1986.

Zhang Dao 張道. *Meihua meng* 梅花夢 (Plum blossom dream). Qiantang: Zhangshi, 1894.

Zhang Huijian 張慧劍. *Ming-Qing Jiangsu wenren nianbiao* 明清江蘇文人年表 (Yearly accounts of activities of Jiangsu literati in the Ming-Qing period). Shanghai: Shanghai guji chubanshe, 1986.

Zhang Lüping 張履平. *Kunde baojian* 坤德宝鑑 (Golden guide to feminine virtues). N.p., 1777. Copy in the Harvard-Yenching Library.

Zhang Xiumin 張秀民. *Zhang Xiumin yinshua shi lunwen ji* 张秀民印刷史论文集 (Essays on the history of printing by Zhang Xiumin). Beijing: Yinshua gongye chubanshe, 1988.

———. *Zhongguo yinshua shi* 中国印刷史 (A history of Chinese printing). Shanghai: Renmin chubanshe, 1989.

Zhang Yan 張研. *Qingdai zutian yu jiceng shehui jiegou* 清代族田与基层社会結构 (Lineage estates and structure of local society in the Qing dynasty). Beijing: Renmin daxue chubanshe, 1991.

Zhang Zengyuan 张增元. "Shibawei Ming-Qing xiqu zuojia de shengping shiliao" 十八位明清戏曲作家的生平史料 (Historical materials on the lives of 18 dramatists from the Ming-Qing period). *Wenxian* 21 (Jan. 1984): 11–19.

Zhao Shijie 趙世杰, comp. *[Jingke] Gujin nüshi* 精刻古今女史 (Lady scholars from the past and present, deluxe edition). 12 *juan*. N.p., 1628. Copy in the Naikaku bunko.

Zhao Xingqin 趙兴勤. "Cai yu mei: Mingmo Qingchu xiaoshuo chutan" 才与美: 明末清初小说初探 (Talent and beauty: a preliminary investigation from novels in the late Ming-early Qing period). In *Ming-Qing xiaoshuo luncong* (Studies in Ming-Qing fiction), vol. 4. Shenyang: Chunfang wenyi chubanshe, 1986.

Zhao Yi 趙翼. *Gaiyu congkao* 陔余丛考 (Miscellaneous investigations during retirement). 1790. Reprinted—Shanghai: Shangwu, 1957.

Zheng Guangyi 郑光仪, ed. *Zhongguo lidai cainü shige jianshang cidian* 中国历代才女诗歌鉴赏辞典 (A critical explanatory guide to poetry by talented women through the dynasties). Beijing: Zhongguo gongren chubanshe, 1991.

Zheng Xie 鄭燮. *Banqiao ji* 板橋集 (Collected works of Banqiao [Zheng Xie]). Reprinted—Shanghai: Dazhong shuju, 1931.

Zheng Zhenduo 郑振铎, comp. *Zhongguo gudai banhua congkan* 中国古代版画丛刊 (Collections of woodblock prints from the Chinese past). 5 vols. Shanghai: Zhonghua shuju, 1961.

———. *Zhongguo gudai mukehua xuanji* 中国古代木刻画选集 (Selected woodblock prints from the Chinese past). Beijing: Renmin meishu chubanshe, 1985.

Zhi Ruzeng 支如增. "Xiaoqing zhuan" 小青傳 (Biography of Xiaoqing). In Zheng Yuanxun 鄭元勳, comp., *Meiyouge wenyu* 媚幽閣文娛 (Essays for amusement from the Meiyou Pavilion). Ming Chongzhen (1628–44) edition. Copy in the Library of Congress.

Zhong Xing 鍾惺, comp. *Mingyuan shigui* 名媛詩歸 (Poetic retrospective of famous ladies). 36 *juan*. Late Ming edition (ca. 1620). Copies in the Library of Congress and Naikaku bunko.

Zhou Lianggong 周亮工. *Shuying* 书影 (In the shadow of books). Reprinted—Vol. 2, no. 6, of *Zhongguo wenxue cankao ziliao xiao congshu* 中国文学参考資料小丛书 (Pocket-size collectanea of references in Chinese literature). Shanghai: Gudian wenxue chubanshe, 1957.

Zhou Lianggong, comp. *Laigutang mingxian chidu xinchao* 賴古堂名賢尺牘新鈔 (Letters by renowned sages from the Leaning on Antiquity Studio, new edition). Preface dated 1662. Reprinted—Vol. 1, no. 6, of *Zhongguo wenxue zhenben congshu* (Collectanea of gems of Chinese literature). Shanghai: Beiye shanfang, 1935.

Zhou Zhenhe (Zyō Zenho) 周振鶴. "Kōnan kai" 江南解 (On Jiangnan). *Chūgoku tosho* 中国図書 3, no. 5 (May 1991): 2–6, 15.

Zhou Zhenhe and You Rujie 游汝杰. *Fangyan yu Zhongguo wenhua* 方言与中国文化 (Dialects and Chinese culture). Shanghai: Shanghai renmin chubanshe, 1986.

Zhou Zhibiao 周之標, comp. *Nüzhong qi caizi lanke erji* 女中七才子蘭咳二集 (Second collection of orchid gurglings by seven talented scholars among women). 8 *juan*. Suzhou: Baohong tang, preface 1650. Copy in the Naikaku bunko.

Zhu Dongrun 朱東潤. *Chen Zilong jiqi shidai* 陈子龍及其時代 (Chen Zilong and his times). Shanghai: Shanghai guji chubanshe, 1984.

Zhu Jingfan 朱京藩. *Fengliu yuan* 風流院 (Garden of romance). Preface dated 1629. Reprinted—Vol. 2, no. 66, of Guben xiqu congkan biankan weiyuanhui (Editorial committee of collectanea of dramas in their ancient editions), ed., *Guben xiqu congkan* (Collectanea of dramas in their ancient editions). Beijing: Zhonghua shuju, 1957.

Zhu Peichu 朱培初. *Zhongguo de cixiu* 中国的刺绣 (Chinese embroidery). Beijing: Renmin chubanshe, 1987.

Zhu Qiqian 朱啟鈐. *Nügong zhuanzheng lue* 女紅傳徵略 (Brief biographies of embroiderers). In idem, comp., *Xiupu* 繡譜 (Manuals of embroidery). Vol. 1, no. 32, of *Yishu congbian* 藝術叢編 (Collectanea in fine arts), in Yang Jialuo, ed., *Zhongguo xueshu mingzhu* 中國學術名著 (Famous works of Chinese scholarship), series 5. Taibei: Shijie shuju, 1962.

Zhuang Lian 莊練. "Wencai fengliu Liu Rushi" 文采風流柳如是 (The literary flair and romance of Liu Rushi). *Mingshi yanjiu zhuankan* 明史研究專刊 5 (Dec. 1982): 323–26.

Zou Liuyi 鄒流綺 [Siyi 斯漪], comp. *Shiyuan baimingjia ji* 詩媛八名家集 (Selections from eight lady masters of poetry). Preface dated 1655. Microfilm copy in Yale University Library.

Zurndorfer, Harriet. *Change and Continuity in Chinese Local History: The Development of Huizhou Prefecture, 800–1800*. Leiden: E. J. Brill, 1989.

Character List

Entries are alphabetized letter by letter, ignoring word and syllable breaks.

Andingjun 安定君
anjian 暗間

"Bairi ji Shen anren wen"
百日祭沈安人文
Ban Zhao 班昭
"Beiqu" 北去
Bencao 本草
Bian Xuanwen 卞玄文
Bianyong wanbao quanshu
便用萬宝全書
"Biaomei Zhang Qianqian zhuan"
表妹張倩倩傳
binü 婢女

cai 才
cainü 才女
caiyuan 才媛
Caiyun cao 裁雲草
cai zuohe, ji weimei 才作合, 技為媒
Cao Cao 曹操
Cao Dagu 曹大家
Cao Hong 曹洪
Cao Jianbing 曹鑑冰
Cao Xuequan 曹學佺
Cao Zhenting 曹震亭
Cao Zhi 曹植

Chai Jingyi 柴靜儀 (Jixian 季嫻)
Chai Shiyao 柴世堯
changhe 唱和
Changsheng dian 長生殿
"Chao nüwu" 嘲女巫
Chaoshengge ji 潮生閣集
Cha shu 茶書
Cheng Qiong 程瓊
Chen Jiru 陳繼儒
Chen Lanxiu 陳蘭修
Chen Tong 陳同
Chen Weisong 陳維崧
Chen Yuanlong 陳元龍
Chen Zilong 陳子龍
chi (Chinese foot) 尺
chi (defilement) 癡
Chishang ke 池上客
choufu 醜婦
chuanqi 傳奇
Chu Hong 褚宏
"Chumen nan" 出門難
Chunbo ying 春波影
churu 出入
chuwai wei nüfu 出外爲女傳
ci 詞
citang 祠堂
cong 從

congliang 從良
congliang zhizhao 從良執照
congyi erzhong, zhisi buer
  從一而終，至死不二
congzi 從姊
cui 瘁
Cundi (Zhunti) 準提
Cunyu cao 存餘草

dajia 大家
Daoxue suru 道學宿儒
daru 大儒
de 德
Deng Hanyi 鄧漢儀
Deng Zhimo 鄧志謨
di 弟
diaolong shou 雕龍手
Ding Qianxue 丁乾學
Ding Shengzhao 丁聖肇
Ding Yuru 丁玉如
Dong Qichang 董其昌
Du Liniang muse huanhun
  杜丽娘慕色還魂
"Du Li Zhuowu *Fenshu* yijue"
  讀李卓吾焚書一絕
duoliang 度量
"Du Xu Yuan shi yu mei Weiyi"
  讀徐媛詩與妹維儀
"Du Ye Qiongzhang yiji"
  讀葉瓊章遺集
"Du Yuanhu Huang Yuanjie shi"
  讀鴛湖黃媛介詩

engong 恩貢
Erqi caotang 二弃草堂
Eryu cao 二餘草

fa 法
"Fan furen *Luowei yin* xu"
  范夫人絡緯吟序

fang 房
fangke 坊刻
Fang Mengshi 方孟式
Fang Weiyi 方維儀
Fang Weize 方維則
Fang Yizhi 方以智
"Fanli" 凡例
"Fanmen qiyulu" 梵門綺語錄
Fanshi jiacheng 范氏家乘
Fan Yunlin 范允臨
Fan Zhongyan 范仲俺
Feicui ji 翡翠集
Fengliu yuan 風流院
Feng Maoyuan 馮茂遠
Feng Menglong 馮夢龍
Fengshen yanyi 封神演義
Feng Xian 馮嫻 (Youling 又令)
"Feng xiaolian Jianshan zhuan"
  馮孝廉兼山傳
Feng Yunjiang 馮雲將
fenhen 憤恨
"Fenhu shiji" 汾湖石記
Fenshu 焚書
Fenyu cao 焚餘草
fu (rhyme-prose) 賦
fu (to attach) 附
fudao wuwen 婦道無文
funü yanhui 婦女宴會
Furen ji 婦人集
Furong xia 芙蓉峽
Fu she 復社
Fusheng liuji 浮生六記
Fuxue 婦學

geji 歌妓
gong 公
Gong Dingzi 龔鼎孳
Gonggui shishi 宮閨詩史
guan 館
Guan Daosheng 管道昇

"Guangling nüer hang"
　廣陵女兒行
guanhua 官話
guanke 官刻
Guifan 閨範
guifang zhixiu 閨房之秀
"Guige xumu" 閨閣序目
guikun 閨閫
Gui Maoyi 歸懋儀
"Guinan kuailu" 歸南快錄
Gui Shufen 歸淑芬
guishu shi 閨塾師
guixiu 閨秀
"Guixiu Wang Yuying *Liuqie ji*
　xu" 閨秀王玉映留篋集序
guizhong yilie 閨中義烈
Gujin mingyuan baihua shiyu
　古今名媛百花詩餘
"*Gujin mingyuan shigui* xu"
　古今名媛詩歸序
Gujin nüshi 古今女史
Gu Kezhen 顧可貞
Gu Lanyu 顧蘭玉
Gu Mei 顧媚
Gu Qiji 顧啟姬 (Si 姒)
guqin 古琴
Gu Ruopu 顧若璞
Gu Ruoqun 顧若群
Gu Shouqian 顧壽潛
Guxianglou ji 古香樓集
Guxiu 顧繡
Guxi Yenü 姑溪野女
Gu Yurui 顧玉蕊
Gu Zhangsi 顧張思

"Haichang leshan pai" 海昌樂山派
hanfu 悍婦
hanshi 寒食
Han Ximeng 韓希孟
Han Yu 韓愈

Hedong 河東
He Shuangqing 賀双卿
He Shugao 何述皋
hezi hui 盒子會
Hong Sheng 洪昇
Hongyu 紅于
Hong Zhize 洪之則
huaben 話本
Huang Chonggu 黃崇嘏
Huang Dezhen 黃德貞
"Huang Jieling *Yueyaocao* tici"
　黃皆令越遊草題詞
Huang Maowu 黃茂梧
Huang Mengwan 黃孟畹
Huangming jingshi wenbian
　皇明經世文編
Huang Ruheng 黃汝亨
"Huangshi Jieling xiaozhuan"
　黃氏皆令小傳
Huang Shuanghui 黃双蕙
Huang Shude 黃淑德
Huang Shugu 黃樹穀
Huang Shusu 黃淑素
Huang Tingjian 黃庭堅
Huang Xiangsan 黃象三
Huang Yuanjie 黃媛介 (Jieling
　皆令)
Huang Yuanzhen 黃媛貞
Huang Yuqi 黃毓祺
Huang Zongxi 黃宗羲
"*Huanhun ji* ba" 還魂記跋
"*Huanhun ji* jishi" 還魂記紀事
"*Huanhun ji* tixu" 還魂記題序
"*Huanhun ji* xu" 還魂記序
Hu Baoyi 胡抱一
Hufang shi 湖舫詩
hui 慧
Hui Baifang 蕙百芳
huishou 會首
"Hun yi" 昏義

"Huo wen" 或問
hutian hudi 胡天胡帝
Hu Xiaosi 胡孝思

ji (prostitute) 妓
ji (to inherit) 繼
jia (family) 家
jia (insincere) 假
jia (to marry a husband) 嫁
jiake 家刻
jian 賤
Jiang Jinde 蔣金德
"Jiaochuang yeji" 蕉牕夜記
Jiaofang 教坊
"Jiao te sheng" 郊特牲
jia'ou 佳偶
Jiao Xun 焦循
jiaqing 假情
jiaren 佳人
jiashu 家塾
"Jiaze" 家則
jiazu 家族
jiefu 節婦
Jie Zhitui 介之推
"Ji Fan furen Wuhu" 寄范夫人蕪湖
"Jifu Pugong wen" 祭夫濮公文
jijiu 祭酒
"Ji Longer wen" 祭龍兒文
"Ji Maojiazi" 寄毛家姊
jin-gen 金根
Jingling 竟陵
jingnü 靜女
Jin Guliang 金古良
Jingzhiju shihua 靜志居詩話
Jinling fansha zhi 金陵梵利志
"Jinling qigai zhuan" 金陵乞丐傳
jinmu 妗母
Jin Sheng 金聲
"*Jinshilu* xu" 金石錄序

jintong yunü 金童玉女
jinü 妓女
"Jinü Qiongzhang zhuan"
    季女瓊章傳
jin-yin 金銀
"Ji shengnü Qiongzhang wen"
    祭甥女瓊章文
Ji Shuye 嵇叔夜 (Kang 康)
"Ji wangnü Xiaoluan wen"
    祭亡女小鸞文
ji yi 寄意
"Ji zhangnü Zhaoqi wen"
    祭長女昭齊文
"Jizi shu" 寄姊書
"Jucun shibi" 居村適筆

kairo 回路
Kaopan ji 考槃集
"Ke *Yinhong ji* xiaoyin"
    刻吟紅集小引
Kong Shangren 孔尚任
"Ku Huang furen Mengwan"
    哭黃夫人孟畹
Kunde baojian 坤德寶鑑
kyōdōtai 共同体
kyōshin 鄉紳

Lai Huimin 賴惠敏
Langye Wangshi pulue
    瑯琊王氏譜略
Lang Yufu 郎玉甫
"Lao zuonie" 老作孽
Lechang 樂昌
Lei Fu 耒復
Lei Jizhi 耒集之
Lezi 泐子
li 理
liang 艮
liangban 艮伴

Liang Hongyu 梁紅玉
Liang Mengzhao 梁孟昭
Liang Ying 梁瑛
Lianhua luo 蓮花落
Liaodu geng 療妒羹
"*Lichui ji* xu" 鸝吹集序
Li Cunwo 李存我
lienü 烈女
Lienü zhuan 列女傳
Lingyun ge 凌雲閣
Lin Tiansu 林天素 (Xue 雪)
linxia zhifeng 林下之風
Lin Yining 林以寧 (Yaqing 亞清)
liqing 丽情
Li Qingzhao 李清照
Li Rihua 李日華
Li Shu 李淑
Liu Jundu 劉峻度
Liu Rushi 柳如是
Liu Xiang 劉向
Liu Xiaochuo 劉孝綽
Liu Yin 柳隱
Liu Yiqing 劉義慶
Liu Zongzhou 劉宗周
Li Xinjing 李心敬
lixue 理學
Liyin ge 離隱歌
Li Yu (r. 961–75) 李煜
Li Yu (1611–80) 李漁
Li Zhi 李贄
Longfu nüshi 龍輔女士
Longyang 龍陽
Lu Guang 陸廣
Lü Kun 呂坤
Luo Rufang 羅汝芳
Luowei yin 絡緯吟
Lu Qingzi 陸卿子
Lu Shengji 陸聖姬 (Wenluan 文鸞)
Lu Xun 魯迅

Lu Yu 陸羽
Lu Zigang 陸子剛

mai qie 買妾
Mao Anfang 毛安芳 (Ti 媞)
Mao Jike 毛際可
Mao Jin 毛晉
Mao Qiling 毛奇齡
Mao Xianshu 毛先舒
Ma Quan 馬荃
Ma Rong 馬融
Ma ruren 馬孺人
Ma Yuandiao 馬元調
mei 美
Meicun jiazang gao 梅村家藏稿
meide 美德
Meihua meng 梅花夢
meinü 美女
meiren 美人
Meishi 梅市
"*Meishi changhe shigao* shuhou"
　　梅市唱和詩稿書後
Mei xiong 媚兄
meng 夢
mengzi 盟姊
Miaozhuang Wang 妙莊王
ming 名
mingji 名妓
mingjian 明間
"Mingmo-Qingchu shizu de xing-
　　cheng yu xingshuai"
　　明末清初士族的形成與興衰
Mingshan jixuan 名山記選
Mingshan tu 名山圖
mingshi 名士
Mingyuan ji'nang 名媛璣囊
Mingyuan shigui 名媛詩歸
Mingyuan shiwei 名媛詩緯
Mizi xia 彌子瑕

"*Mudan ji* ping" 牡丹記評
Mudanting 牡丹亭
Mudanting huanhun ji
　　牡丹亭還魂記

nannü suiyi, aiyu zetong 男女雖異,
　　愛慾則同
Nan Yuan 南園
nanzun nübei 男尊女卑
nei 內
Neixun 內訓
Neize 內則
neizhu 內助
Ningxiang ge shiji 凝香閣詩集
Ni Renji 倪仁吉
Ni Yuanlu 倪元路
Nongzheng quanshu 農政全書
Nü caizi shu 女才子書
nü di 女弟
nüer bufu 女而不婦
Nüfan 女範
nügong 女工, 女紅
Nügong yuzhi 女紅餘志
Nüjie 女誡
"*Nüjing xu*" 女鏡序
Nü lunyu 女論語
nüshen 女身
nüshi 女士
nüshih 女史
nüshi jijiu 女士祭酒
nüshu 女書
Nü sishu 女四書
Nü xiaojing 女孝經
nü zhangfu 女丈夫
Nü zhuangyuan 女狀元

pai 派
paipu 牌譜

"Pi *Caizi Mudanting* xu"
　　批才子牡丹亭序
pinnü 貧女
pojing chongyuan 破鏡重圓
Pu Shiqi 濮士齊

qi 契
qian 乾
Qian Fenglun 錢鳳綸 (Yunyi 雲儀)
qiangzong hanzu 強宗悍族
Qian Liu 錢鏐
Qian Qianyi 錢謙益
Qian Xiyan 錢希言
"Qianyan" 前言
Qian Yi 錢宜
Qian Yinguang 錢飲光
Qian Zhaoxiu 錢肇修
Qi Bansun 祁班孫
"Qibei rongyan" 棲北冗言
Qi Biaojia 祁彪佳
"Qibu" 起步
Qi Deqian 祁德菏 (Xiangjun 湘君)
Qi Deqiong 祁德琼
Qi Deyuan 祁德淵
"Qie boming" 妾薄命
Qi Lisun 祁理孫
qing 情
qingchi 情痴
qingjiao 情教
Qinglou ji 青樓集
Qingshi 情史
Qin Guan 秦觀
qingzhi 情至
Qinlou yigao 琴樓遺稿
Qin Shu 秦淑
Qinzhai yuan 秦齋怨
Qishan cao 期山草
"*Qishan cao* xiaoyin" 期山草小引

Qiyan'ai 圮雁哀
"Qi Zhongmin gong nianpu"
　祁忠敏公年譜
qu 娶
Quan Zhe shihua 全浙詩話
"Quqie nabi lun" 娶妾納婢論
Qu Yuan 屈原

ren 仁
renqing 人情
Renxiaowen 仁孝文
Ren Yuan 任遠
Ren Zhaolin 任兆麟
ru 儒
rujia nü 儒家女
rushi 儒士

sancong 三從
"*Sanfu ping Mudanting* zaji"
　三婦評牡丹亭雜記
Sang Zhenbai 桑貞白
sanhe yuan 三合院
sanqu 散曲
Sanyan 三言
se 色
shangfu 商婦
Shang Jinglan 商景蘭
Shanhai jing 山海經
shen 神
Shen Darong 沈大榮
Shen Fu 沈復
sheng 生
Shen Huaman 沈華鬘
Shen Huiduan 沈蕙端
Shen Jing 沈璟
shenming 神明
Shen Qianjun 沈倩君
Shen Renlan 沈紉蘭

shen-shang 紳商
Shen Xiang 沈纕
Shen Xianying 沈憲英
Shen Yichen 沈奕琛
Shen Yixiu 沈宜修
Shen Yongji 沈永濟
Shen Zhiyao 沈智瑤
Shenzhou nüzi xinshi 神州女子新史
Shen Zibing 沈自炳
Shen Zizheng 沈自徵
shi (grain measure) 石
shi (market) 市
shi (poetry) 詩
Shi Chengjin 石成金
Shiguan 詩觀
Shiji 史記
Shi Jinchen 史搢臣
Shijun zhi 十郡志
shinü 侍女
"Shinü chunxi tu" 仕女春戲圖
Shinü Huang Jieling ji
　士女黃皆令集
Shinüshi 詩女史
Shi Runzhang 施閏章
Shishuo xinyu 世說新語
Shizhai ji 士齋集
Shi Zhenlin 史震林
shizhi qiya, fudi Pan-Yang
　世執契雅，復締潘楊
"Shi zhuer" 示諸兒
"Shou chongsaoshi Shi ruren qishi
　ji zhi Junqian wushi xu"
　壽從嫂氏史孺人七十暨姪雋千五
　十序
Shu jian 書箋
shunü 淑女
Shuofu 說郛
shuopa zimei 手帕姊妹

Shuxiu zongji 淑秀總集
si 私
side 四德
Sima Guang 司馬光
Sima Xiangru 司馬相如
si'nan 嗣男
sizi 嗣子
"Song Fan furen congyi you Dian-
nan" 送范夫人從宦遊滇南
Song Ruozhao 宋若昭
Su Hui 蘇蕙
Suichun 隨春
Su Wanlan 蘇畹蘭
Su Wu 蘇武
Su Xiaoxiao 蘇小小

tang 堂
Tang Bin 湯斌
Tang Shunzhi 唐順之
Tang Shuyu 湯漱玉
Tang Xianzu 湯顯祖
Tan Yangzi 曇陽子
Tan Ze 談則
Taohua shan 桃花扇
Tao Yuanzao 陶元藻
Tao Zhengxiang 陶正祥
tayū 太夫
tianjing 天井
"Tiantai Le fashi lingyi ji"
天台泐法師靈異記
Tian Yiheng 田藝蘅 (Ziyi 子藝)
tianyuan 天緣
Tian Yuyan 田玉燕
tianzi 天姿
Tiaodeng ju 挑燈劇
"Ti Huang Jieling hua"
題黃皆令畫
Tong Guoqi 佟國器

Tonglian xuxie 彤奩續些
tongnian 同年
Tongqiu she mengdi 同秋社盟弟
Tongshu leiju keze daquan
通書类聚剋則大全
Tong tianle 通天樂
tongxin 童心
tongxue 同學
Tufeng lu 土風錄
tuntian 屯田

wai 外
waihao 外號
Wanbao quanshu 萬宝全書
wande 完德
Wang Duanshu 王端淑 (Yuying
玉映; Yingranzi 映然子)
Wang Fengxian 王鳳嫻
Wang Gen 王艮
Wang Hui 王徽
wanglai 往來
Wang Naiqin 王乃欽
Wang Ranming 汪然明
Wang Shaomei 王紹美
"Wangsheng qishi zhuan"
往生奇逝傳
"Wangshi Shen anren zhuan"
亡室沈安人傳
Wan Shizhen 王世貞
Wang Shoumai 王壽邁
Wang Siren 王思任
Wang Wei 王微 (Xiuwei 修微)
Wang Xianji 王献吉
Wang Xizhi 王羲之
Wang Yangming 王陽明
Wang Yuezhuang 王月粧
Wang Zhenyi 王貞儀
Wang Zhideng 王穉登

Wanhua ting 萬花亭
wanlian 婉戀
Wan Shouqi 萬壽祺
wanwu 玩物
Wanzai pian 宛在篇
Weifen ji 未焚集
Wei Xuanwen 韋宣文
Wei Yong 衞泳
Wei Zhongxian 衞忠賢
wen 文
wencai 文采
Wenluan cao 文鸞草
wenrou dunhou 溫柔敦厚
Wen Shu 文俶
Wen Tianxiang 文天祥
Wenxuan 文選
wenzhang 文章
Wen Zhengming 文徵明
wenzi zhiji 文字知己
Wowen Jushi 我聞居士
Woyuexuan ji 臥月軒集
Wu Bai 吳柏
Wu Bing 吳炳
Wu Dilan 吳砥瀾
wufu 五服
Wu Guofu 吳國輔
Wu Hao 吳顥
wuji 舞妓
"*Wumengtang ji* xu" 午夢堂集序
Wumengtang shicao sizhong
　　午夢堂詩鈔四種
wuming 無明
wuqing 無情
Wu Ren 吳人
Wusao ji 吳騷集
Wu Shan 吳山
wusheng zhai 無生債
Wushuang pu 無雙譜

Wutong 五通
Wu Weiye 吳偉業
Wuxia Cishi 無瑕詞史
Wuye tang 無葉堂
Wu Yirong 吳軼容
Wuzazu 五雜組
Wu Zhensheng 吳震生
Wu Zhiyi 吳之藝
Wu Zixu 伍子胥
"Wuzong waiji" 武宗外紀

Xia 夏
Xiang Lanzhen 項蘭貞
Xiang Sheng 向升
Xiang Yu 項羽
xiannü 賢女
Xianqing ouji 閒情偶寄
xianyuan 賢媛
Xiao Baojuan 蕭寶卷
Xiaojiao Guniang 小腳姑娘
xiaopin 小品
Xiaoqing 小青
Xiao Tong 蕭統
Xie Daoyun 謝道韞
Xiefang ji 擷芳集
"Xie jixie" 謝寄鞋
Xie Zhaozhe 謝肇淛
"Xie zhen" 寫真
Xihu erji 西湖二集
Xihu xue 西湖雪
Xiling Shizi 西泠十子
Xinbian shiwen leiju hanmo da-
　　quan 新編事文類聚翰墨大全
xing 興
xingling wenxue 性靈文學
xingwang 興亡
xingzhuang 行狀
Xi Peilan 席佩蘭

xiqu 戲曲

Xiu Mudan 繡牡丹

Xiuyu xucao 繡餘續草

"Xizeng geji Sanli wushou"
　戲贈歌妓三麗五首

Xizi 醯子

xu (to encourage) 勖

xu (to make up for) 續

"Xu" (preface) 序

Xuanzhi ji 玄芝集

Xu Deyan 徐德言

Xu Deyin 徐德音

Xue Lingyun 薛灵雲

Xue Rengui 薛仁貴

Xue Susu 薛素素

Xue Tao 薛濤

Xu Guangqi 徐光啓

Xun Fengqian 荀奉倩

Xu Rundi 徐潤第

Xu Sanchong 徐三重

Xu Shumin 徐樹敏

Xu Tianxiao 徐天嘯

Xu Wei 徐渭

Xu Xuling 徐旭齡

Xu Yejun 徐野君 (Shijun 士俊)

Xu Yuan 徐媛

Xu Zhizhu 徐智珠

"Xuzi Fan furen shi xu"
　徐姊范夫人詩序

Yan Ermei 閻爾梅

Yang Ai 楊愛

Yang Aiai 楊愛愛

Yang Guifei 楊貴妃

Yang Lian 楊漣

Yang Shigong 楊世功

Yang Yuanyin 楊元蔭

Yang Yunyou 楊雲友

Yan Qiongqiong 嚴琼琼

"Yanti lianzhu" 艷體連珠

Yanyuan zalu 硯緣雜錄

Yanzi jian 燕子箋

Yao Lingze 姚令則

Yaoniang 窅娘

yaotai 瑤台

yaren fengzhi 雅人風致

"Ye furen yiji xu" 葉夫人遺集序

Yejia dai 葉家帶

Ye Shaoyuan 葉紹袁

Ye Shicheng 葉世侗

Ye Shirong 葉世傛

Ye Shuchong 葉舒崇

Ye Wanwan 葉紈紈

Ye Xiaoluan 葉小鸞

Ye Xiaowan 葉小紈

yi 儀

yin 隱

yi'nan cao 宜男草

Yinglian 影憐

Yinhong ji 吟紅集

Yirensi 伊人思

Yizhengtang ji 亦政堂集

Yizhong yuan 意中緣

Yonghu nüzi 容湖女子

Yongxing 永興

You 游

Youfu 幼婦

Youju jian 遊具箋

younü 遊女

youqing 有情

youqing zhiwu 有情之物

yu 慾

Yuan Dacheng 阮大鋮

"Yuandan zaigao wangnü Xiao-
　luan wen" 元旦再告亡女小鸞文

Yuanguo tang 員果堂

zhenqing 真情
zhenshen 鍼神
"Zhenxian zhuan" 貞仙傳
Zhongguo funü shenghuo shi
中國婦女生活史
"*Zhongshan xian* xu" 鍾山献序
Zhongxiang ci 衆香詞
Zhong Xing 鍾惺
Zhou Daodeng 周道登
Zhou guan 周官
Zhou Ji 周楫
Zhou Kai 周愷
Zhou Lanxiu 周蘭秀
Zhou li 周禮
Zhou Lianggong 周亮工
Zhou Yifen 周艶芬
Zhu Chusheng 朱楚生
Zhu Derong 朱德蓉
Zhu Jingfan 朱京藩
Zhumengzi 煮夢子

Zhuo Keyue 卓珂月
zhuren 主人
Zhu Rouze 朱柔則
Zhu Shuzhen 朱淑真
Zhu Xi 朱熹
Zhu Yizun 朱彝尊
zi 字
Zizi xiang 字字香
zong 宗
zongfa 宗法
"Zongshi zhuan" 宗室傳
Zou Saizhen 鄒賽貞
"Zouwei chenqi dangyan shi"
奏為陳乞當嚴事
zu 族
zugu 族姑
Zuili erji changhe 檇李二姬唱和
Zuo Fen 左芬
Zuo Shi 左氏
Zuo Si 左思

Index

In this index an "f" after a number indicates a separate reference on the next page, and an "ff" indicates separate references on the next two pages. A continuous discussion over two or more pages is indicated by a span of page numbers, e.g., "57–59." *Passim* is used for a cluster of references in close but not necessarily consecutive sequence.

Library of Congress Cataloging-in-Publication Data

Ko, Dorothy, 1957–
    Teachers of the inner chambers : women and culture in
seventeenth-century China / Dorothy Ko.
        p. cm.
    Includes bibliographical references and index.
    ISBN 0-8047-2358-3 (alk. paper) :   — ISBN 0-8047-2359-1
(pbk. : alk. paper) :
        1. Women — China — Social conditions. 2. China — Civilization —
1644–1912. I. Title.
HQ1767.K6 1994
305.4'0951'09032 — dc20   94-1166
                                                        CIP